PRINCIPLES OF
MACROECONOMICS

FOURTH CANADIAN EDITION

Robert H. Frank
Cornell University

Ben S. Bernanke
Princeton University (affiliated)
Chairman, Board of Governors of the
Federal Reserve System

Lars Osberg
Dalhousie University

Melvin L. Cross
Dalhousie University

Brian K. MacLean
Laurentian University

McGraw-Hill Ryerson
Connect. Learn. Succeed.

The McGraw·Hill Companies

McGraw-Hill
Ryerson
Connect. Learn. Succeed.

Principles of Macroeconomics
Fourth Canadian Edition

ISBN-13: 978-0-07-040145-7
ISBN-10: 0-07-040145-4

1 2 3 4 5 6 7 8 9 10 QDB 1 9 8 7 6 5 4 3 2

Printed and bound in the United States of America.

Care has been taken to trace ownership of copyright material contained in this text; however, the publisher will welcome any information that enables them to rectify any reference or credit for subsequent editions.

Sponsoring Editor: *James Booty*
Marketing Manager: *Jeremy Guimond*
Developmental Editor: *Daphne Scriabin*
Editorial Associate: *Erin Catto*
Supervising Editor: *Jessica Barnoski*
Photo/Permissions Research: *Daphne Scriabin*
Copy Editor: *Julie van Tol*
Proofreader: *Simpson Editorial Services*
Production Coordinator: *Sheryl MacAdam*
Cover Design: *Greg Devitt*
Cover Image: *OJO Images Ltd./Alamy*
Interior Design: *Greg Devitt*
Page Layout: *Laserwords Private Limited*
Printer: *Quad/Graphics Dubuque*

Library and Archives Canada Cataloguing in Publication

Principles of macroeconomics / Robert H. Frank . . . [et al.].—4th Canadian ed.

Includes bibliographical references and index.
ISBN 978-0-07-040145-7

    1. Macroeconomics—Textbooks. I. Frank, Robert H.
HB172.5.P75 2012   339   C2011-906891-5

INSTRUCTORS...

Would you like your **students** to show up for class **more prepared**?
(Let's face it, class is much more fun if everyone is engaged and prepared...)

Want an **easy way to assign** homework online and track student **progress**?
(Less time grading means more time teaching...)

Want an **instant view** of student or class performance?
(No more wondering if students understand...)

Need to **collect data and generate reports** required for administration or accreditation?
(Say goodbye to manually tracking student learning outcomes...)

Want to **record and post your lectures** for students to view online?
(The more students can see, hear, and experience class resources, the better they learn...)

With **McGraw-Hill's Connect,**™

INSTRUCTORS GET:

- Simple **assignment management**, allowing you to spend more time teaching.

- **Auto-graded** assignments, quizzes, and tests.

- **Detailed visual reporting** where student and section results can be viewed and analyzed.

- Sophisticated **online testing** capability.

- A **filtering and reporting** function that allows you to easily assign and report on materials that are correlated to learning objectives and Bloom's taxonomy.

- An easy-to-use **lecture capture** tool.

- The option to **upload course documents** for student access.

ABOUT THE AUTHORS

Professor Frank is the Henrietta Johnson Louis Professor of Management and Professor of Economics at the Johnson Graduate School of Management at Cornell University, where he has taught since 1972. His "Economic View" column appears regularly in *The New York Times*. After receiving his B.S. from Georgia Tech in 1966, he taught math and science for two years as a Peace Corps Volunteer in rural Nepal. He received his M.A. in statistics in 1971 and his Ph.D. in economics in 1972 from The University of California at Berkeley. During leaves of absence from Cornell, he has served as chief economist for the Civil Aeronautics Board (1978-1980), a Fellow at the Center for Advanced Study in the Behavioral Sciences (1992-93), Professor of American Civilization at l'École des Hautes Études en Sciences Sociales in Paris (2000-01), and the Peter and Charlotte Schoenfeld Visiting Faculty Fellow at the NYU Stern School of Business in 2008-09. Professor Frank is the author of a best-selling intermediate economics textbook—*Microeconomics and Behavior*, Eighth Edition (Irwin/McGraw-Hill, 2010). His research has focused on rivalry and cooperation in economic and social behaviour. His books on these themes include *Choosing the Right Pond* (Oxford, 1995), *Passions Within Reason* (W. W. Norton, 1988), *What Price the Moral High Ground?* (Princeton, 2004), *Falling Behind* (University of California Press, 2007), *The Economic Naturalist* (Basic Books, 2007), *The Economic Naturalist's Field Guide* (Basic Books, 2009), and the *Darwin Economy* (Princeton, 2011), and have been translated into 22 languages. *The Winner-Take-All Society* (The Free Press, 1995), co-authored with Philip Cook, received a Critic's Choice Award, was named a Notable Book of the Year by *The New York Times*, and was included in *BusinessWeek*'s list of the 10 best books of 1995. *Luxury Fever* (The Free Press, 1999) was named to the *Knight-Ridder* Best Books list for 1999.

Professor Frank has been awarded an Andrew W. Mellon Professorship (1987-1990), a Kenan Enterprise Award (1993), and a Merrill Scholars Program Outstanding Educator Citation (1991). He is a co-recipient of the 2004 Leontief Prize for Advancing the Frontiers of Economic Thought. He was awarded the Johnson School's Stephen Russell Distinguished Teaching Award in 2004 and 2010 and the School's Apple Distinguished Teaching Award in 2005. His introductory microeconomics course has graduated more than 7,000 enthusiastic economic naturalists over the years.

Professor Bernanke received his B.A. in economics from Harvard University in 1975 and his Ph.D. in economics from MIT in 1979. He taught at the Stanford Graduate School of Business from 1979 to 1985 and moved to Princeton University in 1985, where he was named the Howard Harrison and Gabrielle Snyder Beck Professor of Economics and Public Affairs, and where he served as Chairman of the Economics Department.

Professor Bernanke was sworn in on February 1, 2006, as Chairman and a member of the Board of Governors of the Federal Reserve System. He has also been appointed to a second term, which expires January 31, 2014. Professor Bernanke also serves as Chairman of the Federal Open Market Committee, the System's principal monetary policy-making body. He was appointed as a member of the Board to a full 14-year term, which expires January 31, 2020. Before his appointment as Chairman, Professor Bernanke was Chairman of the President's Council of Economic Advisers, from June 2005 to January 2006.

Professor Bernanke's intermediate textbook, with Andrew Abel and Dean Croushore, *Macroeconomics*, Seventh Edition (Addison-Wesley, 2011), is a best-seller in its field. He has authored more than 50 scholarly publications in macroeconomics, macroeconomic history, and finance. He has done significant research on the causes of the Great Depression, the role of financial markets and institutions in the business cycle, and measuring the effects of monetary policy on the economy. Professor Bernanke has held a Guggenheim Fellowship and a Sloan Fellowship, and he is a Fellow of the Econometric Society and of the American Academy of Arts and Sciences. He served as the Director of the Monetary Economics Program of the National Bureau of Economic Research (NBER) and as a member of the NBER's Business Cycle Dating Committee. In July 2001, he was appointed editor of the *American Economic Review*. Professor Bernanke's work with civic and professional groups includes having served two terms as a member of the Montgomery Township (N.J.) Board of Education.

Lars Osberg is currently McCulloch Professor, and Chair of the Department of Economics at Dalhousie University, but he began life in Ottawa. As an undergraduate, he attended Queen's University in Kingston and the London School of Economics and Political Science. After two years working for the Tanzania Sisal Corporation as a CUSO volunteer, he went to Yale University for his Ph.D. His first book was *Economic Inequality in Canada* (1981), and the most recent is *The Economic Implications of Social Cohesion* (2003). In between, there were eight others. He is also the author of numerous refereed articles in professional journals, book chapters, reviews, reports, and miscellaneous publications. His major fields of research interest have been the extent and causes of poverty and economic inequality, with particular emphasis in recent years on social policy and the implications of working time, unemployment, and structural change. Among other professional responsibilities, he was president of the Canadian Economics Association in 1999–2000. Recent papers can be found at http://myweb.dal.ca/osberg/.

Melvin Cross received an Associate of Arts degree from Dawson Community College in 1968, a B.A. from the University of Montana in 1970, an M.A. from Simon Fraser University in 1972, and a Ph.D. in economics from Texas A&M University in 1976. He is an Associate Professor and Graduate Coordinator in the Department of Economics at Dalhousie University, which he joined in 1975. He held an adjunct appointment in the School of Resource and Environmental Studies, and he was an Associate Fellow in the Foundation Year Program of the University of King's College from 1991 to 2002. Professor Cross has taught as a visitor at Queen's University, the University of Sydney, and Carleton University. His teaching and research interests are in the economics of natural and environmental resources and the history of economic thought. He has taught principles of economics throughout his career. He is an author or co-author of articles in the *Canadian Journal of Fisheries and Aquatic Science*, *Canadian Public Policy*, *History of Political Economy*, *Marine Resource Economics*, and other journals. He is Past President of the Atlantic Canada Economics Association, having served as Vice-President during 2007–09, and then President in 2009–11.

Brian K. MacLean is Professor of Economics at Laurentian University in Sudbury, Ontario, where he has been Chair of the Department of Economics and Director of the Institute for Northern Ontario Research and Development. He was born and raised in Charlottetown, Prince Edward Island, speaks Japanese as a second language, and has been a visiting professor at Hokkaido University in Sapporo, Japan, and Saitama University, just outside of Tokyo, where he returns each summer to deliver a series of lectures. His publications include the prescient edited volume *Out of Control? Canada in an Unstable Financial World* (Lorimer, 1999). His recent research includes topics such as the implications for other economies of Japan's experience of countering the aftermath of a major asset price bubble and the implications for macroeconomics of the global financial crisis and recession. He has served on the Executive of the Canadian Economics Association, as the CEA liaison with the Canadian Women Economists Network, and has been a Steering Committee member of the Progressive Economics Forum for more than a decade.

BRIEF CONTENTS

CONTENTS

PREFACE

The Great Depression of the 1930s was an important example of how the Canadian economy could seriously malfunction, and highlighted the importance of good economic analysis and policy to improve its functioning. Economic events since 2008—the financial crisis on Wall Street; its propagation to financial markets in Europe, Asia, and Canada; commodity price and exchange rate gyrations; and long-term mass unemployment, especially in the United States—have provided a repeat lesson. Enrolment in economics classes is, as a direct result, growing because more and more students want to understand the causes and implications of these events.

Feedback from users supports our conviction that this textbook provides a different and better way to introduce beginning students to macroeconomics. This text continues to emphasize (1) an active, student-centred approach to learning; (2) economic naturalism; (3) the philosophy that evidence matters; and (4) repeated use of core principles.

ACTIVE LEARNING

Active learning by students—that is, learning based on applying new ideas until they are internalized—is an essential part of an effective learning process. By "learning" we do not just mean being able to answer a test question the next day. By the time they reach university, many students have become quite good at quick memorization. But even "A" students never fully internalize a concept unless they use it repeatedly. This textbook has been designed for instructors who strive to stimulate the intellectual curiosity of their students and thereby have an enduring impact on them. We think it useful for instructors to ask themselves, "What do I want my students to retain from this course ten or twenty years from now?" Education research shows that long-term retention depends on students seeing both the value of a concept and *actively* using it. Throughout the book we use a number of devices to foster active learning.

1. **Worked Examples.** New ideas and concepts are introduced by means of simple examples, usually numerical, which are developed step-by-step in the text. These examples display the reasoning process used to reach the economic conclusion or insight, and they provide a model for the student to apply when working on exercises and problems.

EXAMPLE 4.1

Productivity and output per person in Canada, the United States, and China

In 2009, the value of Canadian economic output was approximately C\$1.3 trillion (1300 billion). In the same year, the estimated value of U.S. output was approximately C\$14.1 trillion and that of the People's Republic of China was approximately C\$4.9 trillion. The populations of Canada, the United States, and China in 2009 were about 33.7 million, 307.4 million, and 1.33 billion, respectively, while the numbers of employed workers in the three countries were approximately 16.8 million, 139.9 million, and 813.5 million, respectively.[4]

The output per person and average labour productivity for Canada, the United States, and China in the year 2009 can be determined using the data provided above. Output per person is simply total output divided by the number of people in an economy. Average labour productivity is output divided by the number of employed workers. Doing the math, we get the following results for 2009, the year in question.

---

2. Exercises. Following many examples, and indeed throughout each chapter, we pose exercises in the running text that challenge the student to test and extend his or her understanding of the ideas being discussed. Answers to these exercises are provided at the end of the chapter, allowing immediate feedback.

The price of gold is US$1500/ounce in New York and ¥150 000/ounce in Tokyo. If the law of one price holds for gold, what is the nominal exchange rate between the U.S. dollar and the Japanese yen?

Example 13.5 and Exercise 13.6 illustrate the application of the purchasing power parity theory. According to the **purchasing power parity (PPP)** theory, nominal exchange rates are determined as necessary for the law of one price to hold.

A useful prediction of the PPP theory is that in the long run, the currencies of countries that experience relatively high inflation will tend to depreciate against the currencies of countries that experience relatively low inflation. To see why, we will extend the analysis in Example 13.6.

purchasing power parity (PPP) the theory that nominal exchange rates are determined as necessary for the law of one price to hold

---

3. Anecdotes and Illustrations. Active learning is more likely to take place when students are engaged and motivated. We begin almost every chapter with an anecdote that motivates the discussion, and we illustrate the ideas with memorable cartoons, photographs, and original line drawings. Most important, we have striven to minimize jargon and engage the student with direct, friendly writing.

4. Recap Boxes and Summaries. To keep students focused on the forest as well as the trees, at strategic points in each chapter we have provided "recap boxes." Recaps summarize the main ideas of the previous section. The recap boxes are also reiterated by bulleted end-of-chapter summaries, which are designed to review the most important concepts presented in the chapter.

"We're a natural, Rachel. I handle intellectual property, and you're a content-provider."

RECAP

DETERMINING THE EXCHANGE RATE

- Supply and demand analysis is a useful tool for studying the short-run determination of the exchange rate. Canadian households and firms supply Canadian dollars to the foreign exchange market to acquire foreign currencies, which they need to purchase foreign goods, services, and assets. Foreigners demand Canadian dollars in the foreign exchange market to purchase Canadian goods, services, and assets. The equilibrium exchange rate, also called the *market equilibrium value of the exchange rate*, equates the quantities of dollars supplied and demanded in the foreign exchange market.

- An increased preference for foreign goods, an increase in Canadian real GDP, or an increase in the real interest rate on foreign assets will increase the supply of dollars on the foreign exchange market, lowering the value of the dollar. An increased preference for Canadian goods by foreigners, an increase in real GDP abroad, or an increase in the real interest rate on Canadian assets will increase the demand for dollars, raising the value of the dollar.

- If the Bank of Canada raises the real interest rate, it will tend to increase the demand for Canadian dollars and, thereby, strengthen the Canadian dollar. A stronger dollar reinforces the effects of interest rate hikes on aggregate spending by reducing net exports, a component of aggregate demand. Conversely, if the Bank of Canada lowers the real interest rate, it will tend to weaken the Canadian dollar.

5. **Review Questions and Problems.** Questions for review at the end of each chapter encourage the student to test his or her understanding of the main ideas of the chapter. End-of-chapter problems are carefully crafted to help students internalize and extend core concepts.

ECONOMIC NATURALISM

Economics is fascinating because of its power to explain. As an extension of the active-learning approach, we encourage students to become "economic naturalists" who employ basic economic principles to understand and explain what they see around them in the "laboratory of life."

Studying biology enables people to observe and marvel at the many details of the natural environment that would otherwise have escaped notice. For the naturalist, a walk in a quiet wood becomes an adventure. Similarly, economists can watch basic economic processes in real time, every day, in their real lives. Studying economics can thus enable students to see the world in which they live and work in a new light. Throughout the text, Economic Naturalist examples show students the relevance of economics to their world—how economics can help them to understand the world they live in. The following are just some of the issues raised:

- Does GDP measurement by Statistics Canada ignore the underground economy?

- What is the macroeconomic impact of a sharp drop (or rise) in world oil prices?

- How can a country such as Ireland recover from the 2008–2009 global recession without expansionary macroeconomic policies?

- Is a strong currency a sign of a strong economy?

- How is a trade surplus compatible with a current account deficit?

Through exposure to economic naturalism, students are encouraged to pose and answer applied economic questions on their own, and they become more likely to use economics long after completing their introductory course.

ECONOMIC NATURALIST 10.1

When the Bank of Canada "Ran Out of Ammunition"

The Bank of Canada's overnight rate target was at 4.5 percent when early signs of an impending recession surfaced in the summer of 2007. The Bank of Canada began a series of interest rate cuts. By April 21, 2009, the Bank of Canada announced that it would reduce its key policy rate to 0.25 percent. A key policy rate of 0.25 percent is incredibly low by historical standards. Prior to 2009, the lowest the Bank of Canada's key policy rate had ever been was 1.22 percent, and that was registered way back in July 1958.[11] In cutting the overnight rate target to 0.25 percent, the Bank declared that 0.25 percent was the "effective lower bound" for the overnight rate target. In other words, the Bank was saying that it could not cut its key policy rate any further. Some other central banks found themselves in the same predicament. Because interest rate cuts are what central banks use to fight recession, commentators said that the central banks had "run out of ammunition." Furthermore, the Bank of Canada did not just run out of ammunition, but it was without ammunition for over 13 months.

EVIDENCE MATTERS

Getting students to appreciate the power of economic models is a crucial goal of an introductory course, but students also need to know the empirical evidence. Does real GDP per capita correlate with direct measures of living standards? Do nominal interest rates tend to rise with the inflation rate? Do slowdowns in real GDP growth produce increases in the unemployment rate? Do economies with high inflation experience exchange rate depreciation? Is higher capital per worker associated with higher output per worker? Does average productivity growth necessarily translate into real wage growth? By providing evidence on questions such as these, we encourage students to view economic theories as testable hypotheses, not as unquestionable pronouncements.

REPEATED USE OF CORE PRINCIPLES

A few core principles arise again and again in economics, especially in microeconomics, but also in macroeconomics. By repeating these core principles even in the purely macroeconomic chapters (4 to 16), the text enhances the likelihood that students will leave the course with a thorough appreciation of the principles. A small icon appears in the margin whenever one of the core principles is discussed, thereby reinforcing the principles many times over.

The Cost-Benefit Principle: A rational decision maker will take an economic action if, and only if, the extra benefits from taking the action are greater than the extra costs.

COST-BENEFIT

WHAT IS NEW AND IMPROVED IN THIS EDITION

- The three chapters of Part 1 stress the importance of models in economics while retaining a strong emphasis on the cost-benefit principle (optimization).
- The three chapters of Part 1, identical to the first three chapters of the companion volume *Principles of Microeconomics* in previous editions, are now more concise and more directly relevant to macroeconomics.
- The relevance of macroeconomics for understanding the global recession of 2008–2009 and its aftermath is demonstrated throughout the textbook, including in the Economic Naturalist examples.
- Unconventional monetary policy, a hot topic of debate since 2008, is introduced as a key term in Chapter 4, and explained further in Chapter 9.
- Government budget deficits and debt receive expanded treatment in Chapter 4 and again in Chapter 8.
- Chapter 5 features a much more compact discussion of the income approach to GDP.
- Chapter 6 highlights the significance of the zero bound on nominal interest rates during the 2008–2009 recession.
- The concept of unemployment duration is introduced in Chapter 7.
- Asset price bubbles are discussed in Chapter 8 in connection with concept of the wealth effect.
- The chapter on money and banking now appears before the chapter explaining monetary policy with the Keynesian cross diagram.
- Chapter 9 features a new subsection on the role of the central bank in ensuring the stability of the financial system, and includes an optional appendix on the vertical money supply theory of interest rate determination.
- Chapter 10 explains the challenge faced by a central bank if the interest rate spread widens during a financial crisis.
- Chapter 11 uses the *AD-AS* model to analyze the path to recovery for Euro-zone economies such as Ireland.
- A thorough rewriting of Chapter 12 on inflation and output has made it more accessible to students.

- Through greater emphasis on the supply and demand model of exchange rate determination, Chapter 13 has also been made more accessible.
- Chapter 14 on economic growth gives greater attention to concerns about global warming.
- The detailed section on trade institutions in Chapter 15 has been shortened and simplified.
- Chapters 16 and 17 of the previous edition have been combined into a single chapter on Saving, Capital Formation, and Financial Markets, and concludes with a new subsection on "What type of financial system?"

RETAINED FEATURES

- Active learning approach.
- Emphasis on prediction of real world events and explanation of real world issues.
- Careful presentation of GDP, labour force, and price level measurement issues to provide students with a strong empirical grounding.
- Compact development of the Keynesian cross model.
- Patient, systematic treatment of money and banking.
- Compact development of the traditional *AD–AS* model.
- Development of the Bernanke/Taylor/Romer model of inflation and output determination as a complement to, or substitute for, the traditional *AD–AS* model, depending on instructor choice.
- Thorough, lively coverage of exchange rate issues.
- Solid core chapter on economic growth pitched at a level appropriate for first-year students.
- Detailed application of a supply and demand model to discuss winners and losers from international trade and the impact of tariffs and quotas.
- Solid discussion of the institutions of international trade.
- Frequent references back to earlier chapters so that students get repeated exposure to findings such as the Fisher effect.
- Discussion of savings and investment firmly linked to real-world categories employed by Statistics Canada.
- Widespread use of Statistics Canada data with CANSIM series numbers provided.

THOROUGHLY CANADIAN MACRO

A macro textbook directed to a Canadian audience must confront head-on the interdependence of national economies. Our book places a strong emphasis on *open economy issues*. The role of Canada's flexible exchange rate in amplifying the impact of monetary policy is discussed in Chapters 10, 11, and 12. The causes and consequences of currency appreciation and depreciation are covered in Chapter 13. Chapter 15 discusses international trade institutions, and notes that international trade produces both winners and losers. The historical contribution of non-resident saving to Canadian capital formation and the connection between the current account balance and international capital flows are discussed in Chapter 16.

In addition, a Canadian macroeconomics textbook needs to introduce students to Canadian data, institutions, and policies. Beginning in Chapters 4, 5, and 6, we introduce macroeconomic data on the Canadian economy through the use of figures and tables. For example, we introduce our discussion of international trade in Chapter 15 with an empirical section on Canada's role in the global economy. In analyzing saving and investment in Chapter 16, we link the discussion to Statistics Canada data from the *National Income and Expenditure Accounts*. When we examine net capital inflows in Chapter 16, we employ data from *Canada's Balance of International Payments* and are careful to highlight the distinction between the current account balance and net exports. More generally, we have carefully documented the sources of data, and in most cases data-based figures and tables provide the relevant data series label, not just the table number, from Statistics Canada's CANSIM database. We have also included a data appendix at the end of the textbook, which uses CANSIM time series to show the major trends in the Canadian economy in recent decades. The explanatory notes for the data appendix provide an overview of the meaning and significance of macroeconomic variables that are critical to studying the Canadian economy.

Institutions relating to monetary, fiscal, and trade policy are important to macroeconomics, and we pay particular attention to institutions of monetary policy. For example, to understand Canadian macroeconomic issues today, it is essential to understand how the Bank of Canada operates. We emphasize that the Bank's stated goal is to keep inflation in the range of 1 to 3 percent, and that the instrument the Bank uses to achieve its goal is the overnight rate target.

Relevant examples make the discussion of Canadian data, institutions, and policies come alive for students. Our Economic Naturalist examples dealing specifically with the Canadian economy answer questions such as

- Why was December 2010 probably a good month for a Canadian family to take out a five-year, fixed-rate mortgage, while September 1981 was an incredibly bad month to do so?
- Why did Canadian inflation dramatically escalate during 1973–1974 and during 1980–1981, but not in 2007–2008?
- Why do central banks, including the Bank of Canada, try to achieve low, positive inflation rather than zero inflation?

ORGANIZATION OF TOPICS

Principles of Macroeconomics is divided into four parts. Part 1 (Chapters 1, 2, and 3) demonstrates how economists use models to clarify the essentials of a situation, explains basic concepts such as the cost-benefit principle and the equilibrium principle, and introduces macroeconomic topics such as the production possibilities curve, the circular flow of income and expenditure, and the fallacy of composition. Part 2 then brings the student into the realm of macroeconomic issues and data. Chapter 4 gives an overview of the issues that macroeconomists study. Chapters 5 and 6 focus on issues of measurement. Chapter 5 looks at measures of real economic activity, such as GDP and the unemployment rate, and Chapter 6 considers measures of the price level and inflation. As preparation for our model of output and inflation rate determination, we provide students with a thorough grounding in the terminology they need in order to discuss changes in the inflation rate.

Part 3 studies the short-run behaviour of the economy, including cyclical fluctuations and stabilization policy. Chapter 7 introduces short-term fluctuations and includes descriptions of Canada's experience with recessions and expansions, the characteristic behaviour of unemployment and inflation during business cycles, and the measurement of an economy's output gap. In the short run, changes in aggregate spending can affect output. Chapter 8 looks at the relationship between planned aggregate spending and output in the very short run, when prices are fixed and firms simply meet the demand for their output. In this setting, government policies that affect planned aggregate spending, such as changes in government purchases, can help to eliminate output gaps. Chapter 9 deals with money and banking and how central banks operate as a prelude to Chapter 10, which maintains the short-run focus of Chapter 8 but extends the model to consider monetary policy issues. Chapter 11 dispenses with the modeling assumption of a fixed price level and considers output and price level determination in the context of a traditional model of aggregate demand and supply. Chapter 12 presents a model according to which an output gap substantially different from zero will eventually cause the inflation rate to change. This, in turn (via the central bank's policy reaction function), triggers a mechanism for the elimination of output gaps over time. The chapter also considers other sources of inflation, notably aggregate supply shocks, and the policy dilemmas that these create. Chapter 13 extends the discussion of exchange rates to provide a supply and demand model of exchange rate determination and other topics relating to both flexible and fixed exchange rates.

If macroeconomic stability is achieved, then no topic in economics is more important to living standards than the sources of long-term output and productivity growth. The three chapters of Part 4, therefore, deal primarily with long-term economic performance. Chapter 14 reviews the record of long-term economic growth and discusses the factors (such as rising levels of education, fixed capital formation, and improvements in technology) that have contributed to productivity growth. Chapter 15 analyzes the trade dimension of Canada's role in the global economy. It deals with trade theory, data, and institutions from a macroeconomic perspective. Chapter 16 analyzes how saving (including non-resident saving) is related to economy-wide investment. It discusses factors affecting savings and investment decisions, and it deals both with the role of the financial system and with how bond and stock markets operate.

ALTERNATIVE COURSE STRUCTURES

As our discussion of the organization of topics indicates, there is a well-developed logic to the structure and coverage of this textbook. But, naturally, each instructor will teach the material a bit differently; some will decide to cover less material, and others may prefer to teach the long-run chapters of Part 4 before the short-run chapters of Part 3. The textbook lends itself to these and other course structures. Here we will first discuss options for covering less material, regardless of the sequencing of the chapters, and then we suggest an alternative, "long-run first" path through the chapters.

Covering Less Material   What are the options for covering less material? Part 1 can be skipped if this textbook is employed in the second term of a course that covers microeconomics in the first term. We believe that instructors should cover each of the three chapters of Part 2, otherwise students may fail to develop a good grasp of what the key macroeconomic variables—GDP, the unemployment rate, and the inflation rate—really represent and of how real variables differ from nominal ones. In Part 3, Chapter 9 is mainly concerned with money and banking issues, and although it deals with important matters, the chapter is not strictly required for the chapters that follow it. Indeed, in the previous edition of this textbook, most of the material in Chapter 9 was in the final chapter of Part 3. It should be noted, however, that the Chapter 9 key terms *effective lower bound* and *key policy rate* do crop up in later chapters. Chapters 11 and 12 provide alternative macroeconomic models: Chapter 11 deals with a traditional aggregate demand–aggregate supply model of output and price level determination, whereas Chapter 12 presents a more recent model of output and inflation rate determination. Some instructors will decide to skip one of these two chapters. In Part 4, Chapter 14 on long-run economic growth is the key chapter, and most instructors will also want to cover Chapter 15 on international trade. Chapter 16 deals with topics that many students find fascinating and practical, such as stock and bond price determination, but many topics in Chapter 16 are not emphasized in other widely used textbooks, so some instructors may decide to skip this in the interests of time.

Long-Run First Option   Some Canadian instructors like to cover the "long-run" material early in the course and, in fact, the first two editions of this textbook followed a "long-run first" approach. The usual option for a long-run first approach would be to cover Part 1 (introductory chapters), then Part 2 (measurement chapters) and Part 4 (long-run chapters), and finally Part 3 (short-run chapters). Instructors who follow this approach should be aware that some Economic Naturalist examples in the long-run chapters make reference to terms covered in the short-run chapters—for example, terms such as the Fisher effect and the purchasing power parity theory of exchange rate determination—and Chapter 15 on international trade now has a section that refers back to the short-run macro model of Chapter 8.

CONNECT

McGraw-Hill Connect™ is a web-based assignment and assessment platform that gives students the means to better connect with their coursework, with their instructors, and with the important concepts they will need to know for success now and in the future.

With Connect, instructors can deliver assignments, quizzes, and tests online. Nearly all the questions from the text are presented in an auto-gradeable format and tied to the text's learning objectives. Instructors can edit existing questions and author entirely new problems. Track individual student performance—by question, assignment, or in relation to the class overall—with detailed grade reports. Integrate grade reports easily with Learning Management Systems (LMS) such as WebCT and Blackboard. And much more.

By choosing Connect, instructors are providing their students with a powerful tool for improving academic performance and truly mastering course material. Connect allows students to practice important skills at their own pace and on their own schedule. Importantly, students' assessment results and instructors' feedback are all saved online—so students can continually review their progress and plot their course to success.

Connect also provides 24/7 online access to an eBook—an online edition of the text—to aid them in successfully completing their work, wherever and whenever they choose.

KEY FEATURES

SIMPLE ASSIGNMENT MANAGEMENT

With Connect, creating assignments is easier than ever, so you can spend more time teaching and less time managing.

- Create and deliver assignments easily with selectable end-of-chapter static and algorithmic questions and test bank material
- Streamline lesson planning, student progress reporting, and assignment grading to make classroom management more efficient than ever
- Go paperless with the eBook and online submission and grading of student assignments

SMART GRADING

When it comes to studying, time is precious. Connect helps students learn more efficiently by providing feedback and practice material when they need it, where they need it.

- Automatically score assignments, giving students immediate feedback on their work and side-by-side comparisons with correct answers
- Access and review each response; manually change grades or leave comments for students to review
- Reinforce classroom concepts with practice tests and instant quizzes

INSTRUCTOR LIBRARY

The Connect Instructor Library is your course creation hub. It provides all the critical resources you'll need to build your course, just how you want to teach it.

- Assign eBook readings and draw from a rich collection of textbook-specific assignments
- Access instructor resources, including ready-made PowerPoint presentations and media to use in your lectures
- View assignments and resources created for past sections
- Post your own resources for students to use

eBOOK

Connect reinvents the textbook learning experience for the modern student. Every Connect subject area is seamlessly integrated with Connect eBooks, which are designed to keep students focused on the concepts key to their success.

- Provide students with a Connect eBook, allowing for anytime, anywhere access to the textbook
- Merge media, animation and assessments with the text's narrative to engage students and improve learning and retention
- Pinpoint and connect key concepts in a snap using the powerful eBook search engine
- Manage notes, highlights and bookmarks in one place for simple, comprehensive review

LYRYX ASSESMENT FOR ECONOMICS (LAECON)

lyryx

Based on *Principles of Macroeconomics* by Frank, Bernanke, Osberg, Cross, and MacLean, Lyryx Assessment for Economics is a leading-edge online assessment system, designed to support both students and instructors. The assessment takes the form of a homework assignment called a *lab*. The assessments are algorithmically generated and automatically graded so that students get instant grades and feedback. New labs are randomly generated constantly, providing the student with unlimited opportunities to try a type of each question. After they submit a lab for marking, students receive extensive feedback on their work, thus promoting their learning experience.

FOR THE INSTRUCTOR

The goal of Lyryx is to enable you to use these labs to generate course marks instead of having to create and mark your own labs. The content, marking, and feedback have been developed and implemented with the help of experienced instructors in economics. After registering your courses with us, you can then use LAECON content to create your own unique labs by selecting problems from our bank of questions and setting deadlines for each one of these labs. You have access to all your students' marks and can view their best labs. At any time, you can download the class grades for your own programs.

FOR THE STUDENT

LAECON offers algorithmically generated and automatically graded assignments. Students get instant grades and instant feedback—no need to wait until the next class to find out how well they did! Grades are instantly recorded in a gradebook that the student can view. Students are motivated to do their labs for two reasons: First, because their results can be tied to assessment, and second, because they can try the lab as many times as they wish prior to the due date and have only their best grade recorded. Instructors know from experience that students who do their economics homework will be successful in the course. Recent research regarding the use of Lyryx has shown that when labs are tied to assessment, even if worth only a small percentage of the total grade for the course, students WILL do their homework—and MORE THAN ONCE!! Please contact your iLearning Sales Specialist for additional information on the Lyryx Assessment Economics system. Visit http://laecon.lyryx.com.

SUPERIOR SERVICE

Superior Service   Service takes on a whole new meaning with McGraw-Hill Ryerson and *Principles of Macroeconomics*. More than just bringing you the textbook, we have consistently raised the bar in terms of innovation and educational research—both in economics and in education in general. These investments in learning and the education community have helped us to understand the needs of students and educators across the country, and allowed us to foster the growth of truly innovative, integrated learning.

Integrated Learning   Your Integrated *i*Learning Sales Specialist is a McGraw-Hill Ryerson representative who has the experience, product knowledge, training, and support to help you assess and integrate any of our products, technology, and services into your course for optimal teaching and learning performance. Whether it's helping your students improve their grades, or putting your entire course online, your *i*Learning Sales Specialist is there to help you do it. Contact your *i*Learning Sales Specialist today to learn how to maximize all of McGraw-Hill Ryerson's resources!

iLearning Services   McGraw-Hill Ryerson offers a unique *i*Services package designed for Canadian faculty. Our mission is to equip providers of higher education with superior tools and resources required for excellence in teaching. For additional information, visit www.mcgrawhill.ca/highereducation/iservices.

Teaching & Learning Conference Series   The educational environment has changed tremendously in recent years, and McGraw-Hill Ryerson continues to be committed to helping you acquire the skills you need to succeed in this new milieu. Our innovative Teaching & Learning Conference Series brings faculty together from across Canada with 3M Teaching Excellence award winners to share teaching and learning best practices in a collaborative and stimulating environment. Pre-conference workshops on general topics, such as teaching large classes and technology integration, will also be offered. We will also work with you at your own institution to customize workshops that best suit the needs of your faculty.

Tegrity   Tegrity is a service that makes class time available all the time by automatically capturing every lecture in a searchable format for students to review when they study and complete assignments. With a simple one-click start-and-stop process, you capture all computer screens and corresponding audio. Students can replay any part of any class with easy-to-use browser-based viewing on a PC or Mac. Educators know that the more students can see, hear, and experience class resources, the better they learn. With Tegrity, students quickly recall key moments by using Tegrity's unique search feature. This search helps students efficiently find what they need, when they need it, across an entire semester of class recordings. Help turn all your students' study time into learning moments immediately supported by your lecture. To learn more about Tegrity watch a 2-minute Flash demo at http://tegritycampus.mhhe.com.

Create Online McGraw-Hill's Create Online places the most abundant resource at your fingertips—literally. With a few mouse clicks, you can create customized learning tools simply and affordably. McGraw-Hill Ryerson has included many of its market-leading textbooks within Create Online for eBook and print customization as well as many licensed readings and cases. For more information, please visit www.mcgrawhillcreate.com.

CourseSmart CourseSmart brings together thousands of textbooks across hundreds of courses in an eTextbook format providing unique benefits to students and faculty. By purchasing an eTextbook, students can save up to 50 percent off the cost of a print textbook, reduce their impact on the environment, and gain access to powerful Web tools for learning, including full text search, notes and highlighting, and email tools for sharing notes among classmates. For faculty, CourseSmart provides instant access to review and compare textbooks and course materials in their discipline area without the time, cost, and environmental impact of mailing print examination copies. For further details, contact your *i*Learning Sales Specialist or visit www.coursesmart.com.

Instructor's Resources for Principles of Macroeconomics, Fourth Canadian Edition

- **Instructor's Manual** This manual is extremely useful for all teachers, but especially for those new to the job. It offers suggestions for using the Test Bank and the Economic Naturalist cases. It supplies sample syllabi with assignments, sample exams, and supplemental material. For each chapter, it provides an overview, an outline, teaching objectives, additional Economic Naturalist discussion questions, answers to textbook questions and problems, homework assignments with answers, and sample quizzes with answers.
- **Computerized Test Banks** The test banks (micro and macro) updated by David Sabiston of Mount Royal University ensure maximum flexibility in test preparation, including the reconfiguring of graphing exercises. The test banks contain more than 5000 multiple-choice questions categorized by Learning Objective, Learning Level (knowledge, comprehension, application, analysis), Type (graph, calculation, word problem), and Source (textbook, Web, unique).
- **PowerPoint Slides** Rafat Alam of Grant MacEwan University has updated this package of dynamic slides of the important illustrations in the textbook.

ACKNOWLEDGMENTS

The authors want to thank, first and foremost, James Booty, our Sponsoring Editor, and Daphne Scriabin, our Developmental Editor. The entire team at McGraw-Hill Ryerson deserves credit for keeping the project moving in a timely fashion. And we are grateful for the outstanding work of the McGraw-Hill Ryerson editorial and production teams.

We would like to acknowledge the role played by Mara Storey in updating data for this edition. We are extremely indebted to Teresa Cyrus, Dalhousie University, for the close reading and perceptive comments provided in her technical reviews of the manuscript. We also thank the following teachers and colleagues, whose thorough reviews and thoughtful suggestions led to innumerable substantive improvements:

Khyati Antani, Humber College

Iris Mei Sze Au, University of Toronto

Ron Bianchi, Vanier College

Menouar Boulahfa, Dawson College

Tatjana Brkic, Red River College

Natalya Brown, Nipissing University

Ergete Ferede, Grant MacEwan University

Bruce Hammond, Fanshawe College

Rashid Khan, McMaster University

Michael Leonard, Kwantlen Polytechnic University

Anthony Myatt, University of New Brunswick

C Fiifi Odoom, Douglas College

Geoffrey Prince, Centennial College

Harry Sackey, Vancouver Island University

Greg Tkacz, St. Francis Xavier University

Mary Ann Vaughan, University of Waterloo

Wahida Yasmeen, St. Francis Xavier University

Andrew Wong, University of Alberta

DEDICATION

For Ellen   R. H. F.
For Anna   B. S. B.
For Molly   L. S. O.
For Anna, Nathan, and Thomas, in memory of Carmelita   M. L. C.
For Kathleen and Vera, in memory of Ken   B. K. M.

PART 1

INTRODUCTION

How many students are there in your economics class? Why has the average class size in Canadian universities increased over the last twenty years?

Why does global fossil fuel consumption continue to increase? What policies might be effective in dealing with its implications for the atmosphere's concentration of CO_2 and the resultant global climate change?

Why were summer jobs so much easier to get in 2008—before the financial crisis and recession—than they were a year or two later? What determines the ups and downs of the unemployment rate?

To answer these questions, and many others, you need to know something about economics. And as a discipline of thought, economics is both as old as the hills and as young as last minute's newsflash. Human societies have always depended on a division of labour to produce the goods and services needed to sustain life, and for almost as long people have tried to figure out how the allocation of tasks works and how it could be made to work better. In today's global economy, the range of commodities, the diversity of jobs necessary to produce them, and the complexity of mechanisms of coordination that make our division of labour work are massively more complicated than they were in caveman days. But the same big questions are always there. How can we explain how much is produced and who gets what share? Can we increase total production and improve the division of that output?

Because societies have changed, economics has evolved over time. This text discusses some ideas that have been around for a long time, because the problems they address have long been with us. It also discusses some concepts that are relatively new, because the world has new problems and because some problems have only recently been solved. As an academic discipline, economics is both a subject matter and a *way of thinking* about the world. Over many years, economists have developed principles and models that are useful for understanding a wide range of situations, and the range of issues analyzed by economists has grown enormously. Economic analysis helps us understand practical problems with immediate impacts on our living standards (such as changes in rents and the real estate market) and complex issues with long-term impacts on the world's ecology (such as trends in pollution and greenhouse gas emissions). A major objective of this book is to help you learn these principles and models and how to apply them to a variety of issues.

The three chapters of Part I introduce the subject matter of economics, and demonstrate how economists use models to clarify the essentials of a situation. Chapter 1 provides an overview of what economics is all about and shows that comparing the cost and benefit of choices is a useful approach to economic decision making. Chapter 2 analyzes specialization among individuals in the production of goods and services. A high degree of specialization requires not only trade but also the widespread use of money, prices, and markets, which can be illustrated with the circular flow of income and expenditure. Finally, Chapter 3 presents an overview of the model of supply and demand, perhaps the best-known model in economics.

CHAPTER 1
Why Study Economics?

LEARNING OBJECTIVES

When you have completed this chapter, you will be able to

LO1 Define economics, microeconomics, and macroeconomics.

LO2 Identify John Maynard Keynes, Alfred Marshall, and Adam Smith, and state briefly the influence each of them had on economics.

LO3 State and explain the problem of scarcity and its relation to opportunity cost.

LO4 Explain how a rational decision maker applies the cost–benefit principle.

LO5 State how three pitfalls can undermine rational economic decisions.

LO6 Explain how data are used to evaluate economic theories.

LO7 Distinguish positive economics from welfare economics.

LO8 Define an economic naturalist.

We begin this chapter by explaining the subject matter and characteristics of economics. We include a discussion of the evaluation of economic theories. The organizing idea of this chapter is the cost–benefit principle. This principle will help you understand and explain many patterns of behaviour you observe in the world around you. Understanding the principle can help you avoid three pitfalls that can plague decision makers in everyday life. We will identify and explain these pitfalls. Chapter 1 concludes with a discussion of economic naturalism and basic ways of organizing economic activity. Economic naturalism is a term that indicates an ability to use basic economics to help make sense of observations we encounter in everyday life.

1.1 ECONOMICS AS A SUBJECT

Because humans are curious, people have been trying to explain what makes the economy work for a very long time. The "origins" of economics as a system of thought are thus lost in antiquity. Nevertheless, one of the first widely-accepted definitions of economics was provided by the British economist Lionel Robbins back in 1932: "Economics is the science which studies human behaviour as a relationship between given ends and scarce means which have alternative uses."[1]

economics the study of how people make choices under conditions of scarcity and the results of those choices for society

This definition was attractive in part because it was broad. A similar definition of **economics** would be, "the study of how people make choices under conditions of scarcity and the results of those choices for society." Both this and Robbins's definition refer to scarcity, which simply means that choices among alternatives are necessary. If one chooses to purchase a motorcycle, the same funds cannot be used to pay for a holiday in Europe. A student who enrols for a course and wants to attend lectures cannot take a job during class times. The idea that choices among mutually exclusive alternatives are very often necessary is central to economics, especially microeconomics, the branch of economics that dominated at the time Robbins formulated his definition.

---

1   Lionel Robbins, *An Essay on the Nature and Significance of Economic Science*, 2nd ed. (London: Macmillan, 1940).

ECONOMICS: MICRO AND MACRO

Present-day economics has two main branches: microeconomics and macroeconomics. Economists use the term **microeconomics** to describe the study of choices individuals make under scarcity and the implications of these choices for the behaviour of prices and quantities in individual markets. **Macroeconomics**, by contrast, is the study of the performance of national economies and of the policies that governments use to try to affect that performance. Macroeconomics tries to understand the determinants of such things as the level of national output, the unemployment rate, and the inflation rate. This text will deal somewhat with microeconomics for Chapters 1 to 3, but exclusively with macroeconomics from Chapters 4 to 16.

Until the mid-1930s, there was no widely recognized distinction between macroeconomics and microeconomics. For a remarkably long time, the nineteenth-century textbook, *Principles of Economics* (1890), by **Alfred Marshall**, dominated the teaching of economics.[2] Marshall's influence on microeconomics continues to the present day. Much of the analysis in Chapter 3 of this textbook can be traced to the work of Marshall.

Macroeconomics as we know it today emerged with the publication of **John Maynard Keynes**'s *The General Theory of Employment, Interest, and Money* in 1936, which provided a new framework for thinking about the Great Depression of the 1930s. During the 1930s, previously accepted theories could not satisfactorily explain why many of the leading capitalist economies failed to recover from depressed output and high unemployment. Macroeconomics thus started to develop as a main branch of economics in response to a widespread perception that new ways of thinking about the economy as a whole were needed.

At the introductory level in universities and colleges, students typically study macroeconomics in one term (using this text or another like it) and microeconomics in another term (using the companion text). If they go on to major in economics, students will take additional core courses in microeconomic theory and macroeconomic theory at a more advanced level, courses in quantitative methods such as mathematics and statistics for economics, and a variety of courses in fields such as public finance, labour economics, health economics, international trade, international finance, development economics, environmental economics, money and banking, industrial organization, urban economics, or history of economic thought. Some fields such as health economics and environment economics make much use of microeconomic theory, whereas other fields such as international finance and money and banking tend to make more use of macroeconomic theory.

ECONOMICS AS A SOCIAL SCIENCE

Economists have long been fond of the expression, "economics is the queen of the social sciences." On the one hand, the expression recognizes that economics belongs to a group of disciplines such as political science, sociology, psychology, human geography, and history that study individual and collective aspects of human behaviour. The subject matter that is the focus of each of these disciplines is different—economics is the study of the economy (the production and distribution of goods and services) whereas sociology, for example, is the study of society—but they overlap. Economists learn from and contribute to the other social sciences.

On the other hand, the expression "economics is the queen of the social sciences," contains the controversial suggestion that economics stands above the other social sciences in that, say, its methods are more rigorous and its findings more reliable than those of other social sciences. Whether or not economics should be regarded as the queen of the social sciences aside, it is widely accepted that economics differs from other social sciences for more reasons than just its subject matter.

microeconomics the study of individual choices under scarcity and the implications of these choices for the behaviour of prices and quantities in individual markets

macroeconomics the study of the performance of national economies and the policies that governments use to try to improve that performance

Alfred Marshall (1842–1924) an economist of the nineteenth and early twentieth centuries who published *Principles of Economics* (1890) and whose influence on economics continues to this day

John Maynard Keynes (pronounced "Kains") (1883–1946), a British economist whose *The General Theory of Employment, Interest and Money* (1936) is widely regarded as the seminal work in modern macroeconomics

---

2 You can read five of the six books of Alfred Marshall's *Principles of Economics* online at http://socserv2. socsci.mcmaster.ca/~econ/ugcm/3ll3/marshall/prin/index.html.

One distinguishing feature of economics as a social science is that economic theories are often expressed as abstract models. Indeed, two years after the publication of his *The General Theory of Employment, Interest and Money*, John Maynard Keynes described economics as a "science of thinking in terms of models joined to the art of choosing models that are relevant to the contemporary world."[3]

The term *model* is used to express the idea that thinking clearly about the economy involves abstracting from unnecessary detail—that is, selecting key features of reality to focus on, and ignoring the rest. We need to do this because our minds simply cannot keep track of all possible bits of information, and only some of it is important. When we go to the supermarket, for example, there is music on the public address system, but does that determine what we buy? To analyze grocery sales, economists will typically focus on the prices and quantities of commodities purchased, because economists assume that these are the really crucial variables. Models, in other words, are based upon assumptions. Sometimes models are expressed with mathematical equations (for example, when presented in specialized publications for academic economists), but in introductory textbooks such as this one the models are mostly expressed with a combination of words, tables, and graphs.[4] An **economic model** can be defined as a representation of economic reality that highlights particular variables and the relationships among them.

In addition to the frequent use of abstract models to express theories, another distinguishing feature of economics has been the tendency of economists to assume in their theories that human beings are rational. In economics, a **rational decision maker** has clear objectives and behaves logically to achieve those objectives.

In most market situations, this is taken to mean that the decision maker is self-interested and acts to realize his or her self-interest.[5] This self-interest assumption can be found in *The Wealth of Nations*, probably the most influential economics book ever written, wherein **Adam Smith** famously declared that, "It is not from the benevolence of the butcher, the brewer, or the baker that we expect our dinner, but from their regard to their own interest."[6]

Although economists tend to be more inclined than other social scientists to assume rational decision making, economists generally recognize that the assumption is not always realistic and have explored the consequences of making other assumptions about human behaviour in certain settings. Indeed, while most professors of economics in countries such as Canada and the United States follow a broadly similar approach to their subject, economics is like other social sciences in having different approaches or schools of thought. These schools of thought differ according to the assumptions, such as the rational decision-making assumption, that their theories are most likely to employ.[7] Economists who tend to focus on situations in which economic decision making is less than fully rational have promoted a relatively new and growing approach known as behavioural economics.[8] Research by behavioural economists is reflected, for example, in Section 1.3 later in this chapter. The approach followed by Alfred Marshall, with more of a focus on rational decision making, has been described as neoclassical economics. John Maynard Keynes, whose theories we will cover in later chapters, took a broader view, arguing that investment was often motivated by "animal spirits," and that in negotiating wages workers were often concerned with fairness.

economic model a representation of economic reality that highlights particular variables and the relationships among them

rational decision maker someone with clear objectives who behaves logically to achieve those objectives

Adam Smith (1723–1790) Scottish economist who wrote *The Wealth of Nations* (1776), probably the most influential economics book ever written

---

3 Quoted in Robert Skidelsky, *Keynes: The Return of the Master* (Toronto: Penguin Canada, 2009), p. 58.

4 An example of a specialized publication for academic economists is the *Canadian Journal of Economics*.

5 Note that we are careful not to say that individuals always are purely self-interested. Many important issues (such as the raising of children) cannot plausibly be analyzed solely with reference to purely self-interested behaviour.

6 Adam Smith, *The Wealth of Nations* (New York: Random House, 1969 [original 1776]), Book 1 Chapter II, p. 14. Also found at http://socserv.mcmaster.ca/~econ/ugcm/3ll3/smith/wealth/wealbk01.

7 A common way for economics students to learn about schools of economics is to study the history of economic thought by taking courses in it or by reading books such as Robert Heilbroner, *The Worldly Philosophers: The Lives, Times, and Ideas of the Great Economic Thinkers* 7th edition (New York: Touchstone, 1999).

8 For numerous microeconomic issues for which behavioural economists depart from the rational decision-making assumption, see, for example, Richard Thaler and Cass Sunstein, *Nudge: Improving Decisions About Health, Wealth, and Happiness* (New Haven, Connecticut: Yale University Press, 2008).

RECAP

ECONOMICS AS A SUBJECT

Economics is the study of the production, exchange, and distribution of goods and services. Economics includes both microeconomics and macroeconomics. **Microeconomics** studies individual choices in individual markets and the consequences of that behaviour, especially at the level of particular markets or industries. **Macroeconomics**, by contrast, studies the performance of national economies and of the policies that governments use to try to affect that performance.

Three particularly important figures in the history of economics are Adam Smith (1723–1790), the author of the enormously influential *The Wealth of Nations* (1776); Alfred Marshall (1842–1924), whose *Principles of Economics* (1890) greatly contributed to the spread of neoclassical microeconomics throughout the English-speaking world; and John Maynard Keynes (1883–1946), whose *The General Theory of Employment, Interest and Money* (1936) revolutionized thinking about macroeconomics.

Economics is a social science and as such belongs to a group of disciplines including political science, sociology, and psychology. One distinguishing feature of economics as a social science is that economic theories are often expressed as abstract models. Another distinguishing feature has been the greater tendency of economists over other social scientists to make the assumption that human beings are rational—that is, have clear objectives and behave logically to achieve them. But economists today are more aware than in Alfred Marshall's day of situations for which the assumption of rational decision making may not be the most suitable.

1.2 SCARCITY, RATIONALITY, AND THE COST-BENEFIT PRINCIPLE

If we could always have whatever we wanted, for free, right now, we would never have to choose—all we would ever have to say is "more please," and we would get it. Unfortunately, the real world is not like that. Most things have a cost in time or money or other resources, all of which we have in only limited amounts. As we noted earlier, scarcity means that we have to make choices; having more of one item means choosing less of another.

That such trade-offs are widespread and important is a central problem of economics. We can call this the **scarcity problem**, because it is the simple fact of scarcity that makes trade-offs necessary. Another name for the scarcity problem might be the "no-free-lunch" idea, which comes from the observation that even a lunch that is given to you takes time to eat—time you could have spent doing other useful things.

The Scarcity Problem: The resources available to us, including time, are limited. Scarcity means that we have to make choices—having more of one good thing usually means having less of another.

SCARCITY PROBLEM

Trade-offs require that choices be made. If people have to make economic choices because resources are scarce, how will they make their choices? Microeconomics commonly assumes that decision makers act rationally. Economic decision makers, it is often assumed, will compare costs and benefits and will take an action only if the benefits to them exceed its costs to them. More precisely, a rational decision maker will take an economic action if, and only if, the extra benefits from taking the action are greater than the extra costs. We call this statement the **cost–benefit principle**. It is one of the core principles of economics.

The Cost-Benefit Principle: A rational decision maker will take an economic action if, and only if, the extra benefits from taking the action are greater than the extra costs.

COST–BENEFIT PRINCIPLE

APPLYING THE COST–BENEFIT PRINCIPLE

The cost–benefit principle is a fundamental tool for the study of how rational people make choices. Often the major difficulty in applying the cost–benefit principle is coming up with reasonable measures of all the relevant benefits and costs, especially of the costs. To illustrate how the cost–benefit principle is applied, we begin with a very simple example that puts you in the role of the decision maker.

EXAMPLE **1.1**

Will you walk downtown to save $10 on a $25 computer game?

Imagine you are about to buy a $25 computer game at the nearby campus store when a friend tells you that the same game is on sale at a downtown store for only $15. If the downtown store is a 30-minute trip away, where will you buy the game?

Application of the cost–benefit principle leads to the prediction that you will buy the computer game downtown if the benefit of doing so exceeds the cost. The benefit of taking any action is the dollar value of everything you gain by taking it. Here, the benefit of buying downtown is exactly $10, since that is the amount you will save on the purchase price of the game. The cost of taking any action is the dollar value of everything you give up by taking it. Here, the cost of buying downtown is the dollar value of the time and trouble of making the trip. But how do we estimate that dollar value?

One way is to perform the following hypothetical action. Imagine that a stranger has offered to pay you to do an errand that involves the same trip downtown (perhaps to drop off a letter for her at the post office). If she offered you a payment of, say, $100, would you accept? If so, we know that your cost of walking downtown and back must be less than $100. Now imagine her offer being reduced in small increments until you finally refuse the last offer. For example, if you agree to walk downtown and back for $9 but not for $8.99, then your perceived cost of making the trip is $9. Thus, an economist applying the cost–benefit principle would predict that you would buy the game downtown, because the $10 you save (your benefit) is greater than your $9 cost of making the trip. On the other hand, suppose that your cost of making the trip is greater than $10. In that case, the cost–benefit principle predicts that you would buy the game from the nearby campus store.

Note that if the time it would take to walk downtown and back has a value to you of more than $10, it is perfectly rational to decide *not* to save $10 on the computer game. Economists know that money isn't everything. But in order to compare the sizes of benefits and costs, we need some common unit of measurement. Economists often use dollar values (that is, in economies such as Canada's where the dollar is the currency) to measure costs and benefits because they are a convenient and comparable unit. This, however, does not imply that we will always choose the alternative that costs the least or saves the most money.

OPPORTUNITY COST

Suppose, for example, that the time required for the trip downtown is the only time you have left to study for a difficult test the next day. Or suppose you are watching one of your favourite movies, or that you are tired and would love to take a short nap. In such cases, we say that the **opportunity cost** of making the trip, the value of what you must sacrifice to walk downtown and back, is high and you are more likely to decide against making the trip.

In this example, if watching the last hour of the movie is the most valuable opportunity that conflicts with the trip downtown, the opportunity cost of making the trip is the dollar value you place on pursuing that opportunity—that is, the largest amount you would be willing to pay to avoid missing the end of the movie. Note that the opportunity cost of making the trip is not the combined value of *all* possible activities you could have

opportunity cost the value of the next-best alternative that must be foregone in order to undertake an activity pursued, but only the value of your *best* alternative, the one you would have chosen had you not made the trip.

Notice that opportunity costs can be either *explicit* or *implicit*. An explicit opportunity cost requires an outlay or payment. For example, a bus fare is an *explicit* opportunity cost. An implicit opportunity cost does not involve an actual payment. If it uses up your time to make a trip downtown and you would pay some amount to avoid the trip, then the trip downtown has an implicit opportunity cost of that amount even though you do not actually pay out the cash. The total opportunity cost of any action is the sum of explicit and implicit opportunity costs.

Throughout the text we will pose exercises like the one that follows. You will find that pausing to answer them will help you to master key concepts in economics. Because doing these exercises is not very costly, the cost–benefit principle indicates that it is well worth your while to do them!

You would again save $10 by buying the game downtown rather than at the campus store, but your cost of making the trip is now $12, not $9. Where does the cost–benefit principle predict that you will buy the game?

EXERCISE 1.1

RECAP

SCARCITY, RATIONALITY, AND THE COST-BENEFIT PRINCIPLE

The resources available to us, including time, are limited. Scarcity means that we have to make choices—having more of one good thing usually means having less of another. Cost-benefit analysis is an approach to making choices, and the cost-benefit principle can help us predict the choices made by economic decision makers.

The cost-benefit principle holds that a rational decision maker will take an economic action if, and only if, the extra benefits from taking the action are greater than the extra costs. Applying the cost-benefit principle is facilitated by measuring all benefits and costs in a common monetary unit, such as dollars. The measurement of all relevant costs is aided by the concept of opportunity cost. The opportunity cost of an activity is the value of the next-best alternative that must be foregone to perform the activity.

1.3 THREE IMPORTANT DECISION PITFALLS

Rational people will apply the cost–benefit principle most of the time, although probably in an intuitive and approximate way, rather than through explicit and precise calculation. Knowing that rational people tend to compare costs and benefits enables economists to predict their likely behaviour. Yet researchers have identified situations in which people tend to apply the cost–benefit principle inconsistently. People sometimes tend to ignore certain costs that are relevant to a decision at hand, for example, and sometimes they are influenced by costs that are irrelevant.

Three of the most commonly encountered and important pitfalls concern opportunity costs, sunk costs, and the difference between average and marginal costs. In these situations, the cost–benefit principle may not predict behaviour accurately, but it proves helpful in another way, by identifying specific strategies for avoiding bad decisions. We will examine these three important decision pitfalls in this section. Knowing these pitfalls will help you to deepen your understanding of what economists mean by rational behaviour.[9]

---

9 The examples in this section are inspired by the pioneering behavioural economics research of Daniel Kahneman and the late Amos Tversky. Kahneman was awarded the 2002 Nobel Prize in economics for his achievements in integrating insights from psychology into economics.

PITFALL 1: IGNORING OPPORTUNITY COSTS

Sherlock Holmes, Arthur Conan Doyle's legendary detective, was successful because he saw details that most others overlooked. In *Silver Blaze*, Holmes is called on to investigate the theft of an expensive racehorse from its stable. A Scotland Yard inspector assigned to the case asks Holmes whether some particular aspect of the crime required further study. "Yes," Holmes replies, and describes "the curious incident of the dog in the nighttime." "The dog did nothing in the nighttime," responds the puzzled inspector. But, as Holmes realized, that was precisely the problem. The watchdog's failure to bark when Silver Blaze was stolen meant that the watchdog knew the thief. This clue substantially reduced the number of suspects and eventually led to the thief's apprehension.

Just as we often don't notice when a dog fails to bark, many of us tend to overlook the implicit value of activities that fail to happen. As discussed earlier, however, intelligent decisions require taking the value of foregone opportunities into account. What is not stated may be as important as what is explicitly stated.

Opportunity costs are like dogs that fail to bark in the night.

The opportunity cost of an activity, once again, is the value of all that must be foregone in order to engage in that activity. If buying a computer game downtown means not watching the last hour of a movie, then the value to you of watching the end of the movie is an implicit cost of the trip. Many people make flawed decisions because they tend to ignore the value of such foregone opportunities. To avoid overlooking implicit costs, economists often translate questions like, "Should I walk downtown?" into ones like, "Will I be better off if I walk downtown or watch the end of the movie?"

As the next example makes clear, even people who seem to know that they should weigh the pros and cons of the actions they are contemplating sometimes don't have a clear sense of how to measure the relevant costs and benefits.

EXAMPLE 1.2

Will you walk downtown to save $10 on a $1,020 laptop computer?

You are about to buy a $1,020 netbook computer at the nearby campus store when a friend tells you that the same computer is on sale at a downtown store for only $1,010. If the downtown store is half an hour's walk away, where will you, as a rational decision maker, buy the computer?

Assuming that the netbook is light enough to carry without effort, the structure of this example is exactly the same as that of the earlier example about where to buy the computer game—the only difference is that the price of the netbook is dramatically higher than the price of the computer game. As before, the benefit of buying downtown is the dollar amount you'll save, namely, $10. And since it's exactly the same trip, its cost also must be the same as before. So if you are perfectly rational, you will make the same decision in both cases. Yet when real people are asked what they would do in these situations, the overwhelming majority says they would walk downtown to buy the game but buy the netbook at the campus store. When asked to explain, most of them say something like, the trip was worth it for the game because you save 40 percent, but not worth it for the netbook because you save only $10 out of $1,020.

This is faulty reasoning. The benefit of the trip downtown is not the proportion you save on the original price. Rather, it is the absolute dollar amount you save. Since the benefit of walking downtown to buy the netbook is $10, exactly the same as for the computer game, and since the cost of the trip must also be the same in both cases, the net benefit from making both trips must be exactly the same. And that means that a rational decision maker would make the same decision in both cases. Yet, as noted, most people choose differently.

EXERCISE 1.2   **For someone living in Toronto, which of the following is more valuable, all else equal: saving $100 on a $2,000 plane ticket to Tokyo or saving $90 on a $500 plane ticket to Ottawa?**

The pattern of faulty reasoning in the decision just discussed is one of several decision pitfalls to which people are prone. In the discussion that follows, we will identify two additional decision pitfalls. In some cases, people ignore costs or benefits that they ought to take into account, while on other occasions they are influenced by costs or benefits that are irrelevant.

PITFALL 2: FAILURE TO IGNORE SUNK COSTS

Pitfall one occurs when people ignore opportunity costs. In another common pitfall, the opposite is true: people are influenced by costs that really are not opportunity costs. *The only costs that are relevant to a decision about whether to take an action are the costs that we can avoid by not taking the action.* As a practical matter, however, many decision makers appear to be influenced by **sunk costs**—costs that are beyond recovery at the moment a decision is made. For example, money spent on a nontransferable, nonrefundable airline ticket is a sunk cost.

sunk cost a cost that is beyond recovery at the moment a decision is made

Because sunk costs must be borne *whether or not an action is taken,* they are irrelevant to a rational decision of whether to take the action. Suppose, for example, that you have invested $300,000 in a small manufacturing shop that is still incomplete and worthless in its current state. Things have not gone well, and it will cost another $290,000 to finish the job. But due to a new technological development, you could start a new, equally valuable manufacturing shop from scratch for only $275,000. If one of the two options—finishing off the original shop or starting a new shop from scratch—is rational, which one is it? The key to this decision is that the original $300,000 has already been spent. That money is gone; it is a sunk cost. For the same return, you can either invest an additional $290,000 or invest an additional $275,000. Starting a new shop from scratch is the rational choice.

Indian Summer, an Indian restaurant in Northern Ontario, offers an all-you-can-eat lunch buffet for $9.99. Customers pay $9.99, and no matter how many times they refill their plates there is no additional charge. One day, as a goodwill gesture, the owner of the restaurant tells 10 randomly selected customers that their lunches are on the house. The remaining customers pay the usual price. If all diners are rational, will there be any difference in the average quantity of food consumed by people in these two groups?

EXERCISE 1.3

PITFALL 3: FAILURE TO UNDERSTAND THE AVERAGE-MARGINAL DISTINCTION

As we have seen, rational economic decisions take proper account of opportunity costs. Because sunk costs are not opportunity costs, sunk costs are irrelevant to economic decisions and are not counted when the cost–benefit principle is applied. Further, accurate application of the cost–benefit principle is not possible if marginal costs and benefits are confused with average costs and benefits.

The cost–benefit framework emphasizes that the only relevant costs and benefits in a rational decision about whether to change the amount of an activity are *marginal costs* and *benefits*. Economists define the **marginal cost** of an activity as the increase in total cost that results from carrying out one additional unit of the activity. Similarly, the **marginal benefit** of an activity is the increase in total benefit that results from carrying out one more unit of the activity. In many contexts, however, people seem more inclined to compare **average costs** and **average benefits**—total cost or benefit per unit of activity.

marginal cost the increase in total cost that results from carrying out one additional unit of an activity

marginal benefit the increase in total benefit that results from carrying out one more unit of an activity

To see the importance of the average-marginal distinction, suppose that you are a sales manager in charge of deciding whether to assign a newly hired salesperson to one sales region or another. Suppose also that you wish to assign the new salesperson in a way that maximizes sales. What data would help you to make your decision? A sales manager not familiar with the average-marginal distinction might be satisfied with obtaining data

average cost total cost per unit of activity

average benefit total benefit per unit of activity

on average sales per salesperson in the two regions. The sales manager might then assign the new salesperson to the region where sales per salesperson (i.e., average sales) are highest. But it is not necessarily the case that the region with higher average sales is the region where an additional salesperson will add the most to total sales. In fact, average sales are not useful in determining where to send the new salesperson. Perhaps the new salesperson will add little to total sales in the region with higher average sales because the region is nearly saturated. If the region with lower average sales in underserved, a new salesperson in that region might significantly increase total sales. The relevant question concerns how much the new salesperson will add to total sales in one region versus another. The average sales per salesperson in each of the two regions are not relevant.

E X E R C I S E   1 . 4   **The average-marginal distinction is also relevant to understanding income tax systems. Suppose that for incomes up to $9,999 the marginal income tax is zero. If your income reaches $10,000, however, your marginal income tax rate becomes 15 percent. How much tax would you pay if your income is $10,000? What would be your average income tax rate (income tax paid/income)?**

COST-
BENEFIT

The conclusion that some costs, especially marginal costs and opportunity costs, are important while others, like sunk costs and average costs, are irrelevant to economic decisions is implicit in our original explanation of the *cost–benefit principle* (an action should be taken if, and only if, the extra benefits of taking it exceed the extra costs). Yet the pitfalls of (1) ignoring opportunity costs, (2) considering sunk costs, and (3) confusing average with marginal cost are so important that we enumerate them separately. As a result, a core principle worthy of repeated emphasis emerges:

The Principle of Relevant Costs: In considering whether to produce or consume more of a good, what matters is the cost of one more unit (marginal cost).

RELEVANT
COSTS

> RECAP ↑
>
> ### THREE IMPORTANT PITFALLS
>
> 1. **The pitfall of ignoring opportunity costs.** When performing a cost–benefit analysis of an action, it is important to account for the full opportunity cost of the action. The opportunity cost of an action is the value of the next best alternative that is foregone by taking the action.
>
> 2. **The pitfall of not ignoring sunk costs.** When deciding whether to perform an action, it is important to ignore sunk costs—costs that cannot be avoided even if the action is not taken. Even though a ticket to a game may have cost $30, if you have already bought it and cannot sell it to anyone else the $30 is a sunk cost. If your decision to attend the game is based entirely on the cost–benefit principle, you will ignore the sunk cost.
>
> 3. **The pitfall of using average instead of marginal costs and benefits.** Decision makers often have ready information about the total cost and benefit of an activity, and from these it is easy to calculate the activity's average cost and benefit. However, it is a mistake to increase an activity simply because its average benefit is greater than its average cost. Likewise, it is a mistake to decrease an activity simply because its average benefit is less than its average cost. The cost–benefit principle states that total benefit can be increased by increasing the amount of an activity if, and only if, the benefit of one more unit of the activity is greater than its cost. Likewise, total benefit can be increased by decreasing the activity if, and only if, its *marginal* benefit is less than its *marginal* cost.

1.4 ECONOMIC THEORIES AND THEIR EVALUATION

In economics, how do we know if a theory is useful? How do we evaluate a theory? Should we be concerned about the realism of the assumptions behind our theories?

ALL ELSE EQUAL

In the real world, many things can happen at the same time for many different reasons; therefore, one concept that is absolutely essential in evaluating theories is that of "all other conditions being held constant." The Latin expression for "all else equal" is *ceteris paribus*. Although English-speaking economists these days typically know only a few Latin expressions, nearly all of them know *ceteris paribus*. You should, too.

ceteris paribus a Latin phrase meaning "all else equal"

When economists or other social scientists make predictions, these are seldom unconditional. For example, in our discussions earlier in this chapter of whether to go downtown in order to save money on the purchase of a computer game or a computer, we never mentioned the weather. In the real world, a sudden blizzard or thunderstorm is likely to change people's decisions, but implicitly we assumed that the weather did not change. Typically, our prediction is all else being equal, which is similar to the prediction you were asked about in Exercise 1.1. In that exercise, the cost of a trip downtown increased from $9 to $12, and you were asked for a prediction based on the cost–benefit principle of where you would buy the computer game. In essence, you were asked to say what would happen if one condition (the cost of a trip downtown) changed while other relevant conditions stayed the same. Scientific theories are generally like this; they predict what will happen if there is change in one variable (or possibly a few variables) while all other variables stay the same.

THE REALISM OF ASSUMPTIONS

Many newcomers to economics are concerned with the realism of the assumptions employed in economics. Some of these concerns are more justified than others. For example, people differ in terms of how well their economic decisions can be explained by assuming that they pursue the cost–benefit principle. Someone whose own decisions seem very haphazard compared to the decision making described in Example 1.1 above might be inclined to question the realism of employing the cost–benefit principle for predicting economic behaviour.

Example 1.1, however, was only intended to explain how cost–benefit calculations work. It was framed in terms of an individual decision maker in order to keep matters simple, but in economics we are typically not concerned with predicting the decisions of one specific person. Rather, we are usually interested in predicting outcomes that involve decisions by large groups of people. In macroeconomics, for example, we might be interested in the impact on overall spending in the Canadian economy of a cut to the GST. Such spending is based upon the decisions of millions of people. Not everyone will change their spending because of a cut to the GST, but many will. In a case such as this, the assumption that people apply the cost–benefit principle is less than fully realistic when applied to some of the people, but it can still lead to successful predictions.

On the other hand, some concerns about the realism of assumptions in economics about human behaviour are certainly justified. For example, the influential economists George Akerlof and Robert Shiller have argued that many aspects of the global financial crisis and recession of 2008–2009 are best explained by recognizing some of the ways in which the behaviour of people deviated from strict rationality in years leading up to the crisis.[10]

10 See George Akerlof and Robert Shiller, *Animal Spirits: How Human Psychology Drives the Economy, and Why It Matters for Global Capitalism* (Princeton, N.J.: Princeton University Press, 2009).

Newcomers to economics are sometimes concerned that economic models are not "realistic." But a model is a bit like a map, and no map can possibly replicate an area in all details. Maps necessarily abstract from reality in order to highlight the most important features of concern to the users of the map, and different maps are useful for different purposes (e.g., you may want a map marked with bicycle routes for a cycling vacation, but the public works department needs a map that marks underground wiring and pipes). Model builders ignore influences that they consider relatively unimportant, in order to concentrate attention on the most important influences.

Physicists, for example, who want to predict how quickly a rock dropped from the top of a tower will hit the ground can do a fairly good job even if they ignore (i.e., assume away) the influence of air resistance. Even though the physicist knows perfectly well that air resistance has an influence, it is small enough to be ignored given the force of gravity and the density of a rock, and it makes the calculations much simpler. But if the same physicists were asked how long it would take a feather to fall to the ground, they would know that air resistance *will* make a difference in that case and must be taken into consideration. Choosing the right assumptions makes the difference between a model that performs well and one that does not. Because different assumptions often lead to different conclusions, you should always examine the assumptions upon which economic models are based.

POSITIVE ECONOMICS, WELFARE ECONOMICS, AND EFFICIENCY

Why do people study economics? There is no single answer. For some people, the motivation is simply to understand how the economy works. But others may study economics because they want to use their understanding of economic processes in order to change economic outcomes, which implies that they should have some way to evaluate which outcomes are "better."

Our discussion of economic theory has emphasized the use of economics for prediction. Economic theories that are used to make predictions are examples of *positive economics*. **Positive economics** has two dimensions. First, it offers cause-and-effect explanations of economic relationships. Second, positive economics has an empirical aspect. In principle, data can be used to confirm or refute propositions, or hypotheses, that emerge from positive economics. In principle, data can also be used to measure the magnitude of effects predicted by positive economics; for example, data on overall spending in the economy can be used to evaluate whether a cut in the GST had the impact predicted by an economic model.

While economics shares with physics and other natural sciences the use of theory for predictive purposes, there is more to economics than prediction. A very substantial portion of textbook microeconomics consists of what is known as *welfare economics*. **Welfare economics** is concerned not only with prediction or facts, but it also involves the evaluation of economic outcomes or situations according to ethical or value standards. While it may use many of the same assumptions and models as positive economics, welfare economics is not purely concerned with prediction. It is also concerned with judging whether some outcomes or situations are superior to or better than others. To judge the optimality of outcomes or situations, ethical or value standards must be used. A key argument in favour of welfare economics is that economic policy choices must be made, and it is reasonable to expect that better decisions will be made if costs and benefits of the decision are systematically tallied and evaluated than if decisions are simply made according to the whims of policy makers or some other arbitrary process.

To take a microeconomics example of welfare economics, suppose that a new tax is placed on imports of pork products into the Canadian market. Using positive economics, you could make a prediction about the impact of the tax on the prices of pork products, and some other person could evaluate your prediction independent of any standard of ethical evaluation. Using welfare economics, you could draw a conclusion about whether

positive economics
economic analysis offering cause-and-effect explanations of economic relationships; its propositions or hypotheses can, in principle, be confirmed or refuted by data; in principle, data can also be used to measure the magnitude of effects that it predicts

welfare economics
economic analysis that is concerned not only with prediction or facts but also involves the evaluation of economic outcomes or situations according to ethical or value standards (which may be either explicit or implicit)

the new tax makes Canadians better or worse off. But to reach your conclusion, you will need not just to predict the factual result of the application of the tariff. You will also need to use some ethical criteria, at least implicitly. Suppose that you conclude that the new tax will lead to a reduction in the consumption of pork and that this will make Canadians worse off. A vegetarian who believes that pigs are intelligent creatures that should not be eaten by human beings might accept your prediction about the consequences of the tax for Canadian pork consumption but question the part of your conclusion about Canadians being worse off if they consume less pork. Ultimately, the difference comes down to the fact that the two of you are employing different ethical or value standards.

To take a macroeconomics example, suppose that the government is deciding whether to move from a two percent inflation target to a zero percent inflation target. Using positive economics, an economist could make predictions about the consequences of the change in the inflation rate target for economic growth, the unemployment rate, the exchange rate, the inflation rate itself, and so on. But to come to an overall cost–benefit calculation of whether Canadians would be better or worse off as a result of adopting a zero inflation rate target would require the employment of ethical or value standards. Positive economics may give you the prediction that the move to a zero inflation rate target would make some people a bit richer and many more people a bit poorer. But how do you add together the gains of some people with the losses of the others? That necessarily involves the use of ethical or value standards. It is a matter of welfare economics and not a matter of purely positive economics.

Sometimes the term positive economics is contrasted with the term *normative economics*, where normative economics is said to be explicitly concerned with issues of fairness, equity, or ethics. However, this contrast can mislead people into thinking that economics which is not explicitly concerned with issues of fairness, equity, or ethics must be positive economics. But whether economics is positive or not is solely a matter of whether it is restricted to issues of fact or prediction. Economic evaluations and policy statements do not become positive economics just because the ethical or evaluation standards are implicit or hidden or relatively uncontroversial.

One of the most widely used terms in welfare economics is *efficiency*. The use of the term efficiency in welfare economics, however, can easily lead to confusion. In everyday life, statements about efficiency are usually similar to statements in positive economics. For example, the term "fuel efficiency" with respect to an automobile has a straightforward meaning—the distance the automobile can travel for a given amount of fuel. It says nothing about whether or not higher fuel efficiency is better. The term efficiency is sometimes used in this positive sense in economics. For example, one production process might be described as being more cost-efficient than another. This typically means that the monetary cost of achieving a given output is lower with one production process than with the other. But in its most common use in economics, efficiency relates to optimality; that is, what is best. In this use, it is a term of welfare economics. When a professional economist states that one tax is more efficient than another, for example, it is easy for non-economists and novice economists to assume that the statement comes from positive economics. But usually the professional economist is making a welfare economics statement with the term efficiency.

EVIDENCE AND FALLACIES

Whether economists are making predictions as part of purely positive economics or making statements about desirable public policy based on the predictions of positive economics, they must be concerned, as scientists, with evaluating their predictions using evidence. Often this assessment of predictions with evidence will be somewhat casual, involving, say, the comparison of two variables over time. Other times, it will be more formal and will draw upon techniques from the discipline of statistics. The branch of economics known as **econometrics** involves the application of statistical techniques

econometrics a branch of economics that involves the application of statistical techniques to economic data, and the development of statistical techniques for analyzing such data to economic data, and the development of rigorous statistical techniques for analyzing such data.

In making use of evidence, one of the most important logical errors is to mistake correlation for causation. Just because two variables move together or one variable precedes another does not mean that one is the cause of the other. Correlation does not necessarily indicate causation. Although, for example, the United States spends considerably more per capita on health care than Canada does, Canadians have a longer life expectancy than Americans. Does this imply that spending more money on health care reduces life expectancy? Hardly! If two variables move together but are otherwise unrelated, we have a **spurious correlation**. Cause and effect and correlation are two very different things.

Another significant logical mistake is known as the *fallacy of composition*. The fallacy of composition occurs in everyday life when, for example, the assumption is made that if one fan at a sporting event can get a better view by standing up, then all fans at the event will get a better view if they all stand up at once. The statement, "If one farmer harvests a larger crop he will be better off; therefore, if all farmers harvest larger crops, all farmers will be better off," is another example. If all farmers harvest larger crops, prices may decrease by an amount that would more than offset the benefit of larger harvests. What is true for an individual is not necessarily true for an entire group. The statement, "What is good for business is good for the country," provides yet another example. A tax reduction for large corporations may benefit their shareholders, but it does not necessarily follow that the tax reduction is good for everyone else.

The **fallacy of composition**, therefore, occurs if one argues that what is true for a part must also necessarily be true for the whole. It is the mistake of assuming that what is true for a part (such as an individual consumer or firm) is also necessarily true for the whole (such as the whole market or economy). Although the example of the farmer is a microeconomic one, the issue is particularly important in macroeconomics.

spurious correlation a case in which two variables move together but are otherwise unrelated

fallacy of composition the argument that because something is true for a part, it also is necessarily true for the whole

> **RECAP**
>
> ## ECONOMIC THEORIES AND THEIR EVALUATION
>
> Economic predictions are always subject to the *ceteris paribus* (all else equal) qualification.
>
> Not all concerns about the realism of economics models are justified. Economic models that assume rational behaviour can lead to accurate predictions about the behaviour of large groups of people even if some people do not behave rationally. Models in economics or other disciplines cannot be perfectly realistic, but this is no more of a problem than the fact that a map is not a full-scale reproduction of the area it represents. On the other hand, the predictions of models do depend on the assumptions they are based upon, and choosing the right assumptions makes the difference between a model that performs well and one that does not.
>
> Positive economics offers cause-and-effect explanations of economic relationships. In principle, data can be used to confirm or refute propositions or hypotheses that emerge from positive economics. Welfare economics is concerned with the evaluation of economic outcomes or situations and is not strictly limited to predicting what will happen. It is concerned with judging whether some outcomes or situations are superior to or better than others according to ethical or value standards that may be explicit or implicit.
>
> As scientists, economists must be concerned with evaluating their predictions using evidence in the form of data. Formal evaluation of economic theories and predictions typically involves the application of econometrics. In evaluating statistical evidence, it is important to be aware of possible pitfalls such as the fallacy of composition and the argument that a spurious correlation implies cause and effect. Awareness of the fallacy of composition is particularly relevant for the consideration of macroeconomic issues.

1.5 ECONOMIC NATURALISM

With the rudiments of the cost–benefit framework under your belt, you are now in a position to become an **economic naturalist**, someone who uses insights from economics to help make sense of observations from everyday life. People who have studied biology are able to observe and marvel at many details of nature that would otherwise escape their notice. For example, while the novice may see only trees on a walk in the woods in early April, the biology student notices many different species of trees and understands why some are already in leaf while others are still dormant. Likewise, the novice may notice that in some animal species, males are much larger and more impressive in appearance than females, but the biology student knows that that pattern occurs only in species in which males take several mates. Natural selection favours larger males because their greater size helps them to prevail in the often bloody contests among males for access to females. By contrast, males tend to be roughly the same size as females in monogamous species, where there is much less fighting for mates.

In similar fashion, learning key economic principles and models enables us to see the mundane details of ordinary human existence in a new light. Whereas the uninitiated often fail even to notice these details, the economic naturalist not only sees them but becomes actively engaged in the attempt to understand them by using positive economics. Let's consider an example of the type of questions that economic naturalists might pose for themselves.[11]

economic naturalist someone who uses insights from economics to help make sense of observations from everyday life

---

ECONOMIC NATURALIST 1.1

Why are some places littered with beer containers while others are not?

Arriving in the United Kingdom from Nova Scotia in the summer of 2001, a visiting economic naturalist was surprised to see how much the back alleys of British towns were littered with discarded beer cans. Why did the United Kingdom have this problem of littering when Canada did not?

The beer can litter problem has an easy explanation—in the United Kingdom there was no system of deposits on beverage containers, so they were often thrown away after they were emptied, and aluminum cans accumulated at the roadsides and in back alleys. Although aluminum can be recycled, scrap yards did not pay enough per can to make it worthwhile for people to collect them. By contrast, in Canada, due to provincial government container deposit legislation, consumers pay a deposit on beverage containers; even if they do not bother to return

their empties, the cans and bottles they discard in public places are collected and returned for the refund. The deposit system means that discarded bottles and cans have, effectively, a market value, and recovery rates are high, especially for beer bottles, which have recovery rates of about 98 percent in most provinces.[12]

Although littering is neither legally nor ethically defensible, it is influenced by the basic cost–benefit principle. Therefore, public policy to reduce litter has to try to ensure that the benefits to individuals of reducing litter exceed their costs. In the United Kingdom, government policy did not even try to influence that cost–benefit calculation to make it worthwhile to avoid beer-can littering.[13]

---

11 For a large and fascinating collection of economic naturalist examples, see Robert Frank, *The Economic Naturalist: In Search of Explanations for Everyday Enigmas* (New York: Basic Books, 2008).

12 See Clarissa Marowski, "Who Pays What: An Analysis of Beverage Container Recovery and Costs in Canada," 2004–2005, http://www.bottlebill.org/assets/pdfs/legis/canada/2005-WhoPaysWhat.pdf.

13 For the argument that the United Kingdom needs container deposit legislation, see http://litterheroes.co.uk/bottlebill.htm.

1.6 WHAT WILL BE PRODUCED, HOW, AND FOR WHOM?

Every society always has to answer the same basic economic questions: What goods and services will be produced? How much of each? Who will get to consume these goods and services?

For example, food and housing have to be produced if humans are to survive, and all human societies provide people with some entertainment during their hours of leisure. But how much of our limited time and other resources will we devote to building housing, how much to the production of food, and how much to providing entertainment and other goods and services? What techniques will we use to produce each good? Who will do each specific task? Could we reallocate productive resources and produce more output from the same or fewer inputs?

As we will see in subsequent chapters, these questions about *production* are inextricably linked to the basic question of *distribution*: Who will get more and who will get less? For example, what income will the person who stocks shelves in a grocery store earn? How much will the CEO of the grocery chain receive? Will society make provision for those who cannot work; for example, a taxi driver paralyzed in a car accident?

Since each person's income helps determine his or her demand for the goods and services a society produces, the type and amount of goods produced depends on the distribution of incomes. Production and distribution are thus simultaneously determined. But what *distribution* of income would be fair? Economists concerned about *equity* will therefore also ask, could we reallocate rewards so as to produce a fairer distribution of consumption?

ALTERNATIVE METHODS OF ORGANIZING ECONOMIC ACTIVITY

This chapter and the following two chapters, especially Chapter 3, discuss how markets work, because markets play an important role in organizing economic activity in most modern societies. However, there have been, historically, many societies in which markets played a less important role. Consider the economic units of ancient and medieval times. They were, by modern standards, small, isolated, and relatively self-sufficient. For example, Athens, the largest of the city states in ancient Greece, probably occupied an area less than half the size of Prince Edward Island and had a comparable population of maybe 140,000 people. In such a world as Athens', the economic matters of production, distribution, and prices were determined by authoritative control based on widely accepted rules, customs, and traditions. In the participatory democracy of Greek city states, citizenship was reserved for adult males. Citizens performed jury duty, worked on legislative affairs, and undertook other civic tasks. Slaves and foreigners produced goods and services. Plunder also was used to support the city state. Elsewhere, however, monarchs ruled their kingdoms with nearly absolute power.

This sketch of economic circumstances in ancient times suggests several ways of allocating economic resources. In a *command* system, a central authority—the king, for example—makes most economic decisions. When they reserved some tasks for citizens and then restricted citizenship to males, the Greeks also used *personal characteristics* to allocate certain occupations. If the sons and daughters of slaves also were slaves, *tradition* is being used to allocate economic tasks. As well, the ancient Greeks used *force* to allocate resources when they relied on plunder to take goods and services from non-Greek communities.

These ancient examples do not exhaust the list of possibilities. In modern economies, a *lottery* reallocates resources in favour of the winner and away from all others who participate in the lottery. A queue can be used to allocate items such as tickets for a rock concert or to ration goods on a *first-come, first-served* basis. A *tournament* allocates resources when a contest determines who wins a prize.[14] *Majority rule* can be used to decide resource allocation, as when governments allocate resources among competing uses such a health care, roads, social services, and education. *Command* is another possibility as it can be implemented on a small scale, as in ancient kingdoms or modern family enterprises; on a somewhat larger scale within corporations; or on an immense scale, such as in the central planning of the former Soviet Union.

For much of the twentieth century, in centrally planned communist nations, a central bureaucratic committee established production targets for the country's farms and factories, developed a master plan for how to achieve those targets (including detailed instructions concerning who was to produce what), and set up guidelines for the distribution and use of the goods and services produced.

Although central planning is rare today, so are *pure* market economies. Modern industrial countries are more properly described as *mixed economies,* meaning that goods and services are allocated by a combination of markets, regulation, and other forms of collective control. Still, in Canada, as elsewhere, markets therefore play a crucial role in determining both what is produced and who gets what. Therefore, we need to understand how (and why) markets can often successfully answer these questions, and also how (and why) they may sometimes fail.

---

14 Prizes in athletic tournaments are one example, but a prize to motivate salespersons in a sales contest also allocates resources.

SUMMARY

- Economics is the study of the economy, the production and distribution of goods and services. Economics consists both of microeconomics, which focuses on the consequences of individual behaviour at the level of specific markets, and macroeconomics, which focuses on the performance of national economies and policies to improve that performance. **LO1**

- Economics differs from other social sciences not just by its subject matter but also by a tendency to think in terms of models and a tendency to assume, unless the evidence suggests otherwise, that people behave rationally. **LO1**

- Three particularly important figures in the history of economic thought are Adam Smith (1723–1790), the author of *The Wealth of Nations*; Alfred Marshall (1842–1924), whose influence on microeconomics continues to this day; and John Maynard Keynes (1883–1946), who is associated with Keynesian macroeconomics. **LO2**

- The scarcity problem says that because material and human resources are limited, having more of one good thing usually means making do with less of some other good thing. **LO3**

- The cost–benefit principle says that a rational decision maker will take an action if, but only if, its benefit is at least as great as its cost. The benefit of an action is defined as the largest dollar amount the person will be willing to pay in order to take the action. The cost of an action is defined as the dollar value of everything the person must give up in order to take the action. **LO4**

- Often the question is not whether to pursue an activity but rather how many units of it to pursue. In these cases, the rational actor pursues additional units as long as the marginal benefit of the activity (the benefit from pursuing an additional unit of it) exceeds its marginal cost (the cost of pursuing an additional unit of it). **LO4**

- In using the cost–benefit framework, we need not presume that people choose rationally all the time. Indeed, we identified three common pitfalls that plague decision makers in all walks of life: a tendency to ignore opportunity costs, failing to ignore sunk costs, and a tendency to base decisions on average costs and benefits when it is appropriate to use marginal costs and benefits. **LO5**

- Predictions in economics make use of the *ceteris paribus* assumption, also known as the "all else equal" assumption. **LO6**

- As scientists, economists must be concerned with evaluating their predictions using evidence in the form of data. Formal evaluation of economic theories and predictions typically involves the application of econometrics. **LO6**

- In evaluating statistical evidence, it is important to avoid the fallacy of composition and to be aware that correlation does not imply causation. **LO6**

- Positive economics offers cause-and-effect explanations of economic relationships. In principle, data can be used to confirm or refute propositions, or hypotheses, that emerge from positive economics. Welfare economics is concerned with the evaluation of economic outcomes or situations and is not strictly limited to predicting what will happen. It is concerned with judging whether some outcomes or situations are superior to or better than others according to ethical or value standards that may be explicit or implicit. **LO7**

- An economic naturalist has the ability to use economic principles and models to make sense of observations encountered in everyday life or in the news. **LO8**

CORE PRINCIPLES

The Scarcity Problem
Because material and human resources are limited, having more of one good thing usually means making do with less of some other good thing. (5)

The Cost–Benefit Principle
A rational decision maker will take an action if, and only if, the extra benefits from taking the action are greater than the extra costs. (5)

The Principle of Relevant Costs
In considering whether to produce or consume more of a good, what matters is the cost of one more unit (marginal cost). (10)

KEY TERMS

Adam Smith (4)
Alfred Marshall (3)
average cost (9)
average benefit (9)
ceteris paribus (11)
econometrics (13)
economic model (4)

economic naturalist (15)
economics (2)
fallacy of composition (14)
John Maynard Keynes (3)
macroeconomics (3)
marginal benefit (9)
marginal cost (9)

microeconomics (3)
opportunity cost (6)
positive economics (12)
rational decision maker (4)
spurious correlation (14)
sunk cost (9)
welfare economics (12)

REVIEW QUESTIONS

1. On what grounds does the textbook describe the Robbins definition of economics as a product of its times? **LO1**

2. Who were Adam Smith, Alfred Marshall, and John Maynard Keynes? Of Marshall and Keynes, who is associated with microeconomics and who with macroeconomics? **LO2**

3. Describe the scarcity problem and the cost–benefit principle in your own words. **LO3, LO4**

4. True or false: As a rational decision maker, your willingness to drive downtown to save $30 on a new appliance will depend on what fraction of the total selling price $30 is. Explain. **LO5**

5. Many people think of their air travel as being free when they use frequent-flyer coupons. Explain why these people are likely to make wasteful travel decisions. **LO5**

6. Is the nonrefundable tuition payment you made to your university this semester a sunk cost? How would your answer differ if your university were to offer a full tuition refund to any student who dropped out of school during the first two months of the semester? **LO5**

7. Discuss valid and less valid concerns about the realism of economic assumptions. **LO6**

8. If a government uses cost–benefit analysis to decide whether or not to build a bridge, is the government using positive economics or welfare economics? **LO7**

9. What do the fallacy of composition and spurious correlations have in common? How do they differ? **LO7**

10. What is an economic naturalist? **LO8**

PROBLEMS

1. State which of the following economic issues are primarily microeconomic and which are primarily macroeconomic. **LO1**
   a. The national unemployment rate.
   b. The inflation rate.
   c. Why cell phone service plans in Canada cost more than in Morocco.
   d. Why airline fares rose significantly in 2010.
   e. The causes of the global recession of 2008–2009.

2. The maximum price you would pay for having a freshly washed car when you go out to dinner is $6. The smallest amount for which you would be willing to wash someone else's car is $3.50. You are going out to dinner this evening, and your car is dirty. How much net benefit would you receive from washing it? **LO4**

3. To earn extra money in the summer, you grow tomatoes and sell them at the farmers' market for 30 cents per kilogram. By adding compost to your garden, you can increase your yield as shown in the following table. If compost costs 50 cents per kilogram and your goal is to make as much money as possible, how many kilograms of compost will you add? **LO4, LO5**

Kilograms of compost	Kilograms of tomatoes
0	100.0
1	120.0
2	125.0
3	128.0
4	130.0
5	131.0
6	131.5

4. For each long-distance call anywhere in Canada, a new phone service will charge users 30 cents per minute for the first 2 minutes and 2 cents per minute for additional minutes in each call. Tom's current phone service charges 10 cents per minute for all calls, and his calls are never shorter than 7 minutes. If Tom's dorm switches to the new phone service, what do you predict will happen to the average length of his calls? **LO4, LO5**

5. The meal plan at university A lets students eat as much as they like for a fixed fee of $500 per semester. The average student there eats 125 kg of food per semester. University B charges $500 for a book of meal tickets that entitles the student to eat 125 kg of food per semester. If the student eats more than 125 kg, he or she pays extra. If the student eats less, he or she gets a refund. If students are rational, at which university will average food consumption be higher? At which university is more food likely to be wasted? Explain briefly. **LO4, LO5**

6. A shirt company spends $1000 per week on rent for its factory. Each shirt made at the factory requires $2 worth of cloth and $6 worth of labour and energy. If the factory produces 2000 shirts per week: **LO4, LO5**
   a. What is the average cost of a shirt?
   b. What is the marginal cost of a shirt?

   If the factory produces 3000 shirts per week:
   c. What is the average cost of a shirt?
   d. What is the marginal cost of a shirt?

7. A group has chartered a bus for a trip to Niagara Falls. The driver's fee is $95, the bus rental is $500,

and the fuel charge is $75. The driver's fee is nonrefundable, but the bus rental may be cancelled a week in advance at a charge of $100. At $25 a ticket, how many people must buy tickets a week before so that cancelling the trip definitely will not pay? **LO4, LO5**

8. Sam bought a Trek bicycle for $800 instead of a Cannondale for $1000. Now he finds out that another bike store in town is selling the Cannondale for $800. Mikkel, Sam's friend, offers him $600 for his Trek. If Sam is a rational consumer, will he sell Mikkel his Trek and buy the Cannondale? **LO4, LO5**

9. Which of the following are examples of the use of positive economics and which are examples of welfare economics? **LO7**
   a. The Canadian Centre for Policy Alternatives forecasts that GDP will rise as a consequence of increased government spending to counter the recession.
   b. A cost–benefit study from the C. D. Howe Institute suggests that Canadians would be better off if Canada were to sign a free trade deal with China.
   c. A report from the Department of Finance in Ottawa argues that the current contribution rate for the Canada Pension Plan premiums is high

enough to sustain the benefits paid by the plan for decades into the future.
   d. A paper published in the journal *Canadian Public Policy* claims that a high estate tax in Canada would substantially reduce wealth inequality among Canadians.

10. Which of the following statements represent examples of the fallacy of composition? Which of them represent examples of spurious correlations? Explain. **LO6**
   a. What is good for business is good for the country.
   b. Students at schools that have introduced sex education programs have higher rates of sexual activity. Therefore, sex education programs cause students to engage in more sexual activity.
   c. If one farmer produces a bigger crop, she will be better off. Therefore, if all farmers produce bigger crops they will all be better off.
   d. Every year as the Christmas shopping season reaches its peak in Canada, the amount of cash circulating in the economy increases. The increased cash in the economy is the cause of increased retail spending in Canada during the Christmas shopping season.

ANSWERS TO IN-CHAPTER EXERCISES

1.1 The benefit of buying the game downtown is again $10 but the cost is now $12, so your net benefit from buying it downtown would be $10 − $12 = −$2. Since your net benefit from making the trip would be negative, the rational choice would be to buy at the campus store. **LO4**

1.2 For a rational decision maker, saving $100 is more valuable than saving $90, all else equal. It is true that $90 is a discount of 18 percent on a ticket priced at $500, while $100 is a discount of only 5 percent on a ticket priced at $2000. However, the percentages are irrelevant to a rational economic decision. **LO4, LO5**

1.3 If the diners are rational, whether or not they were randomly selected to have lunch on the house should make no difference in the average quantity of food they consume at the buffet. (Carefully designed experimental research, however, indicates that those who pay out of their own pocket for a buffet may fail to ignore sunk cost and feel that they must get their money's worth. They will tend to consume more than those who are randomly selected to have lunch on the house.) **LO4, LO5**

1.4 If your income is $10,000, you will pay a marginal income tax rate of 15 percent on the $1 of income above $9,999. Your tax bill will be $0.15 (that is, 15 cents). Your average income tax rate would be approximately zero (0.0015 percent). **LO5**

APPENDIX 1A
Working with Equations, Graphs, and Tables

Although many of the examples and most of the end-of-chapter problems in this book are quantitative, none require mathematical skills beyond basic high school algebra and geometry. In this brief appendix, we review some of the skills you will need for dealing with these examples and problems.

The ability to translate simple verbal descriptions into the relevant equations or graphs is important. You will also need to translate tabular information into equations or graphs, and sometimes you will need to translate graphical information into a table or equation. The following examples illustrate all the tools you will need.

1A.1 USING A VERBAL DESCRIPTION TO CONSTRUCT AN EQUATION

We begin with an example that shows how to construct a long-distance telephone billing equation from a verbal description of the billing plan.

EXAMPLE 1A.1

Your long-distance telephone plan charges you $5/month plus 10 cents/minute for long-distance calls. Write an equation that describes your monthly telephone bill.

An **equation** is a simple mathematical expression that describes the relationship between two or more **variables**—quantities that are free to assume different values in some range. The most common type of equation we'll work with contains two types of variables: **dependent variables** and **independent variables**. In this example, the dependent variable is the dollar amount of your monthly telephone bill, and the independent variable is the variable on which your bill depends, namely, the volume of long-distance calls you make during the month. Your bill also depends on the $5 monthly fee and the 10 cents/minute charge. But in this example, those amounts are *constants,* not variables. A **constant**, also called a **parameter**, is a quantity in an equation that is fixed in value, not free to vary. As the terms suggest, the dependent variable describes an outcome that depends on the value taken by the independent variable.

equation a mathematical expression that describes the relationship between two or more variables

variable a quantity that is free to take a range of different values

dependent variable a variable in an equation whose value is determined by the value taken by another variable in the equation

independent variable a variable in an equation whose value determines the value taken by another variable in the equation

constant (parameter) a quantity that is fixed in value

Once you have identified the dependent variable and the independent variable, choose simple symbols to represent them. In algebra courses, X is typically used to represent the independent variable and Y the dependent variable. Many people find it easier to remember what the variables stand for, however, if they choose symbols that are linked in some straightforward way to the quantities that the variables represent. Thus, in this example, we might use B to represent your monthly *bill* in dollars and T to represent the total *time* in minutes you spent during the month on long-distance calls.

Having identified the relevant variables and chosen symbols to represent them, you are now in a position to write the equation that links them:

$$B = 5 + 0.10T, \tag{1A.1}$$

where B is your monthly long-distance bill in dollars and T is your monthly total long-distance calling time in minutes. The fixed monthly fee (5) and the charge per minute (0.10) are parameters in this equation. Note the importance of being clear about the units of measure. Because B represents the monthly bill in dollars, we must also express the fixed monthly fee and the per-minute charge in dollars, which is why the latter number appears in Equation 1A.1 as 0.10 rather than 10. Equation 1A.1 follows the normal convention in which the dependent variable appears by itself on the left-hand side while the independent variable or variables and constants appear on the right-hand side.

Once we have the equation for the monthly bill, we can use it to calculate how much you will owe as a function of your monthly volume of long-distance calls. For example, if you make 32 minutes of calls, you can calculate your monthly bill by simply substituting 32 minutes for T in Equation 1A.1:

$$B = 5 + 0.10(32) = 8.20. \tag{1A.2}$$

Your monthly bill when you make 32 minutes of calls is thus equal to $8.20.

EXERCISE 1A.1

Under the monthly billing plan described in Example 1A.1, how much would you owe for a month during which you made 45 minutes of long-distance calls?

1A.2 GRAPHING THE EQUATION OF A STRAIGHT LINE

The next example shows how to portray the billing plan described in Example 1A.1 as a graph.

EXAMPLE 1A.2

Construct a graph that portrays the monthly long-distance telephone billing plan described in Example 1A.1, putting your telephone charges, in dollars per month, on the vertical axis, and your total volume of calls, in minutes per month, on the horizontal axis.

The first step in responding to this instruction is the one we just took; namely, to translate the verbal description of the billing plan into an equation. When graphing an equation, the normal convention is to use the vertical axis to represent the dependent variable and the horizontal axis to represent the independent variable. In Figure 1A.1, we therefore put B on the vertical axis and T on the horizontal axis. One way to construct the graph shown in the figure is to begin by plotting the monthly bill values that correspond to several different total amounts of long-distance calls. For example, someone who makes 10 minutes of calls during the month would have a

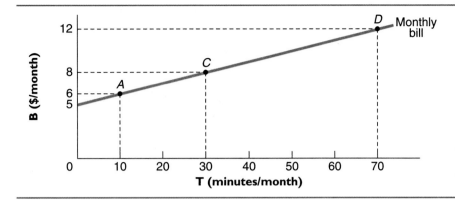

FIGURE 1A.1
The Monthly Telephone Bill in Example 1A.1
The graph of the equation $B = 5 + 0.10T$ is the straight line shown. Its vertical intercept is 5, and its slope is 0.10.

bill of $B = 5 + 0.10(10) = \$6$. Thus, in Figure 1A.1, the value of 10 minutes/month on the horizontal axis corresponds to a bill of \$6/month on the vertical axis (point A). Someone who makes 30 minutes of long-distance calls during the month will have a monthly bill of $B = 5 + 0.10(30) = \$8$, so the value of 30 minutes/month on the horizontal axis corresponds to \$8/month on the vertical axis (point C). Similarly, someone who makes 70 minutes of long-distance calls during the month will have a monthly bill of $B = 5 + 0.10(70) = \$12$, so the value of 70 minutes on the horizontal axis corresponds to \$12 on the vertical axis (point D). The line joining these points is the graph of the monthly billing equation of Example 1A.1.

As shown in Figure 1A.1, the graph of the equation $B = 5 + 0.10T$ is a straight line. The parameter 5 is the **vertical intercept** of the line—the value of B when $T = 0$, or the point at which the line intersects the vertical axis. The parameter 0.10 is the **slope** of the line, which is the ratio of the **rise** of the line to the corresponding **run**. The ratio rise/run is simply the vertical distance between any two points on the line divided by the horizontal distance between those points. For example, if we choose points A and C in Figure 1A.1, the rise is $8 - 6 = 2$ and the corresponding run is $30 - 10 = 20$, so rise/run = 2/20 = 0.10. More generally, for the graph of any equation $Y = a + bX$, the parameter a is the vertical intercept and the parameter b is the slope.

vertical intercept in a straight line, the value taken by the dependent variable when the independent variable equals zero

slope in a straight line, the ratio of the vertical distance the straight line travels between any two points (**rise**) to the corresponding horizontal distance (**run**)

rise vertical distance a straight line travels between any two points

run horizontal distance a straight line travels between any two points

1A.3 DERIVING THE EQUATION OF A STRAIGHT LINE FROM ITS GRAPH

The next example shows how to derive the equation for a straight line from a graph of the line.

EXAMPLE 1A.3

Figure 1A.2 shows the graph of the monthly billing plan for a new long-distance plan. What is the equation for this graph? How much is the fixed monthly fee under this plan? How much is the charge per minute?

The slope of the line shown is the rise between any two points divided by the corresponding run. For points A and C, rise = $12 - 8 = 4$ and run = $40 - 20 = 20$, so the slope equals rise/run = 4/20 = 1/5 = 0.20. And since the horizontal intercept of the line is 4, its equation must be given by

$$B = 4 + 0.20T. \tag{1A.3}$$

FIGURE 1A.2
Another Monthly Long-Distance Plan
The vertical distance between points A and C is $12 - 8 = 4$ units, and the horizontal distance between points A and C is $40 - 20 = 20$, so the slope of the line is $4/20 = 1/5 = 0.20$. The vertical intercept (the value of B when $T = 0$) is 4. So the equation for the billing plan shown is $B = 4 + 0.20T$.

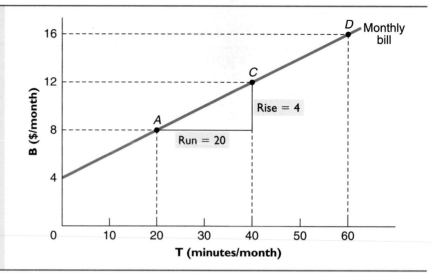

Under this plan, the fixed monthly fee is the value of the bill when $T = 0$, which is $4. The charge per minute is the slope of the billing line, 0.20, or 20 cents/ minute.

EXERCISE 1A.2   **Write the equation for the billing plan shown in the accompanying graph. How much is its fixed monthly fee? its charge per minute?**

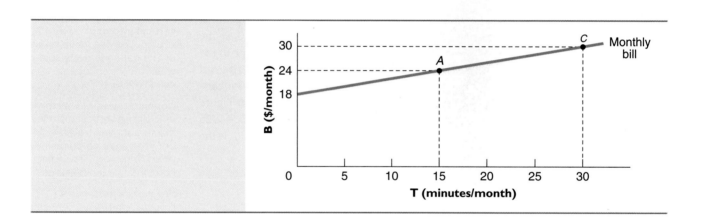

1A.4 CHANGES IN THE VERTICAL INTERCEPT AND SLOPE

Examples 1A.4 and 1A.5 and Exercises 1A.3 and 1A.4 provide practice in seeing how a line shifts with a change in its vertical intercept or slope.

EXAMPLE 1A.4

Show how the billing plan whose graph is in Figure 1A.2 of Example 1A.3 would change if the monthly fixed fee were increased from $4 to $8.

An increase in the monthly fixed fee from $4 to $8 would increase the vertical intercept of the billing plan by $4 but would leave its slope unchanged. An increase in the fixed fee thus leads to a parallel upward shift in the billing plan by $4, as shown in Figure 1A.3. For any given number of minutes of long-distance calls, the monthly

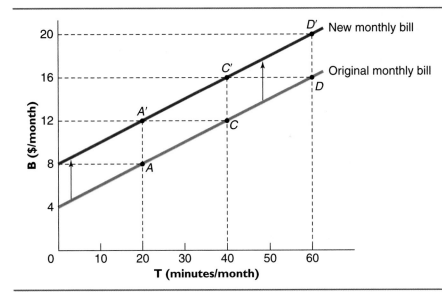

FIGURE 1A.3

The Effect of an Increase in the Vertical Intercept

An increase in the vertical intercept of a straight line produces an upward, parallel shift in the line.

charge on the new bill will be $4 higher than on the old bill. Thus 20 minutes of calls per month cost $8 under the original plan (point *A*) but $12 under the new plan (point *A'*). Forty minutes costs $12 under the original plan (point *C*) and $16 under the new plan (point *C'*). Sixty minutes costs $16 under the original plan (point *D*) and $20 under the new plan (point *D'*).

Show how the billing plan whose graph is in Figure 1A.2 would change if the monthly fixed fee were reduced from $4 to $2.

EXERCISE 1A.3

EXAMPLE 1A.5

Show how the billing plan whose graph is in Figure 1A.2 would change if the charge per minute were increased from 20 cents to 40 cents.

Because the monthly fixed fee is unchanged, the vertical intercept of the new billing plan continues to be 4. But the slope of the new plan, shown in Figure 1A.4, is 0.40, or twice the slope of the original plan. More generally, in the equation $Y = a + bX$, an increase in b makes the slope of the graph of the equation steeper.

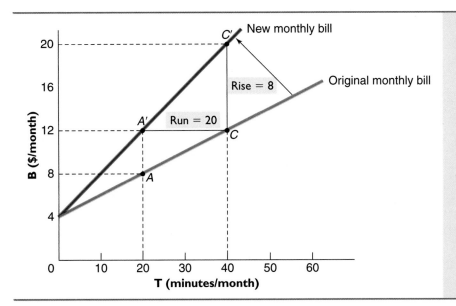

FIGURE 1A.4

The Effect of an Increase in the Charge per Minute

Because the fixed monthly fee continues to be $4, the vertical intercept of the new plan is the same as that of the original plan. With the new charge per minute of 40 cents, the slope of the billing plan rises from 0.20 to 0.40.

EXERCISE 1A.4

Show how the billing plan whose graph is in Figure 1A.2 would change if the charge per minute were reduced from 20 cents to 10 cents.

Exercise 1A.4 illustrates the general rule that in an equation $Y = a + bX$, a reduction in b makes the slope of the graph of the equation less steep.

1A.5 CONSTRUCTING EQUATIONS AND GRAPHS FROM TABLES

Example 1A.6 and Exercise 1A.5 show how to transform tabular information into an equation or graph.

EXAMPLE 1A.6

Table 1A.1 shows four points from a monthly long-distance telephone billing equation. If all points on this billing equation lie on a straight line, find the vertical intercept of the equation and graph it. What is the monthly fixed fee? What is the charge per minute? Calculate the total bill for a month with one hour of long-distance calls.

One approach to this problem is simply to plot any two points from the table on a graph. Since we are told that the billing equation is a straight line, that line must be the one that passes through any two of its points. Thus, in Figure 1A.5 we use *A* to denote the point from Table 1A.1 for which a monthly bill of $11 corresponds to 20 minutes/month of calls (second row) and *C* to denote the point for which a monthly bill of $12 corresponds to 40 minutes/month of calls (fourth row). The straight line passing through these points is the graph of the billing equation.

Unless you have a steady hand, however, or use extremely large graph paper, the method of extending a line between two points on the billing plan is unlikely to be

TABLE 1A.1
Points on a Long-Distance Billing Plan

Long-distance bill ($/month)	Total long-distance calls (minutes/month)
10.50	10
11	20
11.50	30
12	40

FIGURE 1A.5
Plotting the Monthly Billing Equation from a Sample of Points Point *A* is taken from row 2, Table 1A.1, and point *C* from row 4. The monthly billing plan is the straight line that passes through these points.

very accurate. An alternative approach is to calculate the equation for the billing plan directly. Since the equation is a straight line, we know that it takes the general form $B = f + sT$, where f is the fixed monthly fee and s is the slope. Our goal is to calculate the vertical intercept f and the slope s. From the same two points we plotted earlier, A and C, we can calculate the slope of the billing plan as $s = \text{rise/run} = 1/20 = 0.05$.

So all that remains is to calculate f, the fixed monthly fee. At point C on the billing plan, the total monthly bill is $12 for 40 minutes, so we can substitute $B = 12$, $s = 0.05$, and $T = 40$ into the general equation $B = f + sT$ to obtain

$$12 = f + 0.05(40), \tag{1A.4}$$

or

$$12 = f + 2, \tag{1A.5}$$

which solves for $f = 10$. So the monthly billing equation must be

$$B = 10 + 0.05T. \tag{1A.6}$$

For this billing equation, the fixed fee is $10/month, the calling charge is 5 cents/minute ($0.05/minute), and the total bill for a month with one hour of long-distance calls is $B = 10 + 0.05(60) = \$13$, just as shown in Figure 1A.5.

The following table shows four points from a monthly long-distance telephone billing plan.

EXERCISE 1A.5

Long-distance bill ($/month)	Total long-distance calls (minutes/month)
20	10
30	20
40	30
50	40

If all points on this billing plan lie on a straight line, find the vertical intercept of the corresponding equation without graphing it. What is the monthly fixed fee? What is the charge per minute? How much would the charges be for one hour of long-distance calls per month?

See Connect for a brief discussion of how simultaneous equations can be used to decide which of two different long-distance billing plans is best for your purposes. As you read this book, you also will find that equations and graphs play a principal role in economics. Supply and demand graphs and equations appear in Chapter 3 as only one of many examples. Supply and demand can be expressed as simultaneous equations in the same way that two long-distance billing plans can be expressed as simultaneous equations.

KEY TERMS

constant (21)
dependent variable (21)
equation (21)
independent variable (21)

parameter (21)
rise (23)
run (23)
slope (23)

variable (21)
vertical intercept (23)

ANSWERS TO IN-APPENDIX EXERCISES

1A.1 To calculate your monthly bill for 45 minutes of calls, substitute 45 minutes for T in Equation 1A.1 to get $B = 5.00 + 0.10(45) = \$9.50$. **LO1A.1, LO1A.2**

1A.2 Calculating the slope using points A and C, we have rise $= 30.00 - 24.00 = 6.00$ and run $= 30.00 - 15.00 = 15.00$, so rise/run $= 6/15 = 2/5 = 0.40$. And since the horizontal intercept of the line is 18, its equation is $B = 18 + 0.40T$. Under this plan, the fixed monthly fee is \$18, and the charge per minute is the slope of the billing line, 0.40, or 40 cents/minute. **LO1A.3**

1A.3 A \$2 reduction in the monthly fixed fee would produce a downward, parallel shift in the billing plan by \$2. **LO1A.4**

1A.4 With an unchanged monthly fixed fee, the vertical intercept of the new billing plan continues to be 4. The slope of the new plan is 0.10, half the slope of the original plan. **LO1A.1, LO1A.5**

1A.5   Let the billing equation be $B = f + sT$, where f is the fixed monthly fee and s is the slope. From the first two points in the table, calculate the slope $s = $ rise/run $= 10/10 = 1$. To calculate f, we can use the information in row 1 of the table to write the billing equation as $20 = f + 1(10)$ and solve for $f = 10$. So the monthly billing equation must be $B = 10 + 1.0T$. For this billing equation, the fixed fee is \$10/month, the calling charge is \$1/minute, and the total bill for a month with one hour of long-distance calls is $B = 10 + 1(60) = \$70$. **LO1A.6**

CHAPTER 2
Comparative Advantage: The Basis for Exchange

During a stint as a volunteer teacher in rural Nepal, a young economic naturalist employed a cook named Birkhaman, who came from a remote Himalayan village in neighbouring Bhutan. Although Birkhaman had virtually no formal education, he was spectacularly resourceful. His primary duties, preparing food and maintaining the kitchen, he performed with competence and dispatch. But he also had many other skills. He could thatch a roof, butcher a goat, and repair shoes. An able tinsmith and a good carpenter, he could sew, fix a broken alarm clock, and plaster walls. On top of all that, he was a local authority on home remedies.

Birkhaman's range of skills was broad even by Nepalese standards. But even the least skilled Nepalese villager can perform a wide range of tasks that most Canadians hire others to perform. The alternative to a system in which everyone is a jack of all trades is one in which people *specialize* in particular goods and services, and then satisfy their needs by trading among themselves.

Our task in this chapter is to explain some specific reasons why exchange and specialization can increase economic output. In doing so, we will explore why people choose to exchange goods and services in the first place, rather than having each person produce his own food, cars, clothing, shelter, and the like.

A major focus of this chapter is a simple model of what economists call *comparative advantage*. Roughly speaking, a person has a comparative advantage at producing a particular good or service, let's say haircuts, if that person is *relatively* more productive at providing haircuts than at providing other goods or services. Under certain conditions, our model leads to the prediction that specialization according to comparative advantage can lead to increased output of goods and services.

This chapter will also introduce two means of visualizing an economy. One is the *production possibilities curve,* which is a graphical method of describing the combinations of goods and services that an economy can produce. The other is the *circular flow diagram*, an illustration of exchange relationships in a monetary economy highlighting the mutual dependence of incomes and expenditures in an economy.

Photo courtesy of Robert H. Frank

Did this man perform most of his own services because he was poor, or was he poor because he performed most of his own services?

2.1 EXCHANGE AND OPPORTUNITY COST

Time is a scarce resource, and the fact that there is never enough time to do everything implies that the opportunity cost of spending more time on any one activity is having less time available to spend on others. As the following example makes clear, this helps explain why some can earn more income by concentrating on those activities in which they excel.

EXAMPLE 2.1

Can Eddie Greenspan earn more income if he hires someone to write his own will?

Eddie Greenspan is one of Canada's top criminal defence lawyers. He has defended against charges ranging from drunk driving to murder, and his list of extremely rich clients has included notables such as Garth Drabinsky (the theatre producer convicted in 2009 for fraud and forgery) and Conrad Black (the publisher convicted in 2007 in a U.S. court for fraud).

Although Greenspan spends virtually all of his working hours practicing criminal law,[1] he may also be competent to perform a broader range of legal services. Suppose, for the sake of argument, that he could prepare his own will in one hour, only half as long as it would take any other lawyer. Despite this, can Greenspan make more income if he hires someone to write his own will?

Suppose that on the strength of his reputation as a criminal lawyer, Greenspan can earn more than $1000 an hour practicing criminal law. Therefore, the opportunity cost of any time he spends preparing his will would be more than $1000 per hour. Lawyers who specialize in wills and estate law typically earn considerably less than that amount. Although in our example Greenspan is able to prepare his will in one hour, suppose that he nevertheless engages a competent wills and estates lawyer who prepares the will in two hours and charges a fee of $700. By not preparing his own will, Greenspan can use the hour he has saved to earn $1,000—he can be $300 richer if he employs the wills and estates lawyer to write the will and then spends the hour saved to bill for criminal law work.[2]

Will a top lawyer make more income if he prepares his own will?

Notice two things in the preceding example. First, if Greenspan's skills enable him to write a will in less time than a wills and estates lawyer, economists would say that Greenspan has an *absolute advantage* at preparing his will. A person has an **absolute advantage** over another person if he or she takes less time to perform a task than the other person does. It also follows that, compared to Greenspan, the wills and estates lawyer has an absolute disadvantage in writing wills.

Second, because Greenspan can earn $1000 per hour in criminal law work, the opportunity cost of his time is $1000 per hour. The opportunity cost of the wills and estates lawyer's time is $350 per hour. Because the opportunity cost of the wills and estates lawyer's time is $350 per hour, the wills and estates lawyer has a *comparative advantage* in preparing wills. A person has a **comparative advantage** over another if his or her opportunity cost of performing a task is lower than the other person's opportunity cost. As the logic of Example 2.2 below shows, it also follows that Greenspan has a comparative advantage in criminal law.

absolute advantage the advantage of taking fewer hours to perform a task than another person does

comparative advantage the advantage of having a lower opportunity cost of performing a task than another person does for the same task

---

1 According to Andy Halloway, "Eddie Greenspan," *Canadian Business*, 31, January 2005.

2 Notice that, in addition to the assumptions explicitly mentioned here, it is implicitly assumed that Greenspan bills by the hour and always has the option of working an additional hour at criminal law at his full hourly rate. Also, lawyers and other highly skilled experts become experts through years of practice. It is extremely unlikely that a lawyer who has specialized in criminal law for decades would be able to prepare a will in less time than a lawyer who prepares wills on a regular basis.

THE PRINCIPLE OF COMPARATIVE ADVANTAGE

Example 2.1 points to the key insight that a simple model of specialization according to comparative advantage can offer: when the opportunity costs of performing various tasks are different for different people, they can increase the total output of available goods and services by trading with one another. The following example is a numerical illustration of the logic behind this model.

EXAMPLE **2.2**

Will Rikke be more productive if she updates her own Web page?

Consider the case of Rikke and Beth. Rikke can update a Web page in 20 minutes or repair a bicycle in 10 minutes. Beth can update a Web page in 30 minutes or repair a bicycle in 30 minutes. Table 2.1 summarizes the data: Rikke clearly possesses an absolute advantage over Beth in both activities.

TABLE 2.1
Productivity Information for Rikke and Beth

	Time to update a Web page	Time to complete a bicycle repair
Rikke	20 minutes	10 minutes
Beth	30 minutes	30 minutes

Time used to update a Web page cannot be used to repair a bicycle, and vice versa. Thus each woman incurs an opportunity cost whenever she updates a Web page instead of repairing a bicycle. If Rikke spends 20 minutes updating a Web page, she sacrifices the opportunity to use the same 20 minutes for repairing two bicycles. The opportunity cost of each Web page that Rikke updates is therefore two bicycle repairs. If Beth were to use 30 minutes to update a Web page, she sacrifices the opportunity to use the same 30 minutes to repair a bicycle. The opportunity cost of each Web page that Beth updates is only one bicycle repair. Table 2.2 summarizes the data on the opportunity costs. The left-hand column shows that Beth's opportunity cost of updating a Web page is half the amount of Rikke's. Like the wills and estates lawyer who has a *comparative* advantage over the trial lawyer in writing wills, Beth has a *comparative* advantage over Rikke in updating Web pages.

TABLE 2.2
Opportunity Costs for Rikke and Beth

	Opportunity cost of updating a Web page	Opportunity cost of repairing a bicycle
Rikke	2 bicycle repairs	0.5 Web-page update
Beth	1 bicycle repair	1 Web-page update

The same reasoning will provide each woman's opportunity cost of repairing bicycles. Since it takes Rikke 20 minutes to update a Web page and only 10 minutes to fix a bicycle, each bicycle repair she does prevents Rikke from updating one half of a Web page; that is, the opportunity cost of each bicycle that Rikke repairs is half a Web-page update. Similarly, the opportunity cost of each bicycle that Beth repairs is one Web-page update. For each woman, the opportunity cost of one bicycle repair is the *reciprocal* of her opportunity cost of updating a Web page. The right-hand column of Table 2.2 shows each woman's opportunity cost of one bicycle repair. Notice that Rikke has a comparative advantage over Beth in bicycle repairs.

Suppose that the community where Rikke and Beth live wants 16 Web-page updates per day. If neither person specializes, and Rikke spends one half of her eight-hour workday repairing bicycles and one half updating Web pages, she can update 12 Web pages and repair 24 bicycles. Suppose Beth provides four more updates by spending two hours on Web pages, for a total 16 updates per day between them. With her remaining six hours, Beth can repair 12 bicycles. Together, Rikke and Beth repair 36 bicycles per eight-hour day. These data are summarized in Part A of Table 2.3.

TABLE 2.3
The Gains When Rikke and Beth Specialize

Part A: Without Specialization				
	Time spent updating Web pages	Number of updated Web pages	Time spent repairing bicycles	Number of bicycles repaired
Rikke	4 hours	12	4 hours	24
Beth	2 hours	4	6 hours	12
Total output		16		36

Part B: With Specialization According to Comparative Advantage				
	Time spent updating Web pages	Number of updated Web pages	Time spent repairing bicycles	Number of bicycles repaired
Rikke	0 hours	0	8 hours	48
Beth	8 hours	16	0 hours	0
Total output		16		48
Net gain with specialization		0		12

Suppose each woman had specialized according to comparative advantage. In eight hours Beth would update 16 Web pages and Rikke would repair 48 bicycles. Part B of Table 2.3 summarizes these data. With specialization, 12 more bicycles are repaired, and there is no reduction in the number of Web page updates. Specialization reduces the opportunity cost of the 16 Web page updates the community wants. Therefore, specialization creates 12 additional bicycle repairs!

Rikke is *not* better off if she updates her own Web page, even though she is a better programmer than Beth. Because she has a comparative advantage in repairing bicycles, Rikke will be better off if she specializes in repairing bicycles and hires Beth to update her Web page.

"We're a natural, Rachel. I handle intellectual property, and you're a content-provider."

The details of Example 2.2 include the number of minutes each person needs to complete each task. However, the information necessary to compute the opportunity cost of one good in terms of another can be presented as each person's *productivity* in each task. **Productivity** is units of output per hour divided by units of input per hour. Because the information can be presented in either of these two ways, one must pay careful attention to the form in which it is presented.

productivity units of output per hour divided by units of input per hour

Exercise 2.1 below provides data on the labour *productivity* of Mina and Barb. Like Beth and Rikke of Example 2.2, both have skills as computer programmers and bicycle mechanics. Each woman's labour is an input to a production process. Her labour productivity is her output per hour of labour time. Thus Barb's productivity when she repairs bicycles is three repairs per hour. Barb also can update three Web pages per hour. Barb has a greater productivity in both tasks that gives her an absolute advantage over Mina in both tasks: *greater productivity* confers an *absolute* advantage. However, Barb has a *comparative* advantage in only one task because she has a lower opportunity cost than Mina does in only one task. A *lower opportunity cost* confers a *comparative* advantage. Work through Exercise 2.1 to see how to proceed when information is presented in this alternative format.

EXERCISE 2.1

Will Barb be better off if she updates her own Web page?

The following table shows the productivity rates for Barb and Mina in HTML programming and repairing bicycles. Does the fact that Barb can program faster than Mina imply that Barb will be better off if she updates her own Web page?

	Productivity in programming	Productivity in bicycle repair
Mina	2 Web-page updates per hour	1 repair per hour
Barb	3 Web-page updates per hour	3 repairs per hour

The prediction of the model illustrated by Examples 2.1 and 2.2 is so important that we state it formally as one of the core principles:

COMPARATIVE
ADVANTAGE

The Principle of Comparative Advantage: Total output is largest when each person concentrates on the activities for which his or her opportunity cost is lowest.

Indeed, the gains made possible from specialization based on comparative advantage constitute one rationale for market exchange. They partially explain why each person does not devote 10 percent of his or her time to producing cars, 5 percent to growing food, 25 percent to building housing, 0.0001 percent to performing brain surgery, and so on. By concentrating on those tasks at which we are relatively most productive, together we can produce vastly more than if we all tried to be self-sufficient.

In Chapter 1 you were introduced to the idea that economic models are based upon assumptions. Do you notice any specific assumptions behind the numerical illustration involving Beth and Rikke specializing according to comparative advantage?

One simplification was that the example avoided the possibility that after specialization, the output of one service decreased while the output of the other increased. In the example, the output of one service (Web-page updates) stayed the same while the output of the other service (bicycle repairs) increased. In this special case, we would say that total output went up without knowing the prices of the services. If the output of one service went up and the output for the other went down, however, we would have had no way of expressing total output without knowing the prices of the services. In general, if we wish to aggregate different services we need to know their prices. With prices and quantities for services, we can calculate the value of output; for example, 16 Web-page updates times $100 per page plus 48 bicycle repairs at $2 per repair would give output of $1696. Using prices to aggregate the output of various goods and services is covered in Chapter 5.

A second assumption behind the model is that, both before Beth and Rikke specialize and after they specialize, they each work eight hours per day. Neither of them can be underemployed or unemployed. But, as we will see in the final section of Chapter 5 where we discuss the measurement of unemployment, and in the chapters of Part 3 of this textbook where we examine economic fluctuations, it is often important to recognize unemployment as a serious issue.

A third assumption is that Beth and Rikke produce their services with only their labour. Usually, however, we produce goods and services using at least tools, and the tools can make a huge difference in how productive we are. The same person, for example, can be much more productive updating web pages with a high-powered, state-of-the-art computer than with some outdated computer that is constantly crashing due to memory constraints. In Chapters 14 and 16, we will examine how investment in machinery, equipment, and other durable goods used in production is critical for the growth of labour productivity.

A fourth assumption is that the comparative advantages of Beth and Rikke are relatively innate or at least difficult to change. If the highly productive Rikke can update a Web page in 20 minutes and complete a bicycle repair in 10 minutes because of short training programs she attended, and if Beth could be as productive as Rikke in both tasks if she attended the same training programs, there could be greater gains in output from having Beth attend the training programs than by just moving to a system of specialization that leaves Beth as a low-productivity updater of Web pages. In Chapter 14, we analyze the role of education and training in enhancing labour productivity growth.

RECAP

EXCHANGE AND OPPORTUNITY COST

Gains from exchange are possible if trading partners have comparative advantages in producing different goods and services. An individual has a comparative advantage when his or her opportunity cost—measured in terms of other production opportunities foregone—is smaller than the corresponding opportunity costs of his or her trading partners. Under certain assumptions, the model of comparative advantage predicts that maximum output can be achieved if each person specializes by producing the good or service in which she has the lowest opportunity cost (the principle of comparative advantage). Comparative advantage can make specialization worthwhile even if one trading partner has an absolute advantage in each activity.

2.2 COMPARATIVE ADVANTAGE AND PRODUCTION POSSIBILITIES

Comparative advantage and specialization allow an economy to produce more than if each person tries to produce a little of everything. In this section, we first examine an imaginary economy with only one person and then note how economic possibilities change as additional people join the economy. Along the way, we introduce a useful graph called the *production possibilities curve*, which is used to describe the combinations of goods and services that a particular economy can produce.

PRODUCTION POSSIBILITIES IN A ONE-PERSON ECONOMY

We begin with a hypothetical economy consisting of a single worker (Susan) who lives on a small island. Susan's options are limited to producing sugar cane and Macadamia nuts. The more time she spends cutting sugar cane, the less time she has available for picking nuts. If she wants more sugar cane, then she must make do with a smaller amount of nuts. Knowing how productive she is at each activity, we can easily summarize the various combinations of sugar cane and nuts she can harvest each day if she makes full use of her available working time (eight hours). This menu of possibilities is known as the **production possibilities curve**.

As the following example illustrates, constructing the production possibilities curve for a one-person economy is a straightforward matter.

EXAMPLE **2.3**

What is the production possibilities curve for an economy in which Susan is the only worker?

Susan has to allocate her production time between sugar cane and nuts. Each hour per day that she devotes to cutting sugar cane yields 1.5 kg of cane, and each hour she devotes to harvesting nuts yields 3 kg of nuts. If Susan works a total of eight hours per day, her production possibilities curve is the graph that displays, for each level of sugar cane she cuts, the maximum amount of nuts that she can pick.

The vertical axis in Figure 2.1 shows Susan's daily production of sugar cane, and the horizontal axis shows her daily production of nuts. It is easiest to understand this graph if we start by looking at two extreme allocations of her time. If she works the full eight hours of her working day cutting sugar cane at the rate of 1.5 kg of sugar cane per hour, she would pick (8 hours/day)(1.5 kg/hour) = 12 kg per day of sugar cane and 0 kg of nuts. That combination of sugar cane and nuts is represented by point A in Figure 2.1, the vertical intercept of Susan's production possibilities curve.

Now suppose, instead, that Susan devoted all her time to picking nuts. Picking at a rate of 3 kg of nuts per hour, her total daily production would be (8 hours/day)(3 kg/hour) = 24 kg of nuts and 0 kg of sugar cane. That combination is represented by point B in Figure 2.1, the horizontal intercept of Susan's production possibilities curve.

Because Susan's production of each good is exactly proportional to the amount of time she devotes to that good, the remaining points along her production possibilities curve will lie on the straight line that joins A and B. For example, suppose that Susan devotes six hours each day to cutting sugar cane and two hours to picking nuts. She will then produce (6 hours/day)(1.5 kg/hour) = 9 kg of sugar cane and (2 hours/day)(3 kg/hour) = 6 kg of nuts per day, which is the point labelled C in Figure 2.1. Alternatively, if she devotes two hours to sugar cane and six hours to nuts, she will get (2 hours/day)(1.5 kg/hour) = 3 kg of sugar cane and (6 hours/day)(3 kg/hour) = 18 kg of nuts per day. This alternative combination is represented by point D in Figure 2.1.

In this simple example, we have assumed that there is no change in Susan's output per hour, whether she spends more or less time producing nuts or sugar cane. This implies that Susan's production possibilities curve (PPC) is a straight line, with a constant slope. If Susan changes her allocation of time and moves from Point C to Point D, she will give up 6 kgs of sugar cane in order to produce 12 more kilograms of nuts—the slope of Susan's PPC is the ratio of vertical "rise" to horizontal "run"; that is, 6 kg of sugar cane/12 kg of nuts. *Figure 2.1 thus shows graphically that Susan's opportunity cost of an additional kilogram of nuts is 1/2 kg of sugar cane.*

How much sugar cane does Susan give up when she produces more nuts? The opportunity cost (OC) of nuts can be expressed as the following simple formula:

$$OC_{nuts} = \frac{\text{loss in sugar cane}}{\text{gain in nuts}}.$$

One could equally well express the same tradeoff in terms of Susan's opportunity cost of sugar cane:

$$OC_{sugar\ cane} = \frac{\text{loss in nuts}}{\text{gain in sugar cane}}.$$

To say that Susan's opportunity cost of an additional kilogram of nuts is 1/2 kg of sugar cane is exactly equivalent to saying that her opportunity cost of 1 kg of sugar cane is 2 kg of nuts.

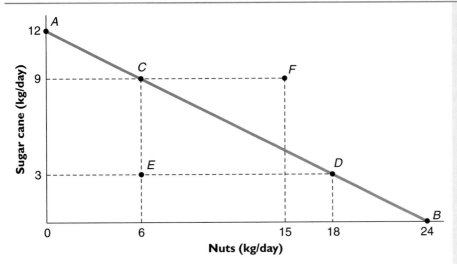

FIGURE 2.1

Attainable and Efficient Points on Susan's Production Possibilities Curve
Points that lie either on the production possibilities curve (for example, *A*, *C*, *D*, and *B*) or to its left (for example, *E*) are said to be attainable. Points that lie to the right the production possibilities curve (for example, *F*) are unattainable. Points that lie on the curve are said to be efficient, while those that lie within the curve are said to be inefficient (for example, *E*).

The production possibilities curve shown in Figure 2.1 is an example of the scarcity problem—when resources are limited, having more of one good or service generally means having to settle for less of another (see Chapter 1). Although in everyday life the "price" of a commodity is usually expressed in dollar terms, economists think of the concept of price in more general terms—what a person has to give up in order to gain something. If Susan wants an additional kilogram of sugar cane she can have it, but only if she is willing to give up 2 kg of nuts. The opportunity cost of producing sugar is, in effect, its price (2 kg of nuts).

Any point that lies either on the production possibilities curve or to the left of it is said to be an **attainable point**, meaning that it can be produced with currently available resources. In Figure 2.1, for example, points *A*, *B*, *C*, *D*, and *E* are attainable points. Points that lie to the right of the production possibilities curve are said to be **unattainable** because they cannot be produced using currently available resources. In Figure 2.1, *F* is an unattainable point because Susan cannot produce 9 kg of sugar cane per day *and* 15 kg of nuts.

Points that lie within the curve are said to be *inefficient*, because existing resources would allow for production of more of at least one good without sacrificing the production of any other good. At *E*, for example, Susan is producing only 3 kg of sugar cane per day and 6 kg of nuts, which means that she could increase her harvest of sugar cane by 6 kg per day without giving up any nuts (moving from *E* to *C*). Alternatively, Susan could pick as many as 12 additional kilograms of nuts each day without giving up any sugar cane (moving from *E* to *D*). So a point such as *E* is called an **inefficient point**. An **efficient point** is one that lies on the production possibilities curve. At any such point, more of one good can be produced only by producing less of the other.[3]

Note that in distinguishing between *attainable* and *unattainable* levels of production per day, we assumed that a workday is composed of eight working hours. In this example, we assumed Susan could work eight hours per day because we wanted to specify a working day that could be sustained over time—that was attainable in the longer run and not just for short periods of time. Clearly, if Susan were to work 18 hours per day, she could produce both more nuts and more sugar cane. But she could not expect to keep this up for too long, since sleeping, eating and other "personal maintenance" activities take time.

attainable point any combination of goods that can be produced using currently available resources

unattainable point any combination of goods that cannot be produced using currently available resources

inefficient point any combination of goods for which currently available resources enable an increase in the production of one good without a reduction in the production of the other

efficient point any combination of goods for which currently available resources do not allow an increase in the production of one good without a reduction in the production of the other

3 Some authors use the terminology **technically inefficient point** and **technically efficient point** to emphasize that the idea of efficiency involved is a purely technical one of maximum output for given input in a positive economics sense, rather than an idea of efficiency in terms of optimality in a welfare economics sense.

Why might Susan be at point *E*? It is never in her self-interest to use an inefficient technique, but perhaps she has mistakenly adopted an inferior technology (for example, using a glove, which slows her down). By switching to an efficient technique, she gets more of both goods.

FACTORS THAT INFLUENCE THE PRODUCTION POSSIBILITIES CURVE

To see how the slope and position of the production possibilities curve depend on an individual's productivity, let's compare Susan's PPC to that of a person who is less productive in both activities.

EXAMPLE **2.4**

How do changes in productivity affect the opportunity cost of nuts?

Suppose Tom can harvest nuts at a rate of 0.75 kg per hour and sugar cane at 0.75 kg per hour. If Tom lives alone on an island, describe the economy's production possibilities curve.

We can construct Tom's PPC the same way we did Susan's. Note first that if Tom devotes an entire workday (8 hours/day) to cutting sugar cane, he harvests (8 hours/day)(0.75 kg/hour) = 6 kg of sugar cane per day and 0 kg of nuts. Therefore, the vertical intercept of Tom's PPC is *A* in Figure 2.2. If instead he devotes all his time to picking nuts, he gets (8 hours/day)(0.75 kg/hour) = 6 kg of nuts per day and no sugar cane. That means the horizontal intercept of his PPC is *B* in Figure 2.2. As before, because Tom's production of each good is proportional to the amount of time he devotes to it, the remaining points on his PPC will lie along the straight line that joins these two extreme points.

FIGURE 2.2
Tom's Production Possibilities Curve
The less productive a person is, the closer his PPC will be to the origin.

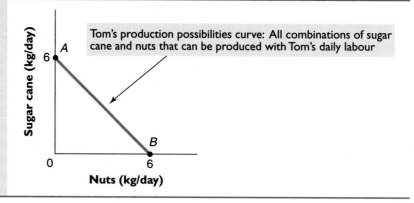

How does Tom's PPC compare with Susan's? Because Tom is less productive than Susan at both activities, the horizontal and vertical intercepts of Tom's PPC lie closer to the origin than do Susan's (see Figure 2.3). For Tom, the opportunity cost of an additional kilogram of nuts is 1 kg of sugar cane, which is twice Susan's opportunity cost of nuts. This difference in opportunity costs shows up as a difference in the slopes of their PPCs—the absolute value of the slope of Tom's PPC is 1, whereas Susan's is 1/2.

While Tom is absolutely less productive than Susan at harvesting sugar cane, his opportunity cost of sugar cane is only half Susan's. Whereas Susan must give up 2 kg of nuts to cut an additional kilogram of sugar cane, Tom must give up only 1 kg. This difference in opportunity costs illustrates the concept of comparative advantage. Although Susan has an absolute advantage in harvesting both sugar cane and nuts, Tom has a *comparative* advantage in sugar cane because his opportunity cost of cutting sugar cane is less than Susan's.

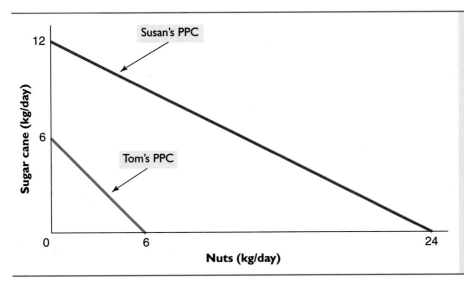

FIGURE 2.3
Individual Production Possibilities Curves Compared
Though Tom is less productive in both activities than Susan, Tom's opportunity cost of cutting sugar cane is only half that of Susan's.

Notice that the principle of comparative advantage is a relative concept—one that makes sense only when the relative productivities of two or more people (or countries) are being compared. To cement this idea, work through the following exercise.

Suppose Susan's output remains the same (she can harvest 1.5 kg of sugar cane per hour or 3 kg of nuts per hour) but Tom develops his skills such that he can pick 0.75 kg of sugar cane per hour or 2.25 kg of nuts per hour. What is Susan's opportunity cost of picking a kilogram of nuts? What is Tom's opportunity cost of picking a kilogram of nuts? Where does Susan's comparative advantage now lie?

EXERCISE 2.2

PRODUCTION POSSIBILITIES IN A TWO-PERSON ECONOMY

As the next examples illustrate, a comparative advantage arising from disparities in individual opportunity costs can create gains for everyone.

EXAMPLE **2.5**

How does the one-person economy's PPC change when a second person is added?

Suppose Susan and Tom decide to live on the same island. Susan can harvest 1.5 kg of sugar cane or 3 kg of nuts per hour, and Tom can harvest 0.75 kg of sugar cane or 0.75 kg of nuts per hour. If they are the only two people in the economy and each works eight hours per day, describe the production possibilities curve for the economy as a whole.

To understand the PPC for a two-person economy, we can start by asking how much sugar cane they would have if both Susan and Tom worked full-time harvesting sugar cane. The answer is 18 kg per day (12 kg from Susan and 6 kg from Tom), so point A in Figure 2.4 is the vertical intercept of the PPC. On the other hand, if Susan and Tom both worked full-time picking nuts, they would pick 30 kg of nuts per day (24 kg from Susan and 6 kg from Tom), which gives us point B in Figure 2.4, the horizontal intercept of the PPC.

In contrast to the PPC for the one-person economy, however, the PPC for the two-person economy is not a straight line joining the two extreme points. To see why, suppose Susan and Tom were initially devoting all their time to harvesting sugar cane but then decide they want some nuts. If Susan starts to pick nuts they can both

FIGURE 2.4

The PPC for a Two-Person Economy

If Tom and Susan want to consume nuts, it makes sense for them to rely initially on Susan, because her opportunity cost of producing nuts is lower than Tom's. Only after Susan is fully occupied picking nuts (point D) will additional nut production start to rely on Tom.

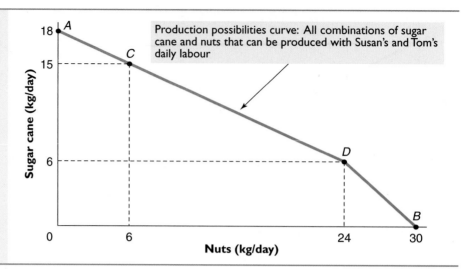

Production possibilities curve: All combinations of sugar cane and nuts that can be produced with Susan's and Tom's daily labour

be better off, because her opportunity cost of picking nuts is only half Tom's. For example, if Susan spent two hours picking nuts while Tom continued to devote all his time to sugar cane, they would lose 3 kg of sugar cane but gain 6 kg of nuts each day. Point C in Figure 2.4 represents this combination.

If Susan devotes all her time to picking nuts while Tom continues to spend all his time on sugar cane, they will be at D in Figure 2.4, which represents 6 kg of sugar cane and 24 kg of nuts per day. If they want to expand nut production any further, Tom will have to take some of his time away from sugar cane. But in doing so, they gain only one additional kilogram of nuts for each kilogram of sugar cane they lose. Notice in Figure 2.4 how the slope of the PPC changes at point D. To the right of point D, the slope of the PPC reflects Tom's opportunity cost of sugar cane, not Susan's.

EXERCISE 2.3   **To the left of point D in Figure 2.4, what is the slope of the production possibilities curve, and what opportunity cost does this slope represent?**

The PPC for the two-person economy bends outward (is concave to the origin) because of individual differences in opportunity costs. As the following example shows, this distinctive shape represents expanded opportunities for both Susan and Tom.

EXAMPLE **2.6**

What is the best way to achieve a given production goal?

Tom and Susan want 15 kg of sugar cane per day and 6 kg of nuts. If their productive abilities are as described in Example 2.5, what is the most effective way of dividing their labour?

Although Tom has a comparative advantage in harvesting sugar cane, even if he spends all his time harvesting sugar cane he can cut only (8 hours/day)(0.75 kg/hour) = 6 kg per day. So Susan will have to harvest the additional 9 kg of sugar cane to achieve their production target of 15 kg. Since Susan is capable of harvesting (8 hours/day)(1.5 kg/hour) = 12 kg of sugar cane per day, she will need only six hours per day to harvest 9 kg. She can spend the remaining two hours picking nuts, which is exactly the amount of time she needs to pick their production target of 6 kg. In terms of their two-person production possibilities curve, this allocation of labour puts Susan and Tom at point C in Figure 2.4. At the optimal division of labour (point C), Tom specializes completely in sugar cane because his opportunity cost of harvesting sugar cane is less than Susan's. Susan, whose opportunity cost of harvesting sugar cane is higher than Tom's, harvests only as much sugar cane as is needed to complete their production target. This allocation of labour enables the desired quantity of sugar to be produced with the minimum possible sacrifice of nuts. It also illustrates **The Principle of Increasing Opportunity Cost:** that when increasing the production of any good, first employ those resources with the lowest opportunity cost. Only when all of the lowest cost resources are employed does it make economic sense to use resources that have higher opportunity costs.

The Principle of Increasing Opportunity Cost: When increasing the production of any good, first employ those resources with the lowest opportunity cost. Only when all of the lowest cost resources are employed does it make economic sense to use resources that have higher opportunity costs.

INCREASING
OPPORTUNITY
COST

A PRODUCTION POSSIBILITIES CURVE FOR A MANY-PERSON ECONOMY

The process of constructing a production possibilities curve for an economy with many workers is conceptually similar to those already shown. Consider again an economy in which the only two goods are sugar cane and nuts, with sugar cane again on the vertical axis and nuts on the horizontal axis. We can still ask how much sugar cane could be produced if all available workers worked full-time picking sugar cane, and this is still given by the vertical intercept of the economy's PPC. For the hypothetical economy in Figure 2.5, the maximum attainable amount of sugar cane production is 100 000 kg per day (an amount chosen arbitrarily, for illustrative purposes). The horizontal intercept of the PPC is the amount of nuts that could be gathered if all available workers worked full-time gathering nuts, shown for this same economy as 80 000 kg per day (also an amount chosen arbitrarily). Unlike the earlier examples involving one or two workers, the PPC shown in Figure 2.5 looks like a smooth curve that is bowed out from the origin. If we could zoom in on it, we would see that the curve is really made up of many small line segments, each corresponding to one of many workers. But the key point of Figure 2.5 is the same as the key point of Figure 2.4—the opportunity cost of nuts increases as the economy produces more of them. When the economy moves from A, where it is producing only sugar cane, to B, 20 000 kg of nuts per day are gained by giving up only 5000 kg per day of sugar cane. When nut production is increased still further, however—for example, by moving from B to C—the economy gives up 5000 kg per day of sugar cane, yet gains only 10 000 additional kilograms of nuts. This pattern of increasing opportunity cost persists over the

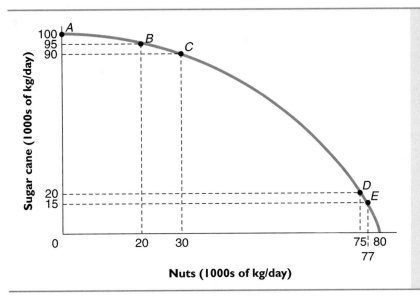

FIGURE 2.5
Production Possibilities Curve for a Large Economy
For an economy with millions of workers, the PPC bows outward from the origin.

entire length of the PPC. In moving from *D* to *E*, the economy again gives up 5000 kg per day of sugar cane but now gains only 2000 kg of nuts per day. Note that the same pattern of increasing opportunity cost applies to sugar cane. Thus, as progressively more sugar cane is produced, the opportunity cost of producing additional sugar cane, as measured by the amount of nuts that must be sacrificed, also increases.

Why is the PPC for the multi-person economy bow shaped? As we keep reassigning workers from cutting sugar cane to picking nuts, it makes sense to start by transferring the people who are not very good at cutting sugar cane. However, sooner or later we must reassign even sugar specialists like Tom. Indeed, we must eventually reassign others whose opportunity cost of producing nuts is far higher than his.

The shape of the production possibilities curve shown in Figure 2.5 illustrates the principle of increasing opportunity cost: *when increasing the production of any good, first employ those resources with the lowest opportunity cost.* This strategy will provide increased amounts of one good at the smallest possible sacrifice of other goods. In the context of our examples, using the principle of increasing opportunity cost allows each additional kilogram of nuts to be obtained with the smallest possible sacrifice of sugar cane, and vice versa.

THE CAUSES OF SHIFTS IN THE ECONOMY'S PRODUCTION POSSIBILITIES CURVE

The production possibilities curve of Figure 2.5 provides a summary of the production options available at a point in time to an economy producing sugar cane and nuts with the labour of many workers. At any given moment, the PPC shown in Figure 2.5 is a graphical representation of a fundamental trade-off confronting that hypothetical economy – the only way people can produce more nuts is to produce less sugar cane.

Economists often use PPC diagrams to represent the choices of real world economies where output is imagined to consist of millions of goods and services but they are organized into two categories, one represented on the horizontal axis (such as civilian goods and services) and the other on the vertical axis (such as military goods and services). They also recognize that goods and services are not produced with labour alone, and that productivity depends upon factors such as the *capital goods* people have to work with and the education and training that people have. **Capital goods (physical capital)** are durable, long-lasting assets produced by the economy and used as inputs to the production process. They include machinery and equipment, for example.

For convenience, let us stick to an economy producing the two goods of sugar cane and nuts but recognize the variety of factors that affect productivity in the economy. In constructing the PPC of Figure 2.6 labelled "Original PPC," we have implicitly held all these factors constant. However, over time, it is possible to increase production of all goods and services—this is what is meant by economic growth. As shown in Figure 2.6, economic growth can be represented as an outward shift in the economy's production possibilities curve from the original PPC (showing points *B* and *C*) to the new PPC (showing *D*). Growth could come from a larger workforce, improvements in the skills of the workforce, additions to the stock of capital goods, improved technology, and so on. The study of the determinants of economic growth is a major topic in macroeconomics. If maintained over long periods of time, economic growth can greatly enhance standards of living, as will be discussed briefly in Chapter 4 and in detail in Chapter 14.

In Figure 2.6, *A* represents an inefficient level of output. Because *A* lies within the PPC, it shows that, even without changing technology or total labour force or other factors, the economy could produce more of both goods just by moving to the PPC (for example, moving from *A* to either *B* or *C*).

Why, you may ask, might an economy ever be at *A*? One possibility is that some resources are involuntarily unemployed. The conditions under which recessions occur, causing labour and other resources to be idle, is another important topic in

---

capital goods (physical capital) durable, long-lasting assets produced by the economy and used as inputs to the production process

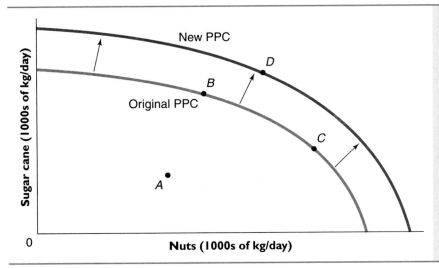

FIGURE 2.6
Economic Growth: An Outward Shift in the Economy's PPC
Increases in productive resources (such as labour and capital equipment) or improvements in knowledge and technology cause the PPC to shift outward. They are the main factors that drive economic growth.

macroeconomics. Whatever the reason, if an economy is operating at any point within its production possibilities curve, it is being productively inefficient because it is not using all of its economic resources in their technically most effective way. Any point on a possibility curve represents a state of *productive efficiency*. **Productive efficiency** occurs when an economy is using all of its economic resources in their technically most effective way.

Even if both *B* and *C* are on the PPC and *productively efficient*, what combination of output of nuts or sugar cane would people prefer? At both *B* and *C*, more of one commodity can only be obtained at the sacrifice of some of the other. Often a majority of the people would prefer one point or the other. In an extreme hypothetical case, it might be that the economy is at point *C*, producing a relatively large amount of nuts and relatively little sugar cane, but people's tastes are such that everybody could be made happier if the economy were at *B*, with fewer nuts and more sugar cane. If resources could be reallocated so that everybody would be better off if the economy moved *along* the PPC to a different point on the curve, then the economy is said to be in a state of *allocative inefficiency*. If it is impossible to reorganize economic resources so that at least one person is better off while nobody is worse off, the economy has accomplished a state of **allocative efficiency**. Allocative efficiency is a concept employed in welfare economics.

productive efficiency occurs when an economy is using all of its economic resources in their technically most effective way

allocative efficiency occurs when it is impossible to reorganize economic resources so that at least one person is better off while nobody is worse off

RECAP

COMPARATIVE ADVANTAGE AND PRODUCTION POSSIBILITIES

For an economy that produces two goods, the *production possibilities curve* describes the maximum amount of one good that can be produced for every possible level of production of the other good. *Attainable points* are those that lie on or within the curve, and technically *efficient points* are those that lie along the curve. The slope of the production possibilities curve tells us the opportunity cost of producing an additional unit of the good measured along the horizontal axis. The principle of increasing opportunity cost tells us that the slope of the production possibilities curve becomes steeper as we move downward to the right.

Economic growth can be represented by an outward shift of the production possibilities curve. It can arise from an increase in the amount of productive resources available to an economy, from improvements in knowledge and technology, and from formation of physical capital.

2.3 SPECIALIZATION AND STANDARDS OF LIVING

Specialization enhances standards of living in different ways, not just through people specializing according to comparative advantage. The model of comparative advantage behind the previous numerical illustrations in this chapter is usually attributed to David Ricardo (1772–1823), an English economist who explained the model in 1817 using an example involving England and Portugal producing wine and cloth.

But Adam Smith, the Scottish economist first mentioned in Chapter 1, analyzed specialization independently of Ricardo's specialization according to comparative advantage. Smith noted, for example, that specialization eliminates the switching and start-up costs incurred when people have to move back and forth among numerous tasks. These gains apply not only to people but also to the tools and equipment they use. Breaking a task down into simple steps, each of which can be performed by a different machine, greatly multiplies the productivity of individual workers. Smith's description of specialized work in an eighteenth-century Scottish pin factory is one of the most famous passages in the history of economic thought:

> One man draws out the wire, another straightens it, a third cuts it, a fourth points it, a fifth grinds it at the top for receiving the head; to make the head requires two or three distinct operations . . . I have seen a small manufactory of this kind where only ten men were employed . . . [who] could, when they exerted themselves, make among them about twelve pounds of pins in a day. There are in a pound upwards of four thousand pins of middling size. Those ten persons, therefore, could make among them upwards of forty-eight thousand pins in a day. Each person, therefore, making a tenth part of forty-eight thousand pins, might be considered as making four thousand eight hundred pins in a day. But if they had all wrought separately and independently, and without any of them having been educated to this peculiar business, they certainly could not each of them have made twenty, perhaps not one pin in a day.[4]

Specialization also allows people to develop skills through practice and experience. In the past, people have had an exaggerated view of the importance of "talent" in explaining performance differences among individuals. Views about the importance of innate talent, however, are changing, in part because of the impact of bestselling books such as Malcolm Gladwell's *Outliers* (2008) and Geoff Colvin's *Talent is Overrated* (2008). Both of these books call attention to the research by psychologist Anders Ericsson and others in the Expert Performance Movement about the role of practice and experience in explaining individual performance.[5]

If specialization can lead to dramatic gains in productivity and thereby improve living standards, why have come countries been slow to specialize? One example is provided by Nepal in the 1960s, the home country of the jack of all trades named Birkhaman mentioned in the introduction to this chapter. Specialization in Nepal was limited by relatively low population density and especially by Nepal's rugged terrain. Exchanging goods and services with residents of other villages was difficult, because the nearest village in most cases could be reached only after trekking several hours over treacherous Himalayan trails. This extreme isolation helped account for Nepal's failure to benefit from widespread specialization.

---

4 Adam Smith, *The Wealth of Nations* (New York: Random House, 1969 [original 1776]), Book I, Chapter I.

5 To learn more about deliberate practice and expert performance, and thereby form an accurate view of the role of talent in explaining performance differences, you are encouraged to read Stephen Dubner and Stephen Levitt, "A Star is Made," *New York Times*, May 7, 2006, http://www.nytimes.com/2006/05/07/magazine/07wwln_freak.html.

CAN WE HAVE TOO MUCH SPECIALIZATION?

As in any issue in economics, however, if we want to analyze specialization we should think about both costs and benefits. The mere fact that specialization boosts productivity does not mean that more specialization is always better than less, for specialization also entails costs. For example, most people appear to enjoy variety in the work they do, but variety tends to be one of the first casualties as workplace tasks become ever more narrowly specialized.

Charlie Chaplin's 1936 film, *Modern Times,* paints a vivid portrait of the psychological costs of repetitive factory work. As an assembly worker, Chaplin's only task, all day every day, is to tighten the nuts on two bolts as they pass before him on the assembly line. Finally, he snaps and walks zombie-like from the factory, wrenches in hand, tightening every nut-like protuberance he encounters.

Modern Times was filmed nearly eighty years ago, and since then industrial engineers have realized that good job design involves finding the right balance between the benefits and costs of specialization. Modern factory designers recognize that excessive specialization will hurt the motivation of workers to produce high-quality output and may cost more in the long run, so now there is a conscious effort to avoid inefficient specialization.

2.4   THE CIRCULAR FLOW OF INCOME AND EXPENDITURE

We started the discussion of a production possibilities curve with the example of Susan living alone on an island. For her, there is no trade or exchange, only her own production and consumption. In a one-person economy, there can be no gains from specialization. In the next example, which concerned a two-person economy (Tom and Susan), the PPC showed that specialization could increase total production. Moreover, exchange is simple in a two-person, two-good economy. If either Tom or Susan want to consume amounts of sugar and nuts different from what they each produce themselves, they can trade and only with each other. In a hypothetical two-person, two-good economy, exchange is simple—nuts can be bartered for sugar cane or vice versa.

In a real economy, millions of people are employed in hundreds of thousands of categories of specialized jobs, and hundreds of thousands of commodities are bought and sold. Complex specialization and exchange are inextricably linked. A doctor who spends most of the day with patients must depend on someone else to grow her food, weave the cloth for her clothes, and manufacture her car. Accountants and car mechanics similarly

Drawing by Gini Kennedy

depend on someone else to produce their electricity, teach their children, and so on. In rich nations, because we are highly specialized in our work, we depend on the cooperation of many other individuals to obtain the things we need and desire.

The complexity of a large, modern economy means that barter is rarely feasible. In our simplified two-person example, if Susan wants to trade macadamia nuts for sugar cane at exactly the same time and place that Tom wants to trade sugar cane for nuts, then barter can work; but this "mutual coincidence of wants" is rare in a modern economy. Most of us instead sell our labour in return for money that we can then spend to obtain the goods and services we want, when we want them.

As we exchange goods and services for money, each of us, every day, engages in a sequence of economic transactions, and every one of which can be viewed from two angles. When a student buys a coffee before class, that transaction is a purchase from the student's point of view and a sale from the point of view of the coffee shop. When an employer pays a student for working a part-time job, the payment is an expenditure for the employer and income for the student. These transactions are interdependent—students are able to buy coffee if they have the money, which they may get from their part-time jobs, and coffee shop owners need to make sales in order to have the money to pay their part-time staff. More generally, labour earnings enable households to make consumption expenditures, and consumer spending provides the revenue that enables firms to hire workers and pay wages.

One way to visually represent this interdependence of spending is a *circular flow diagram*, as is shown in Figure 2.7. In general, a **circular flow diagram** provides an illustration of exchange relationships in a monetary economy, highlighting the mutual dependence of incomes and expenditures. Figure 2.7 can be made much more realistic, but the simplest version of the circular flow diagram is sufficient for our purposes here. It represents a very simple economy that has no government, no financial sector, and does not engage in foreign trade.

Despite being a simplification, Figure 2.7 can represent the main idea of the circular flow of expenditure and exchange. Each transaction is represented by two flows: money (marked in red) and goods or services (marked in blue). Individuals, living in households, sell their labour services to firms. Firms use the labour they hire to produce goods and services that they sell to households. The blue arrows in the upper half of Figure 2.7 indicate the flow of labour through the labour market to firms. The blue arrows in the lower

circular flow diagram an illustration of exchange relationships in a monetary economy highlighting the mutual dependence of incomes and expenditures

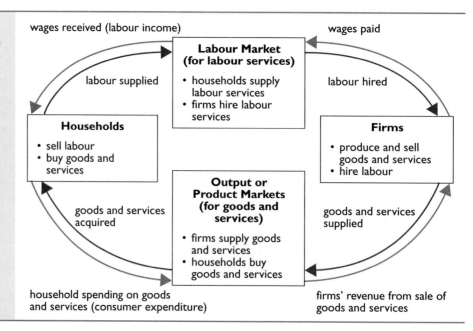

FIGURE 2.7

The Circular Flow of Income and Expenditure

This diagram links income and expenditure in a highly simplified model of the economy. The outer set of arrows in red indicates money or dollar flows in the economy. The inner set of arrows in blue indicates the flows of real inputs and goods and services.

wages received (labour income)   wages paid

labour supplied   labour hired

Labour Market (for labour services)
- households supply labour services
- firms hire labour services

Households
- sell labour
- buy goods and services

Firms
- produce and sell goods and services
- hire labour

goods and services acquired   goods and services supplied

Output or Product Markets (for goods and services)
- firms supply goods and services
- households buy goods and services

household spending on goods and services (consumer expenditure)   firms' revenue from sale of goods and services half indicate the flow of goods and services from firms through markets for goods and services to households. Thus, the blue inner arrows indicate a flow of real (or physical) units. The outer red lines represent money flows.

As indicated by the red arrows in the upper half of Figure 2.7, wages and salaries are expenditures that flow from firms through the labour market to households, where they are received as income. Red arrows in the lower half show the payments flowing from households through markets for goods and services to firms. The expenditures of households are the income of firms, and the expenditures of firms are the incomes of households. Because the red outer arrows represent monetary flows in the economy, in general, one party's expenditure is always somebody else's income.[6]

We will present a more elaborate version of the circular flow diagram in Chapter 5 when we take up the topic of explaining how we measure the output of an economy. It turns out that there are two major approaches to achieving the same measure of output—the expenditure approach and the income approach—and the circular flow diagram helps to explain how they are related.

RECAP

Incomes and expenditures are mutually dependent. Every transaction has two sides—one person's expenditure always is another person's income. A *circular flow diagram* can be used to illustrate exchange relationships in a monetary economy.

6 This two-sided nature of every transaction produces an important result. If we sum *sales* of all final goods and services and then sum *purchases* of all final goods and services, the two totals are identical. *The two sums must tally to the same number!*

SUMMARY

- One person has an *absolute* advantage over another in the production of a good if she can produce more of that good than the other person. One person has a *comparative* advantage over another in the production of a good if she is relatively more efficient than the other person at producing that good, meaning that her opportunity cost of producing it is lower than her counterpart's. Specialization based on comparative advantage is one basis for economic exchange. The model of comparative advantage predicts that output can be increased if each person specializes in the task at which she is relatively most efficient. The model is based on multiple assumptions. **LO1**

- The production possibilities curve is a simple device for summarizing the possible combinations of output that a society can produce if it employs its resources efficiently. In a simple economy that produces only sugar cane and nuts, the PPC shows the maximum quantity of sugar cane production (vertical axis) possible at each level of nut production (horizontal axis). The slope of the PPC at any point represents the opportunity cost of nuts at that point, expressed in kilograms of sugar cane. **LO2, LO4**

- All production possibilities curves slope downward because of the scarcity problem, which implies that the only way to obtain more of one good is to accept less of another. In a nut/sugar cane economy whose workers have different opportunity costs of picking nuts, the slope of the PPC becomes steeper with increasing production of nuts and movement down the curve. This change in slope illustrates the principle of increasing opportunity cost, which states that in expanding the production of any good, a society minimizes its opportunity cost by first employing those resources that are relatively efficient at producing that good. Only when all of the lowest cost resources are employed does it make economic sense to use resources that have higher opportunity costs. **LO3**

■ One reason for an economy to be operating at a technically inefficient point inside its PPC is the existence of unemployment. **LO4**

■ Economic growth can be represented by an outward expansion of the PPC curve. Factors that would cause an economy's PPC to shift outward include an increase in the size of the labour force and its skills, additions to the stock of capital goods, and improvements in technology. Economic growth improves an economy's ability to produce goods and services. **LO5**

■ Specialization can enhance standards of living in different ways, not just through people specializing according to comparative advantage. For example, specialization can eliminate the switching and start-up costs incurred when people have to move back and forth among numerous tasks, and specialization allows people to develop skills through practice and experience. **LO5**

■ The circular flow of income and expenditure emphasizes that every transaction is two sided. One party's sale (or income) always is another party's expenditure. The circular flow also emphasizes the interdependence of the individuals who live and work in an economy. **LO6**

CORE PRINCIPLES

 The Principle of Comparative Advantage
Total output is largest when each person concentrates on the activities for which his or her opportunity cost is lowest. (34)

 The Principle of Increasing Opportunity Cost
In expanding the production of any good, first employ those resources with the lowest opportunity cost. Only when all of the lowest cost resources have been employed does it make economic sense to use resources that have higher opportunity costs. (41)

KEY TERMS

absolute advantage (31)   comparative advantage (31)   production possibilities curve (36)
allocative efficiency (43)   efficient point (37)   productivity (34)
attainable point (37)   inefficient point (37)   unattainable point (37)
capital goods (42)   physical capital (42)
circular flow diagram (46)   productive efficiency (43)

REVIEW QUESTIONS

1. Explain what having a comparative advantage at producing a particular good or service means. What does having an absolute advantage at producing a good or service mean? **LO1**

2. What are four assumptions behind the simple model of comparative advantage? **LO1**

3. How will a reduction in the number of hours worked each day affect an economy's production possibilities curve? **LO5**

4. How will technological innovations that boost labour productivity affect an economy's production possibilities curve? **LO5**

5. Why does saying that people are poor because they do not specialize make more sense than saying that people perform their own services because they are poor? **LO4**

6. What are some factors that would cause an economy's production possibilities curve to shift outward? **LO5**

7. What are two sources of gains from specialization in addition to specialization according to comparative advantage? **LO5**

8. Why does every purchase of a good or service represent both expenditure and income? **LO6**

PROBLEMS

1. Consider a society whose only worker is Helen, who allocates her production time between cutting hair and baking bread. Each hour per day she devotes to cutting hair yields 4 haircuts, and each hour she devotes to baking bread yields 8 loaves of bread. If Helen works a total of 8 hours per day, graph her production possibilities curve. **LO4**

2. Refer to Problem 1. Which of the points listed below is efficient? Which is attainable? **LO4**
   a. 28 haircuts/day, 16 loaves/day
   b. 16 haircuts/day, 32 loaves/day
   c. 18 haircuts/day, 24 loaves/day

3. Determine whether the following statements are true or false, and briefly explain why. **LO1, LO4**
   a. Toby can produce 5 L of apple cider or 70 g of feta cheese per hour. Kyle can produce 3 L of apple cider or 42 g of feta cheese per hour. Therefore, Toby and Kyle cannot benefit from specialization and trade.
   b. A doctor who can vacuum her office faster and more thoroughly than a commercial cleaner is better off if she cleans her office herself.
   c. In an economy in which millions of workers each have different opportunity costs of producing two goods, the principle of comparative advantage implies that the slope of the production possibilities curve decreases in absolute value as more of the goods on the horizontal axis are produced.

4. Nancy and Bill are auto mechanics. Nancy takes 4 hours to replace a clutch and 2 hours to replace a set of brakes. Bill takes 6 hours to replace a clutch and 2 hours to replace a set of brakes. If Bill and Nancy open a motor repair shop: **LO1, LO4**
   a. both will be better off if Nancy works only on clutches, and Bill works only on brakes.
   b. Bill has a comparative advantage at replacing brakes.
   c. Nancy has an absolute advantage at replacing clutches.

   d. Nancy has a comparative advantage at replacing clutches.
   e. all but one of the above statements are correct.

5. Bob and Stella are a married couple. Bob takes 10 minutes to change a light bulb and 2 minutes to fix a broken fuse. Stella takes 3 minutes to change a light bulb and 30 seconds to fix a broken fuse. Which of the following statements is true? **LO1, LO4**
   a. Stella has a comparative advantage at fixing fuses, because she can do it faster than Bob.
   b. Stella has a comparative advantage at changing light bulbs and fixing fuses, because she can do both of them faster than Bob.
   c. Stella has an absolute advantage at changing light bulbs and fixing fuses, because she can do both of them faster than Bob.
   d. Bob has a comparative advantage at fixing fuses, because Stella has a comparative advantage at changing light bulbs.
   e. Stella has a comparative advantage at changing light bulbs.

6. Kamal and Filipe are stranded together on a desert island. The raw materials on the island are suitable only for making beer and pizza, but their quantities are unlimited. What is scarce is labour. Filipe and Kamal each spend 10 hours a day making beer or pizza. The following table specifies *how much beer and pizza Filipe and Kamal can produce per hour.*

	Beer	Pizza
Filipe	1 bottle per hour	0.2 pizzas per hour
Kamal	1.5 bottles per hour	0.5 pizzas per hour

   a. Draw the daily production possibilities curves (PPCs) for Filipe and Kamal.
   b. Who has an absolute advantage in making pizza? in brewing beer?
   c. Who has a comparative advantage in making pizza? in brewing beer?

Now suppose their preferences are as follows: Filipe wants 2 beers and as much pizza as he can eat each day, and Kamal wants 2 pizzas and as much beer as he can drink each day. **LO4**

d.   If each man is self-reliant, how much beer and pizza will Filipe and Kamal eat and drink?

e.   Suppose the two men decide to trade with each other. Draw their joint PPC, and give an example of a trade that will make each of them better off.

7. Rework Problem 6 with the following changes: **LO1, LO4**

a.   Each individual's productivity is shown in the table that follows, *which specifies the number of hours each man needs to produce a single unit of beer and pizza.*

b.   Filipe wants 6 beers and as much pizza as he can eat each day, while Kamal wants 2 pizzas and as much beer as he can drink each day.

	Production time for 1 beer	Production time for 1 pizza
Filipe	5/4 hours	5/3 hours
Kamal	5 hours	5/2 hours

8. Suppose Filipe and Kamal's production possibilities curves from Problem 7 are combined. What would be the maximum number of pizzas available to Filipe and Kamal if they could buy or sell in a world market in which 1 beer could be exchanged for 1 pizza? What would be the maximum number of beers available to them? **LO2**

9. Kate and William both can produce oranges and olive oil. Kate can produce up to 10 kg of oranges per week or 5 bottles of olive oil, or any combination of oil and oranges along a straight-line production possibilities curve linking those two points. William can produce up to 50 kg of oranges per week or 1 bottle of olive oil, or any combination along a straight-line production possibilities curve linking those points. **LO1, LO2, LO3**

a.   Does the principle of increasing opportunity cost apply in either of these two economies? Why or why not?

b.   Suppose Kate and William agree that each will specialize in the production of either oil or oranges. According to the principle of comparative advantage, who will specialize in which commodity?

c.   If Kate and William agree to trade oranges and olive oil with each other, what are the maximum

and minimum prices that can prevail for oranges, in terms of bottles of olive oil?

10. Jay, Kay, and Dee are marooned on the Greek island of Skorpios. They must find a way to provide themselves with food and drinking water. The following table shows how many hours each person takes to produce one unit of food or one unit of water. **LO2, LO4**

	Production time for 1 unit of food	Production time for 1 unit of drinking water
Jay	1 hour	2 hours
Kay	2 hours	1 hour
Dee	4 hours	6 hours

a.   If each person can work for 12 hours a day and each person provides only for himself or herself, draw their individual PPCs.

b.   Suppose Jay, Kay, and Dee decide to produce food and water cooperatively so they can gain from trade. Draw their combined production possibilities curve.

c.   If the trio wants, in aggregate, to consume 15 units of food and 12 units of water, who will specialize in food production? Who will specialize in water production? Will anyone divide his or her time between food and water production?

d.   If the trio wants, in aggregate, to consume 6 units of water and as much food as possible, who will specialize in food and who will specialize in water? Will anyone divide his or her time between food and water production? How much food will be produced?

e.   Suppose production is as in (c). Dee suggests dividing the output equally among the three of them. Assuming that the amounts of food that Jay and Kay get under this arrangement are exactly what each would have chosen if he or she had lived and worked alone, is each of them strictly better off when they share? Explain.

11. Why does each of the following transactions represent both income and expenditure? **LO6**

a.   A reckless driver pays a fine of $1,000 for stunt driving.

b.   A worker receives a paycheque on payday.

c.   A student pays the bookstore $800 for textbooks.

d.   The Canadian government spends $50 billion for new F35 airplanes.

e.   A gambler wins $100 000 at the casino.

ANSWERS TO IN-CHAPTER EXERCISES

2.1

	Productivity in programming	Productivity in bicycle repair
Mina	2 Web-page updates per hour	1 repair per hour
Barb	3 Web-page updates per hour	3 repairs per hour

The entries in the table tell us that Barb has an absolute advantage over Mina in both activities. While Barb can update three Web pages per hour, Mina can update only two. Barb's absolute advantage over Mina is even greater in the task of fixing bicycles—three repairs per hour versus Mina's one.

But, as in Example 2.2, the fact that Barb is a better programmer than Mina does not imply that Barb will be better off if she updates her own Web page. Barb's opportunity cost of updating a Web page is one bicycle repair, whereas Mina must give up only half a bicycle repair to update a Web page. Mina has a comparative advantage over Barb at programming, and Barb has a comparative advantage over Mina at bicycle repair. **LO2**

2.2 Susan's opportunity cost of picking a kilogram of nuts is 1/2 kg of sugar cane. But Tom's opportunity cost of picking a kilogram of nuts is now only 1/3 kg of sugar cane. So Tom has a comparative advantage at picking nuts, and Susan has a comparative advantage at cutting sugar cane. **LO2**

2.3 The slope to the left of D (in absolute value) is 1/2 kg of sugar cane per kilogram of nuts, which is Susan's opportunity cost of picking nuts. **LO2**

CHAPTER 3
Supply and Demand: An Introduction

LEARNING OBJECTIVES

When you have completed this chapter, you will be able to:

LO1 Explain the nature of an economic model and give examples of at least two economic models.

LO2 Explain the slope of a market supply curve and how it summarizes the behaviour of many sellers.

LO3 Explain the slope of a market demand curve and how it summarizes the behaviour of many buyers.

LO4 Draw and label a supply and demand diagram and use it to explain how the supply and demand curves determine equilibrium price and quantity.

LO5 Define the equilibrium principle and explain why the equilibrium principle does not prove that one equilibrium is better than another.

LO6 Explain how shifts in supply and demand curves change prices and quantities.

LO7 State the assumptions behind the supply and demand model and explain why it best applies to markets where many buyers interact with many sellers of a uniform product.

In Toronto, as in any other Canadian city, the stock of food-stuffs on hand at any moment in grocery stores, restaurants, and private kitchens is sufficient to feed the city's 2.5 million residents for a week at most. Almost no food is produced within the city, yet most of Toronto's residents have nutri-tionally adequate and highly varied diets. Provisioning Toronto requires millions of kilograms of food to be deliv-ered throughout the city every day. Somehow, the system must not only deliver enough food to satisfy Torontonians' discriminating palates, but it must also deliver the *right kinds* of food: there must not be too much bacon and too few eggs, or too much caviar and not enough canned tuna, and so on. Similar judgments must be made *within* each category of food and drink: there must be the right amount of Swiss cheese and the right amounts of provolone, Gorgonzola, and feta, not too much basmati rice and not too little risotto, and a different variety of herbs and seasonings for each ethnic-ity of cuisine. Moreover, someone must decide how much of each type of food will be delivered to *each* of the thousands of restaurants and grocery stores in the city. Someone must determine whether the deliveries will be made in big trucks or small ones, arrange that the trucks be in the right place at the right time, and ensure that fuel and qualified drivers are available.

Thousands of individuals will play a role in this collec-tive effort. Some people must drive food delivery trucks, rather than trucks that deliver lumber. Others must become mechanics who fix these trucks, rather than carpenters who build houses. Others must become farmers, rather than architects or bricklayers. Still others must become chefs in upscale restaurants, or at McDonald's, instead of becoming plumbers or electricians.

A great number of complex tasks must be coordinated in order to provide Torontonians with food every day. Nevertheless, the citizens of that city are able to obtain what they need fairly easily and consistently. In Canada, the overwhelmingly majority of daily decisions in the food supply chain are coordinated through markets. The remark-able fact that Torontonians are able to obtain what they need fairly easily and consistently is primarily due to the incentives that market prices establish. Yes, a grocery store will occasionally run out of flank steak, or a waiter must sometimes tell a diner that someone else has just ordered the last serving of roast duck, but such episodes remain in memory only because they are rare.

In this chapter, we will use economic models to explore how markets allocate food, housing, and other goods and services. An economic model, as we noted in Chapter 1, is a representation of economic reality that highlights particular variables and the relationships among them. The term economic model may sound impressive but, as the definition states, it really just means providing an explicit description of the relationship between two or more variables. In Chapter 2, for example, we used a model to explain the idea of comparative advantage. The model was presented in the form of a numerical example involving Rikke and Beth updating Web pages and repairing bicycles. It was a model of an economy consisting of two people producing two services. Making certain assumptions, we used the model to show that they could increase their total output by specializing according to their comparative advantage. In this chapter, we will use similar specific examples to illustrate one specific model of how some markets function.

A particular economic model may work well for analyzing one type of market, but not another. For example, the market for pizzas is quite different from the market for electricity. Many restaurants in Toronto will deliver pizzas, but each house in Toronto has only one line that delivers electricity. Thus a model designed to analyze the market for pizzas will not provide a good understanding of the market for electricity, and vice versa. Since there is often more than one economic model that could be used to analyze a particular market, economists have to choose between competing models, using evidence on the actual accuracy of each model's predictions. Nevertheless, when markets work well, they are effective in allocating a complex array of goods, services, and resources. To be sure, markets are by no means perfect. In microeconomics, economists analyze under which circumstances markets function smoothly, and they also discuss how markets, when left to themselves, cannot be expected to function well.

This chapter provides an introductory overview of how economists analyze markets with many buyers and sellers of standardized products. It uses a model based on supply and demand, two concepts that we soon will define carefully. Most of microeconomics is directly concerned with analyses of individual markets, while macroeconomics focuses on national economies as entire units. Nevertheless, individual markets—labour markets, financial markets, and foreign exchange markets—also play a central role in macroeconomics. And macroeconomic models, although they are quite distinct from the model of supply and demand, are much easier to understand for those who have studied the supply and demand model than for those who haven't studied it.

In capitalist, or market, economies, people decide for themselves which careers to pursue and which products to produce or buy. However, there are few, if any, *pure* market economies today. Modern industrial countries are more properly described as *mixed economies*, meaning that goods and services are allocated by a combination of markets, regulation, and other forms of collective control.

3.1 MARKETS AND PRICES

Beginning with some basic concepts and definitions, we will explore how the interactions between buyers and sellers in markets determine the prices and quantities of the various goods and services traded in those markets. By definition, the **market** for any good is the context in which potential buyers and sellers of that good can negotiate exchanges. For any good, we specify the time and the place at which it is bought and sold. So, for example, the market for hamburgers on a given day in a given place is just the set of people (or other economic actors, like firms) potentially able to buy or sell hamburgers at that time and location.

market the context in which potential buyers and sellers of a good or service can negotiate exchanges

In the market for hamburgers, sellers comprise the individuals and companies that either sell or might sell hamburgers, under the right circumstances. Similarly, buyers in this market include all individuals who buy, or might buy, hamburgers. How is the market price of hamburgers determined?

Some people might think it depends on the cost of production; others, the value to the consumer. Writing in the late nineteenth century, the British economist Alfred Marshall declared, "We might as reasonably dispute whether it is the upper or the under blade of a pair of scissors that cuts a piece of paper, as whether value is governed by utility or cost of production."[1] Our task in the pages ahead will be to explore Marshall's insights and gain some practice in applying them. As a first step, we introduce the two main components of Marshall's analysis: the supply curve and the demand curve.

THE SUPPLY CURVE

supply curve a curve or schedule showing the total quantity of a good of uniform quality that sellers want to sell at each price during a particular period of time provided that all other things are held constant

quantity supplied the total amount of a good of uniform quality that all sellers are willing to produce and sell at a single, specific price during a particular period of time

In the market for hamburgers, the **supply curve** of hamburgers is a simple schedule, or graph, that tells us, for each possible price of hamburgers, the total quantity of hamburgers of uniform quality that all hamburger sellers together would be willing to supply per period of time at that price, provided that all other things are held constant. Notice that the definition of the supply curve refers to the *quantities* of hamburgers that sellers are *willing* to *supply* at specific prices. Although they are related, the *supply curve* and the *quantity supplied* are two different concepts. **Quantity supplied** is the total amount of a good of uniform quality that all sellers together are willing to produce and sell *at a single, specific price* during a particular period of time.

What does the supply curve of hamburgers look like? People will be willing to produce and sell hamburgers as long as, *and only as long as*, the price they receive for them is sufficient to cover their opportunity costs of supplying them (what they could have earned if they had spent their time and invested their money in some other way). Figure 3.1 provides an illustration. It portrays a single supply curve showing the relationship between *price* and *quantity supplied*. Many points lie on this single curve. Each point on a supply curve identifies a specific quantity supplied and a corresponding, specific price. Figure 3.1 indicates that if the price is $2, the quantity of hamburgers supplied will be 8000. If the price is higher, the quantity is greater; for example, at a price of $3 each, 12 000 will be supplied.

Economists know perfectly well that some hamburgers are bigger and better than others (and consequently sell for a higher price), but we want to focus on the role played by prices in the market. Hence we simplify by making the assumption that we can draw a supply curve for a particular type of hamburger of uniform quality; for example, one made with six ounces of well-done, grade A beef and garnished with relish.

FIGURE 3.1
The Daily Supply Curve of Hamburgers in Downtown Toronto
At higher prices, sellers generally offer more units for sale. The supply curve is upward sloping.

1 Alfred Marshall, *Principles of Economics* (1920), 8th ed., (London: Macmillan & Co Ltd, 1964), p. 290.

The definition of quantity supplied also refers to a particular period of time. A quantity supplied of 8000 hamburgers per day is quite different from a quantity of 8000 hamburgers per month. Because, to be meaningful, our definition must specify the period of time during which a quantity is supplied, the label on the horizontal axis of Figure 3.1 indicates quantity supplied *per day*.

Why is the supply curve for hamburgers upward sloping? When the price of hamburgers is low, say, $2 per hamburger, only those people who can sell hamburgers for a very low cost will be willing to supply them. For the supply curve shown in Figure 3.1, the quantity supplied at a price of $2 will be 8000 hamburgers per day, which is the total quantity of hamburgers supplied by people whose cost of selling hamburgers is $2 per hamburger or less. If the price of a hamburger were to rise above $2, additional sellers would find it worthwhile to offer hamburgers for sale. For example, at a price of $3, Figure 3.1 shows that the quantity of hamburgers supplied is 12 000 per day, while at a price of $4 the quantity supplied is 16 000. The higher the price is, the more people find it worthwhile to supply hamburgers.

Finally, a supply curve (or schedule) holds constant all things other than price and quantity supplied. The Latin term *ceteris paribus* (other things constant) is often used to indicate this assumption, one which allows us to focus on the impact of price on quantity supplied. Many things could affect actual supply in the real world. If, for example, a sudden blizzard dumped a metre of snow on the city, it would be impossible for most people to get to work until the streets were plowed, and the supply of hamburgers (and much else) would be disrupted. We will ignore such possibilities and impose the assumption of *ceteris paribus* in order to show how supply and demand determine the price and quantity traded. Later, we will relax the assumption of *ceteris paribus* to see the effects of factors other than price.

BOX 3.1

Supply as an Equation

There are many possible ways to express economic ideas. An economic model can be explained with words, described with graphs, or represented by mathematical equations. If we choose to use the language of mathematics, the supply curve pictured in Figure 3.1 could also be written algebraically as

$$Q_s = a + bP_s.$$

Algebraically, we use Q_s to mean quantity supplied in *thousands* of units and P_s to mean supply price. In general, the parameter a is the horizontal intercept, and the parameter b is the reciprocal of the slope of the supply curve. The plus sign indicates a direct, positive relationship between quantity supplied and price. In the specific example of the supply schedule portrayed graphically in Figure 3.1, $a = 0$ and $b = 4$, so the supply curve also can be written algebraically as

$$Q_s = 4P_s.$$

If we measure quantity supplied in thousands of hamburgers per day and price in dollars, we can state the relationship between price and quantity supplied in any of three ways. Both the graphical representation of Figure 3.1 and the algebraic statement $Q_s = 4P_s$ are equivalent to the verbal statement, "If price increases by one dollar, quantity supplied will increase by 4000 hamburgers." The mathematical statement says the same thing as either the figure or the words, just more compactly.[2]

---

2 The reader may be perplexed by the economist's practice of placing price, the independent variable, on the vertical axis. The practice stems from Alfred Marshall, who treated quantity as the independent variable because he wanted to investigate the effect of changes in quantity on price. Such was Marshall's influence that ever since he published *Principles of Economics* in 1890, economists have placed price on the vertical axis.

THE DEMAND CURVE

The supply curve, by itself, does not tell us how many hamburgers will be sold in downtown Toronto on a given day, or at what price those hamburgers will sell. To find the prevailing price and quantity, we also need the *demand curve* for hamburgers in this market. The **demand curve** for hamburgers is a graph that tells us the total quantity of hamburgers that buyers want to buy at each price.[3]

demand curve a curve or schedule showing the total quantity of a good of uniform quality that buyers want to buy at each price during a particular period of time provided that all other things are held constant

Figure 3.2 graphs the daily demand for a hypothetical market for hamburgers in Toronto. It shows a relationship between *price* and *quantity demanded*. Typically, a demand curve is downward sloping. The demand curve in Figure 3.2 shows that when price is high, buyers as a group are willing to purchase fewer hamburgers. Like the supply curve, the demand curve is composed of many points. Each point on the demand curve identifies a specific quantity demanded at the corresponding price. Thus, a single demand curve plots many different quantities demanded and many prices. When the price is $4, quantity demanded is 8000 hamburgers per day. When the price is $3, the quantity demanded is 12 000 hamburgers per day, and so on.

FIGURE 3.2

The Daily Demand Curve for Hamburgers in Downtown Toronto
The demand curve for any good is a generally downward-sloping function of its price. At lower prices, buyers generally want to purchase more units.

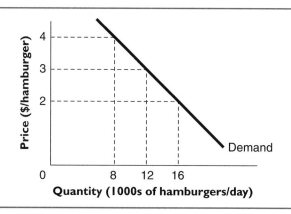

We define the demand curve in the same terms as we do the supply curve. The demand curve pertains to a good of uniform quality. Quantity demanded is specified as an amount per period of time, so the label on the horizontal axis of Figure 3.2 indicates that quantity is measured in thousands of hamburgers *per day*. Finally, the assumption of *ceteris paribus* pertains to demand just as it does to supply. A single demand curve shows the relationship between quantity demanded and price, provided that all things other than price and quantity are held constant. Therefore, we define **quantity demanded** as the total amount purchased by all buyers at a single, specific price. We will return to the question of what happens to demand when things other than price and quantity change, but first we develop the concept of market equilibrium.

quantity demanded the total amount of a good of uniform quality purchased at a single, specific price by all buyers during a particular period of time

BOX 3.2

Demand as an Equation

Demand, like supply, can be analyzed with words, with graphs, or by using equations. A linear demand curve can be represented algebraically by an equation of the form

$$Q_D = c - dP_D.$$

3 To be truly precise, we have to specify "hamburgers of uniform quality during a particular period of time, in downtown Toronto, provided that all other things are held constant." But the key idea is fairly simple: how many would people want to buy, at each price?

Quantity demanded is represented by Q_D, while P_D represents demand price. In general, the parameter c represents the horizontal intercept; that is, the quantity of hamburgers that would be consumed if the price is zero (if hamburgers were free). The minus sign indicates an indirect, negative relationship between quantity demanded and price. In the specific case of the demand curve that is graphed in Figure 3.2, the demand curve can be written as the equation

$$Q_D = 24 - 4P_D.$$

In this case, Q_D represents quantity demanded in *thousands* of units, $c = 24$, and $d = -4$. Again, one could express it verbally: if price increases by one dollar, quantity demanded will decrease by 4000 hamburgers. Some people find it easiest to understand the relationship between quantity demanded and price when it is expressed verbally, while others prefer algebra or graphs. All are equally valid—they are just different ways of saying the same thing.

MARKET EQUILIBRIUM

The concept of *equilibrium* is employed in both the physical and social sciences and is of central importance in economic analysis. We use the term **equilibrium** to denote a state of rest.

In general, a system in equilibrium has no tendency to change. In physics, for example, a ball hanging from a spring is said to be in equilibrium when the spring has stretched so that the upward force it exerts on the ball is exactly counterbalanced by the downward force of gravity. In economics, the supply curve states that when price *increases*, the quantity supplied also *increases*; the two are *directly* related. The demand curve states that when price *increases*, quantity demanded *decreases*; the two are *inversely* related. A market is said to be in equilibrium when supply and demand are exactly counterbalanced so that no participant in the market has any desire to alter his or her behaviour. In equilibrium, there is no tendency for price and quantity to change.

If we want to determine the final position of a ball hanging from a spring, we need to find the point at which the forces of gravity and spring tension are exactly counterbalanced and the system is in equilibrium. Similarly, if we want to find the price at which a good will sell (the **equilibrium price**) and the quantity of it that will be sold (the **equilibrium quantity**), we need to find the equilibrium in the market for that good. The price and quantity at which the supply and demand curves for the good intersect is the equilibrium. For the hypothetical supply and demand curves for hamburgers in downtown Toronto, the equilibrium price will therefore be $3 per hamburger, and the equilibrium quantity of hamburgers sold will be 12 000 per day, as shown in Figure 3.3, which combines Figures 3.1 and 3.2.

equilibrium a state that occurs when all of the forces that act on all the variables in a system are in balance, exactly offsetting each other so that none of the variables in the system has any tendency to change

equilibrium price and **equilibrium quantity** the price and quantity of a good at the intersection of the supply and demand curves for the good

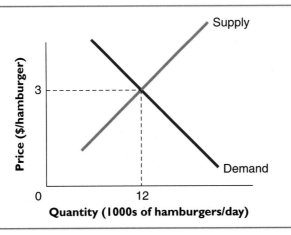

FIGURE 3.3

The Equilibrium Price and Quantity of Hamburgers in Downtown Toronto
The equilibrium quantity and price of a product are the values that correspond to the intersection of the supply and demand curves for that product.

In Figure 3.3, note that at the equilibrium price of $3 per hamburger, both sellers and buyers are *satisfied* in the following sense: buyers are buying exactly the quantity of hamburgers they want to buy at that price (12 000 per day) and sellers are selling exactly the quantity of hamburgers they want to sell (also 12 000 per day) at that same price. In this **market equilibrium**, both buyers and sellers are satisfied in that neither group faces any incentives to change their behaviour.

market equilibrium occurs when all buyers and sellers are satisfied with their respective quantities at the market price

Note the limited sense of the term *satisfied* in the definition of market equilibrium. It does not mean that sellers would be displeased to receive a price higher than the equilibrium price. Rather, it means only that they are able to sell all they wish to sell at the equilibrium price. Similarly, to say that buyers are satisfied at the equilibrium price does not mean that they would not like to have a higher income or that they would not be happy to pay less than the equilibrium price. Rather, it means only that, given their incomes, they are able to buy exactly as many units of the good as they want to at the equilibrium price.

Note also that if the price of hamburgers in our downtown Toronto market was anything other than $3, either buyers or sellers would not be satisfied. Suppose, for example, that the price of hamburgers was $4, as shown in Figure 3.4. At that price, buyers want to buy only 8000 hamburgers per day, but sellers want to sell 16 000. Since no one can force someone to buy a hamburger against his or her wishes, this means that buyers will buy only the 8000 hamburgers they want to buy. So when the price exceeds the equilibrium price, sellers will be dissatisfied. At a price of $4 in this example, the quantity supplied exceeds the quantity demanded by 8000 hamburgers. Therefore, sellers are left with an **excess supply**, or **surplus**.

excess supply, or surplus the difference between the quantity supplied and the quantity demanded when the price of a good exceeds the equilibrium price; leaves some sellers dissatisfied

Conversely, suppose that the price of hamburgers in the downtown Toronto market was less than the equilibrium price, say $2 per hamburger. As shown in Figure 3.5, buyers want to buy 16 000 hamburgers per day at that price, whereas sellers want to sell only 8000. This time the buyers will be dissatisfied, because sellers cannot be forced to sell hamburgers against their wishes. At a price of $2, in this example, the quantity demanded exceeds the quantity supplied by 8000 hamburgers. Therefore, buyers experience an **excess demand**, or **shortage**.

excess demand, or shortage the difference between the quantity supplied and the quantity demanded when the price of a good lies below the equilibrium price; leaves some buyers dissatisfied

Markets for goods and services often tend toward their respective equilibrium prices and quantities, provided that many buyers and sellers are competing in the market. The mechanisms by which this happens are implicit in our definitions of excess supply and excess demand. Suppose, for example, that the price of hamburgers in our hypothetical market was $4, leading to excess supply, as shown in Figure 3.4. Sellers are dissatisfied

FIGURE 3.4
Excess Supply
When price exceeds the equilibrium price, there is excess supply, or surplus, that is equal to the difference between quantity supplied and quantity demanded.

FIGURE 3.5
Excess Demand
When price lies below the equilibrium price, there is excess demand or shortage—the difference between quantity demanded and quantity supplied.

because they provide more hamburgers than buyers want to buy, so they have an incentive to take whatever steps they can to increase their sales. A simple strategy is for them to cut their price slightly. Thus, if one seller reduced his price from $4 to, say, $3.95 per hamburger, he could attract some of the buyers who otherwise would have had to pay $4 for hamburgers. Those sellers, to recover their lost business, would then have an incentive to match the price cut. But notice that if all sellers lowered their prices to $3.95, there would still be considerable excess supply in the hamburger market. So sellers would face continuing incentives to cut their prices. This pressure to cut prices will not go away until the price falls all the way to $3. At $3, excess supply is zero.

Conversely, suppose that the price starts out less than the equilibrium price; say, $2 per hamburger. This time it is the buyers who are dissatisfied. A person who cannot get all the hamburgers she wants at a price of $2 has an incentive to offer a higher price, hoping to obtain hamburgers that would otherwise have been sold to other buyers. And sellers, for their part, will be only too happy to post higher prices as long as queues of dissatisfied buyers remain.

The upshot is that price has a tendency to move to its equilibrium level under conditions of either excess supply or excess demand. And when price reaches its equilibrium level, both buyers and sellers are satisfied simultaneously, since they are able to buy or sell precisely the amounts they choose, given their incomes.

We emphasize that the mere fact that buyers and sellers are satisfied in this sense does not mean that markets automatically result in the best of all possible worlds. For example, a poor person may buy one hamburger each day at a price of $3, but still be hungry. In this case, he is satisfied only in the limited sense that with his available income he either cannot buy a second hamburger or prefers buying something else.

It is also important to emphasize that the equilibrating process depends on competition among many buyers and sellers, all of whom are small relative to the size of the market. If all sellers are small, no seller has the ability to increase the price of hamburgers above the equilibrium price by restricting the quantity supplied. For example, if all sellers are small, no seller can raise the price of hamburgers to $4 by restricting the quantity to 8000 hamburgers per day. Why? Because at $4, other sellers will be perfectly willing to compete for buyers by increasing the quantity of hamburgers, while offering a somewhat lower price.

Similarly, if all buyers are small, no buyer can reduce price below the equilibrium price, say to $2, by announcing that they will pay no more than $2 for a hamburger. Why? Because at $2, only 8000 hamburgers per day will be supplied, and other buyers will compete for hamburgers by offering a somewhat higher price.

BOX **3.3**

Market Equilibrium: Supply Equals Demand

When a market is in equilibrium, no buyer or seller wants to change their behaviour, so none of the variables in the system tend to change. Figure 3.3 presents a graphical representation of equilibrium in a simple system of supply and demand—the intersection of the supply and demand curves. The intersection of supply and demand curves is the only place where quantity supplied, Q_S, equals quantity demanded, Q_D. It, therefore, identifies the equilibrium quantity, which we will call Q^*. Because the supply price, P_S, equals demand price, P_D, at this intersection point, the intersection also identifies the equilibrium price, which we will call P^*.

We can represent equilibrium algebraically by using the equations for supply and demand that appear in the previous boxes. In market equilibrium, we have that $P_S = P_D = P^*$ and $Q_S = Q_D = Q^*$. Therefore, by setting $Q_S = Q_D$ we can solve for P^*:

$$a + bP^* = c - dP^*.$$

The equation for supply (from Box 3.1) is on the left-hand side of the equal sign, and the equation for demand (from Box 3.2) is on the right.

Solving for P^* we have that

$$P^* = \frac{(c-a)}{(b+d)}.$$

We can substitute P^* into either the equation for demand or for supply to determine Q^*. Using the demand equation, we have

$$Q^* = c - d \times \left(\frac{c-a}{b+d}\right).$$

Therefore, the equilibrium condition states that supply is equal to demand. The equilibrium quantity is Q^*. By definition, $Q_S = Q_D = Q^*$, where quantity supplied and quantity demanded are represented by Q_S and Q_D, respectively, as they were in the earlier two boxes.

If we insert the values for the parameters as stated in the two earlier boxes, we can rewrite the equilibrium condition:

$$0 + 4P^* = 24 - 4P^*.$$

Since this is one equation with one unknown, we can solve for P^* and find that $P^* = \$3$. The equilibrium value for price can be substituted into either the equation for supply or the equation for demand to determine that the equilibrium quantity is 12. Remember that Q^* is measured in thousands of units. Therefore, the equilibrium quantity actually is 12 000 hamburgers. The values for equilibrium price and quantity are consistent with what is shown in Figure 3.3.

As demonstrated here, an equilibrium of supply and demand involves the simultaneous solution of two equations. See Connect for additional discussion of how two simultaneous equations are solved.

MARKETS, EQUILIBRIUM, AND FAIRNESS

When a market is out of equilibrium, it is always possible to identify mutually beneficial, but unrealized, exchanges. When people have failed to take advantage of all mutually beneficial exchanges, we often say that there is "cash on the table"—the economist's metaphor for unexploited opportunities. When the price in a market is below the equilibrium price, there is cash on the table because it will always be possible for a supplier to produce an additional unit at a cost that is lower than the price buyers are willing to pay. This leads to an important result, which we will state as a core principle.

The Equilibrium Principle: A market in equilibrium leaves no unexploited opportunities for trade between individuals.

EQUILIBRIUM

Equilibrium in a supply and demand model means there is no tendency for price and quantity to change. Equilibrium, then, is a concept of positive economics that of itself says nothing about whether one equilibrium outcome is better than another. In welfare economics, economists examine considerations relevant to judging that one equilibrium outcome is superior to another. One such consideration, which is relatively easy to understand and explain, is the distribution of income.

Is an equilibrium solution also a fair solution?

Equilibrium and fairness are two very different concepts. Consider two societies. The first consists of a few wealthy people and many who are poor. The second society is more equal—almost everyone is middle class. Wealthy people can afford to buy mansions, the middle class have enough income to buy small houses, and poor people can only afford one room shacks. Therefore, the demand for mansions in the first society will be greater than the demand for mansions in the second society. Likewise, the two societies will have different demands for modest houses and shacks. Because the two societies have different patterns of demand, when the market for houses is in equilibrium in each society, the equilibrium combination of mansions, modest homes, and shacks in the first society will differ from the equilibrium combination in the second society. In general, whenever the distribution of assets differs between one society and another, the equilibrium consumption of commodities will also differ. *Each different distribution of wealth will produce a different equilibrium solution for prices and quantities produced.* The equilibrium principle has nothing to say about whether any particular initial distribution of assets is fair, and it thus leaves unexamined an important ethical question: is one distribution of wealth "better" than another?

> **RECAP** ↑
>
> **MARKETS AND PRICES**
>
> The *market* for a good or service is the context in which potential buyers and sellers of the good or service can negotiate exchanges. For any given price, the *supply curve* shows the total quantity that suppliers of the good would be willing to sell, and the *demand curve* shows the total quantity that demanders would be willing to buy. Suppliers are willing to sell more at higher prices (supply curves slope upward) and demanders are willing to buy less at higher prices (demand curves slope downward).
>
> *Market equilibrium,* the situation in which all buyers and sellers are satisfied with their respective quantities at the market price, occurs at the intersection of the supply and demand curves. The corresponding price and quantity are called the *equilibrium price* and the *equilibrium quantity.*
>
> Prices and quantities tend to be driven toward their equilibrium values by the competitive actions of buyers and sellers. If the price is initially too high, resulting in excess supply, dissatisfied sellers will compete for buyers by cutting their prices to sell more. If the price is initially too low, resulting in excess demand, competition among buyers drives the price upward. This process continues until equilibrium is reached. The equilibrating process depends on competition among large numbers of small buyers and sellers.
>
> A market in equilibrium means that all opportunities for individuals to make exchanges that are privately beneficial to both parties have been realized.
>
> If each individual starts with an initial endowment of assets, and all individuals are free to make mutually beneficial exchanges, each different initial distribution of assets will in general produce different market equilibrium of commodity production and prices. The equilibrium principle has nothing to say about whether the initial endowment of wealth is "fair."

FIGURE 3.6

An Increase in the Quantity Demanded versus an Increase in Demand

Panel (a): An increase in quantity demanded is represented by a downward movement along the demand curve as price falls. Panel (b): An increase in demand is represented by an outward shift of the demand curve.

3.2 EXPLAINING CHANGES IN PRICES AND QUANTITIES

If we know how the factors that govern supply and demand curves are changing, we can make informed predictions about how prices and the corresponding quantities will change. But when describing changing circumstances in the marketplace, we must take care to recognize some important terminological distinctions. For example, we must distinguish between the meanings of the seemingly similar expressions *change in the quantity demanded* and *change in demand*. When we speak of a **change in the quantity demanded**, we mean the change in quantity that people want to buy that occurs in response to a change in price. For instance, Figure 3.6(a) depicts an increase in the quantity demanded that occurs in response to a reduction in the price of tuna. When the price falls from $5 to $4 per can, the quantity demanded rises from 2000 to 4000 cans per day. By contrast, when we speak of a **change in demand**, we mean a *shift in the entire demand curve*. For example, Figure 3.6(b) depicts an increase in demand, meaning that at every price the quantity demanded is higher than before. In summary, a change in the quantity demanded refers to a movement *along* the demand curve, and a change in demand means a *shift* of the entire curve.

A similar terminological distinction applies on the supply side of the market. A **change in supply** means a shift in the entire supply curve, whereas a **change in the quantity supplied** refers to a movement along the supply curve. Why might the demand curve shift? Why might the supply curve shift? Shifts in either the supply curve or demand curve happen because of changes in some of the factors we have held constant up until now. We can use the framework of supply and demand to analyze the implications of changes in these factors.

Alfred Marshall's supply and demand model is a useful tool for an economic naturalist. Once we understand the forces that govern the placements of supply and demand curves, we are in a position to make sense of a host of interesting observations in the world around us.

SHIFTS IN THE SUPPLY CURVE

To get a better feel for how the supply and demand model enables us to predict and explain price and quantity movements, it is helpful to begin with a few simple examples. Because the supply curve is based on costs of production, anything that changes production costs will shift the supply curve and hence will result in a new equilibrium quantity and price.

change in quantity demanded a movement along the demand curve that occurs in response to a change in price

change in demand a shift of the entire demand curve

change in supply a shift of the entire supply curve

change in quantity supplied a movement along the supply curve that occurs in response to a change in price

EXAMPLE **3.1**

What will happen to the equilibrium price and quantity of new houses if the price of lumber declines?

Suppose the initial supply and demand curves for new houses are as shown by the curves S and D in Figure 3.7, resulting in an equilibrium price of $160 000 per house and an equilibrium quantity of 40 houses per month. A decline in the price of lumber reduces the cost of making new houses, and this means that, for any given price of houses, more builders can profitably serve the market than before. Diagrammatically, this means a rightward shift in the supply curve of houses, from S to S'. (A rightward shift in the supply curve can also be described as a downward shift.)

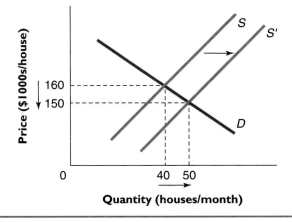

FIGURE 3.7
The Effect on the Market for New Houses of a Decline in the Price of Lumber
When input prices fall, supply shifts right, causing equilibrium price to fall and equilibrium quantity to rise.

If we assume that the decline in the price of lumber has no impact on incomes in the lumber industry and hence on the demand for homes, then a decline in the price of lumber produces a significant rightward shift in the supply curve of houses, but no perceptible shift in the demand curve. We see from Figure 3.7 that the new equilibrium price, $150 000 per house, is lower than the original price, and the new equilibrium quantity, 50 houses per month, is higher than the original quantity.

Example 3.1 involved changes in the cost of an input in the production of a good, lumber, in the production of houses. We have modified the assumption of *ceteris paribus*, all other things equal, to now mean all other things equal but one (i.e., the price of lumber). As the following case illustrates, supply curves also shift when technology changes.

Changes in *input* prices and technology are two of the most important factors that give rise to shifts in supply curves. **Inputs** are those items used in a production process to produce a good or service. In Example 3.1, lumber is an input used in the production of houses. The supply curve for houses in Figure 3.7 shifted to the right, or increased, because the price of lumber fell, thus reducing the cost of an input in building houses. Consider another example. Because petroleum is an input used in plastics production, a decrease in the price of petroleum shifts the supply curve of plastic garbage cans to the right. Garbage cans are now cheaper to produce, so there will be an increase in quantity supplied at each particular price. Generally, a reduction in the price of an input into the production of a good will increase the supply of that good. An increase in the price of an input will have the opposite effect.

Technology is the stock of knowledge, useful in producing goods and services, that is available to a society. An improvement in technology means that an increase in the stock of available knowledge has made it possible to produce more of at least one good or

inputs goods or services used in the process of producing a different good or service

technology the stock of knowledge, useful in producing goods and services, that is available to a society

Why has the consumption of French fries increased substantially during the last 35 years?

Commercial techniques for peeling, cutting, cooking, and storing French fries are much more sophisticated now than they were 35 years ago. Today, raw potatoes are processed into French fries in a few large plants, frozen, and shipped to restaurants and consumers. Once in restaurants and homes, French fries are easily cooked. In the United States, consumption of potatoes has increased by about 30 percent since 1977, most of it because Americans are eating more French fries and potato chips.[4]

In Figure 3.8, the curves labelled S and D depict the supply and demand curves for French fries during the late 1970s. The curve S' represents the supply curve today. The increase in supply is the result of technological improvements in the production of French fries. As the graph shows, the equilibrium quantity of French fries has increased and the price has decreased.

FIGURE 3.8
The Effect of Technological Change on the Market for French Fries
When new technology reduces the cost of production, supply shifts right, causing the equilibrium price to fall and the equilibrium quantity to rise.

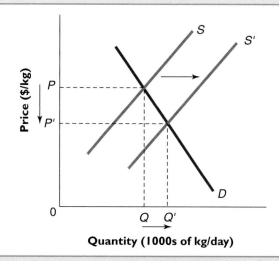

service from a given set of inputs. In the case given in Economic Naturalist 3.1, the stock of knowledge concerning the production of French fries increased, causing an increase in the supply of French fries.

In the real world, many other factors can cause supply to shift. When we think about a change in something other than price and quantity, we are modifying the assumption of *ceteris paribus*. If we do this one thing at a time, we can analyze the impact of each change. For example, weather conditions have a major impact on the yield of crops and the supply of foodstuffs (and on the supply of other goods and services, too). If we introduce changes in the weather as a factor, we are allowing more than just price and quantity to change.

Expectations of future changes can also affect supply curves. Suppose that a drought causes an expectation that harvests at the end of the current growing season will be small. Suppliers are likely to withhold supplies from existing stocks on the *expectation* that whatever is withheld now can be sold at a higher price later. The supply curve for the current period will shift to the left, which is a reduction of supply. Supply in the current period is reduced even though the existing stock of wheat is not affected by the drought. Because suppliers *expect* a smaller harvest in the future, they reduce supply now.

4 David M. Cutler, Edward L. Glaeser, and Jesse M. Shapiro, "Why have Americans Become More Obese?" *Journal of Economic Perspectives, 17* (2003), p. 94.

An increase in a subsidy can also shift a supply curve to the right, as can an increase in the number of firms serving a market. A reduction in a subsidy or the number of firms in a market would shift a supply curve to the left.

SHIFTS IN DEMAND

The preceding examples involved changes that gave rise to shifts in supply curves. Next, we'll look at what happens when demand curves shift. In the following example, the shift in demand results from events outside the particular market itself.

EXAMPLE **3.2**

What will happen to the equilibrium price and quantity of tennis balls if court rental fees decline?

Let the initial supply and demand curves for tennis balls be as shown by the curves S and D in Figure 3.9, where the resulting equilibrium price and quantity are $1 per ball and 40 million balls per month, respectively. Tennis courts and tennis balls are what economists call **complements**—goods that are more valuable when used in combination than when used alone. Tennis balls, for example, would be of less value if there were no tennis courts on which to play. (Tennis balls would still have *some* value even without courts; for example, to the parents who pitch them to their children for batting practice.) As tennis courts become cheaper to use, people will respond by playing more tennis, and this will increase their demand for tennis balls. A decline in court rental fees will, thus, shift the demand curve for tennis balls rightward to D'. (A rightward shift of a demand curve can also be described as an upward shift.)

complements a relationship between two goods such that an increase in the price of one causes a leftward shift in the demand curve for the other

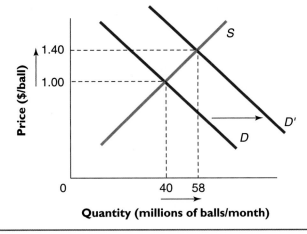

FIGURE 3.9
The Effect on the Market for Tennis Balls of a Decline in Court Rental Fees
When the price of a good's complement falls, demand for the good shifts right, causing equilibrium price and quantity to rise.

Note in Figure 3.9 that, for the demand shift shown, the new equilibrium price of tennis balls, $1.40, is higher than the original price, and the new equilibrium quantity, 58 million balls per month, is higher than the original quantity.

EXAMPLE **3.3**

What will happen to the equilibrium price and quantity of overnight letter delivery service as more people gain access to the Internet?

Suppose that the initial supply and demand curves for overnight letter deliveries are as shown by the curves S and D in Figure 3.10 and that the resulting equilibrium price and quantity are denoted P and Q. Email messages and overnight letters are examples of **substitutes**, meaning that the two, in many applications at least, serve

substitutes a relationship between two goods such that an increase in the price of one causes a rightward shift in the demand curve for the other

FIGURE 3.10
The Effect on the Market for Overnight Letter Delivery of a Decline in the Price of Internet Access
When the price of a substitute for a good falls, demand for the good shifts left, causing equilibrium price and quantity to fall.

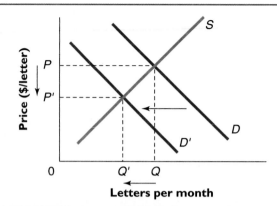

similar functions for people. When two goods or services are substitutes, a decrease in the effective price of one will cause a leftward shift in the demand curve for the other. (A leftward shift in a demand curve can also be described as a downward shift.) An increase in Internet access is, in effect, a decline in the price of a substitute for overnight delivery for affected users. Diagrammatically, this means a leftward shift in the demand curve for overnight delivery service to D' in Figure 3.10.

As the figure shows, both the new equilibrium price P' and the new equilibrium quantity Q' are lower than the initial values P and Q. More widespread Internet access probably will not put Purolator and UPS out of business, but it will definitely cost them many customers.

To summarize, economists define goods as substitutes if an increase in the price of one causes a rightward shift in the demand curve for the other. By contrast, goods are complements if an increase in the price of one causes a leftward shift in the demand curve for the other. The concepts of substitutes and complements enable you to answer questions like the one posed in the following exercise.

EXERCISE 3.1   **How will a decline in airfares affect intercity (or long-distance) bus fares and the price of hotel rooms in resort communities serviced by airlines?**

Demand curves are shifted not just by changes in the prices of substitutes and complements but also by other factors that change the amounts that people are willing to pay for a given good or service. One of the most important such factors is household income.

ECONOMIC NATURALIST 3.2

When the price of oil rises, why do prices for houses in Calgary rise?

Calgary's economy is heavily dependent on the oil industry. If the price of oil rises, oil companies respond by exploring for more oil and by developing existing oil fields more intensively. As oil companies increase their activity, more people will be drawn to Calgary, some to work in the oil industry, others to supply more goods and services to the oil industry as it expands, and still others to supply goods and services to Calgary's rising population. (For example, if more families move to Calgary, more teachers will be required.) In addition, wages and salaries will tend to be bid up to attract more workers, there will be more opportunities to work overtime, and so on. Thus, individuals will tend to have higher incomes because of the oil boom. Because of a larger population and because at least some individuals will have higher incomes, and now may be able to afford to move out of apartments into houses, the demand curve for houses will shift to the right, as shown by the demand curve labelled D' in Figure 3.11. As a result, the equilibrium price and quantity of houses, P' and Q', will be higher than before.

FIGURE 3.11
The Effect of an Increase in the Price of Oil on the Price of Houses in Calgary
An increase in income shifts demand for a normal good to the right, causing equilibrium price and quantity to rise.

Two factors caused the demand curve for houses in Calgary to shift to the right when the price of oil rose: the population of the city increased, and the income of individuals increased. Either factor by itself would have caused the demand curve to shift to the right; together, they reinforce each other. When incomes increase, the demand curves for most goods will shift to the right. In recognition of that fact, economists have chosen to call such goods **normal goods**.

Not all goods are normal goods, however. In fact, the demand curves for some goods actually shift leftward when income goes up, and such goods are called **inferior goods**. When would having more money tend to make you want to buy less of something? In general, this will happen in the case of goods for which there are attractive substitutes that sell for only slightly higher prices. Ground beef with high fat content is an example of an inferior good. For health reasons, many people prefer ground beef with low fat content, and when they do buy high-fat meats it is usually a sign of budgetary pressure. When people in this situation receive higher incomes, they switch to leaner grades of meat, which causes the demand curve for high-fat hamburger meat to shift leftward.

normal good a good whose demand curve shifts rightward when the incomes of buyers increase

inferior good a good whose demand curve shifts leftward when the incomes of buyers increase

Normal and inferior goods were defined in terms of how their demand curves are affected by an increase in income. How will a decrease in income affect the demand for a normal good? How will it affect an inferior good?

EXERCISE 3.2

Preferences, or tastes, are another important factor that determines whether a given good will meet the cost–benefit test. Think about the car advertisements on TV or elsewhere that you have seen recently. A few of them convey market information; that is, they tell consumers the price or technical features of a particular brand of automobile. But the ads that feature beautiful women and handsome men driving through impossibly romantic scenery are all about creating brand image and, thereby, increasing the likelihood that you will buy that particular car, at any given price. The main role of the advertising industry is to shape preferences, thereby *shifting* to the right the demand curves of consumers for the client's product.

Expectations can also influence demand. For example, if there are clear reasons to expect that the price of a product will rise in the near future, some buyers may wish to increase their purchases now, before the anticipated price rise.

FOUR SIMPLE RULES

For supply and demand curves that have the conventional slopes (upward sloping for supply curves, downward sloping for demand curves), the preceding examples illustrate

FIGURE 3.12
Four Rules Governing the Effects of Supply and Demand Shifts

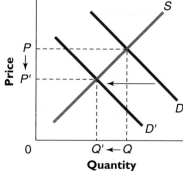

An increase in demand will lead to an increase in both the equilibrium price and quantity.

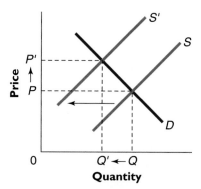

A decrease in demand will lead to a decrease in both the equilibrium price and quantity.

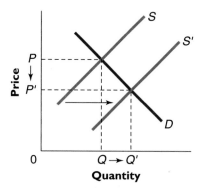

An increase in supply will lead to a decrease in the equilibrium price and an increase in the equilibrium quantity.

A decrease in supply will lead to an increase in the equilibrium price and a decrease in the equilibrium quantity.

the four basic rules that govern how shifts in supply and demand affect equilibrium prices and quantities. These rules are summarized in Figure 3.12.

The qualitative rules summarized in Figure 3.12 hold for supply or demand shifts of any magnitude, provided the curves have their conventional slopes. Although it is easy enough for textbook authors to invent examples where only one thing is happening in a market, in the real world we often observe simultaneous changes in demand and supply. As the next example demonstrates, when both supply and demand curves shift at the same time, the direction in which equilibrium price or quantity changes will depend on the relative magnitudes of the shifts.

EXAMPLE 3.4

How do shifts in *both* demand and supply affect equilibrium quantities and prices?

What will happen to the equilibrium price and quantity in the corn–tortilla chip market if both of the following events occur: (1) researchers discover that the oils in which tortilla chips are fried are harmful to human health, and (2) the price of corn-harvesting equipment falls?

The discovery regarding the health effects of the oils will shift the demand for tortilla chips to the left, because many people who once bought chips in the belief that they were healthful will now switch to other foods. The decline in the price of harvesting equipment will shift the supply of chips to the right, because additional

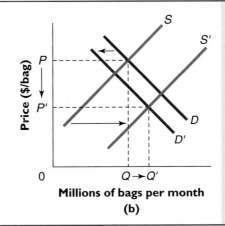

FIGURE 3.13

The Effects of Simultaneous Shifts in Supply and Demand
When demand shifts left and supply shifts right, equilibrium price falls, but equilibrium quantity may either fall, as shown in panel (a), or rise, as show in panel (b).

farmers will now find it profitable to produce corn. In Figure 3.13(a) and (b), the original supply and demand curves are denoted by *S* and *D,* while the new curves are denoted by *S'* and *D'*. Note that in both parts, the shifts lead to a decline in the equilibrium price of chips.

But note also that the effect of the shifts on equilibrium quantity cannot be determined without knowing their relative magnitudes. Taken separately, the demand shift causes a decline in equilibrium quantity, whereas the supply shift causes an increase in equilibrium quantity. The net effect of the two shifts thus depends on which of the individual effects is larger. In Figure 3.13(a), the demand shift dominates, so equilibrium quantity declines. In Figure 3.13(b), the supply shift dominates, so equilibrium quantity goes up.

The following exercise asks you to consider a simple variation on the problem posed in Example 3.4.

What will happen to the equilibrium price and quantity in the corn-tortilla chip market if both the following events occur: (1) researchers discover that a vitamin found in corn helps protect against cancer and heart disease and (2) a swarm of locusts destroys part of the corn crop?

EXERCISE 3.3

ECONOMIC NATURALIST 3.3

Why do the prices of some goods, like airline tickets to Europe, go up during the months of heaviest consumption while others, like sweet corn, go down?

Seasonal price movements for airline tickets are primarily the result of seasonal variations in demand. Thus, ticket prices to Europe are highest during the summer months because the demand for tickets is highest during those months, as shown in Figure 3.14(a) (where the *w* and *s* subscripts denote winter and summer values, respectively).

By contrast, seasonal price movements for sweet corn are primarily the result of seasonal variations in supply. The price of sweet corn is lowest in the summer months because its supply is highest during those months, as shown in Figure 3.14(b).

FIGURE 3.14
Seasonal Variation in the Air Travel and Corn Markets
Panel (a): Prices are highest during the period of heaviest consumption and are the result of high demand.
Panel (b): Prices are lowest during the period of heaviest consumption when heavy consumption is the result of high supply.

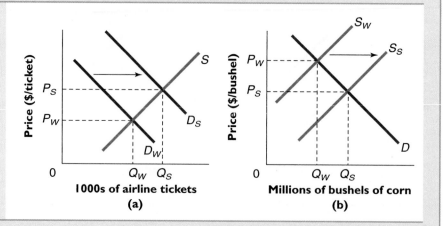

RECAP

EXPLAINING CHANGES IN PRICES AND QUANTITIES

FACTORS CAUSING AN INCREASE IN SUPPLY (SUPPLY CURVE SHIFTS RIGHT)

1. A decrease in the cost of materials, labour, or other inputs used in the production of the good or service.

2. An improvement in technology that reduces the cost of producing the good or service.

3. An increase in a subsidy provided by government.

4. An increase in the number of firms.

    When these factors move in the opposite direction, supply will shift left.

FACTORS CAUSING AN INCREASE IN DEMAND (DEMAND CURVE SHIFTS RIGHT)

1. A decrease in the price of complements to the good or service.

2. An increase in the price of substitutes for the good or service.

3. An increase in income (for a normal good).

4. An increased preference by demanders for the good or service.

5. An increase in the population of potential buyers.

    When these factors move in the opposite direction, demand will shift left. When both supply and demand shift, it is often necessary to know the relative magnitudes of the shifts to determine if equilibrium price and equilibrium quantity increase or decrease.

BOX 3.4

Supply Increases: A New Market Equilibrium

In Box 3.3 we showed how algebra can be used to calculate equilibrium in a simple system of supply and demand. We can use the same algebraic system to calculate a new equilibrium when either supply or demand shifts. For this, the terms will remain defined as they were in the previous boxes.

Recall that in Box 3.1 the supply of hamburgers was represented by

$$Q_S = 4P_S.$$

Now suppose that a hamburger vendor discovers a new technique enabling him to flip six patties at one time and transfer them all to buns simultaneously with a second flip. Other vendors watch and discover they can learn the new technique quickly. Soon the six-burger flip has permeated the entire market, and vendors provide hamburgers more quickly than they were before. A technological improvement has occurred.

How can technological improvement be represented graphically? A downward shift, or to the right, of the supply curve can be represented by increasing the horizontal intercept of the equation for supply. This implies a new equilibrium price and quantity. Suppose the horizontal intercept increases from zero to one. The equation for supply then becomes

$$Q_S = 1 + 4P_S.$$

The equation for demand remains what it was in the previous box,

$$Q_D = 24 - 4P_D$$

At the market equilibrium, $Q_S = Q_D = Q^*$ (equilibrium quantity) and $P_S = P_D = P^*$ (equilibrium price). We can use the supply equation, the demand equation, and the equation for market equilibrium to write

$$1 + 4P^* = 24 - 4P^*.$$

Notice that, once again, the algebra is just a mathematical expression demonstrating the same thing as the verbal statement that supply equals demand, which must be the case when the system is in equilibrium. The equation for supply, appearing to the left of the equal sign, has changed, but the expression is otherwise unchanged from what appears in Box 3.3.

Solving the expression reveals that $P^* = \$2.875$. (We can assume that vendors round their prices to \$2.88.) Substituting \$2.875 into either the equation for demand or the new equation for supply reveals that $Q^* = 12.5$. Because quantity is measured in thousands, the equilibrium quantity is 12 500 hamburgers per day. A comparison of this equilibrium quantity and price with those calculated in Box 3.3 reveals that the new quantity is larger and the new price is lower. This is consistent with the lower left-hand panel of Figure 3.12, which pertains to an increase in supply.

Changes in the values of the parameters could represent changes in either demand or supply. For example, an increase in demand can be represented by an increase in the horizontal intercept of the demand curve. A change in the slope of the demand curve can be introduced by changing the parameter that represents slope. The slope of the supply curve can be changed in the same way. Smaller or larger changes in parameters can be used to represent smaller or larger changes to demand or supply.

3.3   WHEN IS THE SIMPLE SUPPLY AND DEMAND MODEL APPROPRIATE?

This chapter has argued that a model based on supply and demand can help us to understand and predict events in some markets. But which markets? To explain, we should emphasize that we have made some important assumptions:

1. All participants in the market are so small that no single buyer or seller can influence price. Moreover, it is not possible for any buyers or sellers to form combinations that can influence price.
2. All suppliers provide an identical product; quality is uniform. Thus, no buyer has reason to prefer the product of one supplier over that of another.
3. All buyers know the price and quality of the product that is being supplied on the market. If information is available to one buyer or seller, it is available to all buyers and sellers.
4. Transactions can occur easily. It is not difficult for buyers and sellers to meet and conduct transactions.

These conditions are met strictly by only a small percentage of the markets in the Canadian and other economies. If the markets roughly satisfy these conditions, however, then economists will often use a supply and demand model to examine at least some aspects of the market. But in many markets, one of the four conditions is so seriously violated that the supply and demand model is clearly inappropriate. As we noted earlier, most of us depend on a single electrified line to obtain our electricity, which is a violation of the first condition, and the supply and demand model is hardly appropriate for a market with a single seller. Other important markets also are not well described by the four conditions listed above. Microeconomics goes beyond the supply and demand model to consider models that are more suitable for analyzing markets for which these four conditions do not apply. Macroeconomics often assumes that most markets are much slower to respond to changes in demand than the supply and demand model suggests.

Having introduced the supply and demand model, this textbook will now move on to purely macroeconomic chapters, beginning with three chapters dealing with the measurement of key macroeconomic variables such as the economic growth rate, unemployment rate, inflation rate, exchange rate, trade balance, and government budget balance. The supply and demand model will be used again in Chapter 12 to deal with explaining changes in exchange rates. And knowledge of how the supply and demand model works will help you to understand macroeconomic models such as the basic Keynesian model introduced in Chapter 8 that, like the supply and demand models, has two curves or lines and an equilibrium condition.

SUMMARY

- An economic model describes results that stem from the relationships it portrays; it also provides hypotheses about what will happen if any of the variables change. The comparative advantage model of Chapter 2 is one example of a model. The supply and demand model of this chapter is another. **L01**

- Alfred Marshall's model of supply and demand explains why neither cost of production nor value to the purchaser (as measured by willingness to pay) by itself is sufficient to explain why some goods are cheap and others are expensive. To explain variations in price, we must examine the interaction of cost and willingness to pay. As we saw in this chapter, uniform goods and services sold in markets with many buyers and sellers differ in price because of differences in their respective supply and demand curves. **L02, L03, L04**

■ The demand curve is a downward-sloping line that tells what quantity buyers will demand at any given price in a market with many buyers. The supply curve is an upward-sloping line indicating the quantity sellers will offer at any given price in a market with many sellers. The market equilibrium occurs when the quantity buyers demand at the market price is exactly the same as the quantity that sellers offer. The equilibrium price–quantity pair is the one at which the demand and supply curves intersect. In equilibrium, market price measures both the value of the last unit sold to buyers and the cost of the resources required to produce it. **LO2, LO3, LO4**

■ The equilibrium principle states that a market in equilibrium leaves no unexploited opportunities for exchanges among individuals. Equilibrium is a concept of positive economics that of itself says nothing about whether one equilibrium outcome is better than another. For example, each different distribution of wealth will produce a different equilibrium solution for prices and quantities produced. The equilibrium principle has nothing to say about whether any particular distribution of wealth or income is fair. **LO5**

■ When the price of a good lies above its equilibrium value, there is an excess supply, or surplus, of that good. Excess supply motivates sellers to cut their prices, and price continues to fall until the equilibrium price is reached. When price lies below its equilibrium value, there is excess demand, or shortage. With excess demand, dissatisfied buyers are motivated to offer higher prices, and the upward pressure on prices persists until equilibrium is reached. The equilibrating process depends on competition among many small buyers and sellers. **LO4**

■ The basic supply and demand model is a useful tool of the economic naturalist. Changes in the equilibrium price of a good, and in the amount of it traded in the marketplace, can be predicted on the basis of shifts in its supply or demand curves. The following four rules hold for any good with a downward-sloping demand curve and an upward-sloping supply curve:

• An increase in demand will lead to an increase in equilibrium price and quantity.

• A reduction in demand will lead to a reduction in equilibrium price and quantity.

• An increase in supply will lead to a reduction in equilibrium price and an increase in equilibrium quantity.

• A decrease in supply will lead to an increase in equilibrium price and a reduction in equilibrium quantity. **LO6**

■ Incomes, tastes, population, and the prices of substitutes and complements are among the factors that shift demand schedules. Supply schedules, in turn, are primarily governed by such factors as technology, input prices, and, for agricultural products, the weather. Changes in expectations can also shift supply and demand schedules. **LO6**

■ The supply and demand model is not a general model of markets. It applies best to markets with specific characteristics such as many buyers and many sellers of a uniform product. There are other models for markets with other characteristics. Macroeconomics often assumes that markets are much slower to respond to changes in demand than the supply and demand model might suggest. **LO7**

CORE PRINCIPLES

The Equilibrium Principle

A market in equilibrium leaves no unexploited trading opportunities for personal gain for individual . Equilibrium is based on an underlying distribution of wealth. (However, the equilibrium principle does not say whether one equilibrium is better than another one.) (61)

KEY TERMS

change in demand (62)
change in quantity
  demanded (62)
change in quantity supplied (62)
change in supply (62)
complements (65)
demand curve (56)
equilibrium (57)

equilibrium price (57)
equilibrium quantity (57)
excess demand (58)
excess supply (58)
inferior good (67)
inputs (64)
market (53)
market equilibrium (58)

normal good (67)
quantity supplied (54)
quantity demanded (56)
shortage (58)
substitutes (65)
supply curve (54)
surplus (58)
technology (64)

REVIEW QUESTIONS

1. Give two examples of economic models. Do economic models always give correct predictions? If not, why not? **LO1**

2. Why isn't knowing how much it costs to produce a good sufficient to predict its market price? **LO2, LO3, LO4**

3. Distinguish between the meaning of the expressions "change in demand" and "change in the quantity demanded." **LO3**

4. Distinguish between the meaning of the expressions "change in supply" and "change in the quantity supplied." **LO2**

5. Explain why, in a market suitable to analysis with the demand and supply model, a price set below the market equilibrium price would be predicted to cause

a gap between quantity demanded and quantity supplied. Also, state the term or terms used by economists to describe such a gap. **LO4**

6. If supply increases at the same time as demand increases, what does the supply and demand model predict about equilibrium price and quantity? **LO6**

7. Explain why, in unregulated markets with many buyers and sellers, the equilibrium principle suggests that excess demand and excess supply tend to be fleeting. **LO4, LO5**

8. Explain why the equilibrium price and quantity in a particular market, say, for an inferior good, will depend upon the distribution of income. **LO5**

9. Why is the supply and demand model not a general model of markets? **LO7**

PROBLEMS

1. If the market price is kept below the equilibrium price by a regulation, what does the demand and supply model predict about the gap between quantity demanded and quantity supplied? If, in the real world, there is a gap between quantity demanded and quantity supplied, does it necessarily imply that a regulation is keeping the market price below the equilibrium price? **LO4**

2. State whether the following pairs of goods are likely to be complements or substitutes. (If you think a pair is ambiguous in this respect, explain why.) **LO3, LO4, LO6**
   a. tennis courts and squash courts
   b. squash racquets and squash balls
   c. ice cream and chocolate
   d. cloth diapers and disposable diapers

3. How would each of the following affect the Canadian market supply curve for wheat? **LO2, LO6**
   a. A new and improved crop rotation technique is discovered.
   b. The price of fertilizer falls.
   c. The government offers new tax breaks to farmers.
   d. The Prairies suffer a drought.

4. Indicate how you think each of the following would affect demand in the indicated market: **LO3, LO6**
   a. An increase in family income on the demand for winter vacations in the Caribbean
   b. A study linking beef consumption to heart disease on the demand for hamburgers
   c. A relaxation of immigration laws on the demand for elementary-school places

    d.   An increase in the price of audiocassettes on the demand for CDs

    e.   An increase in the price of CDs on the demand for CDs

5. A student at the University of Regina claims to have spotted a UFO outside Regina. How will his claim affect the supply of binoculars in Regina stores? **LO2, LO3, LO6**

6. What will happen to the equilibrium price and quantity of oranges if the price of fertilizer used for growing oranges rises? **LO6**

7. How will an increase in the birthrate affect the equilibrium price of land? **LO6**

8. What will happen to the equilibrium price and quantity of fish if it is discovered that fish oils help prevent heart disease? **LO6**

9. What will happen to the equilibrium price and quantity of beef if the price of chicken feed increases? **LO6**

10. Use supply and demand analysis to explain why hotel room rental rates near your campus during parents' weekend and graduation weekend might differ from the rates charged during the rest of the year. **LO6**

11. Suppose the current issue of *The Globe and Mail* reports an outbreak of mad cow disease in Manitoba, as well as the discovery of a new breed of chicken that gains more weight from the same amount of food than existing breeds. How will these developments affect the equilibrium price and quantity of chicken sold in Canada? **LO6**

12. What will happen to the equilibrium quantity and price of potatoes if population increases and a new, higher yielding variety of potato plant is developed? **LO6**

13. What will happen to the equilibrium price and quantity of apples if apples are discovered to help prevent colds and a fungus kills 10 percent of existing apple trees? **LO6**

14. What will happen to the equilibrium quantity and price of corn if the price of butter increases and the price of fertilizer decreases? **LO6**

15. Tofu was available 25 years ago only from small businesses operating in Chinese quarters of large cities. Today tofu has become popular as a high-protein health food and is widely available in supermarkets throughout Canada. At the same time, production has evolved to become factry based, using modern food-processing technologies. Draw a diagram with demand and supply curves depicting the market for tofu 25 years ago and the market for tofu today. Given the information above, what does the demand–supply model predict about changes in the quantity of tofu sold in Canada between then and now? What does it predict about changes in the price of tofu? **LO6**

16. State whether the following statement is true, false, or uncertain and explain why: All goods and services should be provided through markets because markets in equilibrium leave no unexploited opportunities for individuals. **LO5**

17. Suppose that this is a single seller of electricity and that the government reduces the price that the seller is allowed to charge. Is it appropriate to apply the supply and demand model to analyze this scenario? Explain. **LO7**

ANSWERS TO IN-CHAPTER EXERCISES

3.1   Travel by air and travel by bus are substitutes, so a decline in airfares will shift the demand for bus travel to the left, resulting in lower bus fares and fewer bus trips taken. Travel by air and the use of resort hotels are complements, so a decline in airfares will shift the demand for resort hotel rooms to the right, resulting in higher hotel rates and an increase in the number of rooms rented. **LO6**

3.2   A decrease in income will shift the demand curve for a normal good to the left and will shift the demand curve for an inferior good to the right. **LO6**

3.3   The vitamin discovery shifts the demand for chips to the right, and the crop losses shift the supply of bags of chips to the left. Both shifts result in an increase in the equilibrium price of bags of chips. But depending on the relative magnitude of the shifts, the equilibrium quantity of bags of chips may either rise, as in panel (a) of the figure, or fall, as in panel (b). **LO6**

Millions of bags per month
(a)

Millions of bags per month
(b)

PART 2

MACROECONOMICS: ISSUES AND DATA

This section introduces you to *macroeconomics*, the study of the performance of *national* economies. *Macroeconomics* looks at issues such as why some economies grow more rapidly than others, and why economies can experience *severe* slumps.

Unlike microeconomics, which focuses on the behaviour of individual households, firms, and markets, macroeconomics takes a bird's-eye view of the economy. It looks at the forest, so to speak, and not just the trees, because sometimes the whole is *more than the sum of the parts*. So while microeconomists might study the determinants of consumer phone-call spending, macroeconomists analyze the factors that determine aggregate, or total, consumer spending. Experience has shown that the macroeconomic perspective is essential for the analysis of issues such as unemployment, inflation, and economic growth.

Chapter 4 begins our discussion of macroeconomics by introducing you to some of the key macroeconomic issues and questions. These include the search for the factors that cause economies to grow, productivity to improve, and living standards to rise over long periods of time. Macroeconomists also study shorter-term fluctuations in the economy (called recessions and expansions), unemployment, inflation, and the economic interdependence among nations, among other topics. Macroeconomic policies—government actions to alter the overall performance of the economy—are of particular concern to macroeconomists, as the quality of macroeconomic policy-making is a major determinant of a nation's economic health.

To study phenomena like economic growth scientifically, economists must have accurate measurements. Chapters 5 and 6 continue the introduction to macroeconomics by discussing how some key macroeconomic concepts are measured and interpreted. Chapter 5 discusses two important measures of the level of economic activity: the gross domestic product and the unemployment rate. Besides describing how these variables are constructed in practice, that chapter will also discuss how these measures are related to the living standard of the average person. Chapter 6 concerns the measurement of the price level and inflation, and it includes a discussion of the impacts that different types of price-level changes have on the economy. When you have completed Part 2, you will be familiar not only with the major questions that macroeconomists ask but also with some of the most important tools that they use in search of answers.

CHAPTER 4
Macroeconomics:
The Bird's-Eye View of the Economy

LEARNING OBJECTIVES

When you have completed this chapter, you should be able to:

LO1 Explain the major issues that macro-economists study.

LO2 Discuss the different forms of macro-economic policy and their function.

LO3 Describe aggregation and explain how macroeconomists use it, and relate aggregation to the fallacy of composition.

In 1929, the Great Depression began in the United States and quickly turned into a global economic slump. With its high level of dependence on exports, Canada was hit hard by the global downturn. Between 1929 and 1933, Canada's real output declined by almost 30 percent, consumer prices fell by 23 percent, and the unemployment rate soared from 3 percent to 19.3 percent. Large numbers of Canadians became dependent on government relief for survival.

Economic conditions were even worse in some other countries. In Germany, for example, nearly a third of the labour force could not find work, and many families lost their savings as major banks collapsed. Indeed, the desperate economic situation was a factor behind Adolf Hitler's rise to power in 1933.

How could such an economic catastrophe have happened? One often-heard hypothesis is that the Great Depression in the United States was caused by wild speculation on Wall Street, which provoked the stock market crash. But though U.S. stock market prices were unrealistically high in 1929, other factors must have been involved to produce an economic catastrophe as drastic as the Great Depression. A severe crash of U.S. housing prices since 2007, as well as subsequent financial panic and a stock market crash, produced a severe recession that at first followed a path comparable to that of the U.S. economy during the Great Depression. But economic growth resumed in 2009, and although the U.S. economy appears poised for a period of slow growth, it does not appear destined to experience a replay of the Great Depression. Canada, too, experienced a sharp recession in 2008–2009, but after three quarters of negative growth, the economy returned to positive growth.

Another explanation for the Depression has been that capitalist economies like the United States and Canada are naturally unstable and prone to long periods of economic depression. This explanation, however, fails to account for why the Great Depression was so much worse than earlier economic slumps. It also fails to explain why the "mixed" capitalist economies that emerged from the Second World War have avoided a depression comparable to that experienced by the capitalist economies of the 1930s.

Why did the United States, Canada, and other economies experience such severe and prolonged stagnation during the Great Depression, then? Obviously there were triggering factors, but today most economists who have studied the period attribute a substantial portion of the blame to *poor economic policy-making* in the major capitalist countries. Of course, policy-makers did not set out to transform an economic downturn into a decade-long economic catastrophe. Rather, they fell prey to misconceptions of that time concerning how the economy worked. In other words, the Great Depression *could have been greatly mitigated* if only the state of economic knowledge had been better. From today's perspective, the Great Depression was to macroeconomic policy-making what the voyage of the *Titanic* was to ocean navigation.

One of the few benefits of the Great Depression was that it forced economists and policy-makers of the 1930s to recognize that there were major gaps in their understanding of how the economy works. This recognition led to the development of a new sub-field within economics, called *macroeconomics*. As mentioned in Chapter 1, *macroeconomics* is the study of the performance of national economies and the policies governments use to try to improve that performance.

This chapter will introduce the subject matter and some of the tools of macroeconomics. Understanding episodes like the Great Depression remains an important concern of macroeconomists, and economists are now researching the global recession of 2008–2009 and its aftermath. But the field of macroeconomics has expanded to include the analysis of many other aspects of national economies. Among the issues macroeconomists study are the sources of long-run economic growth and development, the causes of high unemployment, and the factors that determine the rate of inflation. Appropriately enough, in a world in which economic "globalization" preoccupies business people and policy-makers, macroeconomists also study how national economies interact. Since the performance of the national economy has an important bearing on the availability of jobs, the wages workers earn, the prices they pay, and the rates of return they receive on their savings, it's clear that macroeconomics addresses bread-and-butter issues that affect virtually everyone.

In light of the world's experience during the Great Depression, macroeconomists are particularly concerned with understanding how *macroeconomic policies* work and how they should be applied. **Macroeconomic policies** are government actions designed to affect the performance of the economy as a whole (as opposed to policies intended to affect the performance of the market for a particular good or service, such as lumber or haircuts). The hope of many macroeconomists is that by improving knowledge about how government policies affect the economy, they can help current or alternative policy-makers do a better job and avoid serious mistakes, such as those that were made during the Great Depression. On an individual level, educating people about macroeconomic policies and their effects will make for a better-informed citizenry, capable of making well-reasoned decisions in the voting booth.

macroeconomic policies
government actions designed to affect the performance of the economy as a whole

4.1 THE MAJOR MACROECONOMIC ISSUES

We have defined macroeconomics as the study of the performance of the national economy as well as the policies used to improve that performance. Let's now take a closer look at some of the major economic issues that macroeconomists study.

ECONOMIC GROWTH AND LIVING STANDARDS

Although the wealthy industrialized countries (such as Canada, the United States, Japan, and the countries of Western Europe) are certainly not free from poverty, hunger, and homelessness, the typical person in those countries enjoys a standard of living better than at any previous time or place in history. By *standard of living*, we mean the degree to which people have access to goods and services that make their lives easier, healthier, safer, and more enjoyable. People with a high living standard enjoy more and better consumer goods: the latest audio and video equipment, smart phones, and the like. But they also benefit from a longer life expectancy and better general health (the result of high-quality medical care, good nutrition, and good sanitation), higher literacy rates (the result of greater access to education), more time and opportunity for cultural enrichment and recreation, more interesting and fulfilling career options, and better working conditions. Of course, the *scarcity problem* means that even for the citizens of a rich country, having more of one good thing means having less of another. But higher incomes make these choices much less painful than they would be otherwise. Choosing between a larger apartment and a nicer car is much easier than choosing between feeding your children adequately and sending them to school, the kind of hard choice people in the poorest nations face.

Canadians sometimes take their standard of living for granted. But we should realize that the way we live today is radically different from the way people have lived throughout most of history. The current standard of living in Canada is the result of sustained economic growth through several generations, a long upward trend in the quantity and quality of the goods and services the economy can produce, and policies to ensure that the gains from growth have been shared. The basic equation is simple: provided that there are mechanisms to ensure that the gains from growth are widely shared, the more we can produce, the more we can consume, whether it be private goods, social spending, or leisure.

To get a sense of the extent of economic growth over time, examine Figure 4.1, which shows how the output of the Canadian economy has increased since 1926. (We discuss the measure of output used here, real gross domestic product, in Chapter 5.) Although output fluctuates at times, the overall trend has been unmistakably upward. Indeed, in 2010, the output of the Canadian economy was about 19 times what it was in 1926 and more than eight times its level in 1950. What caused this remarkable economic growth? Can it continue? Should it? These are some of the questions macroeconomists try to answer.

One reason for the growth in Canadian output over the past century has been the rapid growth of the Canadian population, and hence the number of workers available. Because of population growth, increases in *total* output cannot be equated with improvements in the general standard of living. Although increased output means that more goods and services are available, increased population implies that more people are sharing those goods and services. Because the population changes over time, output *per person* is a better indicator of the average living standard than total output.

Figure 4.2 shows output per person in Canada since 1926 (the blue line). Note that the long-term increase in output per person is smaller than the increase in total output shown in Figure 4.1 because of population growth. Nevertheless, the gains made over this long period are still impressive: in 2010, the value of output per Canadian resident was about 5.5 times the value produced per Canadian resident back in 1926. To put this increase into perspective, Canadians no longer rely upon horse and buggy for everyday travel—according to recent estimates, 83 percent of Canadian households owned or

FIGURE 4.1

Output of the Canadian Economy, 1926–2010

The output of the Canadian economy has increased by 19 times since 1926 and by more than 8 times since 1950.

SOURCE: Adapted from the Statistics Canada CANSIM database, http://cansim2.statcan.gc.ca, series v41707175 and from series F55 of Historical Statistics of Canada, 11-516-XWE1983001, July 1999.

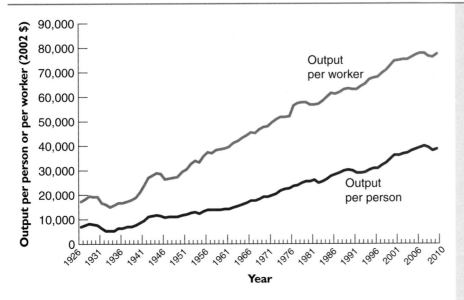

FIGURE 4.2

Output per Person and per Worker in the Canadian Economy, 1926–2010
The red line shows output per worker in the Canadian economy since 1926, and the blue line shows output per person. Relative to 1926, output per person is about 5.5 times greater, and output per worker is 4.5 times greater. SOURCE: Adapted from Statistics Canada, CANSIM series v2461119, v466668, v41707175, and from series D129, A1 and F55 of Historical Statistics of Canada, 11-516-XWE1983001.

leased one or more vehicles (automobiles, trucks, or vans). Television ownership is taken for granted, with about 66 percent of households subscribing to cable and 24 percent to satellite. About 82 percent of Canadian households have a computer at home, and 78 percent of all households access the Internet from home.[1]

Nor has the rise in output been reflected entirely in increased availability of consumer goods. In health, for example, great strides have been made. The mortality rate for infants has plummeted from about 100 per 1000 live births in the 1920s to about 5 per 1000 live births. Average life expectancy has risen from 59 to 81 years (78 years for males and 83 years for females). In education, as late as 1951 over half of the Canadian population aged 15 and over had less than a Grade 9 education, while only a few percent (mostly men) had university degrees. By 1996, adults with university degrees had become more numerous than adults with less than Grade 9, and the share of degrees earned by women had surpassed 50 percent. By 2008, almost half of the population aged 25 to 64 had obtained a college or university education.[2]

www.statcan.gc.ca
Statistics Canada

PRODUCTIVITY

While growth in output per person is closely linked to changes in what the typical person can *consume,* macroeconomists are also interested in changes in what the average worker can *produce.* Figure 4.2 shows how output per employed worker (that is, total output divided by the number of people working) has changed since 1926 (red line). The figure shows that in 2010, a Canadian worker could produce about 4.5 times the value of goods and services produced by a worker back in 1926, despite the fact that the workweek is now shorter.

Economists define **average labour productivity** as output per employed worker.[3] As Figure 4.2 shows, average labour productivity and output per person are closely related. This relationship makes sense—as we noted earlier, the more we can produce, the more

average labour productivity
output per employed worker

1 Figures on household equipment are taken from Statistics Canada, *Spending Patterns in Canada* 2009 (Ottawa: Statistics Canada, December 2010), Catalogue no. 62-202-X, Table 7, p. 45.

2 Detailed information about education attainment in Canada can be found in Statistics Canada, *Education Indicators in Canada: An International Perspective* (Ottawa: Statistics Canada, 2010), Catalogue no. 81-604-X.

3 For some purposes, such as productivity comparisons between the United States and Europe, it is useful to recognize that average labour productivity can also be measured as output divided by the number of hours worked. A country with relatively long average hours of work, such as the United States, comes out higher in international average labour productivity rankings if countries are ranked by average output per employed worker than if they are ranked by average output per hour worked.

we can consume. Because of this close link to the average living standard, average labour productivity and the factors that cause it to increase over time are of major concern to macroeconomists.

It should be noted that although the typical household is more likely to experience better wages and living conditions when average labour productivity is rising, the process is not automatic. In some countries, there have been whole decades during which the value of goods and services that typical households could buy actually stagnated despite rising average labour productivity. (For further information, see Figure 6.1.) During such periods, there is a shift in the income distribution from low- and middle-income households to high-income households.

Although the long-term improvement in output per worker is impressive, the *rate* of improvement has slowed somewhat since the 1970s. Between 1950 and 1973 in Canada, output per employed worker increased by 2.4 percent per year. But from 1973 to 2010, the average rate of increase in output per worker was only 1 percent per year, despite a noticeable upsurge during the 1997–2000 period. Slowing productivity growth leads to less rapid improvement in living standards, since the supply of goods and services cannot grow as quickly as it does during periods of rapid growth in productivity. Identifying the causes of productivity slowdowns and speed-ups is thus an important challenge for macroeconomists.

The current standard of living in Canada is not only much higher than in the past but also much higher than in many other nations today. Why do many of the world's countries, including both the developing nations of Asia, Africa, Latin America, and some countries of Eastern Europe, not enjoy living standards comparable to those of Western countries? How can these countries catch up? Once again, these are questions of keen interest to macroeconomists.

EXAMPLE 4.1

Productivity and output per person in Canada, the United States, and China

In 2009, the value of Canadian economic output was approximately C$1.3 trillion (1300 billion). In the same year, the estimated value of U.S. output was approximately C$14.1 trillion and that of the People's Republic of China was C$4.9 trillion. The populations of Canada, the United States, and China in 2009 were about 33.7 million, 307.4 million, and 1.33 billion, respectively, while the numbers of employed workers in the three countries were approximately 16.8 million, 139.9 million, and 813.5 million, respectively.[4]

The output per person and average labour productivity for Canada, the United States, and China in the year 2009 can be determined using the data provided above. Output per person is simply total output divided by the number of people in an economy. Average labour productivity is output divided by the number of employed workers. Doing the math, we get the following results for 2009, the year in question.

	Canada	United States	China
Output per person (C$)	$39 657	$ 45 934	$3 734
Average labour productivity (C$)	$79 334	$100 936	$6 127

Note that the larger population and hence greater number of employed workers of the United States provides a partial explanation of why U.S. output was larger than Canadian output in 2009. But U.S. output was also higher because average labour

---

4 The statistics in the example are from each country's official agencies, and the output statistics are converted to a common basis using average annual exchange rates for each country. Economists often adjust the output of the Chinese economy upward by a very large amount to reflect what Chinese output would be if valued at prices prevailing in the rest of the world. They sometimes adjust Chinese employment numbers upward by a moderate amount to reflect alleged undercounting of the employed in China.

productivity was higher in that country. On the other hand, China's output was greater than Canada's solely because of China's greater population and employment figures. China's average labour productivity was much lower. But in recent years China's output has been growing much more rapidly than those of high-income countries, and China's population growth has been relatively slow in the same period. This means that the average labour productivity gap between China and high-income countries will shrink rapidly for as long as current trends continue.

When we closely examine the data, the average labour productivity gap between China and, for example, Canada is substantial and associated with significant differences in more direct measures of living standards. For example, according to the latest *Human Development Report* published by the United Nations, average life expectancy at birth is several years longer in Canada than in China, about 7 percent of the adult Chinese population is classified as illiterate compared to less than 1 percent in Canada, and about 15 percent of the Chinese population is classified as living on US$1.25 or less a day.[5] (For additional evidence of how average labour productivity differences among countries are associated with differences in direct measures of living standards, see Table 5.4.)

RECESSIONS AND EXPANSIONS

Economies do not always grow steadily; sometimes they go through periods of unusual strength or weakness. A look back at Figure 4.1 shows that although output generally grows over time, it does not always grow smoothly. (Figure 7.2, which shows growth of output per capita directly, provides a sharper picture of the often rough process of output growth.) Particularly striking is the decline in output during the Great Depression of the 1930s, followed by the sharp increase in output during the Second World War (1939–1945). But the figure shows many more moderate fluctuations in output as well.

Pronounced slowdowns in economic growth are called *recessions*. Extraordinarily severe economic slowdowns, like the one that began in 1929, are called *depressions*. In Canada, major recessions occurred in 1981–1982, 1990–1992, and 2008–2009 (find those recessions in Figure 4.1). During recessions, economic opportunities decline: jobs are harder to find, people with jobs are less likely to get wage increases, profits are lower, and more companies go out of business. Recessions are particularly hard on economically disadvantaged people, who are most likely to be thrown out of work and have the hardest time finding new jobs.

Sometimes the economy grows quickly. These periods of economic growth are called *expansions,* and particularly strong expansions are called *booms*. During an expansion, jobs are easier to find, more people get raises and promotions, and most businesses thrive.

The alternating cycle of recessions and expansions raises some questions that are central to macroeconomics. What causes these short-term fluctuations in the rate of economic growth? What can government policy-makers do about them?

UNEMPLOYMENT

The *unemployment rate,* the fraction of the labour force who are looking for a job but can't find work, is a key indicator of the state of the labour market. When the unemployment rate is high, work is hard to find, and people who do have jobs typically find it harder to get promotions or wage increases.

Figure 4.3 shows the unemployment rate in Canada since 1921. Unemployment rises during recessions; note the dramatic spike in unemployment during the Great Depression and the increases in unemployment during the 1981–1982, 1990–1992, and 2008–2009

5 See Human Development Indicators, *Human Development Report 2009,* http://hdr.undp.org/en/, and CIA, *World Factbook, 2009/2010,* https://www.cia.gov/library/publications/the-world-factbook/index.html.

FIGURE 4.3

The Canadian Unemployment Rate, 1921–2010

The unemployment rate measures the unemployed as a percentage of the labour force. This graph of the Canadian unemployment rate shows three major spikes since 1921: during the Great Depression of the 1930s and during the severe recessions of the early 1980s and the early 1990s. The unemployment rate shot up recently during the recession of 2008–2009.

SOURCE: Adapted from the Statistics Canada, CANSIM series v2062815, v2062815, and from series D132 and D127 of Historical Statistics of Canada.

recessions. But even in the so-called good times, such as the 1960s and the last few years of the 1990s, some people are unemployed. Why does unemployment rise so sharply during periods of recession? And why are there always unemployed people, even when the economy is booming?

EXAMPLE 4.2

Increases in unemployment during recessions and an economic slowdown

Find the increase in Canada's monthly unemployment rate from the onset of a recession or economic slowdown to the peak unemployment rate in the three-year period thereafter. Specifically, find the increases in the unemployment rate associated with the recessions beginning in the third quarter of 1981 and the second quarter of 1990, and in the slowdown beginning in mid-2000, and the effects of the recession that began in late 2008.

Unemployment-rate data are published in Statistics Canada's *Labour Force Survey*, which yields the following information:

Unemployment rate at the beginning of recession or slowdown (%)	Peak unemployment rate (%)	Increase in unemployment rate
8.3 (October 1981)	12.9 (December 1982)	+4.6
7.8 (July 1990)	11.8 (June 1993)	+4.0
6.7 (June 2000)	8.0 (January 2002)	+1.3
6.1 (August 2008)	8.7 (August 2009)	+2.6

The unemployment rate reached a higher peak in the 1980s recession and underwent a larger percentage-point increase than in the recession of the 1990s. But the recession of the 1990s was more drawn out, and it took longer for the unemployment rate to peak. The rise in the unemployment rate during the economic slowdown of 2000–2001 was much less pronounced than in the two earlier recessions. The latest recession saw a higher unemployment rate than that of the prior slowdown, but still not as drastic as that of the early 1980s and 1990s.

Though the recessions of the 1980s and 1990s have been the most severe for Canada since the Second World War, they pale in comparison to the Great Depression. Then Canada's unemployment rate increased from an annual rate of 3 percent in 1929 to an annual rate of 19.3 percent in 1933. Clearly, that 16.3-percentage-point increase in the unemployment rate belongs to a class by itself.

One question of great interest to macroeconomists is why unemployment rates differ markedly from country to country. For example, the unemployment rate in Canada prior to 1981 tended to be no higher on average than the U.S. rate. But during the 1980s, the Canadian rate averaged two percentage points higher than the U.S. rate, and in the 1990s, the gap widened to 3.8 points. Since then the situation has changed dramatically.

Find the most recent monthly unemployment rates for Canada and the United States. A useful source is the website (http://www.oecd.org/) of the Organization for Economic Cooperation and Development (OECD), an organization of high-income countries. The OECD produces standardized unemployment rates for making comparisons among its member countries. How does the Canada–U.S. unemployment rate gap today differ from the gap during the 1990s?

EXERCISE 4.1

www.oecd.org
OECD

INFLATION

Another important economic statistic is the rate of *inflation*, which is the rate at which prices in general increase over time. As we discuss in Chapter 6, when the inflation rate changes sharply, it can alter the distribution of income between borrowers and savers. Very high inflation imposes costs on the economy, as does negative inflation (known as deflation).

In recent years, inflation has been relatively low or moderate in Canada, but that has not always been the case (see Figure 4.4 for data on Canadian inflation since 1915). During the early 1930s, deflation was a major problem whereas during the 1970s, inflation was a leading public concern. Why was deflation severe in the early 1930s, why was inflation high in the 1970s, and why has inflation been relatively low or moderate in recent years? What difference does it make to the average person?

FIGURE 4.4
The Canadian Inflation Rate, 1915–2010
Canada experienced double-digit inflation near the end of WWI (1917–1918 and 1920), for two years following WWII (1948 and 1951), and in the mid-1970s and early 1980s. Inflation rates have been low during the past decade but not as low as during 1930–1933, Great Depression years characterized by deflation (negative inflation or a falling price level).
SOURCE: Adapted from Statistics Canada, CANSIM series v41690973.

Inflation and unemployment are often linked together in policy discussions. One reason for this linkage is the oft-heard argument that unemployment can be reduced only at the cost of higher inflation and that inflation can be reduced only at the cost of higher unemployment. Another impact of inflation is that interest rates tend to be higher in periods of high inflation. The link between inflation and interest rates is discussed in Chapter 6.

ECONOMIC INTERDEPENDENCE AMONG NATIONS

National economies do not exist in isolation but are increasingly interdependent. Canada, always a trading nation, became sharply more dependent on trade during the 1990s. By 2010, Canadian exports amounted to about 29 percent of Canadian output and imports to 31 percent.

Sometimes international flows of goods and services become a matter of political concern. The Canada–U.S. Free Trade Agreement (FTA) implemented in January 1989 and the North American Free Trade Agreement (NAFTA) entered into by Canada, the United States, and Mexico in January 1994 have been the subject of intense policy debate in Canada. What are the implications—for economic growth, jobs, and income distribution—of trade agreements in which countries agree to reduce taxes or quotas on the international flow of goods and services?

A related issue is the phenomenon of *trade imbalances,* which occur when the quantity of goods and services that a country sells abroad (its *exports*) differs significantly from the quantity of goods and services its citizens buy from abroad (its *imports*). Figure 4.5 shows Canadian exports and imports since 1961, measured as a percentage of the economy's total output. Except for a brief time following the implementation of the Canada–U.S. Free Trade Agreement and, more recently, since the recession of 2008–2009, Canadian exports have typically outstripped imports, creating a situation called a *trade surplus.* Given the timing of events, the *trade deficits* of the early 1990s might seem to stem from the FTA, but many economists point more to the role of the then-strong Canadian dollar, which hampered exports and encouraged imports.

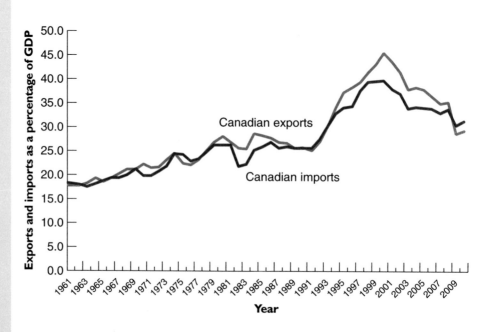

FIGURE 4.5
Exports and Imports as Shares of Canadian Output, 1961–2010
The red line shows Canadian exports as a percentage of Canadian output. The blue line shows imports relative to output. In recent decades, Canada has exported more than it has imported, though imports outstripped exports during the period 1991–1992 (when the Canadian dollar was strong and the Canada–U.S. Free Trade Agreement was being implemented) and again during the recession of 2008–2009.
SOURCE: Adapted from Statistics Canada, CANSIM series v646957, v646954 and v646937.

FIGURE 4.6
Canada's Exchange Rate, 1971 to 2011
The red line expresses the value of the Canadian dollar relative to the U.S. dollar from January 1971 to January 2011. The declining value of the Canadian dollar from the early 1990s until 2002 was a source of controversy in Canada. More recently, the high value of the Canadian dollar has become a source of controversy. SOURCE: Pacific Exchange Rate Service, http://fx.sauder.ubc.ca/.

While Canada has tended to run trade surpluses in most years of recent decades, imports to the United States have exceeded exports since the 1970s, with the U.S. trade deficit in 2000 reaching a record high of 3.7 percent of GDP. Macroeconomists debated whether U.S. trade deficits of this magnitude were sustainable and whether the deficits pointed to an eventual weakening of the U.S. dollar. Starting in 2003, the U.S. dollar has weakened against most major currencies, including the Canadian dollar. The U.S. dollar strengthened during the initial phase of the global recession of 2008–2009, but then weakened again.

The value of one currency relative to another, known as the foreign exchange rate, is another aspect of the economic interdependence among nations. Figure 4.6 illustrates the large swings in the value of the Canada–U.S. foreign exchange rate in recent decades. Exchange rate issues are discussed in detail in Chapter 12.

RECAP

THE MAJOR MACROECONOMIC ISSUES

- *Economic growth and living standards* Over the past century, the industrialized nations have experienced remarkable economic growth and improvements in living standards. Macroeconomists study the reasons for this extraordinary growth and try to understand why growth rates vary markedly among nations.

- *Productivity* Average labour productivity, or output per employed worker, is a crucial determinant of living standards. Macroeconomists ask, "What causes slowdowns and speed-ups in the rate of productivity growth?"

- *Recessions and expansions* Economies experience periods of markedly slower or negative growth (recessions) and more rapid growth (expansions). Macroeconomists examine the sources of these fluctuations and the government policies that attempt to moderate them.

- *Unemployment* The unemployment rate is the fraction of the labour force who are looking for a job but can't find work. Unemployment rises during recessions but there are always unemployed people, even during good times. Macroeconomists study the causes of unemployment, including the reasons why it sometimes differs markedly across countries.

- *Inflation* The inflation rate is the rate at which prices in general are increasing over time. Questions macroeconomists ask about inflation include the following: Why does inflation vary over time and across countries? Must a reduction in inflation be accompanied by an increase in unemployment, or vice versa?

- *Economic interdependence among nations* Modern economies are highly interdependent. Related issues studied by macroeconomists include the desirability of new trade agreements, the causes and effects of trade imbalances, and exchange-rate determination.

4.2 MACROECONOMIC POLICY

We have seen that macroeconomists are interested in why different countries' economies perform differently and why a particular economy may perform well in some periods and poorly in others. Although many factors contribute to economic performance, government policy is surely among the most important. Understanding the effects of various policies and helping government officials develop better policies are important objectives of macroeconomists.

TYPES OF MACROECONOMIC POLICY

We have defined macroeconomic policies as government policies that affect the performance of the economy as a whole, as opposed to the market for a particular good or service. There are three major types of macroeconomic policy: *monetary policy, fiscal policy,* and *structural policy.*

The term **monetary policy** refers in normal times to central bank management of interest rates in order to achieve macroeconomic objectives. For reasons that we will discuss in later chapters, most economists agree that changes in interest rates affect other important economic variables, including the international value of the dollar, national output, employment, and inflation. In virtually all countries, monetary policy is controlled by a government institution called the *central bank.* In Canada, the central bank is called the Bank of Canada. It corresponds to the Federal Reserve System in the United States.

In abnormal times, such as a financial panic or a severe recession, monetary policy may consist not only of central bank management of interest rates but also a variety of other central bank policy measures such as loaning money to troubled financial institutions and buying long-term government debt. Such measures have been employed by many central banks to achieve their macroeconomic objective since the onset of the 2008–2009 global recessions, and they have been referred to by economists and central bankers as **unconventional monetary policy**.

Fiscal policy refers to decisions that determine the government's budget, including the amount and composition of government expenditures and government revenues. The balance between government spending and revenue (mainly from taxes) is a particularly important aspect of fiscal policy known as the **government budget balance**. If revenues are less than expenditures, the government budget balance is negative and described as a **government budget deficit**. If revenues exceed expenditures, the balance is positive and described as a **government budget surplus**.

Figure 4.7 shows Canada's federal government budget deficits and surpluses for the 1984–2010 period. The federal deficit percentage declined from the mid-1980s

monetary policy refers in normal times to central bank management of interest rates to achieve macroeconomic objectives

unconventional monetary policy refers to measures, such as loaning money to troubled financial institutions and buying long-term government debt, that central banks utilize in abnormal times to supplement conventional monetary policy

fiscal policy decisions that determine the government's budget, including the amount and composition of government expenditures and government revenues

government budget balance the difference between government revenues and expenditures; it equals zero when revenues equal expenditures, is positive when revenues exceed expenditures, and is negative when revenues fall short of expenditures

government budget deficit when government revenues fall short of expenditures; that is, the government budget balance is negative

government budget surplus when government revenues exceed expenditures; that is, the government budget balance is positive

FIGURE 4.7

The Federal Government Budget Balance as a Percentage of Output, Canada, 1984–2010

The red line shows the federal government budget balance as a percentage of Canadian output. The federal deficit percentage declined from the mid-1980s until the onset of the early 1990s recession, which caused it to rise again. Recovery from the recession and major federal expenditure cuts in the mid-1990s reduced deficits and eventually produced surpluses towards the end of the 1990s. In 2009 the budget balance moved back into deficit.

SOURCE: Fiscal Reference Tables, http://www.fin.gc.ca/frt-trf/2010/frt-trf-10-eng.pdf. Department of Finance, Canada, October 2010. Reproduced with the permission of the Minister of Public Works and Government Services, 2011.

Note: The year shown is the fiscal year ending in that year; e.g., 2010 stands for fiscal year 2009–2010.

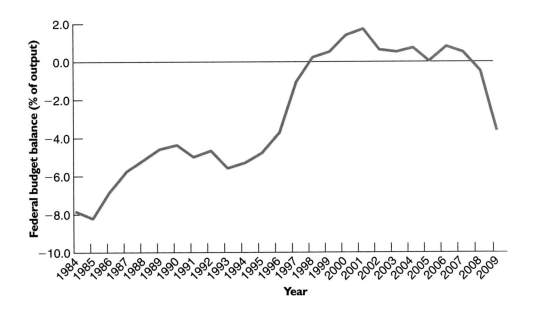

until the early 1990s recession, which caused it to rise again. Recovery and major federal expenditure cuts in the mid-1990s reduced deficits and produced surpluses by the end of the decade. Federal income tax cuts in 2000 reduced the surpluses as did the economic slowdown of 2000–2001. GST cuts in mid-2006 and early 2008 and corporate tax cuts worked in the direction of reducing the surplus, and the recession of 2008–2009 saw the small surplus replaced by a deficit of 3.6 percent of GDP by fiscal year 2009–2010.

As with monetary policy, economists generally agree that fiscal policy can have important effects on the overall performance of the economy. For example, many economists believe that contractionary fiscal policy in the 1930s contributed to the severity of the Great Depression in Canada and many other countries, and expansionary fiscal policy in Canada and other countries softened the global recession of 2008–2009, helping to prevent a second Great Depression.

Government deficits and surpluses are *flows*—measured over time, much as we measure our income over, say, a month or a year. If there are deficits, they are financed by borrowing. The federal government borrows by issuing bonds. In general, a flow measured over time has a counterpart measured at a point in time that is classified as a *stock*. The total of all federal government bonds outstanding is the federal *government debt*.

government debt the sum of past government deficits and surpluses; a stock measure that is calculated at a point in time

Government debt is a stock measure that reflects the sum of past government deficits and surpluses. It is calculated at a point in time such as, say, March 31 2012. Deficits add to the government debt; surpluses reduce the government debt.

Knowledge of government debt is relevant to understanding fiscal policy because governments are concerned to control their ratios of debt relative to the size of the economy. As a result of the global recession of 2008–2009 and efforts to combat it, government deficits have increased around the world, and government debt to output ratios have risen sharply in many countries. Figure 4.8 shows the federal government debt to output ratio for Canada. It has risen since the recession of 2008–2009 but is far below the peak experienced in the mid-1990s. In Chapter 8 we will analyze fiscal policy, including government budget balances and government debt, at greater length.

structural policy government policies aimed at changing the underlying structure, or institutions, of the nation's economy

A final type of macroeconomic policy is **structural policy**, which includes government policies aimed at changing the underlying structure or institutions of the nation's economy. Structural policies come in many forms, from minor tinkering to ambitious overhauls of the entire economic system. The move away from central planning and toward a more market-oriented approach in many formerly communist countries, such as Poland, the Czech Republic, and Hungary, is a large-scale example of structural policy. Many developing countries have tried structural reforms at the urging of the International Monetary Fund. Supporters of structural policy typically claim that, by changing the basic characteristics of the economy or by remaking its institutions, the reforms can stimulate economic growth and improve living standards.

Monetary, fiscal, and structural policies are always controversial, and economists often differ regarding what they view as the appropriate policies at any given time. Economists differ in their policy recommendations either because they have different values or because they make different predictions about the impacts of particular policies, such as changes in interest rates, changes in government spending or taxation, or

FIGURE 4.8
The Federal Government Debt (Accumulated Deficit) as a Percentage of Output, Canada, 1961–2010
The red line shows the accumulated federal government debt as a percentage of the output of the Canadian economy. The debt to output ratio fell from the early 1960s (indeed from the end of WW II, though the 1940s and 1950s are not covered by the figure) until the mid-1970s and then climbed until the mid-1990s. From the mid-1990s, the debt to output ratio fell until the 2008–2009 recession, and rose thereafter.
SOURCE: See Figure 4.7.

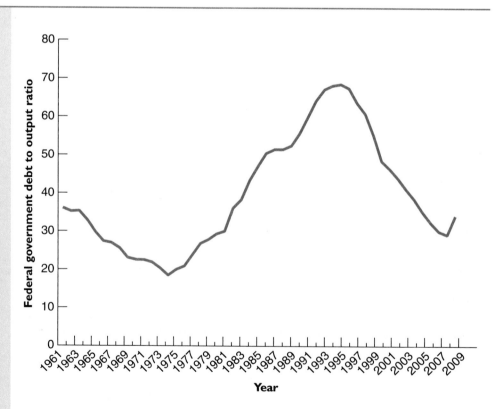

structural policies such as new trade agreements. Economists may make different predictions either because they use different economic models or because they have different assessments of the evidence.

During and since the recession of 2008–2009, for example, a common view among macroeconomists in the high-income countries has been that combating the recession and its aftermath required active use of monetary and fiscal policy, and that larger government deficits and higher government debt-to-GDP ratios had to be accepted as a cost of preventing prolonged high unemployment rates and economic stagnation. Other macroeconomists, however, warned against the possibility that active use of monetary and fiscal policy to simulate the economy would produce higher inflation and unsustainable government debt-to-GDP ratios.

> **RECAP**
>
> ## MACROECONOMIC POLICY
>
> *Macroeconomic policies* affect the performance of the economy as a whole. The three types of macroeconomic policy are monetary policy, fiscal policy, and structural policy.
>
> *Monetary policy,* which in Canada is under the control of the Bank of Canada, usually refers to interest rate changes made by the central bank. Since the beginning of the global recession of 2008–2009, many central banks have supplemented their interest rate changes with *unconventional monetary policy* measures, such as loans to troubled financial institutions and purchases of long-term government debt. *Fiscal policy* involves decisions about the government budget, including its expenditures and tax collections. *Structural policy* refers to government actions to change the underlying structure or institutions of the economy. Structural policy can range from minor tinkering to a major overhaul of the economic system, as with the formerly communist countries that are attempting to convert to market-oriented systems.
>
> All three forms of macroeconomic policy are controversial, and there are important differences among macroeconomists about the appropriate policy actions at any given time.

4.3 AGGREGATION

In Chapter 1, we discussed the difference between macroeconomics, the study of national economies, and microeconomics, which studies both individual economic entities (such as households and firms) and the markets for specific goods and services. The main difference between the fields is one of perspective: macroeconomists take a bird's-eye view of the economy, ignoring the fine details to understand how the system works as a whole. Microeconomists work instead at "ground level," studying the economic behaviour of individual households, firms, and markets. Both perspectives are essential to understanding what makes an economy work.

EXERCISE 4.2

Which of the following questions would be studied primarily by macroeconomists? by microeconomists? Explain.

 a. **Did increased government spending act to offset the rise of the unemployment rate during the 2008–2009 recession?**

 b. **Does Microsoft's dominance of the software industry harm consumers?**

 c. **Should the Bank of Canada and the Department of Finance raise the midpoint of the inflation-control target range from 2 percent to something higher?**

 d. **Why did Canada's average rate of personal saving rise during the 2008–2009 recession?**

e. Does the increase in the number of consumer products being sold over the Internet threaten the profits of conventional retailers, such as Canadian Tire?

aggregation the adding up of individual economic variables to obtain economy-wide totals

Although macroeconomics and microeconomics take different perspectives on the economy, the basic tools of analysis are much the same. In the chapters to come, you will see that macroeconomists apply some of same core principles (see Chapters 1–3) as microeconomists. But macroeconomists must pay particular attention to issues of **aggregation**, the adding up of individual economic variables to obtain economy-wide totals.

For example, explaining trends in movie theatre ticket sales relative to spending on DVD rentals is a topic for microeconomics, not macroeconomics. Instead, macroeconomists add up consumer spending on all goods and services during a given period to obtain *aggregate,* or total, consumer spending. And they explore connections between aggregate consumer spending and variables such as aggregate income and unemployment.

Sometimes, sensible aggregation involves more than just suppressing details in order to see the bigger picture; it requires recognizing that the whole can be more than the sum of the parts. In other words, sensible aggregation may require avoiding the mistake known as the *fallacy of composition*, a concept from Chapter 1 that is worth reviewing here.

fallacy of composition the argument that because something is true for a part, it is also true for the whole

The fallacy of composition occurs when, for example, the assumption is made that if one fan at a sporting event can get a better view by standing up, then all fans at the event will get a better view if they all stand up at once. In economics, the **fallacy of composition** occurs when it is falsely assumed that what is true at the level of a particular individual, household, firm, or industry is necessarily true at a higher aggregate level. An awareness of the fallacy of composition is particularly important in macroeconomics, where aggregation across the whole economy is involved. Some conclusions that might be valid at the level of microeconomics, for example, many not be valid at the level of macroeconomics.

For a macroeconomic example of the fallacy of composition, suppose that one Canadian becomes rich because the government of Canada issues a cheque for $1 million to compensate him for wrongful imprisonment on a murder charge. Would it be logical to generalize that everyone in Canada could become rich if the government issued cheques for $1 million to every man, woman, and child? Macroeconomists would identify such a generalization as an example of the fallacy of composition. The total value of the cheques would exceed the current dollar value of Canada's economic output 30 times over. The government would have to pay for the cheques by printing and issuing a tremendous amount of additional Canadian currency. In normal times, the price level for the Canadian economy would soar and the value of the currency would plummet—one Canadian dollar would at most buy what a few pennies would buy today. It is true that there would be some redistribution of income. Students with loans, for example, would be able to pay them off more easily. But the average Canadian would not become richer.

> **RECAP**
>
> **AGGREGATION**
>
> Macroeconomics, the study of national economies, differs from microeconomics, the study of individual economic entities (such as households and firms) and the markets for specific goods and services. Macroeconomists take a bird's-eye view of the economy. To study the economy as a whole, macroeconomists make frequent use of *aggregation,* the adding up of individual economic variables to obtain economy-wide totals.
>
> A cost of aggregation is that the fine details of the economic situation are obscured. Sensible aggregation sometimes requires recognizing that the whole can be more than the sum of its parts. Sensible aggregation may require avoiding the mistake known as the *fallacy of composition*.

4.4   STUDYING MACROECONOMICS: A PREVIEW

This chapter introduced many of the key issues of macroeconomics. In the chapters to come, we will look at each of these issues in more detail. The next two chapters (Chapters 5 and 6) cover the *measurement* of economic performance, including key variables like the level of economic activity, extent of unemployment, and rate of inflation. Obtaining quantitative measurements of the economy, against which theories can be tested, is the crucial first step in answering basic macroeconomic questions like those raised in this chapter.

In Part 3 we will study short-term economic fluctuations. In this part we will develop three distinct formal macroeconomic models. These models serve a very different purpose than the supply and demand model of perfect competition in microeconomics, but familiarity with the building of the supply and demand model with its two curves (supply and demand) and an equilibrium condition is helpful for understanding these macroeconomic models, which also feature two or three curves and an equilibrium condition.

Chapter 7 provides background on what happens during recessions and expansions, as well as some historical perspective. Chapter 8 discusses one important source of short-term economic fluctuations; that is, variations in aggregate spending. The chapter also shows how, by influencing aggregate spending, fiscal policy may be able to moderate economic fluctuations. The second major policy tool for stabilizing the economy, monetary policy, is the subject of Chapter 9. Chapter 10 develops a model of the simultaneous determination of the price level and of the level of output. Chapter 11 brings inflation into the analysis and discusses the circumstances under which macroeconomic policy-makers may face a short-term trade-off between inflation and unemployment.

Chapter 12 fleshes out our analysis of exchange rates between national currencies. We will discuss in detail how exchange rates are determined and how they affect the workings of the economy and macroeconomic policy. The role played in the economy by money and banks is covered in Chapter 13. This chapter supplements the preceding chapters on monetary policy and exchange rates and provides a bridge to the long-run chapters that follow.

In Part 4 we look at economic behaviour over relatively long periods of time. Chapter 14 examines economic growth and productivity improvement, the fundamental determinants of the average standard of living in the long run. International trade, which has played an important role in Canada's development, is the focus of Chapter 15. Chapter 16 deals with the role of the financial system in the economy. It covers topics such as saving, investment in new capital goods, the pricing of bonds and stocks, and international capital flows.

Finally, throughout your textbook you will see figures similar to the ones in this chapter that are based upon data from Statistics Canada. At the back of your textbook, after the index, you will find a data section that covers data series on 28 key macroeconomic variables from 1976 to 2010. The first part of the data section is a table of the series titled "Canadian Macroeconomic Data Table, 1976–2010." The second part consists of explanatory notes dealing with the meaning and significance of key variables. For each variable, the data label for the CANSIM database from Statistics Canada is provided so that you can use the data label to access the data yourself.

SUMMARY

- Macroeconomics is the study of the performance of national economies and the policies governments use to try to improve that performance. Some of the broad issues macroeconomists study are
  - sources of economic growth and improved living standards;
  - trends in *average labour productivity,* or output per employed worker;
  - short-term fluctuations in the pace of economic growth (recessions and expansions);
  - causes and cures of unemployment and inflation;
  - economic interdependence among nations. **LO1**

- To help explain differences in economic performance among countries, or in economic performance in the same country at different times, macroeconomists study the implementation and effects of macroeconomic policies. *Macroeconomic policies* are government actions designed to affect the performance of the economy as a whole. Macroeconomic policies include *monetary policy,* central bank management of interest rates; *fiscal policy,* relating to decisions about the government's budget; and *structural policy,* aimed at affecting the basic structure and institutions of the economy. **LO2**

- Macroeconomics is distinct from microeconomics, which focuses on the behaviour of individual economic entities and specific markets. Macroeconomists make heavy use of *aggregation,* which is the adding up of individual economic variables into economy-wide totals. Aggregation allows macroeconomists to study the "big picture" of the economy, while ignoring fine details about individual households, firms, and markets. Sensible aggregation sometimes requires recognition that the whole can be more than the sum of the parts. **LO3**

KEY TERMS

aggregation (92)
average labour productivity (81)
fiscal policy (88)
government budget balance (88)

government budget deficit (88)
government budget surplus (88)
government debt (90)
macroeconomic policies (79)

monetary policy (88)
structural policy (90)
unconventional monetary policy (88)

REVIEW QUESTIONS

1. How did the experience of the Great Depression motivate the development of the field of macroeconomics? **LO1**

2. How has Canadian economic performance differed from U.S. economic performance in recent decades? **LO1**

3. Why is average labour productivity a particularly important economic variable? **LO1**

4. True or false, and explain: Economic growth within a particular country generally proceeds at a constant rate. **LO1**

5. True or false, and explain: Differences of opinion about economic policy recommendations can always be resolved by objective analysis of the issues. **LO2**

6. If one computer-chip maker increases output, it will realize increased revenue. If all computer-chip makers increase output, prices will tend to fall, and this could result in reduced revenue. What is the term used for the mistake of assuming that what is true for one acting alone is also true for all acting together? **LO3**

7. What type of macroeconomic policy (monetary, fiscal, structural) might include each of the following actions: **LO2**

    a. A broad government initiative to shift from a high-energy-use economy to a low-energy-use economy.

    b. A government spending program to improve roads and other infrastructure during a recession.

    c. A series of interest rate cuts by the central bank to stimulate spending in the economy.

    d. An attempt to reduce the government budget deficit by raising taxes.

    e. Central bank provision of additional cash to the banking system during a financial crisis.

    f. A decision by a developing country to impose controls on international capital flows.

PROBLEMS

1. Visit the Bank of Canada website (http://www.bankofcanada.ca/en/index/html) and search for information about unconventional monetary policy. Give at least two examples of unconventional monetary policy. Has the Bank of Canada adopted any unconventional monetary policy measures since the onset of the recession of 2008–2009? Explain. **LO2**

2. Is it possible for average living standards to rise during a period in which average labour productivity is falling? Discuss, using a numerical example for illustration. **LO2**

3. The Bureau of Economic Analysis, or BEA, is a U.S. government agency that collects a wide variety of statistics about the U.S. economy. From the BEA's home page (http://www.bea.gov) find data for the most recent year available on U.S. exports and imports of goods and services. (Hint: look at the annual data in an Excel file with monthly and annual data under U.S. economic accounts/International/Trade in goods and services). Is the United States running a trade surplus or deficit? Explain. How did the trade balance change from 2008 to 2009? Explain. **LO3**

4. From the fiscal reference tables (http://www.fin.gc.ca/pub/frt-trf/index-eng.asp) published by the Canadian Department of Finance, we can find that federal government revenues for the fiscal year 2007–2008 were $242.4 billion. Federal government expenditures were $232.8 billion. What was the federal budget balance for fiscal year 2007–2008? Was the balance a deficit or a surplus? **LO2**

5. Which of the following would be studied by a macroeconomist? by a microeconomist? **LO1**

    a. The global operations of Barrick Gold Corporation.

    b. The factors behind the proliferation of payday loan companies in Canada.

    c. The impact of falling commodity prices on inflation and growth in the Canadian economy.

    d. The impact of copyright laws on the prices of university textbooks in different countries.

    e. The effects of tax cuts on the federal budget deficit.

6. Use an Internet search engine such as Google to find information about the "paradox of thrift." Describe the paradox of thrift. Which fallacy does the paradox of thrift illustrate? Which famous economist of the first half of the twentieth century called attention to the paradox of thrift? Under what conditions is the paradox of thrift most likely to occur? **LO3**

7. Chapter 1 of your textbook introduced the distinction between positive economics and welfare economics. The distinction between positive economic statements and welfare economic statements applies to macroeconomics as well as to microeconomics. Each of the following statements might well have appeared in the business pages of a Canadian newspaper. Label each statement as positive or welfare (normative). Note the key word or words that lead to your conclusion. **LO2**

    a. If economic growth turns negative next year, the federal government budget deficit will increase.

    b. A moderate inflation rate is better than a low inflation rate.

    c. When oil prices decline month after month, the value of the Canadian dollar tends to fall relative to the U.S. dollar in the foreign exchange market.

    d. The output of China is greater than that of Japan.

    e. Canadians will be better off with a government debt-to-GDP ratio of zero.

ANSWERS TO IN-CHAPTER EXERCISES

4.1   The answer depends on current statistics, but in 2009 and 2010 the U.S. unemployment rate was higher than the Canadian rate. **LO1**

4.2   **LO1, LO3**

a. Macroeconomists. Government spending and the unemployment rate are aggregate concepts pertaining to the whole economy.

b. Microeconomists. Microsoft, though large, is an individual firm.

c. Macroeconomists. Relevant evidence would relate to the links between inflation and other macroeconomic variables.

d. Macroeconomists. Average saving is an aggregate concept.

e. Microeconomists. The focus is on a relatively narrow set of markets and products rather than on the economy as a whole.

CHAPTER 5
Measuring Economic Activity: GDP and Unemployment

"Total economic activity was unchanged in this month, after edging up 0.1 percent last month."

"The unemployment rate held at 8.0 percent for the fourth consecutive month."

News headlines like these fill the airwaves—some TV and radio stations carry nothing else. In fact, all kinds of people are interested in economic data. The average person hopes to learn something that will be useful in a business decision, a financial investment, or a career move. The professional economist depends on economic data in much the same way that a doctor depends on a patient's vital signs—pulse, blood pressure, and temperature—to make an accurate diagnosis. To understand economic developments and to be able to give useful advice to policy-makers, business people, or union leaders, an economist simply must have up-to-date, accurate data.

Measurement of the economy dates back to the mid-seventeenth century. Not until the twentieth century, though, did economic measurement come into its own, and not until the Second World War were the foundations of modern economic measurement in place.

The Second World War was an important catalyst for the development of economic statistics since its very outcome depended on mobilization of economic resources. In the United Kingdom, for example, Richard Stone contributed to wartime planning by pioneering a comprehensive system for measuring the economy's output. He did so by making use of macroeconomic concepts developed in the 1930s by John Maynard Keynes, possibly the most influential economist of the twentieth century. In Canada, the foundations for modern-day economic statistics were established by a 1945 White Paper on Employment and Income.[1]

In this chapter and the next, we will focus on the measurement of three basic macroeconomic variables that arise in almost any discussion of the economy: the *gross domestic product* (or GDP), the *unemployment rate*, and the *inflation rate*. This chapter deals primarily with the first two of these statistics. Chapter 6 deals with the inflation rate.

GDP can be expressed in three different but equivalent ways: by production (or value added), expenditure, and income approaches. This chapter begins with the production

1 *Employment and Income With Special Reference to the Initial Period of Reconstruction*, (Ottawa: King's Printer, April 1945).

approach to GDP measurement, the approach followed in the Statistics Canada publication *Gross Domestic Product by Industry*. The key source of GDP measurements for Canada, however, is a Statistics Canada publication called the *National Income and Expenditure Accounts*. The words "expenditure" and "income" in the title refer to the two major ways Statistics Canada obtains the same number for GDP: by adding up different categories of expenditure in the economy, or by adding up the incomes earned in producing the economy's output. The incomes earned in producing GDP, in turn, are associated with employment as defined in the *Labour Force Survey*, the source for unemployment-rate statistics.

By the end of this chapter, you will understand how official measures of output and unemployment are constructed and will have gained some insight into their strengths and limitations. Understanding the strengths and limitations of economic data is necessary background for the economic analysis in the chapters to come.

www.statcan.gc.ca
Gross Domestic Product by
Industry

5.1 GROSS DOMESTIC PRODUCT: MEASURING THE NATION'S OUTPUT

Chapter 4 discussed the link between an economy's output and its living standard. We noted that high levels of output per worker are associated with a high standard of living. A "worker" is someone engaged in paid employment as measured by the *Labour Force Survey*.[2] But what, exactly, does "output" mean? To study economic growth and productivity scientifically, we need to be more precise about how economists define and measure an economy's output.

The most commonly used measure of an economy's output is called the *gross domestic product*, or *GDP*. GDP is intended to measure how much an economy produces in a given period, such as a quarter (three months) or a year. More precisely, **gross domestic product (GDP)** is the market value of the final goods and services produced in a country during a given period. To understand this definition, let's take it apart and examine each of its parts separately. The first key phrase in the definition is "market value."

gross domestic product (GDP) the market value of the final goods and services produced in a country during a given period

MARKET VALUE

A modern economy produces many different goods and services, from dental floss (a good) to acupuncture (a service). To be able to talk about total output as opposed to the output of specific items like dental floss, economists need to *aggregate* the quantities of many different goods and services into a single number. We have a ready means of adding them up if they are exchanged for money, and hence also have *market prices*.

A simple example will illustrate the process. In the imaginary economy of Orchardia, total production is 4 million apples and 6 million pears.[3] One could add the number of apples to the number of pears and conclude that the total output is 10 million pieces of fruit. But would Orchardia's output then just equal the output of an economy producing 10 million blueberries? And what if Orchardia also produced 3 million pairs of shoes? What is a sensible way of adding apples and pears to shoes?

Suppose, however, we know that apples have a market price of $0.25 each, pears of $0.50 each, and shoes of $20 a pair. Then we can say that the market value of this economy's production, or its GDP, is equal to

2 Someone engaged in paid employment can be an employee, an employer, or a self-employed worker without employees. A tiny fraction, less than half a percentage point, of the employment involved in the production of Canadian GDP consists of unpaid family labour on farms and in small businesses. For ease of expression, we will generally ignore this unpaid employment.

3 To keep things simple, we are assuming that apples and pears in this imaginary economy are each of a single type. In reality, adding together, say, Spartan apples with Macintosh apples or Bartlett pears with Anjou pears requires a similar procedure to adding apples to pears.

$$\left(4 \text{ million apples} \times \frac{\$0.25}{\text{apple}}\right) + \left(6 \text{ million pears} \times \frac{\$0.50}{\text{pear}}\right)$$

$$+ \left(3 \text{ million pairs of shoes} \times \frac{\$20}{\text{pair}}\right) = \$64 \text{ million.}$$

Notice that when we calculate total output this way, the more expensive items (the shoes) receive a higher weighting than the cheaper items (the apples and pears). But this weighting is not a subjective judgment about the relative values of apples, pears, and shoes; the weights are market prices that large numbers of people have been willing to pay in millions of transactions.

EXAMPLE **5.1**

Orchardia's GDP

Suppose Orchardia were to produce 3 million apples, 3 million pears, and 4 million pairs of shoes at the same market prices as in the preceding text. What is its GDP now?
Now the Orchardian GDP is equal to

$$\left(3 \text{ million apples} \times \frac{\$0.25}{\text{apple}}\right) + \left(3 \text{ million pairs} \times \frac{\$0.50}{\text{pair}}\right)$$

$$+ \left(4 \text{ million pairs of shoes} \times \frac{\$20}{\text{pair}}\right) = \$82.25 \text{ million.}$$

Notice that Orchardian GDP is higher in Example 5.1 than in the previous text, even though two of the three goods (apples and pears) are being produced in smaller quantities than before. The reason is that the good whose production has increased (shoes) is much more valuable than the goods whose production has decreased (apples and pears).

Now suppose Orchardia produces the original quantities of the three goods at the original prices ($0.25/apple, $0.50/pear, and $20/pair of shoes). In addition, suppose Orchardia produces 5 million peaches at $0.30 each. What is the GDP of Orchardia now?

EXERCISE 5.1

Market prices provide a convenient way to add together, or aggregate, the many different goods and services produced in a modern market economy. Market prices even provide the basis for valuing public-sector services, such as healthcare and education, provided to the public without charge.

There are no market prices for public services provided without charge, but the paid labour and other inputs used to produce them are purchased in markets; thus, non-marketed public services are valued in GDP according to the market value of the inputs used to produce them. This practice is followed by statistical agencies around the world. And if it were not followed, there would be a large category of employment as measured by the *Labour Force Survey* without a corresponding measure of output in GDP.

But the use of market prices of goods and services (or the use of market prices of inputs) does not provide a solution to all aggregation problems. For example, in a predominantly agricultural society where relatively few goods and services are traded in markets and much of agricultural production goes towards the farm households' own subsistence, an economic aggregate based only on market transactions would seriously understate the level of economic activity.[4]

Even in modern market economies, it is important to recognize that the expansion of marketed and public-sector output may come about in part through the incorporation

---

4 One way to deal with this problem is to impute a value to agricultural output produced by farm households for their own consumption. The statistical agencies of many countries include such an imputation in their calculation of GDP.

of activities that had previously taken place outside of paid employment. For example, the growth of paid housekeeping and childcare services may represent in part a conversion of unpaid household activities into marketed output or into publicly provided services.

The opposite process can also take place. That is, reductions in marketed and public-sector output may be associated with the expansion of non-market household activity. For example, the extension of the average age of completing education results in young people spending less time in paid employment and more time studying. Or a trend to early retirement from paid employment might reduce GDP but result in an increase in, say, recreational gardening.[5]

While GDP for Canada is calculated from market values the way we have done for the imaginary economy of Orchardia, not all goods and services with market value go into the GDP total. As we will see next, the GDP total includes only those goods and services that are the end products of the production process, called *final goods and services*. Otherwise, there would be a problem of counting some goods and services two or more times.

FINAL GOODS AND SERVICES

Many goods are used in the production process. Before a baker can produce a loaf of bread, grain must be grown and harvested. Then the grain must be ground into flour and, together with other ingredients, baked into bread. Of the three major goods that are produced during this process—grain, flour, and bread—only the bread is used by consumers. Because producing the bread is the ultimate purpose of the process, the bread is called a *final good*. In general, a **final good or service** is the end product of a process, the product or service that consumers actually use. The goods or services produced on the way toward making the final product—here, the grain and the flour—are called **intermediate goods or services**.

Since we are interested in measuring only those items that are of direct economic value, *only final goods and services are included in GDP*. Intermediate goods and services are *not* included. To illustrate, suppose that the grain from the previous example has a market value of $0.50 (the price the milling company paid for the grain). The grain is then ground into flour, which has a market value of $1.20 (the price the baker paid for the flour). Finally, the flour is made into a loaf of fine French bread, worth $2 at the local store. In calculating the contribution of these activities to GDP, would we want to add together the values of the grain, the flour, and the bread? No, because the grain and flour are intermediate goods, valuable only because they can be used to make bread. So, in this example the total contribution to GDP is $2, the value of the loaf of bread, the final product.

Example 5.2 illustrates the same distinction but this time with a focus on services.

final goods or services consumed by the ultimate user; because they are the end products of the production process, they are counted as part of GDP

intermediate goods or services used up in the production of final goods and services and therefore not counted as part of GDP

EXAMPLE 5.2

The hair stylist and her assistant

Your hair stylist charges $20 for a haircut. In turn, she pays her assistant $4 per haircut in return for sharpening the scissors, sweeping the floor, and other chores. For each haircut given, what is the total contribution of the hair stylist and her assistant, taken together, to GDP?

The answer to this problem is $20, the price of the haircut. The haircut is counted in GDP because it is the final service, the one that actually has value to the final user. The services provided by the assistant have value only because they contribute to the production of the haircut, and thus they are not counted as a final service in GDP.

A process that is equivalent to adding together the value of all final goods and services is adding up the *value added* by all firms in the production process. The **value added** by

value added for any firm, the market value of its product or service minus the cost of inputs purchased from other firms

5 Time spent in unpaid housekeeping, child care, studying, and recreational gardening is not measured by the *Labour Force Survey* or by GDP. But statistics on non-market uses of time by the working-age population have been collected intermittently by Statistics Canada through the *General Social Survey*. (Catalogue no. 89F0115XWE).

TABLE 5.1
Value Added in Bread Production

Firm	Revenue − Cost of intermediate goods = Value added		
Grain supplier	$0.50	$0.00	$0.50
Flour miller	$ 1.20	$0.50	$0.70
Bakery	$2.00	$ 1.20	$0.80
Total			$2.00

any firm equals the market value of its product or service minus the cost of inputs purchased from other firms. Table 5.1 provides the relevant data from the simple example of the $2-per-loaf French bread. The value added by the grain supplier was $0.50 because the grain was sold to the flour miller for $0.50 and was assumed to require no intermediate goods for its production. The value added by the flour miller was $0.70, the difference between the value of the flour sold to the bakery and the cost of the grain used to produce the flour. Finally, the value added by the bakery was $0.80, the difference between the price for which the bread was sold as a final good and the cost to the bakery of purchasing the flour (assumed to be the sole intermediate good utilized by the bakery). Notice that the sum of value added by the three firms is $2, which equals the market value of the bread.

A special type of good that is difficult to classify as intermediate or final is a *capital good*. As previously explained in Chapter 2, a capital good is a long-lived good, which is itself produced and used only to produce other goods and services. Factories and machines are examples of capital goods. Capital goods do not fit the definition of final goods, since their purpose is to produce other goods. On the other hand, they are not used up during the production process, except over a very long period, so they are not exactly intermediate goods either. For purposes of measuring GDP, statistical agencies have agreed to classify newly produced capital goods as final goods. Otherwise, a country that invested in its future by building modern factories and buying new machines would be counted as having a lower GDP than a country that devoted all its resources to producing consumer goods.

We have now established that GDP is equal to the market value of final goods and services. Let's look at the last part of the definition: "produced within a country during a given period."

PRODUCED WITHIN A COUNTRY DURING A GIVEN PERIOD

The word *domestic* in the term *gross domestic product* tells us that GDP is a measure of economic activity within a given country. Thus, only production that takes place within the country's borders is counted. For example, the GDP of Canada includes the market value of all cars produced within Canadian borders, even though the cars are made in foreign-owned plants. Looked at in another way, cars produced in Canada by a U.S.–based company like General Motors are *not* counted in U.S. GDP.

We have seen that GDP is intended to measure the amount of production that occurs during a given period, normally the calendar year. For this reason, only goods and services that are actually produced during a particular year are included in the GDP for that year. Example 5.3 and Exercise 5.2 illustrate.

EXAMPLE 5.3

The sale of a house and GDP

A 20-year-old house is sold to a young family for $100 000. The family pays the real estate agent a 6 percent commission. What is the contribution of this transaction to GDP?

Because the house was not produced during the current year, its value is *not* counted in this year's GDP. (The value of the house was included in the GDP 20 years earlier, the year the house was built.) In general, purchases and sales of existing assets, such as old houses or used cars, do not contribute to the current year's GDP. However, the $6000 fee paid to the real estate agent represents the market value of the agent's services in helping the family find the house and make the purchase. Since those services were provided during the current year, the agent's fee *is* counted in current-year GDP.

EXERCISE 5.2   **A financial investor sells 100 shares of stock in corporate stock for $50 per share. She pays her broker a 2 percent commission for executing the sale. How does the financial investor's transaction affect the current-year GDP?**

RECAP

MEASURING GDP

Gross domestic product (GDP) equals

the market value
GDP is basically an aggregate of the market values of the many goods and services produced in the economy. The services provided by government employees are typically not provided at market prices, so they are included in GDP at the government's cost of producing them. Goods and services produced by unpaid household labour for use within the household, everything from meal preparation to mowing the lawn, are not included in GDP.

of final goods and services
Final goods and services, which include capital goods such as factories and machines, are counted in GDP. Intermediate goods and services, which are used up in the production of final goods and services, are not counted.

In practice, the value of final goods and services is determined by the value-added method. The value added by any firm equals the firm's revenue from selling its product, minus the cost of inputs purchased from other firms. Summing the value added by all firms in the production process yields the value of the final good or service.

produced in a country during a given period
Only goods and services produced within a nation's borders are included in GDP, and only those produced during the current year, or the portion of the value produced during the current year, are counted as part of the current-year GDP.

5.2 THE EXPENDITURE METHOD FOR MEASURING GDP

GDP is a measure of the quantity of goods and services *produced* by an economy. But any good or service that is produced will also be *purchased* and used by some economic agent—a consumer buying Christmas gifts or a firm investing in new machinery, for example. For many purposes, knowing not only how much is produced, but who uses it and how, is important.

Economic statisticians divide the users of the final goods and services that make up the GDP for any given year into four categories: *households, firms, governments,* and the *foreign sector* (i.e., foreign purchasers of domestic products). They assume that all the final goods and services that are produced in a country in a given year will be purchased and used by members of one or more of these four groups. Furthermore, the amounts that purchasers spend on various goods and services should be equal to the market values of those goods and services. As a result, GDP can also be measured by adding up the total amount spent by each of the four groups on final goods and services and subtracting spending on imported goods and services.

Corresponding to the four groups of final users are four components of expenditure: consumption, private-sector investment, government purchases, and net exports. That is, households consume, firms engage in private-sector investment, governments make government purchases, and the foreign sector buys the nation's exports. Table 5.2 gives the dollar values for each of these components for the Canadian economy in 2010. As the table shows, GDP for Canada in 2010 was over $1.6 trillion, which is roughly $48 000 per person. Detailed definitions of the components of expenditure and their principal subcomponents follow. As you read through them, refer to Table 5.2 to get a sense of the relative importance of each type of spending.

Consumption, or personal expenditure, is spending by households on goods and services, such as food, clothing, and entertainment. Consumption is divided into four subcomponents:

consumption spending by households on goods and services, such as food, clothing, and entertainment

- *Durable goods*, or consumer durables, are long-lived goods such as cars and furniture purchased for household use. Note that new houses are not treated as consumer durables but as part of private-sector investment.
- *Semi-durable goods* are consumer goods that would typically be used on multiple occasions and be expected to last for a year or more. Examples are clothing and footwear.
- *Non-durable goods* are consumer goods that would typically be used only once, or be expected to last less than a year. Examples are food, gasoline, and heating fuel purchased by households.
- *Services*, a large component of consumer spending, include everything from haircuts and taxi rides to legal and financial services.

Not all personal spending is counted as consumption in GDP. For example, if you give change to a homeless person, the act is considered a private transfer, reducing your income and increasing the income of the homeless person, not as a payment for goods or services received. Similarly, allowances paid by parents to children are considered transfers, not payments for services rendered.

Private-sector investment, sometimes called business investment or simply investment, is spending by firms on final goods and services, primarily capital goods and housing. Private-sector investment is divided into three subcomponents:

private-sector investment spending by firms on final goods and services, primarily capital goods and housing

- Investment in *non-residential structures and equipment*, or non-residential gross fixed capital formation, is the purchase by firms of new capital goods such as machinery, factories, office buildings, shopping malls, and transportation equipment. (Remember that for the purposes of calculating GDP, long-lived capital goods are treated as final goods rather than as intermediate goods.) Firms buy capital goods to increase their capacity to produce. A new car will be treated as a consumer durable falling under consumption if purchased for family use but as an investment in equipment if purchased by a taxi company as an addition to its fleet.
- Investment in *residential structures*, or housing investment, refers to purchases of new dwellings, regardless of whether the dwelling is a new house purchased by a family for personal use or a new apartment building purchased by a landlord to earn rental income. In many respects, purchases of new houses by families are like their purchases of consumer durables and could be classified as consumption. But national accounting experts have decided otherwise, as a matter of convention. For GDP accounting purposes, residential investment is treated as an investment by the business sector.
- *Business investment in inventories*, or inventory investment, refers to changes in company inventories. The goods a firm produces but does not sell during the current period are treated, for accounting purposes, as if the firm had bought those goods from itself. This is a smart accounting twist for making sure that production equals

TABLE 5.2
Expenditure Components of Canadian GDP, 2010 ($billions)

Component and Principal Subcomponent Names	Principal Subcomponent Values	Component Values	Macroeconomic Symbols	Percentage of GDP
Consumption		941.4	**C**	**58.1%**
Durable goods	114.0			
Semi-durable goods	71.4			
Non-durable goods	224.4			
Services	531.6			
Private-Sector Investment		291.4	**I**	**18.0%**
Non-residential structures and equipment	177.6			
Residential structures	111.8			
Business investment in inventories	2.0			
Government Purchases		420.0	**G**	**25.9%**
Net government current expenditure on goods and services	352.7			
Government gross fixed capital formation	67.3			
Net exports		−30.8	**NX**	**−1.9%**
Exports	476.5			
Imports	−507.3			
Statistical discrepancy	−0.5	−0.5		**−0.03%**
Total:				
Gross Domestic Product	1621.5	1621.5	**Y**	**100%**

SOURCE: Adapted from the Statistics Canada CANSIM database, http://cansim2.statcan.gc.ca. Table 380-0002 and from the Statistics Canada website, http://www40.statcan.gc.ca/l01/cst01/ECON04-eng.htm. Extraction date May 10, 2011. Note: The statistical discrepancy is used to reconcile GDP from the expenditure approach with GDP from the income approach. If one approach leads to a higher estimate than the other, then half of the difference between the two is added to the lower value and half is subtracted from the higher value. The table omits government inventory investment, which is so small that its GDP share rounds to zero. Components do not add to totals exactly as a result of rounding and this minor omission.

expenditure—that all the goods produced are also sold. Inventory investment will take a negative value if the value of inventories on hand falls over the course of a year. Inventories of a firm tend to build up (positive inventory investment) if there is an unanticipated decline in sales and tend to run down (negative inventory investment) when there is an unanticipated increase in sales.

People often refer to purchases of financial assets, such as stocks or bonds, as investments. For an individual buying a stock or bond with the hope of financial gain, the stock or bond may seem like an investment promising to yield a financial return. But for the economy as a whole, the stock or bond is a piece of paper or a computer entry representing an asset for the buyer and a liability for the seller. Its purchase is not equivalent to the formation of *new* physical capital or inventories that we have labelled private-sector investment. The everyday use of the term investment for purchases of financial assets, then, is very different from the definition of investment employed in GDP. Whereas economists usually use the term "real" to distinguish inflation-adjusted values from "nominal" ones, as explained below, they also use the term "real investment" to describe this formation of new physical capital or inventories and to contrast it with "financial investment."

Government purchases are purchases by federal, provincial/territorial, and municipal governments of final goods (such as computers) and services (such as teaching in public schools). Government purchases in GDP are a subset of all spending recorded in government budgets. Government purchases do *not* include *government transfer payments*, which are payments made by the government in return for which no current goods or services are received. Examples of transfer payments (which, again, are *not* included in government purchases but are included in government budgets) are old age security benefits, employment insurance benefits, and social assistance payments. Interest paid on the public debt is another type of transfer. It is also excluded from government purchases in GDP but is recorded, of course, in government budgets.

Government purchases are divided into two major subcomponents:

- *Net government current expenditure on goods and services* consists of purchases of office supplies and the services of government employees. Department of National Defence spending on warships, military aircraft, weapons, and the like also falls into this category.
- *Government gross fixed capital formation*, or government investment in fixed capital, corresponds to government purchases of new structures and equipment, including waterworks, sewage systems, roads, harbours, and airports. It includes the portion of Department of National Defence spending on durable assets that could be used for civilian purposes, such as docks, roads, hospitals, and transport aircraft.

For some purposes, it is useful to combine private-sector investment and government investment into a single total. For example, in discussing economy-wide saving and capital formation in Chapter 16, we will examine how Statistics Canada combines private-sector investment and government investment into a category of economy-wide investment called *gross investment*. This gross investment includes both replacement investment and *net investment*. **Net investment** refers to investment that adds to the total capital stock of the economy. If net investment is zero, the total capital stock is unchanged from one year to the next. If net investment is positive, as it usually is in the Canadian economy, then the capital stock grows from one year to the next.

Our fourth and final major expenditure category is **net exports**, which equal exports minus imports, where

- *exports* are domestically produced final goods and services that are sold abroad (or to visiting tourists), and
- *imports* are purchases by domestic buyers of goods and services that were produced abroad. Imports are subtracted from exports to find the net amount of spending on domestically produced goods and services.

A country's net exports reflect the net demand by the rest of the world for its goods and services. Net exports can be negative, since imports can exceed exports in any given year. The annual net exports of the United States, for example, have been consistently negative for over two decades. As Table 5.2 showed, Canada's net exports were negative in 2010, but Figure 4.5 showed that Canada's net exports have traditionally been positive.

The relationship between GDP and expenditures on goods and services can be summarized by an equation. Let

$$Y = \text{gross domestic product, or output}$$
$$C = \text{consumption expenditure}$$
$$I = \text{private-sector investment}$$
$$G = \text{government purchases}$$
$$NX = \text{net exports}$$

Using these symbols, we can write that GDP equals the sum of the four types of expenditure algebraically:

$$Y = C + I + G + NX.$$

government purchases purchases by federal, provincial, and municipal governments of final goods and services; does not include government transfer payments or interest paid on the public debt

net investment investment that adds to the total capital stock of the economy

net exports exports minus imports

EXAMPLE **5.4**

Measuring GDP by production and by expenditure

Suppose that an economy produces 1 000 000 automobiles valued at $15 000 each. Of these, 700 000 are sold to consumers, 200 000 are sold to businesses, 50 000 are sold to the government, and 25 000 are sold abroad. No automobiles are imported. The automobiles left unsold at the end of the year are held in inventory by the auto producers. Find GDP in terms of (a) the market value of production and (b) the components of expenditure. You should get the same answer both ways.

The market value of the production of final goods and services in this economy is 1 000 000 autos times $15 000 per auto, or $15 billion.

To measure GDP in terms of expenditure, we must add spending on consumption, private-sector investment, government purchases, and net exports. Consumption is 700 000 autos multiplied by $15 000, or $10.5 billion. Government purchases are 50 000 autos multiplied by $15 000, or $0.75 billion. Net exports are equal to exports (25 000 autos at $15 000, or $0.375 billion) minus imports (zero), so net exports are $0.375 billion.

So what about private-sector investment? Here we must be careful. The 200 000 autos that are sold to businesses, worth $3 billion, count as investment. But notice, too, that the auto companies produced 1 000 000 automobiles but sold only 975 000 (700 000 + 200 000 + 50 000 + 25 000). Hence, 25 000 autos were unsold at the end of the year and were added to the automobile producers' inventories. This addition to producer inventories (25 000 autos at $15 000, or $0.375 billion) counts as inventory investment, which is part of total private-sector investment. Thus, total private-sector investment spending equals the $3 billion worth of autos sold to businesses plus the $0.375 billion in inventory investment, or $3.375 billion.

To recap, in this economy, consumption is $10.5 billion, private-sector investment (including inventory investment) is $3.375 billion, government purchases equal $0.75 billion, and net exports are $0.375 billion. Summing these four components of expenditure yields $15 billion—the same value for GDP that we got by calculating the market value of production.

EXERCISE 5.3   **Extending Example 5.4, suppose that 25 000 of the automobiles purchased by households are imported rather than domestically produced. Domestic production remains at 1 000 000 autos valued at $15 000 each. Once again, find GDP in terms of (a) the market value of production and (b) the components of expenditure.**

RECAP↑

EXPENDITURE COMPONENTS OF GDP

GDP can be expressed as the sum of expenditures on domestically produced final goods and services. The four types of expenditure that are counted in the GDP, and the economic groups that make up each type of expenditure, are as follows:

Who makes the expenditure?	Type of expenditure	Examples
Households	Consumption	Food, clothes, haircuts, new cars
Firms	Private-sector investment	New factories and equipment, new houses, increases in inventory stocks
Governments	Government purchases	New school buildings, roads, docks, salaries of civil servants
Foreign sector	Net exports, or exports minus imports	Exported manufactured goods, resource exports, financial services provided by domestic residents to foreigners

5.3 GDP AND THE INCOMES OF CAPITAL AND LABOUR

We have seen that the GDP can be thought of equally well as a measure of total value added or as a measure of total expenditure. Either method of calculating GDP gives the same final answer. A third way to think of GDP is in terms of the incomes it can be broken down into. Broadly speaking, GDP can be divided into labour income and capital income.

Statistics Canada divides income into more than just two broad categories, but the details of GDP in terms of income are unimportant for macroeconomics compared to the details of GDP in terms of expenditure. The following list of four major components of GDP in terms of income will give you a good sense of what is involved.[6] Of the four components, the first corresponds closely to labour income, and the other three correspond roughly to capital income (though the third component also includes labour income):

- *Wages, salaries, and supplementary labour income* are the largest single income component of income-based GDP. Supplementary labour income is another word for the monetary value of fringe benefits.
- *Corporate and like profits before taxes* is a term we have used to group together the net earnings of private-sector corporations and government business enterprises after deducting an allowance (see *capital consumption allowances* below) for the consumption of fixed capital. This category includes corporate income paid out as dividends.
- *Net farm and small business income* is a term we have used to group together the net income of farmers and net income of unincorporated businesses. This category also includes most rental income.
- *Interest and miscellaneous investment income* is basically interest and other investment income (excluding dividends), less net investment income received from abroad, less interest on the public debt.

Figure 5.1 will help you visualize the three equivalent ways of thinking about GDP: the market value of production, the total value of expenditure, and the sum of labour income and capital income. Figure 5.1 also, roughly, captures the relative importance of the components of expenditure and of income.

FIGURE 5.1
The Three Faces of GDP
The GDP can be expressed equally well as (1) the market value of production, (2) total expenditure (consumption, private-sector investment, government purchases, net exports), or (3) total income (labour income and capital income).

---

6 If you are interested in the details and actual data on Canadian GDP in terms of income, see Statistics Canada website, http://www40.statcan.gc.ca/l01/cst01/ECON03-eng.htm.

Income and expenditure are equal in magnitude. Recall that there is a circular flow relationship between them. Figure 2.7 presented the circular flow of income and expenditure in a highly simplified model of the economy featuring labour as the only input and consumer goods and services as the only output. The revenue that firms received from selling consumer goods and services depended on the expenditure of households, which in turn depended on the wages that households received from firms. Figure 5.2 provides a circular flow diagram with more detail than was given in Figure 2.7. It is still a simplified model in that it does not take into account, for example, financial markets and the

---

FIGURE 5.2

The Circular Flow of Income and Expenditure Revisited

This diagram links income and expenditure in a model of the economy that includes firm, household, government, and rest of the world (foreign) sectors. The red arrows indicate money or dollar flows in the economy. The blue arrows indicate the flow of real inputs and goods and services.

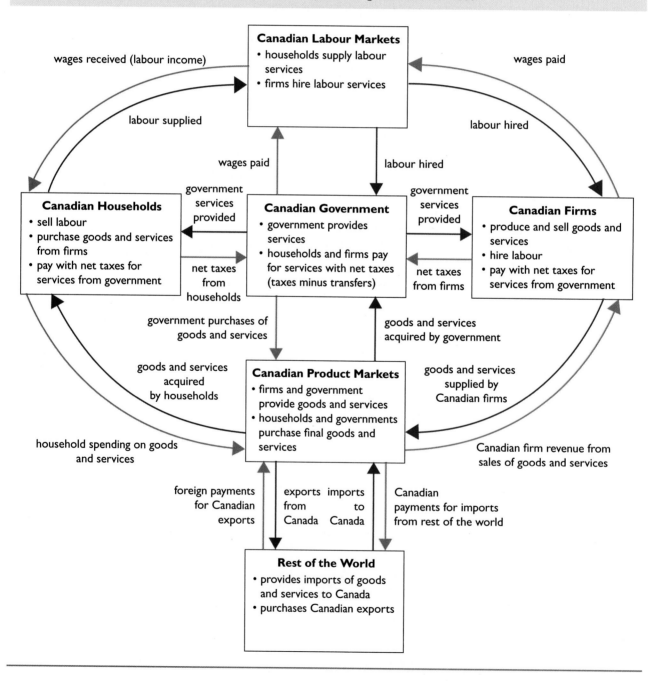

sources of income (interest and dividends) associated with bonds, stocks, and other financial instruments. (Financial markets are discussed in Part 4.) But in addition to households and firms, Figure 5.2 accounts for the government sector and the rest of the world (or foreign sector) and thereby deals with additional flows of income and expenditure. Although the income and expenditure approaches to GDP measurement provide a more realistic representation of the economy than Figures 2.7 and 5.2, they too are based upon the circular flow of income and expenditure.

ECONOMIC NATURALIST 5.1

Does GDP measurement ignore the underground economy?

It is commonly assumed that economic activities conducted "underground" in order to evade tax officials or law enforcement officers are not captured in GDP. It is true that GDP does not capture all underground activity, but a careful Statistics Canada study concluded that measured underground activity could make up as much as 1.5 percent of official Canadian GDP.[7] This is not surprising if you understand the basics of GDP measurement, such as that GDP can be measured by three different approaches, and that even the income approach is not only based upon tax returns.

For example, the method of estimating residential rents is to multiply the stock of rented dwellings by the average monthly rent paid by tenants, based upon answers to questions about rent asked in the monthly *Labour Force Survey*. Even if a high percentage of landlords cheated on their tax returns, the value of rents recorded in GDP would be quite accurate.

GDP will also pick up some underground transactions because of the way intermediate goods and services are treated in the national accounts. Suppose

that a contractor pays an electrician under the table to wire a house. The electrician will not declare the income, and the value added by the electrician will be underestimated. But the house will still be sold for its market value, so the value added by the contractor will be overestimated. Provided Statistics Canada has good statistics on housing sales, the estimate of total value added will be correct.

In other cases, the underground activity may require significant amounts of an input that is measured in GDP. Suppose that someone grows marijuana at home using electric lamps for artificial light and then sells the marijuana in underground transactions. GDP will not pick up the marijuana sales directly. If the extra electricity usage is billed for (rather than stolen), however, it will be misclassified as personal consumption rather than as an intermediate input for producing marijuana. Still, the electricity consumption will add to the GDP total and serve as a rough proxy for the marijuana production.

5.4 NOMINAL GDP VERSUS REAL GDP

As a measure of the total production of an economy over a given period, such as a particular year, GDP is useful in comparisons of economic activity in different places. For example, GDP data for the year 2012, broken down by province, could be used to compare aggregate production in Ontario and Quebec or in British Columbia and Alberta during that year. However, economists are interested in comparing levels of economic activity not only in different *locations* but *over time* as well.

Using GDP to compare economic activity at two different points in time may give misleading answers, however, as the following example shows. Suppose for the sake of illustration that the economy produces only chicken salads and garden salads. The prices and quantities of the two goods in the years 2002 and 2012 are shown in Table 5.3.

---

7 Statistics Canada, *The Size of the Underground Economy in Canada*, Catalogue 13-603E, No. 2. For an update of the original study, see Berouk Terefe, Conrad Barber-Dueck and Marie-Josée Lamontagne, *Estimating the Underground Economy in Canada*, 1992–2008, Income and Expenditure Accounts Division, Statistics Canada, June 2011.

If we calculate GDP in each year as the market value of production, we find that GDP for 2002 is

$$\left(10 \text{ chicken salads} \times \frac{\$10}{\text{chicken salad}}\right) + \left(15 \text{ garden salads} \times \frac{\$5}{\text{garden salad}}\right)$$

The GDP for 2012 is

$$\left(20 \text{ chicken salads} \times \frac{\$12}{\text{chicken salad}}\right) + \left(30 \text{ garden salads} \times \frac{\$6}{\text{garden salad}}\right)$$

Comparing the GDP for the year 2012 to the GDP for the year 2002, we might conclude that it is 2.4 times greater ($420/$175).

TABLE 5.3
Prices and Quantities in 2002 and 2012

	Quantity of chicken salads	Price of chicken salads	Quantity of garden salads	Price of garden salads
2002	10	$10	15	$5
2012	20	$12	30	$6

But look more closely at the data given in Table 5.3. Can you see what is wrong with this conclusion? The quantities of both chicken salads and garden salads produced in the year 2012 are exactly twice the quantities produced in the year 2002. If economic activity, as measured by actual production of both goods, exactly doubled over the 10 years, why do the calculated values of GDP show a greater increase?

The answer, as you also can see from the table, is that prices as well as quantities rose between 2002 and 2012. Because of the increase in prices, the *market value* of production grew more over those 10 years than the *physical volume* of production. So in this case, GDP is a misleading gauge of economic growth during the 2002–2012 period, since the physical quantities of the goods and services produced in any given year, not the dollar values, are what determine people's economic well-being. Indeed, if the prices of chicken salads and garden salads had risen 2.4 times between 2002 and 2012, GDP would have risen 2.4 times as well, with no increase in physical production! In that case, the claim that the economy's (physical) output had more than doubled during the 10-year period would obviously be wrong.

As this example shows, if we want to use GDP to compare economic activity at different points in time, we need some method of excluding the effects of price changes. In other words, we need to adjust for inflation. To do so, economists use a common set of prices to value quantities produced in different years. The standard approach is to pick a particular year, called the *base year,* and use the prices from that year to calculate the market value of output. When GDP is calculated using the prices from a base year, rather than the current year's prices, it is called **real GDP**, to emphasize its concern with real physical production. Real GDP is also called constant-dollar GDP. It is GDP adjusted for inflation. To distinguish real GDP, in which quantities produced are valued at base-year prices, from GDP valued at current-year prices, economists refer to the latter measure as **nominal GDP**.

real GDP a measure of GDP in which the quantities produced are valued at the prices in a base year rather than at current prices

nominal GDP a measure of GDP in which the quantities produced are valued at current-year prices; measures the *current dollar value* of production

EXAMPLE **5.5**

Calculating the change in real GDP over the 2002–2012 period

Using data from Table 5.3, and assuming that 2002 is the base year, find real GDP for the years 2012 and 2002. By how much did real output grow between 2002 and 2012?

To find real GDP for the year 2012, we must value the quantities produced that year using the prices in the base year, 2002. Using the data in Table 5.3,

Year 2012 real GDP = (year 2012 quantity of chicken salads × year 2002 price of
 chicken salads) + (year 2012 quantity of garden salads ×
 year 2002 price of garden salads)
 = (20 × $10) + (30 × $5)
 = $350.

The real GDP of this economy in the year 2012 is $350. What is the real GDP for 2002?

By definition, the real GDP for 2002 equals 2002 quantities valued at base-year prices. The base year in this example happens to be 2002, so real GDP for 2002 equals 2002 quantities valued at 2002 prices, which is the same as nominal GDP for 2002. In general, in the base year, real GDP and nominal GDP are the same. We already found nominal GDP for 2002, $175, so that is also the real GDP for 2002.

We can now determine how much real production has actually grown over the 10-year period. Since real GDP was $175 in 2002 and $350 in 2012, the physical volume of production doubled between 2002 and 2012. This conclusion makes good sense, since Table 5.3 shows that the production of both chicken salads and garden salads exactly doubled over the period. By using real GDP, we have eliminated the effects of price changes and obtained a reasonable measure of the actual change in real production over the 10-year span.

Of course, the production of all goods will not necessarily grow in equal proportion, as in Example 5.5. Exercise 5.4 asks you to find real GDP when chicken salad and garden salad production grow at different rates.

EXERCISE 5.4

Suppose production and prices of chicken salads and garden salads in 2002 and 2012 are as follows:

	Quantity of chicken salads	Price of chicken salads	Quantity of garden salads	Price of garden salads
2002	10	$10	15	$5
2012	30	$12	30	$6

These data are the same as those in Table 5.3, except that chicken salad production has tripled rather than doubled between 2012 and 2002. Find real GDP in 2002 and 2012, and calculate the growth in real output over the 10-year period. (Continue to assume that 2002 is the base year.)

If you complete Exercise 5.4, you will find that the growth in real GDP between 2002 and 2012 reflects a sort of average of the growth in physical production of chicken salads and garden salads. Real GDP therefore remains a useful measure of overall production, even when the production of different goods and services grows at different rates.

The method of calculating real GDP just described was followed for many years by Statistics Canada. However, as of May 2001, Statistics Canada switched to more complicated method for determining real GDP called the *chain Fisher real GDP method*. The new method, which updates prices each quarter, makes the official real GDP data less sensitive to the particular base year chosen. But the results obtained by the two methods are generally similar.

The older method carried out not just for two goods as in our example but for all of GDP, involves the calculation of what Statistics Canada calls a fixed-weight GDP price index. The newer method involves the calculation of what is called an implicit chain price index. Each of these price indexes is what economists call a **GDP deflator**, a measure of

GDP deflator a measure of the price level of goods and services included in GDP the price level of goods and services included in GDP. The reason for the term *deflator* is that the price index is used to deflate nominal GDP in order to get real GDP, as the following formula shows:

$$\text{Real GDP} = \frac{\text{Nominal GDP}}{\text{GDP deflator}} \times 100$$

RECAP

NOMINAL GDP VERSUS REAL GDP

Nominal GDP is calculated using current-year prices. Real GDP, also called constant-dollar GDP, is GDP adjusted for inflation; it may be thought of as measuring the volume of production. Comparisons of economic activity at different times should always be done using real GDP, not nominal GDP.

5.5   REAL GDP IS INAPPROPRIATE AS THE SOLE ECONOMIC GOAL

Financial commentators in the news media frequently talk as if the maximum possible growth of GDP is the single appropriate goal for economic policy. Even some politicians talk this way.

Statisticians engaged in GDP accounting, however, emphasize that real GDP is not a magic number showing the level of society's well-being. Real GDP provides a measure of marketed output (and the market value of public services) that fits with the measure of employment in the *Labour Force Survey*. Such a measure is important for a number of reasons, one of which is that it provides data on something people care about—the goods and services they receive from market transactions or from the public sector. But people care about many other things as well. Because GDP is only intended to measure the market value of some things that people care about, most economists would argue that maximizing real GDP is not always the right goal for economic policy-makers.

The issue of the appropriate goals for economic policy-makers is by its very nature a normative or welfare economics one; that is, involving value judgments. Any two reasonable people with the same understanding of positive economics may differ about appropriate goals for economic policy-makers because the two of them have different values. Nevertheless, in Canada there is considerable agreement among economists on the normative or welfare economics of why maximizing growth of real GDP should not be the sole goal. To understand why, it is useful to consider two general issues: (1) shortcomings of using total GDP as a measure of the benefits people derive from the output of the economy, and (2) shortcomings of common proposals to increase GDP at the expense of other things that people value.

THE GDP TOTAL AND THE BENEFITS OF FINAL GOODS AND SERVICES

Real GDP has some shortcomings as an indicator of benefits that the average person or household derives from the output of the economy. These are not shortcomings of the way GDP is measured, but of the way some analysts interpret it.

A widely understood shortcoming of total real GDP is that the benefits people derive from economic output depend on what is available to them as individuals or households. Benefits are not primarily related to a total that would increase if the population increased while the amounts available per individual or household were held constant. This shortcoming is readily remedied by dividing GDP by the population to get GDP per capita (as we noted in Chapter 4).

A related shortcoming is that the benefits people derive from economic output depend upon the distribution of income among individuals, households, or other groups. For example, GDP per capita tells little about the benefits received by average households if a relatively small number of rich households control most of the GDP. Fortunately, data on the distribution of income among different groups is available from Statistics Canada publications such as *Income in Canada* (Catalogue no. 75-202-XWE).

A third shortcoming is that GDP is a measure of goods and services produced by the residents of a country. An associated concept, **gross national product (GNP)**, measures the market value of goods and services produced by factors of production owned by the residents of a country. For example, the output of a U.S.-owned auto plant is included in Canadian GDP. But while the wages paid to the autoworkers would be included in Canadian GNP, the profits of the plant would not be included. They would be included in U.S. GNP. GNP is more closely related than GDP to the benefits that people in a country receive from economic activity.

> **gross national product (GNP)** the market value of goods and services produced by factors of production owned by the residents of a country; equivalent in magnitude to gross national income (GNI)

Incidentally, partly due to the high degree of foreign ownership of corporations operating in Canada, Canadian GNP has been less than Canadian GDP. (Over the period 1992–2010, for example, Canadian GNP averaged about 97 percent of Canadian GDP and has been over 98 percent more recently.) That is, Canada had negative net foreign investment income: the value of profits, dividends, and interest flowing to foreign residents from Canadian production exceeded the value of the opposite flow. Statistics Canada now gives the GDP concept prominence over the GNP concept, but statistics on GNP are still collected and published. GNP relates to the expenditure side of the national accounts, and the corresponding term on the income side is Gross National Income or GNI. GNI is equal in magnitude to GNP.

Finally, "gross" concepts like GDP or GNP include the value of investment devoted to replacing capital goods that have worn out or become obsolete. While such investment is important, its growth is not necessarily related to the growth of the benefits that people derive from economic output. Thus, net measures, such as net domestic product and net national income, may be better indicators of economic performance than indicators like GDP or GNP. Net national income also has the merit of being free of the third shortcoming listed above.

QUESTIONABLE PROPOSALS FOR INCREASING GDP

Over the years, there have been various proposals to increase GDP wholly or partly at the expense of other things that people value. To be able to evaluate such proposals properly, it is useful to know that GDP is only intended to measure the market value of goods and services.

Non-working time

Most Canadian workers (and workers in other industrialized countries as well) spend many fewer hours at paid employment than did Canadian workers of 100 or more years ago. In those times, industrial workers frequently worked 12 hours a day. Today, a workweek of 40 hours or less is typical in Canada. Indeed, in some European countries a workweek of 35 hours or less has become the norm. The increased non-working time available to workers today as compared to decades ago is something most workers value highly. A proposal to increase the length of the standard workweek in Canada could raise Canadian GDP, but longer hours would not necessarily make the average Canadian employee better off.

Part of the reason employees would not be better off is that they would have less time for rest and relaxation. But during off-work hours, women and men engage in a variety of activities, not just those purely for leisure. They prepare home-cooked meals, engage in volunteer activities, and so on. Longer working hours mean less time for those activities as well.

Environmental quality and resource depletion

Environmental regulations sometimes reduce the level or growth rate of GDP. But clean air, rivers, and lakes, for example, are things most Canadians value highly. To make the case for relaxing regulations designed to maintain air or water quality, it is not enough to prove that their removal would lead to an increase in GDP. Proposals regarding environmental regulation and deregulation need to be assessed by comparing costs and benefits (see Chapter 1 on the *cost–benefit principle*). Placing a dollar value on intangibles, like having a clean lake to swim in, may be difficult. But the fact that the benefits are difficult to measure does not mean that they are unimportant.

COST-
BENEFIT

Proposals to relax environmental regulations regarding exploitation of non-renewable or finite natural resources raise a special issue. At any point in time, a country has non-renewable resources of given value. They are a stock, a form of wealth. Increasing the production and sale of the natural resource will increase GDP, a flow, but the value of the stock will tend to decline.

Quality of daily life and working life

What makes a particular town or city an attractive place in which to live? Many people value such things as minimal traffic congestion, lack of noise pollution, and a low crime rate. Thus, citizens of a suburban area may be justified in opposing the construction of a new shopping centre if it would have a negative effect on their quality of life—even though the new centre may increase GDP.

Similarly, what makes a particular establishment an attractive place to work? Most employees value such things as procedural fairness in job evaluation, task assignment, and dismissals. They value scheduled breaks that allow time for relaxation with co-workers and they appreciate restrictions on involuntary overtime. They appreciate not being worked to their physical limit or beyond. Employment laws and collective agreements have evolved to deal with workplace issues like these. Sometimes, proposals to weaken employment laws or restrict unions are based on the argument that they will increase GDP. Even if a particular proposal would increase GDP, employees would rightly be concerned about the possible impact on the quality of their working lives, and might reasonably oppose it.

5.6 BUT REAL GDP PER CAPITA IS RELATED TO LIVING STANDARDS

Most economists would agree, then, that looking at the effects of a proposed policy only on the growth of real GDP is not a sufficient normative basis on which to evaluate a policy. Sound policy evaluation requires considering additional measures. Nevertheless, real GDP per person *does* tend to be positively associated with many things people value, including more and better goods and services, better health and life expectancies, and better education. Next we discuss some of the ways in which a higher real GDP per capita is associated with a higher standard of living.

AVAILABILITY OF GOODS AND SERVICES

Obviously, citizens of a country with a high real GDP per capita are likely to possess more and better goods and services (after all, that is what GDP measures). On average, people in high per capita GDP countries enjoy larger, better-constructed, and more comfortable homes, higher-quality food and clothing, a greater variety of entertainment opportunities, better access to transportation, better communications and sanitation, and other advantages. While it is easy to take a high standard of material consumption for granted if you have it, the majority of people in the world attach great importance to achieving material prosperity.

HEALTH AND EDUCATION

Beyond an abundance of consumer goods and services, a high GDP per capita brings other more basic advantages. Table 5.4 shows the differences among countries at different levels of real GDP per capita with regard to some important indicators of living standards, including life expectancy, infant mortality rates, births attended by skilled health personnel, and educational opportunity. The columns provide data for (1) Canada; (2) countries belonging to the Organization for Economic Cooperation and Development (OECD), a group of mainly high-income countries; (3) all developing countries; and (4) the least developed countries. Most of the data come from 2007. As the first row of Table 5.4 shows, GDP per capita in Canada and other OECD countries is several times that of the average developing country and over 19 times that of the least developed countries.

How do these large differences in GDP per capita relate to other indicators of living standards? Table 5.4 shows that on the most basic measures of human welfare, the developing countries fare much worse than the OECD countries. A child born in one of the least developed countries has a 9.7 percent (97/1000) chance of dying before reaching the age of one, and a less than 50 percent probability of surviving to age 65. The corresponding figures for the OECD countries are 0.9 percent (9/1000) and about 84 percent, respectively. A child born in an OECD country has a life expectancy of about 78 years,

© Bettman/Corbis

A child born in one of the least developed countries has a 15 percent chance of dying before reaching the age of 5.

TABLE 5.4
GDP and Basic Indicators of Living Standards

Indicator	Canada	OECD countries	All developing countries	Least developed countries
GDP per person (U.S. dollars)	$35 812	$29 197	$5282	$1499
Life expectancy at birth (years)	79.8	77.8	65.5	52.7
Infant mortality rate (per 1000 births)	5	9	57	97
Probability at birth of surviving to age 65 (male)	84.9	80.5	62.6	44.3
Probability at birth of surviving to age 65 (female)	91	89.2	70.3	49.9
Births attended by skilled health personnel (percentage)	98	95	60	35
Secondary enrollment rate (as percentage of age group)	95.2	87	53	27
Female secondary age group enrollment (as percentage of male rate)	99	98	93	81

SOURCE: Statistics are from the United Nations *Human Development Report 2007/2008,* available at http://www.undp.org/. For indicators not reported in the *Human Development Report 2007/2008,* statistics from earlier issues of the *Human Development Report* were used. Since 2009, the Human Development Reports have not provided statistics for the "all developing countries" and "least developed countries" categories.

www.undp.org
Human Development Report

compared to about 53 years for a child born in one of the least developed countries. Superior nutrition, sanitation, and medical services in the richer countries account for these large discrepancies in basic welfare. For example, in OECD countries, 95 percent of births are attended by skilled health personnel compared with only 35 percent in the least developed countries.

On another important dimension of living standards, education rates, countries with high levels of GDP per capita also have the advantage. As Table 5.4 shows, the percentage of children of secondary-school age who are enrolled in school is about 87 percent in OECD countries, compared with about 27 percent in the least developed countries. Note also that in the high-income countries, female youth are almost as likely as male youth to be enrolled in secondary education, whereas in the least developed countries, female youth are only four-fifths as likely as males to be enrolled.

WHY NOT MAKE GDP PER CAPITA INTO A MEASURE OF WELL-BEING?

We have seen that while real GDP per capita is closely associated with many important indicators of living standards, it does not measure everything that people care about. And GDP-related measures are often used in ill-advised ways in public policy discussions, as noted, for example, in the widely discussed 2009 Report of the Commission on Economic Performance and Social Progress (the Sarkozy Report).[8] So why not replace GDP, which only measures and only purports to measure the market value of output, with a broad measure that attempts to measure well-being? Wouldn't this put an end to questionable proposals for increasing GDP at the expense of other things people care about?

Arguments against replacing GDP include the following:

- The GDP accounts have many uses—budget forecasting, testing macroeconomic theories, making international comparisons, and so on. Most day-to-day users of the GDP accounts would not want to see them replaced by something else.
- In particular, as we have emphasized, output in the GDP accounts is closely related to employment in the *Labour Force Survey*. If, for example, the measure of output is expanded to include an estimate of the value created in the time a retiree spends on recreational gardening, then two problems arise. Treating gardening as employment in the *Labour Force Survey* would render meaningless current distinctions between being "employed," "unemployed," and "not in the labour force" (categories discussed later in this chapter). On the other hand, excluding gardening time from the measure of employment while including the value of gardening in the output measure would create a problem for productivity measurement: there would be an output without any corresponding input measure.
- GDP is measured with a high degree of objectivity in accordance with United Nations guidelines. A measure of well-being would lack official international approval and would require a series of more subjective valuations of difficult-to-measure activities.
- GDP can co-exist with other measures the *Human Development Index* of the United Nations and the *Index of Economic Well-Being* (the Osberg-Sharpe index) of the Centre for the Study of Living Standards. Indeed, these other measures include real GDP per capita as an important component. They could not be calculated without the prior calculation of GDP.
- If questionable proposals for increasing GDP at the expense of other things that people care about come from special interests concerned with personal gain, it is unclear that replacing GDP with a broader measure would achieve anything beyond a change in the tactics employed by special interests.

8   The report is available online at http://www.stiglitz-sen-fitoussi.fr/documents/rapport_anglais.pdf.

BOX   5.1

The Index of Economic Well-Being

Canadian economists Lars Osberg and Andrew Sharpe have developed an index of economic well-being based upon four main components:

- effective per capita consumption flows—includes consumption of marketed goods and services, government services, household production, leisure and changes in life span, and subtracts "regrettable necessities" (e.g., activities, such as cleaning up after oil spills, which are measured in GDP but are not viewed by Osberg and Sharpe as adding to human satisfaction)
- societal accumulation of stocks of productive resources—includes, among other things, changes in the value of natural resource stocks and environmental costs
- income distribution—the intensity of poverty and the inequality of income
- economic security from job loss and unemployment, illness, family breakup, and poverty in old age

In one of many applications, the index of economic well-being was recently calculated for fourteen high-income countries—Australia, Belgium, Canada, Denmark, Finland, France, Germany, Italy, the Netherlands, Norway, Spain, Sweden, the United Kingdom, and the United States—over the period 1980–2007. In every country, the index increased over the period, but long-term growth in the index was less than growth in GDP per capita, although to different degrees in different countries.[9]

Note, however, that GDP per capita remains an important component in the index of economic well-being.

Furthermore, some events move *all* components of the index in the same direction, at the same time. In a typical recession, for example, consumption, accumulation, economic equality and economic security *all* fall.

RECAP

REAL GDP AND LIVING STANDARDS

Real GDP is an objective measure of the market value of goods and services. But economists generally agree that maximizing real GDP growth is not appropriate as the sole normative goal for economic policy. In the first place, maximizing real GDP growth per capita makes more sense than maximizing real GDP growth. Moreover, if a policy proposal promoted growth of real GDP per capita at the expense of other things that people care about, then the policy could be evaluated according to the cost–benefit principle.

Although maximizing real GDP growth may not be appropriate as the sole normative goal for economic policy, real per capita GDP is associated with many things that people value, including consumption of more and better goods and services, better health, longer life expectancy, and higher rates of educational attainment.

There are many arguments for not replacing GDP with a broad measure of economic well-being, one of which is that real GDP can be supplemented with other measures without being replaced by them.

---

9   See Lars Osberg and Andrew Sharpe, "New Estimates of the Index of Economic Well-being for Selected OECD Countries, 1980–2007," CSLS Research Report 2009–11, at http://www.csls.ca/reports/csls2009-11.pdf. The most recent data on the index can be found at http://www.csls.ca.

5.7 THE UNEMPLOYMENT RATE

In assessing the level of economic activity in a country, economists look at a variety of statistics. Besides GDP, economists intensely analyze labour force statistics. The measurement of GDP is closely linked to the measurement of the labour force through a common definition of production that links what is counted as output or income in GDP with what is counted as employment in the labour force statistics. Roughly speaking, you are only counted as employed in the labour force statistics if your labour activity produces output as measured by GDP. For example, if you earn your income by mowing grass for a lawn maintenance company you are counted as employed in the labour force statistics and the service you contribute is counted as output in GDP. If you mow your own lawn without pay, however, that is not sufficient for you to be counted as employed nor is the service you provide to yourself or your family counted as output in GDP.

The best-known labour force statistic is the unemployment rate. The unemployment rate is a sensitive indicator of conditions in the labour market. When the unemployment rate is low, jobs are secure and relatively easier to find. Low unemployment is often associated with improving wages and working conditions as well, as employers compete to attract and retain workers.

We will discuss unemployment further in Chapter 7. This section will explain key labour force statistics with particular emphasis on the unemployment rate.

MEASURING UNEMPLOYMENT

Each month, Statistics Canada conducts a *Labour Force Survey* of about 56 000 households.[10] Each person in a household who is 15 years of age or older is placed in one of three categories:

1. *Employed.* A person is considered employed during the survey week if he or she did any paid work (even for a few hours) in the context of an employee–employer relationship or self-employment or did unpaid work contributing directly to the operation of the family farm or business. A person is also considered employed if he or she had a job but was not at work during the survey week due to illness, personal or family responsibilities, vacation, or a labour dispute.

2. *Unemployed.* In general, a person is unemployed if he or she did not work during the preceding week but was available and made some effort to find work (for example, by going to a job interview) in the past four weeks. Persons on temporary layoff and persons with a job to start at a definite date in the future, however, can be counted as unemployed even if they did not actively search (the idea being that a person in either of those two categories is unemployed but is not looking for a job because he or she already has one lined up). Incidentally, the requirement of being available for work means that full-time students currently attending school and seeking full-time work to begin later are not counted as unemployed.

3. *Not in the labour force.* A person is considered to be not in the labour force if he or she did not work in the past week and did not look for work in the past four weeks. In other words, people who are neither employed nor unemployed (in the sense of looking for work but not being able to find it) are "not in the labour force." Full-time students, unpaid homemakers, retirees, and people unable to work because of illness are examples of people who are not in the labour force.

Based on the results of the survey, Statistics Canada estimates how many people in the whole country fit into each of the three categories.

To find the unemployment rate, Statistics Canada must first calculate the size of the *labour force*. The **labour force** is defined as the total number of employed and unemployed

labour force the total number of employed and unemployed people in the economy

10 As of December 2009, the *Labour Force Survey* has a sample of 56 372 households. See http://www.statcan.gc.ca.

people in the economy (the first two categories of respondents to the *Labour Force Survey*). The **unemployment rate** is then defined as the number of unemployed people divided by the labour force. Notice that people who are out of the labour force (because they are in school, have retired, or are seriously disabled, for example) are not counted as unemployed and thus do not affect the unemployment rate. In general, a high rate of unemployment indicates that the GDP growth rate has been low.

Because the *Labour Force Survey* is used to determine the total number of unemployed Canadian residents, the total is *not* a measure of how many Canadian residents are drawing Employment Insurance (EI) benefits. In fact, the number of unemployed workers in any given month is not even approximately equal to the number drawing EI benefits. For example, in August 2010, the number of Canadians receiving regular EI benefits was 671 200, about 44 percent of the 1 510 900 Canadians unemployed during that month. (There are many reasons for why unemployed workers will not receive EI benefits. Some may not apply for benefits even if they are eligible. Most unemployed workers who do not receive the benefits, however, are ineligible. To receive EI benefits, you have to have paid EI premiums and paid them for a specified period of time. Some of the unemployed, such as those seeking a job for the first time, are ineligible for EI benefits because they have not paid premiums ever; others, such as those who have worked in a seasonal job of short duration, are ineligible because have not paid premiums for the specified period of time.)

Another useful particularly important labour force statistic is the **participation rate**, sometimes called the labour force participation rate, which is the percentage of the working-age population in the labour force (that is, the percentage that is either employed or looking for work). The participation rate for women is calculated by dividing the number of women in the labour force by the number of women of working age (aged 15 and over). Similarly, the male participation rate is the male labour force divided by the male working-age population. As Figure 5.3 shows, the gender gap in participation rates has narrowed dramatically since 1976.

A final labour force statistic of note is the **employment rate**. This is a measure of the employed relative to the working-age population. The employment rate is regularly mentioned in Statistics Canada publications on changes in the labour force.

unemployment rate the number of unemployed people divided by the labour force

participation rate the percentage of the working-age population in the labour force

employment rate the percentage of the working-age population that is employed

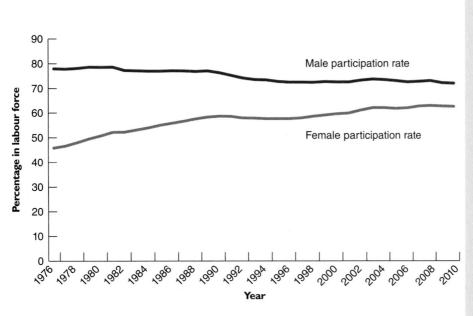

FIGURE 5.3
Male and Female Labour Force Participation Rates, 1976–2010
The participation rate for Canadian women increased sharply from 45.7 percent in 1976 to 58.4 percent in 1990, when the economy fell into a recession. When GDP growth resumed, the female participation rate rose from 57.8 percent in 1997 to a peak of 62.8 percent in 2008. The male participation rate declined gradually from 78.4 percent in 1981 to 71.7 percent in 2009. Both male and female participation rates fell from 2008 to 2010.
SOURCE: Adapted from the Statistics Canada CANSIM database, http://cansim2.statcan.gc.ca, Table 282-0002 series v2461665 and v2461455. Extraction date May 10, 2011.

TABLE 5.5
Canadian Labour Force Data, April 2011 (in thousands)

Employed	17 286.4
Plus:	
Unemployed	1 424.1
Equals: Labour force	18 710.5
Plus:	
Not in the labour force	9204.3
Equals:	
Working-age (15+) population	27 914.8

Unemployment rate = unemployed/labour force = 1 424.1/18 710.5 = 7.6 %; Labour force participation rate = 18 710.5/27 914.8= 67.0%; Employment rate = 17 286.4/ 27 914.8 = 61.9 %

SOURCE: Adapted from Statistics Canada, Labour Force Survey May 2011, Table 1, http:// www.statcan.gc.ca/daily-quotidien/110506/t110506a1-eng.htm.

Table 5.5 illustrates the calculation of key labour force statistics, using data from the *Labour Force Survey* for April 2011. In that month, 7.6 percent of the labour force was unemployed. The participation rate was 67 percent; that is, about two out of every three Canadian residents 15 years of age or older had a paid job or were looking for work. The employment rate, the percentage of the working-age population who were employed, was 61.9 percent.

Figure 5.4 shows the Canadian unemployment rate since 1960. It shows, among other things, that the unemployment rate tends to increase sharply when GDP undergoes a sharp slowdown.

THE COSTS OF UNEMPLOYMENT

Unemployment imposes *economic*, *psychological*, and *social* costs on a country. From an *economic* perspective, the main cost of unemployment is the output that is lost because the workforce is not fully utilized. Much of the burden of the reduced output is borne by

FIGURE 5.4

Canada's Unemployment Rate and Pronounced GDP Slowdowns Since 1960

Canada's unemployment rate—the fraction of the Canadian labour force that is unemployed—is shown by the red line. The vertical lines indicate starting points of periods when the GDP growth rate slowed sharply. A sharp decline in the GDP growth rate produces a sharp rise in the unemployment rate.

SOURCE: Adapted from Statistics Canada, CANSIM series v2062815, and from series D127 of Historical Statistics of Canada.

the unemployed themselves, whose incomes fall when they are not working and whose skills may deteriorate from lack of use. However, society at large also bears part of the economic cost of unemployment. For example, workers who become unemployed are liable to stop paying income taxes and start receiving government support payments, such as employment insurance benefits. This net drain on the government's budget is a cost to all taxpayers.

The *psychological* costs of unemployment are felt primarily by unemployed workers and their families. These psychological costs appear to be most significant during recessions when a substantial number of the unemployed are seeking work for lengthy periods (months and months as opposed to a few weeks). Studies show that lengthy periods of unemployment can lead to a loss of self-esteem, feelings of loss of control over one's life, depression, and even suicidal behaviour.[11] The unemployed worker's family is likely to feel increased psychological stress, compounded by the economic difficulties created by the loss of income.

The *social* costs of unemployment are a result of the economic and psychological effects. People who have been unemployed for a while tend not only to face severe financial difficulties but also to feel anger, frustration, and despair. Not surprisingly, increases in unemployment tend to be associated with increases in crime, domestic violence, alcoholism, drug abuse, and other social problems. The costs created by these problems are borne not only by the unemployed but by society in general, as more public resources must be spent to counteract these problems.

SUPPLEMENTARY MEASURES OF UNEMPLOYMENT

Canada's official unemployment rate is measured with a high level of sophistication in accordance with guidelines established by the International Labour Organization. But the official rate has been criticized, primarily for ignoring *discouraged workers* and *involuntary part-time workers*.

Discouraged workers are people who say they would like to have a job but have not made an effort to find one in the past four weeks because they believe no jobs are available to them. Because they have not engaged in a job search in the past four weeks, they are counted in the *Labour Force Survey* as being not in the labour force.

Involuntary part-time workers are people who say they would like to work full-time but are only able to find part-time work. Because they have jobs, they are counted as employed rather than unemployed.

Statistics Canada has responded to criticisms of the official unemployment rate by publishing several supplementary unemployment rate measures. Figure 5.5 shows Canada's official unemployment rate together with two of the supplementary unemployment rate measures. It also shows the official U.S. unemployment rate.

Notice that the unemployment rate that adjusts the official unemployment rate for the underutilization of labour associated with involuntary part-time workers (represented by the green line) is higher than the official Canadian rate (red line). The percentage point gap between this supplementary measure and the official unemployment rate tends to be higher when the official rate itself is high. But movements in this expanded measure are similar to movements in the official rate.

Statistics Canada also adjusts the official rate to judge what Canada's unemployment rate would be if it were calculated according to U.S. labour force definitions (blue line). Like the other supplementary measures shown in Figure 5.5, it tends to move with the official Canadian rate. The Canadian rate adjusted to U.S. labour force definitions is

discouraged workers people who say they would like to have a job but have not made an effort to find one in the past four weeks

11 For a survey of the literature on the psychological effects of unemployment, see William Darity, Jr., and Arthur H. Goldsmith, "Social Psychology, Unemployment and Macroeconomics," *Journal of Economic Perspectives*, #10, Winter 1996, pp. 121–140. See also Rafael Di Tella, Robert J. MacCulloch, Andrew J. Oswald, "The Macroeconomics of Happiness," *Review of Economics and Statistics*, 2003, vol. 85(4), pp. 809–827.

FIGURE 5.5
Official Canadian U.S. and Supplementary Canadian Unemployment Rates, 1997–2010
Canada's official unemployment rate (red line) is shown together with two supplementary unemployment rate measures (green and blue lines). The supplementary rates tend to move in tune with the official Canadian rate. The official U.S. unemployment rate (purple line) is included for comparison.
SOURCE: Adapted from Statistics Canada, CANSIM series v2170200, v2170201 and v217020, and. U.S. Bureau of Labor Statistics.

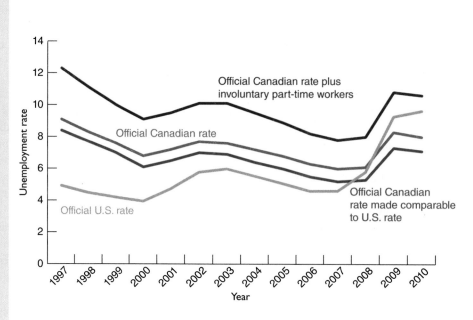

an appropriate one for Canada–U.S. unemployment rate comparisons. It was 4.1 percentage points higher than the official U.S. unemployment rate (purple line) in 1997, when Canadian unemployment still reflected the "Great Slump" of 1990–96 (the severe Canadian recession of 1990–92 followed by a sluggish recovery of Canadian GDP growth). By December 2006, however, the gap between this supplementary rate and the official U.S. rate had been reduced to 0.6 percentage points.

While the various supplementary unemployment rate measures have their uses, the official unemployment rate is the best single indicator of Canadian labour-market conditions. A high official unemployment rate tends to be bad news even for those people who are employed, since raises and promotions are harder to come by in a "slack" labour market. We will discuss the causes and cures of unemployment at some length later.

SUMMARY

- The basic indicator of an economy's output is *gross domestic product (GDP)*. It can be measured as the market value of the final goods and services produced in a country during a given period. Expressing output in terms of market values allows economists to aggregate the millions of goods and services produced in a modern economy. **LO1**

- Only *final goods and services* (which include *capital goods*) are counted in GDP, since they are the only goods and services that directly benefit final users. *Intermediate goods and services,* which are used up in the production of final goods and services, are not counted in GDP, nor are sales of existing assets, such as a 20-year-old house. Summing the value added by each firm in the production process is one of three methods of determining the value of final goods and services. **LO1**

- GDP can also be expressed as the sum of four types of expenditure: *consumption, private-sector investment, government purchases,* and *net exports.* These four types of expenditure correspond to the spending of households, firms, the government, and the foreign sector, respectively. **LO2**

■ A third method of expressing GDP is in terms of income earned from domestic production. Income-based GDP can be broadly divided into labour income and capital income. **LO1**

■ To compare levels of GDP over time, economists must eliminate the effects of inflation. They do so by measuring the market value of goods and services in terms of the prices in a base year. GDP measured in this way is called *real GDP*, while GDP measured in terms of current-year prices is called *nominal GDP*. Real GDP should always be used in making comparisons of economic activity over time. **LO3**

■ Real GDP per person is not intended to be a measure of economic well-being. With a few exceptions, notably government purchases of goods and services (which are included in GDP at their cost of production), GDP includes only those goods and services sold in markets. It does not take into account such matters as time available to people, the value of unpaid or volunteer services, the quality of the environment, quality of life indicators such as the crime rate, or the degree of economic inequality. **LO4**

■ Real GDP per capita is associated with living standards, however. Countries with a high real GDP per person not only enjoy high-quality consumption of goods and services, they also tend to have higher life expectancies, low rates of infant and child mortality, and high rates of school enrollment and literacy. **LO4**

■ The unemployment rate, perhaps the best-known indicator of the state of the labour market, is based on the *Labour Force Survey*. The survey classifies all respondents aged 15 and over as employed, unemployed, or not in the labour force. The *labour force* is the sum of employed and unemployed workers—roughly speaking, people who have a job or are looking for one. The *unemployment rate* is calculated as the number of unemployed workers divided by the labour force. The *participation rate* is calculated as the labour force divided by the working-age population. The employment rate is calculated as the employed divided by the working-age population. **LO5**

■ The costs of unemployment include the economic cost of lost output, the psychological costs borne by unemployed workers and their families, and the social costs associated with problems like increased crime and violence. Critics of the official unemployment rate argue that it understates "true" unemployment by excluding *discouraged workers* and *involuntary part-time workers*. **LO6**

KEY TERMS

consumption (103)
discouraged workers (121)
employment rate (119)
final goods or services (100)
GDP deflator (111)
government purchases (105)

gross domestic product (GDP) (98)
gross national product (GNP) (113)
intermediate goods or services (100)
labour force (118)
net exports (105)
net investment (105)

nominal GDP (110)
participation rate (119)
private-sector investment (103)
real GDP (110)
unemployment rate (119)
value added (100)

REVIEW QUESTIONS

1. Why do economists use market values when calculating GDP? What is the economic rationale for giving high-value items more weight in GDP than low-value items? **LO1**

2. Give examples of each of the four types of aggregate expenditure. Which of the four represents the largest share of GDP in Canada? Can an expenditure component be negative? Explain. **LO2**

3. Does the G in C + I + G + NX represent government spending (total government expenditures) or government purchases? How do government purchases and government spending differ? Does G include government investment? **LO2**

4. Does the I in C+I+ G + NX include purchases of stocks and bonds? Why or why not? **LO2**

5. Does the inventory investment component of I in C+I+G+NX measure inventory or does it measure change in inventory? Explain. **LO2**

6. Al's Shoeshine Stand shined 1000 pairs of shoes last year and 1200 pairs this year. Al charged $4 for a shine last year and $5 this year. If last year is taken as the base year, find Al's contribution to both nominal GDP and real GDP in both years. Which measure would be better to use if you were trying to measure the change in Al's productivity over the past year? Why? **LO3**

7. Why is maximization of real GDP inappropriate as a sole goal for economic policy? **LO4**

8. True or false, and explain: A high participation rate in an economy implies a low unemployment rate. **LO5**

9. How is the measurement of output in GDP accounting related to the measurement of employment in the *Labour Force Survey*? **LO1, LO4, LO5**

PROBLEMS

1. How would each of the following transactions affect the GDP of Canada? **LO1**
   a. The Canadian government pays $1 billion in salaries for government workers.
   b. The Canadian government pays $1 billion to Employment Insurance beneficiaries.
   c. The Canadian government pays a Canadian firm $1 billion for constructing an airport.
   d. The Canadian government pays $1 billion in interest to holders of Canadian government bonds.
   e. The Canadian government pays $1 billion to a U.S. firm for military aircraft.

2. Intelligence Incorporated produces 100 computer chips and sells them for $200 each to Bell Computers. Using the chips and other labour and materials, Bell produces 100 personal computers. Bell sells the computers, bundled with software that Bell licenses from Macrosoft at $50 per computer, to PC Charlie's for $800 each. PC Charlie's sells the computers to the public for $1000 each. Calculate the total contribution to GDP using the value-added method. Do you get the same answer by summing up the market values of final goods and services? **LO1**

3. For each of the following transactions, state the effect both on Canadian GDP and on the four components of aggregate expenditure. **LO2**
   a. Your mother-in-law buys a new car produced in Canada.
   b. Your mother-in-law buys a new car imported from Sweden.
   c. Your mother-in-law's car rental business buys a new car produced in Canada.
   d. Your mother-in-law's car rental business buys a new car imported from Sweden.

4. Here are some data for an economy. Find its GDP. Explain your calculation. **LO2**

Consumption expenditures	$600
Exports	75
Government purchases of goods and services	200
Construction of new homes and apartments	100
Sales of existing homes and apartments	200
Imports	50
Beginning-of-year inventory stocks	100
End-of-year inventory stocks	125
Business fixed investment	100
Government payments to retirees	100
Household purchases of durable goods	150

5. The nation of Potchatoonie produces hockey pucks, cases of root beer, and back rubs. Here are data on prices and quantities of the three goods in the years 2007 and 2012. **LO3**

   Assume that 2007 is the base year. Find nominal GDP and real GDP for both years.

	Pucks		Root beer		Back rubs	
Year	Quantity	Price	Quantity	Price	Quantity	Price
2007	100	$5	300	$20	100	$20
2012	125	$7	250	$20	110	$25

6. The standard assumption is that the GDP deflator will rise over time and be used to reduce (or deflate) nominal GDP to real GDP of a lower dollar amount. But the implicit chain price index form of the GDP deflator dropped from 100 in the first quarter of 1997 to 99.1 by the fourth quarter of 1998. Nominal GDP increased from $870 billion in the first quarter of 1997 to approximately $928.3 billion in the fourth quarter of 1998. Use the GDP "deflator" to calculate real GDP for the fourth quarter of 1998. **LO3**

7. The government is considering a policy to reduce air pollution by restricting the use of "dirty" fuels by factories. In deciding whether to implement the policy, how, if at all, should the likely effects of the policy on real GDP be taken into account? Discuss. **LO4**

8. Here is a hypothetical report from a not-very-efficient survey taker: "There were 65 people in the houses I visited, 10 of them children under 15 and 10 retired; 25 people had full-time jobs, and 5 had part-time jobs. There were 5 full-time homemakers, 5 full-time students aged 15 and over, and 2 people who were ill and cannot work. The remaining people did not have jobs but all said they would like one. One of these people had not looked actively for work for 3 months, however."

Find the labour force, the unemployment rate, and the participation rate implied by the survey taker's report. **LO5**

9. Ellen is downloading labour market data for the most recent month, but her connection is slow and so far this is all she has been able to get:

Unemployment rate	5.0%
Participation rate	62.5%
Not in the labour force	60 million

Find the labour force, the working-age population, the number of employed workers, and the number of unemployed workers for this high-population country. **LO5**

ANSWERS TO IN-CHAPTER EXERCISES

5.1   In the text, GDP was calculated to be $64 million. If in addition Orchardia produces 5 million peaches at $0.30 each, GDP is increased by $1.5 million to $65.5 million. **LO1**

5.2   The sale of stock represents a transfer of ownership of part of the assets, not the production of new goods or services. Hence, the stock sale itself does not contribute to GDP. However, the broker's commission of $100 (2 percent of the stock sale proceeds) represents payment for a current service and is counted in GDP. **LO1**

5.3   As in Example 5.4, the market value of domestic production is 1 000 000 autos multiplied by $15 000 per auto, or $15 billion.

Also as in Example 5.4, consumption is $10.5 billion and government purchases are $0.75 billion. However, because 25 000 of the autos that are purchased are imported rather than domestic, the domestic producers have unsold inventories at the end of the year of 50 000 (rather than 25 000 as in Example 5.4). Thus inventory investment is 50 000 autos times $15 000, or $0.75 billion, and total investment (autos purchased by businesses plus inventory investment) is $3.75 billion. Since exports and imports are equal (both are 25 000 autos), net exports (equal to exports minus imports) are zero. Notice that since we subtract imports to get net exports, it is unnecessary also to subtract imports from consumption. Consumption is defined as total purchases by households, not just purchases of domestically produced goods.

Total expenditure is $C + I + G + NX$ = $10.5 billion + $3.75 billion + $0.75 billion + 0 = $15 billion, the same as the market value of production. **LO2**

5.4   Real GDP in the year 2012 equals the quantities of chicken salads and garden salads produced in the year 2012, valued at the market prices that prevailed in the base year 2002. So real GDP in 2012 = (30 chicken salads × \$10/chicken salad) + (30 garden salads × \$5/garden salad) = \$450.

Real GDP in 2002 equals the quantities of chicken salads and garden salads produced in 2002, valued at 2002 prices, which is \$175. Notice that since 2002 is the base year, real GDP and nominal GDP are the same for that year.

The real GDP in the year 2012 is \$450/\$175, or about 2.6 times what it was in 2002. Hence the expansion of real GDP lies between the threefold increase in chicken salad production and the doubling in garden salad production that occurred between 2002 and 2012. **LO3**

CHAPTER 6
Measuring the Price Level and Inflation

Your grandparents probably remember being able to buy comic books and chocolate sundaes for 25 cents. Today, the same two items might cost $4 or $5. You might conclude from this fact that kids were much better off in "the good old days." But were they really? Without more information we can't tell, because although the prices of comic books and sundaes have gone up, so have allowances. The real question is whether young people's amounts of spending money have increased as much as or more than the prices of the things they want to buy. If so, then they are no worse off today than their grandparents were as youngsters in the days when chocolate bars cost a nickel. In general, our purchasing power increases and we are better off if our income goes up at a faster rate than the overall price level does—that is, if the growth rate of our income exceeds the inflation rate.

An important benefit of studying macroeconomics is learning about the implications of inflation in order to compare changes in economic conditions over time. In this chapter, a continuation of our study of the construction and interpretation of economic data, we will see how inflation is measured and how dollar amounts, such as the price of a comic book or the hourly wage we receive, can be "adjusted" to eliminate the effects of inflation. Quantities that are measured in dollars, or other currency units, and then adjusted for inflation are called real quantities (recall, for example, the concept of real GDP in the last chapter). By working with real quantities, economists can compare real incomes, real wages, or real interest rates.

More important than the implications that inflation has for economic measurement is the impact that it has on the economy. Inflation has consequences for economic growth and income distribution, and the nature of these consequences depends on its level, its rate of change, and whether or not it is anticipated.

6.1 THE CONSUMER PRICE INDEX: MEASURING THE PRICE LEVEL

The **price level** is the overall level of prices at a point in time as measured by a price index. The basic tool economists use to measure the price level in the Canadian economy

price level the overall level of prices at a point in time as measured by a price index such as the CPI

consumer price index (CPI)
for any period, measures the cost in that period of a standard basket of goods and services relative to the cost of the same basket of goods and services in a fixed year, called the base year

is the **consumer price index**, or CPI for short. The CPI for any period measures the cost in that period of a standard set, or basket, of goods and services *relative* to the cost of the same basket of goods and services in a fixed year, called the *base year*.

To illustrate how the CPI is constructed, suppose Statistics Canada has designated 2002 as the base year. (In fact, currently 2002 is the base year but it will change in the future.) Assume for the sake of simplicity that in 2002 a typical Canadian family's monthly household budget consisted of spending on just three items: rent on a two-bedroom apartment, hamburgers, and movie tickets. In reality, of course, families purchase hundreds of different items each month, but the basic principles of constructing the CPI are the same no matter how many items are included. Suppose, too, that the family's average monthly expenditures in 2002, the base year, were as shown in Table 6.1.

TABLE 6.1
Monthly Household Budget of the Typical Family in 2002 (base year)

Item	Cost
Rent, two-bedroom apartment	$500
Hamburgers (60 at $2 each)	120
Movie tickets (10 at $6 each)	60
Total Expenditure	$680

Now let's fast-forward to the year 2012. Over that period, the prices of various goods and services are likely to have changed; some will have risen and some fallen. Let's suppose that by the year 2012 the rent that our family pays for the two-bedroom apartment has risen to $630. Hamburgers now cost $2.50 each, and the price of movie tickets has risen to $7 each. So, in general, prices have been rising.

TABLE 6.2
Cost of Reproducing the 2002 (base year) Basket of Goods and Services in Year 2012

Item	Cost (in 2012)	Cost (in 2002)
Rent, two-bedroom apartment	$630	$500
Hamburgers (60 at $2.50 each)	150	120
Movie tickets (10 at $7 each)	70	60
Total Expenditure	$850	$680

By how much did the family's cost of living increase between 2002 and 2012? Table 6.2 shows that if the typical family wanted to consume the *same basket of goods and services* in the year 2012 as in the year 2002, it would have to spend $850 per month, or $170 more than the $680 per month spent in 2002. In other words, to live the same way in the year 2012 as in the year 2002, the family would have to spend 25 percent more ($170/$680) each month. So, in this example, the cost of living for the typical family rose 25 percent between 2002 and 2012.

Statistics Canada calculates the official consumer price index (CPI) using essentially the same method. The first step in deriving the CPI is to pick a base year and determine the basket of goods and services that were consumed by the typical family during that year. Statistics Canada determines the basket using information obtained from family expenditure surveys. Let's call the basket of goods and services that results the *base-year basket*. Then, each month interviewers operating out of the regional offices of Statistics Canada gather tens of thousands of price quotations on over 600 goods and services. The CPI in any given year is computed using this formula:

www.statcan.gc.ca
Statistics Canada
Consumer Price Index

$$\text{CPI} = \frac{\text{Cost of base-year basket of goods and services in current year}}{\text{Cost of base-year basket of goods and services in base year}} \times 100$$

Returning to the example of the typical family that consumes three goods, we can calculate the CPI in the year 2012 as

$$\text{CPI in year 2012} = \frac{\$850}{\$680} \times 100 = 125.$$

In other words, in this example the cost of living in the year 2012 is 25 percent higher than it was in 2002, the base year. Notice that the base-year CPI is always equal to 100. The CPI for a given period (such as a month or year) measures the cost of living in that period *relative* to what it was in the base year.

EXAMPLE 6.1

Measuring the typical family's cost of living

Suppose that in addition to the three goods and services the typical family consumed in 2002, they also bought four sweaters at $30 each. In the year 2012 the same sweaters cost $50 each. The prices of the other goods and services in 2002 and 2012 were the same as in Table 6.2. Find the change in the family's cost of living between 2002 and 2012.

In the example in the text, the cost of the base-year (2002) basket was $680. Adding four sweaters at $30 each raises the cost of the base-year basket to $800. What does this same basket (including the four sweaters) cost in 2012? The cost of the apartment, the hamburgers, and the movie tickets is $850, as before. Adding the cost of the four sweaters at $50 each raises the total cost of the basket to $1050. The CPI equals the cost of the basket in 2012 divided by the cost of the basket in 2002 (the base year) multiplied by 100, or ($1050/$800) × 100 = 131. We conclude that the family's cost of living rose 31 percent between 2002 and 2012.

Returning to the three-good example in Tables 6.1 and 6.2, find the year 2012 CPI if the rent on the apartment falls from $500 in 2002 to $400 in 2012. The prices for hamburgers and movie tickets in the two years remain the same as in the two tables.

EXERCISE 6.1

The CPI is not itself the price of a specific good or service; it is a *price index*. A **price index** measures the average price of a class of goods or services relative to the price of those same goods or services in a base year. The CPI is an especially well-known price index, one of many that economists use to assess economic trends, but there are several other price indices constructed for the Canadian economy. As we will see in Chapter 10, there is a version of the CPI called the core CPI that is used in monetary policy for assessing the state of the economy. And, for example, because manufacturers tend to pass on increases in the prices of raw materials to their customers, economists use Statistics Canada's *Raw Materials Price Index* (which includes goods not produced in Canada) to forecast changes in the prices of Canadian manufactured goods. Other price indexes supplied by Statistics Canada include the *Industrial Product Price Index* (which measures the prices that producers in Canada receive as their goods leave their production facilities) and the price indexes of the national accounts.[1] One of the price indexes of the national accounts, the *GDP deflator* we mentioned in Chapter 5, is particularly important because it measures the price level of all the goods and services making up GDP.

price index a measure of the average price of a given class of goods or services relative to the price of the same goods and services in a base year

The CPI captures the change in prices affecting average households. Suppose you were to construct a price index to measure changes in the prices facing Canadian university students over the past decade. In general, how would you go about constructing such an index? Why might changes in a price index for university student expenditures differ from changes in the CPI?

EXERCISE 6.2

---

1 Further information on the Raw Materials Price Index and the Industrial Product Price Index can be found at www.statcan.gc.ca/imdb-bmdi/2306-eng.htm and www.statcan.gc.ca/imdb-bmdi/2318-eng.htm respectively.

6.2 INFLATION

rate of inflation the annual percentage rate of change in the price level as measured, for example, by the CPI

The CPI provides a measure of the average *level* of prices relative to prices in the base year. *Inflation*, in contrast, is a measure of how fast the average price level is *changing* over time. The **rate of inflation** is defined as the annual percentage rate of change in the price level, typically as measured by the CPI. For example, the Canadian CPI had a value of 114.7 in August 2009 and a value of 116.7 in August 2010. The inflation rate between August 2009 and August 2010 is the percentage increase in the price level, or 100 times the increase in the price level (116.7 − 114.7 = 2.0) divided by the initial price level (114.7), which is equal to 1.7 percent.

EXAMPLE 6.2

Calculating inflation rates: 1972–1976

The CPIs for the years 1972 through 1976 are shown below. Find the rates of inflation between 1972 and 1973, 1973 and 1974, 1974 and 1975, and 1975 and 1976.

Year	CPI
1972	21.9
1973	23.6
1974	26.2
1975	29.0
1976	31.1

The inflation rate between 1972 and 1973 is the percentage increase in the price level between those years, or

$$\frac{(23.6 - 21.9)}{21.9} = \frac{1.7}{21.9} = 0.0776 = 7.8 \text{ percent.}$$

Do the calculations to confirm that inflation during each of the next three years was 11, 10.7, and 7.2 percent, respectively. During the 1970s, inflation rates were much higher than the 1 to 3 percent annual inflation rates that have prevailed in recent years.

EXERCISE 6.3

Below are CPIs for the years 1929 through 1933. Find the rates of inflation between 1929 and 1930, 1930 and 1931, 1931 and 1932, and 1932 and 1933.

Year	CPI
1929	9.2
1930	9.1
1931	8.2
1932	7.5
1933	7.1

How did inflation rates in the 1930s differ from those of the 1970s?

deflation a situation in which the prices of most goods and services are falling over time so that inflation is negative

The results of the calculations for Exercise 6.3 include some examples of *negative* inflation rates. A situation in which the prices of most goods and services are falling over time so that inflation is negative is called **deflation**. The early 1930s was the last time Canada experienced significant deflation. Japan experienced relatively mild deflation beginning in the late 1990s. In 2008 Japan achieved a decade-high inflation rate of

1.4 percent, which at first appeared to signal the country's long-hoped-for escape from persistent deflation, but with the global recession of 2009 Japan returned to mild deflation, measured as being −1.4 percent inflation.

6.3   ADJUSTING FOR INFLATION

The CPI is an extremely useful tool. Not only does it allow us to measure changes in the *cost of living* (in terms of changes in the price of a fixed basket of goods and services), it can also be used to adjust economic data to eliminate the effects of inflation. In this section, we will see how the CPI can be used to convert quantities measured at current dollar values into real terms, a process called *deflating*. We will also see that the CPI can be used to convert real quantities into current-dollar terms, a procedure called *indexing*. Both procedures are useful not only to economists but to anyone who needs to adjust payments, accounting measures, or other economic quantities for the effects of inflation.

DEFLATING A NOMINAL QUANTITY WITH THE CPI

An important use of the CPI is to adjust **nominal quantities**—quantities measured at their current dollar values—for the effects of inflation. To illustrate, consider a Canadian family with a total income of $50 000 in 2002 and $55 000 in the year 2010. Did the family experience an increase in purchasing power over the eight-year period?

nominal quantity a quantity that is measured in terms of its current dollar value

Without any more information than this, we might be tempted to say yes. After all, the family's income has risen by 10 percent over the period. But prices might also have been rising, as fast or faster than the family's income. In fact, the CPI for Canada rose from 100 in 2002 to 116.5 for 2010. This means that prices rose by 16.5 percent. Since the family's income rose by only 10 percent, the family's purchasing power has declined.

We can make a more precise comparison of the family's purchasing power in 2002 and 2010 by calculating its income in those years in *real terms*. In general, a **real quantity** is one that is measured in base-year dollars, also known as *constant dollars*. To convert a nominal quantity to a real quantity, we must divide the nominal quantity by a price index for the period, as shown in Table 6.3. The calculations in the table show that in *real* or purchasing power terms, the family's income actually *decreased* by $2790, or by about 5 percent of the initial real income of $50 000, between 2002 and 2010.

real quantity a quantity that is measured in constant dollar terms

The problem for this family is that though its income has been rising in nominal (dollar) terms, it has not kept up with inflation. Dividing a nominal quantity by a price index to express the quantity in real terms is called **deflating** the nominal quantity. (Be careful not to confuse the idea of deflating a nominal quantity with deflation, or negative inflation. The two concepts are different.)

deflating (a nominal quantity) the process of dividing a nominal quantity by a price index (such as the CPI) to express the quantity in real terms

Dividing a nominal quantity by the current value of a price index to measure it in real or purchasing power terms is a very useful tool. It can be used to eliminate the effects of inflation from comparisons of any nominal quantity—workers' wages, healthcare expenditures, components of federal or provincial budgets—over time. Why does this method work? In general, if you know both how many dollars you have spent on a given item and the item's price, you can figure out how many of the items you bought (by dividing your expenditures by the price). For example, if you spent $100 on hamburgers last month

TABLE 6.3
Comparing the Real Values of a Family's Income in 2002 and 2010

Year	Nominal family income	CPI	Real family income = Nominal family income/CPI
2002	$50 000	100	$50 000
2010	$55 000	116.5	$47 210

and hamburgers cost $4 each, you can determine that you purchased 25 hamburgers. Similarly, if you divide a family's dollar income or expenditures by a price index, which is a measure of the average price of its purchased goods and services, you will obtain a measure of the real quantity of purchased goods and services. Such real quantities are sometimes referred to as *inflation-adjusted* quantities.

Clearly, in comparing wages or earnings at two different points in time, we must adjust for changes in the price level. Doing so yields the **real wage**—the wage measured in terms of real purchasing power. The real wage for any given period is calculated by dividing the nominal (dollar) wage by the CPI for that period.

real wage the wage paid to workers measured in terms of real purchasing power

EXAMPLE 6.3

Real wages of Canadian hourly paid employees

Hourly paid employees (as distinguished from salaried employees) constituted about half of all Canadian employees in 2010. Statistics Canada reports that the average hourly paid employee earned $16.67 per hour in 2002 and $20.50 per hour in 2010. Determine what happened to the real wages of these employees between these two years.

To find the real wage in 2002 and 2010, we need to know that the CPI was 100 in 2002, the base year, and 116.5 in 2010. In the base year of 2002 the nominal wage equalled $16.67 and, by definition, the real wage was also $16.67. Deflating the 2010 nominal wage of $20.50 by the 2010 CPI, we find that the real wage in 2010 was only $17.60. In real or purchasing power terms, we find that the real hourly wage of paid employees rose by only 5.6 percent between 2002 and 2010 even though the nominal or dollar wage increased by about 23 percent.

Figure 6.1 shows nominal wages and real wages for Canadian hourly paid employees for the period 1983–2010. Notice the dramatic difference between the two trends.

FIGURE 6.1
Nominal and Real Wages of Hourly Paid Employees in Canada, 1983–2010
Although nominal wages of hourly paid employees have risen in Canada over the past two decades, real wages have stagnated. Notice that the real wage and the nominal wage are equal in 2002, the base year.
SOURCE: Adapted from the Statistics Canada, CANSIM series v1809109, v256149 and v41693271.

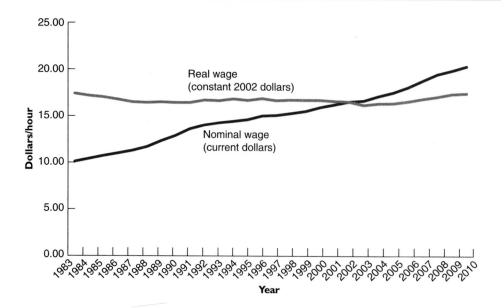

Looking only at nominal wages, one might conclude that hourly paid employees were much better paid in 2010 than in 1983. But once wages are adjusted for inflation, we see that in terms of buying power the wages of hourly paid employees have stagnated at least since 1983. This example illustrates the crucial importance of adjusting for inflation when comparing dollar values over time.

If you worked at job paying the general minimum wage in Ontario in September 2009 you received \$9.50 per hour and if you received the minimum wage in September 2010 you received \$10.25 per hour. The Ontario CPI (with a base year of 2002) was 113.8 in September 2009 and 117.1 in September 2010. What was the percentage increase in your wage in nominal terms? What was the percentage increase in your wage in real terms?

EXERCISE 6.4

DEFLATING BY THE CPI VERSUS DEFLATING BY THE GDP DEFLATOR

The CPI is commonly used to deflate nominal wages and incomes. But the CPI is not the only general price index. In particular, the GDP deflator (discussed in Chapter 5) is a price index for all the goods and services making up GDP, and it can be used to do more than just deflate GDP. For example, while the nominal wage deflated by CPI gives a good measure of the real wage from the standpoint of workers, some economists think that the nominal wage divided by the GDP deflator provides a better measure of the real wage from the standpoint of employers.

Why would it make any difference whether one uses the CPI or the GDP deflator? First, the two can differ because the CPI includes import prices, whereas import prices are excluded from the GDP deflator (since imports are subtracted from exports in calculating GDP). Second, the CPI includes only the prices of consumer goods and services, while the GDP deflator also includes the prices of producer and intermediate goods. The third major difference is that the CPI compares the price of a fixed basket of goods and services today with the price of the same basket in the base year, whereas the composition of the goods and services used to compute the GDP deflator changes regularly.

INDEXING TO MAINTAIN BUYING POWER

The consumer price index can also be used to convert real quantities to nominal quantities. Suppose, for example, that in the year 2002 a married couple with children are divorced, and they reach a settlement by themselves whereby the husband agrees to pay the wife spousal support of \$1000 per month (in addition to child support payments) for eight years. Suppose, too, that their agreement specifies that the spousal support payments should increase to prevent inflation from eroding their purchasing power.[2]

The nominal or dollar amount the husband should pay the wife in the year 2010 to maintain the purchasing power of the spousal support payments depends on how much prices rose between 2002 and 2010. The CPI rose from 100 in 2002 to 116.5 in 2010, or by about 16.5 percent. For the spousal support payments to "keep up with inflation," they would be \$1165 per month in 2010. In general, to keep purchasing power constant, the dollar benefit must be increased each year by the percentage increase in the CPI.

The practice of increasing a nominal quantity according to changes in a price index is called **indexing**. As we will see later in this chapter, indexing is used to some degree in Canada, particularly by the public sector.

indexing the practice of increasing a nominal quantity each period by an amount equal to the percentage increase in a specified price index; prevents the purchasing power of the nominal quantity from being eroded by inflation

---

2 If the couple do not reach their own agreement but require a judge to decide, then the child support payments will be decided by federal or provincial/territorial child support guidelines and will be based upon nominal incomes rather than directly upon the CPI. For details, see Government of Canada, Department of Justice, "About Child Support," http://www.justice.gc.ca/eng/pi/fcy-fea/sup-pen/index.html.

RECAP↑

METHODS TO ADJUST FOR INFLATION

Deflating To correct a nominal quantity, such as a family's dollar income, for changes in the price level, divide it by a price index such as the CPI. This process, called *deflating* the nominal quantity, expresses the nominal quantity in terms of real purchasing power. If nominal quantities from two different years are deflated by a price index with the same base year, the purchasing power of the two deflated quantities can be compared.

    Indexing To ensure that a nominal payment, such as a social insurance benefit, represents a constant level of real purchasing power, increase the nominal quantity each year by a percentage equal to the rate of inflation for that year.

6.4 NOMINAL VERSUS REAL INTEREST RATES

We have seen how to adjust nominal family income for inflation to get real family income and how to adjust nominal wages or salaries to get real wages or salaries. Our next task is to explain how to adjust nominal interest rates to get real interest rates. We will also introduce the hypothesis, known as the Fisher effect, that high inflation rates will tend to produce high nominal interest rates.

    The **nominal interest rate** is the type of interest rate you are apt to see reported in the financial pages of a newspaper or posted on a sign in your bank branch. It can be thought of as the price paid per dollar borrowed per year. If you borrow $1000 now and in a year's time you repay the principal of $1000 plus interest of $100, then your nominal interest rate is 10 percent (the interest payment divided by the principal, all multiplied by 100 for expression as a percentage). Looked at from the standpoint of a lender, the nominal interest rate is the annual percentage increase in the nominal, or current dollar, value of an asset. The **real interest rate**, like the real wage rate, is something we calculate given the inflation rate and the relevant nominal rate.

    More precisely, we can calculate the real interest rate for any financial asset, from a savings account to a government bond, by subtracting the rate of inflation from the market or nominal interest rate on that asset.[3] So if the nominal interest rate on short-term government bonds equals 6 percent and the inflation rate equals 3 percent, then the real interest rate on short-term government bonds is 3 percent. Or if the nominal interest rate on outstanding credit card debt (an asset from the perspective of the lender) is 17 percent and the inflation rate equals 3 percent, then the real rate of interest for credit-card borrowing is 14 percent.

    We can write this definition of the real interest rate in mathematical terms:

$$r = i - \pi,$$

    where r = the real interest rate,
          i = the nominal, or market, interest rate,
         π = the inflation rate.

nominal interest rate the type of interest rate you usually encounter in everyday life—the price paid per dollar borrowed per year

real interest rate the nominal interest rate minus the inflation rate

EXAMPLE **6.4**

Real interest rates in recent decades

Following are interest rates on short-term Canadian federal government bonds for selected years since 1970. Ignoring the impact of taxation, in which of these years did the financial investors who bought government bonds get the best deal? The worst deal?

---

3 An alternative way of calculating the real interest rate takes into account not just the change in the purchasing power of the loan, but also the change in the purchasing power of the interest payments.

Year	Nominal interest rate (%)	Inflation rate (%)	Real interest rate (%)
1970	6.0	3.4	2.6
1975	7.4	10.9	−3.5
1980	12.7	10.1	2.6
1981	17.8	12.4	5.4
1987	8.2	4.4	3.8
1990	12.8	4.8	8.0
1995	7.0	2.2	4.8
2000	5.5	2.7	2.8
2003	2.9	2.8	0.1
2007	4.1	2.2	1.9
2010	0.6	2.0	−1.4

Financial investors and lenders do best when the real (not the nominal) interest rate is high, since the real interest rate measures the increase in their purchasing power. We can calculate the real interest rate for each year by subtracting the inflation rate from the nominal interest rate. The results, as shown in the column above headed "Real interest rate (%)," are 2.6 percent for 1970, −3.5 percent for 1975, 2.6 percent for 1980, 5.4 percent for 1981, 3.8 percent for 1987, 8.0 percent for 1990, 4.8 percent for 1995, 2.8 percent for 2000, 0.1 percent for 2003, 1.9 percent for 2007, and −1.4 percent for 2010.

For purchasers of government bonds, then, the best of these years was 1990, when they enjoyed a real return of 8.0 percent, a higher real return than associated with the whopping 17.8 percent nominal interest rate of 1981. The worst years were 1975 and 2010, when their real return was actually negative. Despite receiving 7.4 percent nominal interest in 1975, financial investors ended up losing buying power in 1975, as the inflation rate exceeded the interest rate on their financial investments. In 2010, the inflation rate was low, but the nominal interest rate was even lower.

Figure 6.2 shows the real interest rate in Canada since 1962, as measured by the nominal interest rate paid on the federal government's short-term bonds minus the

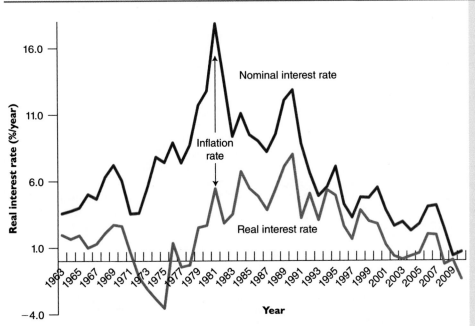

FIGURE 6.2
Real and Nominal Interest Rates in Canada, 1962–2010
The real interest rate (shown by the red line) is the nominal interest rate (blue line) minus the rate of CPI inflation. Real interest rates rose sharply during the 1980s, especially at the end of the decade. They declined after the early 1990s, but until the slowdown of 2001, they still tended to be somewhat higher than during the 1960s.

SOURCE: Adapted from Statistics Canada, CANSIM series v122531 and v41693271.

inflation rate. Note that real interest rates were negative for several years in the 1970s but were high during the 1980s and reached a peak in 1990. They declined after the early 1990s, but until 2001 they still tended to be somewhat higher than during the 1960s.

ANTICIPATED INFLATION AND THE FISHER EFFECT

Economists generally assume that people are forward-looking. People take actions not just in response to past events but in the expectation of future events. To give a simple illustration, Canadian shopping malls regularly enjoy an upsurge in business during November and December due to Christmas shopping. The action of shopping during November and December comes before the event of Christmas on December 25.

People also take actions based upon expectations about uncertain economic outcomes, such as investors buying a company's shares in the hope the shares will go up in value. If expectations turn out to be correct, economists say that the outcome was *anticipated*. If the expectations prove wrong, outcomes are *unanticipated*.

anticipated inflation when the rate of inflation turns out to be roughly what most people had expected

unanticipated inflation when the rate of inflation turns out to be substantially different from what most people had expected

So if the inflation rate for a given period fits with general expectations people had for it in the previous period, economists say that there has been **anticipated inflation**. If the inflation rate proves to be considerably higher or lower than generally expected, there has been **unanticipated inflation**.[4]

With the concepts of anticipated and unanticipated inflation, we can explain why nominal interest rates tend to be high when inflation rates are high and low when inflation rates are low.

ECONOMIC NATURALIST 6.1

Good and bad months to take out a mortgage

Why was December 2010 probably a good month to take out a five-year mortgage to buy a house? A key consideration for whether a particular month is a good one to take out a mortgage is whether the real interest rate over the period of the mortgage turns out to be low by historical standards.[5] The average interest rate for five-year mortgages signed in Canada that month was 5.2 percent, the lowest on record. The CPI had risen 2.4 percent in the 12 months prior to December 2010, not much different from the 2 percent average inflation rate Canada has experienced since the early 1990s. If the nominal interest rate is 5.2 percent and inflation turns out to be 2.4 percent, then the real interest rate is 2.8 (5.2 − 2.4) percent. A real interest rate of 2.8 percent is low by historical standards. Even if the inflation rate were to average 2 percent over the period from December 2010 to December 2015, then real interest rate realized would be 3.2 (5.2 − 2) percent, which is still low by historical standards. It seems, then, that December 2010 will probably

turn out to have been a good month to take out a five-year mortgage.

Now, to take the other extreme, why was September 1981 an incredibly bad month to take out a five-year mortgage? The answer might seem obvious from the average interest rate for five-year mortgages signed in Canada that month—an astounding 21.5 percent. That's about four times as high as the average five-year mortgage rate during December 2010, for example.

But the 21.5 percent rate is a nominal one, and nominal rates tend to be high when inflation rates are high. In late August 1981, Statistics Canada had announced that inflation between July 1980 and July 1981 had been 12.9 percent. So a borrower taking out a mortgage in September 1981 would typically be doing so with the idea that inflation was running at an annual rate of about 12.9 percent. Subtracting 12.9 percent inflation from a 21.5 percent nominal rate yields a real interest rate of 8.6 percent.

---

4 Some economists use these terms differently. They define anticipated inflation as that part of any actual inflation rate that people anticipated and they define unanticipated inflation as the difference between the actual inflation rate that occurs and the inflation rate people had anticipated.

5 Our example ignores complications, such as what will happen to house prices.

It is true that a real interest rate of 8.6 percent on a five-year mortgage is no bargain by historical standards. The average rate over the 1981–2010 period was about 6.1 percent. But real mortgage interest rates have been higher; for example, they hovered around 10 percent for most of 1994.

So why was September 1981 such a bad month to take out a five-year mortgage? Inflation rates dropped to about 4 percent within two years and stayed at about 4 percent through to September 1986. Those who borrowed at 21.5 percent interest knew that their nominal mortgage payments would be high, but they

expected that their nominal incomes would be growing in line with inflation of about 12.9 percent. Instead, inflation rates declined and so did nominal income growth rates. While a 21.5 percent nominal rate corresponded to an 8.6 percent real interest rate in September 1981, for over half of the mortgage period (when inflation averaged 4 percent) it corresponded to a crippling 17.5 percent real rate.

In short, September 1981 was an incredibly bad month to take out a mortgage because borrowers failed to anticipate the sharp *disinflation* (fall in the inflation rate) that followed.

Suppose inflation has recently been high, so borrowers and lenders anticipate that it will be high in the near future. We would expect lenders to raise their nominal interest rate so that their real rate of return will be unaffected. For their part, borrowers are willing to pay higher nominal interest rates when inflation is high, because they understand that the higher nominal interest rate only serves to compensate the lender for the loan being repaid in dollars of reduced real value—in real terms, their cost of borrowing is unaffected by an equal increase in the nominal interest rate and the inflation rate. Conversely, when inflation is low, lenders do not need to charge as high a nominal interest rate to ensure a given real return. Thus, nominal interest rates will be high when anticipated inflation is high and low when anticipated inflation is low. This tendency for nominal interest rates to follow inflation rates is called the **Fisher effect**, after the early twentieth-century American economist Irving Fisher who first pointed out the relationship.

Some evidence for the Fisher effect is shown in Figure 6.3. Nominal interest rates were much lower in the low-inflation 1960s than in the high-inflation 1973–1982 period. Nominal interest rates were also lower in the low-inflation years of 1992–2009 than they were in the moderate-inflation years of 1983–1991. But the relationship between nominal interest rates and the inflation rate is not exact.

One factor contributing to the inexactness of the relationship is that Figure 6.3 shows actual inflation rates not the inflation rates that borrowers and lenders expected. If we

Fisher effect the tendency for nominal interest rates to be high when inflation is high and low when inflation is low

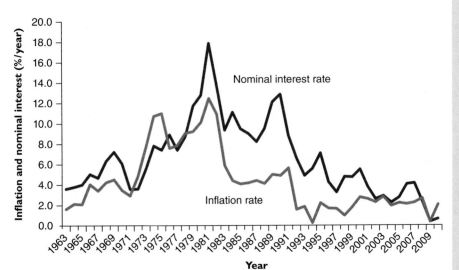

FIGURE 6.3
Inflation and Nominal Interest Rates in Canada, 1962–2010
The tendency for nominal interest rates to be high when the inflation rate is high and low when inflation is low is called the Fisher effect. Some evidence for the Fisher effect is shown in the figure. For example, nominal interest rates were considerably lower in the low-inflation 1960s and the 1996–2010 period than in the high-inflation, 1973–82 period.
SOURCE: Adapted from the Statistics Canada, CANSIM series v122531 and v41693271.

defined the real interest rate as being the nominal interest rate minus the expected rate of inflation, then the Fisher effect would be even more strongly apparent in the data.[6]

6.5 TYPES OF PRICE CHANGES

Economists have developed precise terminology for describing different types of price changes. This terminology is essential for understanding analysis of the consequences of inflation.

THE PRICE LEVEL, RELATIVE PRICES, AND INFLATION

Economists distinguish carefully between the *price level* and the *relative price* of a good or service. The price level is a measure of the overall level of prices at a particular point in time as measured by a price index such as the CPI. Recall that the inflation rate is the percentage change in the price level from year to year. In contrast, a **relative price** is the price of a specific good or service *in comparison to* the prices of other goods and services. In Chapter 3 when we looked at price determination in specific markets using supply and demand diagrams, we were dealing with relative price determination. The diagrams were drawn under the assumption that all else was equal, including the general price level.

How do we measure a relative price change when the price level also changes? For example, if the price of gasoline were to rise by 10 percent while the prices of other goods and services were rising on average by 3 percent, the relative price of gasoline would increase. But if gasoline prices rose by 3 percent while other prices rose by 10 percent, the relative price of gasoline would decrease. That is, gasoline would become cheaper relative to other goods and services, even though it would not become cheaper in absolute terms.

Why is the distinction between relative price changes and changes in the price level important? To illustrate, suppose that the price of gas at the pump increases by 20 percent because of a new tax to reduce carbon emissions from gasoline consumption, but the overall price level is unaffected. Some people might demand that the government do something about this "inflation." But while the increase in gas prices hits the wallets of gasoline consumers, is it an example of inflation? In this example, the overall price level is unaffected so inflation is not an issue. What upsets some gasoline consumers is the change in the relative price of gasoline, particularly compared to the price of labour (wages). By increasing the cost of using gasoline, the increase in the relative price of gasoline makes driving a car more expensive.

In general, changes in relative prices are not the same as a rise in the overall price level. Increases in the prices of some goods could well be counterbalanced by decreases in the prices of other goods, in which case the price level and the inflation rate would be largely unaffected. Conversely, in theory inflation can exist without changes in relative prices. Imagine, for example, that all prices in the economy, including wages and salaries, go up exactly 3 percent each year. The inflation rate is 3 percent, but relative prices are not changing. Indeed, because wages (the price of labour) and other sources of income are increasing by 3 percent per year, people's ability to buy goods and services is unaffected by the inflation.

One reason to distinguish between increases in the average price level (inflation) and increases in the relative prices of specific goods is that the appropriate responses to the two issues may be quite different. To counteract high inflation in an economy that is expanding too rapidly, it may be appropriate (as we will see) for the government to make changes in macroeconomic policies, such as monetary or fiscal policies. But it would not be appropriate for the government to make changes in its macroeconomic policies in response to an increase in gasoline prices caused by the imposition of a carbon tax.

relative price the price of a specific good or service *in comparison* to the prices of other goods and services

---

6 In more advanced discussions of real interest rates, economists distinguish between real interest rates *ex ante* (before the fact; that is, based upon expected inflation) and real interest rates *ex post* (after the fact; that is, based upon realized inflation).

EXAMPLE **6.5**

How to calculate changes in relative prices

Suppose the value of the CPI is 120 in the year 2015, 132 in 2016, and 140 in 2017. Assume also that the price of oil increases 8 percent between 2015 and 2016 and another 8 percent between 2016 and 2017. What is happening to the price level, the inflation rate, and the relative price of oil?

The price level can be measured by the CPI. Since the CPI is higher in 2016 than in 2015 and higher still in 2017 than in 2016, the price level is rising throughout the period. The inflation rate is the percentage increase in the CPI. Since the CPI increases by 10 percent between 2015 and 2016, the inflation rate between those years is 10 percent. However, the CPI increases only about 6 percent between 2016 and 2017 (140 ÷ 132 = 1.06), so the inflation rate decreases to about 6 percent between those years. The decline in the inflation rate implies that although the price level is still rising, it is doing so at a slower pace than the year before.

The price of oil rises 8 percent between 2015 and 2016. But because the general inflation over that period is 10 percent, the relative price of oil—that is, its price relative to all other goods and services—falls by about 2 percent (8 percent − 10 percent = −2 percent). Between 2016 and 2017 the price of oil rises by another 8 percent, while the general inflation rate is about 6 percent. Hence the relative price of oil rises between 2016 and 2017 by about 2 percent (8 percent − 6 percent).

TERMINOLOGY USED TO DESCRIBE OVERALL PRICE CHANGE

The CPI measures the level of overall prices and the inflation rate is typically calculated by the percentage change in the CPI. But the price level and the inflation rate are not the only terms economists use to describe overall price change in the economy. In debates about monetary policy, for example, additional specialized terms are employed.

Figure 6.4 uses hypothetical data to show how change in the CPI is related to the CPI inflation rate and to several specialized terms for describing overall price changes. The blue line shows the value of the CPI in periods from 0 to 12. You can think of the periods as corresponding to calendar years. The red line shows the inflation rate. For any period, it is calculated as

$$100 \times \frac{(\text{CPI current period} - \text{CPI previous period})}{\text{CPI previous period}}.$$

The beige boxes show the specialized terminology used to describe overall price changes in the periods associated with the boxes.

In periods 0 and 1, the CPI is 100. Because the CPI undergoes no change between periods 0 and 1, we calculate an inflation rate of 0 percent for period 1. Economists use the term **zero inflation** to describe a situation like this when the CPI does not change from one period to the next. (Note that we have arbitrarily assumed a value of 0 for the inflation rate in period 0.) In Canadian history, zero inflation prevailed during the period 1926–1930 when the CPI held quite stable at a level of about 9.1 (2002 base year) and the inflation rate fluctuated around 0 (see Figure 4.4 for data on the Canadian inflation rate for the period 1915–2010).

The CPI rises to 104 and 108.2 in periods 2 and 3 respectively. The inflation rate is the same 4 percent in each period. When the CPI rises at a constant rate, we have **stable inflation** or, more precisely, stable positive inflation. Even if the CPI rises by a roughly constant rate (say, 4 percent followed by 5 percent followed by 4 percent), economists tend to say there is stable inflation. For example, the period from 1992 to 2010 when the annual inflation rate averaged less than 2 percent was one of stable inflation.

From period 3 to period 6, the CPI rises from 108.2 all the way to 136.2. Each period-to-period increase is proportionately larger than the one before it. The inflation rate goes

zero inflation when the price level stays roughly constant from one year to the next

stable inflation when the inflation rate stays roughly constant from one year to the next

FIGURE 6.4
The Terminology of Price Change Illustrated
The CPI is shown by the blue line. The CPI inflation rate, shown by the red line, is the percentage change in the CPI.
Zero inflation: the CPI stays the same from one period to the next
Stable inflation: the CPI rises but at a constant rate
Accelerating inflation: the CPI rises at a rate that increases from one period to the next
Disinflation: the CPI rises but at a rate that decreases from one period to the next
Deflation: the CPI falls from one period to the next.

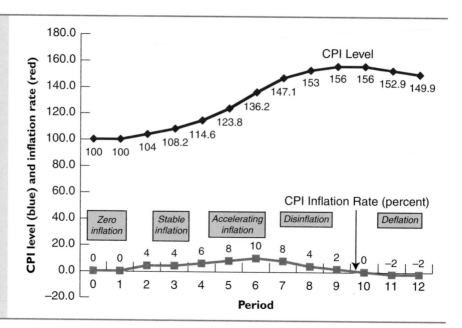

up from 4 percent to 6 percent to 8 percent to 10 percent. When the CPI rises at a rate that increases from one period to the next—in other words, when the inflation rate is rising—we have **accelerating inflation**. Canada experienced accelerating inflation during the period 1971–1975 (when the inflation rate rose from about 3 percent to about 11 percent) and again during the period 1976–1981. Accelerating inflation is often unanticipated.

accelerating inflation when the inflation rate rises from one year to the next

From periods 6 to 10 the CPI increases from 136.2 to 156. But it increases at a decreasing rate. The inflation rate falls from 10 percent all the way to 0 percent. When the inflation rate is falling, but the price level does not drop, we have **disinflation**. Canada experienced disinflation during the recessions of the early 1980s and the early 1990s, and again during the 2008–2009 recession. Between 1981 and 1984, for example, the inflation rate dropped from over 12 percent to just over 4 percent. Like accelerating inflation, disinflation is often unanticipated.

disinflation when the inflation rate falls from one year to the next

Finally, from period 10 to period 12 the CPI drops from 156 to 149.9. The inflation rate turns negative, as it did in Canada during the Great Depression of the 1930s. When the CPI falls from one period to the next, we have negative inflation or *deflation*. In periods 11 and 12 the deflation rate is −2 percent.

EXERCISE 6.5

Flip back to Figure 4.4. Practise using the terms zero inflation, stable inflation, accelerating inflation, disinflation, and deflation to describe how the inflation rate behaved in different periods of Canadian economic history.

Describing the intensity of inflation

It is useful to have terms not just to describe the rate of change of inflation, but also to describe its intensity. If you read research published by the Bank of Canada, for example, you will encounter terms such as those shown in italics in the following sentence: "In the case of Canada, there is evidence that uncertainty about long-run inflation fell considerably between the *high-inflation* period of the 1970s and early 1980s and the subsequent *moderate-inflation* period, and decreased still further in the *low-inflation* period that has been evident since the early 1990s."[7]

Canadian economists have generally described annual inflation in the 1 to 3 percent range that Canada has experienced since 1992 as **low inflation**. Inflation in the range of

low inflation typically means inflation between 1 and 3 percent per year

7   Gerald Stuber, "Implications of Uncertainty about Long-Run Inflation and the Price Level," Working Paper 2001, 16 October 2001. www.bankofcanada.ca/wp-content/uploads/2010/02/wp01-16.pdf.

roughly 3 to 6 percent, as Canada experienced between 1983 and 1991, is often described as **moderate inflation**. Canada's inflation in the 1974–1982 period, when the inflation rate continually exceeded 6 percent, has been described as **high inflation**.

Hyperinflation is used to describe very, very high inflation. While there is no official threshold above which high inflation becomes hyperinflation, inflation rates exceeding 500 percent per year would surely qualify. Several European countries experienced episodes of hyperinflation in the wake of the First and Second World Wars. In the past few decades, episodes of hyperinflation have occurred in several Latin American countries (including Argentina, Bolivia, Brazil, and Peru), in Israel, and in some "transition" economies, including Russia and Yugoslavia (Serbia and Montenegro). More recently, Zimbabwe experienced hyperinflation in the late 2000s.

moderate inflation typically means inflation between 3 and 6 percent per year

high inflation typically means inflation greater than 6 percent per year

hyperinflation typically means inflation greater than 500 percent per year

EXERCISE 6.6

The Bank of Canada has an inflation rate target of 2 percent. Recently Olivier Blanchard, the chief economist of the International Monetary Fund, has argued that some economies would experience better economic performance with an inflation rate target of 4 percent.[8] What term would be used to describe the intensity of inflation associated the Bank of Canada's inflation rate target? What term would be used to describe the intensity of inflation favoured by Olivier Blanchard?

6.6   THE ECONOMIC CONSEQUENCES OF VARIOUS TYPES OF INFLATION

Previous sections of this chapter have dealt with the distinction between inflation and relative price changes. We have also introduced several terms (zero inflation, stable inflation, accelerating inflation, disinflation and deflation) for describing what is happening to the inflation rate. We have explained that both increases in the inflation rate (accelerating inflation) and decreases in the inflation rate (disinflation) are often unanticipated. And we have mentioned some adjectives economists use to describe the intensity of inflation (low, moderate, high, and hyper). We are now in a position to consider the economic *consequences* of various types of inflation. The *sources* of inflation rate change are analyzed in Chapter 12.

As you can now imagine, it is difficult to speak exactly about the consequences of anything so general as "inflation." The consequences of anticipated inflation differ from those of unanticipated inflation. Low inflation may have different consequences than moderate inflation. The consequences of disinflation must be distinguished from those of deflation. Hyperinflation constitutes a category all of its own. For these reasons, we will discuss specific consequences of various types of inflation. Take note that some consequences relate to income distribution, while others relate to economic growth.

UNANTICIPATED INFLATION AND INCOME DISTRIBUTION

One of the most widely accepted statements about inflation is that unanticipated changes in the inflation rate can have consequences for the distribution of income.

Consider a group of unionized workers who have signed a contract setting their wages for the next three years in nominal terms. The inflation rate has been 4 percent in recent years. Expecting inflation to continue along at 4 percent, the employer and representatives of the workers negotiate wages accordingly, providing nominal wage increases of 6 percent per year, and real wage increases of 2 percent per year, for each year of the contract.

8 See Olivier Blanchard, Giovanni Dell'Ariccia, and Paolo Mauro, "Rethinking Macroeconomic Policy," *IMF Staff Position Note*, February 2010. http://www.imf.org/external/pubs/ft/spn/2010/spn1003.pdf.

But then suppose that, to everyone's surprise, there is disinflation and the inflation rate falls to 1 percent for the duration of the contract. The nominal wage increases of 6 percent per year will continue but the inflation-adjusted or real wages of the workers will be higher than before. In the first year, for example, real wages will increase by 5 percent instead of 2 percent. They will be 3 percentage points higher than anyone expected when the contract was negotiated. All else being equal, income will shift from the employer to the employees. Workers will benefit at the expense of the employer provided, of course, the employer does not resort to layoffs or get driven out of business.

The opposite type of situation would occur if, instead of unexpectedly shifting from 4 percent down to 1 percent, the inflation rate unexpectedly rose, say to 6 percent, for the rest of the contract. Then the workers, who had been expecting real wages to increase by 2 percent per year, would instead be getting no real wage increases at all. With nominal wage increases just equal to the inflation rate, their real wages would stagnate, and income would shift to the employer. Of course, depending on the availability of jobs, some workers might quit and seek higher real wages elsewhere.

It is to prevent unexpected changes in the rate of inflation from having an impact on real wages that union contracts are sometimes indexed to the CPI.[9] Indexing can help prevent unanticipated shifts in income between employers and employees as a consequence of unanticipated changes in the rate of inflation. So although unanticipated changes in inflation *can* have consequences for the distribution of income between employers and employees, such consequences are sometimes avoided by the indexing of wages.

Unanticipated changes in the inflation rate can also have consequences for the distribution of income between borrowers (debtors) and lenders (creditors). One illustration of this was provided by Economic Naturalist 6.1, which dealt with why September 1981 was a bad month to take out a mortgage. In general, unexpectedly high inflation rates help borrowers at the expense of lenders, because borrowers are able to repay their loans in less-valuable dollars. Unexpectedly low inflation rates, on the other hand, help lenders and hurt borrowers by forcing borrowers to repay in dollars that are worth more than expected when the loan was made.

Loan contracts, like union wage contracts, can in principle be indexed to the rate of inflation. In practice, full indexing of loans to the CPI is not common in Canada, though the practice is frequently observed in countries with high inflation rates. Even in Canada, however, variable-rate mortgage loans are widespread. To the extent that nominal mortgage interest rates reflect changes in the rate of inflation, variable rate mortgages provide a form of indexing.

ANTICIPATED INFLATION AND INCOME DISTRIBUTION

Economists tend to assume that if people anticipate changes in inflation they will design contracts to prevent inflation from eroding their incomes. As prices of goods and services go up, incomes go up as well, even without indexing. With anticipated inflation, employees and employers are expected to set wages with the inflation rate in mind, just as borrowers and lenders set interest rates in accordance with their expectations about inflation. But many noneconomists tend to be concerned that moderate or high inflation, even if anticipated, would lead to a substantial erosion of their living standards. Are such concerns justified?

Historically, senior citizens on public pensions have been concerned about inflation. Before the early 1970s, public pensions in Canada were not fully indexed to the rate of inflation. When inflation rates picked up in the early 1970s, however, the government of the late Pierre Elliott Trudeau did index public pensions, and they have remained indexed to the CPI ever since.

---

9   Paul Jenkins and Brian O'Reilly, "Monetary Policy and the Economic Well-Being of Canadians," *Review of Economic and Social Progress*, 2001, p. 101. The authors cite evidence that the proportion of Canadian wage settlements with indexing clauses dropped from over 23 percent during 1978–90 to under 11 percent during 1996–2000.

Historically, as well, the income tax system was not fully indexed for inflation, and this meant that inflation could erode the after-tax disposable incomes of taxpayers. Taxpayers would get bumped into tax brackets with higher marginal income tax rates and the value of credits or exemptions would be eroded. Around the time the Trudeau government indexed public pensions, however, it also indexed the federal income tax system. The Brian Mulroney government elected in the 1980s removed full indexing of the income tax system as part of a campaign to reduce federal government deficits. But then in 2000 the Jean Chrétien government, facing large federal budget surpluses, moved to restore the indexing first implemented in the Trudeau years.

In short, both public pensions and the basic features of the federal income tax system are now fully indexed for inflation. On the other hand, private company pensions are a significant source of income for some people, and they are seldom indexed to inflation, at least explicitly. Economists would point out that although anticipated inflation may in special cases result in the erosion of living standards, the income lost by one group is largely gained by another—it does not just go up in smoke. For example, if program spending in some area is eroded by inflation, then program spending in some other area can be increased or, for example, taxes can be cut.

Finally, it is simplistic to just blame inflation when government spending fails to match increases in inflation or when government taxation is higher in real terms when inflation is higher, just as it is simplistic to regard erosion of the minimum wage by inflation as something caused by inflation alone. When inflation is anticipated and governments fail to increase nominal program spending to offset the impact of inflation, then the decline in the real value of program spending is more the result of a government spending decision than it is the result of inflation. Similarly, when the Mulroney government removed full indexing of the tax system in the 1980s, it did so with an understanding that partial removal of indexing would increase government revenues. At most, inflation can help to cloak such decisions.

LOW INFLATION, MODERATE INFLATION, AND ECONOMIC GROWTH

Which is better for economic growth—low inflation or moderate inflation? The question evokes considerable controversy among economists. Here we will simply sketch some of the arguments.

On one side of the debate are economists, such as the ones with the Bank of Canada, who argue that low inflation, perhaps even zero inflation, is optimal for economic growth. A key argument of theirs is that inflation interferes with the information conveyed by price changes. In an economy with negligible inflation, the supplier of a product will recognize an increase in its price as a relative price increase signaling the profitability of bringing more of the product to market. Conversely, demanders will interpret the price increase as a relative price increase signaling that they should economize on their use of the product. But in the presence of inflation, not all price changes represent relative price changes. Participants in a market need to know not only the price of the product sold in the market but also what is happening to the prices of other goods and services. With inflation, then, the signals that are transmitted through the price system may become more difficult to interpret, much in the way that static, or "noise," makes a radio message harder to interpret. According to this **price signal distortion hypothesis**, even moderate inflation creates "noise" in the price system, and thereby impairs the functioning of the economy.

A second argument for little or no inflation is that inflation interferes with the long-term planning of households and firms. Suppose that you want to enjoy a certain standard of living when you retire. How much of your income do you need to save? That depends on what the goods and services you plan to buy will cost 30 or 40 years from now, assuming such goods and services would still be available then. Planning for retirement would be simplest if you knew that the future price level would be pretty much the same as the price level today.

A related argument is that when inflation is negligible and expected to stay negligible, people will tend to sign relatively long-term contracts involving interest rates, wages, and so on. They will avoid wasting time with frequent renegotiation of contracts and the economy will be more efficient as a consequence. By contrast, when inflation is higher and more volatile, people will generally judge long-term contracts as being too risky, and so will endure the time and trouble associated with short-term contracts.

On the other side of the debate are economists who favour moderate inflation over low or zero inflation.[10] Some of these economists argue that low or zero inflation can produce lower economic growth than moderate inflation because low inflation hampers flexibility of real wages. The argument is known as the **downward nominal wage rigidity hypothesis**, and is often attributed to the Nobel Prize-winning economist James Tobin. It states that adjustment generally requires that a decline in the demand for labour in a particular industry results in a reduction in real wages for workers in the industry. Labour demand and supply are discussed in detail in *Principles of Microeconomics*. If the inflation rate is a few percentage points or higher, then the appropriate real wage cuts can typically be achieved without nominal wage cuts. For example, if nominal wages go up by 1 percent, and inflation is 4 percent, then real wages will have fallen by 3 percent. If the inflation rate is zero, however, then a 3 percent cut in real wages requires a 3 percent cut in nominal wages. But workers tend to regard nominal wage cuts as unfair in most situations, so zero or low inflation tends to impair real wage flexibility and hence economic adjustment.

A second argument for moderate inflation is that in fighting past recessions central banks have sometimes had to cut their official interest rates, or key policy rates, by several percentage points. (Details about how central banks use their official interest rates are provided in later chapters.) If the official rate is already very low in line with low inflation (recall the Fisher effect), then macroeconomic policy will be deprived of a key policy lever. In the economics literature, this is known as the **zero bound on nominal interest rates hypothesis**, and it is often credited to Lawrence Summers, an academic economist who served as U.S. Treasury Secretary in the Clinton Administration. One illustration is provided by Japan, where the inflation rate was approximately zero and the official rate of the central bank was only half a percentage point when the economy slipped into recession in 1997. A nominal interest rate cannot be negative, so Japan's official interest rate could not be reduced by even half a percentage point to offset the slump.

In early 2008, as the U.S. financial crisis (associated with the collapse of the housing boom) intensified, concerns were raised by some economists about whether the U.S. central bank would be able to cut interest rates enough to cope with the crisis. And, in fact,

price signal distortion hypothesis the claim that any substantial amount of change in the price level will make it difficult for market participants to interpret the extent to which price changes involve relative price changes

downward nominal wage rigidity hypothesis the claim that low levels of inflation will reduce efficiency because real wage cuts will then typically require nominal wage cuts, which will be resisted

zero bound on nominal interest rates hypothesis the claim that because interest rates cannot go below zero, a central bank may be unable to stimulate the economy with rate cuts if the official interest rate is low to begin with

10 Critics of zero or low inflation dominate. See, for example, contributions to Brian K. MacLean and Lars Osberg, eds., *The Unemployment Crisis* (Montreal: McGill-Queen's, 1996), as well as Lars Osberg and Pierre Fortin, eds., *Hard Money, Hard Times* (Toronto: Lorimer, 1998). Similar arguments were made in 2010 by IMF Chief Economist Olivier Blanchard, as noted in Exercise 6.6.

the central banks of the United States, Canada, and a number of other countries did lower their interest rates to zero as the financial crisis precipitated a global recession, but zero interest rates were not enough to offset the recessionary forces. In these countries, interest rate cuts had to be supplemented by fiscal policy or, in some cases, fiscal policy combined with unconventional monetary policy. (The terms fiscal policy and unconventional monetary policy were introduced in Chapter 4).

DISINFLATION AND ECONOMIC GROWTH

Economists generally agree that the process of getting from high or moderate inflation to low inflation can be very costly in terms of economic growth. In principle, a transition to a lower rate of inflation could be brought about in various ways, such as through an *incomes policy* (a government-initiated attempt to curb inflation by controlling the growth of labour and capital income).[11] But in recent times, disinflation has typically been the product of central bank policy. A central bank tries to produce disinflation by raising its official interest rate. In later chapters we will explain the process by which an increase in the official interest rate can increase interest rates in general and ultimately reduce the growth of overall spending and reduce both economic growth and the rate of inflation. Here it is perhaps sufficient to mention that the two biggest recessions in postwar Canadian economic history, the recessions of the early 1980s and the early 1990s, were both associated with attempts by the Bank of Canada to produce disinflation.

DEFLATION AND ECONOMIC GROWTH

It is easy to get confused about the consequences of deflation if you look at it from a micro perspective rather than a macro perspective. As a consumer seeking to buy a particular good, a fall in the price of that good is a clear benefit. When the prices of goods and services in general fall, which is what occurs under deflation, it might seem obvious that this too is a clear benefit. But to generalize from one consumer gaining from the fall in the price of one good to consumers in general gaining from a fall in the price level is often an example of the *fallacy of composition*. When the overall price level falls, the economy typically gets mired in a severe recession, and consumers' incomes drop by more than the drop in prices—that is, their real incomes fall.

Some columnists for the business sections of newspapers write about the importance of the central bank preserving the purchasing power of the currency. They can make it sound almost like the typical family keeps its life savings in a piggybank and that the value of the money in the piggybank will just go down and down if prices are allowed to rise.

Well, suppose families really did keep their life savings in the form of cash in piggybanks, and that the value of those life savings was the only proper concern of central bankers. Why should central bankers just aim for price stability to preserve the value of money? Why not increase the value of money by bringing about deflation (falling prices)?

To illustrate, suppose that you had $12 706 of Canadian money in a piggybank in 1929. Between 1929 and 1933 the level of the Canadian CPI (2002 base) actually fell from 9.2 to 7.1, a fall of about 23 percent or about 6 percent per year. To buy a basket of goods that cost about $12 960 in 1929 would cost only $10 000 in 1933. The extra $2960 or so is a windfall for the piggybank owner corresponding to a real rate of interest of about 6 percent per year.

While the years 1929–1933 might have been great years for anyone whose standard of living was based upon Canadian money stored in a piggybank, they were the worst years of the Great Depression, as discussed in Chapter 4. Canadian GDP dropped sharply from 1930 to 1933 and the unemployment rate reached a painfully high level never approached before or since.

11 Incomes policies can be compulsory or voluntary, and they may involve controls on prices as well as on income. Canada had a compulsory incomes policy (wage and price controls) during the 1975–78 period when the *Anti-Inflation Act* was in effect.

Deflation has been associated with weak or negative economic growth for some of the same reasons disinflation has, but there are other reasons as well. One of them is suggested by the piggybank example—investors who can earn, say, a tax-free annual return of 6 percent just by holding cash may be reluctant to make their money available for the private-sector investment (in plant and equipment, office buildings, shopping malls, and so on) that would spur employment and productivity increases in the economy. For this and other reasons, very few economists would view deflation as a sensible goal for economic policy, and central banks that target inflation always aim for an inflation rate above zero percent.

HYPERINFLATION AND ECONOMIC GROWTH

One of the most widely accepted findings of research on inflation is that hyperinflation impairs the efficiency of an economy, often severely. Hence, countries experiencing hyperinflation tend to experience lower growth than economies that are comparable on other dimensions.

One reason that hyperinflation is associated with lower economic growth is that it greatly increases the costs of making economic transactions. As an extreme case, think of a shopper needing a wheelbarrow just to transport to the grocery store the cash needed to buy a loaf of bread.[12]

Canada has never experienced a hyperinflation. And annual inflation rates in Canada have never even reached 4 percent in the past two decades let alone the 5000 percent or more observed in several hyperinflations. We will examine hyperinflation in more detail in Chapter 9.

HIGH, ACCELERATING INFLATION AND ECONOMIC GROWTH

Canadian advocates of high and accelerating inflation are few and far between. On the face of it, this might seem odd because Canada's years of high and accelerating inflation in the 1970s were characterized by relatively strong economic growth. Canadian inflation during the period 1971–1981 averaged over 8 percent, but the annual real per capita GDP growth rate for the whole period averaged a healthy 2.7 percent.[13]

By contrast, for the period 1982–1992, inflation averaged under 5 percent through years of disinflation followed by stable inflation and then disinflation again. Real per capita GDP growth for the 1982–1992 period averaged under 1 percent.

High inflation may or may not harm economic growth directly. One problem with high and accelerating inflation, however, is that it typically means that the future inflation rate is difficult to predict and income is thereby arbitrarily redistributed between employers and employees, borrowers and lenders, and so on. Another problem is that if high and accelerating inflation persists it may eventually transform into very high inflation or even hyperinflation.

But perhaps the most serious problem with high and accelerating inflation is political. Because of widely held concerns about redistribution and the risk of hyperinflation, many economists have concluded that high and accelerating inflation will likely create a political consensus in favour of clamping down on inflation, typically through disinflation induced by central bank policies. In turn, such disinflation will mean a recession, a sharp drop in economic growth.

---

12 You may wonder how countries could ever allow themselves to fall into a state of hyperinflation. One common path is for a country to experience economic collapse as a result of war. The government needs revenue but is reluctant or unable to raise the funds through taxation. Instead, it issues extra currency to pay for its purchases. With too much currency chasing too few goods and services, prices soar. People try to hoard goods, and this contributes to accelerating inflation. The government then needs even more currency to pay for its purchases, so it issues more, and eventually the process spins out of control.

13 On the lack of solid international evidence for the view that high inflation harms economic growth, see Jonathan Temple, "The New Growth Evidence," *Journal of Economic Literature*, March 1999, pp. 112–56.

EXERCISE 6.7

Consider the following statement in the pages of a business newspaper:

It increases the real burden of debt for businesses, and causes many of them to go bankrupt. It causes the real wages of currently employed workers to rise, even though their nominal wages have not changed, which in turn may lead to layoffs. And, perhaps worst of all, because nominal interest rates cannot go below zero, it can prevent real interest rates from falling sufficiently to trigger recovery from recession.

What is "it"—moderate inflation, deflation, or accelerating inflation? Explain.

RECAP↑

THE ECONOMIC CONSEQUENCES OF VARIOUS TYPES OF INFLATION

Changes in relative prices (such as the price of bread) should be distinguished from inflation, which is a change in the overall level of prices. The distinction is important because remedies for undesired changes in relative prices and for inflation are different.

It is difficult to draw conclusions about the consequences of anything so general as "inflation." Instead we have examined the consequences of various types of inflation for income distribution and economic growth.

- If inflation is anticipated, it will generally not have major impacts on income distribution, even if indexing is uncommon.
- If inflation is unanticipated (as is often the case for disinflation or accelerating inflation), then it can have major impacts on income distribution, but only in the absence of indexing.
- Deflation has been associated with slow or negative economic growth.
- There is controversy over whether a policy of aiming for low inflation is superior to a policy of tolerating moderate inflation as a means of supporting economic growth.
- High, accelerating inflation can generate political support for a costly disinflation to get inflation back under control.
- Hyperinflation has typically been associated with low or negative economic growth and has often led to economic collapse.

SUMMARY

- The basic tool for measuring inflation is the *consumer price index,* or CPI. The CPI measures the cost of purchasing a fixed basket of goods and services in any period relative to the cost of the same basket of goods and services in a base year. The *inflation rate* is the annual percentage rate of change in the price level as measured by a *price index* such as the CPI. **LO1**

- A *nominal quantity* is a quantity that is measured in terms of its current dollar value. Dividing a nominal quantity, such as a family's income or a worker's wage in dollars, by a price index such as the CPI expresses that quantity in terms of real purchasing power. This procedure is called *deflating* the nominal quantity. If nominal quantities from two different years are deflated by a common price index, the purchasing power of the two quantities can be compared. To ensure that a nominal payment, such as a Canada Pension Plan benefit, represents a constant level of real purchasing power, the nominal payment should be increased each year by a percentage equal to the inflation rate. This method of adjusting nominal payments to maintain their purchasing power is called *indexing*. **LO2**

■ The *real interest rate* is equal to the *nominal,* or *market, interest rate* minus the inflation rate. When inflation is unexpectedly high, the real interest rate is lower than anticipated, which hurts lenders but benefits borrowers. When inflation is unexpectedly low, lenders benefit and borrowers are hurt. To obtain a given real rate of return, lenders must charge a high nominal interest rate when inflation is high and a low nominal interest rate when inflation is low. The tendency for nominal interest rates to be high when inflation is high and low when inflation is low is called the *Fisher effect.* **LO3**

■ It is important to distinguish between increases in the *relative prices* for specific goods and services and increases in the general price level. The distinction is important because the appropriate response to a change in relative prices differs from the appropriate response to inflation. **LO4**

■ Economists employ precise terminology to describe the various types of inflation. Inflation can be *anticipated* or *unanticipated.* Distinctions are drawn between *zero inflation, stable inflation, accelerating inflation, disinflation,* and *deflation.* The intensity of inflation can be described by terms such as *low inflation, moderate inflation, high inflation,* and *hyperinflation.* **LO4, LO5**

■ The various types of inflation have different consequences for income distribution and economic growth. It is almost universally accepted that macroeconomic policy should aim at avoiding the extremes of hyperinflation (which Canada has never experienced) and deflation (which Canada experienced during the Great Depression). It is widely accepted that macroeconomic policy should avoid high and accelerating inflation. **LO6**

KEY TERMS

accelerating inflation (140)
anticipated inflation (136)
consumer price index (CPI) (128)
deflating (a nominal quantity) (131)
deflation (130)
disinflation (140)
downward nominal wage rigidity
　hypothesis (144)
Fisher effect (137)
high inflation (141)

hyperinflation (141)
indexing (133)
low inflation (140)
moderate inflation (141)
nominal interest rate (134)
nominal quantity (131)
price index (129)
price level (127)
price signal distortion
　hypothesis (144)

rate of inflation (130)
real interest rate (134)
real quantity (131)
real wage (132)
relative price (138)
stable inflation (139)
unanticipated inflation (136)
zero bound on nominal interest
　rates hypothesis (144)
zero inflation (139)

REVIEW QUESTIONS

1. Explain why changes in the cost of living for any particular individual or family may differ from changes in the CPI. **LO1**

2. What is the difference between the *price level* and the *rate of inflation* in an economy? **LO1**

3. Why is it important to adjust for inflation when comparing nominal quantities (for example, workers' average wages) at different points in time? What is the basic method for adjusting for inflation? **LO2**

4. Describe how indexing might be used to guarantee that the purchasing power of the wage agreed to in a multiyear collective agreement will not be eroded by inflation. **LO2**

5. How does deflation affect the real return on holding cash? How does positive inflation act as a tax on

criminal gangs holding large quantities of cash to avoid detection by the authorities rather than keeping their money in interest-bearing bank accounts? **LO4**

6. "It's true that unanticipated inflation redistributes wealth from creditors to debtors, for example. But what one side of the bargain loses the other side gains. So from the perspective of society as a whole, there is no real cost." Do you agree? Discuss. **LO6**

7. True or false, and explain: If both the potential lender and the potential borrower correctly anticipate the rate of inflation, inflation will not redistribute wealth from the creditor to the debtor. **LO6**

8. Discuss the different consequences that deflation, high inflation, and hyperinflation have for economic growth. **LO6**

PROBLEMS

1. In the city of Pizzaville, government survey takers determine that typical family expenditures each month in the year designated as the base year are as follows:

   20 pizzas at $10 each
   Rent of apartment, $600 per month
   Gasoline and car maintenance, $100
   Phone service (basic service plus 10 long-distance calls), $50

   In the year following the base year, the survey takers determine that pizzas have risen to $11 each, apartment rent is $640, gasoline and maintenance has risen to $120, and phone service has dropped in price to $40. **LO1**

   a. Find the CPI in the subsequent year and the rate of inflation between the base year and the subsequent year.

   b. The family's nominal income rose by 5 percent between the base year and the subsequent year. Is the family worse off or better off in terms of what its income is able to buy?

2. Here are values of the Canadian CPI for each year over the period 2002–2010. For each year beginning with 2003, calculate the rate of inflation from the previous year. How would you characterize inflation rates over the 2003–2010 period? **LO1**

2002	100.0
2003	102.8
2004	104.7
2005	107.0
2006	109.1
2007	111.5
2008	114.1
2009	114.4
2010	116.5

3. An article in *The Economist* in 2007 reported that agricultural prices have been rising worldwide and that the proportion of the consumer price index taken up by food is much higher in developing countries such as China and India than in developed countries such as the United States.[14]

   Suppose that the share of food in the consumer price index of Canada, China, India, and the United States is as shown in the table below. Suppose also that all four countries are hit by an agricultural price shock that sends the price of food up 10 percent. What impact will this price shock have on the overall price index in each of the four countries, all else

   being equal? Insert your answers in the blank cells of the column titled "Predicted Increase in CPI." **LO2**

Country	Share of Food in CPI (%)[15]	Predicted Increase in CPI
Canada	17	
China	33	
India	46	
United States	14	

4. Suppose a study found that the real entry-level wage for graduates of a certain university declined by 8 percent between 2000 and 2009. The nominal entry-level wage in 2009 was $12.00 per hour. Assuming that the findings are correct, what was the nominal entry-level wage in 2000? Use the CPI data from Problem 2. **LO2**

5. Here is the income tax schedule for a hypothetical country. It is expressed in nominal terms, for the year 2011.

Family income	Taxes due (percent of income)
≤ $20 000	10
$20 001 – $30 000	12
$30 001 – $50 000	15
$50 001 – $80 000	20
>$80 000	25

   The legislature wants to ensure that families with a given real income are not pushed up into higher tax brackets by inflation. The CPI is 175 in 2011 and 185 in 2012. How should the income tax schedule above be adjusted for the year 2012 to meet the legislature's goal? **LO2**

6. In 2007, based upon the Survey of Household Spending of 2005, Statistics Canada announced the following weights for the major spending categories tracked by the CPI.[16]

   Employ the weights given below and suppose that 2002 is the base year with a CPI equal to 100. Suppose also that since 2002 the price of food has increased by 10 percent; the price of housing has increased by 15 percent; and the price of recreation, education, and reading has increased by 20 percent. All other prices are unchanged. Find the CPI for the current year (2012). **LO1**, **LO3**

14 See "Rising food prices; the agonies of agflation," *The Economist*, 25 August 2007, http://www.economist.com/finance/displaystory.cfm?story_id=9707029 (May 2008).

15 Share of food in CPI for China, India, and United States from "Rising food prices" and share of food in CPI for Canada from Statistics Canada, "Weighting Diagram of the Consumer Price Index; 2005 basket at April 2007 Prices, Canada, provinces, Whitehorse and Yellowknife," http://www.statcan.gc.ca/pub/62-001-x/2007005/4183122-eng.htm.

16 Adapted from the Statistics Canada Web site, http://www.statcan.gc.ca/imdb-bmdi/document/2301_D34_T9_V1_B.pdf. The weights do not add up exactly to 100 percent because of rounding.

Food	17.0%	Transportation	19.9%
Shelter	26.6%	Health and personal care	4.7%
Household operations and furnishings	11.1%	Recreation, education, and reading	12.2%
Clothing and footwear	5.4%	Alcoholic beverages and tobacco products	3.1%

ANSWERS TO IN-CHAPTER EXERCISES

6.1 The cost of the family's basket in 2002 remains at $680, as in Table 6.1. If the rent on the apartment falls to $400 in 2012, the cost of reproducing the 2002 basket of goods and services in 2012 is $620 ($400 for rent + $150 for hamburgers + $70 for movie tickets). The CPI for 2012 is accordingly $620/$680, or 0.912. So in this example, the cost of living has fallen nearly 9 percent between 2002 and 2012. **LO1**

6.2 To construct a price index for university student expenditures, you would need to determine the basket of goods and services purchased in the base year. The university student price index in each period would then be defined as the cost of the basket in that period relative to the cost in the base year. To the extent that the mix of purchases of university students differs from that of average households, the university student price index would differ from the CPI. For example, if in the base year university students spent a higher share of their budgets than the average Canadian household on goods and services that have risen relatively rapidly in price (such as tuition fees for post-secondary education), then the inflation rate experienced by university students would be higher than the CPI inflation rate. **LO1**

6.3 The percentage changes in the CPI in each year from the previous year are as follows:

1930	$-1.1 \text{ percent} = 100 \times \dfrac{(9.1 - 9.2)}{9.2}$
1931	-9.9 percent
1932	-8.5 percent
1933	-5.3 percent

Negative inflation is called deflation. The experience of the 1930s, when prices were falling, contrasts sharply with the 1970s, during which prices rose rapidly. **LO1**

6.4 The percentage increase in the nominal value of minimum wage from $9.50 to $10.25 is 7.9 percent. To find the change in the real value of the minimum wage, we must first calculate the real wage in September 2009 and the real wage in September 2010. Deflating the $9.50 minimum wage of September 2009 with the Ontario CPI value of 113.8 gives a real minimum wage of $8.35 in 2002 dollars. Deflating the September 2010 minimum wage of $10.25 by the September 2010 Ontario CPI of 117.1 gives a real minimum wage $8.75 in 2002 dollars. The percentage increase in the real value of the minimum wage is 4.8 percent. **LO2**

6.5 No answer given. **LO4**

6.6 The Bank of Canada aims for *low inflation*. Olivier Blanchard is an advocate of *moderate inflation*. **LO5**

6.7 The paragraph is about *deflation*. Deflation will increase the real burden of nominal debt, raise the real value of a nominal wage, and increase the real interest rate corresponding to any given nominal interest rate. **LO5**

Practise and learn online with Connect.

THE ECONOMY IN THE SHORT RUN

Short-term fluctuations around the long-run average of an economy's growth can be unpleasant. In particular, periods of low or negative economic growth, known as *recessions*, can create significant economic hardship and dissatisfaction for the general population. For example, during the severe recessions of the early 1980s, the early 1990s, and 2008–2009, large numbers of Canadians lost their jobs, and many their homes also, when they were not able to make mortgage payments. In Part 3 of this text we will explore the causes of these short-term fluctuations in key economic variables, including output, unemployment, and inflation, and we will discuss options for stabilizing the economy that are available to government policy-makers.

Chapter 7 provides some necessary background for this study of short-term fluctuations by describing key characteristics and reviewing the historical record of fluctuations in the Canadian economy. In Chapters 8 through 11 we develop a framework for the analysis of short-term fluctuations, and of the alternative policy responses.

Chapter 8 shows how changes in overall spending in the economy may lead to short-run fluctuations in output and employment. The chapter also explains how changes in fiscal policy, those policies related to government spending and taxation, can be used to stabilize spending and output. Chapter 9 considers the roles played in the economy by money, the banking system, and central banks. It provides background knowledge for understanding Chapter 10, which extends the model of Chapter 8 to investigate how interest rate changes by the central bank can be used to stabilize output and employment. Chapter 11 introduces a model that allows us to consider the causes and consequences of changes in the overall price level of the economy. Chapter 12 incorporates inflation into the analysis, discussing both the sources of inflation and the policies that can be used to control it. Finally, Chapter 13 considers the relationship between exchange rate changes and short-term fluctuations in the economy and also the factors determining exchange rates.

CHAPTER 7
Short-Term Economic Fluctuations: An Introduction

LEARNING OBJECTIVES

When you have completed this chapter, you will be able to:

LO1 Identify the four phases of the business cycle.

LO2 Explain the primary characteristics of recessions and expansions.

LO3 Define potential output, measure the output gap, and use these concepts to analyze an economy's position in the business cycle.

LO4 Define the natural rate of unemployment, list its components, and show how it is related to cyclical unemployment.

LO5 Use Okun's law to analyze the relationship between the output gap and cyclical unemployment.

LO6 Discuss the basic differences between how the economy operates in the short run versus the long run.

How would you respond to the following situation? In the very year that you plan to graduate from university and get a full-time job, the economy goes into a serious recession and the unemployment rate soars. Employers have many applicants for every job vacancy, and they prefer qualified applicants with years of work experience over applicants such as you who have just graduated from university.

Some new graduates will stick with their original plan. Typically, they will succeed in finding suitable employment, but it will take months and months of job search instead of the weeks that it would normally take. Other graduates will quickly settle for low-paying jobs for which they are considerably over-qualified. Yet another approach is to apply the *cost–benefit principle* and decide to postpone job hunting until the economy picks up. Some graduates will realize that, because they will not land the high-paying, suitable job they planned for, there will be a low opportunity cost associated with taking a few months to travel the world. So they will pack their bags and go. Other graduates will calculate that there will be a low opportunity cost in spending an extra year at university or college. Indeed, during Canada's last major recession, many universities and colleges saw a jump in enrollment due to students deciding that their time would be better spent in acquiring more education rather than in a frustrating job search in a high-unemployment labour market. For most, especially those who acquired postgraduate degrees and then access to satisfying jobs, this proved to be a wise decision.

This chapter provides insight into, among other things, the economic downturns that force complex decisions on graduating students and often create problems for governing political parties. It is the first of several chapters with a common theme.

In this part of the book we study short-term fluctuations in economic activity, commonly known as *recessions* and *expansions*. We will start, in this chapter, with some background on the history and characteristics of these economic ups and downs. However, the main focus of this part is the causes of short-term fluctuations, as well as the available *policy responses*. Because the analysis of short-term economic fluctuations can become complex and even controversial, we will proceed in a step-by-step fashion. In Chapter 8 we introduce a basic model of booms and recessions, which we will refer to as the *basic Keynesian model* in honour of its principal originator, the British economist

John Maynard Keynes. The basic Keynesian model focuses on the components of aggregate spending, such as consumption spending by households, investment spending by the private sector, investment spending and other purchases by governments, and purchases of our exports by the rest of the world. It considers the effects of changes in this aggregate spending on total real GDP. The basic Keynesian model is a useful starting point. We will build upon it in the later chapters of Part 3.

7.1 RECESSIONS AND EXPANSIONS

As background to the study of short-term economic fluctuations, let's review the historic record of the fluctuations in the Canadian economy. Figure 7.1 shows the path of real GDP in Canada since 1926. As you can see, the growth path of real GDP is not always smooth; the bumps and wiggles correspond to short periods of faster or slower growth.

A period in which the economy is growing at a rate significantly below normal is called a **recession**, or a *contraction*. An extremely severe or protracted recession is called a **depression**. You should be able to pick out the Great Depression in Figure 7.1, particularly the sharp initial decline between 1929 and 1933. But you can also see that the Canadian economy experienced serious recessions in the early 1980s and during 1990–1992.

A popular definition of a recession, one that is often cited by the media, is a period during which real GDP falls for at least two consecutive quarters. This definition is not a bad rule of thumb for most high-income economies such as Canada today. Such economies typically have a normal rate of real growth of a few percentage points or less, and real GDP is likely to fall in such economies when they grow at a rate significantly below normal.

If an economy normally grows at several percentage points a year, however, the economy will be said to experience a recession if its growth rate drops by a few percentage points or more, even if the growth rate is still positive. In an economy where real GDP normally grows at about 10 percent such as China's, for example, the unemployment rate

recession (or contraction) a period in which the economy is growing at a rate significantly below normal

depression a particularly severe or protracted recession

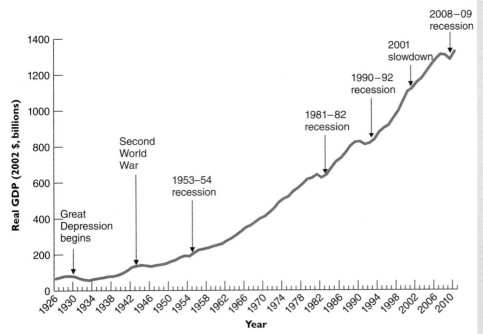

FIGURE 7.1
Fluctuations in Canadian Real GDP, 1926–2010
Real GDP has not grown smoothly but has undergone speed-ups (expansions or booms) and serious slowdowns (recessions or depressions). The most dramatic fluctuations are indicated. Note the contraction from 1929 to 1933 (the first phase of the Great Depression), the boom in 1939–45 (the Second World War), and the recessions of the early 1980s and 1990s, and of 2008–2009.
SOURCE: Adapted from the Statistics Canada, CANSIM series v3860085, and from series F55 of Historical Statistics of Canada.

"Please stand by for a series of tones. The first indicates the official end of the recession, the second indicates prosperity, and the third the return of the recession."

would soar if the growth rate fell to the 6 percent range, as it did in China in the first quarter of 2009, triggering a massive fiscal policy response from the Chinese government. (See also the 1960-1961 Canadian recession in Table 7.1 for an example of a recession with positive growth.)

TABLE 7.1
Canada Recessions 1947–2010

Peak date (start)	Trough date (end)	Approximate duration (months)	Highest unemployment rate (%)	Percentage change in annual real GDP	Duration of subsequent expansion (months)
Sept. 1947	Mar. 1948	6	2.8 (1949)	—	11
Feb. 1949	Jul. 1949	6	3.6 (1950)	—	11
Jun. 1951	Dec. 1951	6	2.9 (1952)	—	16
Apr. 1953	Apr. 1954	12	4.6 (1954)	−1.2 (1953–54)	36
Apr. 1957	Jan. 1958	9	7.0 (1958)	—	25
Feb. 1960	Mar. 1961	13	7.1 (1961)	2.8 (1960–61)	108
Mar. 1970	Jun. 1970	3	6.2 (1971)	—	55
Jan. 1975	Mar. 1975	3	7.0 (1976)	—	59
Feb. 1980	Jun. 1980	4	7.6 (1981)	—	13
Jul. 1981	Oct. 1982	15	11.9 (1983)	−2.9 (1981–82)	90
Apr. 1990	Apr. 1992	24	11.4 (1993)	−1.9 (1990–91)	186
Aug. 2008	Aug. 2009	10	8.7 (2009)	−3.6 (3Q2008–2Q2009)	?

Notes: Highest unemployment rate is the annual rate for the year shown in parentheses—the trough year or the subsequent year, whichever is higher. The percentage change in annual real GDP is measured from the peak year to the following year (as shown in parentheses) for those recessions that lasted 12 months or longer. The 2.8 percent annual real GDP growth associated with the 1960–1961 recession is not a typo. The very high real GDP growth numbers for "good years" in the 1950s and 60s meant that 2.8 percent real GDP growth amounted to a marked slowdown in economic growth.

SOURCE: Adapted from the Statistics Canada CANSIM database, http://cansim2.statcan.gc.ca, Tables 380-0017 series v646957, v646954, and v646937, extraction date May 10, 2011, and the articles "Alternative Measures of Business Cycles in Canada: 1947-1992" and "Year-end review of 2009," *Canadian Economic Observer*, 11-010-XIB, February 1996, appendix and April 2010, Section 3. http://www.statcan.gc.ca/bsolc/olc-cel/olc-cel?catno=11-010-XWE&lang=eng.

Table 7.1 lists the beginning and ending dates of Canadian recessions during the 1947–2009 period, as well as the *duration* (length, in months) of each. The table also gives the highest unemployment rate associated with each recession and the percentage change in real GDP for the longer recessions. (Ignore the last column of the table for now.) The beginning of a recession is called the **peak**, because it represents the high point of economic activity prior to a downturn. The end of a recession, which marks the low point of economic activity prior to a recovery, is called the **trough**.

Table 7.1 shows what is probably the most widely accepted dating of Canadian recessions covering the period since 1947. It does not include the economic slowdown of 2000–2001 because that slowdown was not sufficiently pronounced in Canada to clearly warrant being termed a "recession." As in Figure 7.1, the severity of the early 1980s, the early 1990s, and the 2008–2009 recessions stands out. The 1990–1992 recession featured a milder drop in GDP than the very sharp 1981–1982 recession, but the one in 1990–1992 lasted several months longer. Indeed, at 24 months long, it was by far the longest recession since 1947.

The opposite of a recession is an **expansion**, a period in which the economy is growing at a rate that is significantly *above* normal. Canada has experienced three long expansions in the period since 1947: from 1961 to 1970, from 1982 to 1990, and from 1992 extending into 2008 (provided that the slowdown of 2000–2001 is not counted

peak the beginning of a recession, the high point of economic activity prior to a downturn

trough the end of a recession, the low point of economic activity prior to a recovery

expansion a period in which the economy is growing at a rate significantly above normal

---

FIGURE 7.2

Canada's Real GDP Per Capita Growth Rate, 1927–2010

Growth of real GDP per capita is shown by the jagged red line. It averaged 2.3 percent over the 1927–2010 period, as shown by the long, vertical grey line. During some sub-periods, the real GDP per capita growth rate has differed substantially from its long-term average. On the one hand, the economy registered negative average growth (-1.1 percent) during the Great Depression years of 1929 to 1938 and sluggish average growth (1.2 percent) during the 1980–96 period. On the other hand, real GDP per capita grew at an amazingly strong pace (9.1 percent) during the WW II years of 1940 to 1944, at a rapid pace (3.3 percent) during the 1962–79 period, and at a moderate pace from 1997 to 2005.

SOURCE: Adapted from Statistics Canada, CANSIM series v2461079, v466668 and v41707175 and from series D129, A1 and F55 of Historical Statistics of Canada.

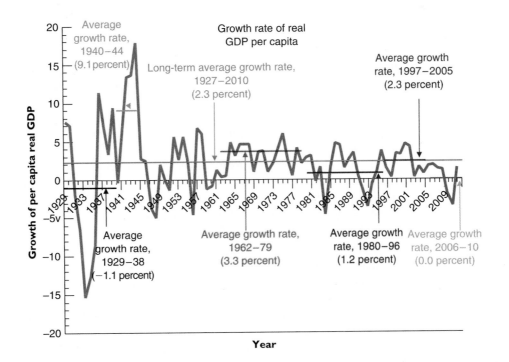

boom a particularly strong and protracted phase of an expansion

as a recession). A particularly strong and protracted phase of an expansion is called a **boom**. The 1997–2000 phase of Canada's most recent long expansion exhibited the characteristics of a boom. In 2003–2007, many Canadian resource industries were enjoying a boom but overall growth was moderate compared to the boom of the late 1990s, in part due to weakness in Canadian manufacturing connected with the strong Canadian dollar.

Figure 7.2 presents another way of showing fluctuations in Canadian economic growth. It depicts year-to-year fluctuations in the growth of real GDP per capita during the 1927–2009 period and thus shows sharper fluctuations than does Figure 7.1, which depicted the level of real GDP. Observe that the Canadian economy produced very low growth rates of real GDP per capita during two long historical periods, the years 1929–1938 and 1980–1996 when the economy went through severe economic downturns.

EXERCISE 7.1

Recessions in the United States invariably have an impact upon certain Canadian industries and usually have a major impact on the Canadian economy as a whole. The most widely accepted dating of U.S. recessions is that determined by the National Bureau of Economic Research. Go to the National Bureau of Economic Research Web site (at the time of writing the most relevant pages on the site are http://www.nber.org/cycles/recessions.html and http://www.nber.org/cycles.html) and find out how much time has elapsed since the last U.S. business cycle peak or trough. Is the U.S. economy currently in recession or expansion? How much time has elapsed since the last peak or trough?

7.2 CHARACTERISTICS OF SHORT-TERM FLUCTUATIONS

Although Figure 7.1 and Table 7.1 show only twenty- and twenty-first-century data, periods of expansion and recession have been a feature of industrial economies since at least the late eighteenth century. Karl Marx and Friedrich Engels referred to these fluctuations, which they called "commercial crises," in their *Communist Manifesto* (1848). In Canada, economists have been studying short-term fluctuations for decades. The traditional term for these fluctuations is *business cycles*, and they are still often referred to as *cyclical fluctuations*. Neither term is very accurate though, since, as Figure 7.1 shows, economic fluctuations are not "cyclical" at all in the sense that they recur at predictable intervals, but instead they are quite *irregular in their length and severity*. This irregularity makes the dates of peaks and troughs extremely hard to predict, despite the fact that professional forecasters have devoted a great deal of effort and brainpower to the task.

Expansions and recessions usually are not limited to a few industries or regions but are *felt throughout the economy*. Indeed, the largest fluctuations may have a global impact. For instance, the Great Depression of the 1930s affected nearly all the world's economies, and the 1981–1982 recession, which originated primarily with the high interest rate policies of the United States, triggered not only recessions in other countries but also a foreign debt crisis affecting a wide range of developing countries. When East Asia suffered a major slowdown in the late 1990s, the effects of that slowdown spilled over into many other regions (including Canada, particularly British Columbia).

Even relatively moderate recessions may strike a number of countries simultaneously. Figure 7.3, which shows the growth rates of real GDP over the period 1999–2010 for Canada, Germany, Japan, the United Kingdom, and the United States, illustrates

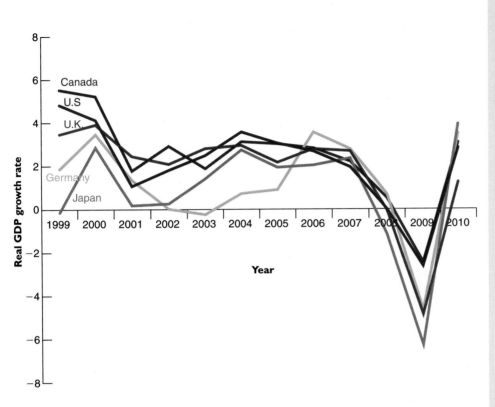

FIGURE 7.3
Real GDP Growth in Five Major Countries, 1999–2010
Annual growth rates for five major industrialized economies show that all the countries except for Japan enjoyed strong, real GDP growth in 1999 and 2000. In 2001 each of these economies experienced an economic slowdown. By 2002 most of them had recovered, and by 2004 all of them had. In 2007 U.S. growth began to falter, and in 2008 each of the five economies went into a sharp recession. SOURCE: International Monetary Fund, *World Economic Outlook Database*, April 2011 http://www.imf.org/external/pubs/ft/weo/2011/01/weodata/index.aspx.

this point. You can see that—except for Japan, which had been suffering special problems related to deflation—all these countries experienced relatively strong growth rates in 1999 and 2000. The 2001 recession lowered the growth rates in all of the countries, with some recovery apparent by 2002 in all of the economies except Germany, which recovered in 2003. In 2007, U.S. growth began to falter and in 2008, each of the five economies went into a sharp recession. By 2010, positive growth had returned to all five economies.

Unemployment is a key indicator of short-term economic fluctuations. The unemployment rate typically rises sharply during recessions and recovers (although more slowly) during expansions. Figure 5.4 showed the Canadian unemployment rate since 1960. You should be able to identify the recessions that began in 1981, 1990, and 2008, for example, by noting the sharp increases in the unemployment rate that began in those years. As we will explain shortly, the part of unemployment that is associated with recessions is called *cyclical unemployment*. Beyond this increase in unemployment, labour market conditions become less favourable to workers during recessions. For example, real wages grow more slowly or even decline, and workers are less likely to receive promotions or bonuses during a recession than during expansionary periods.

Like unemployment, *inflation* follows a typical pattern in recessions and expansions, though it is not so sharply defined. Figure 7.4 shows the Canadian inflation rate since 1960; in the figure, vertical blue lines show the approximate starting dates of periods of recession. Recessions tend to be followed soon after by a decline in the rate of inflation, as indicated by the declines in the inflation rate after the recessions beginning in 1970, 1975,

Unemployment among construction workers rises substantially during recessions.

FIGURE 7.4

Canadian Recessions and Disinflation, 1960–2010

The red line shows the CPI inflation rate and the blue lines indicate when recessions (and the economic downturn of 2000–2001) began. Note that the inflation rate fell after the recessions beginning in 1970, 1975, 1981, 1990, and 2008. The fall in the inflation rate after 1975 is partly due to the Anti-Inflation Act, which imposed wage and price controls during 1975–1978. The fall in the inflation rate after the recession beginning in 1990 was delayed due to the introduction of the GST (which increased consumer prices) and to sharply higher energy prices associated with the Gulf War.

SOURCE: Adapted from Statistics Canada, CANSIM series v41690973.

1981, 1990, and 2008. Furthermore, some recessions have been preceded by increases in inflation, as Figure 7.4 also shows. The behaviour of inflation during expansions and recessions will be discussed more fully in Chapter 12.

Generally, industries that produce *durable goods*, such as cars, houses, and capital equipment, are more affected than others by recessions and booms. In contrast, industries that provide *services* and *non-durable goods* like food are much less sensitive to short-term fluctuations. Thus, an automobile worker or a construction worker is far more likely to lose his or her job in a recession than a hairstylist or a baker is.

> **RECAP**
>
> ### RECESSIONS, BOOMS, AND THEIR CHARACTERISTICS
>
> - A recession is a period in which output is growing more slowly than normal. An expansion is a period in which output is growing more quickly than normal.
>
> - The beginning of a recession is called the peak, and its end (which corresponds to the beginning of the subsequent expansion) is called the trough.
>
> - The sharpest recession in the history f[of]Canada was the initial phase of the Great Depression in 1929–1933. Severe recessions also occurred in

the early 1980s and during 1990–1992. The 2008–2009 recession saw an especially sharp drop in real GDP growth, but the duration of the recession was shorter than that of the early 1990s.

- Short-term economic fluctuations are irregular in length and severity and thus are difficult to predict.

- Expansions and recessions have widespread (and sometimes global) impacts, affecting most regions and industries.

- Unemployment rises sharply during a recession and falls, usually more slowly, during an expansion.

- Recessions tend to be followed by a decline in inflation and are sometimes preceded by an increase in inflation.

- Durable goods industries are more affected by expansions and recessions than other industries. Services and non-durable goods industries are less sensitive to ups and downs in the economy.

7.3 MEASURING FLUCTUATIONS: OUTPUT GAPS AND CYCLICAL UNEMPLOYMENT

If policy-makers are to respond appropriately to recessions and expansions, and economists are to study them, knowing whether a particular economic fluctuation is "big" or "small" is essential. Intuitively, a big recession or expansion is one in which output and the unemployment rate deviate significantly from their normal or trend levels. In this section we will attempt to be more precise about this idea, in preparation for our analysis of the causes and cures of short-run fluctuations. Specifically, we will introduce the concept of the *output gap*, which measures how far output is from its normal level at a particular time, and we will analyze the idea of *cyclical unemployment*, or the deviation of unemployment from its normal level. Finally, we will examine how these two concepts are related.

POTENTIAL OUTPUT AND THE OUTPUT GAP

The concept of *potential output* is a useful starting point for thinking about the measurement of expansions and recessions. **Potential output**, also called *potential GDP* or *full-employment output*, is the amount of output (real GDP) that an economy can produce when using its resources, such as capital and labour, at normal rates. Potential output is not a fixed number but grows over time, reflecting increases in both the amounts of available capital and labour and their productivity. The growth of potential output is very similar to the outward expansion of the production possibilities curve analyzed in Chapter 2. We will discuss the sources of growth in potential output (the economy's productive capacity) at some length in Chapter 14. We will use the symbol Y^* to signify the economy's potential output at a given point in time.

A recession, as we have seen, is a period in which the economy is growing significantly below its normal rate. What causes this slow growth? Logically, there are two possibilities. First, a recession could be a period in which actual output equals potential output, but potential output itself is growing very slowly. Severe soil erosion, for example, would reduce the rate of growth in an agricultural economy, and a decline in the rate of technological innovation might reduce the rate of potential output growth in an industrial economy. Similarly, new technologies, increased capital investment (more precisely, positive net investment), or a surge in immigration that swells the labour force could produce unusually brisk growth in potential output, and thus an economic boom.

The usual explanation for short-term economic fluctuations, however, is that *actual output does not always equal potential output*. For example, potential output may be

potential output (or potential GDP or full-employment output) the amount of output (real GDP) that an economy can produce when using its resources, such as capital and labour, at normal rates growing normally, but for some reason the economy's capital and labour resources may not be fully utilized, so actual output falls below potential output (a recession). Alternatively, capital and labour may be working harder than usual, so actual output expands beyond potential output (a boom). In either of these scenarios, policy-makers face a new problem: how to return actual output to potential. In the next four chapters

ECONOMIC NATURALIST   7.1

Japan's economy: from "bubble economy" to "lost decade" to global recession

The Japanese economy from the late 1980s to the present provides an excellent example of how the distinction between *potential* and *actual* output of an economy illuminates the performance of that economy.

As shown in Figure 7.5, during the latter half of the 1980s, the Japanese economy experienced an unsustainable boom with a large expansionary gap that persisted for about three years. Since the so-called "bubble economy" period of the late 1980s, however, growth in both actual and potential output has slowed significantly. According to the International Monetary Fund, growth of Japan's *potential* output fell from 3.6 percent per year in the 1980s to about 2.2 percent per year since then, due to slower population growth and other factors. But since the early 1990s, *actual* output has only grown at 1.5 percent

a year, considerably less than the potential growth rate.

With growth of actual output typically lagging behind growth of potential output, Japan has had recessionary gaps in many years since the early 1990s. The economic period from 1993 to 2002 has been called the "lost decade" in that country. By 2007, a small expansionary gap had developed due to sustained economic growth since 2003 but during the global recession of 2008-2009, which produced a dramatic reduction in Japanese exports, the recessionary gap widened yet again. The Japanese example illustrates that although recessionary gaps are usually regarded as short-term economic fluctuations, in extreme cases they can persist for at least a decade.

FIGURE 7.5
Output Gap for Japan, 1987–2010
The red line shows Japan's output gap as estimated by the International Monetary Fund. From the late 1980s to the early 1990s, during what has come to be known as the "bubble economy period," Japan experienced a large expansionary gap. From 1992 to 2003, the economy spent most years mired in recession. The global recession of 2008–09 resulted in an especially large recessionary gap. SOURCE: International Monetary Fund, World Economic Outlook Database, April 2011. http://www.imf.org/external/pubs/ft/weo/2011/01/weodata/index.aspx.

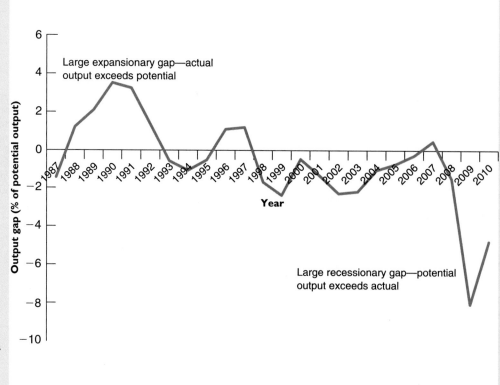

we will discuss policies for *stabilizing* the economy; that is, bringing actual output into line with potential output.

At any point in time, the difference between potential output and actual output is called the **output gap**. Recalling that Y^* is the symbol for potential output and that Y stands for actual output (real GDP), we can express the output gap as $Y - Y^*$. A negative output gap—when actual output is below potential and resources are not being fully utilized—is called a **recessionary gap**. A positive output gap, when actual output is above potential and resources are being utilized at above-normal rates, is referred to as an **expansionary gap**. The usual stated goal of macroeconomic policy-makers is an output gap of zero; that is, an output gap which is neither positive nor negative in sign.[1]

How do output gaps arise? Why doesn't the economy always produce at its potential? Is there anything policy-makers can do about output gaps? These are fundamental questions we will return to frequently in subsequent chapters.

THE OUTPUT GAP AND UNEMPLOYMENT

Recessions typically arise because actual output falls below potential, and they bring bad times. Output falls (or at least grows more slowly), implying reduced living standards. Moreover, recessionary output gaps can be extremely embarrassing for policy-makers because they imply that the economy has the *capacity* to produce more but for some reason is not fully utilizing available resources. In terms of the economy-wide production possibilities curve (PPC) of Chapter 2, the economy is operating at a technically inefficient point inside the PPC.

An important indicator of the low utilization of resources during recessions is the unemployment rate. To take an especially dramatic example, due to the Canadian recession of the early 1990s, the unemployment rate in Toronto soared from 4 percent to 11.5 percent in 1992. In general, a high unemployment rate means that labour resources are not being fully utilized, so output has fallen below potential (a recessionary gap). By the same logic, an unusually low unemployment rate implies that labour is being utilized at a rate greater than normal, so actual output exceeds potential output (an expansionary gap).

As a starting point, it is useful to think of unemployment as being of four broad types: *frictional*, *structural*, *seasonal*, and *cyclical*. We will see shortly that it is also useful to group frictional, structural, and seasonal unemployment together and to contrast them with cyclical unemployment.

Even when jobs are plentiful, some workers with skills in demand where they live will be counted among the unemployed because they are looking for work for a short time before they find it. Days or weeks may go by before, say, a university graduate is able to find suitable work. Short-term unemployment that is associated with the process of matching workers with jobs is called **frictional unemployment**. A certain amount of frictional unemployment is required to allow for good matching of workers with available jobs. So frictional unemployment is, economically, the least costly of the four broad types of unemployment.

Some unemployment occurs because of mismatch—workers are in the wrong place, or do not have the right skills for available jobs. This is usually labelled **structural unemployment**, because it occurs when the structure of demand does not match up with the structure of supply: workers are unable to fill available jobs because they lack the skills or do not live where jobs are available. Perceptions of the extent of structural

output gap (or $Y - Y^*$) the difference between the economy's actual output and its potential output at a point in time

recessionary gap a negative output gap, which occurs when potential output exceeds actual output

expansionary gap a positive output gap, which occurs when actual output is higher than potential output

frictional unemployment the short-term unemployment associated with the process of matching workers with jobs

structural unemployment unemployment that occurs when workers are unable to fill available jobs because they lack the skills, or do not live where jobs are available

---

1 Some sources define an output gap such that a recessionary gap is positive. The approach followed here is more common and is employed, for example, by the Bank of Canada, as in, "A positive output gap means that the economy is operating above its capacity to sustain that level of production owing to excess demand. A negative gap means that there is excess supply—that is to say, spare capacity or slack in the economy—due to weak demand." See Bank of Canada, "The Output Gap," http://www.bankofcanada.ca/about/backgrounders/the-output-gap/.

unemployment are influenced by examples such as Newfoundland outports devastated by the closure of the cod fishery. But the population of such villages makes up a tiny percentage of the Canadian population. Surveys of the labour force as a whole have found that in some years job vacancies in Canada have amounted to 1 percent of the labour force or less.

Canada is a country that experiences climatic extremes. **Seasonal unemployment** results when some jobs come and go with the seasons. This month-to-month variation in employment has predicable patterns (for example, retail stores increase their hiring in November, just in time for the Christmas sales rush, and then usually lay off workers in January). In the past, seasonal variation in employment was much greater in Canada than it is now, in part because sectors such as agriculture that are heavily influenced by the weather are much smaller than they used to be, and in part because sectors like construction have developed effective ways of dealing with the weather. Nevertheless, some impacts of the weather are unavoidable—sunbathing will just never be much fun on a Canadian beach in February—so industries such as tourism remain heavily affected by the seasons.

The fourth type of unemployment increases during recessions (that is, periods of substantially reduced output growth) and is called **cyclical unemployment**. This type of unemployment is also referred to as "demand-deficient" unemployment. The sharp peaks in unemployment that were shown in Figure 5.4 reflect the cyclical unemployment that occurs during recessions. Increases in cyclical unemployment are associated with significant declines in real GDP growth and are therefore quite costly economically.

The natural rate of unemployment is defined as the unemployment that is left when cyclical unemployment is subtracted from total unemployment. It refers to the part of unemployment that is attributable to frictional, structural, and seasonal unemployment. Because the total of frictional, structural, and seasonal unemployment is difficult to measure, however, the **natural rate of unemployment** is typically calculated as the unemployment rate that prevails when the economy has neither a recessionary nor an expansionary gap.

Some economists have used *full-employment rate of unemployment* to describe what we term the natural rate of unemployment, and other economists use *non-accelerating inflation rate of unemployment* (or *NAIRU*). But "natural rate of unemployment" is much more commonly used these days than "full-employment rate of unemployment," and it is simpler than "non-accelerating inflation rate of unemployment."

It is worth mentioning that the adjective "natural" in the natural rate of unemployment may give the false impression that nothing can be done to reduce frictional, structural, and seasonal unemployment. But many things are both "natural" and changeable, such as the number of deaths from malaria. Economists recognize that the amount of frictional, structural, and seasonal unemployment depends upon institutions, structural policies, technology, and other factors. Such factors explain, for example, why natural rates of unemployment vary considerably among countries. Therefore, just as economists recognize that the rate of death from malaria in many developing countries could be substantially reduced by bed nets, medicines, and so on, they also recognize that the natural rate of unemployment in many countries could be lowered by measures such as structural policies.

We will denote the natural rate of unemployment as u^*. Cyclical unemployment, which is the difference between the total unemployment rate and the natural unemployment rate, can thus be expressed as $u - u^*$, where u is the actual unemployment rate and u^* denotes the natural rate of unemployment. Broadly speaking, when the economy experiences a recessionary gap, the actual unemployment rate exceeds the natural unemployment rate, so cyclical unemployment, $u - u^*$, is positive. When the economy experiences an expansionary gap, in contrast, the actual unemployment rate is lower than the natural rate, so cyclical unemployment is negative. This corresponds to a situation in which labour is being used more intensively than normal, so actual unemployment has dipped below its usual frictional, structural, and seasonal levels.

seasonal unemployment unemployment associated with the seasons and/or weather

cyclical unemployment the extra unemployment brought about by periods of recession

natural rate of unemployment (or u*) the part of the total unemployment rate that is attributable to frictional, structural, and seasonal unemployment; equivalently, the unemployment rate that prevails when cyclical unemployment is zero, so the economy has neither a recessionary nor an expansionary output gap

ECONOMIC NATURALIST 7.2

Soaring incarceration rates and the natural rate of unemployment

The percentage of the adult population locked up in prison or in jail, expressed in terms of prisoners to 1000 adults, is known as the incarceration rate. The United States has by far the highest incarceration rate among developed countries. The U.S. incarceration rate doubled between 1985 and 1998, and since then it has continued to grow, reaching almost 8 in 1000 adults in 2010. By comparison, comparable rate for Canada in 2010 was 0.9 per 1000 adults, or about one-tenth the U.S. rate.[2] About 90 percent of those incarcerated in the United States are men. The U.S. incarceration numbers are so dramatic they prompted two leading labour economists to look at the possible impact of the rising incarceration rate on the decline in the natural rate of unemployment among U.S. males since 1985.[3]

Prisoners are counted in neither the numerator (unemployed) nor the denominator (labour force = employed + unemployed) of the unemployment rate. Yet those in jail or prison are likely to have been unemployed prior to arrest and imprisonment. They are disproportionately high-school dropouts under 35 years or age, and like others in that demographic

category, when not in prison, they are prone to structural unemployment, a key component of the natural rate of unemployment.

What happens to the natural rate of unemployment when hundreds of thousands of men prone to structural unemployment are locked up behind bars? According to the calculations of the labour economists, the rising incarceration rate for U.S. males reduced the natural unemployment rate for U.S. males by 0.3 percentage points over a thirteen-year period.

The example of the impact of rising incarceration rates on the natural rate of unemployment for U.S. males illustrates that the natural rate of unemployment depends on social factors. Also, since a substantial fraction of the incarcerated were convicted of drug-related offences that would not be labelled criminal activity in some other countries, the rising incarceration rate in the United States illustrates that policies that reduce the natural rate of unemployment can actually be quite controversial.

OKUN'S LAW

What is the relationship between an output gap and the amount of cyclical unemployment in the economy? We have already observed that, by definition, cyclical unemployment is positive when the economy has a recessionary gap, negative when there is an expansionary gap, and zero when there is no output gap. A more quantitative relationship between cyclical unemployment and the output gap is given by a rule of thumb called *Okun's law*, after Arthur Okun, one of U.S. President John F. Kennedy's chief economic advisers. According to **Okun's law**, each extra percentage point of cyclical unemployment is associated with about a 2-percentage-point decrease in the output gap, measured in relation to potential output.[4] So, for example, if cyclical unemployment increases from 1 to 2 percent of the labour force, the recessionary gap will increase from 2 to 4 percent of potential GDP. Given an estimate of the natural rate of unemployment, Okun's law can be used to infer the value of the output gap. Conversely, given an estimate of the output gap, Okun's law can be used to infer the natural rate of unemployment, as is done in Example 7.1.

Okun's law states that each extra percentage point of cyclical unemployment is associated with about a 2-percentage-point decrease in the output gap, measured in relation to potential output

EXAMPLE **7.1**

Okun's law and Canada's output gap in 2010

In 2010, Canada was still suffering from an 8 percent unemployment rate as the economy recovered from the 2008-2009 recession. Both the Bank of Canada and

---

2 For Canadian incarceration rates, see Statistics Canada, CANSIM series v21536802.

3 See Lawrence Katz and Alan Krueger, "The High-Pressure U.S. Labor Market of the 1990s," *Brookings Papers on Economic Activity*, 1, 1999, pp. 1–88.

4 Mathematically, Okun's law can be expressed as $(Y - Y^*)/Y^* = -2(u - u^*)$. Okun's law as stated above is widely believed to apply to Canada and the United States today. However, the relationship between unemployment and output varies from country to country and from one historical period to another. When Arthur Okun first formulated his law in the 1960s, he suggested that each extra percentage point of U.S. unemployment was associated with about a 3-percentage-point increase in the output gap.

the International Monetary Fund (IMF) published statistics on Canada's output gap. These output gap estimates are shown in column 2 of the table below. We will use them to show that Okun's law can be used to calculate an approximate value of the natural rate of unemployment estimate implied by an output gap estimate.

1.	2.	3.	4.	5.	6.	7.	8.
Source	Output gap (2010 $, billions)	Actual GDP (2010 $, billions)	Potential GDP (2010 $, billions)	Percentage output gap	$u - u^*$ (percentage points)	Unemployment rate, u (%)	Implied natural rate of unemployment, u^* (%)
IMF	39.9	1621.5	1661.4	−2.4	1.2	8.0	6.8
Bank of Canada	29.7	1621.5	1651.2	−1.8	0.9	8.0	7.1

SOURCES: The IMF output gap estimate is from the World Economic Outlook Database, April 2011. The Bank of Canada output gap estimate is the average of the Bank of Canada's quarterly estimates of Canada's output gap as published at http://www.bankofcanada.ca/rates/indicators/capacity-and-inflation-pressures/ as of the 13 June 2011 update. Actual GDP and the actual unemployment rate are from Statistics Canada CANSIM series v646937 and v2062815 respectively.

Column 4 of the table gives the potential GDP estimate formed by adding the output gap estimate from column 2 to actual GDP from column 3. The entries for column 5 are derived by dividing the output gap estimates from column 2 by the corresponding potential GDP estimates from column 4 and multiplying by 100 percent to get the output gap as a percentage of GDP. Okun's law tells us that the percentage output gap is double the percentage-point gap between the actual unemployment rate and the natural rate. In other words, the gap between the actual and natural unemployment rates is half the percentage output gap. So entries in column 6 are derived by dividing the corresponding entries in column 5 by two (ignoring the minus sign). Subtracting the column 6 entries from the column 7 entries gives us the corresponding column 8 entries.

Column 8 indicates the natural rate of unemployment estimates that can be inferred by Okun's law from the output gap estimates in column 2. The lower the output gap estimate, the higher the implied natural rate of unemployment.

It should be noted that even the lowest estimate of the output gap in column 2 (the Bank of Canada one), $39.9 billion, points to the large size of the output losses resulting from recessions. In 2010, Canada had a population of about 34 million people. Hence the output loss per person in that year, according to the lowest estimate in column 2, equalled the output gap of $39.9 billion divided by 34 million people, or about $1174—more than $4694 for a family of four in 2010 dollars. The output losses were even larger, of course, in 2009 when the unemployment rate averaged 8.3 percent. These calculations demonstrate that output gaps and cyclical unemployment have significant costs.

It should also be noted that both the implied natural rates of unemployment stemming from the Bank of Canada and IMF output gap estimates are high compared to what some other economists would estimate as being the natural rate of unemployment for 2010. For example, if the natural rate of unemployment was actually 6 percent, not 6.8 or 7.1 percent, then the actual unemployment rate of 8 percent was 2 percentage points above the natural rate, and the percentage output gap was 4 percent, or almost $68 billion.

CYCLICAL UNEMPLOYMENT AND UNEMPLOYMENT DURATION

Most people find it plausible that if the Canadian unemployment rate soars, say, from 6.1 percent in August 2008 to 8.7 percent in August 2009 as the world economy goes into a global recession, then it is likely that most, if not all, of the rise in the unemployment rate is because of an increase in cyclical unemployment related to the recession. But unless they have some training in economics, people may not have a very good idea about how the rise in the unemployment rate takes place.

Most people recognize that when the economy goes into a recession there will be job losses as a result of businesses going bankrupt or laying off employees because their sales of the business are down. What people may not recognize is that the rise in the unemployment rate is due to factors in addition to job loss.

Remember from Chapter 5 that the working-age population is composed of the unemployed, the employed, and those not in the labour force. Even in the best of times, there will be people leaving employment and becoming unemployed because they lost or quit their jobs. There will also be working-age people (in Canada, those aged 15 and over) becoming unemployed who were previously not in the labour force; for example, full-time students who graduate and starting looking for employment but do not find it right away. What happens during the typical recession is not only that more people become unemployed because they have lost their jobs. What also happens is that during recessions jobs are harder to find and the typical unemployed person takes a longer time to find a job. So during a recession the flow into unemployment speeds up and the flow out of unemployment slows down.

A period during which an individual is continuously unemployed is called an unemployment spell; it begins when the worker becomes unemployed and ends when the worker either finds a job or leaves the labour force, (Remember, working-age people outside the labour force are not counted as unemployed.) The length of an unemployment spell is known as **unemployment duration**. The average duration of unemployment is typically measured in weeks. The duration of unemployment rises during recessions, reflecting the greater difficulty of finding work during those periods.

As Figure 7.6 shows, the average weeks of unemployment duration rose in Canada during and after the early 1990s recession, the 2000–2001 slowdown, and the 2008–2009 recession. From 2008 to 2010, for example, the average unemployment duration rose from 13.7 to 18.4 weeks. Incidentally, unemployment duration differs a lot by the age

unemployment duration the length of a period during which an individual is continuously unemployed

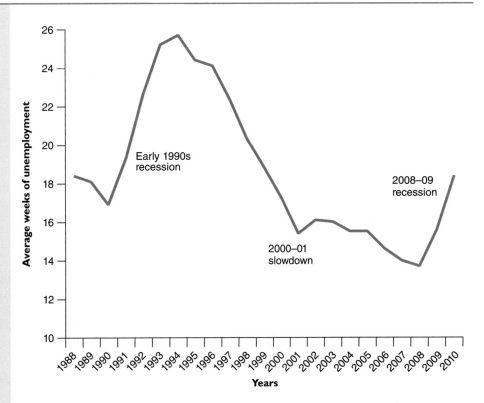

FIGURE 7.6

Average Duration of Unemployment in Canada, Weeks, 1988-2010
This figure shows the average weeks of unemployment in Canada over the years since 1988. The average unemployment duration (length of unemployment spell) increased during and after the early 1990s recession, the 2000–01 slowdown, and the 2008–09 recession. Note that the vertical axis begins at 10 weeks.
SOURCE: Adapted from the Statistics Canada, CANSIM series v2349178

of unemployed workers. In 2009, while the average unemployment spell was 18.4 weeks overall, it was highest for workers aged 55 to 64, for whom it was almost six months.

> **RECAP**
>
> ### OUTPUT GAPS, CYCLICAL UNEMPLOYMENT, AND OKUN'S LAW
>
> *Potential output* is the amount of output (real GDP) that an economy can produce when using its resources, such as capital and labour, at normal rates. The *output gap Y − Y** is the difference between actual output *Y* and potential output *Y**. When actual output is below potential, the resulting output gap is called a *recessionary gap*. When actual output is above potential, the difference is called an *expansionary gap*.
>
> The *natural rate of unemployment u** is the sum of the frictional, structural, and seasonal unemployment rates. It is the rate of unemployment that is observed when the economy is operating at a normal level, with no output gap.
>
> *Cyclical unemployment u-u** is the difference between the actual unemployment rate *u* and the natural rate of unemployment *u**. Cyclical unemployment is positive when there is a recessionary gap, negative when there is an expansionary gap and zero when there is no output gap.
>
> *Okun's law* relates cyclical unemployment and the output gap. According to this rule of thumb, each percentage point increase in cyclical unemployment is associated with about a two-percentage-point increase in the output gap, measured in relation to potential output.
>
> When cyclical unemployment rises in a recession, it is usually not just due to job losses in the economy. It also takes unemployed people longer to find jobs and therefore the length of the typical unemployment spell rises during recessions. Unemployment duration is usually measured in weeks.

7.4 WHY DO SHORT-TERM FLUCTUATIONS OCCUR? A PREVIEW AND A PARABLE

What causes periods of slowdown and expansion? In the previous section, we discussed two possible reasons. First, growth in potential output itself may slow down or speed up, reflecting changes in the growth rates of available capital and labour and in the pace of technological progress. Second, even if potential output is growing normally, actual output may be higher or lower than potential output; that is, expansionary or recessionary output gaps may develop.

We have not yet addressed the question of how output gaps can arise or what policy-makers should do in response. The causes and cures of output gaps will be a major topic of the next four chapters. Here is a brief preview of the main conclusions of those chapters:

1. In a world in which prices are adjusted immediately to balance the quantities supplied and demanded for all goods and services, output gaps might not exist. (See, however, the discussion below about this as possibly a sufficient condition as opposed to a necessary one.) But for many goods and services, the assumption that prices will adjust immediately is not realistic. Instead, many firms adjust the prices of their output only periodically. In particular, rather than changing prices with every variation in demand, firms tend to adjust to changes in demand in the short run by varying the quantity of output they produce and sell. This type of behaviour is known as "meeting the demand" at a preset price.

2. Because in the short-run firms tend to meet the demand for their output at preset prices, changes in the amount that customers decide to spend will affect output. When total spending is low for some reason, output may fall below potential output; conversely, when spending is high, output may rise above potential output. In other

words, *changes in economy-wide spending are the primary cause of output gaps.* Thus, government policies can help to eliminate output gaps by influencing total spending. For example, the government can affect total spending directly simply by changing its own level of purchases.

3. Although firms tend to meet demand in the short run, they will not be willing to do so indefinitely. If customer demand continues to differ from potential output, firms will eventually adjust their prices so as to eliminate output gaps. If demand exceeds potential output (an expansionary gap), firms will raise their prices aggressively, spurring inflation. If demand falls below potential output (a recessionary gap), firms will raise their prices less aggressively or even cut prices, reducing inflation.

4. Eventually price changes by firms and adjustments to wages may work to eliminate output gaps and bring production back into line with the economy's potential output. This process of adjustment is at best slow, however, so that in practice policy-makers, such as central bankers, often take action to speed up the elimination of output gaps.

These ideas will become clearer as we proceed through the next chapters. Before plunging into the details of the analysis, let's consider an example that, while it does not necessarily hold true for the overall economy, illustrates the links between spending and output.

Al's ice cream store produces gourmet ice cream on the premises and sells it directly to the public. What determines the amount of ice cream that Al produces on a daily basis? The productive capacity, or potential output, of the shop is one important factor. Specifically, Al's potential output of ice cream depends on the amount of capital (number of ice cream makers) and labour (number of workers) that he employs, and on the productivity of that capital and labour.

The main source of day-to-day variations in Al's ice cream production is fluctuations in the demand for ice cream by the public. How should Al react to these ebbs and flows in the demand for ice cream? The basic supply and demand model that we introduced in Chapter 3, if applied to the market for ice cream, would predict that the price of ice cream should change with every change in the demand for ice cream. But if Al raised prices in response to increased demand on a hot summer day, say, he could lose customers who would accuse him of "price gouging," raising prices in a way the customers interpret as being unfair (see Economic Naturalist 7.3).[5]

How, then, does Al the ice cream store manager actually deal with changes in the demand for ice cream? Observation suggests that he begins by setting prices based on the best information he has about the demand for his product and the costs of production. Perhaps he prints up a menu or makes a sign announcing the prices. Then, over a period of time, he will keep his prices fixed and serve as many customers as want to buy (up to the point where he runs out of ice cream or room in the store at these prices). This behaviour is what we call "meeting the demand" at preset prices, and it implies that *in the short run*, the amount of ice cream Al produces and sells is determined by the demand for his products.

However, with the passage of time, if the quantity of ice cream the public wants to consume exceeds what Al is able and willing to supply on a normal basis (his potential output in the short run), the situation is quite different.

One possibility is that Al could respond by raising his prices. At higher prices, Al will earn higher profits, and the higher prices will bring the quantity of ice cream demanded closer to Al's normal production capacity. Hiring more employees and expanding the store are other actions Al could take in response to such a situation. Such actions would result in an increase in Al's normal production capacity—a higher level of potential output.

This example illustrates in a simple way the links between spending and output, except, of course, that we must think of this story as applying to the whole economy, not to a single business. The key point is that changes in demand produce a series of responses

---

5 Note that the consequence of decision makers such as consumers, having concerns about fairness, is the sort of departure from narrowly rational behaviour studied by behavioural economics. Strictly "rational" consumers decide by comparing extra costs with extra benefits, not by worrying about whether the price is fair.

ECONOMIC NATURALIST   7.3

Why did the Coca-Cola Company test a vending machine that "knows" when the weather is hot?

According to *The New York Times* (28 October 1999) the Coca-Cola Company quietly tested a pop vending machine that included a temperature sensor. Why would Coca-Cola want a vending machine that "knows" when the weather is hot?

When the weather is hot, the demand for refreshing soft drinks rises, increasing their market-clearing price. To take advantage of this variation in consumer demand, the vending machines that Coca-Cola tested were equipped with a computer chip that gave them the capability to raise pop prices automatically when the temperature climbed. The company's chairman and chief executive, M. Douglas Ivester, described in an interview how the desire for a cold drink increases during a sports championship final held in the summer heat. "So it is fair that it should be more expensive," Mr. Ivester was quoted as saying. "The machine will simply make this process automatic." Company officials suggested numerous other ways in which vending machine prices could be made dependent on demand. For example, machines could be programmed to reduce prices during off-peak hours or at low-traffic machines.

In traditional vending machines, cold drinks are priced in a way analogous to the way Al prices his ice cream: a price is set, and demand is met at the preset price, until the machine runs out of pop. The weather-sensitive vending machine illustrates how technology may change pricing practices in the future. Indeed, increased computing power and access to the Internet have already allowed some firms, such as airline companies, to change prices almost continuously in response to variations in demand.

On the other hand, Coca-Cola's experiments with "smart" vending machines also illustrate the barriers to fully flexible pricing in practice. First, the new vending machines are more costly than the standard model. In deciding whether to use them, the company must decide whether the extra revenues from variable pricing justify the extra cost of the machines. Second, in early tests many consumers reacted negatively to the new machines, complaining that they take unfair advantage of thirsty customers. In practice, customer complaints and concerns about "fairness" make companies less willing to vary prices sensitively with changing demand.

from producers as time passes. At first, producers will typically choose not to change their prices but rather to meet demand at preset prices. Thus, Al's ice cream store enjoys a boom on an unusually hot day, when the demand for ice cream is strong, while an unseasonably cold day brings an ice cream recession. But with the passage of time, prices can adjust. Eventually firms may also add plant and equipment and hire additional workers.

One last point about this ice cream store parable: although macroeconomists argue that inflexibility of prices may be named as a *sufficient* condition to explain short-term economic fluctuations, many Keynesian macroeconomists would argue that it is not a *necessary* condition.[6] It would be an example of the *fallacy of composition* to suppose that because price flexibility eliminates output gaps in micro markets, such as the ice cream market, it would therefore also necessarily eliminate gaps between aggregate demand and aggregate supply at the macro level of the economy. Indeed, many Keynesian economists would argue that downward price flexibility can worsen a recession, as evidenced by the many economies, including Canada's, that experienced deflation without economic recovery during the Great Depression of the 1930s. Recall that in Chapter 6 we noted that deflation, a downward price flexibility at the macro level of the economy, typically has a negative impact on the economy and that central banks around the world therefore work to avoid deflation.

Looking ahead, in Chapters 8 and 9 we develop a short-run model for examining the situation where firms meet demand at preset prices. Chapters 10 and 11 present more complex models based upon a longer time frame.

---

6   See, for example, Greg Hill, "Letter: Misunderstanding Keynes," *The Economists' Voice*, February 2009, vol. 6, no. 4.

SUMMARY

■ Real GDP does not grow smoothly. Periods in which the economy is growing at a rate significantly below normal are called recessions; periods in which the economy is growing at a rate significantly above normal are called expansions. A severe or protracted recession, like the long decline that occurred between 1929 and 1933, is called a depression, while a particularly strong expansion is called a boom. **LO1**

■ The beginning of a recession is called the *peak,* because it represents the high point of economic activity prior to a downturn. The end of a recession, which marks the low point of economic activity prior to a recovery, is called the *trough*. Since the Second World War, Canadian recessions have been shorter on average than booms. **LO1**

■ Short-term economic fluctuations are irregular in length and severity and are thus hard to forecast. Expansions and recessions are typically felt throughout the economy and may even be global in scope. Unemployment rises sharply during recessions (the phenomenon of cyclical unemployment), while inflation tends to fall during or shortly after a recession. Durable goods industries tend to be particularly sensitive to recessions and booms, while services and non-durable goods industries are less sensitive. **LO2**

■ *Potential output,* also called potential GDP or full-employment output, is the amount of output (real GDP) that an economy can produce when it is using its resources, such as capital and labour, at normal rates. The difference between potential output and actual output is the *output gap*. When output is below potential, the gap is called a *recessionary gap;* when output is above potential, the difference is called an *expansionary gap*. Recessions can occur because potential output is growing unusually slowly, but typically occur because actual output is below potential. **LO3**

■ The *natural rate of unemployment* is the part of the total unemployment rate that is attributable to *frictional, structural,* and *seasonal unemployment*. Equivalently, the natural rate of unemployment is the rate of unemployment that exists when the output gap is zero. *Cyclical unemployment,* the part of unemployment that is associated with recessions and expansions, equals the total unemployment rate less the natural unemployment rate. Cyclical unemployment is related to the output gap by *Okun's law,* which states that each extra percentage point of cyclical unemployment is associated with about a 2-percentage-point increase in the output gap, measured in relation to potential output. When cyclical unemployment rises, it is typically associated with a rise in the length of the average unemployment spell. **LO5**

■ In the following chapters, our study of recessions and expansions will focus on the role of economy-wide spending. Changes in economy-wide spending produce a series of responses from producers as time passes. At first, producers will typically choose not to change their prices but rather to meet demand at preset prices. With the passage of time, however, prices can adjust. Eventually firms may add to their plant and equipment and hire additional workers. **LO6**

KEY TERMS

boom (156)
cyclical unemployment (162)
depression (153)
expansion (155)
expansionary gap (161)
frictional unemployment (161)

natural rate of unemployment (or u^*) (162)
Okun's law (163)
output gap (or $Y - Y^*$) (161)
peak (155)
potential output (or potential GDP or full-employment output or Y^*) (159)

recession (or contraction) (153)
recessionary gap (161)
seasonal unemployment (162)
structural unemployment (161)
trough (155)
unemployment duration (165)

REVIEW QUESTIONS

1. Define *recession* and *expansion*. What are the beginning and ending points of a recession called? In postwar Canada, which have been longer on average, recessions or expansions? **LO1, LO2**

2. Why is the traditional term, *business cycles*, a misnomer? How does your answer relate to the ease or difficulty of forecasting peaks and troughs? **LO2**

3. Which firm is likely to see its profits reduced the most in a recession: an automobile producer, a manufacturer of boots and shoes, or a barbershop? Which is likely to see its profits reduced by the least? Explain. **LO2**

4. List four broad types of unemployment and their causes. Which of these types is the least costly, economically? **LO4**

5. How is each of the following likely to be affected by a recession: the natural unemployment rate, the cyclical unemployment rate, the inflation rate? **LO2, LO4**

6. Define *potential output*. Is it possible for an economy to produce an amount greater than potential output? Explain. **LO3**

7. True or false, and explain: When output equals potential output, the unemployment rate is zero. **LO5**

8. If the natural rate of unemployment is 5 percent, what is the overall rate of unemployment if output is 2 percent below potential output? What if output is 2 percent above potential output? **LO5**

9. True or false, and explain: The length of unemployment spells is particularly long for workers in the age group of 15–25 years old. **LO5**

PROBLEMS

1. Given below are data on real GDP and estimates of potential GDP for Canada prepared by the IMF. For each year, calculate the output gap as a percentage of potential GDP, and state whether the gap is a recessionary gap or an expansionary gap, according to the IMF. Also, calculate the year-to-year growth rates of real GDP. **LO1**

Year	Real GDP (2002 $, billions)	Potential GDP (2002 $, billions)
2004	1211	1198
2005	1248	1230
2006	1283	1261
2007	1311	1290
2008	1318	1317
2009	1286	1337
2010	1325	1358

2. Back in 2000, the Canadian unemployment rate averaged 6.8 percent and current dollar GDP reached $1056 billion (or $1.056 trillion). Pierre Fortin, a leading Canadian macroeconomist affiliated with the Université du Québec à Montréal, had estimated Canada's natural rate of unemployment for 2000 as being 5.3 percent. By contrast, one could infer an estimate of a natural rate of unemployment of about 7 percent from official Bank of Canada statements, such as the Bank's claim that the Canadian economy was operating with an expansionary gap for most of 2000 (when the actual unemployment rate was around 6.8 percent in most months).

Using Okun's law, what would be the potential GDP number for 2000 corresponding to a natural unemployment rate of 5.3 percent? What would be the dollar value of the recessionary gap? Also, what would be the potential GDP number corresponding to a natural rate of 7 percent? What would be the dollar value of the expansionary gap? **LO3**

3. Using Okun's law, fill in the four pieces of missing data in the following table. That is, replace (1), (2), (3), and (4) with correct data. **LO3**

Year	Real GDP	Potential GDP	Natural unemployment rate (%)	Actual unemployment rate (%)
2009	7840	8000	(1)	6
2010	8100	(2)	5	5
2011	(3)	8200	4.5	4
2012	8415	8250	5	(4)

ANSWERS TO IN-CHAPTER EXERCISES

7.1   The answer depends on current data. **LO1, LO2**

Practise and learn online with Connect.

CHAPTER 8
Spending and Output in the Short Run

When one of the authors of this book was a small boy, he used to spend some time every summer with his grandparents. A favourite activity of his during these visits was to spend a summer evening on the front porch with his grandmother, listening to her stories.

The early years of Grandma's marriage covered the worst part of the Great Depression. In one of her reminiscences, she remarked that in the 1930s it had been a satisfaction to her to be able to buy her children a new pair of shoes every year. In the town where she and her family lived, many children had to wear their shoes until they fell apart. Her grandson thought this was scandalous: "Why didn't their parents just buy them new shoes?" he demanded.

"They couldn't," said Grandma. "They didn't have the money. Most of the fathers had lost their jobs because of the Depression."

"What kind of jobs did they have?"

"They worked in the shoe factories, which had to close down."

"Why did the factories close down?"

"Because," Grandma explained, "nobody had any money to buy shoes."

The grandson was only 6 or 7 years old at the time, but even he could see that there was something badly wrong with Grandma's logic. On the one side were boarded-up shoe factories and shoe workers with no jobs; on the other, children without shoes. Why couldn't the shoe factories just open and produce the shoes the children so badly needed? Grandma just shrugged and said it didn't work that way.

The story of the closed-down shoe factories illustrates in a microcosm the cost to society of a recessionary gap. In an economy with a recessionary gap, available resources that could be used to produce valuable goods and services are instead allowed to lie fallow. This waste of resources lowers the economy's output and standard of living, compared to its potential.

Grandma's account also suggests how such an unfortunate situation might come about. Suppose factory owners and other producers, being reluctant to accumulate unsold goods on their shelves, produce just enough output to satisfy the demand for their products. And suppose that, for some reason, the public's willingness or ability to spend declines. If spending declines, factories will respond by cutting their production (because they don't want to produce goods they can't sell) and by laying off workers who are no longer needed. And because the workers who are laid off will lose most of their income—a particularly serious loss in the 1930s, in the days before government-sponsored employment insurance—they must drastically reduce their own spending. As their spending declines, factories will reduce their production again, laying off more workers, who in turn reduce their spending, and so on, in a vicious circle. In this scenario, the problem is not a lack of productive capacity, as the factories have not lost their ability to produce, but rather, *insufficient spending* to support the normal level of production.

The idea that a decline in aggregate spending may cause output to fall below potential output was one of the key insights of John Maynard Keynes (1883–1946), who was mentioned in Chapter 1 along with Adam Smith and Alfred Marshall as a key figure in the development of economics. The goal of this chapter is to develop a model of how recessions and expansions may arise from fluctuations in aggregate spending, along the lines first suggested by Keynes. This model, which we call the *basic Keynesian model*, is also known as the *Keynesian cross*, after the diagram that is used to illustrate the theory. In the body of the chapter we will emphasize a numerical and graphical approach to the basic Keynesian model. Appendix 8A to this chapter provides a more general algebraic analysis.

We will begin with a brief discussion of the key assumption of the basic Keynesian model. We will then turn to the important concept of total, or aggregate, *planned spending* in the economy. We will show how, in the short run, planned spending helps to determine the level of output, which can be greater than or less than potential output. In other words, depending on the level of spending, the economy may develop an output gap. "Too little" spending leads to a recessionary output gap, while "too much" creates an expansionary output gap.

An implication of the basic Keynesian model is that government policies that affect the level of spending can be used to reduce or eliminate output gaps. Policies used in this way are called *stabilization policies*. Keynes himself argued for the active use of fiscal policy—policy relating to government spending and taxes—to eliminate output gaps and stabilize the economy. In the latter part of this chapter, we will show why Keynes thought fiscal policy could help to stabilize the economy, and we will discuss the usefulness of fiscal policy as a stabilization tool. Fiscal policy has been the subject of especially heated debates since the onset of the global recession in 2008. In Canada, the use of fiscal policy measures by the federal government to combat the recession has been called Canada's Economic Action Plan.

As we indicated in Chapter 7, the basic Keynesian model is a somewhat simplified model of the economy. It is geared towards showing how an economy suffering from a recessionary gap can raise actual output to the level of potential output. And it is a static model in two respects. First, it treats prices as fixed—firms do not adjust their prices but instead meet the demand forthcoming at preset prices. In other words, a situation of zero inflation is assumed. Second, it treats the level of potential output as fixed. That is, the model deals only with that part of real-world growth that comes about from increasing actual output to its potential level. This means, for example, that fiscal policy is assumed to impact only on actual output and not on potential output, and that the impact of private-sector or government investment on potential output is ignored.

Nevertheless, the basic Keynesian model is a useful one for understanding macroeconomic developments, including macroeconomic commentary in the news media. It is also a key building block of current theories of short-run economic fluctuations and stabilization policies. In subsequent chapters, we will extend the basic Keynesian model to incorporate inflation and other important features of the economy.

John Maynard Keynes
(1883–1946)

8.1 THE KEYNESIAN MODEL'S CRUCIAL ASSUMPTION: FIRMS MEET DEMAND AT PRESET PRICES

The basic Keynesian model is built on a key assumption, highlighted in Box 8.1. This assumption is that firms do not continuously change their prices as supply and demand conditions change; rather, over short periods, firms tend to keep their prices fixed and *meet the demand* that is forthcoming at those prices. As we will see, the assumption that firms vary their production in order to meet demand at preset prices implies that fluctuations in spending will have powerful effects on the nation's real GDP.

BOX 8.1

Key Assumption of the Basic Keynesian Model

In the short run, firms meet the demand for their products at preset prices. Firms do not respond to every change in the demand for their products by changing their prices. Instead, they typically set a price for some period and then *meet the demand* at that price. By meeting the demand, we mean that firms produce just enough to satisfy their customers at the prices that have been set.

The assumption that over short periods of time firms will meet the demand for their products at preset prices is generally realistic. Think of the stores where you shop: the price of a pair of jeans does not fluctuate with the number of customers who enter the store or the latest news about the price of denim. Instead, the store posts a price and sells jeans to any customer who wants to buy at that price, at least until the store runs out of stock.

Firms like these do not change their prices frequently, because doing so would be costly. Economists refer to the costs of changing prices as **menu costs**. The clothing store faces the cost of re-marking all its merchandise if the manager changes prices. But menu costs may also include other kinds of costs, including, for example, the cost of doing a market survey to determine what price to charge and the cost of informing customers about price changes.

menu costs the costs of changing prices

Menu costs will not prevent firms from changing their prices indefinitely. As we saw in Chapter 7, in the case of Al's ice cream store, too great an imbalance between demand and supply, as reflected by a difference between sales and potential output, will eventually lead to a change in price. If no one is buying jeans, for example, at some point the clothing store will mark down its jeans prices. Like other economic decisions, the decision to change prices reflects a *cost–benefit comparison*: prices will be changed if the benefit of doing so, the fact that sales will be brought more nearly into line with the firm's normal production capacity, outweighs the menu costs associated with making the change. As we have stressed, the basic Keynesian model developed in this chapter disregards that prices will eventually adjust, and should therefore be interpreted as applying to the short run.

COST-BENEFIT

8.2 PLANNED AGGREGATE EXPENDITURE

In the Keynesian theory discussed in this chapter, output at each point in time is determined by the amount that people want to spend—what economists call *planned aggregate expenditure*.[1] Specifically, **planned aggregate expenditure (*PAE*)** is total planned

planned aggregate expenditure (*PAE*) total planned spending on final goods and services

---

1 Not all economists and economics textbooks use the term "planned aggregate expenditure." Economists use a variety of synonyms for this concept, with "aggregate expenditure" probably being the most commonly used alternative. Even within this chapter we will sometimes use synonyms for planned aggregate expenditure, such as "planned spending."

spending on final goods and services. Sometimes in economics, total planned spending is called total desired spending.

The four components of total, or aggregate, spending on final goods and services were introduced in Chapter 5:

1. *Consumer expenditure,* or simply *consumption* (*C*), is spending by households on final goods and services. Examples of consumer expenditure are spending on food, clothes, and entertainment, and on consumer durable goods like automobiles and furniture.

2. *Private-sector investment* (*I*) is spending by firms on new capital goods, such as office buildings, factories, and equipment. Spending on new houses and apartment buildings (residential investment) and changes in inventories (inventory investment) are also included. Recall from Chapter 5 that *I* refers to newly created goods, *not* to purchases of financial assets like stocks and bonds.

3. *Government purchases* (*G*) refers to spending by governments (federal, provincial, and municipal) on goods and services. Examples of government purchases include new schools and hospitals, roads, computers, office supplies, military equipment, and the services of public-sector employees, such as teachers, nurses, government office workers, police, and armed forces personnel. Recall from Chapter 5 that government transfer payments, such as Canada Pension Plan and employment insurance benefits, and interest on the public debt are not included in government purchases.

4. *Net exports* (*NX*) equals exports minus imports. Exports are sales of domestically produced goods and services to foreigners; imports are purchases by domestic residents of goods and services produced abroad. Net exports represent the net demand for domestic goods by foreigners.

Some textbooks use the term "investment" rather than "private-sector investment" when referring to *I*, spending by firms on new capital goods, etc. But this can be misleading, because statistical agencies such as Statistics Canada classify a component of government purchases (*G*) as government investment. In other words, there are two types of investment in GDP, private-sector investment and government investment, and *I* only refers to the private-sector type.

Also, some textbooks use the term government expenditures rather than government purchases to refer to *G*, spending by government on goods and services. This can be misleading because government expenditures is widely used to refer to the total of all spending by governments. For example, when we discussed the government budget balance in Chapter 4, we described it as the difference between government expenditures and government revenues. In this commonly used sense, government expenditures includes government transfer payments and government interest payments on government debt, neither of which are included in *G*. In other words, government purchases (*G*) are a subset of what is widely known as government expenditures.

Together these four types of spending—by households, firms, the government, and the rest of the world—sum to total, or aggregate, spending.

PLANNED SPENDING VERSUS ACTUAL SPENDING

In the Keynesian model, output is determined by planned aggregate expenditure, or planned spending for short. Could *planned* spending ever differ from *actual* spending? The answer is yes. The most important case is that of a firm that sells either less or more of its product than expected. As was noted in Chapter 5, additions to the stock of goods sitting in a firm's warehouse are treated in the GDP accounts as inventory investment by the firm. In effect, the GDP accounts are based on the assumption that the firm buys its unsold inventory from itself. The inventory is then counted as part of the firm's investment spending.[2]

---

2 For the purposes of measuring GDP, treating unsold output as being purchased by its producer has the virtue of ensuring that actual production and actual expenditure are equal.

Suppose, then, that a firm's actual sales are less than expected so that part of what it had planned to sell remains in the warehouse. In this case, the firm's actual investment, including the unexpected increases in its inventory, is greater than its planned investment, which did not include added inventory. Suppose we agree to let I^p equal the firm's planned investment, including planned inventory investment. A firm that sells less of its output than planned, and, therefore, adds more to its inventory than planned, will find that its actual investment (including unplanned inventory investment) exceeds its planned investment so that $I > I^p$.

What about a firm that sells more of its output than expected? In that case, the firm will add less to its inventory than planned, so actual investment will be less than planned investment, or $I < I^p$.

Because firms that are meeting the demand for their product or service at preset prices cannot control how much they sell, their actual investment (including inventory investment) may well differ from their planned investment. However, for households, the government, and foreign purchasers, we may reasonably assume that actual spending and planned spending are the same. Thus, from now on we will assume that for consumption, government purchases, and net exports, actual spending equals planned spending.

With these assumptions, we can define planned aggregate expenditure by the equation

$$PAE = C + I^p + G + NX. \tag{8.1}$$

Equation 8.1 says that planned aggregate expenditure is the sum of planned spending by households, firms, governments, and foreigners. We use a superscript p to distinguish planned investment spending by firms, I^p, from actual private-sector investment spending, I. However, because planned spending equals actual spending for households, the government, and foreigners, we do not need to use superscripts for consumption, government purchases, or net exports.

CONSUMER SPENDING AND THE ECONOMY

The largest component of planned aggregate expenditure, about 56 percent of Canadian GDP in recent years, is consumption spending, or C. What determines how much people plan to spend on consumer goods and services in a given period? While many factors may be relevant, a particularly important determinant of the amount people plan to consume is their *disposable income*. **Disposable income** refers to income that includes the addition of transfers (such as employment insurance benefits) and the deduction of taxes (such as employment insurance premiums). All else being equal, households and individuals with higher disposable incomes will consume more than those with lower disposable incomes. Keynes himself stressed the importance of disposable income in determining household consumption decisions, claiming it a "psychological law," that people would tie their spending closely to their incomes.

Disposable income of the private sector is the total production of the economy, Y, less *net taxes*. **Net taxes** refers to taxes minus transfers, including both government transfer payments, such as Canada Pension Plan benefits, and interest on the public debt. So, all else being equal, we can assume that consumption spending (C) increases as *disposable income* ($Y - T$) increases. As already mentioned, other factors may also affect consumption, such as the real interest rate. For now we will ignore those other factors, returning to some of them later.

Note that, although economists sometimes refer to disposable income as after-tax income, this use of the term *after-tax income* can be misleading, because it indicates only the deduction of taxes from income and ignores the addition of transfers to income. Precisely speaking, disposable income is after-taxes-and-transfers income.

disposable income refers to income that includes the addition of transfers and the deduction of taxes

net taxes refers to taxes minus transfers

An equation that captures the link between consumption and disposable income is

$$C = \overline{C} + mpc\,(Y - T). \tag{8.2}$$

This equation, which we will dissect in a moment, is known as a *consumption function*. A **consumption function** relates consumption spending to its determinants, such as disposable income.

Let's look at this consumption function, Equation 8.2, more carefully. The right side of the equation contains two terms, $\overline{C}$ and $mpc\,(Y - T)$. The first term, $\overline{C}$, is a constant term in the equation that is intended to capture factors *other than disposable income* which affect consumption. For example, suppose consumers were to become more optimistic about the future so that they desire to consume more and save less at any given level of their current disposable incomes. An increase in desired consumption at any given level of disposable income would be represented in the consumption function, Equation 8.2, as an increase in the term $\overline{C}$.

We can imagine other factors that may affect the term $\overline{C}$ in the consumption function. For example, suppose there is a boom in the stock market or a sharp increase in house prices making consumers feel wealthier and, thus, more inclined to spend, for a given level of current disposable income. This effect could be captured by assuming that $\overline{C}$ increases. Likewise, a fall in house or stock prices that made consumers feel poorer and less inclined to spend would be represented by a decrease in $\overline{C}$. Economists refer to the effect of changes in asset prices on household wealth and, thus, on their consumption spending as the **wealth effect** of changes in asset prices.

Over the past couple of decades, economists have paid greater attention to the wealth effect due to the importance of *asset price bubbles*. An asset can be financial such as corporate shares or real such as housing or real estate. An **asset price bubble** is said to occur when the price of a financial or real asset or asset category rises much more rapidly than prices in general, and by much more than can be explained by fundamental demand or supply-side factors. Asset price bubbles are usually difficult to identify with absolute certainty as they are unfolding, but, for example, it is usually seen as possible sign of an asset price bubble in apartment buildings if the prices of apartment buildings are rising much more rapidly than the rents that can be earned from owning the apartment buildings. It is usually seen as an asset price bubble in some category of corporate stocks if the prices of the stocks are rising much more rapidly than the earnings of the corporations. Asset price bubbles are typically followed by asset price crashes. The asset price bubbles produce a positive wealth effect, but the asset price crashes produce a negative wealth effect.

The boom in the Canadian economy in the late 1990s was partly due to the positive wealth effect of the soaring stock prices of the information technology companies, such as Nortel, following the so-called dot.com stock market bubble. The 2000–01 slowdown in the Canadian economy was partly due to negative wealth effect produced by the collapse of stock prices when the dot.com bubble burst. The wealth effect is also important for understanding Japan's late 1980s boom and 1900s bust, as well as the global recession of 2008–09, which was partly due to bursting housing bubbles in many countries, particularly the United States.

The second term on the right side of Equation 8.2, $mpc\,(Y - T)$, reflects the effect of disposable income $Y - T$ on consumption. The parameter mpc, a fixed number, is called the *marginal propensity to consume*. The **marginal propensity to consume (mpc)**, is the amount by which consumption rises when current disposable income rises by \$1. Presumably, if people receive an extra dollar of income, they will consume part of the dollar and save the rest. In other words, their consumption will increase but by less than the full dollar of extra income. Thus, we assume that the marginal propensity to consume is greater than 0 (an increase in income leads to an increase in consumption), but less than 1 (the increase in consumption will be less than the full increase in income). These assumptions can be written symbolically as $0 < mpc < 1$.

It is important to recognize that the marginal propensity to consume will generally differ from the *average propensity to consume*. The **average propensity to consume** is calculated by dividing consumption by disposable income.[3] Whereas the marginal propensity to consume is the change in consumption brought about by a change in disposable income, the average propensity to consume is the proportion of all disposable income that is devoted to consumption. The average-marginal distinction, important for understanding the output decisions of firms (see Chapter 1), is also important for understanding the consumption function. For our present purposes, it is the marginal propensity to consume that is the most relevant concept, not the average propensity to consume.

Figure 8.1 shows a hypothetical consumption function, with consumption spending (*C*) on the vertical axis and disposable income ($Y - T$) on the horizontal axis. The intercept of the consumption function on the vertical axis equals the constant term, $\overline{C}$, and the slope of the consumption function equals the marginal propensity to consume, *mpc*.

To see how this consumption function fits reality, compare Figure 8.1 to Figure 8.2, which shows the relationship between aggregate real consumption expenditures and real personal disposable income in Canada for the period 1981 through 2009. In Figure 8.2, a scatter plot, each point on the graph corresponds to a year between 1981 and 2009 (selected years are indicated in the figure). The position of each point is determined by the combination of consumption and personal disposable income associated with that year. As you can see, higher disposable income implies higher consumption.

PLANNED AGGREGATE EXPENDITURE AND OUTPUT

Think back to Grandma's reminiscences recounted in the chapter opening, and recall that an important element of her story involved the links among production, income, and spending. As the shoe factories in Grandma's town reduced production, the incomes of both factory workers and factory owners fell. Workers' incomes fell as the number of hours of work per week were reduced (a common practice during the Depression), workers were laid off, or wages were cut. Factory owners' income fell as profits declined. Reduced incomes, in turn, forced both workers and owners to curtail their spending, which led to still lower production and further reductions in income. This vicious circle led the economy further and further into recession.

The logic of Grandma's story has two key elements: (1) declines in production, which imply declines in the income received by producers, lead to reduced spending; and

average propensity to consume (APC) consumption divided by disposable income

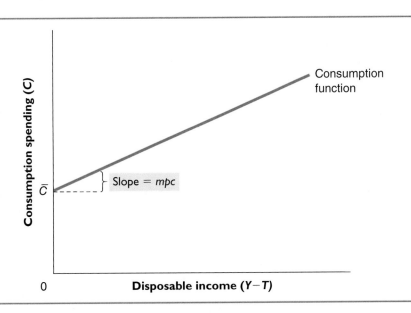

FIGURE 8.1
A Consumption Function
The consumption function relates households' consumption spending, *C* to disposable income, $Y - T$. The vertical intercept of this consumption function is $\overline{C}$, and the slope of the line equals the marginal propensity to consume, *mpc*.

3 The average propensity to consume (APC) can be written as APC = $[\overline{C} + mpc(Y - T)]/(Y - T)$.

FIGURE 8.2
The Canadian Consumption Function, 1981–2009
Each point on this figure represents a combination of aggregate personal expenditure and aggregate personal disposable income for a specific year between 1981 and 2009. Note the strong positive relationship between personal expenditure (consumption) and personal disposable income.
SOURCE: Adapted from the Statistics Canada CANSIM series v646938 and v691566.

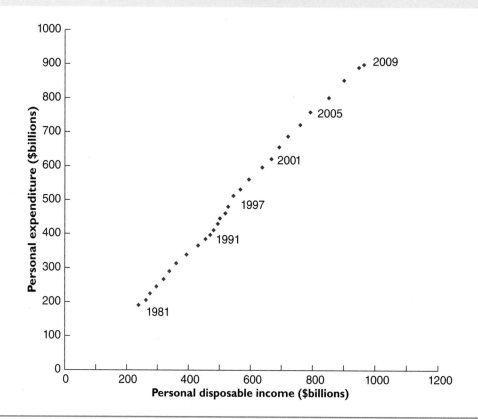

(2) reductions in spending lead to declines in production and income. In this section, we look at the first part of the story, the effects of production and income on spending. We return later in this chapter to the effects of spending on production and income.

Why do changes in production and income affect planned aggregate spending? The consumption function, which relates consumption to disposable income, is the basic source of this relationship. Because consumption spending C is a large part of planned aggregate expenditure, and because consumption depends on output Y, aggregate spending as a whole depends on output. Example 8.1 illustrates this relationship numerically.

EXAMPLE **8.1**

Linking planned aggregate expenditure to output

In a particular economy, the consumption function is

$$C = 620 + 0.8\,(Y - T),$$

so that the intercept term in the consumption function $\overline{C}$, equals 620, and the marginal propensity to consume, mpc, equals 0.8. Also, suppose that we are given that planned private-sector investment spending $I^P = 220$, government purchases $G = 300$, net exports $NX = 20$, and net taxes $T = 250$.

Write a numerical equation linking planned aggregate expenditure *PAE* to output *Y*. How does planned spending change when output, and hence income, change?

Recall the definition of planned aggregate expenditure, Equation 8.1:

$$PAE = C + I^p + G + NX.$$

To find a numerical equation for planned aggregate expenditure, we need to find numerical expressions for each of its four components. The first component of spending, consumption, is defined by the consumption function, $C = 620 + 0.8(Y - T)$. Since net taxes $T = 250$, we can substitute for T to write the consumption function as $C = 620 + 0.8(Y - 250)$. Now plug this expression for C into the definition of planned aggregate expenditure above to get

$$PAE = [620 + 0.8\,(Y - 250)] + I^p + G + NX,$$

where we have just replaced C by its value as determined by the consumption function. Similarly, we can substitute the given numerical values of planned private-sector investment I^p, government purchases G, and net exports NX into the definition of planned aggregate expenditure to get

$$PAE = [620 + 0.8\,(Y - 250)] + 220 + 300 + 20.$$

To simplify this equation, first note that $0.8(Y - 250) = 0.8Y - 200$, then add all the terms that don't depend on output *Y*. The result is

$$PAE = (620 - 200 + 220 + 300 + 20) + 0.8Y$$
$$= 960 + 0.8Y.$$

The final expression shows the relationship between planned aggregate expenditure and output in this numerical example. Note that, according to this equation, a $1 increase in *Y* leads to an increase in *PAE* of (0.8) ($1), or 80 cents. The reason for this is that the marginal propensity to consume, *mpc*, in this example is 0.8. Hence a $1 increase in income raises consumption spending by 80 cents. Since consumption is a component of total planned spending, total spending rises by 80 cents as well.

The solution to Example 8.1 illustrates a general point: planned aggregate expenditure can be divided into two parts, a part that depends on output (*Y*) and a part that is independent of output. The portion of planned aggregate expenditure that is independent of output is called **autonomous expenditure**. In Example 8.1, autonomous expenditure is the constant term in the equation for planned aggregate expenditure, or 960. This portion of planned spending, being a fixed number, does not vary when output varies. By contrast, the portion of planned aggregate expenditure that depends on output (*Y*) is called **induced expenditure**. In Example 8.1, induced expenditure equals 0.8*Y*, the second term in the expression for planned aggregate expenditure. Note that the numerical value of induced expenditure depends, by definition, on the numerical value taken by output. Autonomous expenditure and induced expenditure together equal planned aggregate expenditure.

autonomous expenditure the portion of planned aggregate expenditure that is independent of output

induced expenditure the portion of planned aggregate expenditure that depends on output, *Y*

RECAP

PLANNED AGGREGATE EXPENDTURE

Planned aggregate expenditure (PAE) is total planned spending on final goods and services. The four components of planned aggregate expenditure are consumer expenditure (*C*), planned private-sector investment (*I^p*), government purchases (*G*), and net exports (*NX*). Planned investment differs from actual investment when firms' sales are different from what they expected so that additions to inventory (a component of private-sector investment) are different from what firms anticipated.

> The largest component of planned aggregate expenditure is consumer expenditure, or simply consumption. Consumption depends on disposable income, $Y - T$. The slope of the consumption function equals the marginal propensity to consume, *mpc*. The *marginal propensity to consume*, a number between 0 and 1, is the amount by which consumption rises when disposable income rises by $1.
>
> Increases in output, which imply increases in income, cause consumption to rise. As consumption is part of planned aggregate expenditure, planned aggregate expenditure depends on output as well. The portion of planned aggregate expenditure that depends on output, and hence is determined within the model, is called *induced expenditure*. The portion of planned aggregate expenditure determined outside the model is *autonomous expenditure*.

SHORT-RUN EQUILIBRIUM OUTPUT

Now that we have defined planned aggregate expenditure and seen how it is related to output, the next task is to determine what output will be. Recall the assumption of the basic Keynesian model: that in the short run, producers leave prices at preset levels and simply meet the demand at those prices. In other words, during the short-run period in which prices are preset, firms produce an amount that is equal to planned aggregate expenditure. Accordingly, we define **short-run equilibrium output** as the level of output at which output Y equals planned aggregate expenditure, *PAE*:

short-run equilibrium output the level of output at which output Y equals planned aggregate expenditure; the level of output that prevails during the period in which prices are predetermined

$$Y = PAE. \tag{8.3}$$

Short-run equilibrium output is the level of output that prevails during the period in which prices are predetermined.

We can find the short-run equilibrium output for the economy described in Example 8.1 using Table 8.1. Column 1 in the table gives some possible values for short-run equilibrium output. To find the correct one, we must compare each to the value of planned aggregate expenditure at that output level. Column 2 shows the value of planned spending corresponding to the values of output in column 1. Recall that in Example 8.1, planned spending is determined by the equation

$$PAE = 960 + 0.8Y.$$

Because consumption rises with output, planned aggregate expenditure (which includes consumption) rises also. But if you compare columns 1 and 2, you will see that

TABLE 8.1
Numerical Determination of Short-Run Equilibrium Output

(1) Output Y	(2) Planned aggregate expenditure $PAE = 960 + 0.8Y$	(3) $Y - PAE$	(4) $Y = PAE?$
4000	4160	−160	No
4200	4320	−120	No
4400	4480	−80	No
4600	4640	−40	No
4800	4800	0	Yes
5000	4960	40	No
5200	5120	80	No

when output rises by 200, planned spending rises by only 160. That is, because the marginal propensity to consume in this economy is 0.8, each dollar in added income raises consumption and planned aggregate expenditure by 80 cents.

Again, short-run equilibrium output is the level of output at which $Y = PAE$, or equivalently, $Y - PAE = 0$. Looking at Table 8.1, we can see that there is only one level of output that satisfies that condition, $Y = 4800$. At that level, output and planned aggregate expenditure are precisely equal, so the producers are just meeting the demand.

In this economy, what would happen if output happened to differ from its equilibrium value of 4800? Suppose, for example, that output were 4000. Looking at column 2 of Table 8.1, we can see that when output is 4000, planned aggregate expenditure equals 960 + 0.8(4000), or 4160. Thus, if output is 4000, firms are not producing enough to meet the demand. They will find that as sales exceed the amounts they are producing, their inventories of finished goods are being depleted by 160 per year, and that actual private-sector investment is less than planned private-sector investment. Under the assumption that firms are committed to meeting their customers' demand, firms will respond by expanding their production.

Would expanding production to 4160, the level of planned aggregate expenditure firms faced when output was 4000, be enough? The answer is no, because of induced expenditure. That is, as firms expand their output, aggregate income (wages and profits) rises with it, which in turn leads to higher levels of consumption. Indeed, if output expands to 4160, planned aggregate expenditure will increase as well, to 960 + 0.8(4160), or 4288. So an output level of 4160 will still be insufficient to meet demand. As Table 8.1 shows, output will not be sufficient to meet planned aggregate expenditure until it expands to its short-run equilibrium value of 4800.

What if output were initially greater than its equilibrium value—say, 5000? From Table 8.1 we can see that when output equals 5000, planned aggregate expenditure equals only 4960—less than what firms are producing. So at an output level of 5000, firms will not sell all they produce and will find that their merchandise is piling up on store shelves and in warehouses (actual investment is greater than planned investment). In response, firms will cut their production runs and lay off personnel (who would then cut their spending). As Table 8.1 shows, firms will have to reduce production to its equilibrium value of 4800 before output just matches planned aggregate expenditure.

EXERCISE 8.1

Construct a table like Table 8.1 for an economy like the one we have been working with, assuming that the consumption function is $C = 820 + 0.7 (Y - T)$ and that $I^P = 600$, $G = 600$, $NX = 200$, and $T = 600$.
What is short-run equilibrium output in this economy? (Hint: Try using values for output above 5000.)

Short-run equilibrium output can also be determined graphically, as Example 8.2 shows.

EXAMPLE 8.2

Finding short-run equilibrium output (graphical approach)

Using a graphical approach, find short-run equilibrium output for the economy described in Example 8.1.

Figure 8.3 shows the graphical determination of short-run equilibrium output for the economy described in Example 8.1. Output Y is plotted on the horizontal axis and planned aggregate expenditure PAE on the vertical axis. The figure contains two lines, one of which is a 45° line extending from the origin. In general, a 45° line from the origin includes the points at which the variable on the vertical axis equals the variable on the horizontal axis. In this case, the 45° line represents the equation $Y = PAE$.

FIGURE 8.3
Determination of Short-Run Equilibrium Output (Keynesian Cross)
The 45° line represents the short-run equilibrium condition $Y = PAE$. The line $PAE = 960 + 0.8Y$, referred to as the expenditure line, shows the relationship of planned aggregate expenditure to output. Short-run equilibrium output (4800) is determined at the intersection of the two lines, point E. This and subsequent Keynesian cross diagrams in this textbook are not drawn to scale.

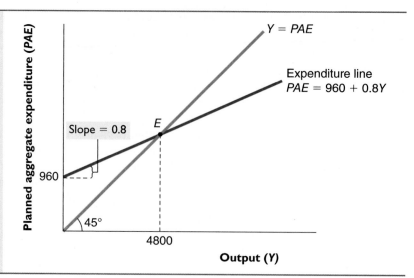

Recall that short-run equilibrium output must satisfy the condition $Y = PAE$. So we know that the value of short-run equilibrium output must lie somewhere on the $Y = PAE$ line.

The second line in Figure 8.3, less steep than the 45° line, shows the relationship between planned aggregate expenditure PAE and output Y. Because it summarizes how total expenditure depends on output, we will call this line the *expenditure line*. In this example, we know that the relationship between planned aggregate expenditure and output (the equation for the expenditure line) is

$$PAE = 960 + 0.8Y.$$

According to this equation, when $Y = 0$, the value of PAE is 960. Thus 960 is the intercept of the expenditure line, as shown in Figure 8.3. The slope of the line relating aggregate demand to output is 0.8, the value of the coefficient of output in the equation $PAE = 960 + 0.8Y$. Where does the number 0.8 come from? (*Hint:* What determines the amount by which aggregate spending increases when output rises by a dollar?)

Only one point in Figure 8.3 is consistent with both the definition of short-run equilibrium output, $Y = PAE$, and the given relationship between planned aggregate expenditure and output, $PAE = 960 + 0.8Y$. That point is the intersection of the two lines, point E. At point E, short-run equilibrium output equals 4800, which is the same value that we obtained using Table 8.1. Notice that at points to the right of E, output exceeds planned aggregate expenditure. Hence, to the right of point E, firms will be producing more than they can sell and will tend to reduce their production. Similarly, to the left of point E, planned aggregate expenditure exceeds output. In that region, firms will not be producing enough to meet demand and will tend to increase their production. Only at point E, where output equals 4800, will firms be producing enough to just satisfy planned spending on goods and services.

The diagram in Figure 8.3 is often called the *Keynesian cross*, after its characteristic shape. The Keynesian cross shows graphically how short-run equilibrium output is determined in a world in which producers meet demand at predetermined prices.

EXERCISE 8.2   **Use a Keynesian cross diagram to show graphically the determination of short-run equilibrium output for the economy described in Exercise 8.1. What are the intercept and the slope of the expenditure line?**

PLANNED SPENDING AND THE OUTPUT GAP

We are now ready to use the basic Keynesian model to show how insufficient planned aggregate expenditure can lead to a recession. To illustrate this idea, we will continue to work with the economy introduced in Example 8.1. We have shown that in this economy, short-run equilibrium output equals 4800. Let's now make the additional assumption that potential output in this economy also equals 4800, or $Y^* = 4800$. In other words, we will assume that, at first, actual output equals potential output so that there is no output gap. Example 8.3 shows, starting from this position of full employment, how a fall in planned aggregate expenditure can lead to a recession.

EXAMPLE 8.3

A fall in planned spending leads to a recession

We found that, for the economy introduced in Example 8.1, short-run equilibrium output Y equals 4800. Assume also that potential output Y^* equals 4800, so that the output gap $Y - Y^*$ equals zero.

Suppose, though, that consumers become more pessimistic about the future, so that they begin to spend less at every level of current disposable income. We can capture this change by assuming that $\overline{C}$, the constant term in the consumption function, falls to a lower level. To be specific, suppose that $\overline{C}$ falls by 10 units, which in turn implies a decline in autonomous expenditure of 10 units. What is the effect of this reduction in planned spending on the economy?

We can see the effects of the decline in consumer spending on the economy using the Keynesian cross diagram. Figure 8.4 shows the original short-run equilibrium point of the model (E), at the intersection of the 45° line, along which $Y = PAE$, and the original expenditure line, representing the equation $PAE = 960 + 0.8Y$. As before, the initial value of short-run equilibrium output is 4800, which we have now assumed also corresponds to potential output Y^*. But what happens when $\overline{C}$ declines by 10, reducing autonomous expenditure by 10 as well?

Originally, autonomous expenditure in this economy was 960, so a decline of 10 units causes it to fall to 950. Instead of the economy's planned spending being described by the equation $PAE = 960 + 0.8Y$, as initially, it is now given by $PAE = 950 + 0.8Y$. What does this change imply for the graph in Figure 8.4? Since the intercept of the expenditure line (equal to autonomous expenditure) has decreased from 960 to 950, the effect of the decline in consumer spending will be to shift the expenditure line down in parallel fashion, by 10 units. Figure 8.4 indicates this downward shift in the expenditure line. The new short-run equilibrium point is at point F, where the new, lower expenditure line intersects the 45° line.

FIGURE 8.4

A Decline in Planned Spending Leads to a Recession

A decline in consumers' willingness to spend at any current level of disposable income reduces planned autonomous expenditure and shifts the expenditure line down. The short-run equilibrium point drops from E to F, reducing output and opening up a recessionary gap.

Point *F* is to the left of the original equilibrium point *E*, so we can see that output and spending have fallen from their initial levels. Since output at point *F* is lower than potential output, 4800, we see that the fall in consumer spending has resulted in a recessionary gap in the economy. More generally, starting from a situation of full employment (where output equals potential output), any decline in autonomous expenditure leads to a recession.

Numerically, how large is the recessionary gap in Figure 8.4? To answer this question, we can use Table 8.2, which is in the same form as Table 8.1. The key difference is that in Table 8.2 planned aggregate expenditure is given by $PAE = 950 + 0.8Y$, rather than by $PAE = 960 + 0.8Y$, as in Table 8.1.

TABLE 8.2
Determination of Short-Run Equilibrium Output after a Fall in Spending

(1) Output Y	(2) Planned aggregate expenditure PAE = 950 + 0.8Y	(3) Y − PAE	(4) Y = PAE?
4650	4670	−20	No
4700	4710	−10	No
4750	4750	0	Yes
4800	4790	10	No
4850	4830	20	No

As in Table 8.1, the first column of the table shows alternative possible values of output *Y,* and the second column shows the levels of planned aggregate expenditure *PAE* implied by each value of output in the first column. Notice that 4800, the value of short-run equilibrium output found in Table 8.1, is no longer an equilibrium; when output is 4800, planned spending is 4790, so output and planned spending are not equal. As the table shows, following the decline in planned aggregate expenditure, short-run equilibrium output is 4750, the only value of output for which $Y = PAE$. Thus a drop of 10 units in autonomous expenditure has led to a 50-unit decline in short-run equilibrium output. If full-employment output is 4800, then the recessionary gap shown in Figure 8.4 is $4800 - 4750 = 50$ units.

EXERCISE 8.3   **In the economy described in Example 8.3, we found a recessionary gap of 50, relative to potential output of 4800. Suppose that in this economy, the natural rate of unemployment u* is 5 percent. If the relationship between the recessionary gap and cyclical unemployment follows Okun's law (as described in Chapter 7), what will be the actual unemployment rate after the recessionary gap appears?**

Example 8.3 showed that a decline in autonomous expenditure arising from a decreased willingness of consumers to spend causes short-run equilibrium output to fall and opens up a recessionary gap. The same conclusion applies to declines in autonomous expenditure arising from other sources. Suppose, for example, that firms become disillusioned with new technologies and cut back their planned investment in new equipment. Another possibility is that firms are suddenly unable to borrow the funds they need to invest. During the fall of 2008, for example, there was a "credit crisis" in many countries during the financial panic triggered by the collapse of the U.S. investment bank Lehman Brothers, and borrowing funds became very difficult for many firms.

"*These are hard times for retailers, so we should show them our support in every way we can.*"

In terms of the model, this reluctance or inability to invest can be interpreted as a decline in planned investment spending, I^P. Under our assumption that planned investment spending is given and does not depend on output, planned investment is part of autonomous expenditure. So a decline in planned investment spending depresses autonomous expenditure and output in precisely the same way that a decline in the autonomous part of consumption spending does. Similar conclusions apply to declines in other components of autonomous expenditure, such as government purchases and net exports, as we will see in later applications.

> Repeat the analysis of Example 8.3, except assume that consumers become more rather than less confident about the future. As a result, $\overline{C}$ rises by 10 units, which in turn raises autonomous expenditure by 10 units. Show graphically that this increase in consumers' willingness to spend leads to an expansionary output gap. Find the numerical value of the expansionary output gap.

EXERCISE 8.4

THE INCOME-EXPENDITURE MULTIPLIER

Note that in Example 8.3, although the initial decline in consumer spending (as measured by the fall in $\overline{C}$) was only 10 units, short-run equilibrium output fell by 50 units. The reason the impact on output and planned aggregate expenditure was greater than the initial change in spending is the "vicious circle" effect suggested by Grandma's reminiscences about the Great Depression. Specifically, a fall in consumer spending not only decreases planned aggregate expenditure, it also reduces the incomes of workers and owners in the industries that produce consumer goods. As their incomes fall, these workers and capital owners reduce their spending, which reduces the output and incomes of *other* producers in the economy. And these reductions in income lead to still further cuts in spending. Ultimately, these successive rounds of declines in spending and income may lead to a decrease in planned aggregate expenditure that is significantly greater than the change in spending that started the process.

The idea that a change in spending may lead to a substantially larger change in short-run equilibrium output is an important feature of the basic Keynesian model. In Example 8.3 we considered the effects of a decrease in spending, but an increase in spending produces the same effect in reverse. For example, if desired consumption had *increased* rather than decreased by 10, it would have set off successive rounds of increases in income and spending, culminating in a final increase of 50 in short-run equilibrium output. The same type of effect also applies to changes in other components of autonomous expenditure. For example, in this hypothetical economy, an increase of 10 in desired investment spending ($\overline{I}$), in government purchases ($\overline{G}$), or in net exports ($\overline{NX}$) would increase short-run equilibrium output by 50. (A bar over a variable indicates that the variable is autonomous.)

The effect on short-run equilibrium output of a one-unit increase in autonomous expenditure is called the **income-expenditure multiplier**, or the *multiplier* for short. In the economy of Example 8.3 the multiplier is 5. That is, each $1 increase in autonomous expenditure leads to a $5 increase in short-run equilibrium output, and each $1 decrease in autonomous expenditure implies a $5 decrease in short-run equilibrium output. Appendix 8B provides more details on the multiplier in the basic Keynesian model, including a formula ($1/[1 - mpc]$) which allows us to calculate the value of the multiplier under specific assumptions about the economy.

We stress that, because our basic Keynesian model omits some important features of an actual economy, it tends to yield unrealistically high values of the multiplier. Indeed, virtually no one believes that the multiplier in the Canadian economy is as high as 5. Real-world estimates typically put the multiplier at less than 2. Also, there is not one unique income-expenditure multiplier: multipliers vary by the type of policy measure the government chooses. Later, we will discuss why our basic Keynesian model tends to overstate the value of a multiplier. Nevertheless, the idea that changes in planned aggregate expenditure can have important effects on short-run equilibrium output remains a central tenet of Keynesian economics and a major factor in modern policy-making.

income-expenditure multiplier the effect of a one-unit increase in autonomous expenditure on short-run equilibrium output

---

RECAP⤴

FINDING SHORT-RUN EQUILIBRIUM OUTPUT

Short-run equilibrium output is the level of output at which output equals planned aggregate expenditure; in symbols, $Y = PAE$. For a specific example economy, short-run equilibrium output can be solved for numerically, as in Table 8.1, or graphically.

The graphical solution is based on a diagram called the Keynesian cross. The Keynesian cross diagram includes two lines: a 45° line that captures the condition $Y = PAE$ and the expenditure line, which shows the relationship of planned aggregate expenditure to output. Short-run equilibrium output is determined at the intersection of the two lines. If short-run equilibrium output differs from potential output, an output gap exists.

Increases in autonomous expenditure shift the expenditure line upward, increasing short-run equilibrium output, and decreases in autonomous expenditure induce declines in short-run equilibrium output. Decreases in autonomous expenditure that drive actual output below potential output are a possible source of recessions.

Generally, a one-unit increase in autonomous expenditure leads to a larger increase in short-run equilibrium output, a result of the *income-expenditure multiplier*. The multiplier arises because a given initial increase in spending raises the incomes of producers, which leads them to spend more, raising the incomes and spending of other producers, and so on.

8.3 STABILIZING PLANNED SPENDING: THE ROLE OF FISCAL POLICY

According to the basic Keynesian model, inadequate spending is an important cause of recessions. To fight recessions, policy-makers must find ways to increase aggregate expenditure. Policies that are used to affect planned spending, with the objective of eliminating output gaps, are called **stabilization policies.**

Policy actions intended to increase planned spending and output are called **expansionary policies**; expansionary policy actions are normally taken when the economy is in recession. It is also possible, as we have seen, for the economy to be "overheated," with output greater than potential output (an expansionary gap). The risk of an expansionary gap, as we will see in more detail later, is that it may lead to an increase in inflation. To offset an expansionary gap, policy-makers will try to reduce spending and output. **Contractionary policies** are policy actions intended to reduce planned spending and output.

The two major types of stabilization policy, *monetary policy* and *fiscal policy*, were introduced in Chapter 4. Recall that monetary policy refers to central bank decisions about interest rates, while fiscal policy refers to decisions about the government's budget—how much the government spends and how much tax revenue it collects. In the remainder of this chapter, we will focus on fiscal policy (monetary policy will be discussed in Chapters 9, 10, and 11). Specifically, we will consider how fiscal policy works in the basic Keynesian model, looking first at the effects of changes in government purchases of goods and services, and then at changes in tax collections. We will conclude the chapter with a discussion of some practical issues that arise in the application of fiscal policy.

stabilization policies
government policies that are used to affect planned aggregate expenditure, with the objective of eliminating output gaps

expansionary policies
government policy actions intended to increase planned spending and output

contractionary policies
government policy actions designed to reduce planned spending and output

GOVERNMENT PURCHASES AND PLANNED SPENDING

Decisions about government spending represent one of the two main components of fiscal policy, the other being decisions about the level and type of taxes. As was mentioned earlier, Keynes himself felt that changes in government purchases were probably the most effective tool for reducing or eliminating output gaps. His basic argument was straightforward: government purchases of goods and services are a component of planned aggregate expenditure, so planned spending is directly affected by changes in government purchases. If output gaps are caused by too much or too little total spending, then the government can help to guide the economy toward full employment by changing its own level of spending. Keynes's views seemed to be vindicated by the events of the 1930s, notably the fact that the Depression did not finally end until governments of several countries greatly increased their spending (especially military spending) in connection with the Second World War.

Example 8.4 shows how increased government purchases of goods and services can help to eliminate a recessionary gap. (The effects of government spending on transfer programs, such as employment insurance benefits, are a bit different. We will return to that case shortly.)

EXAMPLE 8.4

An increase in the government's purchases eliminates a recessionary gap

In Example 8.3, we found that a drop of 10 units in consumer spending creates a recessionary gap of 50 units. How can the government eliminate the output gap and restore full employment by changing its purchases of goods and services G?

In that example, we found that planned aggregate expenditure was initially given by the equation $PAE = 960 + 0.8Y$, so that autonomous expenditure equaled 960. The 10-unit drop in $\bar{C}$ implied a 10-unit drop in autonomous expenditure, to 950.

FIGURE 8.5
An Increase in Government Purchases Eliminates a Recessionary Gap
After a 10-unit decline in the autonomous part of consumer spending, $\overline{C}$, the economy is at point F, with a recessionary gap of 50. A 10-unit increase in government purchases raises autonomous expenditure by 10 units, shifting the expenditure line back to its original position and raising the equilibrium point from F to E. At point E, where output equals potential output ($Y = Y^* = 4800$), the output gap has been eliminated.

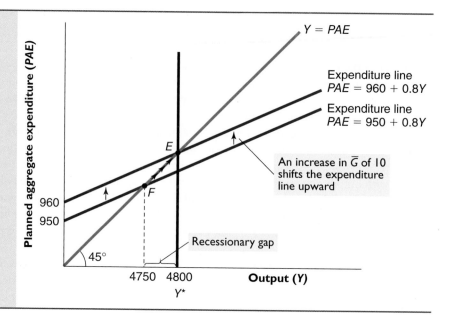

Because the multiplier in that sample economy equalled 5, this 10-unit decline in autonomous expenditure resulted in turn in a 50-unit decline in short-run equilibrium output.

To offset the effects of the consumption decline, the government would have to restore autonomous expenditure to its original value, 960. Under our assumption that government purchases are simply given and do not depend on output, government purchases are part of autonomous expenditure, and changes in government purchases change autonomous expenditure one for one. Thus, to increase autonomous expenditure from 950 to 960, the government should simply increase its purchases by 10 units (for example, by increasing spending on military defence or road construction). According to the basic Keynesian model, this increase in government purchases should return autonomous expenditure and, hence, output to their original levels.

The effect of the increase in government purchases is shown graphically in Figure 8.5. After the 10-unit decline in the autonomous component of consumption spending $\overline{C}$, the economy is at point F, with a 50-unit recessionary gap. A 10-unit increase in government purchases raises autonomous expenditure by 10 units, raising the intercept of the expenditure line by 10 units and causing the expenditure line to shift upward in parallel fashion. The economy returns to point E, where short-run equilibrium output equals potential output, $Y = Y^* = 4800$, and the output gap has been eliminated.

EXERCISE 8.5   **In Exercise 8.4, you considered the case in which consumers become more rather than less confident, leading to an expansionary output gap. Discuss how a change in government purchases could be used to eliminate this output gap. Show your analysis graphically.**

We should point out that in our model a 10-unit increase in private-sector investment, say, or a 10-unit increase in net exports would have exactly the same impact on the recessionary gap as a 10-unit increase in government purchases.

Economic Naturalists 8.1 and 8.2 illustrate the application of fiscal policy in actual economies. Economic Naturalist 8.2 illustrates the idea that a reduction in government purchases could be offset by an increase in net exports.

ECONOMIC NATURALIST 8.1

The Second World War and the end of Canada's Great Depression

During the 1930s, Canada's unemployment rate averaged about 13 percent, with a peak of 19.3 percent in 1933. Although there was some recovery in the late 1930s, the rate still stood at 11.4 percent in 1939. The Great Depression of the 1930s has passed into historical infamy due to the depth and length of its economic downturn, and the social and political turmoil which it produced.

With the wisdom of hindsight, today's economists recognize that the "balanced budget" economic orthodoxy of the time contributed to the severity of The Great Depression. A stock market crash in 1929 and a crisis in the banking system (see Economic Naturalist 13.1) started the downturn. But when tax revenue declined because incomes and sales had fallen, governments tried to avoid deficits and cut their spending, which worsened the situation by depressing planned aggregate expenditure even more.

When war with Nazi Germany came in 1939, Canadian government purchases increased dramatically. They went up from 10 percent of GDP in 1939 to 15 percent in 1940. By 1942, government purchases constituted about 35 percent of GDP (far higher, incidentally, than their roughly 20 percent share of Canadian GDP in recent years). As government purchases increased, Canada's unemployment rate declined sharply. It plummeted from 11.4 percent in 1939 to 2.7 percent in 1942. This historical experience helped convince many Canadian economists of the real-world relevance of Keynes's explanation of how government purchases could eliminate a recessionary gap and sharply reduce the unemployment rate.

ECONOMIC NATURALIST 8.2

Saved by the net exports

With his February 1995 budget, Finance Minister Paul Martin launched the federal government of Canada on a budget deficit reduction crusade that featured major government spending cutbacks. Most provinces followed suit. As a result, government purchases declined from about 22 percent of Canadian GDP in 1994 to 20 percent in 1997. (Government transfer payments, which we will analyze below, also declined as a percentage of GDP.)

Why did the Canadian economy continue to recover from the recession of the early 1990s despite the cutbacks in government purchases? One explanation suggested by our basic Keynesian model is that although the cutbacks acted to slow or stall the economic recovery, they were offset by booming net exports. Both the boom in the U.S. economy (which created demand for Canadian exports) and the weak Canadian dollar (which made Canadian exports relatively cheaper and imports relatively more expensive) contributed to a net export surge during 1994–1997. Canadian net exports had been slightly negative during the 1989–1993 period. But during 1994–1997, net exports surged, averaging about 2 percent of GDP.

In 2009–2010, many European governments found themselves with large budget deficits following the global recession of 2008–2009. Some politicians wished to reduce the budget deficits as rapidly as possible and used the example of Canada's mid-1990s deficit reduction crusade to argue that it would be possible to pursue contractionary fiscal policies without harming the economic recovery process. They tended to ignore the fact that Canada's recovery at that time was saved by the growth of net exports associated with a declining Canadian dollar and a booming U.S. economy.

TAXES, TRANSFERS, AND AGGREGATE SPENDING

Besides making decisions about government purchases of goods and services, fiscal policy-makers also determine the level of tax collections (or, more generally, government revenue) and government transfer payments. Interest on the public debt is a significant transfer from the government to households, but it is largely determined by the stock of outstanding public debt and by market interest rates, rather than by current decisions of fiscal policy-makers. For the sake of simplicity, we will assume that it is constant.

"Your Majesty, my voyage will not only forge a new route to the spices of the East but also create over three thousand new jobs."

Unlike changes in government purchases, changes in taxes or transfer payments do not affect planned spending directly. Instead, they work indirectly by changing disposable income in the household sector. Specifically, either a tax cut or an increase in government transfer payments increases disposable income in the household sector, which, according to the consumption function, should encourage households to spend more on consumer goods and services. In short, changes in taxes and transfer payments affect planned spending only to the extent that they change the level of spending by the household sector. Example 8.5 shows the effect of a tax cut (or an equal-size increase in transfer payments) on spending and output.

EXAMPLE **8.5**

Using a tax cut to close a recessionary gap

In Example 8.3, we found that in our hypothetical economy an initial drop in consumer spending of 10 units creates a recessionary gap of 50. Example 8.4 showed that this recessionary gap could be eliminated by a 10-unit increase in government purchases. Suppose that, instead of increasing government purchases, fiscal policy-makers decided to stabilize planned spending by changing the level of tax collections. By how much should they change taxes to eliminate the output gap?

A common first guess at the answer to this problem is that policy-makers should cut taxes by 10, but that guess is not correct. Let's see why.

The source of the recessionary gap in Example 8.3 is the assumption that households have reduced their consumption spending by 10 units at each level of output Y. To eliminate this recessionary gap, the change in taxes must induce households to increase their consumption spending by 10 units at each output level. However, if net taxes T are cut by 10 units, raising disposable income $Y - T$ by 10 units, consumption at each level of output Y will increase by only 8 units. The reason is that the marginal propensity to consume out of disposable income is 0.8, so consumption spending increases by only 0.8 times the amount of the tax cut. (The rest of the tax cut is saved.)

To raise consumption spending by 10 units, fiscal policy-makers must cut taxes by 12.5 units, reducing $T = 250$ to $T = 237.5$. Because 0.8(12.5) = 10, a tax cut of 12.5 units will spur households to increase their consumption by 10 units at each level of output. That increase will just offset the 10-unit decrease in autonomous consumption $\bar{C}$, restoring the economy to full employment.

Note that since T refers to *net taxes*, or taxes less transfers, the same result could be obtained by increasing transfer payments by 12.5 units. Because households spend

0.8 times any increase in transfer payments they receive, this policy would also raise consumption spending by 10 units at any level of output.

Graphically, the effect of the tax cut is identical to the effect of the increase in government purchases, shown in Figure 8.5. Because it leads to a 10-unit increase in consumption at any level of output, the tax cut shifts the expenditure line up by 10 units. Equilibrium is attained at point *E* in Figure 8.5, where output again equals potential output.

In a particular economy, a 20-unit decrease in planned investment moved the economy from an initial situation of no output gap to a situation with a recessionary gap. Describe two ways, one direct and one indirect, in which fiscal policy could be used to offset this recessionary gap. Assume the marginal propensity to consume equals 0.5. If the government budget is balanced before the decrease in planned investment, does one way of using fiscal policy add more to the government budget deficit than the other?

EXERCISE 8.6

RECAP

FISCAL POLICY AND PLANNED SPENDING

Stabilization policies are policies used to affect planned spending with the objective of eliminating output gaps. *Expansionary polices* are designed to increase planned spending and output and thereby eliminate a recessionary gap. *Contractionary polices* are designed to decrease planned spending and output and thereby eliminate an expansionary gap.

Fiscal policy includes two methods for affecting planned spending: changes in government purchases and changes in taxes or transfer payments. An increase in government purchases increases autonomous expenditure by an equal amount. A reduction in taxes or an increase in transfer payments increases autonomous expenditure by an amount equal to the marginal propensity to consume times the reduction in taxes or increase in transfer payments. The ultimate effect of a fiscal policy change on short-run equilibrium output equals the change in autonomous expenditure times the multiplier. Accordingly, if the economy is in recession, an increase in government purchases, a cut in taxes, or an increase in transfer payments can be used to stimulate spending and eliminate the recessionary gap.

8.4 FISCAL POLICY AS A STABILIZATION TOOL: THREE QUALIFICATIONS

We have shown that the basic Keynesian model provides insights into the impact of fiscal policy on an economy suffering from an output gap such as a recessionary gap. But our discussion has overlooked many fiscal policy issues. Three important fiscal policy issues warrant special mention.

DISCRETIONARY FISCAL POLICY AND AUTOMATIC STABILIZERS

The first issue is that fiscal policy can be discretionary or not. Decisions to change levels of government spending and taxation in order to stabilize planned spending, known as **discretionary fiscal policy**, take time to formulate and implement. But fiscal policy need not take the form of discretionary fiscal policy; fiscal policy can also involve **automatic stabilizers**, provisions in the law that imply *automatic* increases in government spending

discretionary fiscal policy
changes in government spending and taxation deliberately made to stabilize planned aggregate expenditure

automatic stabilizers
provisions in the law that imply automatic increases in government spending or decreases in taxes when real output declines

or decreases in taxes when GDP declines (or even when GDP grows much more slowly than normal). For example, income tax collections fall (because taxable incomes fall) when GDP declines, while employment insurance payments and social assistance payments increase (as more people qualify for income support due to rising unemployment)—all without any explicit new decisions from the federal or provincial governments. These automatic changes in government spending and tax collections help to increase planned aggregate expenditure during recessions and reduce it during expansions, thereby stabilizing the economy (as shown in Problem 10 at the end of this chapter). Note that, because automatic stabilizers move the budget balance in the direction of a deficit during recessions and in the direction of a surplus during expansions, the cumulative impact of automatic stabilizers is that surpluses tend to offset deficits. That is, the working of automatic stabilizers does not necessarily result in a long-term rise in the government debt-to-GDP ratio (or even in the stock of debt itself).

Incidentally, one implication of automatic stabilizers is that if the economy falls into recession, the government's budget balance may turn sharply negative even without any change in the expenditure or tax policies of the government. The average citizen may not understand the operation of automatic stabilizers, so critics of the government may find it convenient to misrepresent the rising government deficit as evidence that the government is engaged in a wild spending (or tax-cutting) spree even when all or most of the deterioration in the budget balance stems from the operation of automatic stabilizers.

Economists tend to support allowing automatic stabilizers to operate and be critical of any balanced budget legislation that would force governments to override automatic stabilizers and actively cut spending or increase taxation in recessions in order to avoid deficits. Some economists tend to be unenthusiastic about discretionary fiscal policy as a means for dealing with anything but the most stubborn recessions, suggesting instead that planned aggregate expenditure be stabilized by monetary policy so that decisions about government spending and taxation can focus on long-term considerations. The role of monetary policy in stabilizing planned aggregate expenditure is the subject of the next chapter. Other economists argue that monetary policy may need to be supplemented by discretionary fiscal policy in certain situations, such as during the Canadian and U.S. slowdowns of 2001. During the severe global recession of 2008–2009, discretionary forms of expansionary fiscal policy measures were adopted by an extremely high percentage of governments, and discretionary fiscal policy was widely supported by economists. In Canada, as noted in the introduction to this chapter, the federal government referred to its fiscal policy measures to combat the recession as Canada's Economic Action Plan.

DEFICITS, DEBT STABILITY, AND DEBT DEFAULT

A second important fiscal policy issue is that fiscal policy-makers generally wish to avoid an ever-rising debt-to-GDP ratio. Recall from Chapter 4 that the government budget deficit is the excess of government expenditure over government revenue. The budget deficit, which is a flow, adds to the stock of government debt (just as water flowing into a bath will fill the tub and continued personal borrowing leads to a larger stock of personal debt). The debt of a government, as with the debt of a household, is best judged in relation to its ability to pay. For a household taking out a mortgage, for example, the amount of debt it can safely carry depends upon its income. For a government, debt is typically measured against the economy's GDP, which gives the government debt-to-GDP ratio that was shown in Figure 4.8.

Government debt stability is the condition that the government debt-to-GDP ratio does not change; that is, the growth of GDP equals the growth of the debt.[4] If the

government debt stability
the condition that the government debt-to-GDP ratio does not change

---

4 It is possible for the government debt-to-GDP ratio to decline even in the face of government deficits if the deficits are sufficiently small that the growth in the government debt is less than the growth in GDP. Indeed, for most of the period from the end of World War II into the early 1970s, Canadian governments tended to run deficits but the debt-to-GDP ratio fell.

government deficit is large and persistent, the government debt will grow more rapidly than GDP, and the government debt-to-GDP ratio will rise. Debt becomes a problem when it gets too large to repay, compared to GDP. So if a country develops an especially high government debt-to-GDP ratio and continues to run large deficits, lenders may become worried that the government will default on its debt, and governments may need to pay especially high interest rates on government borrowing (to compensate lenders for the risk of default). If the interest rates rise dramatically, however, they contribute to the large deficits and the likelihood of default.

At the time of writing in 2011, Greece has been in the news for months as an example of a country with a very high debt-to-GDP ratio that was running very large government deficits, and began having to pay higher and higher interest rates on its borrowing. To prevent the possibility of default, Greece was provided with a large loan in May 2010 from fellow European countries and the International Monetary Fund, on the condition that Greece implement an austerity program consisting of government spending cutbacks and higher tax collections.

In the wake of the global recession of 2008–2009, many governments found themselves with extremely large deficits not just due to the recession, but, in several cases, also to the cost of bailing out lightly regulated banks and other financial sector firms that had taken on enormous risks and then gone bankrupt. These bailout costs were particularly severe in countries in which the failed financial sector was large relative to the overall economy—tiny Iceland being the most extreme example. At the time of writing in 2011, Ireland, which had been running budget surpluses and did not have a particularly high debt-to-GDP ratio prior to the global recession, has been experiencing problems of this sort. It was granted a large loan from the European Union and the International Monetary Fund in November 2010 to deal with concerns that it would default on its debts.

Canada has never reached the point where the federal government has had to pay especially high interest rates, but in the early 1990s, Canada had one of the highest government debt-to-GDP ratios among the G7 countries. Since the mid-1990s, a central objective of Canadian fiscal policy has been to reduce the government debt-to-GDP ratio. Indeed, even though by 2004 Canada had the second lowest government debt-to-GDP ratio among the G7 countries, the 2004 federal budget announced the objective of continuing to reduce the federal government debt-to-GDP ratio—from about 40 percent to 25 percent over the next ten years. The federal debt-to-GDP ratio did decline until fiscal year 2008–2009, but it jumped a few percentage points in 2009–2010, and in the October 2010 fiscal update, the federal Department of Finance predicted that the debt-to-GDP ratio would remain above 30 percent at least until fiscal year 2015–2016.[5] If this projection is correct, it means that the 2004 target will not be achieved on schedule. But Canada would still have an extremely low debt-to-GDP ratio by international standards.[6]

FISCAL POLICY, GROWTH, DISTRIBUTION, AND SECURITY

A third important fiscal policy issue is that changes in government expenditure and taxation have consequences that go beyond short-term fluctuations in the economy; that is, they have consequences for potential output, income distribution, and income security.

For example, in this chapter we have focused on how government purchases, taxes, and transfer payments change planned aggregate expenditure (the demand side of the economy) but we have not discussed how changes in government expenditure (that is, government purchases and government transfer payments) and taxation affect the supply side of the economy, as represented by potential output. But the assumption that fiscal

---

5 See http://www.fin.gc.ca/ec2010/efp-pef-02-eng.asp, Chart 1.5.

6 For precision in international comparisons of government debt-to-GDP ratios, it is necessary to compare the ratio of all Canadian government debt-to-GDP, not just Canadian federal debt-to-GDP.

policy does not affect potential output is often not correct. On the spending side, for example, investments in public capital, such as roads, airports, and schools, can play a major role in the growth of potential output. On the other side of the ledger, tax and transfer programs may well affect the incentives, and thus the economic behaviour, of households and firms. For example, a tax break on new investment may encourage firms to increase their rate of capital formation. An increase in investment will, in turn, affect potential output. Many other examples could be given of how taxes and transfer payments affect economic behaviour and thus potential output. In judging alternative fiscal policies, therefore, it is appropriate to consider their impact not just on planned aggregate expenditure and actual output but also on potential output.

In addition, changes in government expenditure and taxation affect income distribution and income security. Relaxation of the eligibility requirements for employment insurance, for example, tends to equalize the distribution of income and increase income security. On the other hand, personal and corporate income tax cuts generally are of greatest benefit to those with the highest incomes, and the direct consequence of income tax cuts is to make the distribution of household incomes more unequal.

8.5   MORE ON IMPORTS, TAXES, AND MULTIPLIERS

In our presentation of the basic Keynesian model we have made the simplifying assumptions that both net exports and net taxes (taxes minus transfers) are fixed. These are convenient assumptions, and we will continue to hold them for most of our analysis in later chapters of Part 3. In this section, however, we will briefly examine a number of more realistic assumptions about net exports and net taxes, and the effect these have on the income-expenditure multiplier. In a more realistic situation, the income-expenditure multiplier is impacted not only by the marginal propensity to consume but also by the *marginal propensity to import* and the *economy-wide marginal tax rate*.

First consider net exports, the difference between the value of exports and the value of imports. Canadian goods and services that are exported have a value that is relatively independent of Canadian income, but the total value of goods and services that are imported tends to increase as Canadian income increases. This is because our consumption of all goods and services, whether domestically produced or imported, tends to increase when our incomes increase.

marginal propensity to import the amount by which imports rise when income rises by $1

The **marginal propensity to import** is the amount by which imports rise when income rises by $1. Earlier, when we assumed that net exports were fixed, we assumed that the marginal propensity to import was zero. More realistically, however, the marginal propensity to import is greater than zero, but less than one.

How is the multiplier changed when the marginal propensity to import is greater than zero rather than equal to zero? Suppose that exports from Canada increase, for instance, because of increased demand for Canadian resources from China and India. This will increase both output and income in Canada and result in increased consumption expenditure. But because the marginal propensity to import is positive, part of the increased consumption expenditure will be spent on imports. Spending on imports does not directly boost production, jobs, and spending in Canada. The income-expenditure multiplier will therefore be smaller than in the case when the marginal propensity to import was zero. The larger the marginal propensity to import is, the smaller the income-expenditure multiplier will be.

Next, let us reconsider the assumption that net taxes are fixed. This amounts to assuming that as incomes rise the amount of taxes collected by government will stay the same. But income taxes, as the term itself suggests, are income related and will increase with increases in income and expenditure, as will the amount of sales taxes paid. In general, as income goes up so will taxes paid and collected.

The **economy-wide marginal tax rate** is the amount by which taxes rise when income rises by $1. When we assumed that net taxes were fixed, we assumed that the economy-wide marginal tax rate was zero. A more realistic assumption is that this marginal tax rate is greater than zero but less than one.

What are the implications of a positive economy-wide marginal tax rate for the multiplier? Suppose, again, that exports from Canada increase because of increased demand for Canadian resources from China and India. This will increase output and income in Canada. But part of the increase in income will now go to paying extra taxes, so the increase in consumption expenditure and the consequent boost to production, spending, and jobs in Canada will be less than in the case in which the economy-wide marginal income tax rate was zero. (Note that we are following our usual practice of assuming that all else is equal; e.g., we are assuming that despite the increase in tax revenues, government expenditure will stay the same.) The larger the economy-wide marginal tax rate is, the smaller the income-expenditure multiplier will be.

Figure 8.6 illustrates the implications of recognizing a positive marginal propensity to import and a positive economy-wide marginal tax rate for our basic Keynesian model. Panel (a) of Figure 8.6 is very similar to Figure 8.5, which was used to illustrate how an increase in government purchases could be used to eliminate a recessionary gap. At the

economy-wide marginal tax rate the amount by which taxes rise when income rises by $1

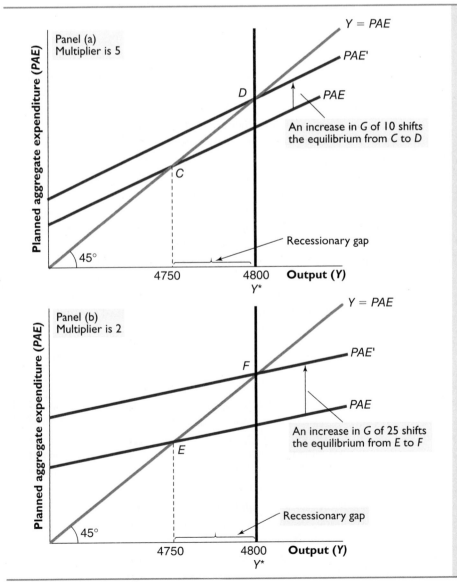

FIGURE 8.6
The Implication of a Small versus a Large Multiplier
Panel (a) represents the case of closing a 50-unit recessionary gap with a 10-unit increase in government purchases when the income-expenditure multiplier is 5.
Panel (b) represents the case of closing a 50-unit recessionary gap with a 25-unit increase in government purchases when the income-expenditure multiplier is 2.

original equilibrium point **C**, actual output is 4750 and potential output is 4800, which implies a recessionary gap of 50 units. The marginal propensity to import and the economy-wide marginal income tax rate are both zero. The income-expenditure multiplier is 5. An increase of 10 units in government purchases raises planned aggregate expenditure by enough to close the recessionary gap and bring the economy to the equilibrium point **D**.

Panel (b) of Figure 8.6 illustrates a situation in which, at the original equilibrium point **E**, actual output is 4750 and potential output is 4800, implying a recessionary gap of 50 units, as in panel (a). In this case, however, the marginal propensity to import and the economy-wide marginal tax rate are both positive, resulting in a smaller income-expenditure multiplier than the multiplier of 5 underlying panel (a). Panel (b) shows a multiplier of 2, which means that a 25-unit increase in government purchases raises planned aggregate expenditure by enough to close the recessionary gap and bring the economy to the equilibrium point **F**.

In short, the income-expenditure multiplier is smaller when either (or both) the marginal propensity to import or the economy-wide marginal tax rate are positive than it is when they are zero. A smaller multiplier means it takes a larger increase in autonomous expenditure to close any given output gap.

SUMMARY

- The basic Keynesian model shows how fluctuations in planned aggregate expenditure, or total planned spending, can cause actual output to differ from potential output. Too little spending leads to a recessionary output gap, while too much spending creates an expansionary output gap. This model relies on the crucial assumption that firms do not respond to every change in demand by changing prices. Instead, they typically set a price for some period, then meet the demand forthcoming at that price. Firms do not change prices continually because changing prices entails costs, called *menu costs*. **LO1**

- *Planned aggregate expenditure* is total planned spending on final goods and services. The four components of total spending are consumption, private-sector investment, government purchases, and net exports. Planned and actual consumption, government purchases, and net exports are assumed to be the same. Actual private-sector investment may differ from planned private-sector investment, because firms may sell a greater or lesser amount of their production than they expected. If firms sell less than they expected, for example, they are forced to add more goods to inventory than anticipated. And because additions to inventory are counted as part of investment, in this case actual investment (including inventory investment) is greater than planned investment. **LO2**

- Consumption is related to disposable income by a relationship called the *consumption function*. The amount by which desired consumption rises when disposable income rises by $1 is called the *marginal propensity to consume (mpc)*. The marginal propensity to consume is always greater than zero but less than one (that is, $0 < mpc < 1$). **LO2**

- An increase in real output raises planned aggregate expenditure, since higher output (and equivalently, higher income) encourages households to consume more. Planned aggregate expenditure can be broken down into two components, autonomous expenditure and induced expenditure. *Autonomous expenditure* is the portion of planned spending that is independent of output. *Induced expenditure* is the portion of spending that depends on output. **LO2**

- At predetermined prices, *short-run equilibrium output* is the level of output that equals planned spending. Short-run equilibrium can be determined numerically by a table that compares alternative values of output and the planned spending implied by each level of output. Short-run equilibrium can be determined graphically in a Keynesian cross diagram, drawn with planned aggregate expenditure on the vertical axis and output on the horizontal axis. The Keynesian cross contains two lines: an expenditure line, which relates planned aggregate expenditure to output, and a 45° line, which represents the condition that short-run equilibrium output equals planned aggregate expenditure. Short-run equilibrium output is determined at the point at which these two lines intersect. **LO3**

■ Changes in autonomous expenditure will lead to changes in short-run equilibrium output. In particular, if the economy is initially at full employment, a fall in autonomous expenditure will create a recessionary gap and a rise in autonomous expenditure will create an expansionary gap. The amount by which a one-unit increase in autonomous expenditure raises short-run equilibrium output is called the *income-expenditure multiplier*. An increase in autonomous expenditure not only raises spending directly, it also raises the incomes of producers, who in turn increase their spending, and so on. Hence the multiplier is greater than one; that is, a one dollar increase in autonomous expenditure raises short-run equilibrium output by more than one dollar. **LO4**

■ To eliminate output gaps and restore full employment, the government employs *stabilization policies*. The two major types of stabilization policy are monetary policy and fiscal policy. Stabilization polices work by changing planned aggregate expenditure, and thus short-run equilibrium output. For example, an increase in government purchases raises planned aggregate expenditure, so it can be used to reduce or eliminate a recessionary gap. Similarly, a cut in taxes or an increase in transfer payments increases the public's disposable income, raising consumption and planned aggregate expenditure. Higher planned aggregate expenditure, in turn, raises short-run equilibrium output. **LO5**

■ There is more to fiscal policy than understanding the magnitude of changes in government purchases, taxes, or transfer payments required to close a particular output gap. First, it is important to distinguish between discretionary fiscal policy and fiscal policy involving automatic stabilizers. Discretionary fiscal policy refers to deliberate decisions to change levels of spending and taxation to stabilize planned spending. Automatic stabilizers are provisions in the law that imply automatic increases in government spending or reductions in taxes when output declines. Second, fiscal policy must take into account the fact that large and persistent deficits would create an ever-rising government debt-to-GDP ratio. Third, fiscal policy may affect potential output, as well as planned spending, and fiscal policy may also affect matters that extend beyond either actual or potential GDP levels, such as the distribution of income or the level of economic security. **LO5**

■ The income-expenditure multiplier is smaller when the marginal propensity to import and/or the economy-wide marginal tax rate are positive than it is when they are zero. The smaller the multiplier is, the larger the increase in autonomous expenditure will need to be in order to close any given output gap. **LO5**

KEY TERMS

asset price bubble (176)
average propensity to consume (APC) (177)
automatic stabilizers (191)
autonomous expenditure (179)
consumption function (176)
contractionary policies (187)
discretionary fiscal policy (191)
disposable income (175)

economy-wide marginal tax rate (195)
expansionary policies (187)
government debt stability (192)
income-expenditure multiplier (186)
induced expenditure (179)
marginal propensity to consume (*mpc*) (176)

marginal propensity to import (194)
menu costs (173)
net taxes (175)
planned aggregate expenditure (*PAE*) (173)
short-run equilibrium output (180)
stabilization policies (187)
wealth effect (176)

REVIEW QUESTIONS

1. What is the key assumption of the basic Keynesian model? Explain why this assumption is needed if one is to accept the view that aggregate spending is a driving force behind short-term economic fluctuations. **LO1**

2. Give an example of a good or service whose price changes very frequently and one whose price changes relatively infrequently. What accounts for the difference? **LO1**

3. Define *planned aggregate expenditure* and list its components. Why does planned aggregate expenditure change when output changes? **LO2**

4. Explain how planned spending and actual spending can differ. Illustrate with an example. **LO2**

5. Sketch a graph of the consumption function, labelling the axes of the graph. Discuss the economic meaning of (a) a movement from left to right along the graph of the consumption function and of (b) a parallel upward shift of the consumption function. **LO2**

6. Sketch the Keynesian cross diagram. Explain in words the economic significance of the two lines graphed in the diagram. Given only this diagram, how could you determine autonomous expenditure, induced expenditure, the marginal propensity to consume, and short-run equilibrium output? **LO3**

7. Define the *income-expenditure multiplier*. In economic terms, why is the multiplier greater than one? **LO4**

8. The government is considering two alternative policies, one involving increased government purchases of 50, the other involving a tax cut of 50. Which policy will stimulate planned aggregate expenditure by more? Why? **LO5**

9. Discuss three reasons why the use of fiscal policy to stabilize the economy is more complex than suggested by the basic Keynesian model. **LO5**

10. How does the size of the income-expenditure multiplier affect the use of government purchases to close a recessionary gap? **LO4**

PROBLEMS

1. Acme Manufacturing is producing $4 000 000 worth of goods this year and is expecting to sell its entire production. It is also planning to purchase $1 500 000 in new equipment during the year. At the beginning of the year, the company has $500 000 in inventory in its warehouse. Find actual investment and planned investment if
   a. Acme actually sells $3 850 000 worth of goods.
   b. Acme actually sells $4 000 000 worth of goods.
   c. Acme actually sells $4 200 000 worth of goods.

   Assuming that Acme's situation is similar to that of other firms, in which of these three cases is output equal to short-run equilibrium output? **LO1**

2. Data on before-tax income, taxes paid, and consumption spending for the Simpson family in various years are given below. **LO2**
   a. Graph the Simpsons' consumption function, and find their household's marginal propensity to consume.
   b. How much would you expect the Simpsons to consume if their income was $32 000 and they paid taxes of $5000?

Before-tax income ($)	Taxes paid ($)	Consumption spending ($)
25 000	3000	20 000
27 000	3500	21 350
28 000	3700	22 070
30 000	4000	23 600

c. Homer Simpson wins a lottery prize. As a result, the Simpson family increases its consumption by \$1000 at each level of disposable income. ("Income" does not include the prize money.) How does this change affect the graph of their consumption function? How does it affect their marginal propensity to consume?

3. An economy is described by the following equations: **LO2**

$$C = 1800 + 0.6(Y - T),$$
$$I^p = \bar{I} = 900,$$
$$G = \bar{G} = 1500,$$
$$NX = \overline{NX} = 100,$$
$$T = \bar{T} = 1500,$$
$$Y^* = 9000.$$

a. Find a numerical equation linking planned aggregate expenditure to output.
b. Find autonomous expenditure and induced expenditure.

4. For the economy described in Problem 3, **LO3**
a. Construct a table like Table 8.1 to find short-run equilibrium output. Consider possible values for short-run equilibrium output ranging from 8200 to 9000.
b. Show the determination of short-run equilibrium output for this economy using the Keynesian cross diagram.
c. What is the output gap for this economy? If the natural rate of unemployment is 4 percent, what is the actual unemployment rate for this economy (use Okun's law)?

5. For the economy described in Problem 3, find the effect on short-run equilibrium output of each of the following changes, taken one at a time:
a. An increase in government purchases from 1500 to 1600.
b. A decrease in net taxes from 1500 to 1400 (leaving government purchases at their original value).
c. A decrease in planned investment spending from 900 to 800.

Assume each of these changes is a change in autonomous expenditure. Take as given that the multiplier for this economy is 2.5. If you have studied Appendix B in this chapter, show why this is so. **LO4**

6. For the following economy, find autonomous expenditure, the multiplier, short-run equilibrium output, and output gap. By how much would autonomous expenditure have to change to eliminate the output gap? **LO4, LO5**

$$C = 3000 + 0.5(Y - T),$$
$$I^p = \bar{I} = 1500,$$
$$G = \bar{G} = 2500,$$
$$NX = \overline{NX} = 200,$$
$$T = \bar{T} = 2000,$$
$$Y^* = 12000.$$

7. An economy has zero net exports ($\overline{NX} = 0$). Otherwise, it is identical to the economy described in Problem 6. **LO3, LO4, LO5**
a. Find short-run equilibrium output.
b. Economic recovery abroad increases the demand for the country's exports; as a result, $\overline{NX}$ rises to 100. What happens to short-run equilibrium output?
c. Repeat part (b), but this time assume that foreign economies are slowing, reducing the demand for the country's exports so that $\overline{NX} = -100$. (A negative value of net exports means that exports are less than imports.)
d. How do your results help to explain the tendency of recessions and expansions to spread across countries?

8. (More difficult.) In a particular economy, planned private-sector investment spending is given by the equation

$$I^p = 300 + 0.1Y.$$

This equation captures the idea that when real GDP rises, firms find it more profitable to make capital investments. Specifically, in this economy, when real GDP rises by a dollar, planned investment spending rises by 10 cents. All the other equations describing this economy are the same as in Problem 6. Find autonomous expenditure, the multiplier, short-run equilibrium output, and the output gap. (Be careful: the multiplier is no longer given by the formula $1/(1 - mpc)$. You will need to calculate directly the effect of a change in autonomous expenditure on short-run equilibrium output.) By how much would autonomous expenditure have to change to eliminate any output gap? **LO3, LO4, LO5**

9. An economy is described by the following equations:
    LO4, LO5

$$C = 40 + 0.8(Y - T),$$
$$I^p = \bar{I} = 70,$$
$$G = \bar{G} = 120,$$
$$NX = \overline{NX} = 10$$
$$T = \bar{T} = 150.$$

a. Potential output Y^* equals 580. By how much would government purchases have to change to eliminate any output gap? By how much would taxes have to change? Show the effects of these fiscal policy changes in a Keynesian cross diagram.

b. Repeat part (a), assuming that $Y^* = 630$.

10. (More difficult.) This problem illustrates the workings of automatic stabilizers. Suppose that the components of planned spending in an economy take their usual forms: $C = \bar{C} + mpc(Y - T)$, $I^p = \bar{I}$, $G = \bar{G}$, and $NX = \overline{NX}$. However, suppose that, realistically, net taxes are not fixed but depend on income as discussed in section 8.5. Specifically, we assume

$$T = tY,$$

where t (a number between 0 and 1) is the fraction of income paid in taxes (the economy-wide marginal tax rate). As we will see in this problem, a tax system of this sort serves as an automatic stabilizer, because taxes collected automatically fall when incomes fall.
LO3, LO4, LO5

a. Find an algebraic expression for short-run equilibrium output in this economy.

b. Find an algebraic expression for the multiplier; that is, the amount that output changes when autonomous expenditure changes by one unit. Compare the expression you found to the formula for the multiplier when net taxes are fixed. Show that making net taxes proportional to income reduces the multiplier.

c. Explain how reducing the size of the multiplier helps to stabilize the economy, holding constant fluctuations in the components of autonomous expenditure.

d. Suppose $\bar{C} = 500$, $\bar{I} = 1500$, $\bar{G} = 2000$, $\overline{NX} = 0$, $mpc = 0.8$, and $t = 0.25$. Calculate numerical values for short-run equilibrium output and the multiplier.

11. (More difficult.) This problem illustrates how much smaller the multiplier can get when both net taxes and net exports depend on income. Let X = exports and M = imports. Assume that the import function is of the form $M = \bar{M} + mY$, where m is a number between 0 and 1. Assume that exports, like private-sector investment and government purchases, are independent of income. Now suppose, as in Problem 10, that $\bar{C} = 500$, $\bar{I} = 1500$, $\bar{G} = 2000$, $mpc = 0.8$, and $t = 0.25$. But also suppose that $\bar{X} = 5000$, $\bar{M} = 1000$, and $m = 0.4$. Calculate numerical values for short-run equilibrium output and the multiplier. **LO3, LO4, LO5**

ANSWERS TO IN-CHAPTER EXERCISES

8.1   First we need to find an equation that relates planned aggregate expenditure (*PAE*) to output. We start with the definition of planned aggregate expenditure and substitute the numerical values given in the problem:

$$PAE = C + I^p + G + NX$$
$$= [\bar{C} + mpc(Y - T)] + I^p + G + NX$$
$$= [820 + 0.7(Y - 600)] + 600 + 600 + 200$$
$$= 1800 + 0.7Y.$$

Using this relationship we construct a table analogous to Table 8.1. Some trial and error is necessary to find an appropriate range of guesses for output (column 1).

Determination of Short-Run Equilibrium Output

(1)	(2)	(3) Planned aggregate expenditure	(4)
Output Y	$PAE = 1800 + 0.7Y$	$Y - PAE$	$Y = PAE$?
5400	5580	−180	No
5600	5720	−120	No
5800	5860	−60	No
6000	6000	0	Yes
6200	6140	60	No
6400	6280	120	No

Short-run equilibrium output equals 6000, as that is the only level of output that satisfies the condition $Y = PAE$. **LO2, LO3**

8.2   The graph below (not drawn to scale) shows the determination of short-run equilibrium output, $Y = 6000$. The intercept of the expenditure line is 1800, and its slope is 0.7. Notice that the intercept equals autonomous expenditure and the slope equals the marginal propensity to consume. **LO2, LO3**

8.3   This problem is an application of Okun's law, introduced in Chapter 7. The recessionary gap in this example is 50/4800, or about 1.04 percent of potential output. By Okun's law, cyclical unemployment is one-half the percentage size of the output gap, or 0.52 percent. As the natural rate of unemployment is 5 percent, the total unemployment rate after the recessionary gap appears will be approximately 5.52 percent. **LO3**

8.4   This exercise is just the reverse of Example 8.3. An increase in $\overline{C}$ of 10 units raises autonomous expenditure and hence the intercept of the expenditure line by 10 units. The expenditure line shifts up, in parallel fashion, by 10 units, leading to an increase in output and an expansionary output gap. As output falls by 50 units in Example 8.3, it rises by 50 units, to 4850, in the case analyzed here. To verify that short-run equilibrium output equals 4850, note that an increase of 10 units in autonomous expenditure implies that PAE rises from $960 + 0.8Y$ to $970 + 0.8Y$. When $Y = 4850$, then $PAE = 970 + 0.8(4850) = 4850$, so that we have $Y = PAE$. **LO4**

8.5   In Exercise 8.4 we saw that a 10-unit increase in $\overline{C}$ increases autonomous expenditure and hence the intercept of the expenditure line by 10 units. The expenditure line shifts upward, in parallel fashion, by 10 units, leading to an expansionary output gap. To offset this gap, the government should reduce its purchases by 10 units, returning autonomous expenditure to its original level. The expenditure line shifts back down to its original position, restoring output to its initial full-employment level. The graph is just the reverse of Figure 8.5, with the expenditure line being shifted up by the increase in consumption and down by the offsetting reduction in government purchases. **LO4, LO5**

8.6   The 20-unit decrease in planned investment is a 20-unit decrease in autonomous expenditure, which will lead to an even greater decrease in short-run equilibrium output. To offset the 20-unit decrease in autonomous expenditure by means of fiscal policy, the government can increase its purchases by 20 units. Alternatively, it could cut taxes (or raise transfers) to increase consumption spending. Since the $mpc = 0.5$, to increase consumption spending by 20 units at each level of output, the government will need to decrease taxes (or increase transfers) by 40 units. At each level of output, a 40-unit tax decrease will increase disposable income by 40 units and cause consumers to increase their spending by $0.5 \times 40 = 20$ units, as needed to eliminate the recessionary output gap.

Based on the information provided, the use of expansionary fiscal policy in the form of government purchases would directly add 20 units to the government budget deficit. The use of expansionary fiscal policy in the form of cutting taxes (or raising transfers) would directly add 40 units to the government budget deficit. **LO4, LO5**

An Algebraic Solution of the Basic Keynesian Model

In this appendix we will show how to find a more general algebraic solution for short-run equilibrium output in the basic Keynesian model. The model we will work with is the same one presented in the main part of the chapter. Start with the definition of planned aggregate expenditure,

$$PAE = C + I^p + G + NX. \tag{8A.1}$$

This equation states that planned aggregate expenditure is the sum of the four types of planned spending: consumption spending by households, C; planned investment spending by firms, I^p; government purchases, G; and net exports purchased by foreigners, NX.

The first component of planned aggregate expenditure, consumption spending, is determined by the *consumption function,* Equation 8A.2:

$$C = \overline{C} + mpc(Y - T). \tag{8A.2}$$

The consumption function says that consumption spending increases when disposable (after-tax-and-transfer) income $Y - T$ increases. Each dollar increase in disposable income raises consumption spending by mpc dollars, where mpc, known as the *marginal propensity to consume,* is a number between 0 and 1. Other factors affecting consumption spending are captured by the term $\overline{C}$. For example, a boom in the stock market that leads consumers to spend more at each level of disposable income (a *wealth effect*) would be represented as an increase in $\overline{C}$.

As in the body of the chapter, we assume that planned private-sector investment, government purchases, net exports, and net tax collections are simply given numbers. A variable whose value is fixed and given from outside the model is called an *exogenous* variable; so in other words, we are assuming that planned private-sector investment, government purchases, net exports, and net tax collections are exogenous variables. Using an overbar to denote the given value of an exogenous variable, we can write this assumption as

$$I^p = \overline{I} \text{ planned private-sector investment,}$$
$$G = \overline{G} \text{ government purchases,}$$
$$NX = \overline{NX} \text{ net exports,}$$
$$T = \overline{T} \text{ net taxes (taxes less transfers).}$$

So for example, $\overline{I}$ is the given value of planned private-sector investment spending, as determined outside the model. In our examples, we will set $\overline{I}$ and the other exogenous variables equal to some particular number.

Our goal is to solve algebraically for *short-run equilibrium output*—the level of output that prevails during the period in which prices are predetermined. The first step is to relate planned aggregate expenditure, *PAE*, to output *Y*. Starting with the definition of planned aggregate expenditure (Equation 8A.1), use the consumption function (Equation 8A.2) to substitute for consumption spending *C*, and replace I^P, *G*, *NX*, and *T* with their exogenous values. With these substitutions, planned aggregate expenditure can be written as

$$PAE = \overline{C} + mpc(Y - \overline{T})] + \overline{I} + \overline{G} + \overline{NX}.$$

Rearranging this equation to separate the terms that do and do not depend on output *Y*, we get

$$PAE = [\overline{C} - mpc\overline{T} + \overline{I} + \overline{G} + \overline{NX}] + mpcY. \tag{8A.3}$$

Equation 8A.3 is an important equation, because it shows the relationship between planned aggregate expenditure *PAE* and output *Y*. The bracketed term on the right side of the equation represents *autonomous expenditure,* the part of planned spending that does not depend on output. The term *mpcY* represents *induced expenditure,* the part of planned spending that does depend on output. Equation 8A.3 is also the equation that describes the *expenditure line* in the Keynesian cross diagram; it shows that the intercept of the expenditure line equals autonomous expenditure and the slope of the expenditure line equals the marginal propensity to consume.

We can illustrate how Equation 8A.3 works numerically by using Example 8.1 in the text. That example assumed the following numerical values: $\overline{C} = 620$, $\overline{I} = 220$, $\overline{G} = 300$, $\overline{NX} = 20$, $\overline{T} = 250$, and $mpc = 0.8$. Plugging these values into Equation 8A.3 and simplifying, we get

$$PAE = 960 + 0.8Y,$$

which is the same answer we found in Example 8.1. Autonomous expenditure in this example equals 960, and induced expenditure equals 0.8*Y*.

The second step in solving for short-run equilibrium output begins with the definition of short-run equilibrium output (Equation 8A.4),

$$Y = PAE. \tag{8A.4}$$

Remember that short-run equilibrium output is the value of output at which output equals planned aggregate expenditure. Using Equation 8A.3 above to substitute for *PAE* in the definition of short-run equilibrium output, we get

$$Y = [\overline{C} - mpc\overline{T} + \overline{I} + \overline{G} + \overline{NX}] + mpcY.$$

The value of *Y* that solves this equation is the value of short-run equilibrium output. To solve for *Y*, group all terms involving *Y* on the left side of the equation:

$$Y - mpcY = [\overline{C} - mpc\overline{T} + \overline{I} + \overline{G} + \overline{NX}]$$

or

$$Y(1 - mpc) = [\overline{C} - mpc\overline{T} + \overline{I} + \overline{G} + \overline{NX}].$$

Dividing both sides of the equation by $(1 - mpc)$ gives

$$Y = (1/(1 - mpc)) [\overline{C} - mpc\overline{T} + \overline{I} + \overline{G} + \overline{NX}]. \tag{8A.5}$$

Equation 8A.5 gives short-run equilibrium output for our model economy in terms of the exogenous values $\overline{C}$, $\overline{I}$, $\overline{G}$, $\overline{NX}$, and $\overline{T}$, and the marginal propensity to consume, *mpc*. We can use this formula to solve for short-run equilibrium output in specific numerical examples. For example, suppose that we once again plug in the numerical values assumed in Example 8.1: $\overline{C} = 620$, $\overline{I} = 220$, $\overline{G} = 300$, $\overline{NX} = 20$, $\overline{T} = 250$, and *mpc* = 0.8. We get

$$Y = \left(\frac{1}{1-0.8}\right)[620 - 0.8(250) + 220 + 300 + 20] = \frac{1}{0.2}(960) = 5(960) = 4800,$$

which is the same answer we found more laboriously using Table 8.1.

Use Equation 8A.5 to find short-run equilibrium output for the economy described in Exercise 8.1. What are the intercept and the slope of the expenditure line?

EXERCISE 8A.1

Equation 8A.5 shows clearly the relationship between autonomous expenditure and short-run equilibrium output. Autonomous expenditure is the first term on the right side of Equation 8A.4, equal to $\overline{C} - mpc\overline{T} + \overline{I} + \overline{G} + \overline{NX}$. The equation shows that a one-unit increase in autonomous expenditure increases short-run equilibrium output by $1/(1 - mpc)$ units. In other words, we can see from Equation 8A.5 that the *multiplier* for this model equals $1/(1 - mpc)$. Further discussion of the multiplier is given in Appendix 8B.

ANSWER TO IN-APPENDIX EXERCISE

8A.1 The equation describing short-run equilibrium output is

$$Y = \frac{1}{(1-mpc)}(\overline{C} - mpc\overline{T} + \overline{I} + \overline{G} + NX). \qquad (8A.5)$$

Using data from Exercise 8.1, set $\overline{C} = 820$, *mpc* = 0.7, $\overline{I} = 600$, $\overline{G} = 600$, $\overline{NX} = 200$, and $\overline{T} = 600$. Plugging these values into Equation (8A.5) we get

$$Y = \left(\frac{1}{1-0.7}\right)[820 - 0.7(600) + 600 + 600 + 200] = 3.33 \times 1800 = 6000,$$

which is the same result obtained in Exercise 8.1. The intercept of the expenditure line is 1800 and the slope is 0.7.

APPENDIX 8B
The Multiplier in the Basic Keynesian Model

This appendix builds on Example 8.3 in the text to give a more complete explanation of the *income-expenditure multiplier* in the basic Keynesian model. In Example 8.3, we saw that a drop in autonomous expenditure of 10 units caused a decline in short-run equilibrium output of 50 units, five times as great as the initial change in spending. Hence the multiplier in this example is 5.

To see why this multiplier effect occurs, note that the initial decrease of 10 in consumer spending (more precisely, in the constant term of the consumption function, $\overline{C}$) in Example 8.3 has two effects. First, the fall in consumer spending directly reduces planned aggregate expenditure by 10 units. Second, the fall in spending also reduces by 10 units the incomes of producers (workers and firm owners) of consumer goods. Under the assumption of Example 8.3 that the marginal propensity to consume is 0.8, the producers of consumer goods will therefore reduce *their* consumption spending by 8, or 0.8 times their income loss of 10. This reduction in spending cuts the income of *other* producers by 8 units, leading them to reduce their spending by 6.4, or 0.8 times their income loss of 8. These income reductions of 6.4 lead still other producers to cut their spending by 5.12, or 0.8 times 6.4, and so on. In principle, this process continues indefinitely, although after many rounds of spending and income reductions the effects become quite small.

When all these "rounds" of income and spending reductions are added, the *total* effect on planned spending of the initial reduction of 10 in consumer spending is

$$10 + 8 + 6.4 + 5.12 + \ldots.$$

The three dots indicate that the series of reductions continues indefinitely. The total effect of the initial decrease in consumption can also be written as

$$10[1 + 0.8 + (0.8)^2 + (0.8)^3 + \ldots].$$

This expression highlights the fact that the spending that takes place in each round is 0.8 times the spending in the previous round (0.8), because that is the marginal propensity to consume out of the income generated by the previous round of spending.

A useful algebraic relationship, which applies to any number x greater than 0 but less than 1, is

$$1 + x + x^2 + x^3 + \ldots = \frac{1}{1-x}.$$

If we set $x = 0.8$, this formula implies that the total effect of the decline in consumption spending on aggregate demand and output is

$$10\left(\frac{1}{1-0.8}\right) = 10\left(\frac{1}{0.2}\right) = 10 \times 5 = 50.$$

This answer is consistent with our earlier calculation, which showed that short-run equilibrium output fell by 50 units, from 4800 to 4750.

By a similar analysis, we can also find a general algebraic expression for the multiplier in the basic Keynesian model. Recalling that *mpc* is the marginal propensity to consume out of disposable income, we know that a 1-unit increase in autonomous expenditure raises spending and income by 1 unit in the first round; by $mpc \times 1 = mpc$ units in the second round; by $mpc \times mpc = mpc^2$ units in the second round; by $mpc \times mpc^2 = mpc^3$ units in the third round; and so on. Thus the total effect on short-run equilibrium output of a 1-unit increase in autonomous expenditure is given by

$$1 + mpc + mpc^2 + mpc^3 + \ldots$$

Applying the algebraic formula given above, and recalling that $0 < mpc < 1$, we can rewrite this expression as $1/(1 - mpc)$. Thus, in a basic Keynesian model with a marginal propensity to consume of *mpc,* the multiplier equals $1/(1 - mpc)$, the same result found in Appendix 8A. Note that if $mpc = 0.8$, then $1/(1 - mpc) = 1/(1 - 0.8) = 5$, which is the same value of the multiplier we found numerically above.

CHAPTER 9
Central Banking, Commercial Banking And Money

In April 2009, with the Canadian economy, still battered from the impact of the global recession, and the unemployment rate at over 8 percent and rising, the Bank of Canada cut the key interest rate it targets to an all-time low of 0.25 percent. It issued a Monetary Policy Report that declared, "In principle, the Bank could lower the policy rate to zero. However, that would eliminate the incentive for lenders and borrowers to transact in markets. . . ."[1] It then stated that 0.25 percent was the effective lower bound for its policy rate, and the rate was not going to go any lower. Some news commentators declared that the Bank of Canada had "run out of ammunition," in the sense that the interest rate was the monetary policy instrument the Bank had been relying upon, and the rate had hit bottom.

But Bank of Canada spokespersons were keen to argue that the situation was under control and that they had more tricks up their sleeves if the need arose. Bank of Canada Governor Mark Carney emphasized that not only had the Bank cut the interest rate to a mere 0.25 percent, but it was committed to holding the rate at 0.25 percent until June 2010. In addition, he stated, if the stimulus provided by the commitment to the 0.25 percent interest rate (and by the expansionary fiscal policy being conducted by the federal, provincial/territorial, and municipal governments) did not provide the economy with sufficient stimulus, the Bank was ready to employ other monetary policy instruments. Additional stimulus, according to Governor Carney, "could be provided through *quantitative easing*, which involves the creation of central bank reserves to purchase financial assets and/or *credit easing*, which includes outright purchases of private sector assets."[2] Some economists, however, were skeptical about the possible effectiveness of the unconventional monetary policy measures mentioned by the Governor.

The global recession and financial crisis of 2008–2009 highlighted two facts about monetary policy. The first is that monetary policy in Canada is primarily about the Bank of Canada using its control over interest rates to achieve its monetary policy objectives.

1   Bank of Canada, *Monetary Policy Report*, April 2009, p. 25. Accessed at http://www.bankofcanada.ca/publications-research/periodicals/mpr/?y=2009.

2   Mark Carney, "Opening Statement," press conference following release of *Monetary Policy Report,* April 23 2009, at http://www.bankofcanada.ca/en/speeches/2009/state09-4.html.

The second is that central banks, particularly in times of crisis, may make use of policy instruments other than control of interest rates.

In Chapter 10, we will concentrate on explaining how the Bank of Canada uses its control over interest rates to stabilize the economy. In this chapter, we will focus on other issues related to monetary policy; issues as varied as how central banks can prevent the collapse of the banking system, unconventional monetary policy, and how in extreme circumstances monetary policy can contribute to hyperinflation. As a prelude to these topics, we discuss the role of money in modern economies: why it is important, and how it is measured. And we explain in detail the solution to the riddle of how commercial banks create money.

9.1 MONEY: ITS EVOLUTION, USES, AND MEASUREMENT

If you visit the Bank of Canada's impressive Currency Museum in Ottawa, you will see that it includes currencies from around the world and from the earliest times to the present. What makes the museum unique, however, is that it traces the evolution of Canadian money, Canadian banking, and the Bank of Canada.[3] It begins with money, as does this chapter. In this section, we will consider the evolution of money, its uses, and then the question of how we measure the quantity of money. Section 9.2 will then consider banking, and section 9.3 will turn to central banking.

EVOLUTION OF MONEY

An early form of money in what is now Canada (and the eastern United States) is called *wampum*, which is an abbreviation by English settlers of an Algonquin word. Wampum refers to strings or belts of cylindrical beads made from polished shells found on the eastern seaboard that were used as currency, for ornamentation, and for ceremonial exchanges. The use of these shell beads by the aboriginal people of the St. Lawrence River was described as early as the 1530s by the French explorer Jacques Cartier.

Wampum came to be used in the fur trade by European traders to purchase beaver pelts from the Iroquois and other native peoples. Wampum was, among other things, a form of money. In everyday language, people use the word *money* to mean "income" or "wealth," as in, "That job pays good money" or, "I wish I had as much money as she does." Economists, however, give a much more specific meaning to the term. To the economist, **money** is any asset that can be used as a means of payment for purchases and settling debts.

One European observer in the mid-1600s stated that the aboriginal people valued wampum "as highly as many Christians do gold, silver, and pearls."[4] At the time, it was common for gold and silver coins to be used as money in Europe. The wampum used in the fur trade as well as the gold and silver coins used in Europe are examples of *commodity money*. **Commodity money** has intrinsic value; commodities that have emerged as money in different societies have typically been storable, easily transportable, and difficult to fake or counterfeit.

Commodity money is distinguished from *fiat money*. **Fiat money** has no (or almost no) intrinsic value or usefulness; its value arises from its widespread acceptance as a means of making purchases and settling debts. New France, the French colony that eventually developed into the province of Quebec, produced a unique form of fiat money. In the late 17th century, the colonial authorities came up with an innovative solution to the shortage

money any asset that can be used as a means of payment for purchases and to settle debts

commodity money an asset with intrinsic value, such as a gold or silver coin, that is generally accepted as a means of payment for purchases and to settle debts

fiat money an asset with no intrinsic value, such as paper currency, that is generally accepted as a means of payment for purchases and to settle debts

3   The Currency Museum maintains a website at http://www.currencymuseum.ca/. Highlights of its collection are presented in the illustrated book *Beads to Bytes: Canada's National Currency Collection* (Ottawa: Bank of Canada, 2008).

4   Quoted in James Powell, *A History of the Canadian Dollar* (Ottawa: Bank of Canada, 2005), p. 3.

of coinage—they issued playing cards with amounts written on the back, and used them to pay soldiers, who then used them for making purchases. Merchants accepted the cards for payments, and the authorities continued to issue new playing card money from time to time until the defeat of France in 1759. When New France came under British control, the card money was redeemed at only a fraction of its face value.

Currency and coins are common examples of money in the modern world. Both are fiat money—the currency is made of paper with no intrinsic value comparable to its face value, and although the coins have metallic content, the value of the metal bears no relation to the value of the coin.

A chequing account balance represents another asset that can be used in making payments (as when you write a cheque to pay the rent for your apartment) and so is also counted as money. In contrast, shares of stock, for example, cannot be used directly in most transactions. Stock must first be sold—that is, converted into cash or a chequing account deposit—before further transactions, such as paying the rent, can be made.

MONEY AND ITS USES

Why do people use money? Money has three principal uses: a *medium of exchange,* a *unit of account,* and a *store of value.*

medium of exchange an asset used in purchasing goods and services

Money serves as a **medium of exchange** when it is used to purchase goods and services, such as when you pay cash for a newspaper or write a cheque to cover your utilities bill. This is perhaps money's most crucial function. Think about how complicated daily life would become if there were no money. Without money, all economic transactions would have to be in the form of **barter,** which is the direct trade of goods or services for other goods or services.

barter the direct trade of goods or services for other goods or services

Barter is highly inefficient because it requires that both parties to a trade have something that the other party wants, a so-called "double coincidence of wants." For example, under a barter system, a musician could get her dinner only by finding someone willing to trade food for a musical performance. Finding such a match of needs, where each party happens to want exactly what the other person has to offer, would be difficult to do on a regular basis. In a world with money, the musician's problem is considerably simpler. First, she must find someone who is willing to pay money for her musical performance. Then, with the money received, she can purchase the food and other goods and services that she needs. In a society that uses money, it is not necessary that the person who wants to hear music and the person who is willing to provide food to the musician be one and the same. In other words, there need not be a double coincidence of wants for trades of goods and services to take place.

© Catherine Karnow/CORBIS

In a world without money, this violinist could eat only by finding someone willing to trade food for a musical performance.

By eliminating the problem of having to find a double coincidence of wants in order to trade, the use of money in a society permits individuals to specialize in producing particular goods or services, as opposed to having every family or village produce most of what it needs. Specialization, including specialization associated with comparative advantage, greatly increases productivity and material standards of living. This usefulness of money in making transactions explains why financial investors hold money, even though money generally pays a low rate of return. Cash, for example, pays no interest at all, and the balances in chequing accounts usually pay a lower rate of interest than could be obtained in alternative financial investments.

COMPARATIVE ADVANTAGE

unit of account a basic measure of economic value

Money's second function is as a *unit of account.* As a **unit of account,** money is the basic yardstick for measuring economic value. In Canada, virtually all prices, including the price of labour (wages) and the prices of financial assets, such as shares of Bombardier stock, are expressed in dollars. Expressing economic values in a common unit of account allows for easy comparisons. For example, gasoline can be measured in litres and coal in tons, but to judge whether 500 litres of gasoline is economically more or less valuable than a ton of coal, we express both values in dollar terms. The use of money as a unit of account is closely related to its use as a medium of exchange; because money is used to buy and sell things, it makes sense to express prices of all kinds in money terms.

As a **store of value**, its third function, money is a way of holding wealth. For example, the miser who stuffs cash in his mattress or buries gold coins under the old oak tree at midnight is holding wealth in money form. Likewise, if you regularly keep a balance in your chequing account, you are holding part of your wealth in the form of money. Although money is usually the primary medium of exchange or unit of account in an economy, it is not the only store of value. There are numerous other ways of holding wealth, such as owning stocks, bonds, or real estate.

For most people, money is not a particularly good way to hold wealth, apart from its usefulness as a medium of exchange. Unlike government bonds and other types of financial assets, most forms of money pay no interest, and there is always the risk of cash being lost or stolen. However, cash has the advantage of being anonymous and difficult to trace, making it an attractive store of value for smugglers, drug dealers, and others who want their assets to stay out of the view of authorities.

MEASURING MONEY

How much money, defined as financial assets usable for making purchases, is there in the Canadian economy at any given time? This question is not simple to answer, because in practice it is not easy to draw a clear distinction between those assets that should be counted as money and those that should not. Dollar bills are certainly a form of money, and a van Gogh painting certainly is not. However, brokerage firms now offer accounts that allow their owners to combine financial investments in stocks and bonds with cheque writing and credit card privileges. Should the balances in these accounts, or some part of them, be counted as money? It is difficult to tell.

Statisticians and economists have skirted the problem of deciding what is or is not money by using several alternative definitions of it that vary in how broadly the concept of money is defined. Historically, considerable attention was paid to a relatively narrow definition called **M1**—that is, the sum of currency outside banks and the balances held in chequing accounts, known as demand deposits. It excluded the balances held in savings accounts, otherwise known as notice deposits.

At one time, it was possible to draw a meaningful line between demand and notice deposits, and the commercial banks were required to hold different percentages of reserves against balances in each of these types of deposits. However, according to the Bank of Canada,

> [F]inancial innovation and the removal of reserve requirements have made the distinction between demand and notice deposits artificial, and it has become increasingly difficult and arbitrary for financial institutions to allocate their deposit accounts between those two categories. Therefore, the reliability of the data needed to create these aggregates has eroded over time.[5]

Based upon this rationale, as of February 2007 the Bank of Canada ceased to construct or publish M1 statistics.

The Bank of Canada continues to publish statistics relating to broader concepts of money such as *M2*.[6] As shown in Table 9.1, **M2** consists of currency outside banks, personal deposits, and non-personal demand and notice deposits. It is prominently featured in the Bank of Canada's weekly *Banking and Financial Statistics*. Notice that currency is a small fraction of M2.

Measures such as M1 and M2 attracted a lot of attention in the late 1970s and early 1980s but do not get a great deal of attention today. The Bank of Canada, for example, once

store of value an asset that serves as a means of holding wealth

M1 sum of currency outside banks and balances held in demand deposits

M2 all the assets in M1 plus some additional assets that are usable in making payments but at greater cost or inconvenience than currency or chequing accounts

---

5 Bank of Canada, "Changes to Monetary Aggregates," at http://www.bankofcanada.ca/tag/monetary-aggregates/.

6 More precisely, the data shown is for M2 (gross), a somewhat broader measure of money supply than the traditional M2 measure. Although the Bank of Canada does not emphasize money supply measures, M2 (gross) receives more attention than the other measures.

TABLE 9.1
Major Components of M2 (gross), December 2010 ($billions)

M2 (gross)	$1013
Currency outside banks	56
Non-personal demand and notice deposits	290
Personal deposits	666

SOURCE: *Bank of Canada Banking and Financial Statistics,* February 2011, Table E1.
Note: The major components do not add exactly to the M2 aggregate primarily due to minor Bank of Canada adjustments not shown. Non-personal notice deposits are deposits of businesses for which banks reserve the right to require notice before a withdrawal is made.

announced targets for the growth of M1 but abandoned the M1 target in 1982. Since the adoption of explicit inflation rate targeting in the early 1990s, the Bank of Canada has at most employed the growth of monetary aggregates as minor indicators of the state of the economy.

Nevertheless, economists at the Bank of Canada and elsewhere recognize that money supply is still significant. For example, a collapse of the money supply, which was a concern in some countries during the financial crisis of 2008–2009 (as discussed in Economic Naturalist 9.1), would have extremely serious recessionary consequences. At the other extreme, a massive increase in the money supply, as occurred in Zimbabwe in 2006–2008 (discussed in Economic Naturalist 9.2), would have extremely serious inflationary consequences.

RECAP

MONEY: EVOLUTION, USES, AND MEASUREMENT

Money is any asset that can be used in making purchases, such as currency or a chequing account. *Commodity money* is money with intrinsic value, such as a gold or silver coin. *Fiat money* is money with no intrinsic value, such as paper currency.

Money serves as a *medium of exchange* when it is used to purchase goods and services. The use of money as a medium of exchange eliminates the need for *barter* and the difficulties of finding a double coincidence of wants. Money also serves as a *unit of account* and a *store of value.*

Two measures of the money supply of considerable historical importance are a narrow measure *M1,* the sum of currency outside banks and the balances held in chequing accounts, and the broader measure *M2,* which consists of currency outside banks, personal deposits, and non-personal demand and notice deposits.

In Canada, measures of the money supply are not watched as closely as they once were. Nevertheless, economists recognize that money supply is still significant in that the collapse of the money supply would have recessionary consequences, and explosion of the money supply would have inflationary consequences.

9.2 COMMERCIAL BANKS AND THE CREATION AND DESTRUCTION OF MONEY

What determines the amount of money in the economy? If the economy's supply of money consisted entirely of currency, the answer would be simple: the supply of money would just be equal to the value of the currency created and circulated by the government. However, as we have seen, in modern economies the money supply consists not only of currency but also of deposit balances held by the public in commercial (that is, private) banks and other financial intermediaries.[7] The determination of the money supply in a modern economy thus depends in part on the behaviour of financial intermediaries and their depositors.

To see how the existence of financial intermediaries affects the money supply, we will use the example of a fictional economy. We assume, initially, that this economy has no financial intermediaries. To make trading easier and to eliminate the need for barter, the government directs the central bank to put into circulation a million identical paper notes, called guilders. The central bank prints the guilders and distributes them to the populace. At this point, the money supply is a million guilders.

However, the citizens are unhappy with a money supply made up entirely of paper guilders, since the notes may be lost or stolen. In response to the demand for safekeeping of money, some entrepreneurs set up a system of commercial banks. At first, these banks are only storage vaults where people can deposit their guilders. When people need to make a payment they can either physically withdraw their guilders or, more conveniently, write a cheque on their account. Cheques give the banks permission to transfer guilders from the account of the person paying by cheque to the account of the person to whom the cheque is made out. With a system of payments based on cheques, the paper guilders need never leave the banking system, although they flow from one bank to another as a depositor of one bank makes a payment to a depositor in another bank. Deposits do not pay interest in this economy; indeed, the banks can make a profit only by charging depositors fees in exchange for safeguarding their cash.

Let's suppose for now that people prefer bank deposits to cash and so deposit all of their guilders with the commercial banks. With all guilders in the vaults of banks, the balance sheet of all of the economy's commercial banks taken together is as shown in Table 9.2.

TABLE 9.2
Consolidated Balance Sheet of the Commercial Banks (Initial)

Assets		Liabilities	
Currency	1 000 000 guilders	Deposits	1 000 000 guilders

The *assets* of the commercial banking system of this fictional economy are the paper guilders sitting in the vaults of all the individual banks. The banking system's *liabilities* are the deposits of the banks' customers, since chequing account balances represent money owed by the banks to the depositors.

Cash or similar assets held by banks are called **bank reserves**. In this example, bank reserves, for all the banks taken together, equal 1 000 000 guilders, the currency listed on the asset side of the consolidated balance sheet. Banks hold reserves to meet depositors' demands for cash withdrawals or to pay cheques drawn on their depositors' accounts. In this example, the bank reserves of 1 000 000 guilders equal 100 percent of banks' deposits, which are also 1 000 000 guilders. A situation in which bank reserves equal 100 percent of bank deposits is called **100 percent reserve banking**.

Bank reserves are held by banks in their vaults, rather than circulated among the public, and thus are *not* counted as part of the money supply. However, bank deposit balances, which can be used in making transactions, *are* counted as money. So, after the introduction of "safekeeper" banks in our fictional economy, the money supply, equal to the value of bank deposits, is 1 000 000 guilders, which is the same as it was prior to the introduction of banks.

After a while, to continue the story, the commercial bankers begin to realize that keeping 100 percent reserves against deposits is not necessary. True, a few guilders flow

bank reserves cash or similar assets held by commercial banks for the purpose of meeting depositor withdrawals and payments

100 percent reserve banking a situation in which banks' reserves equal 100 percent of their deposits

---

7 In Canada, the commercial banks are also known as chartered banks. The big five chartered banks (in order of value of their assets, 2010) are the RBC Royal Bank ($762 billion), TD Canada Trust ($620 billion), Scotiabank ($528 billion), BMO Bank of Montreal ($412 billion), and CIBC ($352 billion).

in and out of the typical bank as depositors receive payments or write cheques, but for the most part the stacks of paper guilders just sit there in the vaults, untouched and unused. It occurs to the bankers that they can meet the random inflow and outflow of guilders to their banks with reserves that are less than 100 percent of their deposits. After some observation, the bankers conclude that keeping reserves equal to only 10 percent of deposits is enough to meet the random ebb and flow of withdrawals and payments from their individual banks. The remaining 90 percent of deposits, the bankers realize, can be lent out to borrowers to earn interest.

So the bankers decide to keep reserves equal to 100 000 guilders, or 10 percent of their deposits. The other 900 000 guilders they lend out at interest to business owners who want to use the money to make improvements to their firms. After the loans are made, the balance sheet of all of the commercial banks taken together has changed, as shown in Table 9.3.

TABLE 9.3

Consolidated Balance Sheet of the Commercial Banks after One Round of Loans

Assets			Liabilities
Currency (= reserves)	100 000 guilders	Deposits	1 000 000 guilders
Loans to farmers	900 000 guilders		

reserve-deposit ratio bank reserves divided by deposits

fractional-reserve banking system a banking system in which bank reserves are less than deposits so that the reserve-deposit ratio is less than 100 percent

After the loans are made, the banks' reserves of 100 000 guilders no longer equal 100 percent of the banks' deposits of 1 000 000 guilders. Instead, the **reserve-deposit ratio**, which is bank reserves divided by deposits, is now equal to 100 000/1 000 000, or 10 percent. A banking system in which banks hold fewer reserves than deposits so that the reserve-deposit ratio is less than 100 percent is called a **fractional-reserve banking system**.

Notice that 900 000 guilders have flowed out of the banking system (as loans to farmers) and are now in the hands of the public. But we have assumed that private citizens prefer bank deposits to cash for making transactions. So ultimately, people will redeposit the 900 000 guilders in the banking system. After these deposits are made, the consolidated balance sheet of the commercial banks is as in Table 9.4.

TABLE 9.4

Consolidated Balance Sheet of the Commercial Banks after Guilders are Redeposited

Assets			Liabilities
Currency (= reserves)	100 000 guilders	Deposits	1 900 000 guilders
Loans to farmers	900 000 guilders		

Notice that bank deposits, and hence the economy's money supply, now equal 1 900 000 guilders. In effect, the existence of the commercial banking system has permitted the creation of new money. These deposits, which are liabilities of the banks, are balanced by assets of 1 000 000 guilders in reserves and 900 000 guilders in loans owed to the banks.

The story does not end here. On examining their balance sheets, the bankers are surprised to see that they once again have "too many" reserves. With deposits of 1 900 000 guilders and a 10 percent reserve-deposit ratio, they need only 190 000 guilders in reserve. But they have 1 000 000 guilders in reserve—810 000 too many. Since lending out their excess guilders is always more profitable than leaving them in the vault, the bankers proceed to make another 810 000 guilders in loans. Eventually these loaned-out guilders are redeposited in the banking system, after which the consolidated balance sheet of the banks is as shown in Table 9.5.

TABLE 9.5
Consolidated Balance Sheet of the Commercial Banks after Two Rounds of Loans and Redeposits

Assets		Liabilities	
Currency (= reserves)	1 000 000 guilders	Deposits	2 710 000 guilders
Loans to farmers	1 710 000 guilders		

Now the money supply has increased to 2 710 000 guilders, equal to the value of bank deposits. Despite the expansion of loans and deposits, however, the bankers find that their reserves of 1 000 000 guilders *still* exceed the desired level of 10 percent of deposits, which is 271 000 guilders. And so yet another round of lending will take place.

Determine what the balance sheet of the banking system of our fictional economy will look like after a third round of lending to farmers and redeposits of guilders into the commercial banking system. What is the size of the money supply at that point?

EXERCISE 9.1

The process of expansion of loans and deposits will only end when reserves equal 10 percent of bank deposits, because as long as reserves exceed 10 percent of deposits, the banks will find it profitable to lend out the extra reserves. Since reserves at the end of every round equal 1 000 000 guilders, for the reserve-deposit ratio to equal 10 percent, total deposits must equal 10 000 000 guilders. Further, since the balance sheet must balance, with assets equal to liabilities, we also know that at the end of the process, loans must equal 9 000 000 guilders. If loans equal 9 000 000 guilders, then bank assets, the sum of loans and reserves (1 000 000 guilders), will equal 10 000 000 guilders, which is the same as bank liabilities (bank deposits). The final consolidated balance sheet is as shown in Table 9.6.

TABLE 9.6
Final Consolidated Balance Sheet of the Commercial Banks

Assets		Liabilities	
Currency (= reserves)	1 000 000 guilders	Deposits	10 000 000 guilders
Loans to farmers	9 000 000 guilders		

The money supply, which is equal to total deposits, is 10 000 000 guilders at the end of the process. We see that the existence of a fractional-reserve banking system has multiplied the money supply by a factor of 10, relative to the economy with no banks or the economy with 100 percent reserve banking. Put another way, with a 10 percent reserve-deposit ratio, each guilder deposited in the banking system can "support" 10 guilders worth of deposits.

To find the money supply in this example more directly, we observe that deposits will expand through additional rounds of lending as long as the ratio of bank reserves to bank deposits exceeds the reserve-deposit ratio desired by banks. When the actual ratio of bank reserves to deposits equals the desired reserve-deposit ratio, the expansion stops. Ultimately, deposits in the banking system satisfy the following relationship:

$$\frac{\text{Bank reserves}}{\text{Bank deposits}} = \text{Desired reserve-deposit ratio.}$$

This equation can be rewritten to solve for bank deposits:

$$\text{Bank deposits} = \frac{\text{Bank reserves}}{\text{Desired reserve-deposit ratio}} \tag{9.1}$$

Since all the currency in our fictional economy flows into the banking system, bank reserves equal 1 000 000 guilders. The reserve-deposit ratio desired by banks is 0.10. Therefore, using Equation 9.1, we find that bank deposits equal (1 000 000 guilders)/0.10, or 10 million guilders, the same answer we found in the consolidated balance sheet of the banks, Table 9.6.

EXERCISE 9.2   **Find deposits and the money supply if the banks' desired reserve-deposit ratio is 5 percent rather than 10 percent. What if the total amount of currency circulated by the central bank is 2 000 000 guilders and the desired reserve-deposit ratio remains at 10 percent?**

THE MONEY SUPPLY WITH BOTH CURRENCY AND DEPOSITS

In our example, we assumed that all money is held in the form of deposits in banks. In reality, of course, people keep only part of their money holdings in the form of bank accounts and hold the rest in the form of currency. Fortunately, allowing for the fact that people hold both currency and bank deposits does not greatly complicate the determination of the money supply, as Example 9.1 shows.

EXAMPLE **9.1**

The money supply with both currency and deposits

Suppose that the citizens choose to hold a total of 500 000 guilders in the form of currency and to deposit the rest of their money in banks. Banks keep reserves equal to 10 percent of deposits. What is the money supply?

The money supply is the sum of currency in the hands of the public and bank deposits. Currency in the hands of the public is given as 500 000 guilders. What is the quantity of bank deposits? Since 500 000 of the 1 000 000 guilders issued by the central bank are being used by the public in the form of currency, only the remaining 500 000 guilders are available to serve as bank reserves. We know that deposits equal bank reserves divided by the reserve-deposit ratio, so deposits are 500 000 guilders/ 0.10 = 5 000 000 guilders. The total money supply is the sum of currency in the hands of the public (500 000 guilders) and bank deposits (5 000 000 guilders), or 5 500 000 guilders.

We can write a general relationship that captures the reasoning of Example 9.1. First, let's write out the assumption that the money supply equals currency plus bank deposits:

Money supply = Currency held by the public + Bank deposits.

We also know that bank deposits equal bank reserves divided by the reserve-deposit ratio that is desired by commercial banks (Equation 9.1). Using that relationship to substitute for bank deposits in the expression for the money supply, we get

$$\text{Money supply} = \text{Currency held by public} + \frac{\text{Bank reserves}}{\text{Desired reserve-deposit ratio}} \tag{9.2}$$

We can use Equation 9.2 to confirm our answer to Example 9.1. In that example, currency held by the public is 500 000 guilders, bank reserves are 500 000 guilders, and the desired reserve-deposit ratio is 0.10. Plugging these values into Equation 9.2, we find that the money supply equals 500 000 + (500 000/0.10) = 5 500 000, the same answer we found before.

EXAMPLE 9.2

Contraction of the money supply

Suppose that people become somewhat worried about the soundness of the banking system and wish to hold more of their wealth in currency and less of it in bank deposits. With no action by the central bank, how would this change in currency holding affect the money supply?

To illustrate with a numerical example, suppose that initially bank reserves are 500, the amount of currency held by the public is 500, and the desired reserve-deposit ratio in the banking system is 0.2. Inserting these values into Equation 9.2, we find that the money supply equals 500 + (500/0.2) = 3000.

Now suppose that, because the public becomes worried about the soundness of the banking system, the public increases its currency holdings to 600 by withdrawing 100 from commercial banks. These withdrawals reduce bank reserves to 400. Using Equation 9.2, we find now that the money supply is 600 + (400/0.2) = 2600. So the public's increased holdings of currency have caused the money supply to drop, from 3000 to 2600. The reason for the drop is that with a reserve-deposit ratio of 20 percent, every dollar in the vaults of banks can "support" $5 of deposits and hence $5 of money supply. However, the same dollar in the hands of the public becomes $1 of currency, contributing only $1 to the total money supply. So when the public withdraws cash from the banks, the overall money supply declines significantly.

A DANGER WITH FRACTIONAL-RESERVE BANKING: THE DESTRUCTION OF MONEY

We have examined a situation in which the public overall suddenly wished to increase its currency holdings, and then the money supply contracted, all else equal. It was a situation in which the public wanted to withdraw some of its money from the banking system, but not all of it. There is a particularly problematic version of this situation, known as a *banking panic*, which can arise under a fractional reserve-banking system. A **banking panic** occurs when depositors, spurred by news or rumours of the imminent bankruptcy of multiple banks, rush to try to withdraw their deposits from the banking system.

A banking panic, incidentally, is broader than a *bank run*. It is a wave of bank runs. A **bank run** takes place when the customers of a particular bank fear that the bank will become insolvent. Customers rush to the bank to take out their money as quickly as possible to avoid losing it. Under fractional-reserve banking, however, even if the fears of the public are initially unfounded, the fears can easily turn into a self-fulfilling prophecy. Under fractional-reserve banking, only a fraction of the depositors' money is going to be held in the vaults of the bank. The rest of it will have been lent out to borrowers. Therefore, if all of the depositors try to take out all of their money, they will fail. It is an example of the fallacy of composition in that if one depositor took out money he or she would succeed in getting it, but if everyone tries to take out his or her money, the bank will run out of money well before everyone can be served.

A banking panic can produce a massive contraction of the money supply. With fewer banks in operation, it will be more difficult for businesses and consumers to borrow, and overall expenditure in the economy will tend to decline, creating a recession or even a depression.

banking panic occurs when there is a rush of withdrawals from the banking system made by depositors responding to news or rumours of impending bankruptcy of multiple banks

bank run occurs when the depositors of a particular bank respond to news or rumours of impending bankruptcy of that particular bank by rushing to withdraw their deposits from the bank

ECONOMIC NATURALIST   9.1

The U.S. banking panic of 1930–1933 and the banking panic of 2008

One of the most dramatic banking panics in world history occurred in the United States during the early stages of the Great Depression, between 1930 and 1933. Although Canada also went through a severe economic downturn in the same period, the country was not gripped by a comparable banking panic, apparently because Canadian banks were large institutions with national networks of branch offices that inspired confidence in Canadian depositors. The U.S. experience with a banking panic, however, is of general relevance as it dramatically illustrates how the public demand for currency and the desired reserve-deposit ratio of banks affect the money supply.

During the 1930–1933 period, approximately one-third of the banks in the United States were forced to close. This near-collapse of the banking system was probably an important reason why the Depression was so severe. With many fewer banks in operation, it was very difficult for small businesses and consumers during the early 1930s to obtain credit. A related important effect of the bank runs was to greatly reduce the nation's money supply. Why should banking panic reduce the national money supply?

During a bank run, people are afraid to keep deposits in a bank because of the risk that the bank will go bankrupt and their money will be lost (this was prior to the introduction of federal deposit insurance). During the 1930–1933 period, many bank depositors withdrew their money from banks, holding currency instead. These withdrawals reduced bank reserves. Each extra dollar of currency held by the public adds one dollar to the money supply; but each extra dollar of bank reserves translates into several dollars of money supply, because in a fractional-reserve banking system, each dollar of reserves can "support" several dollars in bank deposits. Thus, the public's withdrawals from banks, which increased currency holdings by the public but reduced bank reserves by an equal amount, led to a net decrease in the total money supply (currency plus deposits).

In addition, fearing banking panics and the associated withdrawals by depositors, banks increased their reserve-deposit ratios, which reduced the quantity of deposits that could be supported by any given level of bank reserves. This change in reserve-deposit ratios also tended to reduce the money supply.

Data on currency holdings by the public, the reserve-deposit ratio, bank reserves, and the money supply for selected dates are shown in Table 9.7. Notice the increase over the period in the amount of currency held by the public and in the reserve-deposit ratio, as well as the decline in bank reserves after 1930. The last column shows that the U.S. money supply dropped by about one-third between December 1929 and December 1933.[8]

Using Equation 9.2, we can see that increases in currency holdings by the public and increases in the reserve-deposit ratio both tend to reduce the money supply. These effects were so powerful in 1930–1933 that the U.S. money supply, shown in the fourth column of Table 9.7, dropped precipitously, even though currency holdings and bank reserves, taken separately, actually rose during the period.

It is worth noting that although the U.S. banking panic of the 1930s occurred decades ago, it is still relevant to us in the twenty-first century. The Princeton University economist Paul Krugman described the U.S. housing and mortgage financial crisis of 2007–2008 in the following terms in March 2008: "The financial crisis currently under way is basically an updated version of the wave of bank runs that swept the nation three generations ago."[9] In March 2008, fearing a repeat of the 1930s events he studied as an academic economist, Federal Reserve Chairman Ben Bernanke led a decisive move to rescue the near-bank Bear Stearns and have it merged with JP Morgan Chase. The move was made to prevent the possibility of an impending bankruptcy of Bear Stearns, due to losses on mortgage-backed securities, from setting off a chain reaction. In September 2008, based in part on criticism of its rescue of Bear Stearns was a departure from free-market principles, the Fed decided to test whether it could get away with allowing financial institution Lehman Brothers to fail without setting off a chain reaction. The decision proved to be a mistake—a chain reaction was triggered, and the Fed was quickly forced by circumstances to change course.[10]

---

8 In Canada, between 1929 and 1933, the money supply, defined as currency outside the banks and chartered bank deposits, declined by about 15 percent. See Statistics Canada, *Historical Statistics of Canada*, Section J: Banking and Finance, The Supply of Money, Table J1-10, www.statcan.gc.ca/pub/11-516-x/sectionj/J1-10-eng.csv. One view is that the decline in the Canadian money supply was a result of the decline in GDP. Incidentally, during these years, Canada did not have a central bank; the Bank of Canada did not begin operation until 1935.

9 Paul Krugman, "Partying like It's 1929," *New York Times,* 21 March 2008.

10 The quick reversal by the Federal Reserve-led House Financial Services Committee Chairman Barney Frank to jest that, "The national commitment to the free market lasted one day." See Damian Paletta, "Barney Frank Celebrates Free Market Day," *Wall Street Journal*, September 17, 2008, at http://blogs.wsj.com/economics/2008/09/17/barney-frank-celebrates-free-market-day/.

TABLE 9.7
Key U.S. Monetary Statistics, 1929–1933

	Currency held by public	Reserve-deposit ratio	Bank reserves	Money supply
December 1929	3.85	0.075	3.15	45.9
December 1930	3.79	0.082	3.31	44.1
December 1931	4.59	0.095	3.11	37.3
December 1932	4.82	0.109	3.18	34.0
December 1933	4.85	0.133	3.45	30.8

Note: Data on currency, bank reserves, and the money supply are in billions of dollars.
SOURCE: Milton Friedman and Anna J. Schwartz, *A Monetary History of the United States, 1863–1960* (Princeton, N.J.: Princeton University Press, 1963), Table A-1.

Using the data from Table 9.7, confirm that the relationship between the money supply and its determinants is consistent with Equation 9.2. Would the money supply have fallen in 1931–1933 if the public had stopped withdrawing deposits after December 1930 so that currency held by the public had remained at its December 1930 level?

EXERCISE 9.3

RECAP

COMMERCIAL BANKS AND THE CREATION AND DESTRUCTION OF MONEY

Part of the money supply consists of deposits in private commercial banks and other financial intermediaries. Hence, the behaviour of financial intermediaries and their depositors helps to determine the money supply.

Cash or similar assets held by banks are called *bank reserves.* In modern economies, banks' reserves are less than their deposits, a situation called *fractional-reserve banking.* The ratio of bank reserves to deposits is called the *reserve-deposit ratio;* in a fractional-reserve banking system, this ratio is less than one.

The portion of deposits not held as reserves can be lent out by the banks to earn interest. Banks will continue to make loans and accept deposits as long as the reserve-deposit ratio exceeds its desired level. This process stops only when the actual and desired reserve-deposit ratios are equal. At that point, total bank deposits equal bank reserves divided by the desired reserve-deposit ratio, assuming that the money supply equals the currency held by the public plus bank deposits (see Equation 9.2).

If the public overall suddenly wishes to increase its currency holdings, the money supply will contract, all else equal. A *bank run* takes place when the customers of a particular bank fear that the bank will become insolvent. A *banking panic* is a wave of bank runs. A banking panic can cause or deepen a recession.

9.3 THE BANK OF CANADA AND ITS THREE MAJOR RESPONSIBILITIES

Central banks exist in most economies as government agencies. The Bank of Canada, Canada's central bank, opened its doors in March 1935, following the passage of the *Bank of Canada Act* in 1934. Unlike commercial banks, which are private businesses whose principal objective is to make a profit, central banks focus on promoting public goals such as economic growth or moderate inflation or low inflation.

Within the Bank of Canada, decision-making power regarding the achievement of the Bank's goals lies with the governing council, composed of the governor (currently Mark Carney, appointed in February 2008), the senior deputy governor, and four deputy governors. The governor, who is appointed for a term of seven years, is the Bank's chief executive officer. The governor, the senior deputy governor, 12 outside directors, and the deputy minister of finance (who has no vote) constitute a board of directors charged with ensuring that the Bank is managed properly.

The Bank of Canada, like many other central banks, has been criticized for being largely outside of democratic control. It is certainly true that none of the members of either the governing council or the board of directors is elected. But defenders of existing practice note that the Bank of Canada is not completely independent of the elected government. The power of appointing directors to fill vacant seats on the Bank's board rests with the federal minister of finance (who is, of course, elected). The board of directors is responsible for appointing the governor, yet only subject to approval by the federal cabinet. The federal government has a say in the inflation-control targets that have been announced jointly by the Bank and the government every few years since 1991, and these targets make the Bank of Canada accountable to an explicit standard of performance. In addition, the minister of finance can issue a written directive to the governor specifying a change in policy in the case of a profound policy disagreement (in which case the governor would probably resign).

The Bank of Canada, which is based in Ottawa, has also been criticized for its lack of regional representation. Defenders of the Bank point out that it does have regional branch offices in Vancouver, Calgary, Toronto, Montreal and Halifax, and its 12 outside directors represent different regions across Canada. Compared to the U.S. Federal Reserve System, however, the Bank of Canada is highly centralized.

In the remainder of this section we will analyze three major responsibilities of a central bank, taking the Bank of Canada as a concrete example. The analysis builds upon the preceding sections of this chapter.

ISSUANCE OF BANK NOTES

One major responsibility of the Bank of Canada is to issue bank notes. Historically, bank notes have been called paper money, but in early 2011 the Bank of Canada announced its intention to issue polymer bank notes over the next two years, beginning with one hundred dollar bills in November 2011.[11] Bank notes, whether of paper or polymer, make up the largest component of the **currency**, which consists of bank notes and coins. (In Canada, coins are produced by a publicly owned corporation called the Royal Canadian Mint with headquarters in Ottawa.) Because the Bank of Canada is in charge of printing bank notes, it is able to finance itself without a contribution of tax dollars from the federal government and it even produces a tidy profit for the government out of *seigniorage*.

currency refers to bank notes and coins

Seigniorage is a gain to the issuer of bank notes or coins that arises in part because the cost of producing and distributing bank notes and coins is less than their face value and in part because bank notes and coins do not pay interest. In the case of the Bank of Canada, "Seigniorage is the difference between the interest the Bank of Canada earns on a portfolio of Government of Canada securities—which is roughly equal in value to the total value of all bank notes in circulation—and the cost of issuing, distributing, and replacing those notes." As an example, the Bank of Canada notes that it "clears an annual

seigniorage refers to the profit gained from the issue of paper money or coins

11 For the Bank of Canada's economic rationale for moving to polymer banknotes, see Bank of Canada, "Backgrounder on Canada's new polymer bank note series," at www.bankofcanada.ca/wp-content/uploads/2011/06/currency-polymer.pdf.

net revenue of about 95 cents for each \$20 note in circulation."[12] After paying its own expenses, the Bank of Canada has in recent times contributed about \$2 billion per year as profit for the federal government.

STABILITY OF THE FINANCIAL SYSTEM

A second major responsibility of the Bank of Canada is the stability of the financial system, particularly the banking system. At the federal level, the Bank of Canada shares responsibility for financial system stability with other organizations that belong to the Financial Institutions Supervisory Committee, as shown in Figure 9.1.

This is not the place to provide a full explanation of financial system regulation in Canada, but it is worth noting two functions that the Bank of Canada does not perform. The Bank of Canada is not the federal organization with primary responsibility for regulating and supervising deposit-taking institutions and insurance companies—that is the job of the Office of the Superintendent of Financial Institutions.[13] Nor does the Bank of Canada provide *deposit insurance*. **Deposit insurance** is provided to financial institutions, such as banks, so that the deposits of their customers are insured in case the financial institution goes bankrupt. In Canada, deposit insurance of up to \$100 000 per account is provided to member financial institutions by the Canada Deposit Insurance Corporation, a federal Crown (publicly owned) corporation. Among other things, deposit insurance acts to reduce the likelihood of bank runs.

deposit insurance is provided to financial institutions such as banks so that the deposits of their customers are insured in case the financial institution goes bankrupt

---

FIGURE 9.1

The Bank of Canada's Place in Canada's System of Financial Regulation

The Bank of Canada shares responsibility for the stability of the financial system with other federal organizations that make up the Financial Institutions Supervisory Committee: the Department of Finance, the Office of the Superintendent of Financial Institutions, the Canada Deposit Insurance Corporation, and the Financial Consumer Agency of Canada. The Minister of Finance is directly responsible for the Department of Finance, while the Bank of Canada and the other members of the Committee are in an arm's-length relationship to the Minister and the Department of Finance.

SOURCE: Adapted from Office of the Superintendent of Financial Institutions, at http://www.osfi-bsif.gc.ca/osfi/index_e.aspx?ArticleID=2803, extracted May 10, 2011.

---

12 Both quotations are from Bank of Canada, "Seigniorage," at http://www.bankofcanada.ca/en/backgrounders/bg-m3.html. On seigniorage of the Federal Reserve in the United States, see James Hamilton, "How the Federal Reserve earned its profit," *Econobrower* blog, January 17, 2010, at http://www.econbrowser.com/archives/2010/01/how_the_federal.html.

13 For more information on the Office of the Superintendent of Financial Institutions (OSFI), see http://www.osfi-bsif.gc.ca/.

lender of last resort an institution, typically a central bank, that will extend credit to financial institutions during a financial panic to keep the payments system operating smoothly

The unique contribution of the Bank of Canada in maintaining the stability of the financial system stems from its capacity to function as a *lender of last resort*. The strongest meaning of the term **lender of last resort**, one that appeared frequently in the news during the financial crisis of 2007–2009, refers to an organization that will extend credit to financial institutions during a financial panic to keep the payments system operating smoothly and prevent the collapse of the financial system. In modern times, the organization extending the credit is typically the central bank.[14] The capacity of the Bank of Canada to serve as a powerful lender of last resort is rooted in its ability to issue money and in its central role in the payments system, including the Large Value Transfer System that lets financial institutions send large payments to each other with certainty that these payments will settle.

The Bank of Canada's responsibility as a lender of last resort was on display during the financial crisis of 2007–2009. To maintain the smooth functioning of the financial system, the Bank of Canada established what it termed *liquidity* facilities. **Liquidity** refers to ease with which an asset can be converted into cash. Currency is the most liquid asset; a home mortgage held by a financial institution during a housing slump would be an example of an illiquid asset. The liquidity facilities were temporary programs under which the Bank of Canada either accepted a broader than usual range of assets as collateral from financial institutions to which it provided liquid funds, or it provided liquid funds to a broader than usual range of financial institutions, or both.[15] In essence, the Bank of Canada as the lender of last resort provided loans to the financial institutions. The first of the liquidity facility programs was established in late 2007, and new programs were started in the fall of 2008 during the worst phase of the global financial panic. By January 2009, loans from the Bank of Canada to financial institutions amounted to $37 billion. As credit conditions improved in 2009 and into 2010, the temporary programs were phased out. By July 2010, the Bank of Canada's loans to financial institutions amounted to less than $3 billion.

liquidity refers to the ease with which an asset can be converted into cash

Incidentally, it is not only during financial panics that central banks may take action to keep the payments system operating smoothly. For example, the Federal Reserve in the United States implemented a number of measures in response to the September 11, 2001, attacks on the World Trade Center in Manhattan, New York, the home of Wall Street. The Bank of Japan did likewise in response to the earthquake, tsunami, and nuclear power disaster of March 2011.[16]

MONETARY POLICY

The third responsibility of the central bank is for monetary policy. Monetary policy in Canada, as will be discussed in further detail in Chapter 10, centres on the Bank of Canada's setting of its *key policy rate* to attain its objective of achieving a target for annual inflation of 2 percent, which is the midpoint of an inflation control target band of 1 to 3 percent inflation. The **key policy rate** is a general term for the interest rate that the central bank controls to achieve its monetary policy objective or objectives.

key policy rate a general term for the interest rate that the central bank controls to achieve its monetary policy objective

For the Bank of Canada, the specific term used for the key policy rate is the *overnight rate target*, a term that will be discussed in Chapter 10. Starting in December 2000, the Bank of Canada introduced a system of eight pre-specified dates each year for announcing any changes to the overnight rate target. Under special circumstances, the Bank of

14 The Bank of Canada states that it has three roles as a lender of last resort. See http://www.bankofcanada.ca/about/what-we-do/what-is-the-financial-system/. The discussion in this textbook is closest to the third role: "In conditions of severe and unusual stress on the financial system more generally, the Bank has authority to provide liquidity through outright purchases of a wide variety of securities issued by any Canadian or foreign entities, including non-financial firms."

15 The Bank of Canada established a separate website to document the special measures it took to respond to the global financial crisis: http://credit.bank-banque-canada.ca/facilities/about. The site also provides monthly balance sheets for the Bank of Canada.

16 Details of the Federal Reserve's response are covered in a short documentary prepared by the Federal Reserve Bank of San Francisco: "The Federal Reserve Responds to September 11, 2001," at http://www.youtube.com/watch?v=mRo_rSeIAOE.

Canada will change the overnight rate target outside of the fixed dates, as it did in conjunction with the U.S. Federal Reserve on September 17, 2001, the day U.S. financial markets re-opened following the September 11 attacks.

Different central banks have different specific terms for their key policy rates. For example, the U.S. Federal Reserve refers to its key policy rate as the *federal funds rate* target. Moreover, not all central banks have an explicit inflation rate target and may be guided by legislation to recognize other objectives. For example, the United States has a Humphrey–Hawkins Full Employment Act dating from 1978 that, among other things, specifies full employment as a national economic goal. If a central bank does have an inflation target, it is typically no lower than the 2 percent target of the Bank of Canada and no higher than 5 percent.

Although monetary policy in Canada over the past few decades has usually been thought of in terms of central bank manipulation of the key policy rate to achieve its inflation control objective, it is useful to recognize that central banks have other monetary policy measures, besides just key policy rates, at their disposal.

Two such measures are the unconventional monetary policy measures of *quantitative easing* and *credit easing*. Quantitative easing, which had been pioneered by the Bank of Japan in the period 2001–2006, was pursued by central banks in several countries including the United States during and after the global recession of 2008–2009. **Quantitative easing** is the unconventional monetary policy of actively creating central bank reserves for the purchase of financial assets such as government bonds from banks and other financial institutions. It is conducted with a view to providing extra stimulus to economy-wide spending in the context that the economy is in recession and the key policy rate is at the *effective lower bound*. The **effective lower bound** refers to the lowest practically feasible level for a central bank's key policy rate.

The extra stimulus provided by quantitative easing could come about, for example, if the expansion of reserves available to commercial banks causes them to boost their lending to businesses and households. A potential problem for quantitative easing is that with the opportunity cost of holding reserves being low when short-term interest rates are close to zero, and with the risks of lending perceived as being high in the midst of recession (borrowers may go bankrupt and not repay their loans), commercial banks may just hold on to the reserves and not boost their lending by significant amounts.

Credit easing is the unconventional monetary policy of the central bank purchasing private-sector financial assets in order to reduce interest rate spreads in credit markets during a financial panic. The idea is that if the central bank adds to the demand for private-sector financial assets, the issuers of those assets will not have to promise such high rates of interest to sell them. An interest rate spread (sometimes called a credit spread or simply a spread), which will be examined in further detail in Chapter 10, is the difference between a benchmark interest rate such as the overnight rate and the rate on some related, riskier financial asset, such as a corporate bond or a mortgage. During a financial crisis, interest rate spreads can increase, as illustrated in Figure 10.3. If the key policy rate is sufficiently high before the interest rate spread widens, the central bank can offset the rise in the interest rate spread by cutting the key policy rate. If the key policy rate is already at the effective lower bound, however, the conventional monetary policy measure of rate cuts is no longer available, and the central bank may resort to the unconventional monetary policy measure of credit easing.

When the Bank of Canada reduced the overnight rate target to its effective lower bound of 0.25 percent in April 2009, it announced that it would employ the unconventional monetary policy measures of quantitative easing or credit easing if the situation required it. As mentioned previously, however, the Bank of Canada never employed either quantitative easing or credit easing. It did, however, create new liquidity facilities as mentioned above, which have a similar impact to credit easing. Moreover, when the Bank of Canada reduced the overnight rate target to 0.25 percent, it made an unusual commitment with the following words: "Conditional on the outlook for inflation, the target

quantitative easing the unconventional monetary policy of actively creating central bank reserves for the purchase of financial assets

effective lower bound the lowest practically feasible level for a central bank's key policy rate

credit easing the unconventional monetary policy of the central bank purchasing private-sector financial assets in order to reduce interest rate spreads overnight rate can be expected to remain at its current level until the end of the second quarter of 2010. . . ."[17]

In making this announcement, the Bank of Canada was adopting an unconventional policy measure that, like quantitative easing, had been pioneered by the Bank of Japan: a *zero interest rate commitment*. A **zero interest rate commitment** is the unconventional policy measure that the central bank not only reduces the key policy rate to the effective lower bound but it promises to keep the policy rate at the effective lower bound for an extended period. The intention of the central bank in announcing a zero interest rate commitment is that it will provide extra stimulus to economy-wide spending beyond simply reducing the interest rate to zero. For example, economy-wide spending should be higher the lower are longer-term interest rates, and longer-term interest rates should be lower the stronger is the expectation that future short-term interest rates will be low.

zero interest rate commitment *a promise made by a central bank that it will maintain its key policy rate at the effective lower bound for an extended periods*

RECAP ↑

THE BANK OF CANADA AND ITS THREE MAJOR RESPONSIBILITIES

The Bank of Canada is a government agency with decision-making power in the hands of a governing council headed by the Bank of Canada governor. The Bank, like most central banks, is relatively independent of the government.

One major responsibility of the Bank of Canada is to issue bank notes, which is a source of seigniorage for the Bank, and ultimately for the government.

A second major responsibility is for the stability of the financial system, and the Bank of Canada shares this responsibility with other members of the Financial Institutions Supervisory Committee, including the Department of Finance, the Office of the Superintendent for Financial Institutions and the Canadian Deposit Insurance Corporation, The unique responsibility of the Bank of Canada in maintaining the stability of the financial system stems from its capacity to function as a lender of last resort. The Bank's ability to provide liquidity to the financial system is the foundation for its lender of last resort function.

The third major responsibility of the central bank is for monetary policy, and in normal times monetary policy for the Bank of Canada involves adjusting its key policy rate—the overnight rate target—to achieve its inflation control target. However, in response to the persistence of recessionary gaps despite policy rates at the effective lower bound, some central banks have pursued the unconventional monetary policy measures of quantitative easing and credit easing. The Bank of Canada has not pursued these unconventional monetary policy measures, but it did establish special liquidity facilities during the financial crisis to provide tens of billions of dollars of loans to financial institutions. Moreover, when it reduced its key policy rate to the effective lower bound of 0.25 percent, it made a promise, a zero interest rate commitment, to keeping the policy rate at the effective lower bound for an extended period.

9.4   HOW CENTRAL BANKS CAN CHANGE BANK RESERVES

We mentioned that under quantitative easing the central bank increases the reserves available to commercial banks. There are a few different techniques that central banks can use to affect the reserves of commercial banks. We will first explain how three of these techniques could be used to change commercial bank reserves. These techniques are not necessarily

---

17 See Bank of Canada, "Bank of Canada lowers overnight rate target by 1/4 percentage point to 1/4 per cent and, conditional on the inflation outlook, commits to hold current policy rate until the end of the second quarter of 2010," 21 April 2009, http://www.bankofcanada.ca/en/fixed-dates/2009/rate_210409.html.

employed with the intent of changing "the" money supply, but they could be.[18] Then we will consider real-world complications that central banks face in changing the money supply.

AFFECTING THE SUPPLY OF BANK RESERVES: OPEN-MARKET OPERATIONS

Open-market operations occur when the central bank buys or sells financial assets and thereby increases or decreases commercial bank reserves. Suppose, for example, that the central bank buys financial assets, such as short-term government bonds, from the public. Such a purchase of government bonds from the public by the central bank is called an **open-market purchase**. Think of the central bank as paying for the bonds it acquires with newly printed money. Assuming that the public is already holding all the currency that it wants, people will deposit the cash they receive as payment for their bonds in commercial banks. Thus, the reserves of the commercial banking system will increase by an amount equal to the value of the bonds purchased by the central bank. For a given desired reserve-deposit ratio on the part of the banks (that is, assuming that the banks do not just hold onto the reserves as they have done during some episodes of quantitative easing), the increase in bank reserves will lead in turn through the process of lending and redeposit of funds, described in the previous section, to an expansion of bank deposits and the money supply, as summarized by Equation 9.2 in section 9.2.

> **open-market purchase** the purchase of government bonds from the public by the central bank for the purpose of increasing the supply of bank reserves

To reduce bank reserves and thus the money supply, the central bank reverses the procedure. It sells some of the government bonds that it holds (acquired in previous open-market purchases) to the public. The sale of government bonds by the central bank to the public is called an **open-market sale**. Assume that people pay for the bonds by writing cheques on their accounts with commercial banks. Then, when the central bank presents the cheques to the commercial banks for payment, reserves equal in value to the government bonds sold by the central bank are transferred from the commercial banks to the central bank. The central bank retires these reserves from circulation, lowering the supply of bank reserves and, hence, lowering the overall money supply, all else being equal.

> **open-market sale** the sale by the central bank of government bonds for the purpose of reducing bank reserves

Together, open-market purchases and sales are called **open-market operations**. They are a widely used technique of central banking.

> **open-market operations** open-market purchases and open-market sales

AFFECTING THE SUPPLY OF BANK RESERVES: CHANGING RESERVE REQUIREMENTS

Recall that Equation 9.2 relates to a fictional economy where there is only one type of deposit and hence only one definition of the money supply: currency held by the public plus bank deposits. As Equation 9.2 shows, in such an economy, the money supply depends on just three factors: the amount of currency the public chooses to hold, the supply of bank reserves, and the reserve-deposit ratio maintained by commercial banks. For given quantities of currency held by the public and of reserves held by the banks, an increase in the reserve-deposit ratio reduces the money supply, as you can see from Equation 9.2. A higher reserve-deposit ratio implies that banks lend out a smaller share of their deposits in each of the rounds of lending and redeposit described earlier, limiting the overall expansion of loans and deposits.

Suppose that the central bank wished to change the supply of commercial bank reserves in order to change the money supply. Specifically, suppose that the commercial banks maintain a common 3 percent reserve-deposit ratio, and the central bank then wants to contract the money supply. One technique the central bank could use is to force the commercial banks to raise their reserve-deposit ratio.

---

18 As explained later in this chapter, it can be misleading to speak about "the" money supply because there are alternative definitions of the money supply and they differ not just in magnitude but often grow at substantially different rates.

reserve requirements set by some central banks, the minimum values of the ratio of bank reserves to bank deposits that commercial banks are allowed to maintain; the Bank of Canada does not set reserve requirements

Legally required values of the reserve-deposit ratio set by a central bank are called **reserve requirements**. By raising required reserves to, say, 5 percent of deposits, the central bank could force commercial banks to raise their reserve-deposit ratio, at least until it reached 5 percent. As you can see from Equation 9.2, an increase in the reserve-deposit ratio lowers deposits and the money supply, all else being equal.

Note that raising reserve requirements above the desired reserve-deposit ratio of the commercial banks will tend to reduce the money supply, and similarly reducing reserve requirements from a "forced" high level like 5 percent of deposits back down to the desired 3 percent reserve-deposit ratio will tend to increase the money supply. But lowering reserve requirements below the banks' desired reserve-deposit ratio of 3 percent would have no effect—banks would simply hold more reserves than required.

Note also that while some central banks make use of reserve requirements, required reserves were abolished in Canada in the early 1990s. Furthermore, when you read in the news about central banks changing reserve requirements, it does not necessarily mean that they are doing so in order to change some measure of the money supply. For example, in late 2010 China was experiencing rising inflation. According to the analysis of the Bank of Canada, the People's Bank of China, China's central bank, did not want to raise interest rates as that would have put upward pressure on the exchange rate. Instead, the People's Bank of China raised the required reserve ratios for China's commercial banks. The idea was to slow the growth of bank lending—"to contain credit growth," in the words used by the Bank of Canada in analyzing China's monetary policy—and thereby slow the growth of economy-wide opening and ultimately reduce inflationary pressures.[19]

EXAMPLE 9.3
Increasing the money supply by open-market operations

In Shekellia, an economy with a financial system like the fictional one we have been analyzing, currency held by the public is 1000 shekels, bank reserves are 200 shekels, and the desired reserve-deposit ratio is 0.2. What is the money supply? How is the money supply affected if the central bank prints 100 shekels and uses this new currency to buy government bonds from the public? Assume that the public does not wish to change the amount of currency it holds.

As bank reserves are 200 shekels and the reserve-deposit ratio is 0.2, bank deposits must equal 200 shekels/0.2, or 1000 shekels. The money supply, equal to the sum of currency held by the public and bank deposits, is therefore 2000 shekels, a result you can confirm using Equation 9.2.

The open-market purchase puts 100 more shekels into the hands of the public. We assume that the public continues to want to hold 1000 shekels in currency, so people will deposit the additional 100 shekels in the commercial banking system, raising bank reserves from 200 to 300 shekels. As the desired reserve-deposit ratio is 0.2, multiple rounds of lending and redeposit will eventually raise the level of bank deposits to 300 shekels/0.2, or 1500 shekels. The money supply, equal to 1000 shekels held by the public plus bank deposits of 1500 shekels, equals 2500 shekels. So the open-market purchase of 100 shekels, by raising bank reserves by 100 shekels, has increased the money supply by 500 shekels. Again, you can confirm this result using Equation 9.2.

EXERCISE 9.4 **Continuing Example 9.3, suppose that instead of an open-market purchase of 100 shekels, the central bank conducts an open-market sale of 50 shekels' worth of government bonds. What happens to bank reserves, bank deposits, and the money supply? Continue to assume that the public does not wish to change the amount of currency it holds and that the desired reserve-deposit ratio remains as before.**

19 Bank of Canada, *Monetary Policy Report*, January 2011, p. 8. Accessed at http://www.bankofcanada.ca/wp-content/uploads/2011/01/mprjan11.pdf.

AFFECTING THE SUPPLY OF BANK RESERVES: GOVERNMENT DEPOSIT SHIFTING

The government typically maintains deposits in accounts at both the central bank and the commercial banks. The central bank can increase or decrease commercial bank reserves by **government deposit shifting** between itself and the commercial banks.

Suppose that the central bank writes cheques on a government account at the central bank and deposits the cheques into government accounts at the commercial banks. Commercial bank reserves will be increased. For a given desired reserve-deposit ratio on the part of the commercial banks, the increase in bank reserves will lead to an increase in the money supply.

By shifting government deposits in the opposite direction—that is, by shifting government deposits from commercial banks to government accounts with itself—the central bank can decrease bank reserves. With no change in the desired reserve-deposit ratio, the commercial banks will contract their loans, and the money supply will decrease.

government deposit shifting the transfer of government deposits by the central bank between the government's account at the central bank and the government's accounts at commercial banks

REAL WORLD LIMITS TO MONEY SUPPLY CONTROL

In the real world, commercial banks offer various categories of deposits (such as chequing accounts, savings accounts, term deposits, and so on) and members of the public hold deposits not just with commercial banks but also with other financial intermediaries (such as trust companies, credit unions, and caisses populaires in Canada). As a consequence, in the real world we cannot talk about "the" money supply, as if there were only one possible measure of it, but we must recognize that there are many alternative measures of the money supply. These measures differ widely not just in magnitude but also in their annual growth rates. In simplified examples, the money supply either increases or decreases. In a real-world economy like Canada, some measures of the money supply may increase at the same time that others are decreasing. How these measures of the money supply change depends directly upon decisions taken by depositors, borrowers, and lenders in response to changes in income, interest rates, and other economic variables, and only indirectly upon actions by the central bank, the issuer of currency.[20] Indeed, if you visit the Bank of Canada website, you can find statements bluntly declaring that the "Bank of Canada can't directly increase or decrease the money supply at will." By this, the Bank means that it is not able to fine-tune money supply growth targets such as, for example, 5 percent give or take 0.5 percent. But if, very unrealistically speaking, a central bank wished to decimate the money supply and cause a depression, it could do so. It also has the power, in conjunction with the government, to create an astronomical expansion of the money supply and thereby create hyperinflation. This effect of the money supply will be discussed in the next section.

> **RECAP**
>
> ### HOW CENTRAL BANKS CAN CHANGE RESERVES
>
> Central banks can change bank reserves through the techniques of open-market operations, changing reserve requirements, or government deposit shifting. These techniques are not necessarily employed with the intent of changing the money supply, but they could be.
>
> In the real world, we cannot talk about "the" money supply, as if there were only one possible measure of it, but we must recognize that there are many alternative measures of the money supply. These measures differ widely not just in magnitude but also in their annual growth rates.

20 Bruce Montador, "The Implementation of Monetary Policy in Canada," *Canadian Public Policy,* XXI, 1, March 1995, pp. 110–111, notes that, "central banks' views about money supply determination have for a long time been that the money stock is demand determined, and a function of income (and/or wealth) and interest rates."

9.5 THE SIGNIFICANCE OF MONEY SUPPLY

Why is it important to be familiar with how money is created and how the supply of it can, or cannot, be changed? One reason is that such familiarity is relevant to understanding certain economic theories. For example, many intermediate macroeconomics textbooks present a theory of interest rate determination based upon the idea of a money supply curve controlled by the central bank. The material presented in this chapter explains some of the methods that a central bank could use to change the money supply and hence interest rates, according to that theory.

Another reason is for understanding extreme economic events. Economic Naturalist 9.1 detailed how a collapse in the money supply can be associated with a severe economic depression. An understanding of the money supply is also critical to understanding hyperinflation, the extremely high inflation discussed in Chapter 6. This is another clear example of the significance of money supply and the value of a correct understanding of its role. Although hyperinflation has never occurred in Canada, it has occurred in a large number of countries, invariably with dire economic consequences.

The most famous hyperinflation was that of Germany in 1922–1923, often illustrated in history textbooks with a picture of a woman feeding a furnace with banknotes so worthless it was more economical to burn them as fuel than to buy firewood with them.

One of eight hyperinflations that occurred between 1920 and 1947, the German experience of 1922–1923 meets a strict definition for hyperinflation as a situation in which monthly inflation exceeded 50 percent. There were no such hyperinflations between 1947 and the early 1980s, but these events, unfortunately, are not a thing of the past. According to the International Monetary Fund, if hyperinflation is defined as annual inflation exceeding 1000 percent, then, since the early 1980s, some 25 countries have suffered it: 5 Latin American countries, 17 Central and East European or countries of the former Soviet Union, and 3 African countries.[21]

All countries that suffered hyperinflations have one thing in common—during the period of hyperinflation they experienced extremely high rates of growth of their money supply. In fact, their rates of hyperinflation were often close to their rates of money supply growth, something that can be explained by a well-known relationship in economics called the *quantity equation*.

quantity equation an amount of money times its velocity equals nominal GDP; $M \times V = P \times Y$

The **quantity equation** is an identity stating that money (M) times its *velocity* (V) equals the price level (P) times real output (Y). This results in the equation

$$M \times V = P \times Y. \tag{9.3}$$

velocity of money a measure of the speed at which money changes hands in transactions involving final goods and services; $V = (P \times Y)/M$

The price level times real output equals nominal GDP, as discussed in Chapter 6. The **velocity of money**, also known as the rate of circulation of money, can be thought of as a measure of the speed at which money changes hands in the economy. But since the quantity equation is an identity, we can through substitution write

$$V = (P \times Y)/M = Nominal\ GDP/Money\ Supply. \tag{9.4}$$

The velocity of money differs according to which definition of money supply is employed—the broader the definition is, the larger the denominator of the nominal GDP/money supply part of Equation 9.4 is, and the smaller the velocity of money will be as a result.

When explaining hyperinflation, it is common to assume that V and Y are constant. But this is not strictly true; Y tends to fall during hyperinflation and V moves around somewhat. During hyperinflation, however, changes in M are so great relative to changes

21 Sharmini Coorey et al., "Lessons from High Inflation Episodes for Stabilizing the Economy in Zimbabwe," IMF Working Paper, April 2007, at http://www.imf.org/external/pubs/ft/wp/2007/wp0799.pdf (July 2011).

in Y and V that it is reasonable to assume that Y and V are constant throughout, which results in the expression

$$M \times \overline{V} = P \times \overline{Y} \qquad (9.5)$$

where the bars over Y and V indicate that Y and V are assumed to be constant.

If V and Y are constant, it can be derived mathematically from Equation 9.5 that

$$\% \textit{ change in } M = \% \textit{ change in } P. \qquad (9.6)$$

In other words, the rate of growth of the money supply (% change in M) equals the rate of inflation (% change in P).

A word of caution is necessary here. Equation 9.6 has been shown to be a good theory of hyperinflation. There is also evidence that it applies reasonably well to countries with very high inflation, defined as annual inflation of over 100 percent per year.[22] It is not, however, a theory that can explain changes in the inflation rate for a country with low or moderate inflation, as is the case with Canada, the United States, the euro-area countries, Japan, or Britain. As Figure 9.2 shows, money supply growth in Canada has in recent years been a few times higher than the rate of inflation, and fluctuations of money supply

FIGURE 9.2

No Apparent Relationship: Inflation and Money Supply Growth; Canada, 2000–2010

Although hyperinflation is associated with a correspondingly high rate of money supply growth, in countries with low or moderate inflation, growth of the money supply (shown in the figure by the blue line) is not a reliable predictor of changes in the rate of inflation (as shown by the red and green lines). For example, the M2 growth rate in blue is from 2 to over 4 times larger than the inflation rate for the same year, and a noticeable rise in the M2 growth rate, as from 2008 to 2009, is accompanied by a drop rather than a noticeable rise in the inflation rate. SOURCE: Adapted from CANSIM series v41552796 (M2 gross), v1997756 (GDP deflator), and v41690973 (CPI).

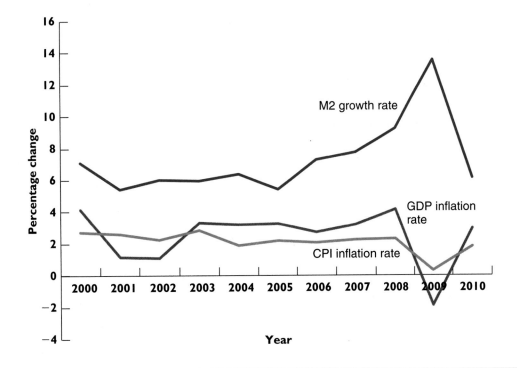

ECONOMIC NATURALIST   9.2

Why did Zimbabwe's annual inflation rate exceed 66 212 percent in early 2008?

According to Zimbabwe's official statistics, which may underestimate the severity of the situation, Zimbabwe's annual inflation rate had reached 66 212 percent by the end of 2007. And it was still rising. In 1980, one Zimbabwe dollar had been worth more than one U.S. dollar, but in early 2008, a $10-million note was not enough to purchase a kilogram of chicken.[23] By April 2009, the situation had become so extreme that Zimbabwe stopped printing the Zimbabwe dollar, and the U.S. dollar and the South African rand were used instead.

Zimbabwe's hyperinflation, as with other hyperinflations, was associated with massive growth in the money supply. Less than two years earlier, in 2006, the inflation rate was several hundred percent, and the annual rate of growth of the money supply was also several hundred percent. Both the rate of growth of the money supply and the inflation rate soared afterwards.

Critics and defenders of the government of then President Robert Mugabe offer different explanations as to why the government resorted to printing money to pay its bills. Critics, for example, emphasize such factors as the loss of government revenue resulting from the collapse of agricultural production that followed Mugabe's controversial farm seizures in 2000. The situation, they say, was made worse by the supply shortages that arose when companies had to stop production of some goods as a result of price controls imposed by the government. Mugabe, on the other hand, blamed the situation on sanctions imposed by the West. Regardless of the reason for firing up the printing presses, however, there is no denying that by printing astronomical amounts of currency to finance its activities, the government created hyperinflation.

If rates of money growth of several hundred percent or more per year lead to hyperinflation, why do countries allow their money supplies to explode? Usually, extremely rapid rates of money growth are the result of governments accumulating large budget deficits that they cover by printing money rather than by selling bonds. Particularly in developing countries or in those suffering from war or political instability, governments sometimes find that they cannot raise sufficient taxes or borrow enough from the public to cover their expenditures. In this situation, if they have direct control over the central bank, they often yield to the temptation to print new money in order to pay their bills. If the resulting increase in the level of inflation is large enough, hyperinflation will follow.

growth and the inflation rate exhibit no perceptible link. Similarly, we note in Chapter 13 that although the purchasing power parity theory of exchange rate determination is useful for explaining exchange rate movements over the long run between countries with very different inflation rates, it is not useful for explaining exchange rate movements between countries with moderate inflation. The theory supporting Equation 9.6 is similar to the purchasing power parity theory in that it is accurate for explaining special situations while at the same time it is irrelevant as an explanation of those that are more commonplace.[23]

RECAP

THE SIGNIFICANCE OF MONEY SUPPLY

- All countries that suffer hyperinflations experience extremely high rates of growth of their money supply.

- *Velocity of money* measures the speed at which money circulates in payments for final goods and services; equivalently, it is equal to nominal GDP divided by the stock of money.

23 "Zimbabwe's Inflation Rate Jumps to Record 66,212%," CBC news, 15 February 2008, at www.cbc.ca/news/business/story/2008/02/15/zimbabwe.html. (July 2011).

- The *quantity equation* states that money times velocity equals nominal GDP, or, in symbols, $M \times V = P \times Y$. If the velocity of money (V) and real GDP (Y) can be assumed to be constant, which is a reasonable assumption when analyzing hyperinflation, the quantity equation implies that a given percentage increase in the money supply leads to approximately the same percentage increase in the price level. In other words, the rate of growth of the money supply approximately equals the rate of hyperinflation.

- Although the *quantity equation* theory successfully explains hyperinflation, it cannot be applied to situations of low or moderate inflation, as is the case in Canada. For such situations the models of Chapters 10, 11, and 12 are relevant instead.

SUMMARY

- *Money* is any asset that can be used in making purchases, such as currency or a chequing account. Commodity money is money with intrinsic value, such as a gold or silver coin. Fiat money is money with no intrinsic value, such as paper currency. **LO1**

- Money has three main functions. (1) It is a medium of exchange, which means that it can be used in transactions. (2) It is a unit of account, in that economic values are typically measured in units of money (e.g., dollars). And (3) it is a store of value, a means by which people can hold wealth. In practice, it is difficult to measure the money supply, since many assets have some money-like features. A relatively narrow measure of money is M1, which includes currency and chequing accounts at commercial banks. A broader measure of money, M2, includes all the assets in M1 plus additional assets that are somewhat less convenient to use in transactions. There are other measures of money as well, and the various measures differ substantially in magnitude. **LO1**

- Because bank deposits are part of the money supply, the behaviour of commercial banks and of bank depositors affects the amount of money in the economy. A key factor is the reserve-deposit ratio chosen by banks. Bank reserves are cash or similar assets held by commercial banks, for the purpose of meeting depositor withdrawals and payments. The reserve-deposit ratio is bank reserves divided by deposits in banks. Modern banking systems have reserve-deposit ratios far below 1, and are called fractional-reserve banking systems. **LO2**

- If the public overall suddenly wishes to increase its currency holdings, the money supply will contract, all else equal. A bank run takes place when the customers of a particular bank fear that the bank will become insolvent. A banking panic is a wave of bank runs. A banking panic can cause or deepen a recession. **LO2**

- The Bank of Canada is a government agency with decision-making power in the hands of a governing council headed by the Bank of Canada governor. The Bank, like most central banks, is relatively independent of the government. **LO3**

- Three major responsibilities of the Bank of Canada are to issue bank notes, to act as the lender of last resort, and to conduct monetary policy. Conventional monetary policy for the Bank of Canada consists of adjusting the key policy rate to achieve the inflation control target. Unconventional monetary policy measures available to central banks at the effective lower bound include quantitative easing, credit easing, and a zero interest rate commitment. **LO3**

- Central banks can affect the reserves available to commercial banks using techniques such as open-market operations, shifting government deposits, and, in some jurisdictions, changes in legal reserve requirements. **LO4**

■ In a real-world economy, some measures of the money supply may increase at the same time that others are decreasing, and for reasons other than the actions of the central bank. Thus, precise control of the money supply may not be possible. **LO4**

■ Hyperinflation is the direct result of massive growth of the money supply, as can be explained by the quantity equation. **LO5**

KEY TERMS

100 percent reserve banking (213)
bank reserves (213)
banking panic (217)
bank run (217)
barter (210)
commodity money (209)
credit easing (223)
currency (220)
deposit insurance (221)
effective lower bound (223)
fiat money (209)

fractional-reserve banking system (214)
government deposit shifting (227)
key policy rate (222)
lender of last resort (222)
liquidity (222)
M1 (211)
M2 (211)
medium of exchange (210)
money (209)
open-market operations (225)

open-market purchase (225)
open-market sale (225)
quantity equation (228)
quantitative easing (223)
reserve-deposit ratio (214)
reserve requirements (226)
seigniorage (220)
store of value (211)
unit of account (210)
velocity of money (228)
zero interest rate commitment (224)

REVIEW QUESTIONS

1. What is *money*? Why do people hold money even though it pays a lower return than other financial assets? **LO1**

2. How does commodity money differ from fiat money? **LO1**

3. How does M2 differ from M1? **LO1**

4. What is fractional-reserve banking? **LO2**

5. What is a banking panic? **LO2**

6. What are three major responsibilities of the Bank of Canada? **LO3**

7. What techniques do central banks employ to change commercial bank reserves? **LO4**

8. What is the quantity equation and how is it used to explain hyperinflation? **LO5**

PROBLEMS

1. During the Second World War, an Allied soldier named Robert Radford spent several years in a large German prisoner-of-war camp. At times, more than 50 000 prisoners were held in the camp, with some freedom to move about within the compound. Radford later wrote an account of his experiences. He described how an economy developed in the camp, in which prisoners traded food, clothing, and other items. Services, such as barbering, were also exchanged. Lacking paper money, the prisoners began to use cigarettes (provided monthly by the Red Cross) as money. Prices were quoted, and payments made, using cigarettes. **LO1**

   a. In Radford's POW camp, how did cigarettes fulfill the three functions of money?

   b. Why do you think the prisoners used cigarettes as money, as opposed to other items of value such as squares of chocolate or pairs of boots?

   c. Do you think a non-smoking prisoner would have been willing to accept cigarettes in exchange for a good or service in Radford's camp? Why or why not?

2. a. In an imaginary economy, bank reserves are 100, the public holds 200 in currency, and the desired reserve-deposit ratio is 0.25. Find deposits and the money supply. **LO2**

   b. The money supply is 500, and currency held by the public equals bank reserves. The desired reserve-deposit ratio is 0.25. Find currency held by the public and bank reserves.

   c. The money supply is 1250, of which 250 is currency held by the public. Bank reserves are 100. Find the desired reserve-deposit ratio.

3. Refer to Table 9.7. Suppose that the Fed had decided to set the U.S. money supply in December 1932 and in December 1933 at the same value as in December 1930. Assuming that the values of currency held by the public and the reserve-deposit ratio had remained as given in the table, by how much more should the Fed have increased bank reserves at each of those dates to accomplish that objective? **LO2**

4. When a central bank increases bank reserves by $1, the money supply rises by more than $1. The amount of extra money created when the central bank increases bank reserves by $1 is called the *money multiplier*. **LO4**

   a. Explain why the money multiplier is generally greater than 1. In what special case would it equal 1?

   b. In an imaginary economy, the initial money supply is $1000, of which $500 is currency held by the public. The desired reserve-deposit ratio is 0.2. Find the increase in money supply associated with increases in bank reserves of $1, $5, and $10. What is the money multiplier in this economy?

   c. Find a general rule for calculating the money multiplier in such an economy.

   d. Explain the difficulties that would arise in calculating a money multiplier for the Canadian economy. Do you think such a multiplier would stay constant from year to year?

5. Suppose that inflation is running at an annual rate of 1000 percent, as it was in Zimbabwe in 2006. **LO5**

   a. Change in which economic variable would lie directly behind this inflation rate? Name and briefly explain the theory that applies to predicting the level of hyperinflation.

   b. If the annual inflation rate is 1000 percent, in what range would you expect to find short-term nominal interest rates? Name and explain the theory that applies to predicting how inflation affects nominal interest rates. (*Hint:* see Chapter 6.)

   c. If the annual inflation rate is 1000 percent, would you expect the market exchange rate to appreciate or depreciate against the U.S. dollar? Name and explain the theory that applies to predicting exchange rate changes between a country with very high inflation and one with low or moderate inflation. (*Hint:* see Chapter 13.)

ANSWERS TO IN-CHAPTER EXERCISES

9.1 Table 9.5 shows the balance sheet of banks after two rounds of lending and redeposits. At that point, deposits are 2 710 000 guilders and reserves are 1 000 000 guilders. Since banks have a desired reserve-deposit ratio of 10 percent, they will keep 271 000 guilders (10 percent of deposits) as reserves and lend out the remaining 729 000 guilders. Loans to farmers are now 2 439 000 guilders. Eventually, the 729 000 guilders lent to the farmers will be redeposited into the banks, giving the banks deposits of 3 439 000 guilders and reserves of 1 000 000 guilders. The balance sheet is as shown in the accompanying table. **LO2**

Assets		Liabilities	
Currency (= reserves)	1 000 000 guilders	Deposits	3 439 000 guilders
Loans to farmers	2 439 000 guilders		

Notice that assets equal liabilities. The money supply equals deposits, or 3 439 000 guilders. *Currency held in the banks as reserves does not count in the money supply.* **LO2**

9.2   Because the public holds no currency, the money supply equals bank deposits, which in turn equal bank reserves divided by the reserve-deposit ratio (Equation 9.1). If bank reserves are 1 000 000 and the reserve–deposit ratio is 0.05, then deposits equal 1 000 000/0.05 = 20 000 000 guilders, which is also the money supply. If bank reserves are 2 000 000 guilders and the reserve-deposit ratio is 0.10, then the money supply and deposits are again equal to 20 000 000 guilders, or 2 000 000/0.10. **LO2**

9.3   Verify directly for each date in Table 9.7 that

$$\text{Money supply} = \text{Currency} + \frac{\text{Bank reserves}}{\text{Desired reserve-deposit ratio}}$$

For example, for December 1929 we can check that 45.9 = 3.85 + 3.15/0.075.
Suppose that the currency held by the public in December 1933 had been 3.79, as in December 1930, rather than 4.85, and that the difference (4.85 − 3.79 = 1.06) had been left in the banks. Then bank reserves in December 1933 would have been 3.45 + 1.06 = 4.51, and the money supply would have been 3.79 + 4.51/0.133 = 37.7. So the money supply would still have fallen between 1930 and 1933 if people had not increased their holdings of currency, but only by about half as much. **LO2**

9.4   If the central bank sells 50 shekels of government bonds in exchange for currency, the immediate effect is to reduce the amount of currency in the hands of the public by 50 shekels. To restore their currency holding to the desired level of 1000 shekels, the public will withdraw 50 shekels from commercial banks, reducing bank reserves from 200 shekels to 150 shekels. The desired reserve-deposit ratio is 0.2, so ultimately, deposits must equal 150 shekels in reserves divided by 0.2, or 750 shekels. (Note that to contract deposits, the commercial banks will have to "call in" or not renew or replace maturing loans, reducing their loans outstanding.) The money supply equals 1000 shekels in currency held by the public plus 750 shekels in deposits, or 1750 shekels. Thus the open-market purchase has reduced the money supply from 2000 to 1750 shekels. **LO4**

APPENDIX 9A
The Vertical Money Supply Theory of Interest Rate Determination

The issue of how central banks control interest rates in an effort to stabilize the economy is a controversial one in macroeconomics. One theory, which we call the vertical money supply theory, is that interest rates are determined by the demand and supply for money. According to this theory, given the money demand curve, the central bank shifts the money supply curve, which is vertical, to bring about changes in interest rates. Most of the remainder of this appendix will explain the vertical money supply theory of interest rate determination. We will, however, conclude with a brief discussion of an alternative theory of interest rate determination, and we will highlight how the two theories share an important conclusion.

9A.1 THE VERTICAL MONEY SUPPLY THEORY OF INTEREST RATE DETERMINATION

To explain this theory, we must consider the demand for money, the supply of money, and money market equilibrium. In thinking about the demand for money, it is useful to recall that money refers to the set of assets, such as cash and chequing accounts, which are usable in transactions. Money is also a store of value, just as stocks, bonds, and real estate are, and, as such, money is a way of holding wealth.

MACROECONOMIC FACTORS THAT AFFECT THE DEMAND FOR MONEY

In any household or business, the demand for money will depend on a variety of individual circumstances. For example, a high-volume retail business that serves thousands of customers each day will probably choose to have more money on hand than a legal firm that bills clients and pays employees monthly. But while individuals and businesses vary considerably in the amount of money they choose to hold, three macroeconomic factors affect the demand for money quite broadly: the nominal interest rate, real output, and the price level. The nominal interest rate affects the cost of holding money throughout the economy, while real output and the price level affect the benefits of money.

Why is the *nominal interest rate* relevant to understanding the cost of holding money? In general, money pays little or no interest. But other financial assets typically yield a return, such as interest on a bond. The interest rate paid on alternatives to money, such as government bonds, determines the opportunity cost of holding money. (The term *opportunity cost* was introduced in Chapter 1.) The higher the prevailing nominal interest rate, the greater the opportunity cost of holding money, and hence the less money individuals and businesses will demand.

In this book, when we talk about "the" nominal interest rate, what we mean is an average measure of interest rates. This simplification is one more application of the macroeconomic concept of aggregation introduced in Chapter 4. It is a reasonable simplification for most purposes in macroeconomics.

The nominal interest rate is a macroeconomic factor that affects the cost of holding money. Two macroeconomic factors that affect the benefit of holding money are

- *Real income or output (Y).* An increase in aggregate real income or output—as measured, for example, by real GDP—raises the quantity of goods and services that people and businesses want to buy and sell. When the economy enters a boom, for example, people do more shopping and stores have more customers. To accommodate the increase in transactions, both individuals and businesses need to hold more money. Thus, higher real output raises the demand for money.
- *The price level (P).* The higher the prices of goods and services, the more dollars (or yen, or euros) are needed to make a given set of transactions. Thus a higher price level is associated with a higher demand for money. Today, when a couple of teenagers go out for a movie and refreshments on Saturday night, they need probably five times as much cash as their parents did 25 years ago. Because the prices of movie tickets and popcorn have risen steeply over 25 years, more money (that is, a larger number of dollars) is needed to pay for a Saturday night date than in the past.

THE MONEY DEMAND CURVE

The economy-wide demand for money can be represented graphically by the money demand curve (see Figure 9A.1). The money demand curve relates the aggregate quantity of money demanded, M, to the nominal interest rate, *i*. The quantity of money demanded, M, is a nominal quantity, measured in dollars (or yen, or euros). Because an increase in the nominal interest rate increases the opportunity cost of holding money, which reduces the quantity of money demanded, the money demand curve slopes down. If we think of the nominal interest rate as the "price" (more precisely. the opportunity cost) of money, and the amount of money people want to hold as the "quantity," the money demand curve is analogous to the demand curve for a good or service (see Chapter 3). As with a standard demand curve, the fact that a higher price of money leads people to demand less of

FIGURE 9A.1

The Money Demand Curve
The money demand curve relates the economy-wide demand for money to the nominal increase rate. Because an increase in the nominal interest rate raises the opportunity cost of holding money, the money demand curve slopes down.

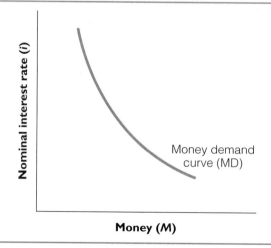

it is captured in the downward slope of the demand curve. Furthermore, as in a standard demand curve, changes in factors other than the price of money (the nominal interest rate) can cause the demand curve for money to shift. Specifically, for a given nominal interest rate, any change that makes people want to hold more money will shift the money demand curve to the right, and any change that makes people want to hold less money will shift the money demand curve to the left.

We have already identified two macroeconomic factors other than the nominal interest rate that affect the economy-wide demand for money: real output and the price level. Because an increase in either of these variables increases the demand for money, it shifts the money demand curve rightward, as shown in Figure 9A.2. Similarly, a fall in real output or the general price level reduces money demand, shifting the money demand curve leftward.

The money demand curve may also shift in response to other changes that affect the cost or benefit of holding money, such as the technological advances of automated banking machines (ABMs). For example, the spread of ABMs would tend to reduce the amount of money people choose to hold (by reducing their demand for cash) and would thus shift the economy-wide money demand curve to the left.

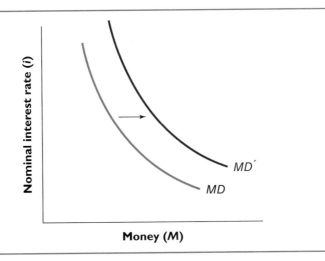

FIGURE 9A.2

A Shift in the Money Demand Curve
At a given nominal interest rate, any change that makes people want to hold more money—such as an increase in the general price level or in real GDP—will shift the money demand curve to the right.

MONEY MARKET EQUILIBRIUM WITH VERTICAL MONEY SUPPLY

The vertical money supply theory maintains that the supply of money is directly controlled by the central bank, and that control over the money supply gives the central bank control over the average interest rate. This theory can be illustrated by Figure 9A.3, which shows the demand for and supply of money in a single diagram. The nominal interest rate is on the vertical axis, and the nominal quantity of money (in dollars) on the horizontal axis. As we have seen, because a higher nominal interest rate increases the opportunity cost of holding money, the money demand curve slopes downward. And because the central bank is assumed to fix the supply of money, we have drawn the money supply curve as a vertical line that intercepts the horizontal axis at the quantity of money chosen by the central bank, denoted M.

As in standard supply and demand analysis, equilibrium in the market for money occurs at the intersection of the supply and demand curves, shown as point E in Figure 9A.3. According to the vertical money supply theory, the equilibrium amount of money in circulation, M, is simply the amount of money the central bank chooses to supply. The equilibrium nominal interest rate, i, is the interest rate at which the quantity of money demanded by the public, as determined by the money demand curve, equals the fixed supply of money made available by the central bank.

What happens if, for example, the nominal interest rate is initially below the equilibrium level in the market for money, for instance, at a value such as i' in Figure 9A.3. At that interest rate, the public's demand for money is M', which is greater than the actual amount of money in circulation, equal to M. How will the public—households and firms—react if the amount of money they hold is less than they would like? To increase their holdings of money, people will try to sell some of the interest-bearing assets they hold, such as bonds. But if there is a widespread move to sell bonds, then the attempt to reduce bond holdings will drive down the price of bonds, in the same way that a glut of apples will drive down the price of apples. A fall in the price of bonds, however, is equivalent to an increase in interest rates. (A detailed explanation of the link between bond prices and the interest rates is provided in Chapter 16). As interest rates rise, the quantity of money held by the public will decline (represented by a right-to-left movement along the money demand curve). When the interest rate reaches its equilibrium value, i in Figure 9A.3, people will be content to hold the quantities of money and other assets that are actually available in the economy.

FIGURE 9A.3

Equilibrium in the Market for Money
Equilibrium in the market for money occurs at point E, where the demand for money by the public equals the amount of money supplied by the central bank. The equilibrium nominal interest rate, which equates the supply of and demand for money, is i.

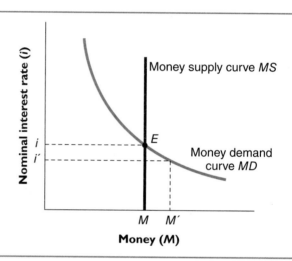

Under the assumption that the central bank fixes the supply of money, Figure 9A.3 shows that the nominal interest rate is determined by equilibrium in the market for money. Now suppose that the central bank decides to lower the interest rate. According to the vertical money supply theory, the central bank lowers the interest rate by increasing the supply of money.

Figure 9A.4 shows the effects of such an increase in the money supply by the central bank. If the initial money supply is M, then equilibrium in the money market occurs at point E in the figure, and the equilibrium nominal interest rate is i. Now suppose the central bank increases the money supply to M′. This increase in the money supply shifts the vertical money supply curve to the right, which shifts the equilibrium in the money market from point E to point F. Note that at point F the equilibrium nominal interest rate has declined, from i to i'. The nominal interest rate must decline if the public is to be persuaded to hold the extra money that has been injected into the economy.

The opposite scenario unfolds if the central bank decides to raise interest rates. To raise interest rates, the central bank must reduce the money supply. With a reduction in the money supply, a higher interest rate is necessary to persuade the public to hold less money.

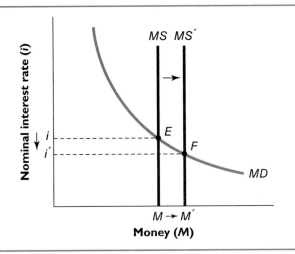

FIGURE 9A.4

The Central Bank Lowers the Nominal Interest Rate
According to the vertical money supply theory, the central bank can lower the equilibrium nominal interest rate by increasing the supply of money. For the given money demand curve, an increase in the money supply from M to M' shifts the equilibrium point in the money market from E to F, lowering the equilibrium nominal interest rate from i to i'.

9A.2 THE MODERN CENTRAL BANKING THEORY OF INTEREST RATE DETERMINATION

The vertical money supply theory has a long history in macroeconomics and is covered in many intermediate macroeconomics textbooks. It is worth knowing. Not all economists, however, think that it is the best theory of interest rate determination.

An alternative to the vertical money supply theory is the modern central banking theory of interest rate determination. It maintains that the supply of money is not directly controlled by the central bank. According to this theory, the central bank does not change market interest rates by changing the money supply. Instead, the money supply responds to changes in interest rates (and other variables, such as the price level). The central bank influences market interest rates directly by changing its key policy rate. When the central bank changes the key policy rate, commercial banks respond by changing their market interest rates.

We will consider the modern central banking theory of interest rate determination in greater detail in Chapter 10. Figure 9A.5 illustrates the theory for the case of a nominal interest rate cut by the central bank. The decision by the central bank to lower the interest rate from i to i' causes the money supply to increase from M to M' (assuming that the money demand curve MD remains stable). Note that, according to the modern central banking theory, the purpose of the interest-rate cut shown in Figure 9A.5 would be to stimulate planned aggregate expenditure, and the increase in the money supply would merely be a side effect.

While the vertical money supply and modern central banking theories differ regarding the nature of money supply, they both accept that central banks can control the nominal interest rate. Either theory can serve as an introduction to our discussion in Chapter 10 of how the Bank of Canada uses control of the interest rate to influence planned aggregate expenditure and the level of output in the economy.

FIGURE 9A.5

Direct Central Bank Manipulation of the Nominal Interest Rate
According to modern central banking theory, the central bank changes the nominal interest rate directly by changing its key policy rate. The purpose of changing the interest rate is to affect planned aggregate expenditure in the economy, but changes in the interest rate also affect the quantity of money demanded and supplied. For example, a reduction of the interest rate from i to i' would, all else being equal, have the side effect of increasing the money demanded and supplied from M to M'.

CHAPTER 10

Stabilizing the Economy: The Role of the Central Bank

Central bank decisions about monetary policy, and especially about the level of interest rates, are subject to intense scrutiny by financial market participants and commentators. In Canada, for example, the business sections of major newspapers speculate intensely about potential Bank of Canada interest rate announcements. Interest rate hikes cause bond prices to drop and can trigger declines in stock prices. When interest rates are cut, the Canadian dollar loses value on the foreign exchange markets. These changes have consequences for financial investors, which is why the business pages pay so much attention to this topic. But interest rate changes also have consequences for the economy as a whole, and that is our main concern as macroeconomists.

In this chapter, we examine conventional monetary policy, one of the two major types of *stabilization policy*. (The other type, fiscal policy, was discussed in Chapter 8.) As we saw in Chapter 8, stabilization policies are government policies that are meant to influence planned aggregate expenditure, with the goal of eliminating output gaps. Both types of stabilization policy are important and have been useful at various times. Both types of stabilization policy can be analyzed with the basic Keynesian model introduced in Chapter 8. In this chapter we will extend that model to take into account the impact of interest rate changes on the economy as a whole.

We begin with a brief discussion of the Bank of Canada, the institution with primary responsibility for monetary policy in Canada. The Bank of Canada and central banking was discussed previously in Chapter 9 where the Bank of Canada's responsibilities for issuing bank notes, ensuring the stability of the financial system, and conducting unconventional monetary policy in extreme circumstances were examined. But in this chapter, the focus is on the conventional monetary policy issue of how the Bank of Canada uses its key policy rate to achieve its inflation-control target. We will examine in detail how the Bank of Canada changes interest rates and how those interest rate changes affect the economy.

LEARNING OBJECTIVES

When you have completed this chapter, you will be able to:

LO1 Describe the Bank of Canada, its monetary policy objective, and its monetary policy instrument.

LO2 Explain the modern central banking theory of interest rate determination through central bank control of the overnight rate.

LO3 Explain how central bank control over nominal interest rates translates into control over real interest rates.

LO4 Use the basic Keynesian model to illustrate both how central banks fight recessions and how central banks prevent inflation.

LO5 Recognize that in implementing monetary policy central banks must be forward looking, and they often face uncertainty.

10.1 THE BANK OF CANADA: CANADA'S CENTRAL BANK

As first mentioned in Chapter 4, and explained in more detail in Chapter 9, the Bank of Canada is Canada's central bank. It is Canada's counterpart to the Federal Reserve in the United States, the European Central Bank, the People's Bank of China, the Bank of Japan, the Bank of England, the Reserve Bank of Australia, the Reserve Bank of India, the Central Bank of Brazil, the Central Bank of Russia, the Riksbank of Sweden, and so on.

Like the Department of Finance, which is the government institution with the greatest responsibility for fiscal policy, the Bank of Canada is based in Ottawa. In contrast to the Department of Finance, which works closely with the government of the day, the Bank of Canada is similar to most central banks in that it possesses a substantial degree of independence from the government. The Bank is headed by a governor who is selected for a seven-year term. At the time of writing (2011), the current governor is Mark Carney, who was appointed in 2008 for a term that ends in 2015.

monetary policy objective
a central bank goal regarding a macroeconomic indicator that the bank influences

Unlike commercial banks, which in Canada are often called chartered banks, the Bank of Canada does not aim for profit maximization. Central banks such as the Bank of Canada have *monetary policy objectives*. A **monetary policy objective** (or policy objective, for short) is a central bank goal regarding a macroeconomic indicator influenced by the bank. The Bank of Canada Act, through which the Bank was established in 1935, indicated that the institution should pursue several policy objectives by stating that the Bank should

> . . . regulate credit and currency in the best interests of the economic life of the nation, to control and protect the external value of the national monetary unit and to mitigate by its influence fluctuations in the general level of production, trade, prices and employment, so far as may be possible within the scope of monetary action, and generally to promote the economic and financial welfare of Canada . . .[1]

In fact, the Bank does not strictly follow the Bank of Canada Act. For example, although the Canadian dollar appreciated sharply against the U.S. dollar from 2003 to 2008, the Bank did not try to control this appreciation and thereby stabilize the exchange rate even though the Bank of Canada Act seems to refer to a goal of exchange rate stability. The rapidly appreciating Canadian dollar had negative consequences for Canada's manufacturing exports and hence manufacturing jobs. In 2007, trade union representatives argued that the strong dollar was the main cause of over 250 000 manufacturing job losses during the 2004 to 2007 period, and they accused the Bank of ignoring its mandate.

inflation-control target
refers either to the range of annual inflation rates within which the central bank aims to keep actual inflation or to the midpoint of the target range

In recent decades, however, the Bank of Canada has claimed that its sole monetary policy objective is to keep the inflation rate low. As was noted in Chapter 6, the goal of low inflation is not universally accepted; some economists, for example, argue for moderate inflation instead. In connection with its policy objective of low inflation, though, the Bank has since the early 1990s signed multi-year agreements with the Government of Canada that specify that the Bank of Canada is to keep annual inflation within a 1 to 3 percent range by aiming for a 2 percent target midpoint. The term **inflation-control target** can refer either to the full inflation target range of the central bank or to the target midpoint.

total CPI synonym for the *CPI* or Consumer Price Index; the adjective "total" emphasizes that is a broad measure of the price level

In controlling inflation, the Bank of Canada uses a distinction between the *total CPI* and the *core CPI*, and a corresponding distinction between *total CPI inflation* and *core CPI inflation*. The term **total CPI** is just another way of saying the CPI (Consumer Price Index), but adding "total" as an adjective emphasizes that is a relatively broad measure of the price level. Specifically, it is a broader measure of the price level than the **core CPI**, which excludes the most volatile components of the CPI. The details of the core CPI vary from economy to economy; for Canada, the core CPI excludes eight components (such as

core CPI measure of the price level that excludes the most volatile components of the total CPI

1   The Bank of Canada Act is available online through the Department of Justice Canada's Web site at http://laws.justice.gc.ca/eng/B-2/page-1.html.

fruit, vegetables, and gasoline) of the total CPI.[2] **Total CPI inflation** refers to the rate of change of the total CPI and **core CPI inflation** refers to the rate of change of the core CPI.

Although the Bank of Canada is ultimately concerned with controlling total CPI inflation, it emphasizes its use of core CPI inflation as an operating guide for monetary policy. The Bank's explanation for using core CPI inflation was an operating guide is that core CPI inflation is less influenced by temporary factors that will reverse of their own accord and more influenced by deeper-rooted factors that the Bank can influence. Moreover, while total CPI and core CPI inflation will differ in the short term, in the medium term and the long term they will tend to be very similar.

Figure 10.1 shows total and core CPI monthly inflation rates from January 2000 to December 2010. It illustrates that the total CPI inflation rate is subject to larger swings than the core CPI inflation rate. The Bank of Canada monitors the monthly inflation rates shown, but its inflation-control target concerns the annual inflation rate, which for both total and core CPI inflation is more stable than the monthly rates shown. The black horizontal lines at 1 percent and 3 percent in Figure 10.1 represent the lower and upper bounds of the inflation-control target range.

total CPI inflation rate of change of the total CPI

core CPI inflation rate of change of the core CPI

FIGURE 10.1
Total CPI Inflation and Core CPI Inflation, Canada, 2000–2010
The figure shows total and core CPI monthly inflation rates from January 2000 to December 2010. The blue line shows the total CPI inflation rate. The total CPI inflation rate is more volatile, subject to larger swings, than the core CPI inflation rate, shown in red. The black horizontal lines at 1 percent and 3 percent are the lower and upper bounds of the inflation-control target range. The Bank of Canada monitors the monthly inflation rates shown, but its inflation-control target concerns the annual inflation rate, which is more stable than the monthly rates shown.
SOURCE: Adapted from Bank of Canada, Consumer Price Index, 2000 to Present, http://www.bankofcanada.ca/rates/price-indexes/cpi/, extracted May 10, 2011.

2 Further details on the core CPI can be found at www.bankofcanada.ca/glossaries/glossary/#term-188.

monetary policy instrument
a tool or technique that a central bank uses to achieve a monetary policy objective

The tools or techniques that a central bank employs to achieve its monetary policy objective (or objectives) are called *monetary policy instruments*. The key **monetary policy instrument** that the Bank of Canada employs to achieve its monetary objective of low inflation is that of changing interest rates as circumstances require. As you will learn in greater detail later in this chapter, lower real interest rates promote more spending in the economy and, hence, tend to produce higher inflation. Conversely, higher real interest rates promote less spending in the economy and tend to result in lower inflation. To achieve its monetary policy objectives, the Bank of Canada makes regularly scheduled announcements about interest rate changes. Eight times a year the Bank of Canada announces whether it will increase, decrease, or leave unchanged its interest rate target.

In Chapter 8 it was noted that in recent decades economists have become more concerned about asset price bubbles and their impact on the stability of economies. Some economists have even argued that central banks should adopt the monetary policy objective of preventing the emergence of asset price bubbles. Most central banks, including the Bank of Canada, have resisted the suggestion that they should target asset prices. They have claimed that it would conflict with the objective of inflation control.[3]

EXERCISE 10.1

Visit the Bank of Canada Web site at http://www.bankofcanada.ca to find answers to the following questions:

a. **In addition to monetary policy, what are three other responsibilities of the Bank of Canada?** (*Hint*: **Look under "About the Bank/Who we are" on the Bank Web site.**)

b. **What are the three "Key Indicators" featured on the lead page of the Bank of Canada Web site?**

c. **In which months of the current year are Bank of Canada interest rate announcements scheduled?** (*Hint*: **Look for "Schedule of key interest rate announcements" on the Bank Web site.**)

d. **List five topics related to the Bank of Canada about which the Bank has prepared brief articles to educate visitors to the Bank of Canada Web site.** (*Hint*: **Look for "About the Bank/Backgrounders"**)

RECAP

THE BANK OF CANADA

The Bank of Canada is Canada's central bank. Like most other central banks, it is relatively independent from the government of the day. The Bank of Canada's key monetary policy objective is inflation control. It has an *inflation-control target* of 1 to 3 percent annual inflation that it seeks to achieve by pursuing 2 percent annual inflation. Although the Bank of Canada is ultimately concerned with controlling *total CPI inflation*, it emphasizes its use of *core CPI inflation* as an operating guide. The key *monetary policy instrument* that the Bank of Canada employs to achieve low inflation is that of changing interest rates. The Bank raises its interest rate target in response to higher inflation and cuts its interest rate target in response to lower inflation. Eight times a year the Bank of Canada makes scheduled announcements regarding whether it will increase, decrease, or leave unchanged its interest rate target.

---

3 The question of whether central banks should target asset prices attracted considerable attention as the dot.com bubble burst in 2000; see, for example, "Central banks, all a-quiver: How should the monetary authorities respond to big misalignments in exchange rates or equity prices?," *Economist,* May 11, 2000, http://www.economist.com/node/348335. The question attracted even more attention after the burst of the U.S. housing bubble in 2006–2007 and the subsequent global recession. See, for example, Martin Wolf, "Central banks must target more than just inflation," *Financial Times,* May 5 2009. http://www.ft.com/cms/s/0/34f7848e-39a7-11de-b82d-00144feabdc0.html.

10.2 THE MODERN CENTRAL BANKING THEORY OF INTEREST RATE DETERMINATION

The **modern central banking theory** of interest rate determination maintains that the central bank influences market interest rates directly by changing an interest rate that it controls. Commercial banks respond by changing their market interest rates. The modern central banking theory is the official view of many central banks, including the Bank of Canada.[4]

According to the Bank of Canada, its main tool for monetary policy—its key monetary policy instrument—is, as noted in Chapter 9, its key policy rate (also called the **official interest rate**). When the Bank changes the key policy rate, "this sends a clear signal about the direction in which it wants short-term interest rates to go. These changes usually lead to moves in the prime rate at commercial banks, which serves as a benchmark for many of their loans."[5]

The essence of the theory is that the central bank, the Bank of Canada, changes its official interest rate, and, in response, commercial banks change the market interest rates (particularly short-term ones) they charge customers—starting with the **prime business rate,** the rate commercial banks charge to their least risky business borrowers. In every month since February 1996, changes in the Bank of Canada's key policy rate have produced changes of the same amount in the prime business rate. More precisely, since February 1996, the prime business rate has been 2 percentage points (200 basis points) above the key policy rate. Both the key policy rate and the prime business rate are referred to as *benchmark rates*. A **benchmark rate** is an interest rate upon which other interest rates are based. Other interest rates are marked up from the benchmark rate.

While the essence of the theory is straightforward, interest rate targeting by the central bank does involve a bit more than just announcing targets. In the Canadian case, starting in December 2000, the Bank of Canada introduced a system of eight pre-specified dates each year for announcing any changes to its key policy rate, which is now the **overnight rate target** (sometimes called the target for the overnight rate). Simply by announcing a change in the overnight rate target, the Bank is able to alter the range in which the *overnight rate* will move. But the Bank takes additional actions—borrowing and lending operations—to ensure that the overnight rate stays very close to the target that the Bank has announced for it.

The **overnight rate** is a market interest rate that large financial institutions (mainly commercial banks) charge one another for overnight loans. The participants in the overnight market are generally financial institutions such as banks. The banks participate in a national system for the clearing and settlement of cheques and electronic funds transfers, the most important component of which is the **Large Value Transfer System (LVTS)**. The LVTS is an electronic wire system that lets financial institutions send large payments to each other with certainty that these payments will settle.[6] Certainty of settlement is guaranteed because net payment obligations are settled from account balances, known as **settlement balances,** held by all LVTS participants at the Bank of Canada. The Bank holds collateral from LTVS participants, and would use it if ever a participating institution could not meet its net payment obligations. As a central bank, the Bank of Canada can supply whatever balances the system may require. In any case, if at the end of the working day, one bank has a surplus of funds it will lend them, overnight, to another bank

modern central banking theory the view that the central bank changes its key policy rate (that is, official interest rate) directly, and commercial banks respond by changing market interest rates

official interest rate a general term for the interest rate which the central bank controls to achieve its monetary policy objective; a term for the key policy rate of a central bank

prime business rate the interest rate that commercial banks charge to their least risky business borrowers; also called the *prime rate*

benchmark rate an interest rate upon which other interest rates are based

overnight rate target the interest rate that the Bank of Canada wants to prevail in the financial market where major Canadian institutions borrow and lend funds to settle daily transactions with one another

overnight rate the market interest rate that financial institutions charge each other for overnight loans

Large Value Transfer System (LVTS) an electronic wire system overseen by the Bank of Canada that allows major financial institutions operating in Canada to send large payments back and forth to each other

settlement balances accounts held at the Bank of Canada by financial institutions for the purpose of settling their net payment obligations to one another

---

4 This theory and the *vertical money supply theory*, an alternative theory of interest rate determination, are compared in Appendix 9A. Both theories reach the general conclusion that central banks can control nominal interest rates.

5 Bank of Canada, "Target for the Overnight Rate," http://www.bankofcanada.ca/en/backgrounders/bg-p9.html.

6 According to the Bank of Canada, as of 2009, the LVTS "processed an average total of about 22,250 payments a day, worth an average total of $153.5 billion." See Bank of Canada, "Large Value Transfer System (LTVS)," http://www.bankofcanada.ca/en/backgrounders/bg-p8.html.

operating band a term used by the Bank of Canada to describe the range of possible overnight interest rates: from 0.25 percentage points below the overnight rate target to 0.25 percentage points above the target

deposit rate the interest rate that the Bank of Canada pays commercial banks for overnight deposits; it corresponds to the lower limit of the Bank of Canada's operating band for the overnight rate

bank rate the interest rate that the Bank of Canada charges commercial banks for overnight loans; it corresponds to the upper limit of the Bank of Canada's operating band for the overnight rate; for decades, it was the Bank's official interest rate

that is short of funds. The borrowing bank will pay the lending bank the overnight rate and their net LVTS positions will be covered.

The Bank of Canada makes sure that the overnight rate stays within an **operating band** of 0.5 percentage points of its overnight rate target (see Figure 10.2). The lower limit of the operating band is 0.25 percentage points below the overnight rate target. The lower limit is a rate (sometimes called the *banker's deposit rate or simply the* **deposit rate**) at which the Bank of Canada will pay interest on overnight funds deposited at the Bank by commercial banks unable to obtain a better rate from other commercial banks. The upper limit of the operating band, called the **bank rate**, is 0.25 percentage points above the overnight rate target. If a commercial bank is not able to borrow overnight funds from another commercial bank at a rate below the upper limit, then the Bank of Canada will lend money overnight to the commercial bank at the upper limit. By standing ready to borrow funds at the lower limit of the operating band and to lend funds at the upper limit, the Bank of Canada is able to keep the overnight rate within the operating band.

But, as is suggested by the closeness of the overnight rate to the overnight target for the days of January 2008 shown in Figure 10.1, the Bank of Canada does not just aim to keep the overnight rate within the operating band—it aims to keep the overnight rate very close to the overnight rate target. In January 2008, for example, the overnight rate only differed from the overnight rate target by more than one **basis point** (one hundredth of a percentage point) for a single day; that is, on January 2, 2008, when it differed by 0.014 percentage points.[7]

FIGURE 10.2

A Downward Shift of the Operating Band for the Overnight Rate, January 2008

The target for the overnight rate (shown in blue) can change at pre-specified dates, as it did on January 22, 2008, when the Bank of Canada lowered it from 4.25 to 4 percent. A lowering of the overnight rate target means that the operating band (shown in beige) shifts downward. The actual overnight rate (shown in red) need not be exactly the same as the overnight rate target, but it is very close. When the Bank of Canada changes the overnight rate target, it is usually by 0.25 percentage points, as shown.

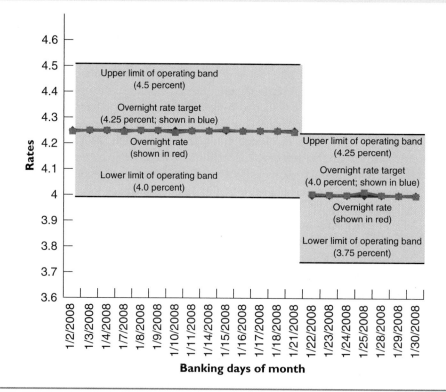

7 Hence, one-quarter of a percentage point equals 25 basis points, one-half of a percentage point equals 50 basis points, one percentage point equals 100 basis points, and so on.

How is the overnight rate kept so close to the overnight rate target? The Bank manages the overnight rate by monitoring the overnight loans market on a daily basis and taking appropriate actions.[8] When the overnight rate is exceeding the overnight rate target, it is because the amount that participants wish to borrow is greater than the amount that other members are willing to lend at that overnight rate target. When this is the case, settlement balances are said to be in deficit. This situation leads the Bank to buy Government of Canada bonds from market participants with an agreement to sell them back at a predetermined price the next business day.[9] The bonds serve as collateral for the Bank of Canada loans, provide liquidity to the market, and bring settlement balances up to zero. Conversely, if overnight funds are trading below the overnight rate target, the Bank of Canada will sell Government of Canada bonds to market participants, with the agreement to buy them back the next business day.[10] The bond sales by the Bank of Canada soak up liquidity in the market and bring settlement balances down to zero.

It is important to recognize that there are limits to Bank of Canada control of the overnight rate. It is certainly true that if the overnight rate is at, say, 4.25 percent, the Bank of Canada can easily bring the overnight rate down very close to 4 percent by cutting the overnight rate target from 4.25 percent to 4 percent. But suppose that the overnight rate target is at 0.5 percent with the actual overnight rate also at 0.5 percent, and the Bank of Canada calculates that to get the economy out of recession and prevent the inflation rate from falling below the inflation-control target it would be necessary for the overnight rate to fall to −0.75 percent. It is just not possible for the Bank of Canada to achieve such a result.

As noted in Chapter 6 in connection with the *zero bound on nominal interest rates hypothesis*, nominal interest rates cannot be negative in financial markets. A negative overnight rate, for example, would mean that a lending bank would lend funds to a borrowing bank overnight, and then the borrowing bank would return to the lending bank an amount *less* than the amount of funds originally lent. So the lowest an overnight rate can go is zero percent, and in some countries this happened during the financial crisis and global recession of 2008–2010. In Canada, however, due to the details of how the Bank of Canada controls the overnight rate, the overnight rate target was cut at its lowest to 0.25 percent (starting in April 2010; see Economic Naturalist 10.1), which the Bank of Canada described as the *effective lower bound*. The **effective lower bound** refers to the lowest feasible level for a central bank's key policy rate.

basis point one hundredth of a percentage point; term often used in describing interest rates

effective lower bound the lowest feasible level for a central bank's key policy rate

---

ECONOMIC NATURALIST 10.1

When the Bank of Canada "Ran Out of Ammunition"

The Bank of Canada's overnight rate target was at 4.5 percent when early signs of an impending recession surfaced in the summer of 2007. The Bank of Canada began a series of interest rate cuts. By April 21, 2009, the Bank of Canada announced that it would reduce its key policy rate to 0.25 percent. A key policy rate of 0.25 percent is incredibly low by historical standards. Prior to 2009, the lowest the Bank of Canada's key policy rate had ever been was 1.22 percent, and that was registered way back in July 1958.[11] In cutting the overnight rate target to 0.25 percent, the Bank declared that 0.25 percent was the "effective lower bound" for the overnight rate target. In other words, the Bank was saying that it could not cut its key policy rate any further. Some other central banks found themselves in the same predicament. Because interest rate cuts are what central banks use to fight recession, commentators said that the central banks had "run out of ammunition." Furthermore, the Bank of Canada did not just run out of ammunition, but it was without ammunition for over 13 months.

---

8 For further details on the approach to monetary policy implementation adopted by the Bank of Canada beginning in February 1999, see Donna Howard, "A Primer on the Implementation of Monetary Policy in the LVTS Environment," *Bank of Canada*, December 2001.

9 The agreement is called a *special purchase and resale agreement*.

10 The agreement is called a *sale and repurchase agreement*.

11 Back in 1958, the key policy rate was the bank rate, not the overnight rate target.

It is worth noting that some advocates of moderate, as opposed to low, inflation had for years warned of the danger of the zero bound on nominal interest rates (as explained in Chapter 6), but economists representing the Bank of Canada had repeatedly argued that the possibility of the Bank ever running out of ammunition was extremely low.[12]

In the abstract, the key policy rate of a central bank can go as low as zero percent. But the Bank of Canada was claiming that for practical purposes 0.25 percent was as low as the overnight rate target and the overnight rate could go. The Bank of Canada kept the overnight rate target at 0.25 percent and the overnight rate at about 0.25 percent until June 1, 2010. During the same time period, however, the corresponding overnight rate in the United States was often at about 0.12 percent and in Japan it was typically at 0.10 percent, so the examples of other countries suggest that perhaps that there was an element of judgment in the Bank of Canada's description of 0.25 percent as the effective lower bound; that is, the rate could possibly have been pushed 10 to 15 basis points lower.

In any case, for the period from April 21, 2009, to June 1, 2010, during which the overnight rate target of the Bank of Canada was maintained at 0.25 percent, the Bank of Canada temporarily changed its operating band for the target. The operating band was reduced from its usual 50 basis points down to 25 basis points. The bank rate was 25 basis points above the overnight rate target, as usual, but the deposit rate, instead of being 25 basis points below the overnight rate target, was set equal to the target. In other words, the overnight rate target was at the bottom of the operating band rather than at the midpoint.[13]

Not all central banks followed the same approach to the operating band during the crisis. The Federal Reserve in the United States, instead of reducing its key policy rate to 0.25 percent like the Bank of Canada did, instead reduced the key policy rate to the range of 0 to 0.25 percent starting on December 16, 2008.[14] The innovative Riksbank, the central bank of Sweden, reduced its deposit rate to −0.25 percent in July 2009 and kept it there until July 2010; that is, instead of offering banks interest for overnight loans the Riksbank offered to "tax" them in the form of a −0.25 percent deposit rate.[15]

RECAP

THE MODERN CENTRAL BANKING THEORY OF INTEREST RATE DETERMINATION

The modern central banking theory claims that when the central bank changes its key policy rate (also called its official interest rate), commercial banks respond by changing market interest rates. In Canada, the key policy rate used to be the bank rate but is now the overnight rate target.

The overnight rate itself is an interest rate that financial institutions charge each other for overnight loans. The Bank of Canada controls the overnight rate through its overnight rate target. The target is the midpoint of an operating band that has the bank rate at its upper bound and the deposit rate at its lower bound. The Bank of Canada monitors the overnight rate on a daily basis and takes whatever actions are necessary to keep the overnight rate very close to the overnight rate target.

Although central banks have a great deal of power to control overnight rates, they are constrained by the zero bound on nominal interest rates. Indeed, according to the Bank of Canada, there is an effective lower bound that is above zero.

---

12 Robert Amano and Malik Shukayev, in "Monetary Policy and the Zero Bound on Nominal Interest Rates," (*Bank of Canada Review*, Summer 2010, p.3) mention sources in which the Bank of Canada downplayed the significance of the zero lower bound.

13 Details are explained in Bank of Canada, "Operating framework for the implementation of monetary policy at the effective lower bound for the overnight interest rate," 21 April 2009, at http://www.bankofcanada.ca/wp-content/uploads/2010/04/rate_210409_1.pdf.

14 See http://www.newyorkfed.org/markets/omo/dmm/fedfundsdata.cfm.

15 See http://www.riksbank.com/templates/Page.aspx?id=12182, and Lars Svensson, "Monetary Policy and Financial Markets at the Effective Lower Bound," *Journal of Money, Credit and Banking*, Supplement to Vol. 42, No. 6 (September 2010), pp. 229–242.

10.3 CAN THE BANK OF CANADA CONTROL THE REAL INTEREST RATE?

The modern central banking theory claims that a central bank, such as the Bank of Canada, has the power to control the economy's *nominal* interest rate. But many important decisions, such as the decisions to consume and invest, depend on the *real* rate of interest. To affect those decisions, a central bank like the Bank of Canada must exert some control over the real interest rate.

Most economists believe that the Bank of Canada can control the real interest rate, at least for some period. To see why, recall the definition of the real interest rate from Chapter 6:

$$r = i - \pi.$$

That is, the real interest rate r equals the nominal interest rate i minus the rate of inflation π. As we have seen, the Bank of Canada can control the nominal interest rate quite precisely. Furthermore, inflation appears to change relatively slowly in response to changes in policy or economic conditions, for reasons we discuss in Chapter 12. Because inflation tends to adjust slowly, action by the Bank of Canada to change the nominal interest rate causes the real interest rate to change by about the same amount. (Additional discussion of interest rates is provided in Chapter 13, where we mention real interest rate determination in an open economy with flexible exchange rates.)

In discussing the Bank of Canada's control over interest rates, we should also recognize that in reality there are many thousands of interest rates in the economy, not just one. Because interest rates tend to move together (allowing us to speak of "the" interest rate), an action by the Bank of Canada to change the overnight rate generally causes other interest rates to change in the same direction. However, the tendency of other interest rates (such as the long-term government bond rate or the rate on bonds issued by corporations) to move in the same direction as the overnight rate is only a tendency, not an exact relationship. In practice, then, the Bank of Canada's control of other interest rates, particularly long-term ones, is somewhat less precise than its control of the overnight rate.

As previously mentioned, the overnight rate is an example of a benchmark rate. Other interest rates are set higher than the benchmark rate. The difference in interest rates between a benchmark rate and a related interest rate is called an **interest rate spread**, a borrowing spread, or, in context, a spread. If interest rate spreads widen, central banks may have to cut their key policy rates more than usual to offset the rise in interest rate spreads. During the period 2007–2010, the turbulent state of financial markets made central bank control of interest rates more challenging than usual, because interest rate spreads rose, as explained in Economic Naturalist 10.2.

interest rate spread the difference, often measured in basis points, between a benchmark interest rate and a related market interest rate (such as between an overnight rate and a mortgage lending rate)

ECONOMIC NATURALIST 10.2

2007–2010: When Central Bank Control of Interest Rates Became More Challenging

Although central bank control over long-term interest rates is less than over short-term interest rates, in normal times there is a fairly consistent response of interest rates charged by banks and other financial institutions to changes in the key policy rate of the central bank (which is the overnight rate target in the case of the Bank of Canada). During the years from 2007 to 2010, however, there was a long stretch of months during which interest rate spreads were much higher than had previously been the case. The rise in interest rate spreads was more severe in some countries than in others.

The usual explanation for the rise in market interest rates relative to the central bank's key policy rate is that market interest rates came to include a premium for the greater risk associated with lending during the financial crisis. For example, prior to the crisis, one major financial institution could lend short term to another major financial institution with little risk that the loan would not be repaid. But during the financial crisis, the lender would often have been very worried that the borrower would go bankrupt before the loan would be repaid and would therefore be unwilling to lend except if the interest rate received would compensate for the greater risk. This explanation was particularly directed to the situation in the United States. There was also a growing sense in financial markets that various forms of lending, most notably mortgage lending, were more risky than previously recognized.

In Canada, the Bank of Canada maintained its ability to control the overnight rate that large financial institutions charge one another for overnight loans. Even over the period of great turbulence in financial markets between September and December 2008, the overnight rate in Canada barely diverged from the Bank of Canada's key policy rate, the overnight rate target.

Beginning in the summer of 2007, however, various short-term interest rates charged by financial institutions rose relative to the overnight rate. David Longworth, then Deputy Governor of the Bank of Canada, touched upon this issue in a speech he delivered in August 2008. He argued that the spread between short-term lending rates charged by financial institutions and the overnight lending rate was lower in Canada than in most other countries during the crisis because Canadian financial institutions were in better financial condition than financial institutions in other countries. Yet even in Canada, he acknowledged, ". . . .the average effective borrowing *spreads* faced by banks, non-financial businesses, and households have increased by about 75 basis points vis-à-vis the overnight rate since the onset of turbulence in financial markets [in the summer of 2007.]"

The rise in the average spread between the overnight rate and a typical market interest rate is illustrated in Figure 10.3, which shows the spread between the overnight rate and typical rate on a

FIGURE 10.3

The Rise and Fall of an Interest Rate Spread, January 2006 to January 2011

The figure shows the interest rate spread between the overnight rate and the typical rate on a one-year mortgage (that is, housing loan). The average spread between the two rates had been 2.3 percentage points (230 basis points) between January 2006 and early July 2007. Over the following year, the average spread rose to 3.15 percentage points. Over the period from early July 2007 to July 2010, the spread averaged almost 3.5 percentage points—over 100 basis points greater than the spread prevailing in the January 2006 to July 2007 period.

SOURCE: Adapted from Statistics Canada CANSIM series v122514 (overnight rate) and v122520 (chartered bank conventional 1-year mortgage).

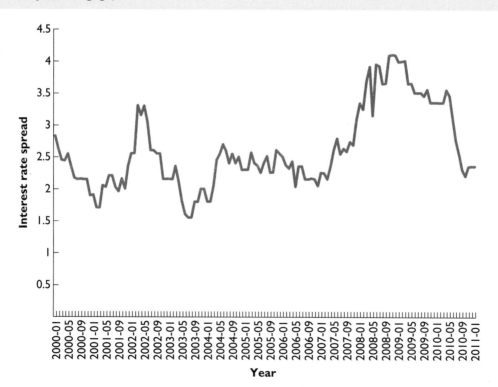

one-year mortgage (that is, housing loan). The average spread between the two rates was 2.3 percentage points (230 basis points) between January 2006 and early July 2007. Over the following year, the average spread rose to 3.15 percentage points, equaling the increase of 75 basis points mentioned by then Deputy Governor Longworth. Over the period from early July 2007 to July 2010, the spread averaged almost 3.5 percentage points, over 100 basis points greater than the spread prevailing in the January 2006 to July 2007 period.

Now, as Longworth noted, if the spread rises but the Bank of Canada still controls the overnight rate through the overnight rate target, the Bank of Canada can offset the rise in the spread by cutting the overnight rate target. The problem created by the rise in the spread illustrated by Figure 10.3 was that the Canadian economy was heading for recession as the spread was rising. The Bank of Canada needed to cut the overnight rate target to offset the forces of recession, forces that became extremely severe in the fall of 2009. The overnight rate target

was at 4.5 percent when early signs of the impending recession surfaced in the summer of 2007. With an effective lower bound of 0.25 percent, that would have left the Bank of Canada with room for 4.25 percentage points of interest rate cuts to stimulate the economy and counteract the recession.

But as events unfolded, over 100 basis points of interest rate cuts were needed merely to offset the rise in the spread between the overnight rate and typical borrowing rates faced by households and businesses. Therefore, less than 3.25 percentage points of interest rate cuts were available to the Bank of Canada to provide additional stimulus with which to fight the worst global recession since the Great Depression. The rise in the spread, then, is an essential part of the story of how the Bank of Canada "ran out of ammunition."

It was because of events such as rising interest rate spreads and coming up against the effective lower bound that many central banks began, during the recession of 2007–2008, to implement unconventional monetary policy, as discussed in Chapter 9.

RECAP

THE CENTRAL BANK AND THE NOMINAL INTEREST RATE

The modern central banking theory claims that the central bank is able to control the nominal interest rate. And because inflation is slow to adjust, in the short run central banks like the Bank of Canada can control the real interest rate (equal to the nominal interest rate minus the inflation rate) as well as the nominal interest rate.

In macroeconomics, we typically assume that interest rates move together, allowing us to speak of "the" interest rate. This simplification abstracts from the fact that central banks generally have better control over short-term interest rates than over long-term ones. It also abstracts from the possibility that during times of financial crisis, interest rate spreads may widen and central banks may have to cut their key policy rates more than usual to offset the rise in interest rate spreads.

10.4 THE EFFECTS OF BANK OF CANADA ACTIONS ON THE ECONOMY

Now that we have seen how the Bank of Canada can influence interest rates (both nominal and real), we can turn to the question of how monetary policy can be used to eliminate output gaps and stabilize the economy. The basic idea is relatively straightforward—planned aggregate expenditure (as we will see) depends on the real interest rate. Specifically, a lower real interest rate encourages higher spending by households and firms, while a higher real interest rate reduces spending. By adjusting the real interest rate, the Bank of Canada can move planned aggregate expenditure in the desired direction. Assuming that firms produce just enough to meet the demand for their output, the stabilization of planned aggregate expenditure leads to stabilization of aggregate output and employment as well. In this section we will first explain how planned aggregate expenditure is related to the real interest rate. Then we will show how the Bank of Canada can use changes in the real interest rate to fight a recession or inflation.

PLANNED AGGREGATE EXPENDITURE AND THE REAL INTEREST RATE

In Chapter 8 we saw how planned spending is affected by changes in real output Y. Changes in output affect the household sector's disposable income, which in turn influences consumption spending, a relationship captured by the consumption function.

A second variable that has potentially important effects on aggregate expenditure is the real interest rate r. The real interest rate influences the behaviour of both households and firms.

For households, the empirical evidence suggests that a higher real interest rate reduces consumption spending. This idea makes sense; think, for example, about people's willingness to buy consumer durables, such as automobiles or furniture. Consumer durables, which are part of consumption spending, are often financed by borrowing from a bank, credit union, or other financial intermediary. When the real interest rate rises, the monthly finance charges associated with the purchase of a car or a piano are higher, and people become less willing or able to make the purchase. Thus, a higher real interest rate reduces people's willingness to spend on consumer goods, assuming disposable income and other factors that affect consumption remain constant.

Besides reducing consumption spending, a higher real interest rate may also discourage firms from making capital investments. For example, upgrading a computer system may be profitable for a manufacturing firm when the cost of the system can be financed by borrowing at a real interest rate of 3 percent. However, if the real interest rate rises to 6 percent, doubling the cost of funds to the firm, the same upgrade may not be profitable and the firm may choose not to invest.[16]

We conclude that *both consumption spending and planned private-sector investment spending decline when the real interest rate increases*. Conversely, a fall in the real interest rate tends to stimulate consumption and investment spending by reducing financing costs. Example 10.1 is a numerical illustration of how planned aggregate expenditure can be related to the real interest rate and output.

When the real interest rate rises, financing a new car becomes more expensive and fewer cars are purchased.

EXAMPLE 10.1

Planned aggregate expenditure and the real interest rate

In a hypothetical version of the Canadian economy, the components of planned spending are given by

$$C = 640 + 0.8(Y - T) - 400r,$$
$$I^P = 250 - 600r,$$
$$G = 300,$$
$$NX = 20,$$
$$T = 250.$$

Find the relationship of planned aggregate expenditure to the real interest rate r and output Y in this economy. Find autonomous expenditure and induced expenditure.

This example is similar to Example 8.1, except that now the real interest rate r is allowed to affect both consumption and planned private-sector investment. For example, the final term in the equation describing consumption, $-400r$, implies that a 1 percent (0.01) increase in the real interest rate, from 4 percent to 5 percent, for example, reduces consumption spending by $400(0.01) = 4$ units. Similarly, the final term in the equation for planned private-sector investment tells us that in this example, a 1 percent increase in the real interest rate lowers planned private-sector investment

---

16 Even if nonresidential business fixed capital formation is relatively insensitive to interest rate changes, as some empirical evidence suggests, overall private-sector investment will tend to be fairly responsive to interest rate changes because of the interest rate sensitivity of the residential investment component of private-sector investment.

by 600(0.01) = 6 units. Thus the overall effect of a 1 percent increase in the real interest rate is to lower planned aggregate expenditure by 10 units, the sum of the effects on consumption and private-sector investment. As in the earlier examples, disposable income $(Y - T)$ is assumed to affect consumption spending through a marginal propensity to consume of 0.8 (see the first equation), and government purchases G, net exports NX, and taxes T are assumed to be fixed numbers.

To find a numerical equation that describes the relationship of planned aggregate expenditure (PAE) to output, we can begin as in Chapter 8 with the general definition of planned aggregate expenditure:

$$PAE = C + I^P + G + NX.$$

Substituting for the four components of expenditure, using the equations describing each type of spending above, we get

$$PAE = [640 + 0.8(Y - 250) - 400r] + [250 - 600r] + 300 + 20.$$

The first term in brackets on the right side of this equation is the expression for consumption, using the fact that taxes $T = 250$, the second bracketed term is planned private-sector investment, and the last two terms correspond to the given numerical values of government purchases and net exports. If we simplify this equation and group together the terms that do not depend on output Y and the terms that do depend on output, we get

$$PAE = [(640 - 0.8 \times 250 - 400r) + (250 - 600r) + 300 + 20] + 0.8Y,$$

or, simplifying further,

$$PAE = [1010 - 1000r] + 0.8Y. \qquad (10.1)$$

In Equation 10.1, the term in brackets is *autonomous expenditure*, the portion of planned aggregate expenditure that does not depend on output. Notice that in this example, *autonomous expenditure depends on the real interest rate r*. Induced expenditure, the portion of planned aggregate expenditure that does depend on output, equals $0.8Y$ in this example.

EXAMPLE 10.2

The real interest rate and short-run equilibrium output

In the economy described in Example 10.1, the real interest rate (r) is set by the Bank of Canada to equal 0.05 (5 percent). Find short-run equilibrium output.

We found in Example 10.1 that, in this economy, planned aggregate expenditure is given by Equation 10.1. We are given that the Bank of Canada sets the real interest rate at 5 percent. Setting $r = 0.05$ in Equation 10.1 gives

$$PAE = [1010 - 1000 \times (0.05)] + 0.8Y.$$

Simplifying, we get

$$PAE = 960 + 0.8Y.$$

So, when the real interest rate is 5 percent, autonomous expenditure is 960 and induced expenditure is $0.8Y$. Short-run equilibrium output is the level of output that equals planned aggregate spending. To find short-run equilibrium output, we could now apply the tabular method used in Chapter 8, comparing alternative values of output with the planned aggregate expenditure at that level of output. Short-run equilibrium output would be determined as the value of output such that output just equals spending, or

$$Y = PAE.$$

However, conveniently, when we compare this example with Example 8.1, we see that the equation for planned aggregate expenditure, $PAE = 960 + 0.8Y$, is identical to what we found there. Thus Table 8.1, which we used to solve Example 8.1, applies to this example as well, and we get the same answer for short-run equilibrium output, which is $Y = 4800$.

Short-run equilibrium output can also be found graphically, using the Keynesian cross diagram from Chapter 8. Again, since the equation for planned aggregate output is the same as in Example 8.1, Figure 8.3 applies equally well here.

EXERCISE 10.2   **For the economy described in Example 10.2, suppose the Bank of Canada sets the real interest rate at 3 percent rather than at 5 percent. Find short-run equilibrium output.**

THE BANK OF CANADA FIGHTS A RECESSION

We have seen that the Bank of Canada can control the real interest rate and that the real interest rate in turn affects planned aggregate expenditure and short-run equilibrium output. Putting these two results together, we can see how Bank of Canada policies can help to stabilize planned aggregate expenditure and output.

Suppose the economy faces a recessionary gap—a situation in which real output is below potential output and planned aggregate expenditure is "too low." To fight a recessionary gap, the Bank of Canada should reduce the real interest rate, stimulating consumption and private-sector investment spending. According to the theory we have developed, this increase in planned aggregate expenditure will increase output, restoring the economy to full employment. Example 10.3 illustrates this point by extending Example 10.2.

EXAMPLE **10.3**

The Bank of Canada fights a recession

For the economy described in Example 10.2, suppose potential output Y^* equals 5000.[17] As before, the Bank of Canada has set the real interest rate equal to 5 percent. At that real interest rate, what is the output gap? What should the Bank of Canada do to eliminate the output gap and restore full employment? You are given that the multiplier in this economy is 5. (Recall from Chapter 8 that real-world income-expenditure multipliers are typically less than 2; we employ 5 here for ease of calculation.)

In Example 10.2 we showed that with the real interest rate at 5 percent, short-run equilibrium output for this economy is 4800. Potential output is 5000, so the output gap $(Y - Y^*)$ equals $4800 - 5000 = -200$. Because actual output is below potential, this economy faces a recessionary gap.

To fight the recession, the Bank of Canada should lower the real interest rate, raising aggregate expenditure until output reaches 5000, the full-employment level. That is, the Bank of Canada's objective is to increase output by 200. Because the multiplier equals 5, to increase output by 200 the Bank of Canada must increase autonomous expenditure by 200/5 = 40 units. By how much should the Bank of Canada reduce the real interest rate to increase autonomous expenditure by 40 units? Autonomous

---

17 For the sake of simplicity, we are assuming that potential output can be precisely estimated. Recall from Chapter 7, however, that potential output is difficult and controversial to estimate and is never known with full certainty, as will be emphasized later in this chapter and again in Chapter 11.

expenditure in this economy is [1010 − 1000r], as you can see from Equation 10.1, so that each percentage point reduction in r increases autonomous expenditure by 1000 × (0.01) = 10 units. To increase autonomous expenditure by 40, then, the Bank of Canada should lower the real interest rate by 4 percentage points, from 5 percent to 1 percent.

In summary, to eliminate the recessionary gap of 200, the Bank of Canada should lower the real interest rate from 5 percent to 1 percent. Notice that the Bank of Canada's decrease in the real interest rate increases short-run equilibrium output, as economic logic suggests.

The Bank of Canada's recession-fighting policy is shown graphically in Figure 10.4. The reduction in the real interest rate raises planned spending at each level of output, shifting the expenditure line upward. When the real interest rate equals 1 percent, the expenditure line intersects the Y = PAE line at Y = 5000, so that output and potential output are equal. A reduction in interest rates by the Bank of Canada, made with the intention of reducing a recessionary gap in this way, is an example of an *expansionary monetary policy*—or, less formally, a *monetary easing*.

Continuing Example 10.3, suppose that potential output is 4850 rather than 5000. By how much should the Bank of Canada cut the real interest rate to restore full employment? You may take as given that the multiplier is 5.

EXERCISE 10.3

THE BANK OF CANADA PREVENTS INFLATION

To this point, we have focused on the problem of stabilizing output, without considering inflation. In Chapter 11, we will see how ongoing inflation can be incorporated into our analysis. For now, we will simply note that one important cause of inflation is an expansionary output gap—a situation in which aggregate expenditure, and hence actual output, exceeds potential output. When an expansionary gap exists, firms find that the demand for their output exceeds their normal rate of production. Although firms may be content to meet the excess demand at previously determined prices for some time, if it persists they will ultimately raise their prices, which means inflation.

Because an expansionary gap stimulates inflation, central banks tend to move to eliminate expansionary gaps as well as recessionary gaps. The procedure for getting rid of an expansionary gap, a situation in which output is "too high" relative to potential

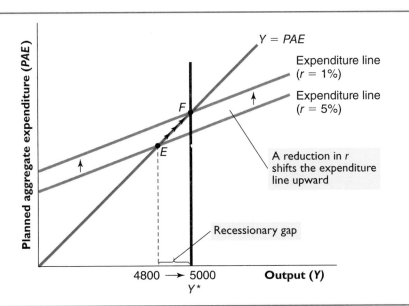

FIGURE 10.4
The Bank of Canada Fights a Recession
When the real interest rate is 5 percent, the expenditure line intersects the Y = PAE line at point E. At that point, output is 4800—below the economy's potential output of 5000 (a recessionary gap of 200). If the Bank of Canada reduces the real interest rate to 1 percent, stimulating consumption and investment spending, the expenditure line will shift upward. At the new point of intersection F, output will equal potential output at 5000.

output, is the reverse of that for fighting a recessionary gap, a situation in which output is "too low." As we have seen, the cure for a recessionary gap is to reduce the real interest rate, an action that stimulates planned spending and increases output. The cure for an expansionary gap is to *raise* the real interest rate, which reduces consumption and planned private-sector investment by raising the cost of borrowing. The resulting fall in planned spending leads, in turn, to a decline in output and a reduction in inflationary pressures.

EXAMPLE 10.4

The Bank of Canada prevents inflation

For the economy studied in Examples 10.2 and 10.3 assume that potential output is 4600 rather than 5000. At the initial real interest rate of 5 percent, short-run equilibrium output is 4800, so this economy has an expansionary gap of 200. How should the Bank of Canada change the real interest rate to eliminate this gap?

In Example 10.3, we were told that the income-expenditure multiplier in this economy is 5. Thus, to reduce total output by 200, the Bank of Canada needs to reduce autonomous expenditure by 200/5 = 40 units. From Equation 10.1, we know that autonomous expenditure in this economy is [1010 − 1000r], so that each percentage point (0.01) increase in the real interest rate lowers autonomous expenditure by 10 units (1000 × 0.01). We conclude that to eliminate the inflationary gap, the Bank of Canada should raise the real interest rate by 4 percentage points (0.04), from 5 percent to 9 percent. The higher real interest rate will reduce planned aggregate expenditure and output to the level of potential output, 4600, thus eliminating inflationary pressures.

The effects of the Bank of Canada's anti-inflation policy are shown in Figure 10.5. With the real interest rate at 5 percent, the expenditure line intersects the $Y = PAE$ line at point E in the figure, where output equals 4800. To reduce planned aggregate expenditure and output, the Bank of Canada raises the real interest rate to 9 percent. The higher real interest rate reduces consumption and private-sector investment spending, moving the expenditure line downward. At the new equilibrium point G, actual output equals potential output at 4600. The Bank of Canada's policy of raising the real interest rate has eliminated the expansionary output gap, and with it, the threat of inflation.

FIGURE 10.5
The Bank of Canada Prevents Inflation
When the real interest rate is 5 percent, the expenditure line intersects the $Y = PAE$ line at point E, where short-run equilibrium output equals 4800. If potential output is 4600, an expansionary output gap of 200 exists. If the Bank of Canada raises the real interest rate to 9 percent, reducing planned aggregate expenditure, the expenditure line shifts downward. At the new intersection point G, actual output equals potential output at 4600, and the expansionary gap is eliminated.

"Personally I liked this roller coaster a lot better before the Federal Reserve Board got hold of it."

OUR KEYNESIAN CROSS MODEL OF MONETARY POLICY COMPARED TO THE BANK OF CANADA'S EXPLANATION

In introducing the Keynesian cross (or basic Keynesian) model, we mentioned that it is highly simplified. In this chapter we have indicated that, despite being highly simplified, the Keynesian cross model is of considerable relevance to understanding real-world monetary policy. This raises the question of how our Keynesian cross model compares to other explanations of real-world monetary policy. For example, how does the simple Keynesian cross model developed in this chapter compare with the explanation of monetary policy provided by the Bank of Canada?

Figure 10.6 depicts the Bank of Canada's view of how its monetary policy actions impact upon the economy. A monetary policy action could be either an increase or a decrease in the overnight rate target. An increase in the overnight rate target, for example, would quickly cause market interest rates to rise and the exchange rate to appreciate. The Canadian dollar would appreciate because Canadian interest rates would rise relative to rates in the United States and other countries, leading to increased demand for Canadian dollars by investors who would need them to purchase Canadian financial assets, particularly bonds. (A full discussion of exchange rate determination will be provided in Chapter 13.)

FIGURE 10.6

The Bank of Canada's View of Monetary Policy

The diagram illustrates that monetary policy actions in the form of changes in the overnight rate target produce changes in market interest rates and the exchange rate that ultimately affect aggregate expenditure growth (either increasing or reducing it) and the rate of inflation.

SOURCE: Adapted from Bank of Canada, www.bankofcanada.ca/en/monetary_mod/mechanism/index.html. Extraction date, May 10, 2011.

Higher market interest rates would gradually slow the growth of consumer spending and private-sector investment and would, hence, slow the growth of aggregate expenditure (spending). The stronger exchange rate would also gradually slow the growth of aggregate expenditure—by reducing the growth of net exports. That is, a stronger Canadian dollar would slow the growth of Canadian exports and stimulate the growth of imports.

The slower growth of aggregate expenditure would translate into slower growth of production (output) and employment. Finally, slower growth would eventually tend to reduce price and cost increases, and result in a lower rate of inflation.

This explanation has much in common with the Keynesian cross explanation underlying Figure 10.5. The basic process is that the Bank of Canada increases the overnight rate target, the higher overnight rate results in higher market interest rates in general, aggregate expenditure is weakened, and inflationary pressure is reduced. Conversely, Figure 10.6 could be used to discuss a decrease in the overnight rate target and the explanation would have much in common with the explanation underlying Figure 10.4.

EXERCISE 10.4   **Based upon Figure 10.6 and the discussion above, describe how the Bank of Canada would view the impact of a decrease in the overnight rate target. That is, describe how a decrease in the overnight rate target would impact market interest rates, the exchange rate, and the inflation rate.**

There are a few noteworthy differences between the Keynesian cross model of Figures 10.4 and 10.5 and the Bank of Canada explanation we have illustrated with Figure 10.6. First, the Bank of Canada explanation emphasizes that changes in the overnight rate target also produce changes in the exchange rate, and hence in net exports. Our Keynesian cross model could be modified to recognize the impact that interest rates have on net exports. Rather than assume that net exports are fixed, we could assume that a rise in the interest rate will decrease net exports and that a fall in the interest rate will increase net exports. Our model would then be more realistic, but the basic result would be the same—an increase in the overnight rate target would lead to a reduction in planned aggregate expenditure.

Second, the Bank of Canada explanation deals with changes in the growth rates of consumer and private-sector investment spending, net exports, aggregate expenditure, and output. Our Keynesian cross model, however, is based upon the assumption that potential output is fixed for the period of analysis. Hence, in the Keynesian cross model, aggregate expenditure and the level of output go up or down relative to a fixed level. In applying the Keynesian cross model to real-world situations, we typically assume that a decrease in the level of aggregate expenditure in the model corresponds to a decrease in the growth rate of aggregate expenditure in the real world. Similarly, we assume that an increase in the level of aggregate expenditure in the model corresponds to an increase in the growth rate of aggregate expenditure in the real world. But the assumption that potential output is fixed is a genuine limitation of the Keynesian cross model that students should recognize. Real-world analysis is typically not about output going up or down relative to a fixed level but about the growth of output increasing or declining relative to the current trend.

Third, the Bank of Canada explanation deals with changes in the rate of inflation. Interest rate increases, for example, will tend, eventually, to decrease the rate of inflation. On the other hand, while the Keynesian cross model can be used to talk about eliminating an expansionary (inflationary) gap and, thereby, preventing the emergence of inflation, the truth is that the Keynesian cross model does not incorporate inflation explicitly. In fact, as explained back in Chapter 8, an underlying assumption of the model is that in the short run, firms meet the demand for their products at preset prices—in other words, zero inflation (see Figure 6.4) is assumed. To consider the more general case where the economy starts from a non-zero rate of inflation, we have to move to the analysis of Chapters 11 and 12.

THE EFFECTS OF BANK OF CANADA ACTIONS ON THE ECONOMY

An increase in the real interest rate reduces both consumption spending and planned private-sector investment spending. Through its control of the real interest rate, the Bank of Canada is thus able to influence planned aggregate expenditure and short-run equilibrium output.

To fight a recession (a recessionary gap), the Bank of Canada should lower the real interest rate, stimulating planned aggregate expenditure and output. Conversely, to fight inflation (an expansionary output gap), the Bank of Canada should raise the real interest rate.

Although the Keynesian cross model employed in this chapter is highly simplified, it allows for an analysis of monetary policy that has much in common with the Bank of Canada's explanation. One limitation of the Keynesian cross model is the assumption that in the short run, firms meet the demand for their products at preset prices, but this limitation will be overcome with the models of Chapters 11 and 12.

10.5   MONETARY POLICY-MAKING AND REAL-WORLD UNCERTAINTY

In this chapter we used a simplified model to explain the basic economics underlying monetary policy. We worked through a number of examples showing the calculation of the real interest rate that is needed to restore output to its full-employment level. While those examples are useful in understanding how monetary policy works, as with our analysis of fiscal policy in Chapter 8, they overstate the precision of monetary policy-making. The real-world economy is highly complex and knowledge of its workings quite imperfect. For example, though we assumed in our analysis that the Bank of Canada knows the exact value of potential output, in reality potential output can be estimated only approximately (and many economists believe that the Bank of Canada is prone to underestimating potential output). As a result, at any given time, the Bank of Canada has only a rough idea of the size of the output gap. Similarly, Bank of Canada policy-makers have only an approximate idea of the effect of a given change in the real interest rate on planned aggregate expenditure, or the length of time before that effect will occur. Because of these uncertainties, the Bank of Canada tends to proceed cautiously. Bank of Canada policy-makers avoid large changes in interest rates and rarely raise or lower the overnight rate target more than 0.25 percentage points (from 3.25 to 3.00 percent, for example) at any one time.

ECONOMIC NATURALIST   10.3

Why did the Bank of Canada raise the overnight rate target 2.5 percentage points in the period from 2004 to 2007?

By the second half of 2004, inflation was running at about 2.3 percent, somewhat above the 2 percent that the Bank of Canada regards as consistent with its objective of maintaining a low inflation rate. The Bank began to judge that the recessionary gap would soon be eliminated and that the economy was on the verge of entering an expansionary gap situation. If an expansionary gap situation did arise, the inflation rate would be expected to rise as well.

The Bank of Canada's judgment that action was required in order to prevent an inflation increase was based on the unemployment rate (we have seen in Chapter 7 that the unemployment rate is linked to the output gap through Okun's law). The unemployment rate had dropped to a low of 6.7 percent at the peak of the economic boom in June 2000, a level that the Bank of Canada viewed as less than or equal to the natural rate of unemployment. After the economic slowdown of late 2000 and 2001, the unemployment rate had reached a high of 7.9 percent in September 2003. But then the unemployment rate began to plummet as the economic recovery took hold. By the end of September 2004, the unemployment rate was down to 7 percent. The Bank of Canada feared that unless it began to raise the overnight target, thereby raising real interest rates and slowing the growth of spending, an expansionary (that is, inflationary) gap would develop and the inflation rate would rise.

The shrinking output gap, however, was not the only factor causing the Bank of Canada to worry about an upsurge in the inflation rate. The Bank was also concerned with already high and still rising energy prices. One indicator of energy prices is the price of gasoline, and, as Figure 10.7 indicates,

from 2002 the price of gasoline rose sharply, relative to price levels in general as measured by the CPI. Energy price increases tend, all else being equal, to generate increases in the CPI, unless offsetting events or deliberate countermeasures take place. (For further explanation, see Chapters 11 and 12.) The Bank of Canada was well aware that energy prices are volatile, which is part of the reason that the Bank relies more upon core CPI inflation than total CPI inflation as an operating guide, but when energy prices rise sharply for several years in a row it starts to look like a trend, not just volatility.

On September 8, 2004, the Bank of Canada announced that it was raising the overnight rate target by 0.25 percentage points, from 2 to 2.25 percent. The press release announcing the interest rate hike stated that "Looking forward, the Bank expects aggregate demand to grow at, or marginally above, the rate of growth of production capacity. With the economy operating close to its capacity, monetary stimulus needs to be reduced to avoid a buildup

FIGURE 10.7

The Gasoline Price Index, 2002–2010

A key concern of the Bank of Canada in the 2004–2008 period was that high and rising energy prices would contribute to more rapid increase in the overall price level. One indicator of the energy prices is the gasoline price index component of the CPI. Over the 2002–2008 period, the CPI rose from 100 to only 114.1, but the gasoline price index rose from 100 to 164.7. Gasoline prices plummeted during the recession of 2008–2009 and then began to rise sharply again as the world economy recovered.
SOURCE: Adapted from Statistics Canada, CANSIM series v41693434 (gasoline) and v41693271 (CPI).

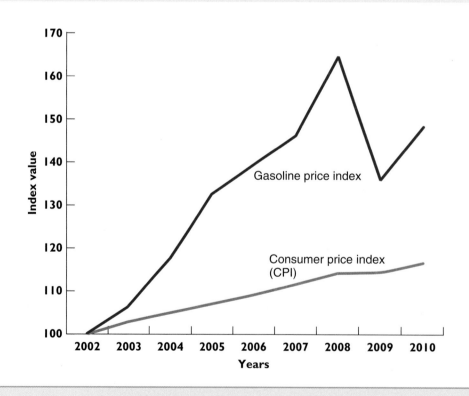

of inflationary pressures. In this context, the Bank decided to raise its target for the overnight rate."[18]

As the unemployment rate continued to fall in 2005 and 2006 (see Figure 4.3), and as energy prices continued to rise at a rapid rate (see Figure 10.7), the Bank of Canada continued to raise the overnight target. By July 10, 2007, the Bank of Canada had raised the overnight rate target to 4.5 percent, a level 2.5 percentage points higher than the rate of three years earlier.

In announcing the interest rate hike on July 10, 2007, however, the Bank of Canada noted that there were some risks connected with its inflation projection; namely, the uncertainty associated with the assessment that the overnight rate should be raised in order to prevent inflation rate increases. It stated, "The main downside risks are related to the higher Canadian dollar and the ongoing adjustment in the U.S. housing sector."[19] From 2003 to 2007, the Canadian dollar had appreciated rapidly against the U.S. dollar, as can be seen in Figure 4.6. A stronger Canadian dollar tends to reduce inflation directly by reducing import prices, which are included in the CPI.

It also tends to reduce inflation indirectly by reducing the growth of net exports, an important component of planned aggregate expenditure, thereby reducing the growth of actual output relative to potential output. (For more on the dollar and exchange rates, see Chapter 13.) The adjustment in the U.S. housing sector refers to a collapse in U.S. housing construction after the dissolving of speculative price bubbles in many U.S. housing markets. (An important sub-component of the investment aspect of planned aggregate expenditure in the U.S., the housing sector corresponds to the "residential structures" line in Table 5.2.) This adjustment threatened to trigger a recession in the United States, and a U.S. recession would impact Canada by reducing U.S. imports from Canada. (Recall the discussion of the marginal propensity to import from section 8.5.)

The U.S. recession proved to be much more severe than most forecasters had predicted, and it triggered a global recession now frequently called the Great Recession. During the Great Recession, unemployment rates rose, energy prices plummeted, and inflation rates declined.

By December of 2007, the period of repeated hikes in the Bank of Canada's overnight rate target had come to an end. The Bank announced what would be the first of a series of overnight rate target decreases. These were designed not just to offset the threat of a U.S. recession, but were intended to help the Canadian economy cope with the impact of a global financial crisis that followed the collapse of the U.S. housing bubble.

18 Bank of Canada, "Press Release, 8 September 2004," http://bankofcanada.ca/en/fixed-dates/2004/rate_080904.html (May 2008).
19 Bank of Canada, "Press Release, 10 July 2007" http://bankofcanada.ca/en/fixed-dates/2007/rate_100707.html (May 2008).

SUMMARY

- Monetary policy is one of two major types of stabilization policy, the other being fiscal policy. Monetary policy influences the state of the economy by changing interest rates. **LO1**

- The Bank of Canada is Canada's central bank. It uses interest rate changes to achieve its monetary policy objective of low inflation. **LO1**

- According to the modern central banking theory, the Bank of Canada changes market interest rates by changing its official interest rate, the overnight rate target. The Bank takes whatever actions are necessary to keep the overnight loans rate close to the overnight rate target. The overnight rate is a reference point or benchmark rate for other market interest rates (particularly short-term interest rates) charged by commercial banks. **LO2**

- The Bank of Canada can control the real interest rate as well as the nominal interest rate. The real interest rate equals the nominal interest rate minus the inflation rate. Because the inflation rate adjusts relatively slowly, the Bank of Canada can change the real interest rate by changing the nominal interest rate. **LO3**

■ The Bank of Canada's actions affect the economy because changes in the real interest rate affect planned aggregate expenditure. Specifically, an increase in the real interest rate raises the cost of borrowing, reducing consumption and planned private-sector investment. Thus, by increasing the real interest rate, the Bank of Canada can reduce planned aggregate expenditure and short-run equilibrium output. Conversely, by reducing the real interest rate, the Bank of Canada can stimulate planned aggregate expenditure and raise short-run equilibrium output. To eliminate a recessionary output gap, the Bank of Canada will lower the real interest rate. To eliminate an expansionary output gap, the Bank of Canada will raise the real interest rate. **LO4**

■ In practice, a central bank's information about the level of potential output and the size and speed of the effects of its actions is imprecise. Thus, monetary policy-making must attempt to cope with real-world uncertainty. **LO5**

KEY TERMS

bank rate (246)
basis point (247)
benchmark rate (245)
core CPI (242)
core CPI inflation (243)
deposit rate (246)
effective lower bound (247)
inflation-control target (242)

interest rate spread (249)
Large Value Transfer System (LVTS) (245)
modern central banking theory (245)
monetary policy instrument (244)
monetary policy objective (242)
official interest rate (245)

operating band (246)
overnight rate (245)
overnight rate target (245)
prime business rate (245)
settlement balances (245)
total CPI (242)
total CPI inflation (243)

REVIEW QUESTIONS

1. Is the Bank of Canada a chartered bank, a commercial bank, or a central bank? **LO1**

2. What is the main policy objective of the Bank of Canada and what are two terms for its main monetary policy instrument? **LO1**

3. Describe the modern central banking theory of how the Bank of Canada manages the overnight rate to change interest rates in the economy. **LO2**

4. You hear a news report that employment growth is lower than expected. How do you expect that report to affect market interest rates? Explain. (*Hint*: Assume that Bank of Canada policy-makers have access to the same data that you do.) **LO2**

5. How does the real interest rate affect planned aggregate expenditure in the Keynesian cross model underlying Figures 10.4 and 10.5? How does the explanation associated with Figures 10.4 and 10.5 compare with the Bank of Canada explanation associated with Figure 10.6? **LO4**

6. The Bank of Canada faces a recessionary gap. How would you expect it to respond? Explain step by step how its policy change is likely to affect the economy. **LO4**

7. Discuss why the analysis of Figures 10.4 and 10.5 overstates the precision with which monetary policy can be used to eliminate output gaps. **LO5**

PROBLEMS

1. Suppose that the Bank of Canada cuts the overnight rate target from, say, 4 percent to 3.75 percent. How would the bank rate change? By how much would you expect the prime business rate to change? **LO2**

2. Suppose that the overnight rate and the overnight rate target are at 4.5 percent. The interest rate spread

between the overnight rate target and typical household and business borrowing is 2 percent. The effective lower bound is 0.25 percent. All of the above rates are in nominal terms and the inflation rate is 2 percent. You are the decision maker for the central bank, and you calculate that to achieve your monetary policy objective the real interest rate for household and business borrowing should be 2.5 percent. **LO1, LO2, LO3**

a. To achieve the real interest rate of 2.5 percent, at what level should you set the overnight rate target?

b. All conditions remain the same as above, but the interest rate spread rises from 2 percent to 3.5 percent. To achieve the real interest rate of 2.5 percent, at what level should you now set the overnight rate target?

c. The interest rate spread remains at 3.5 percent but the inflation rate falls to zero. To achieve the real interest rate of 2.5 percent, at what level should you now set the overnight rate target? Do you have a problem?

3. An economy is described by the following equations: **LO4**

$$C = 2600 + 0.8(Y - T) - 10\,000r,$$
$$I^p = 2000 - 10\,000r,$$
$$G = \overline{G} = 1800.$$

Net exports are zero, net taxes T are fixed at 3000, and the real interest rate r, expressed as a decimal, is 0.10 (that is, 10 percent). Find a numerical equation relating planned aggregate expenditure to output. Using a table or other method, solve for short-run equilibrium output. Show your result graphically using the Keynesian cross diagram.

4. For the economy described in Problem 2: **LO4**

a. Potential output Y^* equals 12 000. What real interest rate should the Bank of Canada set to bring the economy to full employment?

b. Repeat part (a) for $Y^* = 9000$.

5. Here is another set of equations describing an economy: **LO4**

$$C = 14\,400 + 0.5(Y - T) - 40\,000r,$$
$$I^p = 8000 - 20\,000r,$$
$$G = 7000,$$
$$NX = -1800,$$
$$T = 8000,$$
$$Y^* = 40\,000.$$

a. Find a numerical equation relating planned aggregate expenditure to output and to the real interest rate.

b. At what value should the Bank of Canada set the real interest rate to eliminate any output gap? (*Hint:* Set output Y equal to the value of potential output given above in the equation you found in part (a). Then solve for the real interest rate that also sets planned aggregate expenditure equal to potential output.)

6. The Bank of Canada publishes overviews of its monetary policy every quarter. From the Bank of Canada Web site (http://www.bankofcanada.ca), obtain a copy of the latest of these overviews (called *Monetary Policy Report*). In the period covered by the overview, did the Bank of Canada raise interest rates, cut them, or leave them unchanged? What principal developments in the economy did the Bank of Canada say were responsible for its monetary policy stance during the period? **LO1, LO2, LO4, LO5**

ANSWERS TO IN-CHAPTER EXERCISES

10.1 a. In addition to monetary policy, the Bank of Canada has responsibilities for bank notes, the financial system, and funds management. The Bank's responsibilities for bank notes, stability of the financial system, and monetary policy were discussed in Chapter 9. The Bank's responsibility for funds management involves managing the federal government's accounts, debts, and foreign exchange reserves. **LO1**

b. The key indicators are the inflation-control target, the operational guide, and the target for the overnight rate.

The inflation-control target is the Bank of Canada's desired CPI inflation rate target range of 1 to 3 percent. To stay within the target range, the Bank of Canada aims for 2 percent inflation.

The operational guide refers to "core" CPI inflation. According to the Bank, "the Bank uses the core CPI (the CPI excluding eight of the most volatile components as well as the effect of changes in indirect taxes on the remaining components) as a guide to its policy actions. . . . [the] core CPI inflation provides a better measure of the underlying trend of inflation and is, therefore, a more appropriate guide for policy."

The overnight rate, which is analyzed in some detail in this chapter, is a short-term interest rate that influences other interest rates charged by financial institutions, such as mortgage loan rates. The raising and lowering the target for the overnight rate the Bank of Canada influences interest rates and, hence, spending in the economy.

c. The correct answer may vary according to the year in which the question is answered. For 2011, the eight pre-announced dates occur in the months of January, March, April, May, June, September, October, and December. (There is little point in memorizing the months, but for analyzing the economy it can be useful to know not only that there are pre-announced dates but where to find them.)

d. At the time of writing (2011), the Bank of Canada Web site provides visitors with 22 "Backgrounders" (http://www.bankofcanada.ca/en/backgrounders/index.html) on topics related to the Bank's functions, so there are many possible subsets of these 22 topics that would constitute correct answers to this question. The topics include "Monetary Policy," "Target for the Overnight Rate," "How Monetary Policy Works," "Inflation-Control Target," and "Output Gap." LO1

10.2   If $r = 0.03$, then consumption is $C = 640 + 0.8(Y - 250) - 400(0.03) = 428 + 0.8Y$, and planned private-sector investment is $I^p = 250 - 600(0.03) = 232$. Planned aggregate expenditure is given by

$$PAE = C + I^p + G + NX$$
$$= (428 + 0.8Y) + 232 + 300 + 20$$
$$= 980 + 0.8Y.$$

To find short-run equilibrium output, one approach would be to construct a table by trial and error, as shown below.

Determination of short-run equilibrium output

(1)	(2)	(3)	(4)
Output Y	Planned aggregate expenditure PAE = 980 + 0.8Y	Y − PAE	Y = PAE
4500	4580	−80	No
4600	4660	−60	No
4700	4740	−40	No
4800	4820	−20	No
4900	4900	0	Yes
5000	4980	20	No
5100	5060	40	No
5200	5140	60	No
5300	5220	80	No
5400	5300	100	No
5500	5380	120	No

Short-run equilibrium output equals 4900, as that is the only level of output that satisfies the condition $Y = PAE$.

The answer can be obtained more quickly by simply setting $Y = PAE$ and solving for short-run equilibrium output Y. Remembering that $PAE = 980 + 0.8Y$ and substitution for PAE, we get

$$Y = 980 + 0.8Y$$
$$Y(1 - 0.8) = 980$$
$$Y = 5 \times 980 = 4900.$$

So lowering the real interest rate from 5 percent to 3 percent increases short-run equilibrium output from 4800 (as found in Example 10.2) to 4900.

If you have read Appendix 8B on the income-expenditure multiplier, there is yet another way to find the answer. Using Appendix 8B we can determine that the multiplier in this model is 5, since $1/(1 - mpc) = 1/(1 - 0.8) = 5$. Each percentage point reduction in the real interest rate increases consumption by 4 units and planned private-sector investment by 6 units, for a total impact on planned spending of 10 units per percentage point reduction. Reducing the real interest rate by 2 percentage points, from 5 percent to 3 percent, thus increases autonomous expenditure by 20 units. Because the multiplier is 5, an increase of 20 in autonomous expenditure raises short-run equilibrium output by $20 \times 5 = 100$ units, from the value of 4800 we found in Example 10.2 to the new value of 4900. **LO1, LO4**

10.3 When the real interest rate is 5 percent, output is 4800. Each percentage point reduction in the real interest rate increases autonomous expenditure by 10 units. Since the multiplier in this model is 5, to raise output by 50 units the real interest rate should be cut by 1 percentage point, from 5 percent to 4 percent. Increasing output by 50 units, to 4850, eliminates the output gap. **LO4**

10.4 Compare your answer to the Bank of Canada's explanation, at http://www.bankofcanada.ca/publications-research/periodicals/mpr/ about keeping the inflation rate from moving below the target range. **LO5**

APPENDIX 10A
Monetary Policy in the Basic Keynesian Model

This appendix extends the algebraic analysis of the basic Keynesian model that was presented in Appendix 8A to include the role of monetary policy. The main difference from Appendix 8A is that in this analysis the real interest rate is allowed to affect planned spending. We will simply assume that the Bank of Canada can set the real interest rate r at any level it chooses.

The real interest rate affects consumption and planned private-sector investment. To capture these effects, we will modify the equations for those two components of spending as follows:

$$C = \overline{C} + mpc(Y - T) - ar,$$
$$I^p = \overline{I} - br$$

The first equation is the consumption function with an additional term, equal to $-ar$. Think of a as a fixed number, greater than zero, that measures the strength of the interest rate effect on consumption. Thus, the term $-ar$ captures the idea that when the real interest rate rises, consumption declines by a times the increase in the interest rate. Likewise, the second equation adds the term $-br$ to the equation for planned private-sector investment spending. The parameter b is a fixed positive number that measures how strongly changes in the real interest rate affect planned private-sector investment; for example, if the real interest rate rises, planned private-sector investment is assumed to decline by b times the increase in the real interest rate. We continue to assume that government purchases, taxes, and net exports are exogenous variables, so that $G = \overline{G}$, $T = \overline{T}$, and $NX = \overline{NX}$.

To solve for short-run equilibrium output, we start as usual by finding the relationship of planned aggregate expenditure to output. The definition of planned aggregate expenditure is

$$PAE = C + I^p + G + NX.$$

Substituting the modified equations for consumption and planned private-sector investment into this definition, along with the exogenous values of government spending, net exports, and taxes, we get

$$PAE = [\overline{C} + mpc(Y - \overline{T}) - ar] + [\overline{I} - br] + \overline{G} + \overline{NX}.$$

The first term in brackets on the right side describes the behavior of consumption, and the second bracketed term describes planned private-sector investment. Rearranging this equation in order to group together terms that depend on the real interest rate and terms that depend on output, we find

$$PAE = [\overline{C} - mpc\,\overline{T} + \overline{I} + \overline{G} + \overline{NX}] - (a + b)r + mpcY.$$

This equation is similar to Equation 8A.1, in the first appendix to Chapter 8, except that it has an extra term, $-(a + b)r$, on the right side. This extra term captures the idea that an increase in the real interest rate reduces consumption and planned private-sector investment, lowering planned spending. Notice that the term $-(a + b)r$ is part of autonomous expenditure, since it does not depend on output. Since autonomous expenditure determines the intercept of the expenditure line in the Keynesian cross diagram, changes in the real interest rate will shift the expenditure line up (if the real interest rate decreases) or down (if the real interest rate increases).

To find short-run equilibrium output, we use the definition of short-run equilibrium output to set $Y = PAE$ and solve for Y:

$$
\begin{aligned}
Y &= PAE \\
&= [\overline{C} - mpc\overline{T} + \overline{I} + \overline{G} + \overline{NX}] + (a + b)r + mpcY \\
Y(1 - mpc) &= [\overline{C} - mpc\overline{T} + \overline{I} + \overline{G} + \overline{NX}] - (a + b)r \\
Y &= \left(\frac{1}{1 - mpc}\right)[(\overline{C} - mpc\overline{T} + \overline{I} + \overline{G} + \overline{NX})] - (a + b)r]. \quad (10A.1)
\end{aligned}
$$

Equation 10A.1 shows that short-run equilibrium output once again equals the multiplier, $1/(1 - mpc)$, times autonomous expenditure, $\overline{C} - mpc\overline{T} + \overline{I} + \overline{G} + \overline{NX} - (a + b)r$. Autonomous expenditure in turn depends on the real interest rate r. The equation also shows that the impact of a change in the real interest rate on short-run equilibrium output depends on two factors: (1) the effect of a change in the real interest rate on consumption and planned private-sector investment, which depends on the magnitude of $(a + b)$; and (2) the size of the multiplier, $1/(1 - mpc)$, which relates changes in autonomous expenditure to changes in short-run equilibrium output. The larger the effect of the real interest rate on planned spending, and the larger the multiplier, the more powerful will be the effect of a given change in the real interest rate on short-run equilibrium output.

To check Equation 10A.1, we can use it to resolve Example 10.2. In that example we are given $\overline{C} = 640, \overline{I} = 250, \overline{G} = 300, \overline{NX} = 20, \overline{T} = 250, mpc = 0.8, a = 400,$ and $b = 600$. The real interest rate set by the Bank of Canada is 5 percent, or 0.05. Substituting these values into Equation 10A.1 and solving, we obtain

$$Y = \left(\frac{1}{1 - 0.8}\right)[640 - 0.8 \times 250 + 250 + 300 + 20 - (400 + 600) \times 0.05]$$

$$= 5 \times 960 = 4800.$$

This is the same result we found in Example 10.3.

Practise and learn online with Connect.

CHAPTER 11
The Aggregate Demand–Aggregate Supply Model

LEARNING OBJECTIVES

When you have completed this chapter, you will be able to:

LO1 Understand the rationales for each of the three component curves of the aggregate demand–aggregate supply (*AD–AS*) model with a horizontal short-run aggregate supply (*SRAS*) curve.

LO2 Understand the distinction between short-run and long-run equilibrium in the *AD–AS* model with a horizontal *SRAS* curve.

LO3 Be able to apply the *AD–AS* model with a horizontal SRAS curve to real-world topics such as using macroeconomic policy to close output gaps or understanding stagflation.

LO4 Understand the difference between an *AD–AS* model with a horizontal *SRAS* curve and one with an upward-sloping *SRAS* curve.

LO5 Explain the uses of the original Philips curve and the expectations-augmented Philips curve model.

First-year students taking this course today are typically about 19 years old, which means that they were born since the Canadian inflation rate last went above 3 percent for a full year (the inflation rate in 1991 was 5.6 percent). For Canada's current generation of students, rapid inflation—a rapid general increase in the price level—is something they may have read about or heard about, but it is something they have never experienced. For the 12 years from 1998 to 2010, Canada's inflation rate averaged 2.1 percent per year.

Someone taking economics for the first time forty or fifty years ago would have had much the same life experience. Between 1952 and 1965, the Canadian inflation rate averaged 1.4 percent, so undergraduates of the 1960s had much the same personal experience of inflation as undergraduates of today. Economics textbooks of the 1960s rarely talked about inflation. Inflation was simply not the focus of much economic analysis, since there had been so little of it. All that changed dramatically in the 1970s. Inflation in Canada averaged 3.9 percent per year from 1966 to 1972 and then accelerated, averaging 9.6 percent per year from 1973 to 1982. Other industrialized countries experienced a similar pattern.

Economists had to react—their models said very little about changes in the general level of prices, but suddenly the cup of coffee that used to cost a dime cost a quarter. Before much longer, it was fifty cents and still rising. Of course, if the price of coffee had been the only price that was increasing, consumers could just have switched to drinking other beverages, but most prices were increasing at roughly the same rate, so switching was not a solution. The problem was that the purchasing power of a dollar was shrinking as the price level rose.

As we discussed in Chapters 8 and 10, the Keynesian cross model (also called the basic Keynesian model) typically assumes that the price level stays constant for the period of analysis. Though the assumption of a constant price level had never been completely realistic, for many years it was not a bad approximation. In Canada, for example, the price level as measured by the consumer price index (2002 = 100) stood at 9.2 when the Great Depression began in 1929 and did not exceed 9.2 again until 1946, the year of Keynes's death.

There were some increases in the price level just after the Second World War (for example, during the Korean War) but during most of the 1950s and 1960s it stayed pretty constant. The same basket of goods that could be purchased for $16.90 in 1952 would have cost $17.60 in 1957 and had only crept up in price to $20 by 1965. But by the 1970s, assuming a constant price level did not fit well with the experience of most countries, including Canada.

Economists, including economics textbook authors, therefore became open to a new model to supplement the Keynesian cross model of output determination and provide an explanation of price level determination. The *aggregate demand–aggregate supply model* we present in this chapter was the first to achieve widespread acceptance as an answer to that need. The **aggregate demand–aggregate supply (AD-AS) model** shows how economic factors and policies can simultaneously affect the overall price level as well as real output.

aggregate demand–aggregate supply model (*AD-AS*) a model of real output and overall price level determination

Notice that the *AD-AS* model deals with changes in the overall *price level* of the economy. In order to discuss *general* movements in prices, economists have to average all the prices of a typical *market basket* of goods. In this chapter, we will be focusing on the *consumer price index*. In 1964, the consumer price index for Canada was 16.4 and in 1965 it was 16.8—but by 1992 it was 84 and in 2009 it was 114.4. This means that Canadian consumers could buy the same basket of typical consumer goods for $19.52 in 1964 and $20 in 1965, but it would take $100 in 1992 and $136 in 2009 to buy the same basket of goods.

Earlier, we talked about the *annual inflation rate*—which is calculated from data on the price level. If it cost $19.52 to buy a basket of goods in 1964 and $20 to buy the same basket in 1965, then the *percentage change* in prices is 2.5 percent [= (20 − 19.52)/19.52]. The news media often tend to focus on the inflation rate, but the price level and the inflation rate are as different as the speed of a car and its rate of acceleration. As long as a car is going forward, its speed will be greater than zero; but braking or stepping on the gas will cause the car to decelerate or accelerate. Similarly, as long as the price level is rising, the inflation rate will be a positive number. If the economy slows down, and the price level is increasing at a slower rate than before, then the inflation rate goes down (but it is still a positive number). Only if the price level actually declines—which in modern economies seldom happens, even in recessions—will the inflation rate be negative.

In the 1970s, economists focused on the importance of the *price level*, largely because the general level of prices directly determines the purchasing power of money. We will do the same in this chapter.

Of course, the rapid rise in the price level was not the only factor that made economists receptive to a new macroeconomic model. In the mid-1970s, a number of countries, including the United States and Japan, experienced recessions at the same time as they experienced large increases in their price levels. The combination of recession with a sharply rising price level was dubbed "stagflation."

However, stagflation was difficult to explain with the Keynesian cross model. Recall that in our analysis of Chapters 8 and 10, the Keynesian cross model was characterized either by a recessionary gap with actual output below potential output or by an expansionary gap with actual output above potential output and pressure for the price level to rise. The model did not recognize the possibility of a recessionary gap co-existing with a rising price level. Both because of the ever-rising price level and because of the puzzling phenomenon of stagflation, by the 1970s more and more economists had recognized that the Keynesian cross model needed to be supplemented.

Later in this chapter we will examine a Phillips curve model that deals directly with the inflation rate rather than just the overall price level. And Chapter 12 deals with another model that focuses on the inflation rate. But for now we will focus on an aggregate demand–aggregate supply model that deals with determining the price level and real output.

THE THREE COMPONENTS OF THE AGGREGATE DEMAND–AGGREGATE SUPPLY MODEL

11.1

The aggregate demand–aggregate supply model that will be developed in this chapter has three central components: a long-run aggregate supply curve, a short-run aggregate supply curve, and an aggregate demand curve. Each of the curves is related to material covered earlier in the textbook. The aggregate demand curve is derived from the planned aggregate expenditure curve of Chapters 8 and 10. The short-run aggregate supply curve is related to a key assumption underpinning Chapters 8 and 10: in the short run, firms meet demand at existing prices. Later in this chapter we will consider an alternative, upward-sloping version of the short-run aggregate supply curve. The long-run aggregate supply curve is related to the concept of potential output introduced in Chapter 7.

In this section, we will discuss the economic rationale for each of these three curves. In the following section, the three curves will be combined to form the *AD–AS* model, and we will analyze short-run and long-run equilibrium in the context of the model.

AGGREGATE DEMAND

aggregate demand curve
a relationship between overall spending in the economy and the aggregate price level

The **aggregate demand curve** shows the amount of planned aggregate expenditure (and output) at various price levels, as illustrated in the two panels of Figure 11.1.

The aggregate expenditure curve was introduced in Chapter 8. Panel a) of Figure 11.1 represents the idea that the price level is a factor causing shifts in the aggregate expenditure curve. A lower price level (*P′*) causes the planned aggregate expenditure curve to shift upwards compared to the planned aggregate expenditure associated with the pre-existing price level *P*. A higher price level causes the planned aggregate expenditure curve to shift down.

In panel b) the two price levels *P* and *P′* underpinning the two planned aggregate expenditure curves in panel a) are plotted against their respective short-run equilibrium

---

FIGURE 11.1

Planned Aggregate Expenditure (*PAE*) and Aggregate Demand

The two panels show the relationship between the planned aggregate expenditure curve (introduced in Chapter 8) and the aggregate demand curve. Panel a) represents the idea that the price level is a factor causing shifts in the *PAE* curve. A lower price level (*P′*) causes the *PAE* curve to move upwards compared to the *PAE* associated with the pre-existing price level *P*. A higher price level would cause the *PAE* curve to shift down. In panel b) the two price levels *P* and *P′* underpinning the two *PAE* curves in panel a) are plotted against their respective short-run equilibrium output levels *Y* and *Y′*.

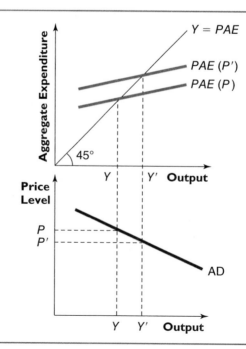

a) Changes in the price level shift planned aggregate expenditure and change real output

b) The aggregate demand schedule shows aggregate output for different price levels output levels Y and Y'. The downward-sloping aggregate demand shown in panel b), then, represents the idea that the price level and output are inversely related.[1]

Historically, two major explanations that have been provided for an inverse relationship between the price level and output, as depicted by a downward-sloping aggregate demand curve, are the *real-balances effect* and the *foreign trade effect*.

The **real-balances effect** is the idea that consumption is positively related to wealth, and that wealth is negatively related to the price level (i.e., that wealth decreases when the price level rises). Why would this be true? One component of wealth is the money held by households and businesses. When the price level rises, the real value of a given stock of money falls. If you had $10 000 in cash and the price level rose by 20 percent, you would be worse off, because the purchasing power of your savings has fallen. In real terms, the value of your cash would have fallen by $2000. If so, you might feel less affluent and less willing to consume. Conversely, when the price level falls, the real value of a given stock of money rises. Since we saw earlier that consumption is a large component of planned aggregate expenditure, anything that influences consumer spending is potentially important—but the empirical question is whether many people actually hold large enough money balances to produce an appreciable impact.

The **foreign trade effect** is based on the assumption that the foreign exchange rate will remain unchanged as the price level changes.[2] (Obviously, this assumption is most reasonable if, as was the case in Canada from 1962 to 1970, the foreign exchange rate is fixed by the central bank at a particular level.) When this assumption is true, then an increase in the price level makes domestic goods and services more expensive relative to foreign goods and services, and tends to result in reduced demand for domestic goods and services. Similarly, a decrease in the price level makes locally produced goods cheaper and produces increased demand for domestic goods and services. As a result, a rise in the price level will reduce net exports (one of the four major components of planned aggregate expenditure) whereas a fall in the price level will increase net exports.

In panel b) of Figure 11.1, we show how, if nothing else were to change, a different price level might affect the level of aggregate demand; that is, we trace out movements *along* a given *AD* curve (which may be caused by any combination of the *real-balances effect* and the *foreign trade effect*).

However, the *AD* curve may also shift its location if the amount of planned expenditure *at a given price level* changes. Panel a) of Figure 11.2 shows a rightward shift of the *AD* curve, which might be caused by increases in autonomous consumption, autonomous private-sector investment, or net exports. It can also be caused by expansionary monetary policy (interest rate cuts) or expansionary fiscal policy (government expenditure increases or tax cuts).

A leftward shift of the *AD* curve, as depicted in panel b) of Figure 11.2, can be caused by decreases in autonomous consumption, autonomous private-sector investment, or net exports. It can also be caused by contractionary monetary policy (interest rate hikes) or contractionary fiscal policy (government expenditure cuts or tax increases).

real-balances effect the hypothesis that overall wealth in the economy will be inversely related to the overall price level, and therefore, that aggregate demand and the price level will be inversely related

foreign trade effect the hypothesis that net exports will be inversely related to the overall price level, and therefore that aggregate demand and the price level will be inversely related

---

1   The downward slope of the aggregate demand curve is *not* based on the same logic that underlies the demand curve for a particular product; i.e., that when prices are higher, people can't afford to buy more goods, and when prices are lower, people can afford to buy more goods. If the prices of goods and services in general go up (as shown by movement up the aggregate demand curve), then the incomes of the people who produce those goods and services will tend to go up in the same proportion. If the prices of goods and services in general go down, then the incomes of the people who produce those goods and services will tend to go down proportionally. To assume that the logic that underpins the downward-sloping demand curve for a particular product also underpins the aggregate demand curve is another example of the *fallacy of composition*.

2   In Chapter 13, we will consider the topic of exchange rate determination. We will present the argument that if the price level in a country rises relative to the price level in other countries, then a flexible exchange rate will tend to depreciate to offset the rise in the price level. The foreign trade effect used to explain the aggregate demand curve assumes that the adjustment of exchange rates to price level changes is either slow or incomplete.

FIGURE 11.2

Shifts of the *AD* curve

Panel a) depicts a rightward shift of the *AD* curve. A rightward shift of the *AD* curve can be caused by such factors as increases in autonomous expenditure and expansionary monetary or fiscal policy. A leftward shift of the *AD* curve, as depicted in panel b), can be caused by such factors as decreases in autonomous expenditure and contractionary monetary or fiscal policy.

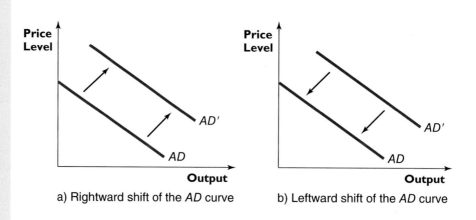

a) Rightward shift of the *AD* curve   b) Leftward shift of the *AD* curve

In other words, *shifts* in the aggregate demand curve of this chapter are explained by the same factors that explained the shift of the aggregate expenditure curve in Chapters 8 and 10.

SHORT-RUN AGGREGATE SUPPLY

The *short-run aggregate supply curve* in Figure 11.3 is drawn as a horizontal line. The **short-run aggregate supply (*SRAS*) curve** represents the idea, previously discussed in connection with the Keynesian cross model, that in the short run, firms supply the output that their customers demand at the prices that they have posted. This version of the curve is sometimes called the Keynesian *SRAS* curve.

short-run aggregate supply (*SRAS*) curve a relationship between real output and the overall price level in the short run; a horizontal version of the curve indicates that firms in the short run meet demand, on average, at existing prices

The horizontal *SRAS* curve of Figure 11.3 will shift in the short run whenever firm costs (such as input prices) change.[3] If costs fall for firms in general, the *SRAS* curve will shift downward, as depicted in panel a) of Figure 11.4. For example, in a computer-intensive economy, if the price of computers (a widely used input) was reduced, the *SRAS* curve would shift downward.

FIGURE 11.3

The Short-Run Aggregate Supply Curve

The horizontal short-run aggregate supply curve represents the idea that, in the short run, firms will supply the output demanded at the fixed price level.

3   The crucial part of Figure 11.3 is that it is horizontal *over the relevant range of outputs*. Very large deviations in output would be likely to force immediate changes in the price level—such as would occur if output were to be cut in half (which would likely produce price cuts), or if output were to increase dramatically above potential output (which would likely only occur in the context of higher prices). However, for fluctuations in output of the size actually observed in recent business cycles, Figure 11.3 is defensible.

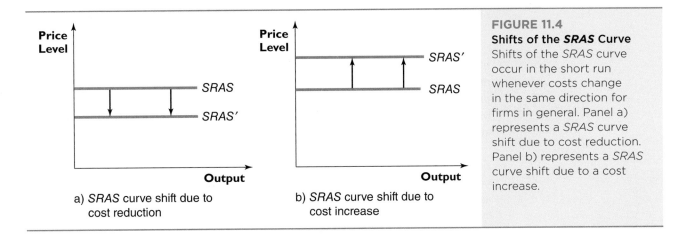

FIGURE 11.4

Shifts of the *SRAS* Curve

Shifts of the *SRAS* curve occur in the short run whenever costs change in the same direction for firms in general. Panel a) represents a *SRAS* curve shift due to cost reduction. Panel b) represents a *SRAS* curve shift due to a cost increase.

If costs rise for firms in general, the *SRAS* curve will shift upwards, as depicted in panel b) of Figure 11.4. For example, in an oil-based economy, if a rise in the price of oil were to occur, the *SRAS* would shift upward.

LONG-RUN AGGREGATE SUPPLY

When we discussed the determinants of the economy's potential output, we mentioned *real inputs* (like labour, capital, and human skills) and the *productivity* with which those inputs are combined in order to produce *real output.* We did not emphasize the money units in which inputs and outputs are measured because these do not affect potential output. Potential output, as first discussed in Chapter 7, is the amount of output (real GDP) that an economy can produce when using its resources, most notably capital and labour, at normal rates. Potential output depends, then, on the amounts of capital, labour, and other inputs, and upon factors that determine the productivity of inputs, such as education levels and technological knowledge—but it is not affected by the general price level. If all the dollar bills (and bank accounts and contracts) in Canada were suddenly multiplied by ten, there would be an extra zero in all contracts and bank accounts and on all dollar bills, but no one in Canada would be able to produce any more or less than before. The **long-run aggregate supply (*LRAS*) curve**, or the relationship between the overall price level of the economy and the economy's potential output, is therefore a vertical line.

The representation of the long-run aggregate supply curve as a vertical line in Figure 11.5 says that the economy's potential output (Y^*) during a given period is independent

long-run aggregate supply (*LRAS*) curve a relationship between potential output and the overall price level; a vertical curve indicating that potential output is independent of the inflation rate

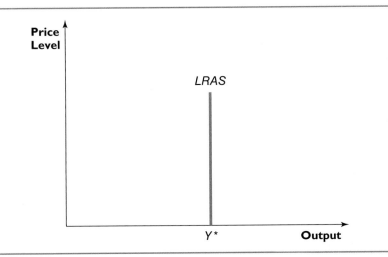

FIGURE 11.5

The Long-Run Aggregate Supply Curve

Drawing the long-run aggregate supply (*LRAS*) curve as a vertical line represents the idea that the economy's potential output (Y^*) during a given period is independent of the price level during that period. If we think of the price level as being represented by the consumer price index (*CPI*), the vertical *LRAS* curve means that neither increases nor decreases in the *CPI* will have any effect on potential output.

of the price level during that period. That is, the vertical *LRAS* curve means that neither increases nor decreases in the CPI will have any effect on potential output.

Remember that when the overall price level rises, which it does as we move up a vertical *LRAS* curve, industries then not only receive higher prices for their output but also must pay higher prices for their inputs. This means that *for the economy as a whole,* higher prices have a different impact than for a given perfectly competitive industry. To generalize from the case of a perfectly competitive industry to the economy as a whole would be an example of the *fallacy of composition.*

If input prices did not go up, then rising prices for output would produce an upward-sloping industry supply curve. But when *all* prices are going up, each firm finds that it is no better off, so there is a vertical long-run supply curve for the economy as a whole, even assuming that the economy is composed entirely of perfectly competitive industries.

To fully understand the *LRAS* curve, we must not just understand movements along the curve—that is, that changes in the price level do not affect potential output—we must also understand the factors that cause the curve to shift. *LRAS* curve shifts are caused by the factors that cause potential output to change.

A rightward shift of the *LRAS* curve, as shown in panel a) of Figure 11.6, signifies an increase in potential output caused by such factors as a rise in the size of the capital stock, an increase in the size of the labour force, or improvements in technology. In modern developed economies, the normal pattern is for potential output to increase from one year to the next.

FIGURE 11.6
Shifts of the *LRAS* Curve
LRAS curve shifts are caused by the factors that cause potential output to change. A rightward shift of the *LRAS* curve is (panel a) an increase in potential output and would be caused by a factor such as improvement in technology. A leftward shift of the *LRAS* curve is a decrease in potential output (panel b). This is rare in modern developed economies and could be caused by a factor such as destruction of the capital stock due to war.

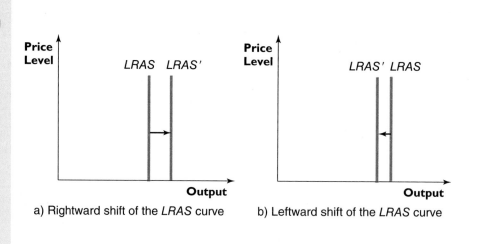

a) Rightward shift of the *LRAS* curve

b) Leftward shift of the *LRAS* curve

A leftward shift of the *LRAS* curve, as shown in panel b), signifies a decrease in potential output. Decreases in potential output could be caused by such factors as destruction of the capital stock due to war or natural disasters, reduction of agricultural capacity due to poor weather, and depletion of natural resources.

In practice, in peacetime it is rare for developed economies, which are typically composed of a diverse collection of industries, to experience decreases in potential output. For example, in 2003 the potential output of the Canadian economy increased somewhat even though Canada was struck by a unusually severe string of disasters—the Canadian beef industry was devastated due to one reported case of "mad cow" disease, the British Columbia forestry industry lost capacity due to massive forest fires, Ontario was struck by an unprecedented power outage, the Toronto tourism industry was temporarily stopped in its tracks by the SARS outbreak, and both Nova Scotia and Prince Edward Island experienced extensive hurricane damage.

THE THREE COMPONENTS OF THE AGGREGATE DEMAND–AGGREGATE SUPPLY MODEL

The *AD–AS* model is represented graphically with the overall price level on the vertical axis and real output on the horizontal axis. The model has three central components: an aggregate demand curve, a short-run aggregate supply curve, and a long-run aggregate supply curve.

The aggregate demand (*AD*) curve is derived from the planned aggregate expenditure curve of Chapters 8 and 10. Two major explanations have been provided for an inverse relationship between the price level and output, as depicted by the downward-sloping aggregate demand curve: the real-balances effect and the foreign trade effect. Increases in autonomous aggregate expenditure or expansionary monetary and fiscal policies cause the *AD* curve to shift to the right. Decreases in autonomous aggregate expenditure or contractionary monetary and fiscal policies cause the *AD* curve to shift to the left. The Keynesian short-run aggregate supply curve (*SRAS*) is drawn as a horizontal line. This represents the idea that in the short run, firms will supply the output demanded at their already posted prices. General increases in the costs of firms will cause firms to revise their posted prices and the *SRAS* curve will shift upwards. General decreases in the costs of firms will cause the *SRAS* curve to shift downwards.

The long-run aggregate supply (*LRAS*) curve is drawn as a vertical line at potential output. It represents the assumption that the potential output of the economy is independent of the overall price level. Potential output depends on the amounts of capital, labour, and other inputs, and on factors that determine the productivity of inputs, such as education levels and technological knowledge. Thus, for example, an increase in capital will cause the *LRAS* curve to shift to the right and a reduction in capital (due to a war, say) will cause the *LRAS* curve to shift to the left.

11.2 SHORT-RUN AND LONG-RUN EQUILIBRIUM IN THE *AD–AS* MODEL

In the short run, actual output is determined by the intersection of the *SRAS* and *AD* curves. If the *SRAS* and *AD* curves intersect at an output level to the left of the *LRAS* curve, actual output falls below potential output and there is a recessionary gap. Panel a) of Figure 11.7 shows how a recessionary gap is represented in the *AD–AS* model with a horizontal, or Keynesian, *SRAS* curve.

a) Recessionary gap: actual output is below potential output ($Y < Y^*$)

b) Expansionary gap: actual output is above potential output ($Y > Y^*$)

FIGURE 11.7

Output Gaps in the *AD–AS* Model

Panel a) shows a recessionary gap with actual output falling below potential output. Panel b) shows an expansionary gap with actual output exceeding potential output.

If the *SRAS* and *AD* curves intersect at an output level to the right of the *LRAS* curve, actual output exceeds potential output and there is an expansionary gap. Panel b) of Figure 11.7 shows an expansionary gap.

Both panels of Figure 11.7 show short-run equilibrium points. They are not, however, long-run equilibrium points. Long-run equilibrium occurs in the *AD–AS* model where the *SRAS* and *AD* curves intersect along the *LRAS* curve.

What brings about long-run equilibrium in the *AD–AS* model?

Let's look first at what happens when aggregate demand (*AD*) produces an output level that is greater than the long-run aggregate supply (*LRAS*) of the economy. As in the Keynesian cross model of Chapters 8 and 10, an expansionary gap will create pressure for the price level to rise. In the *AD–AS* model, the rise in the price level is shown by an upward shift in the *SRAS* curve. In other words, if the *SRAS* and *AD* curves intersect to the right of potential output, there will be pressure for the price level to rise, and the *SRAS* curve will shift upward. When the *SRAS* curve shifts upward enough so that it intersects with the *AD* curve at potential output, there is no longer any pressure for the price level to rise. The model is then in long-run equilibrium.

In panel a) of Figure 11.8, the model is initially at a short-run equilibrium point *A* determined by the intersection of *AD* and *SRAS*. At point *A* there is an expansionary gap, so in the long run, *SRAS* shifts upward to *SRAS'*. Long-run equilibrium is shown by point *B*, where *AD* and *SRAS'* intersect the *LRAS* curve.

FIGURE 11.8
Automatic Elimination of Output Gaps in the *AD–AS* Model
In panel a), the economy is initially experiencing an expansionary gap at point *A*. In the long run, *SRAS* will shift to *SRAS'* and the economy will return to potential output, but with a higher price level as shown by point *B*. In panel b), the economy is initially experiencing a recessionary gap at point *C*. In the long run, *SRAS* will shift to *SRAS'* and the economy will return to potential output but with a lower price level as shown by point *D*.

a) Expansionary gap: actual output is above potential output (Y > Y*)

b) Recessionary gap: actual output is below potential output (Y < Y*)

If, on the other hand, the *AD* curve intersects the *SRAS* curve to the left of the *LRAS* curve, actual output is less than potential output and the economy is experiencing a recessionary gap. In this case, there will be pressure for the price level to drop and for the *SRAS* curve to shift down. When the *SRAS* curve shifts down enough to intersect with the *AD* curve at potential output, there is no longer any pressure for the price level to fall. The model is then in long-run equilibrium.

In panel b) of Figure 11.8, the model is initially at a short-run equilibrium point *C* determined by the intersection of *AD* and *SRAS*. At point *C*, there is a recessionary gap, so in the long run, *SRAS* shifts downward to *SRAS'*. Long-run equilibrium is shown by point *D*, where *AD* and *SRAS'* intersect the *LRAS* curve.

It is at this point that there is controversy among economists. The *AD–AS* model is one of a self-correcting economy. In the short run, actual output can deviate from potential output, but in the long run, the price level adjusts to bring actual output into line with potential output. How long do we have to wait for this long-run result? The model does not specify how long it will take for price level adjustments to eliminate output gaps. It is possible for output gaps, particularly recessionary gaps, to last for years, if monetary or fiscal policies are not used to eliminate them. During the Great Depression of the 1930s, Keynes argued that without government intervention, output gaps would persist, and that there was a strong case for using macroeconomic policy to close the recessionary output gap.

EXAMPLE 11.1

Let us consider a numerical example of short-run output and price determination in the *AD–AS* model. Suppose that the *SRAS* curve is horizontal at a price level of 100. We can represent the *SRAS* curve by the equation Price Level = 100. Suppose also that the *AD* curve can be represented by Price Level = $200 - .02 \times Y$, where Y represents real output. The short-run equilibrium requires that *SRAS* equals *AD*. So set $100 = 200 - .02 \times Y$. That is, $.02 \times Y = 100$, which implies that actual output is equal to 5000. The equilibrium price level, of course, is 100.

EXERCISE 11.1

Suppose that, as in Example 11.1, the *SRAS* curve is horizontal at a price level of 100, but that the *AD* curve shifts to the right and can be represented by the equation Price Level = $220 - .02 \times Y$. What will be the new short-run equilibrium values for real output and the price level?

EXAMPLE 11.2

Let us consider a numerical example of long-run output and price determination in the *AD–AS* model. Suppose the *LRAS* is vertical at 5000. That is, $Y = 5000$. As in Example 11.1, the *AD* curve is represented by Price Level = $200 - .02 \times Y$. In the long run, equilibrium requires that the *AD* equal potential output. So substituting $Y = 5000$ into the *AD* curve equation yields Price Level = $200 - .02 \times 5000 = 200 - 100 = 100$.

EXERCISE 11.2

Suppose that the economy is initially in long-run equilibrium with the *LRAS* curve vertical at a real output of 5000, the *SRAS* curve is horizontal at a price level of 100, and the *AD* curve is given by Price Level = $200 - .02 \times Y$. Then the *AD* curve shifts rightward to $220 - .02 \times Y$. What will be the new long-run equilibrium price level and real output?

RECAP

SHORT-RUN AND LONG-RUN EQUILIBRIUM IN THE *AD–AS* MODEL

In the short run, actual output in the *AD–AS* model is determined by the intersection of the *SRAS* and *AD* curves. If the *SRAS* and *AD* curves intersect at an output level to the left of the *LRAS* curve, actual output falls below potential output and there is a recessionary gap. If the *SRAS* and *AD* curves intersect at an output level to the right of the *LRAS* curve, actual output exceeds potential output and there is an expansionary gap.

The *AD–AS* model is one of a self-correcting economy. In the long run, the price level adjusts to bring actual output into line with potential output—the price level falls to eliminate a recessionary gap or it rises to eliminate an expansionary gap.

11.3 THE *AD-AS* MODEL IN ACTION

Having developed the *AD–AS* model, we can now apply it to policy issues. In this section, we will first explain how macroeconomic policy can be used to close output gaps in the *AD–AS* model, and then we will consider how the *AD–AS* model can be used to explain stagflation.

USING MACROECONOMIC POLICY TO CLOSE OUTPUT GAPS IN THE *AD-AS* MODEL

How can macroeconomic policy be used to close output gaps in the *AD–AS* model? Let us first consider an economy operating with a recessionary gap. In panel a) of Figure 11.9, the economy is experiencing a short-run equilibrium *A* where actual output is below potential output. The use of expansionary monetary policy (interest rate cuts) and/or fiscal policy (government expenditure increases and/or tax cuts) shifts the *AD* curve to *AD'* and results in a new equilibrium point *B* at which the recessionary gap has been eliminated.

The opposite case occurs when the economy is experiencing an expansionary gap. In panel b) of Figure 11.9, the economy is experiencing a short-run equilibrium *C*, where actual output exceeds potential output. The use of contractionary monetary policy (interest rate hikes) and/or fiscal policy (government expenditure cuts and/or tax increases) shifts the *AD* curve to *AD'* and results in a new equilibrium point *D* at which the expansionary gap has been eliminated.

Figure 11.9, of course, makes it look easy—as would be the case if the macroeconomic policy authorities had precise knowledge of the current state of the economy and how the economy responds to macroeconomic policy. However, recall from Chapter 10 that, in practice, macroeconomic policy may not work out so smoothly. If, for example, the potential output of the economy were underestimated, an attempt to eliminate an expansionary gap might go too far, and end up creating a recession.

FIGURE 11.9

Using Macro Policy to Close Output Gaps in the *AD-AS* Model

In panel a) the economy is initially experiencing a recessionary gap. Expansionary macroeconomic policy could be used to shift *AD* rightward to *AD'* and eliminate the recessionary gap. In panel b), the economy is initially experiencing an expansionary gap. Contractionary macroeconomic policy could be used to shift *AD* leftward to *AD'* and eliminate the expansionary gap.

a) Using expansionary macroeconomic policy to close a recessionary gap

b) Using contractionary macroeconomic policy to close an expansionary gap

EXAMPLE 11.3

Suppose that *AD* is given by Price Level = 210 − .02 × *Y* and *SRAS* is given by Price Level = 100. Potential output is equal to 5000. How large will the expansionary gap be? If the macroeconomic policy authorities can change the intercept of the *AD* equation, to what value should they change it to eliminate the expansionary gap?

To find the short-run equilibrium output, set *AD* equal to *SRAS,* which gives 210 − .02 × *Y* = 100 or .02 × *Y* = 110 or *Y* = 5500. That is, actual output of 5500 exceeds potential output of 5000 for an expansionary gap of 500. From Example 11.1, we know that for *SRAS* given by Price Level = 100, *AD* given by *AD* = 200 − .02 × *Y* will give actual output of 5000, which would eliminate the expansionary gap.

Suppose that, as in Example 11.3, *AD* is given by Price Level = 210 − .02 × *Y*, *SRAS* is given by Price Level = 100, and potential output is equal to 5000. The macroeconomic policy authorities wish to eliminate the expansionary gap but their knowledge of the economy is less than perfect, and they engineer a shift of the *AD* curve to Price Level = 190 − .02 × *Y*. What will be the short-run consequence of this shift of the *AD* curve?

EXERCISE 11.3

ECONOMIC NATURALIST 11.1

How will Ireland Recover?

During the global recession of 2008–2009, some economies fell into particularly severe macroeconomic circumstances, and Ireland was among them. Dubbed the Celtic Tiger for its rapid economic growth during the period 1995–2007, Ireland then experienced the collapse of a housing bubble, the bankruptcy and public bailout of its major banks, a sharp decline in economic growth, a doubling of the unemployment rate, and the rapid switch of its government budget balance from a small surplus to a huge deficit (due largely to the operation of automatic stabilizers, which were explained in Chapter 8, and to the public bailout of the banks). The huge deficit combined with the drop in GDP produced an escalation of its government debt-to-GDP ratio that frightened investors and sent interest rates on long-term Irish government bonds from about 5 percent for much of the 2000s to almost 9 percent in late 2010. The Irish government was forced to seek loans from the International Monetary Fund (IMF) and the European Union (EU).[4]

Table 11.1 summarizes key macroeconomic variables for Ireland for the period 2005–2010. In 2009, real GDP dropped almost 8 percent and the

TABLE 11.1
Key Macroeconomic Variables, Ireland, 2005–2010

Macroeconomic Variables	Years					
	2005	2006	2007	2008	2009	2010
Real GDP growth rate	6.0	5.3	5.6	−3.5	−7.6	−1.0
CPI inflation rate	2.2	2.7	2.9	3.1	−1.7	−1.6
Unemployment rate	4.4	4.4	4.6	6.3	11.8	13.6
Government budget balance	1.6	2.9	0.1	−7.3	−14.4	−32.2
Government net debt-to-GDP ratio	15.9	12.2	12.2	23.0	36.4	69.4

SOURCE: Data on Key Macroeconomic Variables from the *World Economic Outlook Database*, April 2011.

---

4 For a quick overview of the Irish situation in 2010, see, for example, Paul Krugman, "Eating the Irish," *New York Times,* November 25, 2010, http://www.nytimes.com/2010/11/26/opinion/26krugman.html and Paul Krugman, "An Irish Mirror," *New York Times*, March 7, 2010, http://www.nytimes.com/2010/03/08/opinion/08krugman.html. For more detail from a leading business journalist, see Michael Lewis, "When Irish Eyes Are Crying," *Vanity Fair*, March 2011, http://www.vanityfair.com/business/features/2011/03/michael-lewis-ireland-201103.

unemployment rate rose 5.5 percentage points from the year before. Obviously the economy was facing a huge recessionary gap. The state of the economy could be likened to that shown by the short-run equilibrium point *C* in panel b) of Figure 11.8 or to the short-run equilibrium point *A* in panel a) of Figure 11.9.

Under ideal circumstances, expansionary monetary policy, expansionary fiscal policy, or some combination of the two might be used to boost aggregate demand and eliminate the recessionary gap. This would correspond to the rightward shift of the *AD* curve to *AD'* in panel a) of Figure 11.9, and the associated shift of the economy to long-run equilibrium point *B* associated with actual output rising to equal potential output, eliminating the recessionary gap.

But Ireland does not set its own monetary policy. It is a eurozone country, and the European Central Bank (ECB) controls its monetary policy. At the time of writing (February 2011), the ECB has had its key policy rate at 1 percent since mid-2009 and shows no signs of cutting the key policy rate any further.

In terms of fiscal policy, the government has been forced into contractionary fiscal policy to try to reduce the budget deficit and bring the debt-to-GDP ratio under control.

It appears that recovery in the Irish economy will not be brought about by expansionary macroeconomic policy but will depend upon a fall in the price level; that is, upon deflation. The Irish CPI fell by 1.7 percent in 2009 and is projected by the IMF to fall 1.6 percent in 2010. In terms of panel b) of Figure 11.8, the fall in the price level corresponds to a drop in the *SRAS* curve. As the *SRAS* curve drops, equilibrium output in the economy rises, all else equal, in part through the foreign trade effect. That is, as prices in Ireland fall relative to prices in other countries, Irish net exports rise because imports to Ireland become more expensive compared to domestic goods and services, and Irish exports become cheaper in foreign markets. In terms of panel b) of Figure 11.8, eventually the *SRAS* curve should drop to *SRAS,'* and the economy should return to potential output at long-run equilibrium point *D*. But many economists predict that this will be a long and very painful process.

USING THE *AD–AS* MODEL TO EXPLAIN STAGFLATION

stagflation the combination of a recessionary gap and a rising price level

As mentioned in the introduction to this chapter, the *AD–AS* model gained acceptance in part because it provided an explanation for the phenomenon of **stagflation**—a recessionary gap combined with a rising price level. Stagflation arises in the context of the *AD–AS* model when some external factor causes the *SRAS* curve to shift upward. Such an external factor is termed an adverse price shock.

The external factor could be an increase in oil prices (because the increase in prices of the 1970s followed shortly after the oil price shock of 1973, this example is not just hypothetical). We will consider the case in which the increase in oil prices shifts the *SRAS* curve upward but does not affect the position of the *LRAS* curve.

Suppose the economy is initially in a state of long-run equilibrium, with the *SRAS* curve intersecting the *AD* curve at potential output, as shown by point *A* in Figure 11.10. When energy prices rise and firms revise their posted prices to reflect their higher level of input costs, the *SRAS* curve shifts upwards to *SRAS'*. As a result, the economy will move to a short-run equilibrium point *B*. Compared with point *A*, point *B* features a lower level of output and a higher price level—stagflation.

In the *AD–AS* model, however, stagflation will not persist if the self-correcting mechanism of the economy is allowed to work. That is, in the long run, the *AD–AS* model predicts that the recessionary gap will cause the *SRAS* curve to shift down, and actual output will return to potential output. In terms of Figure 11.10, in the long run the economy will return to the old equilibrium point *A*.[5]

---

5   Some students may ask, if the country really is self-sufficient in oil, and the recessionary gap is caused by the surge in inflation caused by the increase in the price level set off by increased oil prices, why doesn't the government step in and fix oil prices, keeping the economy at potential output? During the 1970s, Canada's federal government did control oil prices somewhat under the National Energy Program—to the detriment (and intense resentment) of oil-exporting Alberta. Oil prices were later allowed to rise to motivate both greater production and less domestic consumption in the longer run—that is, to increase Canada's net energy exports.

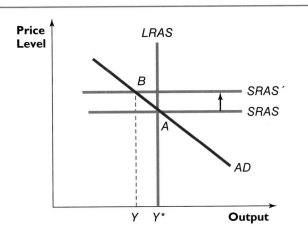

FIGURE 11.10
Stagflation in the *AD–AS* Model
Suppose that the economy is initially in a state of long-run equilibrium with the *SRAS* curve intersecting the *AD* curve at potential output, as shown by point *A*. If the *SRAS* curve shifts upwards to *SRAS'* because of an adverse price shock, the economy will move to a short-run equilibrium point *B*. Compared with point *A*, point *B* features a lower level of output and a higher price level. This amounts to stagflation.

ECONOMIC NATURALIST 11.2

The collapse of oil prices in the latter half of the 1980s and in 2009

The *AD–AS* model became popular in the late 1970s and early 1980s, because economists had to find an explanation for stagflation—the simultaneous combination of rising prices and depressed economic activity. However, the rise of oil prices in the 1970s prompted two economic responses. First, the high price of oil triggered intensified oil exploration that resulted in the discovery of new oil fields and increased oil production. Second, the high price of oil prompted consumers of oil to conserve. The combination of increased supply and reduced demand caused the price of oil to drop. In international markets, the price of a barrel of crude oil plummeted (measured in 2010 U.S. dollars) from US$94 in 1980 to a mere US$27 in 1988, as shown in Figure 11.11.

Just about anyone can understand how lower crude oil prices would translate into lower gasoline prices at the pump. But what macroeconomic impact would a collapse of oil prices have?

Suppose that we examine the situation in the latter part of the 1980s for an economy close to full employment, and we view the decline in crude oil prices arising because of the reduced effectiveness of oil exporting countries at restricting output. Then using our *AD–AS* model, with the economy initially in a position of long-run equilibrium, and assuming that the decrease in the price of oil just shifts the *SRAS* curve downwards without affecting the position of the *LRAS* curve, the macroeconomic impact could be as shown by Figure 11.12.

In Figure 11.12, the economy is initially in long-run equilibrium at point *A*. The drop in oil prices causes the *SRAS'* curve to shift downwards to *SRAS'*. The economy will move to a short-run equilibrium point *B*. Compared with point *A*, point *B* features a higher level of output (*Y* instead of *Y**) and a lower price level (*P'* instead of *P*).

But at point *B* there is an expansionary gap. There will be pressure for the price level to return to *P*. As the price level returns to *P*, output returns to *Y**.

According to our *AD–AS* model, then, the short-run impact of a drop in oil prices is positive. Output goes up and the price level goes down. But there is no long-run macroeconomic impact. In the long run, the price level and output both return to the levels they registered before the oil price drop.

There was also a drop in oil prices from US$97 to US$62 from 2008 to 2009—not as prolonged or a deep a drop as in the latter half of the 1980s, but still rather dramatic. To analyze the drop in oil prices in 2009, however, it is necessary to recognize that, to a very considerable degree, that drop in oil prices was triggered by leftward shifts in the *AD* curves of most countries in the world economy, associated with the financial crisis of 2008. The leftward shift in the *AD* curves created downward pressure on prices generally, including on oil prices. The most relevant figure to explain the situation with an *AD–AS* model would be one such as panel (b) of Figure 11.8.[6]

---

6   A more detailed analysis of the oil price declines in the 1980s and from 2008 to 2009 would recognize, among other things, the role of the early 1980s recessions in bringing down the price of crude oil in the early 1980s, and perhaps the role of the collapse of commodity price speculation, as factors in the decline of oil prices from 2008 to 2009.

FIGURE 11.11

Crude Oil Prices, 1970–2010, Annual Data

The average price of crude oil rose dramatically in the 1970s, reaching a peak of over US$94 in 1980 (expressed in 2010 dollars). This rise in the price of crude oil is what economists call an upward aggregate price shock. But the crude oil price then fell dramatically in the 1980s, reaching US$27 in 1988. The drop in the price of crude oil during the 1980s was what economists call a downward aggregate price shock.

The crude oil price rose sharply again after 2002, reaching US$98 in 2008. It plummeted to US$63 in 2009 due to the global recession before rising again in 2010.

SOURCE: Adapted from data on Crude Oil Prices from *International Monetary Fund, International Financial Statistics,* 2011, and U.S. Bureau of Labor Statistics, Consumer Price Index.

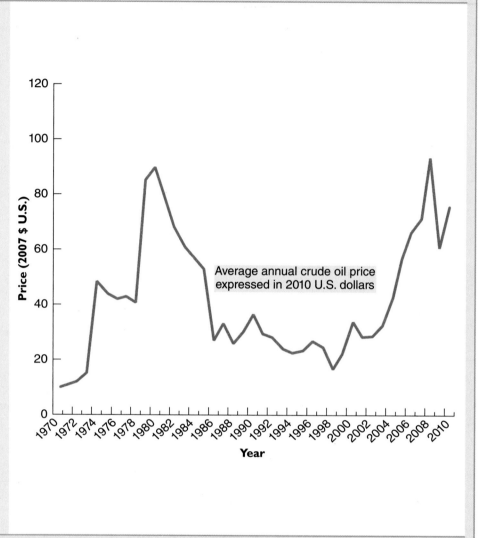

Average annual crude oil price expressed in 2010 U.S. dollars

FIGURE 11.12

A Downward Oil Price Shock in the AD–AS Model

Suppose that the economy is initially in a state of long-run equilibrium, with the *SRAS* curve intersecting the *AD* curve at potential output and price level *P*, as shown by point *A*. If the *SRAS* curve shifts downwards to *SRAS'* because of a favourable oil price shock, the economy will move to a short-run equilibrium point *B*. Compared with point *A*, point *B* features a higher level of output (*Y*) and a lower price level (*P'* instead of *P*). But the expansionary gap associated with point *B* will cause the price level to return to *P*.

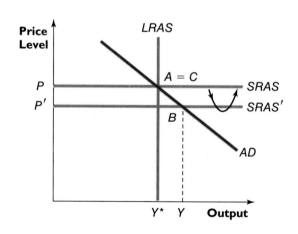

RECAP

THE *AD-AS* MODEL IN ACTION

In the *AD-AS* model, macroeconomic policy can be used to speed up the return to long-run equilibrium. Expansionary macroeconomic policy can be used to eliminate a recessionary gap, and contractionary macroeconomic policy can be used to eliminate an expansionary gap.

The *AD-AS* model can also be used to explain stagflation. Suppose the economy experiences an upward price shock, causing the *SRAS* curve to shift upwards. The new short-run equilibrium will then feature both a higher price level and a lower level of real output.

11.4 AN ALTERNATIVE VERSION OF THE *AD-AS* MODEL

In the previous sections of this chapter, we have presented an *AD–AS* model in which the short-run aggregate supply (*SRAS*) curve is drawn as a horizontal line to indicate that in the short run, firms will supply the output that their customers demand at the prices the firms have posted.

Some economists, however, present an alternative version of the *AD–AS* model in which the *SRAS* curve is upward sloping, as shown in Figure 11.13. The alternative version of the *AD–AS* model also has a different explanation of what causes the *SRAS* curve to shift in response to output gaps.

According to the alternative version of the *AD–AS* model, the upward-sloping *SRAS* curve represents how the aggregate quantity of output supplied by firms will increase with a rise in the price level (or decrease with a fall in the price level). Suppose that firms face a price level that is 2 percent higher than before, because the output prices of firms are 2 percent higher. Will firms increase their output? It depends on what happens to their input prices (that is, their costs). If input prices, such as wages, also increased by 2 percent, firms would not have a profit incentive to increase output. But if wages did not increase immediately when prices increased, the firms could increase their profits by expanding output. The upward-sloping *SRAS* curve, then, represents the assumption that wages lag behind output prices and that this lag gives firms a profit incentive to raise output when the price level rises (and to lower output when the price level falls).

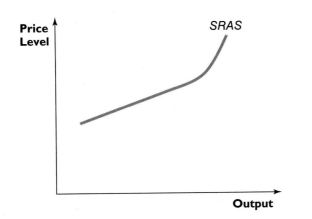

FIGURE 11.13

An Upward-Sloping *SRAS* Curve

An alternative version of the *AD-AS* model features an upward-sloping *SRAS* curve. The assumption behind the upward slope is that when the price level rises, input prices lag behind, which provides firms with a profit incentive to expand output in the short run. Conversely, when the price level falls, input prices again lag behind, which provides firms with a profit incentive to contract output in the short run.

What difference does it make if the *SRAS* curve is upward-sloping? Panel a) of Figure 11.14 shows the alternative version of the *AD–AS* model for the case when an economy initially operating at potential output is subjected to an *increase* in aggregate demand. At the initial equilibrium point A, *AD = SRAS = LRAS*. A rightward shift of *AD* to *AD′* produces a short-run equilibrium B with both a higher price level (*P′* instead of *P*) and a higher output level (*Y′* instead of *Y**). In the long run, the *SRAS* curve shifts leftward to *SRAS′* and the economy moves to point C where output has returned to *Y** and the price level has increased even further, from *P′* to *P″*. In terms of results, the only difference with the *AD–AS* model presented earlier in this chapter is that in this case the price level rises even in the short run.

Panel b) of Figure 11.14 shows the alternative version of the *AD–AS* model for the opposite case when an economy initially operating at potential output is subjected to a decrease in aggregate demand. The initial equilibrium point is D, but a leftward shift of *AD* to *AD′* produces a short-run equilibrium E with both a lower price level (*P′* instead of *P*) and a lower output level (*Y* instead of *Y**). The leftward shift in *AD* produces a recessionary gap. In the long run, the *SRAS* curve shifts rightward to *SRAS* and the economy moves to point F, where output has returned to *Y** and the price level has fallen even further, from *P′* to *P″*. In terms of results, the difference from the *AD–AS* model presented earlier is that the price level falls even in the short run.

In less abstract terms, if there was a sharply increased demand for Canadian resource exports to Asia, this initial change would be represented in terms of a rightward shift of the *AD* curve in an *AD–AS* model. The full analysis in terms of our *AD–AS* model with an upward-sloping *AS* curve would be as is shown in panel a) of Figure 11.14.

If there was sharply reduced demand for Canadian lumber exports to the United States because of a collapse in U.S. housing markets, this initial change would be represented in terms of a leftward shift of the *AD* curve in an *AD–AS* model. The full

FIGURE 11.14

An Alternative Version of the *AD–AS* Model in Action

In panel a), the economy is initially in long-run equilibrium at point A, with price level P, and output equal to potential output Y*. A shift of AD rightward to AD′ moves the economy to point B in the short run. Output rises to Y and the price level rises to P′. In the long run, the SRAS curve shifts leftward to SRAS′ and the economy moves to point C.

In panel b), the economy is initially in long-run equilibrium at point D, with price level P and output equal to Y*. A shift of AD leftward to AD′ moves the economy to point E in the short run. Output falls to Y and the price level falls to P′. In the long run, the SRAS curve shifts rightward to SRAS′ and the economy moves to point F.

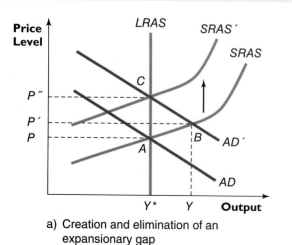

a) Creation and elimination of an expansionary gap

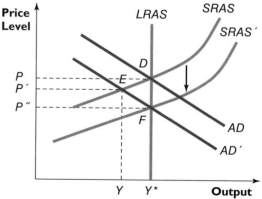

b) Creation and elimination of a recessionary gap

analysis of this event with an upward-sloping AS curve would be as shown in panel b) of Figure 11.14.

Note that panel b) predicts that the price level will fall in the short run, and fall even further in the long run. But in reality this is unlikely as the price level in Canada, as measured by the CPI, has not fallen on an annual basis during the lifetime of the typical reader of this textbook.

RECAP

AN ALTERNATIVE VERSION OF THE *AD–AS* MODEL

In one version of the *AD–AS* model, the *SRAS* curve is upward sloping, not horizontal. The *SRAS* curve would be upward sloping if the overall level of wages adjusted more slowly than the rate of the overall price-level adjustment.

If the *SRAS* curve is upward sloping, and the economy is initially operating at potential output, a rightward shift of the *AD* curve produces a short-run equilibrium with both a higher price level and a higher level of output. In the long run, the *SRAS* curve experiences a leftward shift, which produces an even higher price level, but actual output matches potential output.

Conversely, given the same initial conditions for the model, a leftward shift of the *AD* curve would result in both a lower price level and a lower level of output in the short run. The model predicts an even lower price level and a return of actual output to the level of potential output, in the long run.

11.5 THE EXPECTATIONS-AUGMENTED PHILLIPS CURVE MODEL AS A SUPPLEMENT TO THE *AD–AS* MODEL

The *AD–AS* model arose to explain *stagflation*—a phenomenon not easily handled by the Keynesian cross model. The key merit of the *AD–AS* model as compared with the Keynesian cross model is that both the price level and the output level are directly represented. However, progress in economics proceeds in steps, and over time it became apparent that the *AD–AS* model was only partially satisfactory.

In the first place, as the discussion at the start of the chapter implicitly recognized, for most purposes it is the inflation rate—the rate of *change* of the price level—that interests people. And although the *AD–AS* model gives the impression that the price level and nominal wages decline during recessions, in most recessions the price level and nominal wages continue to rise, *just at a slower rate*—disinflation. The rate of inflation typically declines during a recession, but the price *level* does not actually fall. Deflation does not occur.

One way to deal with the problem that the *AD–AS* model does not deal directly with the rate of inflation is to supplement the model with a model of the Phillips curve. The *Phillips curve* is named after A. W. Phillips, an economist who used British data to link unemployment rates to inflation in a famous paper published in 1958.[7] Phillips found that unemployment rates and wage inflation rates were inversely related. Studies were conducted for other countries in the 1960s, and they usually linked the overall inflation rate to the unemployment rate. Today the term **Phillips curve** is typically used to indicate a statistical relationship between the inflation rate and the unemployment rate. Panel a) of Figure 11.15 shows a Phillips curve for Canadian data from the 1960s—during the 1960s many economists estimated the inflation/unemployment relationship and thought of it as representing a "trade-off" in economic policy.

Phillips curve a term that typically refers to a statistical relationship between the inflation rate and the unemployment rate

---

FIGURE 11.15

Scatterplots of Inflation and Unemployment Rates, Canada, 1960–69 and 1970–2010

Panel a) is a scatterplot of Canadian unemployment and inflation rates for the 1960s. Notice that there is a clear inverse relationship between the two variables. Years are indicated with two digits; for example, 1960 is shown as 60. Panel b) is a similar scatterplot for the 1970–2010 period. For the longer 1970–2010 period, there is no apparent statistical relationship between the two variables.

SOURCE: Adapted from Statistics Canada, CANSIM series v2062815 and v41690973.

a)

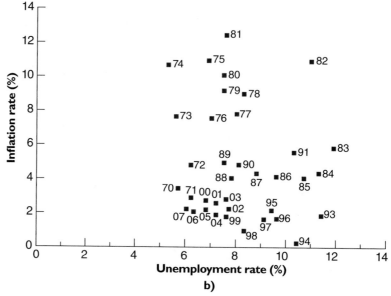

b)

But in more recent decades, the inverse relationship between inflation and unemployment rates observed in the 1960s has broken down. Panel b) of Figure 11.15 shows a scatterplot of annual inflation rates and unemployment rates for Canada between 1970 and 2010. Note that there is no obvious way to fit a curve through the scatterplot of data points.

Why did the simple Phillips curve model of the relationship between inflation and unemployment work well in, say, the 1960s but not in, say, the 1980s? One possible explanation is because of changing expectations of inflation. Recall that at the start of this chapter we noted that the Canadian inflation rate between 1952 and 1965 was on average 1.4 percent. On this basis, it was reasonable for Canadians in the mid-1960s to expect little inflation. But between 1973 and 1982, Canada's inflation rate averaged 9.6 percent, so expecting little change in prices was, by the early 1980s, becoming pretty unreasonable. The *expectations-augmented Phillips curve model* has become widely used as an explanation for why the Phillips curve estimated for the 1960s does not fit the data for later decades. The **expectations-augmented Phillips curve model** distinguishes between a *short-run Phillips curve* and a *long-run Phillips curve* and argues that short-run Phillips curves shift when expectations about the inflation rate change. Figure 11.16 provides a graphical representation of the model.

expectations-augmented Phillips curve model

distinguishes between a short-run and a long-run Phillips curve and argues that the short-run version shifts when expectations about the inflation rate change

A key assumption of the model is that there is a vertical long-run Phillips curve at the natural rate of unemployment. In other words, the **long-run Phillips curve** represents the hypothesis that the natural rate of unemployment is independent of changes in the inflation rate.

According to the expectations-augmented Phillips curve model, at any point in time, people have some set of expectations about future inflation. The **short-run Phillips curve** (*SRPC*) shows an inverse relationship between the inflation rate and the unemployment rate *given* expectations about inflation. But if people expect some change in the rate of inflation, the short-run Phillips curve will shift. If people had expected inflation to be low and they change to expecting inflation to be high, the short-run Phillips curve shifts up. A change in inflationary expectations may occur because actual experience has changed; that is, because inflation has picked up recently, or perhaps because something happens (like an oil embargo) that people have good reason to believe will produce an increase in inflation. Either way, the **short-run Phillips curve** shifts up when people expect inflation to increase.

Conversely, if people had expected inflation to be high and they change to expecting inflation to be low (say, because inflation has declined in recent months), the short-run Phillips curve shifts down.

What determines expectations of inflation? According to the Phillips curve model, people have *adaptive expectations* about inflation. **Adaptive expectations of inflation** means that people adapt their expectations about the future rate of inflation based upon their recent experience with inflation. If inflation has been high, people expect inflation to be high in the future. If inflation has been low, they expect inflation to be low in the future.

How is this model used to explain the scatterplot of inflation and unemployment rates in panel b) of Figure 11.15? The idea is that the scatterplot fits several different short-run Phillips curves rather than a single one. For example, given the fact that inflation had been very low between 1952 and 1965, one might think that if people expected that low inflation to continue, there would be one short-run Phillips curve for the 1960s. Since inflation accelerated during the 1970s, and people's expectations of inflation changed, there would be a different short-run Phillips curve for the 1970s and the 1980s (i.e., a shift

long-run Phillips curve a relationship between the inflation rate and the unemployment rate in the long run; the vertical curve is drawn at the natural rate of unemployment

short-run Phillips curve (*SRPC*) a relationship between actual unemployment and the inflation rate for given inflationary expectations

adaptive expectations of inflation a method of forming expectations about the inflation rate that involves looking to past experience, especially recent past experience

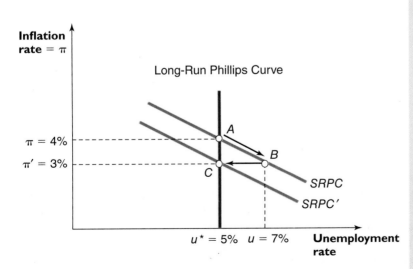

FIGURE 11.16
Lowering the Inflation Rate in the Phillips Curve Model
The economy is initially in equilibrium at point *A*, with actual unemployment equal to the natural rate *u*, and inflation equal to π. The central bank wishes to bring inflation down to π′, so it implements contractionary monetary policy, moving the economy down the short-run Phillips curve to point *B*, where the actual unemployment rate (*u*) exceeds the natural rate, and inflation is at π′. Eventually, inflationary expectations adapt to the new environment, and the short-run Phillips curve shifts to move the equilibrium to *C*, where inflation equals π′ and the unemployment rate has returned to the natural rate.

up in the **short-run Phillips curve**). During the 1990s, expectations changed again, and as a result, the short-run Phillips curve shifted again (downward).

As a hypothetical example, suppose that, initially, the economy is at point *A* in Figure 11.16, which is drawn to represent the idea that the economy is at the natural rate of unemployment (estimated to be 5 percent) and the inflation rate is 4 percent.[8] Suppose also that the central bank wishes to reduce the inflation rate to 3 percent. The central bank will take action, that is, raise interest rates, to create a recessionary gap. When there is a recessionary gap, the actual unemployment rate will be above the natural rate. The recessionary gap and the higher actual unemployment rate will produce a lower inflation rate. So in the short run, the economy will have moved from point *A* to point *B* with a higher rate of unemployment (the cost of the policy of reducing the inflation rate) and a lower rate of inflation (the goal of the policy). In the hypothetical example of Figure 11.16, the actual unemployment rate has increased from 5 percent to 7 percent and the inflation rate has been reduced from 4 percent to 3 percent. In the short run, the economy moves along the short-run Phillips curve (*SRPC*).

But at point *B*, people in the economy are experiencing a lower rate of inflation than before. If they have adaptive expectations, they will come to expect lower inflation, and the short-run Phillips curve will shift downward. If the central bank succeeds in creating a recessionary gap just large enough to realize its inflation target of 3 percent, then the short-run Phillips curve will shift to *SRPC'*.

Notice that the expectations-augmented Phillips curve model is, like the *AD–AS* model, a model of a self-correcting economy. In the short run, the actual unemployment rate can be above or below the natural rate of unemployment. But in the long run, the actual unemployment rate will return to the natural rate of unemployment.

RECAP ↑

THE EXPECTATIONS-AUGMENTED PHILLIPS CURVE MODEL AS A SUPPLEMENT TO THE *AD–AS* MODEL

The expectations-augmented Phillips curve model is used to supplement the *AD–AS* model because the *AD–AS* model does not deal directly with the rate of inflation. The Phillips curve model is represented graphically with the inflation rate on the vertical axis and the unemployment rate on the horizontal axis. The short-run Phillips curve shows a trade-off between the inflation rate and the actual unemployment rate. But the long-run Phillips curve is drawn vertically at the natural rate of unemployment. The expectations-augmented Phillips curve model is, like the *AD–AS* one, a model of a self-correcting economy. One implication of the expectations-augmented Phillips curve model is that if a central bank wishes to achieve a lower rate of inflation it will have to bring about an actual rate of unemployment higher than the natural rate for some period of time.

11.6 CONCLUSION

One approach to dealing with the limitations of the Keynesian cross model is to supplement it with the *AD–AS* model and the expectations-augmented Phillips curve model. In the next chapter, however, we will build on this approach and address more directly the idea that it is the *rate of change of prices* (i.e., inflation) that is the focus of economic policy, not the *level* of prices, and the fact that the central bank changes monetary policy in response to changes in inflation.

---

8 Figure 11.16 embodies the assumption that, at the natural rate of unemployment, the economy is operating with actual output equal to potential output.

One idea behind the *AD–AS* model is that the decline in the price level will boost aggregate demand (because of real balances and foreign trade effects) and thereby raise actual output—but could this actually happen in Canada, for example?

It seemed to be happening in the Irish economy in 2009–2010, as noted in Economic Naturalist 11.2. But Ireland does not have its own central bank. Countries with their own central banks have central banks that are opposed to domestic deflation as a matter of policy. Typically, they would like to keep the inflation rate low or moderate, but they do not want the price level to fall (for reasons that were mentioned in the discussion of inflation in Chapter 6). In Canada, the mid-point of the Bank of Canada's inflation target range is 2 percent and the lower bound is 1 percent, which means that the Bank of Canada aims to have the price level rise by 2 percent a year on average and to never increase it by less than 1 percent a year. The Bank of Canada is so convinced that the self-correcting mechanism of the *AD–AS* model would be slow to do the job that they are unwilling to accept even a year of deflation. So the Bank changes its setting of interest rates to try to keep Canada's inflation rate in the 1 percent to 3 percent range.

To explore the implications of this, we will develop a third macroeconomic model. This macroeconomic model, the subject of Chapter 12, relates real output not to the price level but to the inflation rate, under the assumption that the central bank targets the inflation rate and uses its key policy rate for inflation rate control.

SUMMARY

- The aggregate demand–aggregate supply (*AD–AS*) model was developed to supplement the Keynesian cross model. The *AD–AS* model is designed to analyze how shifts in aggregate demand and supply can affect not just output but also the overall price level. Thus, the model is represented graphically with the overall price level on the vertical axis and real output on the horizontal axis. The *AD–AS* model has three central components: a long-run aggregate supply curve, a short-run aggregate supply curve, and an aggregate demand curve. **LO1**

- The long-run aggregate supply (*LRAS*) curve is drawn as a vertical line at potential output. It represents the assumption that the potential output of the economy is independent of the overall price level. Potential output depends on the amounts of capital, labour, and other inputs, and upon factors determining the productivity of inputs. **LO1**

- The Keynesian short-run aggregate supply curve (*SRAS*) is drawn as a horizontal line. This represents the idea that in the short run, firms will supply the output demanded at their posted prices. General changes in the costs of firms will cause firms to revise their posted prices and the *SRAS* curve to shift. **LO1**

- Two major explanations have been provided for an inverse relationship between the price level and output, as depicted by the downward-sloping aggregate demand (*AD*) curve: the real-balances effect and the foreign trade effect. Changes in autonomous aggregate expenditure or in monetary and fiscal policies cause the *AD* curve to shift. **LO1**

- In the short run, actual output is determined by the intersection of the *SRAS* and *AD* curves, and recessionary or expansionary gaps can result. In the long run, the price level adjusts to bring actual output into line with potential output. Macroeconomic policy, however, can be used to speed up the return to long-run equilibrium. **LO2**

■ The *AD–AS* model can be used to explain stagflation. Suppose the economy experiences an adverse price shock, causing the *SRAS* curve to shift upwards. The new short-run equilibrium will then feature both a higher price level and a lower level of real output. **LO3**

■ One version of the *AD–AS* model features an upward-sloping *SRAS* curve. In this alternative version of the model, shifts in *AD* will produce price-level changes even in the short run. **LO4**

■ The expectations-augmented Phillips curve model, which is used to supplement the *AD–AS* model, is represented graphically with the inflation rate on the vertical axis and the unemployment rate on the horizontal axis. The short-run Phillips curve shows a trade-off between the inflation rate and the actual unemployment rate, but the long-run Phillips curve is drawn vertically at the natural rate of unemployment. **LO5**

KEY TERMS

adaptive expectations of inflation (287)
aggregate demand curve (270)
aggregate demand–aggregate supply model (*AD-AS*) (269)
expectations-augmented Phillips curve model (286)

foreign trade effect (271)
long-run aggregate supply (*LRAS*) curve (273)
long-run Phillips curve (287)
Phillips curve (285)
real-balances effect (271)

short-run aggregate supply (*SRAS*) curve (272)
short-run Phillips curve (287)
stagflation (280)

REVIEW QUESTIONS

1. What does stagflation mean? Why is it difficult to explain stagflation with a Keynesian cross diagram? **LO1**

2. "If a rise in the price of a good causes firms in an industry to produce more of the good, then a rise in the overall price level must produce higher output for the economy as a whole." What is the term for the logical fallacy committed in this quotation? According to the hypothesis of a vertical long-run aggregate supply curve, what impact does a rise in the overall price level have on potential output? **LO1**

3. What type of firm behaviour would justify a horizontal short-run aggregate supply curve? **LO1**

4. True or false, and explain: The downward-sloping aggregate demand curve is explained by the law of demand. **LO1**

5. Given that the *AD–AS* model is one of a self-correcting economy, how could the *AD–AS* model be used to justify expansionary macroeconomic policy to eliminate a recessionary gap? **LO2, LO3**

6. How can stagflation be explained with an *AD–AS* model? **LO3**

7. Is the rationale for an upward-sloping *SRAS* curve the same as the rationale for an upward-sloping industry supply curve in microeconomics? Explain. **LO4**

8. What does the short-run Phillips curve indicate? **LO5**

9. According to the expectations-augmented Phillips curve model, does a central bank face a trade-off if it wishes to lower the inflation rate? Explain. **LO5**

PROBLEMS

1. Suppose you had $1000 in cash in a base year and the price level increased by 10 percent. What would happen to the real value of your cash? **LO1**

2. (More difficult) "The multiplier for an increase in autonomous aggregate expenditure in the basic Keynesian model equals the multiplier for the *AD–AS* model in the short run. In the long run, the multiplier for the *AD–AS* model equals the short-run multiplier if the shift in *AD* is just large enough to close a recessionary gap. But the long-run multiplier for the *AD–AS* model equals zero if the economy is initially operating at potential output." Explain using diagrams. **LO1, LO2**

3. For each of the following events, state whether the impact would be to shift the aggregate demand curve, the short-run aggregate supply curve, or both curves. Also state in which direction the curves would shift. **LO1, LO2**
   a. increased demand by Japan for Canadian lumber.
   b. an increase in the Bank of Canada's overnight rate target.
   c. an increase in the GST.

   d. a sharp drop in world oil prices.
   e. a sharp appreciation of the Canadian dollar.

4. Suppose that an economy is initially at long-run equilibrium, with the horizontal *SRAS* curve intersecting the *AD* curve at potential output. Use an *AD–AS* diagram to show the impact on the price level and real output of an autonomous increase in consumption spending. Distinguish between the short-run impact and the long-run impact. **LO3**

5. Suppose policy-makers are faced with an economy with an actual rate of unemployment above the natural rate. Use the expectations-augmented Phillips curve model to analyze two alternatives: a) policy-makers implement expansionary macroeconomic policy to move the actual rate to the natural rate and b) policy-makers allow the economy to self-correct. **LO5**

6. Assume that the price level is initially equal to 100. Is there a difference between a 2-percentage-point drop in the price level and a 2-percentage-point drop in the inflation rate? Explain. **LO5**

ANSWERS TO IN-CHAPTER EXERCISES

11.1 For the new short-run equilibrium, *AD* must equal *SRAS*. So $100 = 220 - .02Y$. That is, $.02Y = 120$, which implies that real output is equal to 6000. **LO2**

11.2 In long-run equilibrium, *AD* must equal potential output. So substituting $Y = 5000$ into the *AD* curve equation yields Price Level $= 220 - .02 \times 5000 = 220 - 100 = 120$. The *SRAS* curve will shift up and will be horizontal at a price level of 120. **LO2**

11.3 For the new short-run equilibrium, *AD* must equal *SRAS*. So $100 = 190 - .02Y$. That is, $.02Y = 90$, which implies that real output is equal to 4500. The short-run consequence of the macroeconomic policy authorities shifting the *AD* too far to the left would be a recessionary gap of 500. **LO3**

 Practise and learn online with Connect.

CHAPTER 12
Inflation and Output

During the year 2000, the Canadian economy had been booming. The Bank of Canada had raised its key policy rate, the overnight rate target, a few times in the early months of the year to a peak of 5.75 percent in May. Even though total CPI inflation ran at about 3 percent for much of the year, the Bank of Canada refrained from any further increases in the overnight rate. Press releases from the Bank noted core CPI inflation remained well within the Bank's inflation control target range, and explained that total CPI inflation was being driven by temporary gas price increases. But the Bank of Canada faced criticism, notably from analysts with the C.D. Howe Institute who, in the fall of 2000, criticized the Bank's focus on core inflation, and argued for tighter monetary policy.[1]

Not only did the Bank ignore the calls for tighter monetary policy, but on January 23, 2001, noting the slowdown in the U.S. economy that would contribute to weaker growth in Canada, the Bank of Canada cut the overnight rate by a quarter of a percentage point. It was the last interest rate announcement from then Governor Gordon Thiessen before the end of his term as Governor. In the following months, under the new Governor David Dodge, the Bank of Canada implemented eight additional interest rate cuts that would take the overnight rate target to 2.25 percent by the end of the year.

Did the Bank of Canada make the correct judgment in ignoring the criticism of the C.D. Howe Institute? It would appear so: the U.S. economy entered into a full-blown recession in 2001 but thanks in part to the Bank of Canada's cuts to the overnight rate target, the Canadian economy experienced a significantly milder slowdown. And annual inflation in Canada remained within the Bank's 1 to 3 percent target range.

The Bank of Canada interest rate cuts illustrate the difficult and important policy choices that government officials face year after year. In this chapter, we will examine

---

1 See William Robson and Shay Aba, "Stop the Press! Rapid Money Growth May Bring Higher Inflation," *C.D. Howe Institute Commentary*, No. 144, September 2000, and David Laidler and Shay Aba, "It's Time to Ignore Core Inflation," *C.D. Howe Institute Backgrounder*, November 2000.

those choices in further detail. To do this, we develop and apply the *aggregate demand-inflation adjustment model*. This model is an extension of the basic Keynesian model to allow for ongoing inflation. Using this extended analysis, we will be able to show how macroeconomic policies affect inflation as well as output, illustrating in the process the difficult trade-offs policy-makers sometimes face. We start by building the model step by step. We then put the model to work by analyzing expansionary gaps and recessionary gaps.

12.1 INFLATION, SPENDING, AND OUTPUT: OVERVIEW AND THE AGGREGATE DEMAND (*ADI*) CURVE

OVERVIEW

The model developed in this chapter is one of the workhorse models in macroeconomics.[2] It is useful because it shows how output and inflation are determined simultaneously in both the short run and long run. It thus allows us to show what an economy is doing at a particular point in time and lets us predict where the economy is going in the future including where the economy will go in response to fiscal and monetary policy choices.

Figure 12.1 shows the diagram we will use in applying the model to real-world situations. The current inflation rate is on the vertical axis and the current level of output, Y, is on the horizontal axis. The *aggregate demand/inflation* curve, or *aggregate demand* curve for short, is described as the *ADI* curve, and it is downward sloping from left to right to represent the idea that lower rates of inflation lead to higher levels of spending. The inflation-adjustment (*IA*) curve is horizontal to represent the idea that inflation exhibits inertia—that is, a tendency, all else equal, for periods of low inflation to be followed by periods of low inflation and for periods of moderate inflation to be followed by periods of moderate inflation, and so on. The vertical line labelled the long-run aggregate supply curve (*LRAS*) represents the idea that the level of potential output Y does not change with the rate of inflation. The intersection of the three curves, *ADI*, *IA*, and *LRAS*, shows the economy in long-run equilibrium with actual output equal to potential output.

Can any or all of the curves shift? Why are the curves sloped the way that they are? Can the economy be at a point away from long-run equilibrium? If the economy is away from potential output, will it return to its long-run equilibrium? What role can government policy play in returning the economy to long-run equilibrium? To answer questions such as these, and to put this *ADI–IA* model to work, we need to dig into the details of the *ADI*, *IA*, and *LRAS* curves, and short-run equilibrium and long-run equilibrium in the model.[3]

INTRODUCTION TO THE AGGREGATE DEMAND (*ADI*) CURVE

Our first step in digging into the details of the *ADI–IA* model is to consider the economics behind the *aggregate demand/inflation curve*. The **aggregate demand (*ADI*) curve** is based on the relationship between short-run equilibrium output Y and the rate of inflation, denoted π. The name of the curve reflects that, as we have seen, short-run equilibrium output is determined by the total planned spending, or demand, in the economy.

aggregate demand (*ADI*) curve shows the relationship between short-run equilibrium output Y and the rate of inflation π

2 The graphical analysis used in this chapter was initially developed by Ben Bernanke, now chairman of the U.S. Federal Reserve, and it closely follows the approach recommended by David Romer in his work "Keynesian Macroeconomics Without the LM Curve," *Journal of Economic Perspectives*, Spring 2000, pp. 149–170. It is similar to the approach followed by Stanford University economist John Taylor in textbooks and articles, including his "Teaching Modern Macroeconomics at the Principles Level," *American Economic Review*, May 2000, pp. 90–94. It provides a strong foundation for students who go on to study the short-run analysis in intermediate macroeconomics textbooks such as that of Charles Jones, *Macroeconomics*, *2nd ed.* (New York: Norton, 2011).

3 We refer to the *ADI*, *IA*, and *LRAS* "curves" even though they are shown as straight lines.

FIGURE 12.1

The Aggregate Demand (*ADI*)/ Inflation Adjustment (*IA*) Diagram
The *ADI* curve indicates that lower rates of inflation lead to higher levels of spending. The *IA* curve represents the finding that inflation exhibits inertia. The *LRAS* curve shows potential GDP *Y**. The intersection of *ADI, IA,* and *LRAS* corresponds to the economy in long-run equilibrium with actual output equal to potential output.

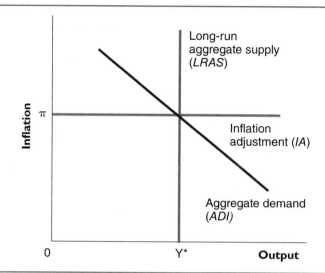

Indeed, by definition, short-run equilibrium output *equals* planned aggregate expenditure, so we could just as well say that the *ADI* curve shows the relationship between inflation and spending.

It is important to distinguish the *ADI* curve from both the expenditure line, introduced as part of the Keynesian cross diagram in Chapter 8, and from the aggregate demand (*AD*) curve, which you might be familiar with from the *AD–AS* analysis of Chapter 10. The upward-sloping expenditure line of the Keynesian cross diagram shows the relationship between planned aggregate expenditure and output. The *AD* curve of the *AD–AS* analysis of Chapter 10 shows the relationship between short-run equilibrium output and the price level. But the *ADI* curve shows the relationship between short-run equilibrium output (which equals planned spending) and the inflation rate (the rate of change of the price level). The *ADI* curve incorporates the very important influence of the central bank's monetary policy on aggregate demand and the consistent way that the Bank of Canada reacts to changes in the *inflation rate*.

We will see shortly that, all else being equal, *an increase in the rate of inflation tends to reduce both aggregate demand and short-run equilibrium output.* Therefore, in a diagram such as Figure 12.1 showing inflation (π) on the vertical axis and output (Y) on the horizontal axis, the *ADI* curve is downward sloping.

Why does higher inflation lead to a lower level of aggregate demand? As we will see next, one important reason is the central bank's response to increases in inflation.

INFLATION, THE BANK OF CANADA, AND AGGREGATE DEMAND

One of the primary responsibilities of the Bank of Canada, or of any central bank, is to control the rate of inflation. For example, in recent years the Bank of Canada has tried to keep inflation in Canada in the range of 1 to 3 percent. There is some disagreement among economists about this inflation control target. For example, as noted in Chapter 6, some economists argue that the Bank of Canada should aim for moderate rather than low inflation. But there is no questioning that the Bank does target low inflation and that low inflation has been achieved.

What can the Bank of Canada do to keep inflation low? As we have already mentioned, one situation that is likely to lead to increased inflation is an expansionary output gap, in which aggregate demand exceeds potential output. When aggregate demand exceeds potential output, firms must produce at above-normal capacity to meet the demands of their customers. Like Al's ice cream store described in Chapter 7, firms may be willing to do so for a time, but eventually they will raise their prices, contributing to inflation. To control inflation, then, the Bank of Canada needs to dampen aggregate demand when it threatens to exceed potential output.

How can the Bank of Canada restrain aggregate demand? As we saw in Chapter 9, the Bank of Canada can reduce private spending, and hence aggregate demand, by raising the real interest rate. This behaviour by the Bank of Canada underlies the link between inflation and aggregate demand that is summarized by the *ADI* curve. When inflation is high, the Bank of Canada responds by raising the real interest rate. The increase in the real interest rate reduces consumption and private-sector investment spending and, hence, aggregate demand.[4] Because higher inflation leads, through the Bank of Canada's actions, to a reduction in aggregate demand, the *ADI* curve is downward sloping, as Figure 12.1 shows. We can summarize this chain of reasoning symbolically as follows:

$$\pi \uparrow \Rightarrow r \uparrow \Rightarrow \text{autonomous expenditure} \downarrow \Rightarrow Y \downarrow$$

where, recall, π is inflation, r is the real interest rate, and Y is output.

The same reasoning applies when inflation falls:

$$\pi \downarrow \Rightarrow r \downarrow \Rightarrow \text{autonomous expenditure} \uparrow \Rightarrow Y \uparrow$$

The downward slope of the *ADI* curve, therefore, depends critically on the Bank of Canada setting high real interest rates when the inflation rate is high and low real interest rates when the inflation rate is low. Economists find it convenient to summarize this type of central bank behaviour in terms of a *monetary policy rule*. A **monetary policy rule** describes how the action a central bank takes depends on the state of the economy.[5] Here action is the central bank's choice of the real interest rate, and the state of the economy is given by the inflation rate.

Table 12.1 presents a monetary policy rule that assumes the Bank of Canada reacts only to inflation. According to the monetary policy rule given in the table, the higher the rate of inflation, the higher the real interest rate set by the Bank of Canada. This relationship is consistent with the idea that the Bank of Canada responds to an expansionary gap (which threatens to lead to increased inflation) by raising the real interest rate. Figure 12.2 shows a graph of this monetary policy rule. The vertical axis of the graph shows the real interest rate chosen by the Bank of Canada; the horizontal axis shows the rate of inflation. The upward slope of the monetary policy rule captures the idea that the Bank of Canada reacts to increases in inflation by raising the real interest rate.

What determines the shape of the Bank of Canada's monetary policy rule? A key consideration is how aggressively the Bank plans to pursue its inflation target. To illustrate,

monetary policy rule describes how the action a central bank takes in response to changes in the state of the economy depends on the state of the economy

TABLE 12.1
A Hypothetical Monetary Policy Rule for the Bank of Canada

Rate of inflation (π)	Real interest rate set by Bank of Canada (*r*)
0.00 (= 0%/year)	0.02 (= 2%)
0.01	0.03
0.02	0.04
0.03	0.05
0.04	0.06

4 As previously noted, an increase in the real interest rate will tend to strengthen the exchange rate and reduce net exports, which will add to the reduction of aggregate demand. Exchange rate issues are examined in Chapter 13.

5 An alternative term, employed in earlier editions of this textbook, is "central bank policy reaction function."

FIGURE 12.2

An Illustration of a Bank of Canada Monetary Policy Rule

This illustration of a monetary policy rule for the Bank of Canada shows the real interest rate the Bank sets in response to any given value of the inflation rate. The upward slope captures the idea that the Bank of Canada raises the real interest rate when inflation rises. The numerical values in the figure are from Table 12.1.

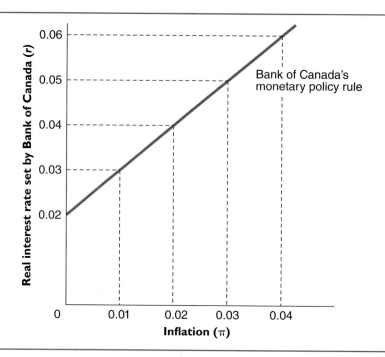

suppose that the Bank of Canada's monetary policy rule were represented with a flatter (less steep) line than the one in Figure 12.2, implying that the Bank changes the real interest rate rather modestly in response to increases or decreases in inflation. In that case, we would conclude that the Bank of Canada does not intend to be as aggressive in its attempts to offset movements of inflation away from the target level. This would roughly correspond to the Bank of Canada adopting a broader inflation-control target range; say, from 0 to 4 percent instead of from 1 to 3 percent, but with the same medium-term target of 2 percent. (As we will see later in this chapter, the adoption of a different inflation target would be shown by a shift of the Bank of Canada's monetary policy rule.)

DERIVING THE AGGREGATE DEMAND (*ADI*) CURVE

To reinforce the preceding explanation of the *ADI* curve, it is useful to derive the *ADI* curve graphically. Figure 12.3 consists of four panels. Panel (a), the lower right panel, shows the *ADI* curve. What we want to explain is the movement from *A* to *B* along the *ADI* curve in panel (a). The movement from *A* to *B* represents the inflation rate rising from π_1 to π_2 and output consequently falling from Y_1 to Y_2. Why does output drop when the inflation rate rises?

Panel (b), the lower left panel, merely serves to show that the rise in the inflation rate from π_1 to π_2 as measured along the vertical axis of panel (a) is exactly equal to the rise in the inflation rate from π_1 to π_2, as measured along the horizontal axis of panel (c).

Panel (c), the upper left panel, shows that when the inflation rate rises from π_1 to π_2, the Bank of Canada responds according to its monetary policy rule by raising the real interest rate from r_1 to r_2. There is a movement along the monetary policy rule line from *A* to *B*.

Panel (d), the upper right panel, shows that when the real interest rate rises from r_1 to r_2, the expenditure line shifts down. Equilibrium output, determined by the intersection of the 45 degree line and the expenditure line, had been Y_1 when the interest rate was r_1. But when the interest rate rose to r_2, the equilibrium output dropped to Y_2. There is a movement along the 45 degree line from *A* to *B*.

Returning to panel (a), we now see that the equilibrium output levels of Y_1 and Y_2 correspond exactly to the equilibrium output levels shown in panel (d).

FIGURE 12.3
Deriving the *ADI* Curve Graphically

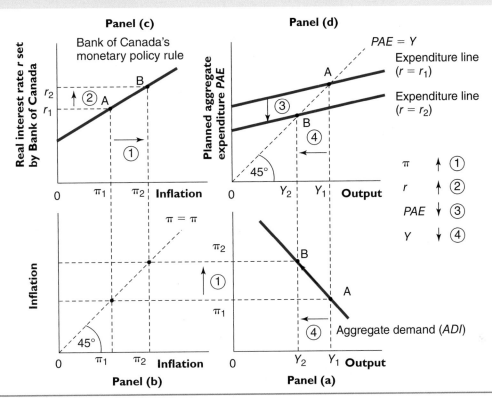

In conclusion, the movement along the *ADI* curve in panel (a) from *A* to *B* summarizes the combined impact of the movement along the monetary policy rule from *A* to *B* in panel (c) and the movement along the 45 degree line in panel (b) from *A* to *B*. In other words, it represents the chain of causation from an increase in inflation to an increase in the real interest rate (implemented by the Bank of Canada), from an increase in the real interest rate to a drop in planned aggregate expenditure, and from a drop in planned aggregate expenditure to a drop in output.

SHIFTS OF THE AGGREGATE DEMAND (*ADI*) CURVE

The downward slope of the *ADI* curve shown in Figure 12.1 and panel (a) of Figure 12.3 reflects the fact that, *all other factors held constant*, a higher level of inflation will lead to lower planned spending and lower short-run equilibrium output. However, inflation is not the only thing that can affect aggregate demand. Even if inflation is held constant, planned spending and short-run equilibrium output can change for other reasons.

Graphically, we represent the impact of these other factors as causing the *ADI* curve to shift. Specifically, for a given level of inflation, if there is a change in the economy that *increases* short-run equilibrium output, the *ADI* curve will shift to the *right*. If, on the other hand, the change *reduces* short-run equilibrium output at any given level of inflation, the *ADI* curve will shift to the *left*. Two sorts of changes can shift the aggregate demand *ADI* curve: (1) changes in spending caused by factors other than output or interest rates, which we will refer to as *autonomous* changes in spending; and (2) changes in the Bank of Canada's monetary policy, as reflected in a shift in the Bank of Canada's monetary policy rule.

Changes in Spending

We have seen that planned aggregate expenditure depends both on income (through the consumption function) and on the real interest rate (which affects both consumption and planned investment). However, many factors besides income and the real interest rate can affect planned aggregate expenditure. If, for example, if the government gets involved in a war (in Afghanistan, for example) it will have to spend more on armaments; a change in government spending that can be seen as a change in *fiscal policy*. As well, changes in consumer confidence can affect consumption spending, new technological opportunities may lead firms to increase their planned investment, or an increased willingness of foreigners to purchase domestic goods may raise net exports. We will refer to changes in planned spending that are not caused by changes in output or the real interest rate as *exogenous* changes in spending.

For a given inflation rate (and thus for a given real interest rate set by the Bank of Canada), an exogenous increase in spending raises short-run equilibrium output, for the reasons we discussed in Chapters 8 and 10. Because it increases output at each level of inflation, *an exogenous increase in spending shifts the ADI curve to the right.* This result is illustrated graphically in Figure 12.4. Imagine, for example, that there is a rise in the stock market because of optimism about new technologies and that this increase in wealth makes consumers more willing to spend. Then, for each level of inflation, aggregate spending and short-run equilibrium output will be higher, a change which is shown as a shift of the *ADI* curve to the right, from *ADI* to *ADI′*.

Similarly, at a given inflation rate, an exogenous decline in spending—for example, a fall in government purchases resulting from a more restrictive fiscal policy, or a decline in consumer spending caused by a collapse in stock prices—will cause short-run equilibrium output to fall. We conclude that *an exogenous decrease in spending shifts the ADI curve to the left.*

EXERCISE 12.1   **Determine how the following events would affect the *ADI* curve:**

a. **Due to widespread concerns about future weakness in the economy, businesses reduce their spending on new capital.**
b. **The federal government increases infrastructure spending.**

Changes in the Bank of Canada's Monetary Policy Rule

Recall that the Bank of Canada's monetary policy rule describes how the Bank of Canada sets the real interest rate at each level of inflation. This relationship is built into the *ADI* curve—indeed, it accounts for the curve's downward slope. As long as the Bank of Canada sets the real interest rate according to this monetary policy rule, its adjustments in the real rate will not cause the *ADI* curve to shift.

FIGURE 12.4

Effect of an Increase in Exogenous Spending

The *ADI* curve is seen both *before* (*ADI*) and *after* (*ADI′*) an increase in exogenous spending—specifically, an increase in consumption spending resulting from a rise in the stock market. If the inflation rate and the real interest rate set by the Bank of Canada are held constant, an increase in exogenous spending raises short-run equilibrium output. As a result, the *ADI* curve will shift to the right, from *ADI* to *ADI′*.

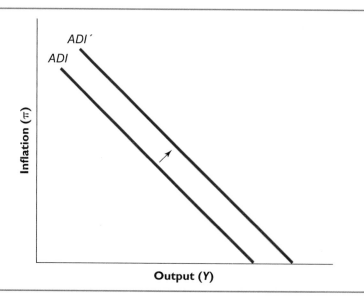

However, on occasion the Bank of Canada may choose to be "tighter" or "easier" than normal, given the rate of inflation. For example, if inflation is too high and has stubbornly refused to decrease, the Bank of Canada might choose a tighter monetary policy, setting the real interest rate higher than normal, given the rate of inflation. This change of policy can be interpreted as an upward shift in the Bank of Canada's monetary policy rule, as shown in Figure 12.5(a). A decision by the Bank of Canada to set the real interest rate at a higher level for each given rate of inflation reduces planned expenditure and, thus, short-run equilibrium output at each rate of inflation also. Why might the Bank of Canada do this? The objective of such a change in policy is to reduce the long-run target level of inflation. An important example of such a shift in the monetary policy rule occurred in 1988 when the Bank of Canada lowered its target rate of inflation. Because an upward shift of the Bank of Canada's monetary policy rule—a tightening of monetary policy—decreases aggregate demand and output at any given rate of inflation, the *ADI* curve shifts to the left, as in Figure 12.5(b).

Similarly, if the economy is experiencing an unusually severe and stubborn recession, the Bank of Canada may choose to stimulate the economy by setting the real interest rate lower than normal, given the rate of inflation. This change in policy can be interpreted as a downward shift of the Bank of Canada's monetary policy rule. Given the rate of inflation, a lower-than-normal setting of the real interest rate will increase aggregate demand and output. Therefore, a downward shift of the Bank of Canada's monetary policy rule—an easing of monetary policy—causes the *ADI* curve to shift to the right.

Note that the terms "tightening" and "easing" are generally used more broadly than they are used here. In general, any lowering of interest rates by the Bank of Canada, even down an existing monetary policy rule, would be termed easing, and any raising of interest rates by the Bank, even up an existing monetary policy rule, would be termed tightening. Tightening and easing in the sense of movements along the existing monetary policy rule are much, much more common that shifts of the monetary policy rule. The two clear shifts of the monetary policy rule of the Bank of Canada in recent decades occurred at the beginning of the 1980s under Governor Bouey and again in the late 1980s under Governor Crow.

FIGURE 12.5

A Tightening of Monetary Policy

A tightening of monetary policy implies that at any given inflation rate, the Bank of Canada sets a higher value of real interest rate than normal. Graphically, this change corresponds to an upward movement in the Bank's monetary policy rule, as in panel (a). A tightening of monetary policy shifts the *ADI* curve to the left, shown in panel (b).

(a)

(b)

EXERCISE 12.2   **What is the difference, if any, between the following?**

a. **An upward shift in the Bank of Canada's monetary policy rule.**
b. **A response by the Bank of Canada to higher inflation, for a given monetary policy rule.**

How does each scenario affect the *ADI* curve?

RECAP

THE AGGREGATE DEMAND (*ADI*) CURVE

- The *ADI* curve shows the relationship between aggregate demand (equal to short-run equilibrium output) and inflation. Higher inflation leads the Bank of Canada to raise the real interest rate, which reduces aggregate demand and short-run equilibrium output. Therefore, the *ADI* curve slopes downward.

- An increase in exogenous spending raises short-run equilibrium output at each value of inflation and so shifts the *ADI* curve to the right. Conversely, a decrease in exogenous spending shifts the *ADI* curve to the left.

- An easing of monetary policy, as reflected by a downward shift in the Bank of Canada's monetary policy rule, shifts the *ADI* curve to the right. A tightening of monetary policy, as reflected by an upward shift in the Bank of Canada's monetary policy rule, shifts the *ADI* curve to the left.

- Changes in inflation correspond to movements *along* the *ADI* curve; they do not shift the *ADI* curve.

12.2 INFLATION AND AGGREGATE SUPPLY: UNDERSTANDING THE *IA* AND *LRAS* CURVES

Until this point in the chapter, we have focused on how changes in inflation affect aggregate demand and short-run equilibrium output, a relationship captured by the *ADI* curve. The next steps are to explain the inflation-adjustment (*IA*) and long-run aggregate supply (*LRAS*) curves. We will begin with the *IA* curve, but first we must consider the topics of *inflation inertia* (which underpins the horizontal nature of the *IA* curve) and *how inflation responds to output gaps* (which underpins upward and downward shifts of the *IA* curve).

INFLATION INERTIA

In low-inflation industrial economies like that of Canada since the early 1990s, inflation tends to change relatively slowly from year to year, a phenomenon that is sometimes referred to as *inflation inertia*.[6] If the rate of inflation in one year is 1.5 percent, it may be 2 percent or even 2.5 percent in the next year. But unless the country experiences a very unusual economic shock, inflation is unlikely to rise to 4 percent or fall to 0 percent in the following year. This relatively sluggish behaviour contrasts sharply with the behaviour of economic variables such as stock or commodity prices, which can change rapidly from day to day. For example, oil prices might well rise by 20 percent over the course of a year and then fall 20 percent over the next year.

---

6 The term *inflation inertia* in economics is derived from the term *inertia* in physics. The laws of physics say that a body will tend to keep moving with a constant speed and direction unless it is acted upon by some outside force, a tendency referred to as *inertia*.

Why does inflation tend to adjust relatively slowly in modern industrial economies? To answer this question we must consider two closely related factors that play an important role in determining the inflation rate: the behaviour of the public's *inflation expectations* and the existence of *long-term wage and price contracts*.

Inflation Expectations

Let's first consider the public's expectations about inflation. In negotiating future wages and prices, both buyers and sellers take into account the rate of inflation they expect will prevail in the next few years. As a result, today's *expectations* of future inflation, in and of themselves, may help to determine the future inflation rate. Suppose, for example, that office worker Fred and his boss Colleen agree that Fred's performance this past year justifies an increase of 2 percent in his real wage for next year. What nominal wage increase should they agree on? If Fred believes that inflation is likely to be 3 percent over the next year, he will ask for a 5 percent increase in his nominal wage to obtain a 2 percent increase in his real wage. If Colleen agrees that inflation is likely to be 3 percent, she should be willing to go along with a 5 percent nominal increase, knowing that it implies only a 2 percent increase in Fred's real wage. Thus, the rate at which Fred and Colleen *expect* prices to rise affects the rate at which at least one price, Fred's nominal wage, *actually* rises.[7] A similar dynamic affects the contracts for production inputs other than labour.

Economy-wide, then, the higher the expected rate of inflation, the more nominal wages and the cost of other inputs will rise. But if wages and other costs of production grow rapidly in response to expected inflation, firms will have to raise their prices rapidly as well to cover their costs. Thus, a high rate of expected inflation tends to lead to a high rate of actual inflation. By the same logic, a moderate rate of expected inflation tends to produce a moderate rate of actual inflation, and a low rate of expected inflation tends to contribute to a low rate of actual inflation.

Assume that employers and workers both agree that real wages should rise by 2 percent next year and intend to sign collective agreements that have that effect.

a. **If the inflation rate is expected to be 2 percent next year, what will happen to nominal wages next year?**
b. **If inflation is expected to be 4 percent next year, rather than 2 percent, what will happen to nominal wages next year?**
c. **Use your answers from parts (a) and (b) to explain how an increase in expected inflation will tend to affect the following year's actual rate of inflation.**

EXERCISE 12.3

The conclusion that actual inflation is partially determined by expected inflation raises the question of what determines inflation expectations. To a great extent, people's expectations are influenced by their recent experience. If inflation has been low for some time, people are likely to expect it to continue to be low. But if inflation has recently been high, people will expect it to continue to be high. If inflation has been unpredictable, alternating between low and high levels, the public's expectations will likewise tend to be volatile, rising or falling with news or rumours about economic conditions or economic policy.

Figure 12.6 illustrates schematically how, for example, moderate inflation may tend to be self-perpetuating. As the figure shows, if inflation has been moderate for some time, people will continue to expect moderate inflation. Increases in nominal wages and other production costs will thus tend to be moderate. If firms raise prices only by enough to cover costs, then actual inflation will be moderate, as expected. This moderate actual rate

---

7 If you find the reasoning in this paragraph difficult to follow, you should review the discussion of nominal versus real variables in Chapter 6.

FIGURE 12.6

A Feedback Loop of Moderate Inflation and Moderate Expected Inflation

Moderate inflation leads people to expect moderate inflation in the future. As a result, they agree to accept moderate increases in wages and the prices of the goods and services they supply, which keeps inflation, and expected inflation, moderate.

will in turn promote moderate expected inflation, perpetuating the feedback loop. The same logic applies in an economy with high inflation and also, of course, in an economy with low inflation such as the Canadian economy since the early 1990s.

Long-Term Wage and Price Contracts

The role of inflation expectations in the slow adjustment of inflation is strengthened by a second key element, the existence of *long-term wage and price contracts*. Union wage contracts, for example, often extend for three years into the future. Likewise, contracts that set the prices manufacturing firms pay for parts and raw materials often cover a few years. Long-term contracts serve to "build in" wage and price increases that depend on inflation expectations at the time the contracts were signed.

To summarize, in the absence of external shocks, inflation tends to remain relatively stable over time, at least in low-inflation industrial economies like Canada's. In other words, inflation is *inertial*. Inflation tends to be inertial for two main reasons. The first is the behaviour of people's expectations of inflation. All else being equal, a low or moderate inflation rate leads people to expect low or moderate inflation in the future, which results in reduced pressure for wage and price increases. Similarly, a high inflation rate leads people to expect high inflation in the future, resulting in more rapid increases in wages and prices. The effects of expectations are reinforced by the existence of long-term wage and price contracts, which is the second reason inflation tends to be stable over time. Long-term contracts tend to build in the effects of people's inflation expectations.

Earlier in this chapter, in sketching an overview of the *ADI–IA* diagram, we stated that the *IA* curve is horizontal to represent the idea that inflation exhibits inertia. Now you have a fuller understanding of what inflation inertia means. Although the rate of inflation is inertial, it does, of course, change over time. We next discuss a key factor that causes the inflation rate to change, and hence for the *IA* curve to shift.

THE OUTPUT GAP AND INFLATION

An important factor that influences the rate of inflation is the output gap, or the difference between actual output and potential output $(Y - Y^*)$. We have seen that, in the short run, firms will meet the demand for their output at previously determined prices. For example, Al's ice cream shop will serve ice cream to any customer who comes into the shop, at the prices posted behind the counter. The level of output that is determined by aggregate demand at preset prices is called short-run equilibrium output.

At a particular time, the level of short-run equilibrium output may happen to equal the economy's long-run productive capacity, or potential output. But as we have seen, that is not necessarily the case. Output may exceed potential output, giving rise to an expansionary gap, or it may fall short of potential output, producing a recessionary gap. Let's consider what happens to inflation in each of these three possible cases: no output gap, an expansionary gap, and a recessionary gap.

When the output gap is zero, firms are satisfied in the sense that their sales equal their normal production rates. As a result, firms have no incentive either to reduce or increase their prices *relative* to the prices of other goods and services. However, the fact that firms are satisfied with their sales does *not* imply that inflation—the rate of change in the overall price level—is zero.

To see why, let's go back to the idea of inflation inertia. Suppose that inflation has recently been steady at 2 percent per year so that the public has come to expect an inflation rate of 2 percent per year. If the public's inflation expectations are reflected in the wage and price increases agreed to in long-term contracts, then firms will find their labour and materials costs are rising at 2 percent per year. To cover their costs, firms will need to raise their prices by 2 percent per year. Note that if all firms are raising their prices by 2 percent per year, the *relative* prices of various goods and services—say, the price of ice cream relative to the price of a taxi ride—will not change. Nevertheless, the economy-wide rate of inflation equals 2 percent, the same as in previous years. We conclude that, *if the output gap is zero, the rate of inflation will tend to remain the same.*

Suppose instead that an expansionary gap exists so that most firms' sales exceed their normal production rates. As we might expect in situations in which the quantity demanded exceeds the quantity firms desire to supply, firms will respond by trying to increase their relative prices. To do so, they will increase their prices by *more* than the increase in their costs. If all firms behave this way, then the general price level will begin to rise more rapidly than before. Thus, *when an expansionary gap exists, the rate of inflation will tend to increase.* This is why economists sometimes refer to an expansionary gap as an inflationary gap.

Finally, if a recessionary gap exists, firms will be selling less than their capacity to produce, and they will have an incentive to cut their relative prices so they can sell more. In this case, firms will raise their prices less than needed to cover fully their increases in costs, as determined by the existing inflation rate. As a result, *when a recessionary gap exists, the rate of inflation will tend to decrease.*

These important results are summarized in Box 12.1. (Note that the real-world behaviour of inflation in response to output gaps may not be as precise as suggested by Box 12.1. For example, the inflation rate may be slow to decline in response to a recessionary output gap. As well, potential output, as mentioned in Chapter 7, cannot be measured with the same precision as actual output—credible estimates of potential output can differ by tens of billions of dollars. So "no output gap" can only mean that actual and potential output are roughly equal, not that they are exactly equal.)

BOX 12.1

The output gap and inflation

Relationship of output to potential output	Behaviour of inflation
1. No output gap: $Y = Y^*$	Inflation remains unchanged
2. Expansionary gap: $Y > Y^*$	Inflation rises: $\pi \uparrow$
3. Recessionary gap: $Y < Y^*$	Inflation falls: $\pi \downarrow$

GRAPHING THE INFLATION-ADJUSTMENT CURVE AND ITS SHIFTS

We can now graph the way that inflation adjusts to the output gap with the *inflation-adjustment (IA) curve*. The **inflation adjustment (IA) curve**, as mentioned at the beginning of section 12.1, is a horizontal line that shows the current rate of inflation in the

inflation adjustment (IA) curve a horizontal line showing the current rate of inflation, as determined by past expectations and pricing decisions

FIGURE 12.7

The Inflation Adjustment Curve and its Shifts

The figure shows an inflation adjustment curve (*IA*) representing the current rate of inflation (π) with output gap (*Y* = *Y**). If the economy were experiencing an expansionary gap (*Y* > *Y**), however, the *IA* curve and the inflation rate would move upwards in the direction of the dashed *IA'* line. On the other hand, if the economy were experiencing a recessionary gap (*Y* < *Y**), the *IA* curve and the inflation rate would move downwards in the direction of the dashed *IA"* line.

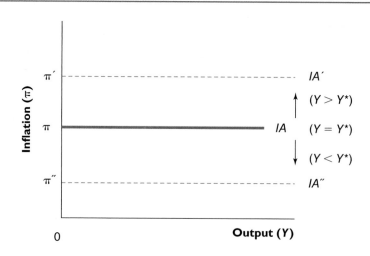

economy. We can think of the current rate of inflation as having been determined by past expectations of inflation and past pricing decisions. The inflation adjustment curve is horizontal because, in the short run, producers supply whatever output is demanded at preset prices. The *IA* curve can be viewed as a short-run aggregate supply curve for the economy was a whole.

Figure 12.7, drawn with inflation π on the vertical axis and real output *Y* on the horizontal axis, shows an inflation adjustment curve *IA* representing the current rate of inflation π when there is no output gap; that is, actual output *Y* equals potential output *Y**. If the economy were experiencing an expansionary gap (with actual output *Y* greater than potential output) however, the *IA* curve and the inflation rate would move upwards in the direction of the dashed *IA'* line. On the other hand, if the economy were experiencing a recessionary gap (with actual output less than potential output), the *IA* curve and the inflation rate would move downwards in the direction of the dashed *IA"* line.

We have now explained in detail the economics behind the *ADI* and *IA* curves, two of the three curves making up the *ADI–IA* diagram. The next step is to explain the economics behind the *LRAS* curve. Of the three curves, it is the easiest to explain.

GRAPHING LONG-RUN AGGREGATE SUPPLY AND ITS SHIFTS

Potential output, as first discussed in Chapter 7, is the amount of output (real GDP) that an economy can produce when using its resources, most notably capital and labour, at normal rates. Potential output depends, then, on the amounts of capital, labour, and other inputs, and upon factors that determine the productivity of inputs, such as education levels and technological knowledge. The representation of the **long-run aggregate supply curve** (*LRAS*) as a vertical line in Figure 12.8 says that the economy's potential output (*Y**) during a given period is independent of the inflation rate during that period. That is, the vertical *LRAS* curve means that neither increases nor decreases in the inflation rate will have any effect on potential output.

To fully understand the *LRAS* curve, we must not just understand movements along the curve (that is, that changes in the inflation rate do not affect potential output), we must also understand the factors that cause the curve to shift. *LRAS* curve shifts are caused by the factors that cause potential output to change.

A rightward shift of the *LRAS* curve, as shown in of Figure 12.8 by a shift from *LRAS* in the direction of *LRAS'*, signifies an increase in potential output caused by such factors as a rise in the size of the capital stock, an increase in the size of the labour force, or

long-run aggregate supply (LRAS) curve a relationship between potential output and the inflation rate; a vertical curve indicating that potential output is independent of the inflation rate improvements in technology. In modern developed economies, the normal pattern is for potential output to increase from one year to the next. In applying the *ADI–IA* model, it is usual to abstract from the ongoing increase in potential output and to assume, unless stated otherwise, that potential output is fixed for the period of analysis.

A leftward shift of the *LRAS* curve, as shown in Figure 12.8 by a shift from *LRAS* in the direction of *LRAS"*, signifies a decrease in potential output. Decreases in potential output could be caused by such factors as destruction of the capital stock due to war or natural disasters, reduction of agricultural capacity due to poor weather, and depletion of natural resources. Though they occur from time to time for particular towns or cities or regions (such as the northeastern region of Japan's main island, which was devastated by the earthquake, tsunami, and nuclear plant damage of March 2011), reductions of potential output for large, high-income, post-industrial economies such as Canada have been rare at the economy-wide level. What is more common is for disasters to slow the rate of growth of potential output.

FIGURE 12.8
The Long-Run Aggregate Supply Curve and its Shifts
Drawing the long-run aggregate supply (*LRAS*) curve as a vertical line represents the idea that the economy's potential output (*Y**) during a given period is independent of the inflation rate during that period. A rightward shift of the *LRAS* curve, such as the shift from *LRAS* in the direction of *LRAS'*, represents an increase in potential output, and would be caused by a factor such as improvement in technology. A leftward shift, such as the shift from *LRAS* in the direction of *LRAS"*, represents a decrease in potential output, and would be caused by a rare event such as a war that decreased the population and the capital stock.

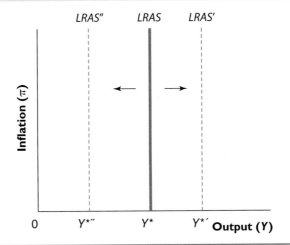

12.3 PUTTING IT ALL TOGETHER: EQUILIBRIUM IN THE *ADI–IA* MODEL

We can now put the *ADI* curve, the *IA* curve, and the *LRAS* curve together and analyze how inflation and output are determined simultaneously. Let's return to Figure 12.1. This diagram shows the economy in **long-run equilibrium**, which is the situation where actual output *Y* is equal to potential output. Graphically, this is shown where the *ADI*, *AS* curve, and *LRAS* curves intersect at a single point.

The economy does not have to be in long-run equilibrium at every point in time. The *ADI* curve and the *IA* curve can intersect at levels of output that are above or below potential output; this is called a **short-run equilibrium**. That is, the economy is in a short-run equilibrium when there is either an expansionary gap or a recessionary gap. An economy can be in short-run equilibrium, but it will not remain there. Let's examine both an expansionary gap and a recessionary gap to see why this is the case.

long-run equilibrium
a situation in which actual output equals potential output and the inflation rate is stable; graphically, occurs when the *ADI* curve, the *IA* curve, and the *LRAS* line all intersect at a single point

short-run equilibrium
a situation in which inflation equals the value determined by past expectations and pricing decisions, and output is consistent with output of that inflation rate; graphically, the intersection of the *ADI* curve and the *IA* curve

A RECESSIONARY GAP

Figure 12.9 illustrates the *ADI–IA* model of how an economy adjusts over time when it begins with a recessionary gap. The economy is initially in equilibrium at point *A* with actual output *Y* and actual inflation π. At this point, there is a recessionary gap since actual output is less than potential output. The *ADI* curve will remain at *ADI* as long as there is no change in the Bank of Canada's monetary policy rule and there are no exogenous changes in spending. The *LRAS* curve will not shift as long as there are no changes in the factors determining potential output. If the *ADI* and *LRAS* curves do not shift, how will long-run equilibrium be restored?

When a recessionary gap exists, firms are not selling as much as they would like to, and so they slow down the rate at which they increase their prices. With prices increasing more slowly, the inflation rate declines. Because of inflation inertia (caused by the slow adjustment of the public's inflation expectations and the existence of long-term contracts), inflation adjusts downward only gradually. As inflation declines, the *IA* curve moves downward, from *IA* to *IA'*. According to the Bank of Canada monetary policy rule that underlies the *ADI* curve, the central bank responds to declines in the inflation rate with interest rate cuts that stimulate consumption and private-sector investment spending. As long as a recessionary gap exists, inflation will continue to fall. The *IA* curve will move downward until it intersects the *ADI* curve at point *B* in the figure. At that point, actual output equals potential output, and the recessionary gap has been eliminated. Because there is no further pressure on inflation at point *B*, the inflation rate stabilizes at the lower level.

To recap, Figure 12.9 illustrates the important point that when a recessionary gap exists, inflation will tend to fall. It also shows that as inflation declines, short-run equilibrium output rises, increasing gradually from *Y* to *Y** as the short-run equilibrium point moves down the *ADI* curve. The source of this increase in output is the behaviour of the Bank of Canada, which lowers the real interest rate as inflation falls, stimulating aggregate demand. As output rises, cyclical unemployment, which by Okun's law (introduced in Chapter 7) is proportional to the output gap, also declines.

AN EXPANSIONARY GAP

What happens if, instead of a recessionary gap, the economy has an expansionary gap, with output greater than potential output? An expansionary gap would cause the rate of inflation to *rise* as firms respond to high demand by raising their prices more rapidly than

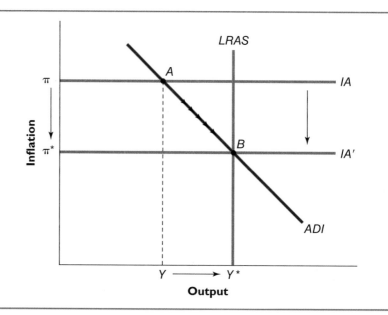

FIGURE 12.9

The Adjustment of Inflation When a Recessionary Gap Exists

At the initial short-run equilibrium point *A*, a recessionary gap exists, putting downward pressure on inflation. As inflation falls gradually, the *IA* curve moves downward until it reaches *IA'* and actual output equals potential output (point *B*). Once the recessionary gap has been eliminated, inflation stabilizes at π*, and the economy settles into long-run equilibrium at the intersection of *ADI*, *LRAS*, and *IA'* (point *B*).

their costs are rising. In graphical terms, an expansionary gap would cause the *IA* curve to move upward over time. Inflation and the *IA* curve would continue to rise until the economy reached long-run equilibrium, with actual output equal to potential output. This process is illustrated in Figure 12.10. Initially, the economy is in short-run equilibrium at point *A*, where $Y > Y^*$ (an expansionary gap). The expansionary gap causes inflation to rise over time; graphically, the inflation adjustment curve moves upward, from *IA* to *IA'*. As the *IA* curve rises, short-run equilibrium output falls, the result of the Bank of Canada's monetary policy rule of increasing the real interest rate when inflation rises. Eventually the *IA* curve intersects the *ADI* curve and *LRAS* line at point *B*, where the economy reaches long-run equilibrium, with no output gap and stable inflation.

A SELF-CORRECTING ECONOMIC MODEL?

Our analysis of Figures 12.9 and 12.10 suggests that if the monetary policy rule of the central bank is stable, the *ADI–IA* model may be *self-correcting* in the long run.[8] In other words, given enough time, output gaps generally tend to disappear as a result of a mechanism built into the model. Inflation rate changes trigger Bank of Canada interest rate changes via the Bank of Canada's given monetary policy rule. Hence expansionary output gaps tend to be eliminated by rising inflation, while recessionary output gaps tend to be eliminated by falling inflation.

This result differs somewhat from the basic Keynesian model, which does not include a self-correcting mechanism. The difference in results is explained by two facts. First, the basic Keynesian model concentrates on the short-run period, during which prices do not adjust; it does not take into account the changes in the inflation rate that occur over a longer period. Second, the basic Keynesian model does not incorporate the Bank of Canada's monetary policy rule.

Does the self-correcting character of our economic model rule out the need for active manipulation of monetary policy (that is, shifting of the central bank's monetary policy rule) or fiscal policy? The usual answer to this question has been that it depends crucially on the speed with which the self-correction process takes place. If self-correction takes place very slowly so that actual output differs from potential output for protracted periods, then active use of monetary and fiscal policies will help to stabilize output. (Recall that

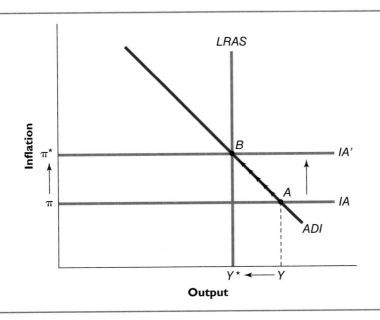

FIGURE 12.10

The Adjustment of Inflation When an Expansionary Gap Exists

At the initial short-run equilibrium point *A*, an expansionary gap exists. Inflation rises gradually (the *IA* curve moves upward), and output falls. The process continues until the economy reaches long-run equilibrium at point *B*, where inflation stabilizes and the output gap is eliminated.

8 Note that it is the model incorporating the central bank monetary policy rule that is self-correcting, not the market economy itself.

many economists, as mentioned in Chapters 8 and 10, believe that policy-makers should generally give active monetary policy a try before resorting to active fiscal policy.) But if self-correction is rapid, then the case for active stabilization policies is weaker. Indeed, if the economy returns to full employment quickly, then attempts by policy-makers to influence aggregate demand would cause actual output to "overshoot" potential output.

The speed with which a particular economy eliminates an output gap depends on a variety of factors. However, a reasonable conclusion is that the greater the initial output gap, the longer it will take for the gap to be eliminated. This observation suggests that active stabilization policies are required to remedy large gaps—such as when the unemployment rate is high. The Canadian economy, for example, recovered very slowly from the 1990–1992 recession.

The recession of 2008–2009 highlighted another answer to the question of whether the self-correcting character of the model rules out the need for active fiscal policy. During 2009, the key policy rate of the Bank of Canada, that is, the overnight rate target, was reduced to the effective lower bound. If the key policy rate is as low as it can go, then the *ADI–IA* model is no longer self-correcting in the face of a recessionary gap. The inflation rate can fall but the central bank cannot respond with interest rate cuts. In such a situation, the case for active fiscal policy is considerably strengthened.[9]

EXERCISE 12.4

Using the *ADI–IA* diagram, illustrate the short-run and long-run effects of a fall in consumer spending on inflation. How does the decline in consumer spending affect output in the short run and in the long run?

RECAP

ADI–IA AND THE SELF-CORRECTING MECHANISM

The economy is in *short-run equilibrium* when inflation equals the value determined by past expectations and pricing decisions, and when output equals the level of short-run equilibrium output that is consistent with that inflation rate. Graphically, short-run equilibrium occurs at the intersection of the *ADI* curve and the *IA* curve.

The economy is in *long-run equilibrium* when actual output equals potential output (there is no output gap) and the inflation rate is stable. Graphically, long-run equilibrium occurs when the *ADI* curve, the *IA* curve, and the *LRAS* line intersect at a common point.

Inflation adjusts gradually and, in conjunction with the Bank of Canada's monetary policy rule, this adjustment tends to bring the economy into long-run equilibrium. Hence expansionary output gaps are eliminated by rising inflation (which triggers interest rate increases by the Bank of Canada), while recessionary output gaps are eliminated by falling inflation (which triggers interest rate cuts by the Bank).

The more rapid this self-correction process, the less need there is for active stabilization policies to eliminate output gaps. In practice, attempts to eliminate output gaps through shifting the *ADI* curve are more likely to be helpful when the output gap is large than when it is small.

In unusual circumstances, the self-correction process will not work. In particular, if the key policy rate of the Bank of Canada is at the effective lower bound, the Bank cannot reduce interest rates in the face of a recessionary gap and declines in the inflation rate. In such circumstances, the case for active fiscal policy is considerably strengthened.

---

9 As briefly mentioned in earlier chapters, if neither conventional monetary policy (interest rate cuts) nor adequately expansionary fiscal policy is available, policy-makers may turn to unconventional monetary policy, as did central banks such as the U.S. Federal Reserve in the wake of the 2008–2009 recession. Unconventional monetary policy is discussed in Chapter 9.

12.4 OTHER SOURCES OF CHANGE IN INFLATION

We have seen that inflation can rise or fall in response to an output gap. But are there other factors besides output gaps that can affect the inflation rate? In this section we use the *ADI–IA* diagram to explore two other sources of inflation rate changes: *inflation shocks* and *potential output shocks*. Sharp changes in potential output and inflation shocks are both referred to as **aggregate supply shocks**.

INFLATION SHOCKS

In late 1973, at the time of the Yom Kippur War between Israel and a coalition of Arab nations, the Organization of Petroleum Exporting Countries (OPEC) sharply cut its supplies of crude oil to the industrialized nations, quadrupling world oil prices. The sharp increase in oil prices was quickly transferred to the prices of gasoline, heating oil, and goods and services that were heavily dependent on oil, such as air travel. (Figure 11.11 covers average crude oil prices from 1970 to the present.) The effects of the oil price increase, together with agricultural shortages that increased the price of food, contributed to a significant rise in the overall Canadian inflation rate in 1973–1974.[10]

The increase in inflation in 1973–1974 is an example of what is referred to as an *inflation shock*. An **inflation shock** is a sudden change in the normal behaviour of inflation, unrelated to the economy's output gap. An inflation shock that causes an increase in inflation, like the large rise in oil prices in 1973, is called an **upward inflation shock**. An inflation shock that reduces inflation, such as the sharp decline in oil prices that occurred in 1986 or the sharp decline that began in mid-2008 and continued into early 2009, is called a **downward inflation shock**.[11] Economic Naturalist 12.1 gives more details on the economic effects of inflation shocks.

aggregate supply shock either an inflation shock or a shock to potential output

www.opec.org

inflation shock a sudden change in the normal behaviour of inflation, unrelated to the nation's output gap

upward inflation shock a sudden increase in the inflation rate, unrelated to the economy's output gap

downward inflation shock a sudden decrease in the inflation rate, unrelated to the economy's output gap

---

ECONOMIC NATURALIST 12.1

Why did Canadian inflation dramatically escalate during 1973–1974 and during 1980–1981, but not in 2007–2008?

Although Canada's inflation rate increased somewhat over the 1960s, averaging around 4 percent in the latter part of the decade, the inflation rate dropped to about 3 percent in 1970 and 1971. Then Canada's inflation rate jumped to almost 8 percent in 1973 and to almost 11 percent in 1974. After subsiding to the single-digit range during 1975–1979 (following the recession of 1975 and the imposition of wage and price controls for 1975–1978), inflation surged back to double-digit levels during 1980–1981. Why did inflation increase so much during 1973–1974 and 1980–1981?

We have already described the quadrupling of oil prices in 1973 and the sharp increases in agricultural prices at about the same time, which together constituted an upward inflation shock. A second inflation shock occurred in 1979, when the turmoil of the Iranian Revolution restricted the flow of oil from the Middle East and doubled oil prices yet again.

Figure 12.11 shows the effects of an upward inflation shock on a hypothetical economy. Before the inflation shock occurs, the economy is in long-run equilibrium at point *A*, at the intersection of *ADI*,

---

10 In Chapter 6, we distinguished between relative price changes (changes in the prices of individual goods) and inflation (changes in the overall price level). In the 1973–1974 episode, changes in the price of individual categories of goods, such as energy and food, were sufficiently large and pervasive that the overall price level was significantly affected. Thus these relative price changes carried an inflationary impact as well.

11 An upward inflation shock is sometimes called an *adverse inflation shock* and a downward inflation shock is sometimes called a *favourable inflation shock*. There terms, however, not only sound normative but they are also counterintuitive in some situations. For example, if a country is suffering from deflation, an upward inflation shock (depending on circumstances) might be considered favourable, not adverse, and a downward inflation shock might be considered unfavourable.

FIGURE 12.11

The Effects of an Upward Inflation Shock

Starting from long-run equilibrium at point *A*, an upward inflation shock directly raises current inflation, causing the *IA* curve to shift upward to *IA'*. At the new short-run equilibrium, point *B*, inflation has risen to π' and output has fallen to Y', creating a recessionary gap. Without a shift in monetary policy, eventually the economy will return to point *A*, restoring the original inflation rate but suffering a long recession. The Bank of Canada could ease monetary policy, shifting the *ADI* curve to *ADI'* and restoring full employment more quickly at point *C*. The cost of this strategy is that inflation remains at its higher level.

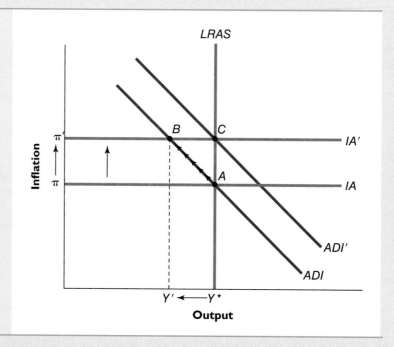

LRAS, and *IA*. At point *A*, actual output is equal to potential output Y^*, and the inflation rate is stable at π. However, an adverse inflation shock directly increases inflation so that the *IA* curve shifts rapidly upward to *IA'*. A new short-run equilibrium is established at point *B*, where *IA'* intersects the aggregate demand curve, *ADI*. In the wake of the inflation shock, inflation rises to π' and output falls from Y^* to Y'. Thus, an inflation shock creates the worst possible scenario: higher inflation coupled with a recessionary gap. The combination of inflation and recession has been referred to as stagflation, or stagnation plus inflation. The Canadian economy experienced stagflation in 1975, after the first oil shock, and again in 1980, after the second oil shock.

An upward inflation shock poses a difficult dilemma for macroeconomic policy-makers. To see why, suppose monetary and fiscal policies were left unchanged following an inflationary shock. In that case, inflation would eventually abate and return to its original level. Graphically, the economy would reach its short-run equilibrium at point *B* in Figure 12.11 soon after the inflation shock. However, because of the recessionary gap that exists at point *B*, eventually inflation would begin to drift downward, until finally the recessionary gap was eliminated. Graphically, this decline in inflation would be represented by a downward movement of the *IA* curve, from *IA'* back to *IA*. Inflation would stop declining only when long-run equilibrium was restored, at point *A* in the figure, where inflation is at its original level of π and output equals potential output.

However, although a "do nothing" policy approach would ultimately eliminate both the output gap and the surge in inflation, it would also put the economy through a deep and protracted recession, as actual output remains below potential output

until the inflation adjustment process is completed. To avoid such an economically and politically costly outcome, policy-makers might opt to eliminate the recessionary gap more quickly. By easing monetary policy, for example, the central bank could shift the *ADI* curve to the right, from *ADI* to *ADI'*, taking the economy to a new long-run equilibrium, point *C* in Figure 12.11. This expansionary policy would help to restore output to the full-employment level more quickly, but as the figure shows, it would also allow inflation to stabilize at the new, higher level.

We have explained why Canadian inflation dramatically escalated during 1973–1974 and during 1980–1981. But why did it not escalate dramatically in 2007–2008, contrary to what you might expect from examining the oil price increases in Figure 11.11? One possible reason is that production in the Canadian economy is less energy-intensive than it was three or more decades ago, so increases in oil prices now have less of an impact on other costs and, hence, other prices in the economy than in the 1970s and 1980s. Many developing countries certainly experienced notably higher inflation in 2007–2008 than Canada, where annual inflation remained within the Bank of Canada's target range. Another possible reason, one that would be favoured by proponents of inflation rate targeting, is that because of the Bank of Canada's system of inflation rate targeting, Canadians have come to trust that the Bank of Canada will keep inflation under control; even if inflation surges, people tend to expect it to be temporary and do not act as though it will become accelerating inflation. Yet another reason is that the financial crisis of 2008 sharply reduced aggregate demand in the Canadian economy before inflation could gather much force.

EXERCISE 12.5

Inflation shocks come in two kinds—upward and downward. In the 1970s, international oil prices increased dramatically, as they did in the early 1990s and the 2002–2008 period. But for most of the 1980s and 1990s, oil prices declined in real terms (as shown in Figure 11.11), and in late 2008, for example, oil prices plummeted for many months. In general, what effect would a decrease in oil prices have on output and inflation?

SHOCKS TO POTENTIAL OUTPUT

In analyzing the effects of increased oil prices on the Canadian economy in the 1970s, we assumed that potential output was unchanged in the wake of the shock. This assumption would not be reasonable for a large net exporter of oil like Saudi Arabia, for which a major oil price increase would constitute a positive shock to potential output. Nor would it be reasonable for an economy such as Japan's, which is almost totally dependent on imports for its oil supplies, and experiences a major oil price increase as a negative shock to potential output. For Japan, as oil prices rose, for example, many companies retired less energy-efficient equipment or scrapped older, gas-guzzling vehicles. This reduced the capital stock, and a smaller capital stock implied lower potential output with no offsetting increase in potential output due to the increased value of oil resources.

For an economy such as Japan's, in which increases in oil prices clearly reduced potential output, their inflationary impact would have been compounded.[12] Figure 12.12 illustrates the effects on the economy of a sudden decline in potential output. For the sake of simplicity, the figure includes only the effects of the reduction in potential output and not the direct effect of the inflation shock. (Problem 6 at the end of the chapter asks you to combine the two effects.)

Suppose once again that the economy is in long-run equilibrium at point A. Then potential output falls unexpectedly from Y^* to $Y^{*\prime}$, shifting the long-run aggregate supply line leftward from $LRAS$ to $LRAS'$. After this decline in potential output, is the economy

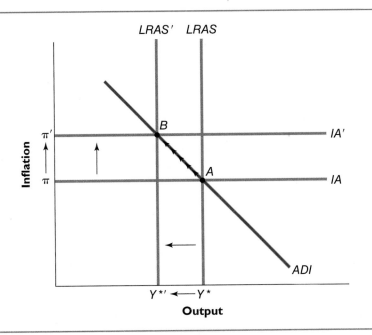

FIGURE 12.12

The Effects of a Negative Shock to Potential Output
The economy is in long-run equilibrium at point A when a decline in potential output from Y^* to $Y^{*\prime}$ creates an expansionary gap. Inflation rises, and the inflation adjustment curve shifts upward from IA to IA'. A new long-run equilibrium is reached at point B, where actual output equals the new, lower level of potential output $Y^{*\prime}$ and inflation has risen to π'. Because it is the result of a fall in potential output, the decline in output is permanent.

12 In 1974 the Canadian real growth rate fell a few percentage points to 4 percent and the inflation rate rose a few percentage points to 11 percent, whereas the Japanese real growth rate dropped over 9 percentage points to -1.4 percent and Japanese inflation almost doubled from 12 percent to 23 percent. These outcomes for the Canadian and Japanese economies had numerous causes and can be partly explained by the oil price shock substantially reducing Japan's potential output but not Canada's, hence compounding the inflationary impact for Japan.

still in long-run equilibrium at point *A*? The answer is no, because output now exceeds potential output at that point. In other words, an expansionary gap has developed. This gap reflects the fact that although planned spending has not changed, the capacity of firms to supply goods and services has been reduced.

As we have seen, an expansionary gap leads to rising inflation. In Figure 12.12, increasing inflation is represented by an upward movement of the *IA curve*. Eventually the inflation adjustment curve reaches *IA′*, and the economy reaches a new long-run equilibrium at point *B*. At that point output has fallen to the new, lower level of potential output *Y*′* and inflation has risen to *π′*.

Incidentally, a big question for macroeconomists has been to explain why the inflation shock from the rise in crude oil (see Figure 11.11) and other international commodity prices in the 2003–2008 period did not have the nearly as much impact on inflation rates in countries such as Canada as did the inflation shocks of the early and late 1970s. One explanation is that the composition of consumption in high-income countries has shifted to services and become more energy efficient so that increases in international commodity prices have less impact on the CPI. In the Canadian case, another explanation is that rising commodity prices contributed to a sharp increase in value of the Canadian currency relative to many other currencies, and hence the stronger Canadian dollar reduced the cost to Canadians of many imported goods, thereby partially offset the commodity price increases.

RECAP

OTHER SOURCES OF CHANGE IN INFLATION

In addition to falling due to recessionary gap and rising due to an expansionary gap, the inflation rate may change in response to inflation shocks or shocks to potential output; that is, due to aggregate supply shocks.

An inflation shock is a sudden change in the normal behaviour of inflation, unrelated to the nation's output gap. An example of an inflation shock is a major run-up or decrease in energy and food prices large enough to change the overall inflation rate. In the *ADI–IA* model, an upward inflation shock creates stagflation, a combination of recession and higher inflation. Stagflation poses a difficult dilemma for policy-makers. If they make no shifts in policy, eventually inflation will subside and output will recover, but in the interim the economy may suffer a protracted period of recession. If they shift monetary or fiscal policy to increase aggregate demand, they will shorten the recession but will also lock in the higher level of inflation. In the *ADI–IA* model, a downward inflation shock results in higher output and lower inflation.

A *shock to potential output* is a sharp change in potential output. Like an upward inflation shock, a negative shock to potential output results in both higher inflation and lower output. In the *ADI–IA* model, a positive shock to inflation results in both lower inflation and higher output

12.5 INFLATION CONTROL AND CANADIAN RECESSIONS

The *ADI–IA* model, which includes the assumption that the Bank of Canada follows a monetary policy rule of using interest rates to control inflation, is a useful device for explaining Canadian recessions and slowdowns. In recent decades, the Canadian economy experienced recessions in the early 1980s and the 1990–1992 period, a slowdown in 2000–2001, and another recession in 2008–2009. The role of Bank of Canada in the early 1980s and early 1990s recessions was quite different from its role in the 2000–2001 slowdown and 2008–2009 recession. The major cause the early 1980s and early 1990s recession was the role of the Bank of Canada in trying to bring the inflation rate down.

But the major cause of the 2000–2001 slowdown and 2008–2009 recession was the decline of exogenous spending.

Recessions with Monetary Tightening as the Major Cause

What can a central bank do when it decides the inflation rate is too high, as the Bank of Canada did in the early 1980s and again in the early 1990s? As Example 12.1 will show, inflation can be slowed by policies that shift the aggregate demand curve leftward. Unfortunately, if the economy is not experiencing an expansionary gap that is the cause of the high inflation, such policies are likely to impose significant short-run costs in the form of lost output and increased unemployment.

EXAMPLE **12.1**

The effects of anti-inflationary monetary policy

Suppose that, although the economy is at full employment, the inflation rate is 12 percent—too high in the estimation of policy-makers. The central bank decides to tighten monetary policy to reduce the inflation rate to 4 percent. What will happen to output, unemployment, and inflation in the short run? What will happen over the long run?

The economic effects of a monetary tightening are very different in the short run and long run. Figure 12.13(a) shows the short-run effect. Initially, the economy is in long-run equilibrium at point A, where actual output equals potential output. But at point A the inflation rate, 12 percent, is high as indicated by the inflation adjustment curve, IA.

To bring inflation down to 4 percent, what can policy-makers do? To get "tough" on inflation, the central bank must set the real interest rate at a level higher than normal, given the rate of inflation. In other words, the central bank must shift its monetary policy rule upward, as in Figure 12.5(a). At a constant rate of inflation, an increase in the real interest rate set by the central bank will reduce consumption and private-sector investment, lowering aggregate demand at every inflation rate. As we

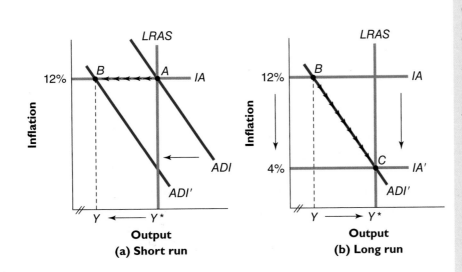

(a) Short run

(b) Long run

FIGURE 12.13

The Short-Run and Long-Run Effects of a Monetary Tightening

(a) Initially the economy is at point A, with actual output equal to potential and the inflation rate at 12 percent. If a monetary tightening by the Bank of Canada shifts the ADI curve to the left, from ADI to ADI', the economy will reach a new short-run equilibrium at point B, at the intersection of ADI' and IA. As short-run equilibrium output falls to Y, a recessionary gap opens up. (b) The recessionary gap eventually causes inflation to decline. The inflation adjustment curve moves downward, from IA to IA'. Long-run equilibrium is restored at point C. In the long run, real output returns to potential and inflation stabilizes at 4 percent.

saw earlier in the chapter, this monetary tightening by the central bank causes the *ADI* curve to shift leftward, from *ADI* to *ADI'* in Figure 12.13(a).

After the central bank's action, the *ADI'* curve and the *IA curve* intersect at point *B* in Figure 12.13(a), the new short-run equilibrium point. At point *B*, actual output has fallen to *Y*, which is less than potential output *Y**. In other words, the central bank's action has allowed a recessionary gap to develop—one result of which will be that unemployment will exceed the natural rate. At point *B*, however, the inflation rate has not changed, remaining at 12 percent. We conclude that, in the short run, a monetary tightening pushes the economy into recession but has little or no effect on the inflation rate because of inflation inertia.

The short-run effects of the monetary tightening—lower output, higher unemployment, and little or no reduction of inflation—are, to say the least, not very encouraging, and they explain why tight monetary policies tend to be particularly unpopular in their early stages. We have not reached the end of the story, however, because the economy will not remain at point *B* indefinitely. The reason is that the existence of a recessionary gap at that point eventually causes inflation to decline, as firms become more reluctant to raise their prices in the face of weak demand.

Graphically, the eventual decline in inflation that results from a recessionary gap is represented by the downward movement of the inflation-adjustment curve, from *IA* to *IA'* in Figure 12.13(b). Inflation will continue to fall until the economy returns to long-run equilibrium at point *C*. At that point, actual output has returned to potential and the inflation rate has stabilized at 4 percent. So we see that, according to our model, a tight monetary policy imposes a potentially large but temporary cost (a bout of depressed output and higher unemployment) for achieving the benefit of a lower equilibrium level of inflation. Similar results arise if fiscal rather than monetary policy is used to reduce aggregate demand.

We have phrased the discussion surrounding Figure 12.13(b) in abstract terms about a central bank reducing inflation from 12 percent to 4 percent. However, the facts roughly fit the disinflation in Canada during the early 1980s under Bank of Canada Governor Gerald Bouey, when inflation was brought down from almost 12 percent to about 4 percent. With different inflation numbers, Figure 12.13 could also be used to analyze Canada's disinflation of the early 1990s, when the Bank of Canada under Governor John Crow reduced Canada's inflation rate from a trend rate of about 4 percent to a trend rate of about 2 percent. In both cases, real GDP growth turned negative during the recession and the annual unemployment rate soared from 7.5 percent before the period of disinflation to a peak of over 11 percent.

The Crow disinflation, incidentally, was much more controversial than the Bouey disinflation for two reasons. First, the reduction of the trend inflation rate from about 4 percent to 2 percent under Crow was widely seen as much less desirable than the reduction of inflation from about 12 percent to 4 percent under Bouey. The extent of the reduction in the inflation rate is measured by the size of the downward shift of the *IA* curve in Figure 12.13. Second, the Crow disinflation was associated with a longer recession than the Bouey disinflation. In terms of Figure 12.13, a longer recession means that the *IA* takes a longer time to shift down to the new long-run equilibrium, meaning that the cumulative amount of lost output is greater for any given shift of the *ADI* curve.

A Downturn and a Recession with Changes in Exogenous Spending as the Major Cause

Prior to the 2000–2001 downturn and the 2008–2009 recession, the Bank of Canada did not launch an inflation-reduction campaign with a new monetary policy rule as it had done in the early 1980s and again in the early 1990s.[13] The key factor in the 2000–2001

---

13 The Bank of Canada did raise interest rates in advance of the downturn in 2000–2001 and the recession of 2008–2009, but in accordance with its given monetary policy rule. It is common for central banks near the peak of a boom to judge that the economy is experiencing or is on the verge of experiencing an expansionary gap and that interest rate hikes are required. This is what the U.S. economist Rudiger Dornbusch had in mind when he declared in 1997 that, "None of the U.S. expansions of the past 40 years died in bed of old age; every one was murdered by the Federal Reserve."

slowdown was the drop in private-sector investment (associated with a slowdown in the global economy and a stock market crash), and the key factors in the 2008–2009 recession were the slowdown in private investment spending and the drop in net exports.[14] The 2000–2001 slowdown and the 2008–2009 recession can both be illustrated with a figure similar to Figure 12.13. The difference from Example 12.1 would be that the leftward shift of the *ADI* curve in Figure 12.13 (a) was not the result of the Bank of Canada changing to a more anti-inflation monetary rule, but due to a reduction in exogenous spending led by a reduction in private-sector investment in 2000–2001, and a reduction in both private-sector investment and net exports in 2008–2009. The reduction in exogenous spending creates a recessionary gap and downward pressure on the inflation rate. The Bank of Canada responded to the 2000–2001 recession with interest rate cuts, as explained in the anecdote that begins this chapter. In the 2008–2009 recession, interest rate cuts were limited by the effective lower bound, and monetary policy was supplemented by discretionary fiscal policy pursued by the Department of Finance.

RECAP

INFLATION CONTROL AND CANADIAN RECESSIONS

Inflation can be reduced by policies that shift the *ADI* curve leftward, such as a move to a tighter monetary policy (an upward shift in the monetary policy rule). In the short run, the effects of an anti-inflationary monetary policy are felt largely on output, so that a disinflation (a substantial reduction in inflation) may create a significant recessionary gap. These predictions appear to have been borne out during the Bouey disinflation of the early 1980s and the Crow disinflation of the early 1990s.

Recessions can also be caused by reductions in exogenous spending that shift the *ADI* curve leftward. For example, the 2008–2009 recession was associated with sharp reductions in private-sector investment and net exports. The leftward shift of the *ADI* curve creates a recessionary gap, downward pressure on the inflation rate, and interest rate cuts by the Bank of Canada that serve to reduce the recessionary gap.

ECONOMIC NATURALIST 12.2

Why do central banks aim for positive, not zero, inflation?

As mentioned numerous times in this textbook, the Bank of Canada has an inflation target of 2 percent. The Bank would be alarmed if Canada's inflation rate were to drop below 1 percent and would take vigorous countermeasures to bring inflation back up to 2 percent. Other central banks with explicit inflation targets, such as those of the United Kingdom, Australia, South Korea, China and Brazil generally have inflation targets of 2 percent or higher. For example, in 2008 those of South Korea, Brazil, and China were 3, 4.5, and 4.8 percent respectively. A similar pattern of low to moderate positive inflation targets seems to hold for most major central banks without explicit inflation targets, such as the U.S. Federal Reserve. The Bank of England's inflation target of 2 percent is on the low side, and its governor, Mervyn King, had been aggressive through the 2000s in keeping inflation low. Yet even King has referred to those who are obsessed with inflation fighting, which would presumably include advocates of zero inflation, as "inflation nutters."[15]

---

14 The data appendix at the back of this textbook provides information on the shares of consumption, private-sector investment, government purchases, and net exports in Canadian GDP for the years from 1976 through to 2010.

15 Governor King's use of the phrase "inflation nutters" was cited approvingly by U.S. Federal Reserve Chairman (then governor) Ben Bernanke in "A Perspective on Inflation Targeting," Annual Washington Policy Conference of the National Association of Business Economists, 25 March 2003, http://www.federalreserve.gov/Boarddocs/Speeches/2003/20030325/default.htm.

But why shouldn't a central bank's inflation target be zero? At least three reasons have been offered.

One is that some economists believe that positive inflation is necessary to "grease" the economic engine. Technological change and shifts in product demand may require real wages in some industries or occupations to fall, even as real wages in other industries are rising, in order to facilitate economic adjustment. If inflation is positive, a worker's real wage will fall whenever the worker's nominal wage rises by less than the rate of inflation. If, for example, the worker's nominal wage rises by 2 percent but inflation is 3 percent, then the worker's real wage has fallen. If, however, inflation is zero, the only way in which the worker's real wage can fall is if the worker's nominal wage itself falls. Some evidence suggests that workers will resist cuts in their nominal wage much more strenuously than they will cuts in their real wage. Consequently, inflation can provide the "grease" for reducing real wages in some industries and occupations, thereby facilitating economic adjustment. This justification for a positive inflation target was mentioned in Chapter 6 and referred to as the downward nominal wage rigidity hypothesis.

A second reason for not having an inflation target of zero is that there are times when the central bank may wish to counteract negative shocks to the economy with a negative real interest rate, and this requires that inflation be greater than zero. Recall that the real interest rate is the nominal interest rate minus the rate of inflation. Thus, a negative real interest rate requires setting a nominal interest rate at less than inflation. If inflation is zero or less than zero, however, a negative real interest rate would require a negative nominal interest rate. With extremely rare exceptions, banks will hold onto their funds rather than lend them out at a negative nominal interest rate (which is like paying people to borrow from you). Consequently, a negative real interest rate must be accompanied by inflation greater than zero. This argument for a positive inflation target was discussed in Chapter 6 in connection with the zero bound on nominal interest rates hypothesis. The argument was also mentioned in Chapter 10 and earlier in this chapter in connection with the Bank of Canada's effective lower bound on the overnight rate target.

A third argument against a zero inflation target acknowledges that, since hitting the target at all times is impossible in practice, having an inflation target of zero (as opposed to 2 percent or higher) greatly increases the risk that the economy will experience periods of deflation (negative inflation). The deflationary experiences of Canada and other countries in the Great Depression of the 1930s and more recently in Japan, illustrate that deflation can be difficult to stop once it starts, and it can lead to painfully slow or negative economic growth. (See Economic Naturalist 7.1 on Japan's "lost decade.") For these reasons, central banks prefer to reduce the risk of deflation by choosing an inflation target safely above zero percent.

12.6 LIMITATIONS OF THE *ADI–IA* MODEL

As mentioned in the introduction to this chapter, our aggregate demand–inflation adjustment (*ADI–IA*) model is a major improvement on the basic Keynesian model of Chapters 8 and 10, primarily because it allows us to analyze the process of inflation. Still, our *ADI–IA* model has a number of possible limitations. We will discuss three of them.

First, the *LRAS* curve may not always be best represented by a thin vertical line (see Figure 12.14). One question relates to the width of the vertical *LRAS* line. Depicting *LRAS* as a thin line amounts to saying that potential output (Y^* in Figure 12.14) can be precisely estimated. But, as we saw in Chapter 7, there is no single, widely accepted calculation of the level of Canada's potential output for any given year. Instead, different economists, even economists in different branches of the same government, support different estimates of potential output, with the estimates possibly differing by tens of billions of dollars or more (see Example 7.1). The fact that potential output cannot be precisely estimated suggests that it might be better to think of *LRAS* not as a thin vertical line but as a thick line or band, as shown in Figure 12.14. If this is the case, there may be a range of levels of actual output that are compatible with inflation rate stability. Figure 12.14 also illustrates the possibility that the *LRAS* curve may not be vertical above a high threshold level of inflation or below a low threshold. The arguments that an exceptionally high rate of inflation or an exceptionally low rate of inflation (e.g., deflation) could have a negative impact on the productive capacity of the economy were mentioned in Chapter 6.

FIGURE 12.14

Questions about the Traditional Vertical *LRAS* Curve

Citing the imprecision of potential output estimates, some economists have questioned the practice of representing *LRAS* by a thin vertical line as opposed to a band. It has also been argued that as inflation enters a very high range, further increases in the rate may reduce potential output. Similarly, when inflation enters a very low range, potential output may be reduced if it decreases further.

Another limitation of our *ADI–IA* model is that the assumption of fixed potential output complicates the task of applying the model to actual economic events. In the model, the "short run" is the time period during which inflation inertia prevails. If inflation inertia no longer prevails, then the inflation adjustment curve shifts, and "long run" analysis applies. The level of potential output, however, is fixed not just in the short run, when inflation inertia prevails, but also in the long run, during which output gaps are eliminated by the self-correcting mechanism.

What complication arises from the assumption that potential output is fixed? In the real world, inflation inertia may apply for periods of more than a year, and it may take as much as two years for an economy to move out of a recession. But potential output changes from year to year and even from quarter to quarter. For example, International Monetary Fund estimates show Canada's potential output expanding at an annual rate of 2.5 percent in recent years. So, because potential output changes continually, our *ADI–IA* model suffers from one of the same limitations as our simple Keynesian model (a limitation noted in Chapter 10). That is, both models deal with actual output going up or down relative to a fixed level of potential output. But real-world economic policy debates are about the growth of actual output increasing or declining relative to a positive-trend rate of potential output growth.[16]

Recognizing the significance of the fixed potential output assumption in the *ADI–IA* model helps to explain why recessionary gaps typically persist much longer than do traditionally defined recessions. A recession is typically defined as a period in which the real GDP growth of an economy declines for at least two consecutive quarters; the subsequent recovery is considered to have commenced when real GDP growth picks up again. But a recessionary gap exists any time that actual output falls below potential output. So even after real GDP growth has picked up again, it may take some years of relatively faster growth (at rates that exceed the continuing expansion of potential output) before the recessionary gap is fully closed.

For example, the Canadian economy entered a recession in 1990 when real GDP growth fell to 0.3 percent. The economy sank deeper into recession in 1991 when real GDP fell by −1.9 percent, and it was still in recession during much of 1992 when the real GDP growth rate was 0.9 percent. By 1993, the real GDP growth rate was 2.3 percent and

www.imf.org
International
Monetary Fund

16 This type of *ADI–IA* model can be modified so that real GDP on the horizontal axis is expressed as percentage deviation from potential GDP, which is not assumed to be fixed. See John Taylor and David Johnson, *Principles of Macroeconomics*, Canadian edition, (Toronto: Nelson, 1997), Chapter 30.

the economy was no longer in recession. But a recessionary gap still persisted for a few more years (at least according to the International Monetary Fund). Similarly, in 2010 the Canadian economic growth had recovered from the recession of 2008–2009 but the unemployment rate still stood at 8 percent.

Indeed, since potential output is growing all the time (thanks to population growth and technological advances), a recessionary gap can open up even when no recession has taken place. If real GDP continued to grow, but at an unusually slow rate that was less than the ongoing growth of potential output, then a recessionary gap would gradually emerge between actual and potential output. Once again, a sustained period of faster-than-normal growth would be required to close the gap.

Finally, a third limitation of the *ADI–IA* model is that the way that the Bank of Canada responds to changes in inflation is somewhat more complex than we have recognized with the *ADI–IA* model. For example, we have not distinguished total CPI inflation from core inflation but, as noted in Chapter 10, the Bank of Canada states that is uses core inflation as an operating guide to its monetary policy decisions. In addition, and this was also noted in Chapter 10, the Bank of Canada's interest rate changes operate on aggregate demand with a lag, so the Bank of Canada does not respond just to current inflation but also to its projections about inflation in the coming months.

> **RECAP**
>
> ### LIMITATIONS OF THE *ADI–IA* MODEL
>
> Representing the LRAS curve as a thin vertical line is a possible limitation of the *ADI–IA* model. Because potential output cannot be precisely estimated, it might be better to think of *LRAS* not as a thin vertical line but as a thick line or band. Also, above some high threshold level the *LRAS* might bend upward to the left, and below some low threshold level it might bend downward to the left.
>
> A second limitation of the *ADI–IA* model is its assumption that potential output is fixed. In the real world, potential output continues to expand during a recession as the economy stagnates. To close the recessionary gap, it is not sufficient to bring actual output back to the level of potential output prevailing before the recession. It is necessary to bring actual output to the economy's current level of potential output, which has kept growing from year to year.
>
> A third limitation of the *ADI–IA* model is that the model as presented in this chapter has ignored the distinction between total and core CPI inflation, and it has ignored the distinction between current and projected inflation.

SUMMARY

- The *aggregate demand (ADI) curve* shows the relationship between aggregate demand and inflation. Because short-run equilibrium output is equal to planned spending, the aggregate demand curve also relates short-run equilibrium output to inflation. Since increases in inflation reduce both planned spending and short-run equilibrium output, the aggregate demand curve is downward sloping in a diagram with inflation on the vertical axis and output on the horizontal axis. **LO1**

- The inverse relationship of inflation and short-run equilibrium output is the result of the behaviour of the Bank of Canada. To keep inflation low, the Bank of Canada reacts to rising inflation by increasing the real interest rate. A higher real interest rate reduces consumption and planned private-sector investment, lowering planned aggregate expenditure and thus short-run equilibrium output. **LO1**

- For a given value of inflation, an autonomous increase in spending (that is, an increase in spending at given levels of output and the real interest rate) raises short-run equilibrium output, shifting the *ADI* curve to the right. The *ADI* curve can also be shifted by a change in the Bank of Canada's monetary policy rule. If the Bank of Canada gets "tougher," choosing a higher real interest rate at each level of inflation, the aggregate demand curve will shift to the left. If the Bank of Canada gets "easier," setting a lower real interest rate at each level of inflation, the *ADI* curve will shift to the right. **LO1**

■ In an industrial economy like Canada's, inflation tends to be inertial, or slow to adjust to changes in the economy. This inertial behaviour reflects the fact that inflation depends in part on people's expectations of future inflation, which in turn depend on their recent experience with inflation. Long-term wage and price contracts tend to "build in" the effects of people's expectations for multiyear periods. Reflecting inflation inertia, the *inflation adjustment (IA) line* is a horizontal line that shows the current rate of inflation, as determined by past expectations and pricing decisions. **LO2**

■ Although inflation is inertial, it does change over time in response to output gaps. An expansionary gap tends to raise the inflation rate, because firms raise their prices more quickly when they are facing demand that exceeds their normal productive capacity. In the presence of an expansionary gap, the *IA* line shifts upward. A recessionary gap tends to reduce the inflation rate, as firms become more reluctant to raise their prices. In the presence of a recessionary gap, the *IA* line shifts downward. **LO2**

■ Drawing the long-run aggregate supply (*LRAS*) curve as a vertical line represents the idea that the economy's potential output (*Y**) during a given period is independent of the inflation rate during that period. *LRAS* curve shifts are caused by the factors that cause potential output to change. A rightward shift of the *LRAS* curve is an increase in potential output and would be caused by a factor such as improvement in technology. A leftward shift of the *LRAS* curve is a decrease in potential output. **LO2**

■ In the *ADI–IA* model, the economy is in *short-run equilibrium* when inflation equals the value determined by past expectations and pricing decisions, and output equals the level of short-run equilibrium output that is consistent with that inflation rate. Graphically, short-run equilibrium occurs at the intersection of the *ADI* curve and the *IA* curve. If an output gap exists, however, the inflation rate will adjust in a way that promotes the elimination of the gap. Graphically, the *IA* curve moves upward or downward as needed to restore output to its full-employment level. When the inflation rate is stable and actual output equals potential output, the economy is in *long-run equilibrium*. Graphically, long-run equilibrium corresponds to the common intersection point of the *ADI* curve, the *IA* curve, and the *LRAS* line. **LO3**

■ If an economic model tends to move toward long-run equilibrium as a result of factors incorporated into the model, it is said to be self-correcting. The more rapid the self-correction process, the smaller the need for active fiscal policies (or shifts in the central bank's monetary policy rule) to eliminate output gaps. In practice, the larger the output gap, the stronger the case for implementing active monetary or fiscal policies. The case for expansionary fiscal policy is strong in the unusual instance, as experienced in Canada in 2009, that there is a recessionary gap and the Bank of Canada's key policy rate is at the effective lower bound. **LO3**

■ One source of changing inflation is the existence of output gaps: recessionary gaps cause inflation to fall, expansionary gaps cause inflation to rise. Aggregate supply shocks are another source. *Aggregate supply shocks* include both *inflation shocks*—sudden changes in the normal behaviour of inflation—and shocks to potential output. **LO4**

■ To achieve a lower inflation target, as the Bank of Canada sought to do prior to the recessions of the early 1980s and early 1990s, policy-makers typically must shift the aggregate demand curve to the left; for example, through "tight" monetary policy. In the short run, the main effects of a reduction in aggregate demand are reduced output and higher unemployment, as the economy experiences a recessionary gap. Recessions can also arise, as in 2008–2009, because of reductions in exogenous spending. **LO5**

■ The *ADI–IA* model of this chapter has at least three possible limitations. First, the representation of the *LRAS* curve by a thin vertical line may be questioned. The range of actual output levels corresponding to the situation of "no output gap" may be wide. Second, the *LRAS* curve may not be vertical above a high threshold level of inflation or below a low threshold. In the *ADI–IA* model, potential output is fixed in the "long run" during which a recessionary gap will tend to be eliminated by a self-correcting process, but in the real world potential output will be expanding noticeably while the correcting process is taking place. Third, the model as presented in this chapter has ignored the distinction between total and core CPI inflation, and it has ignored the distinction between current and projected inflation. **LO6**

KEY TERMS

aggregate demand (*ADI*) curve (293)
aggregate supply shock (309)
downward inflation shock (309)

inflation adjustment (*IA*) curve (303)
inflation shock (309)
long-run aggregate supply (*LRAS*) curve (304)

long-run equilibrium (305)
monetary policy rule (295)
short-run equilibrium (305)
upward inflation shock (309)

REVIEW QUESTIONS

1. What two variables are related by the aggregate demand (*ADI*) curve? Give an economic explanation of the slope of the curve. **LO1**

2. State how each of the following affects the *ADI* curve, and explain. **LO1**
   a. An increase in government purchases.
   b. A cut in taxes.
   c. A decline in planned investment spending by firms.
   d. A decision by the Bank of Canada to lower the real interest rate at each level of inflation.

3. Recent years have seen sharp increases in oil and grain prices. Why does the overall rate of inflation tend to adjust more slowly than prices of commodities, such as oil or grain? **LO2**

4. Discuss the relationship between output gaps and inflation. How is this relationship captured in the aggregate demand–inflation adjustment diagram? **LO2, LO3**

5. Sketch an aggregate demand–inflation adjustment diagram depicting an economy away from long-run equilibrium. Indicate the economy's short-run equilibrium point. Discuss how the economy reaches long-run equilibrium over a period of time. Illustrate the process in your diagram. **LO3**

6. True or false, and explain: The existence of a central bank monetary policy rule makes active use of stabilization policy unnecessary. **LO3**

7. What factors led to increased inflation in Canada during 1973–1974 and 1980–1981? **LO4**

8. Why does an upward inflation shock pose a particularly difficult dilemma for policy-makers? **LO4**

9. How does a very tight monetary policy, such as that conducted by the Bank of Canada in the late 1980s and early 1990s, affect output, inflation, and the real interest rate in the short run? In the long run? **LO5**

10. Summarize three limitations of the *ADI–IA* model. **LO6**

PROBLEMS

1. We saw in Chapter 10 that short-run equilibrium output falls when the Bank of Canada raises the real interest rate. Suppose the relationship between short-run equilibrium output Y and the real interest rate r set by the Bank of Canada is given by

$$Y = 1000 - 1000r.$$

Suppose also that the Bank of Canada's monetary policy rule is the one shown in Table 12.1. For whole-number inflation rates between zero and 4 percent, find the real interest rate set by the Bank of Canada and the resulting short-run equilibrium output. Graph the aggregate demand curve numerically. **LO1**

2. For the economy in Problem 1, suppose that potential output $Y^* = 960$. From the monetary policy rule in Table 12.1, what can you infer about the Bank of Canada's objective for the inflation rate in the long term? **LO1**

3. An economy's aggregate demand curve (the relationship between short-run equilibrium output and inflation) is described by the equation

$$Y = 13\ 000 - 20\ 000\pi.$$

Initially, the inflation rate is 4 percent, or $\pi = 0.04$. Potential output Y^* equals 12 000. **LO3**
   a. Find inflation and output in short-run equilibrium.
   b. Find inflation and output in long-run equilibrium.

Show your work.

4. (More difficult.) This problem asks you to trace out the adjustment of inflation when the economy starts off with an output gap. **LO3**
   a. Suppose that the economy's aggregate demand curve is

$$Y = 1000 - 1000\pi,$$

where Y is short-run equilibrium output and π is the inflation rate, measured as a decimal. Potential output Y^* equals 950, and the initial inflation rate is 10 percent ($\pi = 0.10$). Find output and inflation for this economy in short-run equilibrium and in long-run equilibrium.
   b. Suppose that, each quarter, inflation adjusts according to the following rule:

This quarter's inflation = Last quarter's inflation − 0.0004 × Last quarter's output gap.

Starting from the initial value of 10 percent for inflation, find the value of inflation for each of the next four quarters. Does inflation come close to its long-run value?

5. For each of the following, use an *ADI–IA* diagram to show the short-run and long-run effects on output and inflation. Assume the economy starts in long-run equilibrium. **LO3, LO4, LO5**
   a. An increase in autonomous consumption.
   b. A reduction in taxes.
   c. An easing of monetary policy by the Bank of Canada (a downward shift in the monetary policy rule).
   d. A sharp drop in oil prices.
   e. A war that raises government purchases.

6. Suppose that a permanent increase in oil prices both creates an inflationary shock and reduces potential output. Use an *ADI–IA* diagram to show the effects of the oil price increase on output and inflation in the short run and the long run, assuming that there is no policy response. What happens if the Bank of Canada responds to the oil price increase by tightening monetary policy? **LO4, LO5**

ANSWERS TO IN-CHAPTER EXERCISES

12.1 a. At the current level of inflation, output, and the real interest rate, an exogenous reduction in business spending on new capital will reduce planned investment, causing a decline in overall aggregate expenditures, and a reduction in short-run equilibrium output. Because output has fallen for a given level of inflation, the decrease in business spending leads to a leftward shift in the *ADI* curve. **LO1**

   b. At the current level of inflation, output, and the real interest rate, an increase in infrastructure spending amounts to an increase in *G*, government purchases. The increase in G increases overall aggregate expenditures and leads to an increase in short-run equilibrium output. Because output has increased for a given level of inflation, the increase in infrastructure spending leads to a rightward shift in the *ADI* curve. **LO1**

12.2 a. An upward shift in the Bank of Canada's monetary policy rule means that the Bank of Canada is raising the real interest rate associated with a given level of inflation. An increase in the real interest rate causes both consumption and planned private-sector investment spending to fall, reducing overall aggregate expenditures and short-run equilibrium output. Thus, a shift in the Bank of Canada's monetary policy rule causes the output level to fall for a given level of inflation, resulting in a leftward shift in the *ADI* curve. **LO1**

b. The Bank of Canada's monetary policy rule illustrates that the Bank of Canada responds to rising inflation rates by raising the real interest rate (a move *along* the monetary policy rule), which causes a reduction in overall aggregate expenditures and short-run equilibrium output. However, in this case the Bank of Canada's response to higher inflation causes a *move along* a given *ADI* curve. **LO1**

Note that while the two actions may appear to be similar, there is a key difference. In the first case the Bank of Canada is changing its policy rule for a *given inflation rate,* while in the second case the Bank of Canada is responding to a *changing inflation rate.* Changes in aggregate spending for a given inflation rate shift the *ADI* curve, while changes in aggregate spending resulting from Bank of Canada policy responses to a rise or fall in inflation lead to moves along a given *ADI* curve.

12.3 a. If inflation is expected to be 2 percent next year and workers are expecting a 2 percent increase in their real wages, then they will expect, and ask for, a 4 percent increase in their nominal wages. **LO2**

b. If inflation is expected to be 4 percent next year, rather than 2 percent, workers will expect, and ask for, a 6 percent increase in their nominal wages. **LO2**

c. If wage costs rise, firms will need to increase the prices of their goods and services to cover their increased costs, leading to an increase in inflation. In part b, when expected inflation was 4 percent, firms will be faced with larger increases in nominal wages than in part a, when expected inflation was only 2 percent. Thus, we can expect firms to raise prices by more when expected inflation is 4 percent than when expected inflation is 2 percent. From this example, we can conclude that increased inflationary expectations lead to higher inflation. **LO2**

12.4 The effects will be illustrated in a figure similar to Figure 12.13. Beginning in a long-run equilibrium with output equal to potential output and stable inflation (that is, where the *ADI* curve intersects both the *IA* and *LRAS* lines, the fall in consumption spending will initially lead to a leftward shift in the *ADI* curve and the economy moves to a new, lower, short-run equilibrium output level at the same inflation rate. The shift in *ADI* creates a recessionary gap, since Y is now less than Y^*. The immediate effect of the decrease in consumption spending is only to reduce output. However, over time inflation will fall because of the recessionary gap. As inflation falls the *IA* curve will shift downward. The Bank of Canada responds to the fall in inflation by reducing real interest rates, leading to an increase in aggregate expenditure and output, a move down along the new *ADI* curve. When inflation has fallen enough (and real interest rates have fallen enough) to eliminate the output gap, the economy will be back in long-run equilibrium where output equals potential output, but the inflation rate will be lower than before the fall in consumption spending. **LO3**

12.5 A decrease in oil prices is an example of a downward inflation shock and the economic effects of such a shock are the reverse of those illustrated in Figure 12.11. In this case, starting from a long-run equilibrium where output equals potential output, a downward inflation shock reduces current inflation, causing the *IA* curve to shift downward. The downward shift in the *IA* curve leads to a short-run equilibrium with lower inflation and higher output, creating an expansionary gap. If the Bank of Canada does nothing, eventually the *IA* will begin to shift upward and the economy will return to its original inflation and output levels. However, the Bank of Canada may instead choose to tighten its monetary policy by shifting up its monetary policy rule, raising the current real interest rate, shifting the *ADI* curve to the left and restoring equilibrium at potential GDP, but at the new, lower inflation rate. **LO4**

APPENDIX 12A
The Algebra
of the *ADI–IA* Model

In this appendix we will derive the aggregate demand (*ADI*) curve algebraically. Then we will show how together the *ADI* and the inflation adjustment curve determine the short-run and long-run equilibrium points of the economy.

THE *ADI* CURVE

In the appendix to Chapter 10, Equation 10A.1 showed that short-run equilibrium output depends on both exogenous components of expenditure and the real interest rate:

$$Y = \left(\frac{1}{1 - mpc}\right)[\overline{C} - mpc\overline{T} + \overline{I} + \overline{G} + \overline{NX} - (a + b)r],$$

where $1/(1 - mpc)$ is the multiplier, $\overline{C} - mpc\overline{T} + \overline{I} + \overline{G} + \overline{NX}$ is the exogenous component of planned spending, the term in brackets is autonomous expenditure, and a and b and are positive numbers that measure the effect of changes in the real interest rate on consumption and planned private-sector investment, respectively.

The *ADI* curve incorporates the behaviour of the Bank of Canada, as described by its monetary policy rule. According to its monetary policy rule, when inflation rises, the Bank of Canada raises the real interest rate. Thus the Bank of Canada's monetary policy rule can be written as an equation relating the real interest rate r to inflation π:

$$r = \overline{r} + g\pi, \tag{12A.1}$$

where $\overline{r}$ and g are positive constants chosen by Bank of Canada officials. This equation states that when inflation π rises by 1 percentage point—say, from 2 to 3 percent per year—the Bank of Canada responds by raising the real interest rate by g percentage points. So, for example, if $g = 0.5$, an increase in inflation from 2 to 3 percent would lead the Bank of Canada to raise the real interest rate by 0.5 percentage points. The intercept term $\overline{r}$ tells us at what level the Bank of Canada would set the real interest rate if inflation happened to be zero (so that the term $g\pi$ dropped out of the equation).

We can combine the equation for short-run equilibrium output with the equation for the monetary policy rule by substituting the right-hand side of Equation 12A.1 for the real interest rate r in the above-mentioned Equation 10A.1:

$$Y = \left(\frac{1}{1 - mpc}\right)[\overline{C} - mpc\overline{T} + \overline{I} + \overline{G} + \overline{NX} - (a + b)(\overline{r} + g\pi)]. \tag{12A.2}$$

This equation, which is the general algebraic expression for the *ADI* curve, summarizes the link between inflation and short-run equilibrium output, as shown graphically in Figure 12.1. Equation 12A.2 implies that an increase in inflation π reduces short-run equilibrium output Y, so that the *ADI* curve is downward sloping.

For a numerical illustration of this equation, we can assume that $\overline{C} = 640$, $\overline{T} = 250$, $\overline{I} = 250$, $\overline{G} = 300$, $\overline{NX} = 20$, $mpc = 0.8$, $a = 400$, and $b = 600$. To derive the *ADI* curve, we also need the parameters for the Bank of Canada's monetary policy rule. Table 12.1 related the Bank of Canada's choice of the real interest rate to the inflation rate. To express the relationship in the table in the form of an equation, note that when inflation π equals zero, the real interest rate r equals 2 percent. Therefore the constant term in the Bank of Canada's monetary policy rule, $\bar{r}$, equals 2 percent, or 0.02. Second, Table 12.1 shows that the real interest rate rises one point for each point that inflation rises; therefore the slope of the reaction function, g, equals 1.0. Substituting these numerical values into Equation 12A.2 and simplifying, we get the following numerical equation for the *ADI* curve:

$$Y = 5[640 - 0.8(250) + 250 + 300 + 20 - (400 + 600)(0.02 + \pi)]$$
$$= 4950 - 5000\pi. \tag{12A.3}$$

Note that, in this equation, higher values of inflation imply lower values of short-run equilibrium output.

SHIFTS OF THE *ADI* CURVE

Recall that exogenous changes in spending or changes in the Bank of Canada's monetary policy rule will shift the *ADI* curve. These results follow directly from Equation 12A.2. First, the equation shows that, for a given rate of inflation π, an increase in exogenous spending, $\overline{C} - mpc\overline{T} + \overline{I} + \overline{G} + \overline{NX}$ will raise short-run equilibrium output Y. Thus, an increase in exogenous spending shifts the *ADI* curve to the right; conversely, a decrease in exogenous spending shifts the *ADI* curve to the left.

A shift in the Bank of Canada's monetary policy rule can be captured by a change in the intercept term $\bar{r}$ in Equation 12A.1. For example, suppose the Bank of Canada tightens monetary policy by setting the real interest rate 1 percent higher than before at every level of inflation. Such a change is equivalent to raising the intercept term in the monetary policy rule $\bar{r}$ by 0.01. If you look at Equation 12A.2, you will see that with the level of inflation held constant, an increase in $\bar{r}$ reduces short-run equilibrium output. Thus a tightening of monetary policy shifts the *ADI* curve to the left; conversely, an easing of monetary policy (represented by a decline in $\bar{r}$) shifts the *ADI* curve to the right.

EXERCISE 12A.1

a. **For the economy described above, find an algebraic equation for the *ADI* curve after an exogenous increase in spending (say, in planned private-sector investment) of 10 units.**

b. **For the economy described above, find an algebraic equation for the *ADI* curve after a tightening of monetary policy which involves setting the real interest rate 1 percent higher at each level of inflation.**

SHORT-RUN EQUILIBRIUM

Recall that in short-run equilibrium, inflation is equal to its previously determined value, and the *IA* curve is horizontal at that value. At that level of inflation, the level of output in short-run equilibrium is given by the aggregate demand curve, Equation 12A.2. For instance, in the economy of Equation 12A.3, suppose the current value of inflation is 3 percent. The value of short-run equilibrium output is therefore

$$Y = 4950 - 5000\pi = 4950 - 5000(0.03) = 4800.$$

LONG-RUN EQUILIBRIUM

Recall that in long-run equilibrium, actual output Y equals potential output Y^*. Thus, in long-run equilibrium, the inflation rate can be obtained from the equation for the *ADI* curve by substituting Y^* for Y. To illustrate, let's write the equation for the *ADI* curve in equation 12A.3 once again:

$$Y = 4950 - 5000\pi.$$

Suppose, in addition, that $Y^* = 4900$. Substituting this value for Y in the aggregate demand equation yields

$$4900 = 4950 - 5000\pi.$$

Solving for the inflation rate π, we get

$$\pi = 0.01 = 1\%.$$

When this economy is in long-run equilibrium, then, the inflation rate will be 1 percent. If we start from the value of inflation in short-run equilibrium, 3 percent, we can see that the inflation adjustment curve must shift downward until inflation reaches 1 percent before long-run equilibrium can be achieved.

ANSWER TO IN-APPENDIX EXERCISE 12A.1

12A.1   The algebraic solutions for the *ADI* curves in each case, obtained by substituting the numerical values into the formula, are given below.
     a. $Y = 5000 - 5000\pi.$
     b. $Y = 4900 - 5000\pi.$

CHAPTER 13
Exchange Rates and the Open Economy

LEARNING OBJECTIVES

When you have completed this chapter, you will be able to:

LO1 Define the nominal exchange rate and apply the terms appreciation and depreciation to movements in the nominal exchange rate.

LO2 Use supply and demand to analyze how the nominal exchange rate is determined under a flexible exchange rate system.

LO3 Use supply and demand to analyze how the nominal exchange rate is maintained under a fixed exchange rate system.

LO4 Distinguish between flexible and fixed exchange rates and discuss the advantages and disadvantages of each system.

LO5 Understand the real exchange rate and the law of one price, and apply the purchasing power parity theory of exchange rates to exchange rate determination between economies with large differences in their rates of inflation.

LO6 Discuss the impact of monetary policy with a flexible exchange rate.

Two tourists visiting London many years ago were commiserating over their problems understanding English currency. "Pounds, shillings, tuppence, thruppence, bob, and quid; it's driving me crazy," said the first tourist. "This morning it took me twenty minutes to figure out how much to pay the taxi driver."

The second tourist was more upbeat. "Actually," he said, "since I adopted my new system, I haven't had any problems at all."

The first tourist looked interested. "What's your new system?"

"Well," replied the second, "now, whenever I take a taxi, I just give the driver all the English money I have. And would you believe it, I have got the fare exactly right every time!"

Dealing with unfamiliar currencies, and translating the value of foreign money into one's domestic currency, is a problem every international traveller faces.[1] The traveller's problem is complicated by the fact that *exchange rates*—the rates at which one country's money trades for another—may change unpredictably. Thus, the number of British pounds, Russian rubles, Japanese yen, or U.S. dollars that a Canadian dollar can buy may vary over time, and sometimes quite a lot.

The economic consequences of variable exchange rates are much broader than their impact on travel and tourism, however. For example, the competitiveness of Canadian exports depends in part on the prices of Canadian goods in terms of foreign currencies, which, in turn, depend on the exchange rate between the Canadian dollar and those currencies. Likewise, the prices Canadians pay for imported goods depend in part on the value of the dollar relative to the currencies of the countries that produce those goods. Exchange rates also affect the value of financial investments made across national borders. For countries that are heavily dependent on trade and international capital flows—the majority of the world's nations—fluctuations in the exchange rate may have a significant economic impact.

---

1   However, British money today is less complicated than suggested by this introductory story. In 1971, the British switched to a decimal monetary system, under which each pound is worth 100 pence. At that time, the traditional British system, under which a pound equalled 20 shillings and each shilling equalled 12 pence, was abandoned.

This chapter discusses exchange rates and the role they play in open economies. We will start by examining the *nominal exchange rate*—the rate at which one national currency trades for another. We then show how exchange rates affect the prices of exports and imports, and thus the pattern of trade.

Next we employ a supply-and-demand model to analyze how exchange rates are determined. Exchange rates may be divided into two broad categories: flexible and fixed. The value of a *flexible* exchange rate is determined freely in the market for national currencies, known as the *foreign exchange market.* Flexible exchange rates vary continually with changes in the supply of and demand for national currencies. In contrast, the value of a *fixed* exchange rate is set by the government at a constant level. Because many large, high-income economies, including Canada's, have a flexible exchange rate, we focus on that case first. We show that a country's monetary policy plays a particularly important role in determining the exchange rate. Furthermore, in an open economy with a flexible exchange rate, the exchange rate becomes a tool of monetary policy, in much the same way as the real interest rate.

Although many large, high-income economies have a flexible exchange rate, other economies fix their exchange rates, so we will consider the case of fixed exchange rates as well. We explain first how a country's government (usually, its central bank) goes about maintaining a fixed exchange rate at the officially determined level. We then discuss the relative merits of fixed and flexible exchange rates.

In the latter part of the chapter, we consider the *real exchange rate*—the nominal exchange rate between the currencies of two countries, adjusted for changes in the relative price levels between the two countries since a base year. And we consider the purchasing power parity theory of exchange rate determination. We close the chapter by summarizing the effect of the exchange rate on the economy.

13.1 EXCHANGE RATES

Trade *between* nations usually involves dealing in different currencies. So, for example, if a Canadian resident wants to purchase an automobile manufactured in South Korea, she (or more likely, the automobile dealer) must first trade dollars for the Korean currency, called the won. The Korean car manufacturer is then paid in won. Similarly, an American who wants to purchase shares in a Canadian company (a Canadian financial asset) must first trade his U.S. dollars for Canadian dollars and then use the Canadian dollars to purchase the shares.

NOMINAL EXCHANGE RATES

Because international transactions generally require that one currency be traded for another, the relative values of different currencies are an important factor in international economic relations. The rate at which two currencies can be traded for each other is called the **nominal exchange rate**, or more simply, the *exchange rate* between the two currencies. For example, if one Canadian dollar can be exchanged for 100 Japanese yen, the nominal exchange rate between the Canadian and Japanese currencies is 100 yen/dollar. Each country has many nominal exchange rates—one corresponding to each currency against which its own currency is traded. Thus, the Canadian dollar's value can be quoted in terms of U.S. dollars, euros, British pounds, Chinese yuan, or dozens of other currency units. Table 13.1 gives exchange rates between the Canadian dollar and selected other currencies as of noon in Toronto on February 21, 2011.

As Table 13.1 shows, exchange rates can be expressed either as the amount of foreign currency needed to purchase one Canadian dollar (left column) or as the number of dollars needed to purchase one unit of the foreign currency (right column). These two ways of expressing the exchange rate are equivalent: each is the reciprocal of the other.

nominal exchange rate
the rate at which two currencies can be traded for each other

TABLE 13.1
Nominal Exchange Rates for the Canadian Dollar

Country	Foreign currency/dollars	Dollars/foreign currency
United States (dollar)	1.0165	0.9838
Euro zone countries (euro)	0.7433	1.3454
United Kingdom (pound)	0.6263	1.5967
Japan (yen)	84.531	0.0118
China (yuan)	6.6756	0.1498
India (rupee)	45.662	0.0219
Brazil (real)	1.6935	0.5905
Russia (ruble)	29.638	0.0337
Mexico (peso)	12.256	0.0816
Switzerland (Swiss franc)	0.9623	1.0392

*rates current as of February 21, 2011, at noon EST.
SOURCE: Adapted from the Bank of Canada. http://www.bankofcanada.ca/en/rates/rss_fx.html. The numbers in the dollar/foreign currency column are the reciprocals of the corresponding numbers in the foreign currency/dollar column. The table ignores differences between buying and selling rates for currencies.

For example, on February 21, 2011, the Canadian-U.S. exchange rate could have been expressed either as 1.0165 U.S. dollars per Canadian dollar or as 0.9838 Canadian dollars per U.S. dollar, where 0.9838 = 1/1.0165.

Note that when it costs more than a dollar U.S. to buy a dollar Canadian, the Canadian dollar is said to be stronger than the U.S. dollar. In more technical language, the Canadian dollar is said to be trading above *parity* (or *par*, for short) with the U.S. dollars. In everyday language, parity refers to equality or equivalence. In the context of exchange rates between two different dollar currencies, **parity** refers to the situation when one unit of one currency (such as the Canadian dollar) trades on the foreign exchange market for one unit of another currency (such as the U.S. dollar). For example, if the exchange rate is US$1.0165 per Canadian dollar, the Canadian dollar is said to be trading nearly at parity or, more precisely, slightly above parity (or par). Over the period 1976–2010 covered by the data appendix at the end of the textbook, the only year in which the Canadian dollar traded above par was in 1976. The year in which the Canadian dollar traded furthest below par was 2002, when it cost US$0.64 to buy a Canadian dollar.

parity refers to the situation when one unit of one currency trades on the foreign exchange market for one unit of another currency; frequently abbreviated to "par"

EXAMPLE **13.1**

Nominal exchange rates

Based on Table 13.1, find the exchange rate between the U.S. and British currencies. Express the exchange rate in both pounds per U.S. dollar and U.S. dollars per pound.

From Table 13.1, we see that 0.6263 British pounds will buy a Canadian dollar, and that 1.0165 U.S. dollars will buy a Canadian dollar. Therefore, 0.6263 British pounds and 1.0165 U.S. dollars are equal in value:

0.6263 pounds = 1.0165 U.S. dollars.

Dividing both sides of this equation by 1.0165, we get

0.6161 pounds = 1 U.S. dollar.

In other words, the British-U.S. exchange rate can be expressed as 0.6161 pounds per U.S. dollar. Alternatively, the exchange rate can be expressed as 1/0.6161 = 1.6230 U.S. dollars per pound.

EXERCISE 13.1

From the business section of the newspaper or an online source (try the Bank of Canada link provided in Table 13.1), find recent quotations of the value of the Canadian dollar against the U.S. dollar, and for the Canadian dollar against the euro. Based on these data, find the exchange rate between the U.S. dollar and the euro. Express the exchange rate you derive in two ways (e.g., both as euros per U.S. dollar and as U.S. dollars per euro).

Figure 13.1 shows the nominal exchange rate for the Canadian dollar for 1971 to May 2011, relative to the U.S. dollar. You can see from Figure 13.1 that the Canadian dollar's value has fluctuated over time, sometimes increasing (as in the periods 1986–1992, 2003–2008, and 2009–2011) and sometimes decreasing (as in 1992–2002). An increase in the value of a currency relative to another currency is known as an **appreciation**; a decline in the value of a currency relative to another currency is called a **depreciation**.[2] So we can say that the Canadian dollar appreciated in 1986–1992, 2003–2008, and 2009–2011, and depreciated in 1992–2002. We will discuss the reasons a currency may appreciate or depreciate later in this chapter.

appreciation an increase in the value of a currency relative to another currency

depreciation a decrease in the value of a currency relative to another currency

FIGURE 13.1

Canada's Nominal Exchange Rate, January 1971–May 2011

The figure expresses the value of the Canadian dollar relative to the U.S. dollar from 1971 to May 2011. The declining value of the Canadian dollar from the early 1990s until 2002 was a source of controversy in Canada. More recently, the sharply appreciating value of the Canadian dollar has been controversial.

SOURCE: Pacific Exchange Rate Service, http://fx.sauder.ubc.ca/.

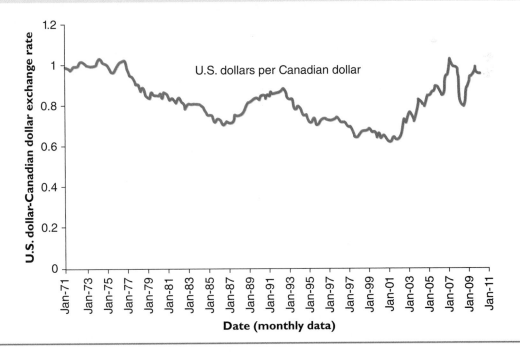

2 More precisely, as explained later in the chapter after we have considered the distinction between fixed and flexible exchange rates, the terms used to describe changes in the exchange rate differ according to whether the exchange rate is flexible or fixed. The terms *appreciation* and *depreciation* are used in connection with changes in the value of a flexible currency.

ECONOMIC NATURALIST 13.1

Does a strong currency imply a strong economy?

Politicians and the public sometimes take pride in the fact that their national currency is "strong," meaning that its value in terms of other currencies is high or rising. Likewise, policy-makers sometimes view a depreciating ("weak") currency as a sign of economic failure. Does a strong currency necessarily imply a strong economy?

There are times, such as in 2006 in Canada, when the national currency is strong, real GDP growth is substantial, and the unemployment rate is low by historical standards. But contrary to popular opinion, there is no simple connection between the strength of a country's currency and the strength of its economy. For example, Figure 13.1 shows that the value of the Canadian dollar relative to the U.S. dollar was greater in the year 1992 than in the year 2000, though Canadian economic performance was considerably better in 2000 than in 1992, a period of deep recession and rising unemployment.

One reason a strong currency does not necessarily imply a strong economy is that an appreciating currency may hurt a country's net exports. For example, if the Canadian dollar strengthens against the U.S. dollar (that is, if a Canadian dollar buys more U.S. dollars than before), U.S. goods will become cheaper in terms of Canadian dollars. The result may be that Canadians prefer to buy U.S. goods rather than goods produced at home. Likewise, a stronger dollar implies that each U.S. dollar buys fewer Canadian dollars, so exported Canadian goods become more expensive to U.S. buyers. As Canadian goods become more expensive in terms of yen, the willingness of U.S. buyers to purchase Canadian exports declines. A strong Canadian dollar may therefore imply lower sales and profits for Canadian industries that export, as well as for Canadian industries that compete with foreign exporters for a share of the domestic Canadian market.

In this chapter, we will use the symbol *e* to stand for a country's nominal exchange rate. Although the exchange rate can be expressed either as foreign currency units per unit of domestic currency, or vice versa, as we saw in Table 13.1, let's agree to define *e* as *the number of units of the foreign currency that the domestic currency will buy*. For example, if we treat Canada as the "home" or domestic country and the United States as the foreign country, *e* will be defined as the number of U.S. dollars that one Canadian dollar will buy (for example, 1.02 U.S. dollars per Canadian dollar). Defining the nominal exchange rate this way implies that an *increase* in *e* corresponds to an *appreciation,* or a strengthening, of the home currency, while a *decrease* in *e* implies a *depreciation,* or weakening, of the home currency.

FLEXIBLE VERSUS FIXED EXCHANGE RATES

flexible exchange rate an exchange rate whose value is not officially fixed but varies according to the supply of and demand for the currency in the foreign exchange market

foreign exchange market the market on which currencies of various nations are traded for one another

fixed exchange rate an exchange rate whose value is set by official government policy

As we saw in Figure 13.1, the exchange rate between the Canadian dollar and the U.S. dollar isn't constant, but rather varies continually. Indeed, changes in the value of the Canadian dollar occur daily, hourly, or even minute by minute. Such fluctuations in the value of a currency are normal for countries, like Canada, which have a *flexible* or *floating exchange rate.* The value of a **flexible exchange rate** is not officially fixed but varies according to the supply of and demand for the currency in the **foreign exchange market**—the market on which currencies of various nations are traded for one another. We will discuss the factors that determine the supply of and demand for currencies shortly.

Some economies do not allow their currency values to vary with market conditions but instead maintain a *fixed exchange rate.* The value of a **fixed exchange rate** is set by official government policy. (A government that establishes a fixed exchange rate typically determines the exchange rate's value independently, but sometimes exchange rates are set according to an agreement among a number of governments.) Some economies fix their exchange rates in terms of the U.S. dollar (Hong Kong, for example), but there are other possibilities. Many

African economies fix the value of their currencies in terms of the euro, the currency of the European Union. Under the gold standard, which many economies used until its collapse during the Great Depression, currency values were fixed in terms of ounces of gold.

RECAP

EXCHANGE RATES

- The *nominal exchange rate* between two currencies is the rate at which the currencies can be traded for each other. More precisely, the nominal exchange rate e for any given country is the number of units of foreign currency that can be bought for one unit of the domestic currency.

- An *appreciation* is an increase in the value of a currency relative to other currencies (a rise in e); a *depreciation* is a decline in a currency's value (a fall in e).

- An exchange rate can be either *flexible,* meaning that it varies freely according to supply and demand for the currency in the foreign exchange market, or *fixed,* meaning that its value is fixed by official government policy.

13.2 DETERMINATION OF FLEXIBLE EXCHANGE RATES: SUPPLY AND DEMAND ANALYSIS

Countries that have flexible exchange rates, such as Canada, see the international values of their currencies change continually. What determines the value of the nominal exchange rate at any point in time? In this section we use supply and demand analysis to answer this question.[3] Our focus for the moment is on flexible exchange rates, whose values are determined by the foreign exchange market. Later in the chapter we discuss the case of fixed exchange rates, the costs and benefits of each type of exchange rate, and the consequences for exchange rates when the inflation rates of economies are very different.

A SUPPLY AND DEMAND ANALYSIS

In this section, we analyze the foreign exchange market and discuss the factors that affect the supply and demand for dollars, and thus the U.S. exchange rate. As we will see, Canadian dollars are demanded in the foreign exchange market by foreigners who seek to purchase Canadian goods and assets, and they are supplied by Canadian residents who need foreign currencies to buy foreign goods and assets. The equilibrium exchange rate is the value of the dollar that equates the number of dollars supplied and demanded in the foreign exchange market. In this section, we will discuss the factors that affect the supply of and demand for dollars, and thus the Canadian exchange rate.

The Supply of Canadian Dollars

Anyone who holds Canadian dollars is a potential supplier of them to the foreign exchange market. In practice, however, the principal suppliers of dollars to the foreign exchange market are Canadian households and firms. Why would a Canadian household or firm want to supply dollars in exchange for foreign currency? There are two major reasons. First, a Canadian household or firm may need foreign currency to purchase foreign goods or services. For example, a Canadian electronics retailer may need U.S. dollars to

---

3 For now we will assume that the inflation rates in the economies being analyzed are approximately the same.

FIGURE 13.2
The Supply and Demand for Canadian Dollars in the U.S. Dollar–Canadian Dollar Market
The supply of Canadian dollars to the foreign exchange market is upward sloping, because an increase in the number of U.S. dollars offered for each Canadian dollar makes U.S. goods, services, and assets more attractive to Canadian buyers. Similarly, the demand for Canadian dollars is downward sloping, because holders of U.S. dollars will be less willing to buy Canadian dollars the more expensive they are in terms of U.S. dollars. The equilibrium exchange rate e^* equates the quantities of Canadian dollars supplied and demanded.

purchase U.S. computers, or a Canadian tourist may need U.S. dollars to make purchases in New York. Second, a Canadian household or firm may need foreign currency to purchase foreign assets. For example, a Canadian mutual fund may wish to acquire stocks issued by U.S. companies, or an individual Canadian saver may want to purchase U.S. government bonds. Because U.S. assets are priced in U.S. dollars, the Canadian household or firm will need to trade Canadian dollars for U.S. dollars to acquire these assets.

The supply of Canadian dollars to the foreign exchange market is illustrated in Figure 13.2. We will focus on the market in which Canadian dollars are traded for U.S. dollars, but bear in mind that similar markets exist for every other pair of traded currencies. The vertical axis of the figure shows the Canadian-U.S. exchange rate as measured by the number of U.S. dollars that can be purchased with each Canadian dollar. The horizontal axis shows the number of Canadian dollars being traded in the U.S. dollar–Canadian dollar market.

Note that the supply curve for Canadian dollars is upward sloping. In other words, the more U.S. dollars each Canadian dollar can buy, the more Canadian dollars people are willing to supply to the foreign exchange market. Why? At given prices for U.S. goods, services, and assets, the more U.S. dollars a Canadian dollar can buy, the cheaper those goods, services, and assets will be in Canadian-dollar terms, and vice versa. For example, if a wooden hockey stick costs $30 in the U.S., and a Canadian dollar can buy one U.S. dollar, the Canadian-dollar price of the hockey stick will be $30. However, if a Canadian dollar can buy only US$0.75, then the Canadian-dollar price of the same hockey stick will be $40. Assuming that lower Canadian-dollar prices will induce Canadians to increase their expenditures on U.S. goods, services, and assets (and vice versa), a higher U.S. dollar–Canadian dollar exchange rate (e) will increase the supply of dollars to the foreign exchange market. Thus, the supply curve for dollars is upward sloping.

The Demand for Canadian Dollars

In the U.S. dollar–Canadian dollar foreign exchange market, demanders of Canadian dollars are those who wish to acquire Canadian dollars in exchange for U.S. dollars. Most demanders of Canadian dollars in the U.S. dollar–Canadian dollar market are U.S. households and firms, although anyone who happens to hold U.S. dollars is free to trade them for Canadian dollars. Why demand dollars? The reasons for acquiring Canadian dollars are analogous to those for acquiring U.S. dollars. First, households and firms that hold U.S. dollars will demand Canadian dollars so that they can purchase Canadian goods and services. For example, a U.S. firm that wants to license Canadian-produced software needs Canadian dollars to pay the required fees, and a U.S. student studying in a Canadian university must pay tuition in Canadian dollars. The firm or the student can acquire the necessary Canadian dollars only by offering U.S. dollars in exchange. Second, households and firms demand Canadian dollars in order to purchase Canadian assets. The purchase of Toronto real estate by a U.S. company or acquisition of Bombardier stock by a U.S. pension fund are two examples.

The demand for dollars is represented by the downward-sloping curve in Figure 13.2. The curve slopes downward because the more U.S. dollars a U.S. citizen must pay to acquire a Canadian dollar, the less attractive Canadian goods, services, and assets will be. Hence, the demand for dollars will be low when Canadian dollars are expensive in terms of U.S. dollars and high when Canadian dollars are cheap in terms of U.S. dollars.

The Market Equilibrium Value of the Canadian Dollar

As mentioned earlier, Canada maintains a flexible, or floating, exchange rate, which means that the value of the Canadian dollar is determined by the forces of supply and demand in the foreign exchange market. In Figure 13.2, the equilibrium value of the dollar is e^*, the U.S. dollar–Canadian dollar exchange rate at which the quantity of dollars supplied equals the quantity of dollars demanded. The equilibrium value of the exchange rate is also called the **market equilibrium value of the exchange rate**. In general, the equilibrium value of the dollar is not constant but changes with shifts in the supply of and demand for dollars in the foreign exchange market.

market equilibrium value of the exchange rate (or equilibrium exchange rate) the exchange rate that equates the quantities of the currency supplied and demanded in the foreign exchange market

CHANGES IN THE SUPPLY OF CANADIAN DOLLARS

Recall that people supply Canadian dollars to the U.S. dollar–Canadian dollar foreign exchange market in order to purchase U.S. goods, services, and assets. Factors that affect the desire of Canadian households and firms to acquire U.S. goods, services, and assets will therefore affect the supply of Canadian dollars to the foreign exchange market. Some factors that will *increase* the supply of Canadian dollars, shifting the supply curve for Canadian dollars to the right, include the following:

- An increased preference for U.S. goods. For example, suppose that U.S. firms produce some popular new consumer electronics, such as tablet computers. To acquire the U.S. dollars needed to buy these goods, Canadian importers will increase their supply of Canadian dollars to the foreign exchange market.
- An increase in Canadian real GDP. An increase in Canadian real GDP will raise the incomes of Canadians, allowing them to consume more goods and services (recall the consumption function introduced in Chapter 8). Some part of this increase in consumption will take the form of goods imported from the U.S. (recall the discussion of the marginal propensity to import in Chapter 8). To buy more U.S. goods, Canadians will supply more Canadian dollars to acquire the necessary U.S. dollars.
- An increase in the real interest rate on U.S. assets. Recall that Canadian households and firms acquire U.S. dollars in order to purchase U.S. assets as well as goods and services. Other factors such as risk held constant, the higher the real interest rate paid by U.S. assets, the more U.S. assets Canadians will choose to hold. To purchase additional U.S. assets, Canadians households and firms will supply more Canadian dollars to the foreign exchange market.

Conversely, reduced demand for U.S. goods, a lower Canadian GDP, or a lower real interest rate on U.S. assets will *reduce* the number of U.S. dollars Canadians need, in turn reducing their supply of dollars to the foreign exchange market and shifting the supply curve for dollars to the left. Of course, any shift in the supply curve for dollars will affect the equilibrium exchange rate, as Example 13.2 shows.

EXAMPLE 13.2

Hockey sticks, the U.S. dollar, and the Canadian dollar

Suppose U.S.-based firms come to dominate the hockey stick market with sticks of increased quality relative to those produced in Canada. All else being equal, how will this change affect the relative value of the U.S. dollar and the Canadian dollar?

FIGURE 13.3
An Increase in the Supply of Canadian Dollars Lowers the Value of the Canadian Dollar
Increased Canadian demand for U.S. hockey sticks forces Canadians to supply more Canadian dollars to the foreign exchange market to acquire the U.S. dollars they need to buy the sticks. The supply curve for Canadian dollars shifts from S to S', lowering the value of the Canadian dollar in terms of the U.S. dollar. The market equilibrium value of the exchange rate falls from e^* to $e^{*'}$.

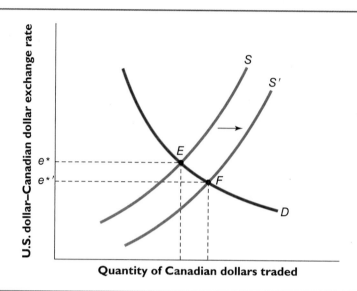

The increased quality of U.S. hockey sticks will increase the demand for the sticks in Canada. To acquire the U.S. dollars necessary to buy more U.S. hockey sticks, Canadian importers will supply more Canadian dollars to the foreign exchange market. As Figure 13.3 shows, the increased supply of dollars will reduce the value of the dollar. In other words, a Canadian dollar will buy fewer U.S. dollars than it did before. At the same time, the U.S. dollar will increase in value: a given number of U.S. dollars will buy more Canadian dollars than it did before.

EXERCISE 13.2   **Canada goes into a recession, and real GDP falls. All else being equal, how is this economic weakness likely to affect the value of the Canadian dollar?**

CHANGES IN THE DEMAND FOR CANADIAN DOLLARS

The factors that can cause a change in the demand for dollars in the foreign exchange market, and thus a shift of the dollar demand curve, are analogous to the factors that affect the supply of dollars. Factors that will *increase* the demand for dollars include

- An increased preference for Canadian goods. For example, U.S. executives might decide to buy more Bombardier planes. To buy the Canadian aircraft, U.S. firms would demand more Canadian dollars on the foreign exchange market.
- An increase in real GDP abroad, which implies higher incomes abroad and thus more demand for imports from Canada.
- An increase in the real interest rate on Canadian assets, which would make those assets more attractive to foreign savers. To acquire Canadian assets, U.S. savers would demand more Canadian dollars.

MONETARY POLICY AND THE FLEXIBLE EXCHANGE RATE

Of the many factors that could influence a country's exchange rate, among the most important is the monetary policy of the country's central bank. As we mentioned in

FIGURE 13.4

An Increase in the Real Interest Rate Strengthens the Canadian Dollar

When the Bank of Canada raises the real interest rate, it increases the demand for Canadian assets by foreign investors. An increased demand for Canadian assets in turn increases the demand for Canadian dollars. The demand curve shifts from D to D', leading the exchange rate to appreciate from e^* to $e^{*'}$.

earlier chapters, monetary policy affects the exchange rate primarily through its effect on the real interest rate.

Suppose the Bank of Canada is concerned about inflation and raises real interest rates in response. The effects of this policy change on the value of the Canadian dollar are shown in Figure 13.4. Before the policy change, the equilibrium value of the exchange rate is e^*, at the intersection of supply curve S and the demand curve D (point E in the figure). The increase in the Canadian real interest rate, r, makes Canadian assets more attractive to foreign financial investors. The increased willingness of foreign investors to buy Canadian assets increases the demand for dollars, shifting the demand curve rightward from D to D' and the equilibrium point from E to F. As a result of this increase in demand, the equilibrium value of the dollar rises from e^* to $e^{*'}$.

In short, an increase in the real interest rate engineered by the Bank of Canada raises the demand for Canadian dollars, causing the Canadian dollar to appreciate. By similar logic, a reduction of the real interest rate by the Bank of Canada would weaken the demand for the Canadian dollar, causing it to depreciate.

In an economic model with fixed net exports, monetary policy affects aggregate demand solely through the real interest rate. For example, by raising the real interest rate, a tight monetary policy reduces consumption and private-sector investment spending. However, if net exports are not fixed, the real interest rate affects the exchange rate so that the exchange rate serves as another channel for monetary policy—one that reinforces the effects of the real interest rate.

To illustrate, suppose that policy-makers are concerned about inflation and decide to restrain aggregate demand. To do so, they increase the real interest rate, reducing consumption and private-sector investment spending. But, as Figure 13.4 shows, the higher real interest rate also increases the demand for Canadian dollars, causing the dollar to appreciate. The stronger dollar, in turn, further reduces aggregate demand. Why? As we saw in discussing the real exchange rate, a stronger dollar reduces the cost of imported goods, increasing imports. It also makes Canadian exports more costly to foreign buyers, which tends to reduce exports. Recall that net exports—exports minus imports—is one of the four components of aggregate demand. Thus, by reducing exports and increasing imports, a stronger dollar (more precisely, a higher real exchange rate) reduces aggregate demand.

In sum, when the exchange rate is flexible, a higher real interest rate reduces net exports (through a stronger dollar) as well as consumption and private-sector investment spending (through a higher real interest rate). Conversely, a lower real interest rate weakens the dollar and stimulates net exports, reinforcing the effect of the lower real interest rate on consumption and private-sector investment spending. Thus, relative to the case of a closed economy that we emphasized earlier, *monetary policy is more effective in an open economy with a flexible exchange rate.*

It is widely recognized that real interest rates (particularly long-term ones) in small open economies like Canada's will be influenced by foreign interest rates. It is worth noting that a flexible exchange rate is typically seen as increasing the power of the central bank in a small open economy like Canada's to maintain a real interest rate different from the real foreign interest rate—say, the U.S. rate. When the central bank of a small open economy raises the domestic real interest rate, for example, net capital inflows (a concept discussed further in Chapter 16) will tend to increase and push up the value of the domestic currency. But as the value of the domestic currency rises, investors will start judging both that the currency is above its normal level and that it will eventually depreciate. The higher domestic real interest rate will be seen as a premium associated with the risk of currency depreciation, and this perception will slow net capital inflows and hence slow the return of the real interest rate back toward its original level.[4]

RECAP

DETERMINING THE EXCHANGE RATE

- Supply and demand analysis is a useful tool for studying the short-run determination of the exchange rate. Canadian households and firms supply Canadian dollars to the foreign exchange market to acquire foreign currencies, which they need to purchase foreign goods, services, and assets. Foreigners demand Canadian dollars in the foreign exchange market to purchase Canadian goods, services, and assets. The equilibrium exchange rate, also called the *market equilibrium value of the exchange rate,* equates the quantities of dollars supplied and demanded in the foreign exchange market.

- An increased preference for foreign goods, an increase in Canadian real GDP, or an increase in the real interest rate on foreign assets will increase the supply of dollars on the foreign exchange market, lowering the value of the dollar. An increased preference for Canadian goods by foreigners, an increase in real GDP abroad, or an increase in the real interest rate on Canadian assets will increase the demand for dollars, raising the value of the dollar.

- If the Bank of Canada raises the real interest rate, it will tend to increase the demand for Canadian dollars and, thereby, strengthen the Canadian dollar. A stronger dollar reinforces the effects of interest rate hikes on aggregate spending by reducing net exports, a component of aggregate demand. Conversely, if the Bank of Canada lowers the real interest rate, it will tend to weaken the Canadian dollar.

13.3 FIXED EXCHANGE RATES

So far we have focused on the case of flexible exchange rates, the relevant case for many high-income economies such as Canada's today. However, the alternative approach, fixing the exchange rate, has been quite important historically. Towards the end of World War II, leading countries led by the United States and the United Kingdom devised an international monetary system, known as the **Bretton Woods system**, under which most

Bretton Woods system an international monetary system under which most countries pegged their currencies to the U.S. dollar; it operated from the end of World War II until 1971

4 In the early 1990s when the Canadian dollar was strong relative to the U.S. dollar, for a few years the real interest rate on Canadian long-term government bonds exceeded the rate on comparable U.S. bonds by about 2 percentage points.

countries pegged their currencies to the U.S. dollar. The system lasted until 1971. Under this system, Canada had a fixed exchange rate with the U.S. dollar until 1950, and then again between 1962 and 1970 when the Canadian dollar was worth US$0.925.[5]

Fixed exchange rates are still used in many economies, especially developing and small ones. In this section, we will see how our conclusions change when the nominal exchange rate is fixed rather than flexible. One important difference is that when a country maintains a fixed exchange rate, its ability to use monetary policy as a stabilization tool is reduced.

HOW TO FIX AN EXCHANGE RATE

In contrast to a flexible exchange rate, whose value is determined solely by supply and demand in the foreign exchange market, the value of a fixed exchange rate is determined by the government (in practice, usually the finance ministry or treasury department, with the cooperation of the central bank). Today, the value of a fixed exchange rate is usually set in terms of a major currency (for instance, between 1996 and 2005 and between 2008 and 2010, China pegged its currency to the U.S. dollar), or relative to a "basket" of currencies, typically those of the country's trading partners. Historically, currency values were often fixed in terms of gold or other precious metals, but in recent decades precious metals have rarely, if ever, been used for that purpose.

Once an exchange rate has been fixed, the government usually attempts to keep it unchanged for some time.[6] However, sometimes economic circumstances force the government to change the value of the exchange rate. A reduction in the official value of a currency is called a **devaluation**; an increase in the official value is called a **revaluation**. The devaluation of a fixed exchange rate is analogous to the depreciation of a flexible exchange rate; both involve a reduction in the currency's value. Conversely, a revaluation is analogous to an appreciation.

The supply and demand diagram we used to study flexible exchange rates can be adapted to analyze fixed exchange rates. Rather than use a completely hypothetical example, let's call the country with the fixed exchange rate China. China is now the world's second largest economy and for most of the period from 1995 to 2010 it had a fixed exchange with the U.S. dollar. China's currency is called the renminbi and the primary unit of the currency is the yuan.[7] Figure 13.5 shows the supply of and demand for the Chinese yuan in the foreign exchange market. Yuan are *supplied* to the foreign exchange market by Chinese households and firms who want to acquire foreign currencies to purchase foreign goods and assets. Yuan are *demanded* by holders of foreign currencies who need yuan to purchase Chinese goods and assets. The numbers employed are hypothetical.

Figure 13.5 shows that the quantities of yuan supplied and demanded in the foreign exchange market are equal when a yuan equals US$0.10 (10 yuan to the U.S. dollar). Hence US$0.10 per yuan is the *market equilibrium value* of the yuan. If China had a flexible-exchange-rate system, the yuan would trade at 10 yuan to the U.S. dollar in the foreign exchange market.

devaluation a reduction in the official value of a currency (in a fixed-exchange-rate system)

revaluation an increase in the official value of a currency (in a fixed-exchange-rate system)

---

5   See James Powell, *A History of the Canadian Dollar* (Ottawa: Bank of Canada, 2005), http://www.bankofcanada.ca/publications-research/books-and-monographs/history-canadian-dollar/. For a convenient graphical summary of key developments, see CBC News, "A history of the Canadian dollar since 1950," http://www.cbc.ca/news/interactives/map-history-dollar/.

6   There are exceptions to this statement. Some countries employ a *crawling peg* system, under which the exchange rate is fixed at a value that changes in a preannounced way over time. For example, the government may announce that the value of the fixed exchange rate will fall 2 percent each year. Other countries use a *target zone* system, in which the exchange rate is allowed to deviate by a small amount from its fixed value. To focus on the key issues, we will assume that the exchange rate is fixed at a single value for a protracted period.

7   For more on the distinction between renminbi and yuan, see Stephen Mulvey, "Why China's currency has two names," *BBC News*, June 26, 2010, http://www.bbc.co.uk/news/10413076, and Paul Krugman,"What's in a name," *New York Times,* October 23, 2009, http://krugman.blogs.nytimes.com/2009/10/23/whats-in-a-name-3/.

FIGURE 13.5
An Overvalued
Exchange Rate
The renminbi's official value, US$0.125, is shown as greater than its market equilibrium value, US$0.10, as determined by supply and demand in the foreign exchange market. Thus the yuan is overvalued. To maintain the fixed value, the government must purchase yuan in the quantity *AB* each period.

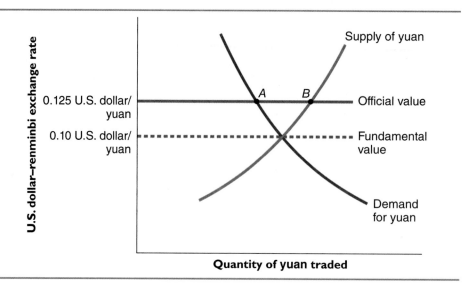

overvalued exchange rate an exchange rate that has an officially fixed value greater than its market equilibrium value

undervalued exchange rate an exchange rate that has an officially fixed value less than its market equilibrium value

capital controls taxes or rules such as constraints on foreign exchange transactions that impede money flows between economies; they are sometimes used to prevent exchange rate fluctuations

But let's suppose that China has a fixed exchange rate and that the government has decreed the value of the Chinese yuan to be 8 yuan to the U.S. dollar, or US$0.125 per yuan. This official value of the yuan, US$0.125, is indicated by the solid horizontal line in Figure 13.5. Notice that it is greater than the market equilibrium value, corresponding to the intersection of the supply and demand curves. When the officially fixed value of an exchange rate is greater than its market equilibrium value, the exchange rate is said to be **overvalued**. The official value of an exchange rate can also be lower than its market equilibrium value, in which case the exchange rate is said to be **undervalued**. (Most experts would argue that China in recent years has actually had an undervalued currency, but the situation of overvaluation depicted in Figure 13.5 could correspond to the Chinese currency situation during the Asian currency crisis discussed in Economic Naturalist 13.2.)

In this example, China's commitment to hold the yuan at 8 to the U.S. dollar is inconsistent with the market equilibrium value of 10 to the U.S. dollar, as determined by supply and demand in the foreign exchange market (the Chinese yuan is overvalued). How could the Chinese government deal with this inconsistency? There are several possibilities.

First, China could simply devalue its currency, from US$0.125 per yuan to US$0.10 per yuan, which would bring the renminbi's official value into line with its market equilibrium value. As we will see, devaluation is often the ultimate result of an overvaluation of a currency. However, a country with a fixed exchange rate will be reluctant to change the official value of its exchange rate every time the market equilibrium value changes. If a country must continually adjust its exchange rate to market conditions, it might as well switch to a flexible exchange rate.

As a second alternative, China could try to maintain its overvalued exchange rate by restricting international transactions. Raising tariffs, tightening quotas on imports, and/or making it more difficult for domestic households and firms to acquire foreign assets would effectively reduce the supply of yuan to the foreign exchange market, raising the market equilibrium value of the currency. An even more extreme action would be to prohibit Chinese from exchanging the renminbi for other currencies without government approval, a policy that would effectively allow the government to determine directly the supply of yuan to the foreign exchange market. Such measures might help to maintain the official value of the renminbi. Indeed, economies with fixed exchange rates are more likely than economies with flexible exchange rates to employ *capital controls*. **Capital controls** are taxes or rules such as constraints on foreign exchange transactions that impede money flows between economies. However, trade restrictions and capital controls have drawbacks to the economy.

A third and most widely used approach to maintaining an overvalued exchange rate is for the government to become a demander of its own currency in the foreign exchange market. Figure 13.5 shows that at the official exchange rate of US$0.125 per yuan, the private-sector supply of yuan (point *B*) exceeds the private-sector demand for yuan (point *A*). To keep the renminbi from falling below its official value, in each period the Chinese government could purchase a quantity of yuan in the foreign exchange market equal to the length of the line segment *AB* in Figure 13.5. If the government followed this strategy, then at the official exchange rate of US$0.125 per yuan, the total demand for yuan (private demand at point *A* plus government demand *AB*) would equal the private supply of yuan (point *B*). This situation is analogous to government attempts to keep the price of a commodity, like grain or milk, above its market level. To maintain an official price of grain that is above the market-clearing price, the government must stand ready to purchase the excess supply of grain forthcoming at the official price. In the same way, to keep the "price" of its currency above the market-clearing level, the government must buy the excess yuan supplied at the official price.

To be able to purchase its own currency and maintain an overvalued exchange rate, the government (usually the central bank) must hold foreign currency assets, called **international reserves**, or simply *reserves*. For example, the Chinese central bank may hold U.S.-dollar deposits in banks or U.S. government debt, which it can trade for yuan in the foreign exchange market as needed. In the situation shown in Figure 13.5, to keep the renminbi at its official value, in each period the Chinese central bank will have to spend an amount of international reserves equal to the length of the line segment *AB*.

Because a country with an overvalued exchange rate must use part of its reserves to support the value of its currency in each period, over time its available reserves will decline. The net decline in a country's stock of international reserves over a year is called its **balance-of-payments deficit**. Conversely, if a country experiences a net increase in its international reserves over the year, the increase is called its **balance-of-payments surplus**.

international reserves foreign currency assets held by a government for the purpose of purchasing the domestic currency in the foreign exchange market

balance-of-payments deficit the net decline in a country's stock of international reserves over a year

balance-of-payments surplus the net increase in a country's stock of international reserves over a year

EXAMPLE 13.3

China's balance-of-payments deficit

The demand for and supply of Chinese yuan in the foreign exchange market are

$$\text{Demand} = 25\,000 - 50\,000e,$$

$$\text{Supply} = 17\,600 + 24\,000e,$$

where the Chinese exchange rate e is measured in U.S. dollars per yuan. Officially, the value of the yuan is US$0.125. Find the market equilibrium value of the yuan and the Chinese balance-of-payments deficit, measured in both yuan and U.S. dollars.

To find the market equilibrium value of the yuan, equate the demand and supply for yuan:

$$25\,000 - 50\,000e = 17\,600 + 24\,000e.$$

Solving for e, we get

$$7400 = 74\,000e$$
$$e = 0.10.$$

So the market equilibrium value of the exchange rate is US$0.10 per yuan, as in Figure 13.5.

At the official exchange rate, US$0.125/yuan, the demand for yuan is $25\,000 - 50\,000(0.125) = 18\,750$, and the supply of yuan is $17\,600 + 24\,000(0.125) = 20\,600$. Thus, the quantity of yuan supplied to the foreign exchange market exceeds the quantity of yuan demanded by $20\,600 - 18\,750 = 1850$ yuan. To maintain the fixed rate, the Chinese government must purchase 1850 yuan per period, which is the Chinese balance-of-payments deficit. Since yuan are purchased at the official rate of 8 yuan to the U.S. dollar, the balance-of-payments deficit in U.S. dollars is (1850 yuan) × (US$0.125/yuan) = US$(1850/8) = US$231.25.

EXERCISE 13.3   **Repeat Example 13.3 under the assumption that the fixed value of the yuan is US$0.15/yuan. What do you conclude about the relationship between the degree of currency overvaluation and the resulting balance-of-payments deficit?**

Although a government can maintain an overvalued exchange rate for a time by offering to buy back its own currency at the official price, there is a limit to this strategy, since no government's stock of international reserves is infinite. It should be noted, however, that if a government has very large international reserves, it may be able to maintain an overvalued exchange rate for quite some time. For reasons discussed in Economic Naturalist 13.3 and Box 13.1 later in this chapter, since the late 1990s a number of developing economies with fixed exchange rates have accumulated massive international reserves. Table 13.2 shows the international reserves of a range of economies. China tops the list with international reserves valued at almost US$2.9 trillion. Economies that do not manage their exchange rates, such as the United States and Canada, have international reserves that are small relative to the scale of their economies.

EXERCISE 13.4   **Diagram a case in which a fixed exchange rate is undervalued rather than overvalued. Show that, to maintain the fixed exchange rate, the central bank must use domestic currency to purchase foreign currency in the foreign exchange market. With an undervalued exchange rate, is the country's central bank in danger of running out of international reserves? (*Hint*: Keep in mind that a central bank is always free to print more of its own currency.)**

TABLE 13.2
International Reserves, 2010–2011, Billions of U.S. Dollars

People's Republic of China	$ 2850 (Dec 2010)
Japan	$ 1092 (Jan 2011)
Eurozone	$ 753 (Sep 2010)
Russia	$ 497 (Nov 2010)
Saudi Arabia	$ 445 (Dec 2010)
Republic of China (Taiwan)	$ 383 (Sept 2010)
Brazil	$ 305 (Feb 2011)
India	$ 301 (Feb 2011)
South Korea	$ 291 (Dec 2010)
Hong Kong	$ 266 (Sep 2010)
Singapore	$ 226 (Dec 2010)
Thailand	$ 174 (Feb 2011)
United States	$ 129 (July 2010)
Mexico	$ 113 (Dec 2010)
Malaysia	$ 106 (Nov 2010)
Canada	$ 60 (Feb 2011)

SOURCES: Wikipedia, "Foreign exchange reserves," at http://en.wikipedia.org/wiki/International_reserves; Bank of Canada, http://beta.bankofcanada.ca/rates/related/international-reserves/. Extraction date, May 15, 2011.

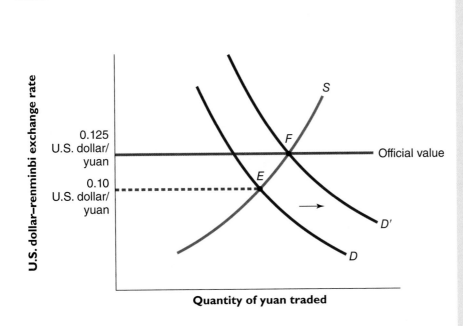

FIGURE 13.6

An Increase in the Real Interest Rate Eliminates an Overvaluation

With the demand for the yuan given by D and the supply given by S, equilibrium occurs at point E and the market equilibrium value of the yuan equals US$0.10 per yuan—below the official value of US$0.125 per yuan. The central bank can eliminate the overvaluation of the yuan by raising the domestic real interest rate, making domestic assets more attractive to foreign financial investors. The resulting increase in demand for the yuan, from D to D', raises the renminbi's market equilibrium value to US$0.125 per yuan, the official value. The yuan is no longer overvalued.

MONETARY POLICY AND THE FIXED EXCHANGE RATE

We have seen that there is no really satisfactory way of maintaining a fixed exchange rate above its market equilibrium value for an extended period. A central bank can maintain an overvalued exchange rate for a time by using international reserves to buy up the excess supply of its currency in the foreign exchange market. But a country's international reserves are limited and may eventually be exhausted by the attempt to keep the exchange rate artificially high.

An alternative to trying to maintain an overvalued exchange rate is to take actions that increase the market equilibrium value of the exchange rate. If the exchange rate's market equilibrium value can be raised enough to equal its official value, then the overvaluation problem will be eliminated. The most effective way to change the exchange rate's market equilibrium value is through monetary policy. As we saw earlier in the chapter, a monetary policy that raises the real interest rate will increase the demand for the domestic currency, as domestic assets become more attractive to foreign financial investors. Increased demand for the currency will in turn raise its market equilibrium value.

The use of monetary policy to support a fixed exchange rate is shown in Figure 13.6. At first, the demand for and supply of the Chinese yuan in the foreign exchange market are given by the curves D and S, so the market equilibrium value of the yuan equals US$0.10 per yuan—less than the official value of US$0.125 yuan. Just as before, the yuan is overvalued. This time, however, the Chinese central bank uses monetary policy to eliminate the overvaluation problem. To do so, the central bank increases the domestic real interest rate, making Chinese assets more attractive to foreign financial investors and raising the demand for yuan from D to D'. After this increase in the demand for yuan, the market equilibrium value of the yuan equals the officially fixed value, as can be seen in Figure 13.6. Because the yuan is no longer overvalued, it can be maintained at its fixed value without loss of international reserves or fear of "speculative attack" (see below). Conversely, a reduction of the real interest rate by the central bank could be used

"It's just a flesh wound. I got it defending the dollar."

to remedy an undervaluation, in which case the official exchange rate is below the market equilibrium value.

Although monetary policy can be used to keep the market equilibrium value of the exchange rate equal to the official value, using monetary policy in this way has some drawbacks. In particular, *if monetary policy is used to set the market equilibrium value of the exchange rate equal to the official value, it is no longer available for stabilizing the domestic economy.* Suppose, for example, that the Chinese economy were suffering a recession due to insufficient aggregate demand at the same time that its exchange rate is overvalued. The Chinese central bank could lower the real interest rate to increase spending and output, or it could raise the real interest rate to eliminate overvaluation of the exchange rate, *but it cannot do both.* Hence, if Chinese officials decide to maintain the fixed exchange rate, they must give up any hope of fighting the recession using monetary policy. The fact that a fixed exchange rate limits or eliminates the use of monetary policy for the purpose of stabilizing aggregate demand is one of the most important features of a fixed-exchange-rate system.

The conflict monetary policy-makers face, stabilizing the exchange rate versus stabilizing the domestic economy, is most severe when the exchange rate is under a *speculative attack.* A **speculative attack** involves massive selling of domestic currency assets by both domestic and foreign financial investors. A speculative attack lowers the market equilibrium value of the exchange rate still further by increasing the supply of the currency in the foreign exchange market. To stop a speculative attack, the central bank must raise the market equilibrium value of the currency a great deal, which requires a large increase in the real interest rate. (In a famous episode in 1992, the Swedish central bank responded to an attack on its currency by raising the short-term interest rate to 500 percent!) However, because the increase in the real interest rate that is necessary to stop a speculative attack reduces aggregate demand, it can cause a severe economic slowdown. Economic Naturalist 13.2 describes a real-world example of this phenomenon.

speculative attack
a massive selling of domestic currency assets by financial investors

www.riksbank.com
Swedish Central Bank

What were the causes and consequences of the East Asian crisis of 1997–1998?

During the past three decades, the countries of East Asia have enjoyed impressive economic growth and stability. But the "East Asian miracle" seemed to end in 1997 when a wave of speculative attacks hit the region's currencies. Thailand, which had kept a constant value for its currency in terms of the U.S. dollar for more than a decade, was the first to come under attack, but the crisis spread to other countries, including South Korea, Indonesia, and Malaysia. Each of these countries was ultimately forced to devalue its currency. What caused this crisis, and what were its consequences?

Because of the impressive economic record of the East Asian countries, the Asian currency crisis was not expected by most policy-makers, economists, and financial investors. With the benefit of hindsight, however, we can identify some of its causative factors.

One is that the U.S. dollar strengthened from mid-1995 to 1997, particularly against the Japanese yen, and this caused the East Asian currencies pegged to it to strengthen and their trade deficits to widen. If an economy with a fixed exchange rate is running large trade deficits, currency traders often judge that the currency is overvalued, so larger trade deficits triggered speculation against certain East Asian currencies, particularly the Thai baht. Thailand used its foreign currency reserves to defend the baht, but eventually it was forced to devalue. Then panic struck currency markets. Financial investors became increasingly fearful of other devaluations in the region, speculative attacks intensified, and several other East Asian economies were eventually forced to devalue.

Many of the countries forced to devalue had abandoned controls of international capital flows in the early 1990s. But China and Vietnam, which had never abandoned capital controls, were able to withstand the speculative attacks. Also, both China and Hong Kong were aided in withstanding attacks by their massive holdings of foreign currency reserves.[8]

The International Monetary Fund (IMF) provided emergency loans to several East Asian countries (see Box 13.1), but some economists believe that the conditions attached to the loans worsened the situation. In an attempt to raise the market equilibrium values of their exchange rates and stave off additional devaluation, several of the countries increased their real interest rates sharply, at IMF urging. However, the rise in real interest rates depressed aggregate demand, contributing to sharp declines in output and rising unemployment.

Fortunately, by 1999 most East Asian economies had begun to recover. Still, the crisis impressed the potential dangers of fixed exchange rates quite sharply in the minds of policy-makers in developing countries.

BOX 13.1

The International Monetary Fund

The International Monetary Fund (IMF) was established after the Second World War. An international agency, the IMF is controlled by a 24-member executive board. Eight executive board members represent individual countries (China, France, Germany, Japan, Russia, Saudi Arabia, the United Kingdom, and the United States); the other 16 members each represent a group of countries. A managing director oversees the IMF's operations and its approximately 2600 employees.

The original purpose of the IMF was to help manage the system of fixed exchange rates, called the Bretton Woods system, put in place after the war. Under Bretton Woods, the IMF's principal role was to lend international reserves to member countries that needed them so that those countries could maintain their exchange rates at the official values. However, by 1973, the United States, the United Kingdom, Germany, and most other industrial nations had abandoned fixed exchange rates for flexible rates, leaving the IMF to find a new mission. Since 1973, the IMF has been involved primarily in lending to developing countries. It lent heavily to Mexico when that country experienced speculative attacks in 1994, and it made loans to East Asian countries during the 1997–1998 crisis. Other countries that received large IMF loans in recent years include Russia and Brazil.

8 For further analysis of the East Asian currency crisis, see Brian MacLean, ed., "The Transformation of International Economic Policy Debate, 1997–98," in *Out of Control: Canada in an Unstable Financial World* (Lorimer: Toronto, 1999), pp. 67–94.

The IMF's performance in the crises of the 1990s has been especially controversial. Many observers credit the IMF with helping Mexico, the East Asian nations, and others to recover quickly from the effects of speculative attacks, and contend that the IMF plays a vital role in maintaining international economic stability. However, some critics have charged that the IMF has required recipients of its loans to follow economic policies, such as tight monetary policies and fiscal cutbacks, that have turned out to be ill-advised. In particular, some believe that the IMF's policies were aimed at keeping Wall Street investors happy, rather than at providing economic stability. They have claimed that the IMF's loans help foreign financial investors and the richest people in the countries receiving loans, rather than the average person.

The IMF has also come into conflict with the World Bank, a separate international institution that was set up at about the same time as the IMF. The World Bank, whose mission is to provide long-term loans to help poor nations develop their economies, has complained that IMF interventions in poor countries interfered with World Bank programs and objectives. In 2000, a report commissioned by the U.S. Congress recommended reducing the IMF's powers (as well as, incidentally, those of the World Bank).

A strategy followed by many developing countries over the past several years has been to accumulate massive foreign exchange reserves in order to be able to prevent currency crises and thereby avoid the need to call on the IMF for loans. As a consequence, the IMF loan portfolio (that is, credit outstanding) shrank from US$117 billion in late 2003 to just $16 billion in early 2008. In 2008, the IMF itself was running deficits and was forced to make major cuts to its staff. The global recession and financial crisis of 2008–2009, however, created new opportunities for the IMF, including loans to so-called peripheral European countries such as Greece and Ireland.

RECAP

FIXED EXCHANGE RATES

- The value of a fixed exchange rate is set by the government. The official value of a fixed exchange rate may differ from its market equilibrium value, as determined by supply and demand in the foreign exchange market. An exchange rate whose officially fixed value exceeds its market equilibrium value is overvalued; an exchange rate whose officially fixed value is below its market equilibrium value is undervalued.

- For an overvalued exchange rate, the quantity of the currency supplied to the foreign exchange market at the official exchange rate exceeds the quantity demanded. The government can maintain an overvalued exchange rate for a time by using its international reserves (foreign currency assets) to purchase the excess supply of its currency. The net decline in a country's stock of international reserves during the year is its balance-of-payments deficit.

- If a country's international reserves are quite limited, it cannot maintain an overvalued exchange rate for very long. Moreover, if financial investors fear an impending devaluation of the exchange rate, they may launch a speculative attack, selling domestic currency assets and supplying large amounts of the country's currency to the foreign exchange market—an action that exhausts the country's reserves even more quickly. One response to this situation is for economies with fixed exchange rates to accumulate massive international reserves during periods when their exchange rates are undervalued.

> - By raising the real interest rate, a central bank raises the demand for the currency and hence its market equilibrium value. By raising a currency's market equilibrium value to its official value, higher interest rates can eliminate the problem of overvaluation and stabilize the exchange rate. However, if monetary policy is used to set the market equilibrium value of the exchange rate, it is no longer available for stabilizing the domestic economy.

13.4 SHOULD EXCHANGE RATES BE FIXED OR FLEXIBLE?

Should countries adopt fixed or flexible exchange rates? In briefly comparing the two systems, we will focus on two major issues: (1) the effects of the exchange rate system on monetary policy and (2) the effects of the exchange rate system on trade and economic integration.

On the issue of monetary policy, we have seen that the type of exchange rate a country has strongly affects the central bank's ability to use monetary policy to stabilize the economy. A flexible exchange rate actually strengthens the impact of monetary policy on aggregate demand. But a fixed exchange rate prevents policy-makers from using monetary policy to stabilize the economy, because they must instead use it to keep the exchange rate's market equilibrium value at its official value (or else risk speculative attack).

In large economies like those of the United States and Japan, and also in medium-sized developed economies like Canada and Australia, giving up the power to stabilize the domestic economy via monetary policy makes little economic sense. Thus, for such economies there is a very strong case for employing a flexible exchange rate. However, in very small economies, giving up this power may have benefits that exceed the costs. The benefits may be particularly large for small developing economies that have a history of very high and damaging rates of inflation. A fixed exchange rate may help such economies achieve low or moderate rates of inflation.

The second important issue is the effect of the exchange rate on trade and economic integration. Proponents of fixed exchange rates argue that fixed rates promote international trade and cross-border economic cooperation by reducing uncertainty about future exchange rates. For example, a firm that is considering building up its export business knows that its potential profits will depend on the future value of its own country's currency relative to the currencies of the countries to which it exports. Under a flexible-exchange-rate regime, the value of the home currency fluctuates with changes in supply and demand and is, therefore, difficult to predict far in advance. Such uncertainty may make the firm reluctant to expand its export business. Supporters of fixed exchange rates argue that if the exchange rate is officially fixed, uncertainty about the future exchange rate is reduced or eliminated.

One problem with this argument, which has been underscored by episodes like the East Asian crisis, is that fixed exchange rates are not guaranteed to remain fixed forever. Although they do not fluctuate from day to day as flexible rates do, a speculative attack on a fixed exchange rate may lead suddenly and unpredictably to a large devaluation. Thus, a firm that is trying to forecast the exchange rate 10 years into the future may face as much uncertainty if the exchange rate is fixed as if it is flexible.

The potential instability of fixed exchange rates caused by speculative attacks has led some countries to try a more radical solution to the problem of uncertainty about exchange rates: the adoption of a common currency. Economic Naturalist 13.3 describes an important instance of this strategy.

ECONOMIC NATURALIST   13.3

Why have 17 European countries adopted a common currency?

Effective January 1, 1999, eleven Western European nations, including France, Germany, and Italy, adopted for some purposes a new currency called the euro, irrevocably fixed the exchange rates between their currencies, and transferred key functions from their central banks to the European Central Bank (ECB). A twelfth country, Greece, joined this arrangement in 2001, and in January 2002, the various countries began to call in their domestic currencies and replace them with euro currency. Since then, five additional countries have joined the "eurozone" and adopted the euro. Why have these economies adopted a common currency?

For some decades, the nations of Western Europe have worked to increase economic cooperation and trade among themselves. European leaders believed that a unified and integrated European economy would be more productive and perhaps more competitive with the North American economy than a fragmented one. As part of this effort, these countries established fixed exchange rates under the auspices of a system called the European Monetary System (EMS). Unfortunately, the EMS did not prove stable. Numerous devaluations of the various currencies occurred, and in 1992 severe speculative attacks forced several economies, including Great Britain, to abandon the fixed-exchange-rate system.

In December 1991, in Maastricht in the Netherlands, the member countries of the European Community (EC) adopted a treaty popularly known as the Maastricht Treaty. One of the major provisions of the treaty, which took effect in November 1993, was that member countries would strive to adopt a common currency. This common currency, known as the euro, was formally adopted on January 1, 1999. The advent of the euro mean the that Europeans would no longer have to change currencies when trading with other European countries, much as Canadians from different provinces can trade with each other without worrying that a "Nova Scotia dollar" will change in value relative to a "British Columbia dollar." The euro has helped to promote European trade and cooperation, while eliminating the problem of speculative attacks on the currencies of individual countries.

Because Western Europe now has a single currency, it also must have a common monetary policy. The EC members agreed that European monetary policy would be put under the control of a new European Central Bank (ECB), a multinational institution located in Frankfurt, Germany. One problem with having a single monetary policy for 17 different economies is that different countries may face different economic conditions, so a single monetary policy cannot respond to all of them. What can the ECB do, for example, if Ireland is suffering from a recession (which requires an easing of monetary policy) while Germany is worried about inflation (which requires a tightening)? This problem was brought to the fore by the global recession and financial crisis of 2008–2009.[9]

ECONOMIC NATURALIST   13.4

Why has China stopped pegging the renminbi to the U.S. dollar?

From mid-1995 to mid-2005, the Chinese renminbi (also known as the yuan) was pegged to the U.S. dollar. Although this practice was often criticized by U.S. politicians who wished for a stronger renminbi in order to prevent rising Chinese trade surpluses with the United States, to many Chinese politicians and economists the fixed exchange rate seemed to be a key component in the package of policies that consistently produced very high real GDP growth rates for China. Why then, in mid-2005, did the Chinese government finally allow the renminbi to appreciate against the U.S. dollar?

One explanation emphasizes the impact of a depreciating exchange rate on the growth of aggregate demand in China. Since about 2002–2003, the United States dollar had been depreciating against almost all other major currencies. When it was pegged to the U.S. dollar, the renminbi also depreciated against other major currencies. For example, the red line of Figure 13.7 shows the appreciation of the euro against the yuan, and thus against the U.S. dollar to which the renminbi was pegged, beginning in 2002. This gave a strong stimulus to China's net exports and, hence, to aggregate demand growth in China. But the aggregate demand growth of China, according to this explanation, was already sufficient without depreciation of the renminbi. The depreciating renminbi caused actual GDP growth to exceed potential GDP growth. And if actual GDP growth exceeds potential GDP growth, the inflation rate tends to rise, as is explained in Chapter 11. To combat rising inflation from excessive aggregate demand growth, the renminbi, therefore, was allowed to appreciate.

---

9   See, for example, Paul Krugman, "Greek End Game," *New York Times*, May 5, 2010, at http://krugman.blogs.nytimes.com/2010/05/05/greek-end-game/.

A related explanation, which has been advanced by *The Economist* newsweekly, is that China allowed the renminbi to appreciate in order to offset an increase in domestic inflation due to, among other things, a surge in the prices of imported foods, particularly grains and fuel. The argument is that a stronger renminbi will act to reduce the prices of imports and, thereby, counteract the rise of domestic inflation as measured by the consumer price index. China's consumer price index includes the prices of imports consumed by households, as does the Canadian consumer price index, explained in Chapter 6.

A final explanation for allowing the appreciation is that China wished to stem the excessive growth of the country's international reserves (official foreign exchange reserves). Some economists believe that the renminbi became increasingly undervalued during much of the period it was pegged to the U.S. dollar. As discussed earlier in this chapter, if a country with a fixed exchange rate has an undervalued currency, it can expect to accumulate international reserves. Conversely, if it revalues

its currency or allows the currency to appreciate, the accumulation of international reserves should be slowed or stopped as a result. International reserves are desirable, up to a point, because they allow a country to defend its exchange rate against speculative attacks. But China's reserves are truly massive, more than double those of Japan, the economy with the world's second largest international reserves. The bulk of China's foreign exchange reserves, as with the majority of those from most countries, are held in the form of U.S.-dollar, short-term government bonds. And as the U.S. dollar began to depreciate against most other currencies, many economists have pointed to the risk China faces by holding so much of its wealth in U.S. dollars.

In the fall of the 2008, China went back to a fixed exchange rate to prevent any appreciation of its currency as the global recession unfolded and commodity prices plummeted. But in the summer of 2010, with solid economic growth restored to the Chinese economy and rising inflation as a concern, China once again allowed its exchange rate to float.

FIGURE 13.7

The Chinese Renminbi, January 1994–May 2011

From mid-1995 to mid-2005, the Chinese renminbi was pegged to the U.S. dollar at about US$0.1208 per yuan (or about 8.3 yuan per dollar). During this period, however, the renminbi fluctuated very substantially against other currencies, such as the euro. The renminbi, for example, appreciated against the euro from the inception of the euro until the latter half of 2002. From mid-2005, the renminbi was allowed to appreciate substantially against the U.S. dollar. It was pegged against the U.S. dollar during the global recession that began in the latter half of 2008, but it has been allowed to appreciate again since 2010.
SOURCE: Monthly average exchange rate data from the Pacific Exchange Rate Service, http://fx.sauder.ubc.ca/.

www.ecb.int
European Central Bank

13.5   INFLATION RATE DIFFERENCES AND EXCHANGE RATE DETERMINATION

In this section, we discuss the implications for the exchange rate between two countries should the inflation rates of the countries be very different. In our supply and demand analysis, we assumed both that the dollar price of Canadian goods and the foreign currency price of foreign goods (for example, the price of Apple iPads in U.S. dollars) did not change. If the inflation rates of the two countries, Canada and the United States, are very different, however, we would definitely need to relax this assumption. The theory we shall use to discuss the impact of inflation rate differences on the exchange rate is called the theory of *purchasing power parity*. In order to explain this theory, we must first introduce the real exchange rate.

THE REAL EXCHANGE RATE

The nominal exchange rate tells us the price of the domestic currency in terms of a foreign currency. The *real exchange rate* is the nominal exchange rate between the currencies of two countries, adjusted for changes in the relative price levels between the two countries since a base year. Adjusting a nominal exchange rate to get a real exchange rate is comparable to adjusting nominal GDP to get real GDP (covered in Chapter 5), adjusting nominal incomes or wages to get real incomes or wages (Chapter 6), or adjusting a nominal interest rate to get a real interest rate (Chapter 6). We will also see that a country's real exchange rate has implications for its ability to sell its exports abroad.

To provide background for discussing the real exchange rate, imagine you are in charge of purchasing for a Canadian corporation that is planning to acquire a large number of new trucks. The company's transportation specialist has identified two models, one Japanese made and one Canadian made, that meet the necessary specifications. Since the two models are essentially equivalent, the company will buy the one with the lower price. However, since the trucks are priced in the currencies of the countries of manufacture, the price comparison is not so straightforward. Your job is to determine which of the two models is cheaper.

To complete your assignment, you will need three pieces of information: the nominal exchange rate between the Canadian dollar and the yen and the prices of the two models in terms of the currencies of their countries of manufacture. Example 13.4 shows how you can use this information to determine which model is cheaper.

EXAMPLE 13.4

Comparing prices expressed in different currencies

A Canadian-made truck costs $24 000, and a similar Japanese-made truck costs ¥1 875 000. If the nominal exchange rate happens to be 75 yen per dollar, which truck is the better buy?

To make this price comparison, we must measure the prices of both trucks in terms of the same currency. To make the comparison in dollars, we first convert the Japanese truck's price into dollars. The price in terms of Japanese yen is ¥1 875 000 (the symbol ¥ means "yen"), and we are told that ¥75 = $1. To find the dollar price of the truck, then, we observe that for any good or service,

$$\text{Price in yen} = \text{Price in dollars} \times \text{Value of dollar in terms of yen.}$$

Note that the value of a dollar in terms of yen is simply the yen-dollar exchange rate. Making this substitution and solving, we get

$$\text{Price in dollars} = \frac{\text{Price in yen}}{\text{Yen} - \text{dollar exchange rate}}$$
$$= \frac{¥1\,875\,000}{¥75/\$1} = \$25\,000.$$

Notice that the yen symbol appears in both the numerator and the denominator of the ratio, so it cancels out. Our conclusion is that the Canadian truck at $24 000 is $1000 cheaper than the Japanese truck, which is $25 000. The Canadian truck is the better deal.

Continuing Example 13.4, compare the prices of the Japanese and Canadian trucks by expressing both prices in terms of yen.

In Example 13.4, the fact that the Canadian truck was cheaper implied that your firm would choose it over the Japanese-made truck. In general, a country's ability to compete in international markets depends in part on the prices of its goods and services *relative* to the prices of foreign goods and services, when the prices are measured in a common currency. In the hypothetical example of the Japanese and Canadian trucks, the price of the domestic (Canadian) good relative to the price of the foreign (Japanese) good is $24 000/$25 000, or 0.96. So the Canadian truck is 4 percent cheaper than the Japanese truck, putting the Japanese product at a competitive disadvantage.

More generally, economists ask whether *on average* the goods and services produced by a particular country are expensive relative to the goods and services produced by other countries. This question can be answered by the country's *real exchange rate*. Specifically, a country's **real exchange rate**, as mentioned previously, is the nominal exchange rate between the currencies of two countries adjusted for changes in the relative price levels in the two countries since a base year.

To obtain a formula for the real exchange rate, recall that e equals the nominal exchange rate (the number of units of foreign currency per dollar) and that P equals the domestic price level, as measured, for example, by the consumer price index. Similarly, let P^f equal the foreign price level.

The real exchange rate equals the price of the average domestic good or service relative to the price of the average foreign good or service. It would not be correct, however, to define the real exchange rate as the ratio P/P^f, because the two price levels are expressed in different currencies. As we saw in Example 13.4, to convert foreign prices into Canadian dollars we must divide the foreign price by the exchange rate. By this rule, the price in dollars of the average foreign good or service equals P^f/e. Now we can write the real exchange rate as

$$\text{Real exchange rate} = \frac{P}{P^f/e}$$

To simplify this expression, multiply the numerator and denominator by e to get

$$\text{Real exchange rate} = \frac{eP}{P^f} \qquad (13.1)$$

which is the formula for the real exchange rate.

Because both P and P^f are indexes, the real exchange rate for an economy is necessarily an index. The most frequently analyzed real exchange rate for the Canadian dollar is the U.S. dollar–Canadian dollar real exchange rate, and it is usually set equal to 1.0 for 1973. Back in 1973, the U.S. and Canadian dollars traded at par, meaning it cost one U.S. dollar to buy a Canadian dollar, or that e was equal to 1.0. For the real exchange rate to equal 1.0 when e is equal to 1.0, the ratio of P and P^f must also be set to equal 1.0. Some economists set the ratio of the Canadian CPI to equal the U.S. CPI, whereas other economists set the ratio of the Canadian GDP deflator to equal the U.S. GDP deflator.

The real exchange rate, an overall measure of the cost of domestic goods and services relative to foreign goods and services, can be an important economic variable. When the real exchange rate rises, domestic goods become more expensive relative to foreign goods (when priced in the same currency). An increase in the real exchange rate implies that domestic producers will have greater difficulty exporting to other countries (domestic goods have become "overpriced"), while foreign goods will sell well in the home country (because imported goods have become cheaper relative to goods produced at home).

real exchange rate the nominal exchange rate between the currencies of two countries adjusted for changes in the relative price levels in the two countries since a base year.

Since a higher real exchange rate tends to reduce exports and increase imports, we conclude that *net exports will tend to decrease when the real exchange rate increases.* Conversely, if the real exchange rate declines, then the home country will find it easier to export (because its goods are priced lower relative to those of foreign competitors), while domestic residents will buy few imports (because imports have become more expensive relative to domestic goods). Thus *net exports will tend to increase when the real exchange rate decreases.*

Equation 13.1 also shows that the real exchange rate tends to move in the same direction as the nominal exchange rate *e* (since *e* appears in the numerator of the formula for the real exchange rate). To the extent that real and nominal exchange rates move in the same direction, we can conclude that net exports will be hurt by a high nominal exchange rate and helped by a low nominal exchange rate. In recent decades, the inflation rates of Canada and the United States have been fairly similar, so for looking at the Canada-U.S. dollar exchange rate it is usually adequate to focus on the nominal exchange rate.

A SIMPLE THEORY OF EXCHANGE RATES: PURCHASING POWER PARITY (PPP)

The concept that the real exchange rate is useful for understanding a long-standing theory of how nominal exchange rates are determined is called *purchasing power parity,* or PPP. To understand this theory, we must also discuss a fundamental economic concept called *the law of one price.* The **law of one price** states that if transportation costs are relatively small, the price of an internationally traded commodity will be the same in all locations. For example, if transportation costs are not too large, the price of a ton of wheat ought to be the same in Bombay, India, and Sydney, Australia. Suppose that were not the case— that the price of wheat in Sydney was only half of the price in Bombay. In that case, grain merchants would have a strong incentive to buy wheat in Sydney and ship it to Bombay, where it could be sold at double the price of purchase. As wheat left Sydney, reducing the local supply, the price of wheat in Sydney would rise, while the inflow of wheat into Bombay would reduce the price in Bombay. According to the *equilibrium principle* (Chapter 3), the international market for wheat would return to equilibrium only when unexploited opportunities to profit had been eliminated—specifically, only when the prices of wheat in Sydney and in Bombay became equal or nearly equal (with the difference being less than the cost of transporting wheat from Australia to India).

If the law of one price were to hold for all goods and services (which is not a realistic assumption, as we will see shortly), then the value of the nominal exchange rate would be determined, as Example 13.5 illustrates.

law of one price
if transportation costs are relatively small, the price of an internationally traded commodity will be the same in all locations

EQUILIBRIUM

EXAMPLE **13.5**

How many Indian rupees equal one Australian dollar? (1)

Suppose that a ton of wheat costs 5 Australian dollars in Sydney and 150 rupees in Bombay. If the law of one price holds for wheat, what is the nominal exchange rate between Australia and India?

Because the market value of a ton of wheat must be the same in both locations, we know that the Australian price of wheat must equal the Indian price of wheat so that

5 Australian dollars = 150 Indian rupees.

Dividing by 5, we get

1 Australian dollar = 30 Indian rupees.

So the nominal exchange rate between Australia and India should be 30 rupees per Australian dollar.

The price of gold is US\$1500/ounce in New York and ¥150 000/ounce in Tokyo. If the law of one price holds for gold, what is the nominal exchange rate between the U.S. dollar and the Japanese yen?

Example 13.5 and Exercise 13.6 illustrate the application of the purchasing power parity theory. According to the **purchasing power parity (PPP) theory**, nominal exchange rates are determined as necessary for the law of one price to hold.

A useful prediction of the PPP theory is that in the long run, *the currencies of countries that experience relatively high inflation will tend to depreciate against the currencies of countries that experience relatively low inflation.* To see why, we will extend the analysis in Example 13.6.

purchasing power parity (PPP) the theory that nominal exchange rates are determined as necessary for the law of one price to hold

EXAMPLE 13.6

How many Indian rupees equal one Australian dollar? (2)

Suppose India experiences very high inflation so that the price of a bushel of wheat in Bombay rises from 150 to 300 rupees. Australia has no inflation, so the price of wheat in Sydney remains unchanged at 5 Australian dollars. If the law of one price holds for wheat, what will happen to the nominal exchange rate between Australia and India?

As in Example 13.5, we know that the market value of a bushel of wheat must be the same in both locations. Therefore,

5 Australian dollars = 300 rupees.

Equivalently,

1 Australian dollar = 60 rupees.

The nominal exchange rate is now 60 rupees/Australian dollar. Before India's inflation, the nominal exchange rate was 30 rupees/Australian dollar (Example 13.5). So in this example, high inflation has caused the rupee to depreciate against the Australian dollar. Conversely, Australia, with no inflation, has seen its currency appreciate against the rupee.

This link between high inflation and depreciation makes economic sense. High inflation implies that a nation's currency is losing purchasing power in the domestic market. Analogously, exchange rate depreciation implies that the nation's currency is losing purchasing power in international markets.

Figure 13.8 shows annual rates of inflation and nominal exchange rate depreciation for the 10 largest South American countries from 1995 to 2001, a period during which several of these countries experienced high inflation. Inflation is measured as the annual rate of change in the country's consumer price index; depreciation is measured relative to the U.S. dollar. As you can see, inflation varied greatly among South American countries during the period. For example, Argentina's inflation rate was essentially the same as that of the United States, while Venezuela had inflation of 37 percent per year and Ecuador's inflation was 45 percent per year. (Since 2001, inflation rates have fallen substantially for many of these countries, and factors such as those examined in the supply and demand analysis of exchange rate determination have been more relatively more important in explaining their exchange rates.)

Figure 13.8 shows that, as the PPP theory implies, countries with the highest inflation during the 1995–2001 period tended to experience the most rapid depreciation of their currencies.

SHORTCOMINGS OF THE PPP THEORY

Empirical studies have found that the PPP theory is useful for predicting some of the change in nominal exchange rates over the relatively long run. However, the theory is less

FIGURE 13.8

Inflation and Currency Depreciation in South America, 1995–2001

The annual rates of inflation and nominal exchange-rate depreciation (relative to the U.S. dollar) in 10 South American countries varied considerably during 1995–2001. High inflation was associated with rapid depreciation of the nominal exchange rate. SOURCES: International Monetary Fund, International Financial Statistics, and authors' calculations.

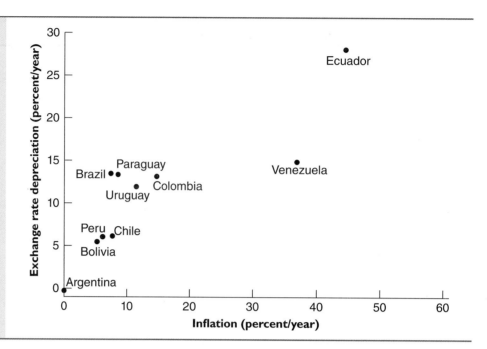

successful in predicting short-run movements in exchange rates, except where very high inflation causes rapid depreciation of a country's exchange rate, as shown in Figure 13.8.

A particularly dramatic failure of the PPP theory occurred in Canada beginning in the 1990s. As Figure 13.1 indicates, between 1992 and 2002 the value of the Canadian dollar fell nearly 30 percent relative to the U.S. dollar. This strong depreciation could be explained by PPP theory only if inflation were considerably higher in Canada than in the U.S. In fact, inflation was slightly lower in Canada than in the United States throughout the period.

Another example is the recent behaviour of the Brazilian real, one of the currencies shown in Figure 13.8. Over the 2004–2007 period, Brazilian inflation exceeded U.S. inflation by about 2 percentage points per year; inflation in Brazil averaged 5.3 percent compared to 3 percent in the United States. But over this same period, the Brazilian real appreciated strongly against the U.S. dollar, moving from 2.85 reais per U.S. dollar in January 2004 to 1.79 reais per U.S. dollar in December 2007.

Why does the PPP theory work less than perfectly at best, and less well in the short run (say, under a decade) than in the long run? Recall that this theory relies on the law of one price, which says that the price of an internationally traded commodity must be the same in all locations. The law of one price works well for goods such as wheat or gold, which are standardized commodities that are traded widely. However, *not all goods and services are traded internationally,* and *not all goods are standardized commodities.*

Many goods and services are not traded internationally, because the assumption underlying the law of one price—that transportation costs are relatively small—does not hold for them. For example, for Indians to export haircuts to Australia, they would need to transport an Indian barber to Australia every time a Sydney resident desired a trim. Because transportation costs prevent haircuts from being traded internationally, the law of one price does not apply to them. Thus, even if the price of haircuts in Australia were double the price of haircuts in India, market forces would not necessarily influence prices toward equality in the short run. (Over the long run, some Indian barbers might emigrate to Australia.) Other examples of non-traded goods and services are agricultural land, buildings, heavy construction materials (whose value is low relative to their transportation costs), and highly perishable foods. In addition, some products use non-traded goods and services as inputs: A McDonald's hamburger served in Moscow has both a tradable component (frozen hamburger patties) and a non-tradable component (the labour of counter workers). In general, the greater the share of non-traded goods and services in a nation's output, the less precisely the PPP theory will apply to the country's exchange rate.[10]

The second reason the law of one price and the PPP theory sometimes fail to apply is that not all internationally traded goods and services are perfectly standardized commodities, like grain or gold. For example, Canadian-made automobiles and Japanese-made automobiles are not identical; they differ in styling, horsepower, reliability, and other features. As a result, some people strongly prefer one nation's cars to another's. Thus, if Japanese cars cost 10 percent more than Canadian cars, Canadian automobile exports will not necessarily flood the Japanese market, since many Japanese will still prefer Japanese-made cars even at a 10-percent premium. Of course, there are limits to how far prices can diverge before people will switch to the cheaper product. But the law of one price, and hence the PPP theory, will not apply exactly to non-standardized goods.

www.economist.com/markets/
bigmac/index.cfm

> **RECAP**
>
> ### EXCHANGE RATE DETERMINATION IN THE LONG RUN
>
> - The *real exchange rate* is nominal exchange rate between the currencies of two countries adjusted for changes in the relative price levels in the two countries since a base year. An increase in the real exchange rate implies that domestic goods and services are becoming more expensive relative to foreign goods and services, which tends to reduce exports and increase imports. Conversely, a decline in the real exchange rate tends to increase net exports.
>
> - A useful formula for the real exchange rate is eP/P^f, where e is the nominal exchange rate, P is the domestic price level, and P^f is the foreign price level.
>
> - The *purchasing power parity (PPP)* theory of nominal exchange rate determination is based on the law of one price. The *law of one price* states that if transportation costs are relatively small, the price of an internationally traded commodity must be the same in all locations. According to the PPP theory, the nominal exchange rate between two currencies can be found by setting the price of traded commodities in one currency equal to the price of the same commodities expressed in the second currency.
>
> - A useful prediction of the PPP theory is that the currencies of countries with relatively high inflation will tend to depreciate against the currencies of countries that experience relatively low inflation. However, the fact that many goods and services are non-traded, and that not all traded goods are standardized, reduces the applicability of the law of one price, and hence, of the PPP theory. Thus the theory has severe shortcomings for short-run analysis.

13.6 THE IMPACT OF MONETARY POLICY WITH A FLEXIBLE EXCHANGE RATE: A RESTATEMENT

This chapter has been primarily about the economic factors that determine fluctuations in flexible exchange rates and the economic policies necessary to maintain fixed exchange rates. To close the chapter, however, let us re-emphasize the point that changes in the exchange rate do have an important effect on the Canadian economy. In particular,

---

10 Trade barriers such as tariffs and quotas also increase the costs associated with shipping goods from one country to another. Thus, trade barriers reduce the applicability of the law of one price in much the same way that physical transportation costs do.

FIGURE 13.9
Lower Interest Rates and a Lower Value of the Currency Raise GDP
Falling interest rates in Canada raise GDP both through a lower cost of borrowing, increasing private-sector investment and consumption, and through a fall in the real exchange rate, increasing net exports.

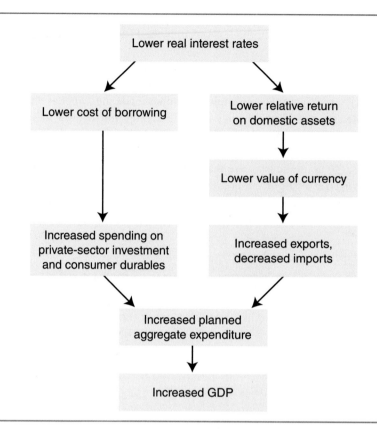

exchange rate changes that result from monetary policy changes (increases or decreases in the key policy rate by the Bank of Canada) tend to intensify the impact of monetary policy.

Figure 13.9 shows how a reduction in real interest rates by the Bank of Canada results in a rise in GDP, through two channels. First, as we saw in Chapter 10, falling interest rates reduce the cost of borrowing for firms and households, which encourages private-sector investment spending (particularly residential investment) and consumer durables spending. Second, as this chapter shows, falling interest rates lower the return on Canadian assets, making them less attractive relative to foreign assets. This reduces the value of the Canadian dollar, raising exports and lowering imports. The increases in private-sector investment, consumption, and net exports pull up planned aggregate expenditure, causing GDP to rise.

SUMMARY

- The *nominal exchange rate* between two currencies is the rate at which the currencies can be traded for each other. A rise in the value of a currency relative to another currency is called an *appreciation*; a decline in the value of a currency is called a *depreciation*. **LO1**

- Exchange rates can be flexible or fixed. The value of a *flexible exchange rate* is determined by the supply of and demand for the currency in the *foreign exchange market*, the market on which currencies of various nations are traded for one another. The government sets the value of a *fixed exchange rate*. **LO1**

- Supply and demand analysis is a useful tool for studying the determination of exchange rates in the short run. The equilibrium exchange rate, also called the *market equilibrium value of the exchange rate,* equates the quantities of the currency supplied and demanded in the foreign exchange market. A currency is supplied by domestic residents who wish to acquire foreign currencies to purchase foreign goods, services, and assets. An increased preference for foreign goods, an increase in the domestic GDP, or an increase in the real interest rate on foreign assets will all increase the supply of a currency on the foreign exchange market and thus lower its value. A currency is demanded by foreigners who wish to purchase domestic goods, services, and assets. An increased preference for domestic goods by foreigners, an increase in real GDP abroad, or an increase in the domestic real interest rate will all increase the demand for the currency on the foreign exchange market and thus increase its value. **LO2**

- If the exchange rate is flexible, by raising the real interest rate the central bank will tend to increase the demand for the currency and cause it to appreciate. The stronger currency reinforces the effects of the tight monetary policy on aggregate demand by reducing net exports. Conversely, by lowering the real interest rate, the central bank weakens the currency, which in turn stimulates net exports. **LO2**

- The value of a fixed exchange rate is officially established by the government. A fixed exchange rate whose official value exceeds its market equilibrium value in the foreign exchange market is said to be *overvalued.* An exchange rate whose official value is below its market equilibrium value is *undervalued.* A reduction in the official value of a fixed exchange rate is called a *devaluation;* an increase in its official value is called a *revaluation.* **LO3**

- For an overvalued exchange rate, the quantity of the currency supplied at the official exchange rate exceeds the quantity demanded. To maintain the official rate, the country's central bank must use its *international reserves* (foreign currency assets) to purchase the excess supply of its currency in the foreign exchange market. Because a country's international reserves are limited, it cannot maintain an overvalued exchange rate indefinitely. **LO3**

- By raising the real interest rate and thereby raising the market equilibrium value of the exchange rate, a central bank can eliminate the problem of overvaluation. However, if monetary policy is used to set the market equilibrium value of the exchange rate equal to the official value, it is no longer available for stabilizing the domestic economy. Thus, under fixed exchange rates, monetary policy has little or no power to affect domestic output and employment. **LO3**

- Because a fixed exchange rate implies that monetary policy can no longer be used for domestic stabilization, most large and medium-sized developed countries employ a flexible exchange rate. A fixed exchange rate may benefit a small country with a poor inflation record by forcing its central bank to follow the monetary policies of the country to which it has tied its rate. Advocates of fixed exchange rates argue that they increase trade and economic integration by making the exchange rate more predictable. However, the threat of speculative attacks greatly reduces the long-term predictability of a fixed exchange rate. **LO4**

- The *real exchange rate* is the price of the average domestic good or service *relative* to the price of the average foreign good or service, when prices are expressed in terms of a common currency. An increase in the real exchange rate implies that domestic goods and services are becoming more expensive relative to foreign goods and services, which tends to reduce exports and increase imports. Conversely, a decline in the real exchange rate tends to increase net exports. **LO5**

- A long-standing theory of nominal exchange rate determination, the *purchasing power parity* (PPP) theory, is based on the law of one price. The *law of one price* states that if transportation costs are relatively small, the price of an internationally traded commodity must be the same in all locations. According to the PPP theory, we can find the nominal exchange rate between two currencies by setting the price of commodities in one of the currencies equal to the price of the commodities in the second currency. The PPP theory correctly predicts that the currencies of countries that experience very high inflation will tend to depreciate. However, the fact that many goods and services are not traded internationally, and that not all traded goods are standardized, makes the PPP theory less useful for explaining other situations, particularly short-run changes in exchange rates. **LO5**

■ With a flexible exchange rate, exchange rate changes that result from monetary policy changes (increases or decreases in the key policy rate by the Bank of Canada) tend to intensify the impact of monetary policy. **LO6**

KEY TERMS

appreciation (329)
balance-of-payments deficit (339)
balance-of-payments surplus (339)
Bretton Woods system (336)
capital controls (338)
depreciation (329)
devaluation (337)
fixed exchange rate (331)

flexible exchange rate (331)
foreign exchange market (331)
international reserves (339)
law of one price (350)
market equilibrium value of the
    exchange rate (333)
nominal exchange rate (327)
overvalued exchange rate (338)

parity (328)
purchasing power parity
    (PPP) (351)
real exchange rate (349)
revaluation (337)
speculative attack (342)
undervalued exchange rate (338)

REVIEW QUESTIONS

1. Japanese yen trade at 100 yen/Canadian dollar and Mexican pesos trade at 10 pesos/Canadian dollar. What is the nominal exchange rate between the yen and the peso? Express in two ways. **LO1**

2. Why do Canadian households and firms supply dollars to the foreign exchange market? Why do foreigners demand dollars in the foreign exchange market? **LO2**

3. Under a flexible exchange rate, how does a reduction of the real interest rate by the central bank affect the value of the exchange rate? Does this change in the exchange rate tend to weaken or strengthen the effect of the monetary ease on output and employment? Explain. **LO2**

4. Define *overvalued exchange rate*. Discuss four ways in which government policy-makers of an economy with a fixed exchange rate can respond to

an overvaluation. What are the drawbacks of each approach? **LO3**

5. Contrast fixed and flexible exchange rates in terms of how they affect (a) the ability of monetary policy to stabilize domestic output and (b) the predictability of future exchange rates. **LO4**

6. Define *nominal exchange rate* and *real exchange rate*. How are the two concepts related? **LO1, LO5**

7. Would you expect the law of one price to apply to crude oil? to fresh milk? to taxi rides? Explain your answer in each case. **LO5**

8. Describe the impact of a hike in the central bank's key policy rate on an economy with a flexible exchange rate. In your description, include the impact of net exports. (*Hint*: This is the opposite case to the one shown in Figure 13.9). **LO6**

PROBLEMS

1. Using the data in Table 13.1, find the nominal exchange rate between the British pound and the Japanese yen. Express in two ways. How do your answers change if the pound appreciates by 10 percent against the dollar while the value of the yen against the dollar remains unchanged? **LO1**

2. Suppose a French bottle of champagne costs 20 euros. **LO1, LO2**

   a. If the euro-Canadian dollar exchange rate is 0.8 euro per Canadian dollar, so that a dollar can buy 0.8 euro, how much will champagne cost in Canadian dollars?

b. If the euro-Canadian dollar exchange rate rises to 1 euro per dollar, how much will the champagne cost in Canadian dollars?

3. How would each of the following be likely to affect the value of the dollar, all else being equal? Explain. **LO2**

   a. Canadian stocks are perceived as having become much riskier financial investments.

   b. European computer firms switch from Canadian-produced software to software produced in India, Israel, and other nations.

   c. As East Asian economies grow, international financial investors become aware of many new, high-return investment opportunities in the region.

   d. The Canadian government imposes a large tariff on imported automobiles.

   e. The Bank of Canada reports that it is less concerned about inflation and more concerned about an impending recession in Canada.

   f. Canadian consumers increase their spending on imported goods.

4. The demand for and supply of shekels in the foreign exchange market is

$$\text{Demand} = 30\ 000 - 8000e,$$
$$\text{Supply} = 25\ 000 + 12\ 000e,$$

   where the nominal exchange rate is expressed as Canadian dollars per shekel. **LO2, LO3**

   a. What is the market equilibrium value of the shekel?

   b. The shekel is fixed at 0.30 Canadian dollars. Is the shekel overvalued, undervalued, or neither? Find the balance-of-payments deficit or surplus in both shekels and dollars. What happens to the country's international reserves over time?

   c. Repeat (b) for the case in which the shekel is fixed at 0.20 Canadian dollars.

5. Eastland's currency is called the eastmark, and Westland's currency is called the westmark. In the market in which eastmarks and westmarks are traded for each other, the supply of and demand for eastmarks is given by

$$\text{Demand} = 25\ 000 - 5000e + 50\ 000(r_E - r_W).$$
$$\text{Supply} = 18\ 500 + 8000e - 50\ 000(r_E - r_W).$$

   The nominal exchange rate e is measured as westmarks per eastmark, and r_E and r_W are the real interest rates prevailing in Eastland and Westland, respectively. **LO2, LO3**

   a. Explain why it makes economic sense for the two real interest rates to appear in the demand and supply equations in the way they do.

   b. Initially, $r_E = r_W = 0.10$, or 10 percent. Find the market equilibrium value of the eastmark.

   c. The Westlandian central bank grows concerned about inflation and raises Westland's real interest rate to 12 percent. What happens to the market equilibrium value of the eastmark?

   d. Assume that the exchange rate is flexible and that Eastland does not change its real interest rate following the increase in Westland's real interest rate. Is the action of the Westlandian central bank likely to increase or reduce aggregate demand in Eastland? Discuss.

   e. Now suppose that the exchange rate is fixed at the value you found in (b). After the action by the Westlandian central bank, what will the Eastlandian central bank have to do to keep its exchange rate from being overvalued? What effect will this action have on the Eastlandian economy?

   f. In the context of this example, discuss the effect of fixed exchange rates on the ability of a country to run an independent monetary policy.

6. A British-made automobile is priced at £20 000 (20 000 British pounds). A comparable U.S.-made car costs US$26 000. One pound trades for US$2 in the foreign exchange market. Which country's cars are more competitively priced? **LO5**

7. Between last year and this year, the CPI in Blueland rose from 100 to 110 and the CPI in Redland rose from 100 to 105. Blueland's currency unit, the blue, was worth CDN$1 last year and is worth 90 cents (Canadian) this year. Redland's currency unit, the red, was worth 50 cents (Canadian) last year and is worth 45 cents this year. Find the percentage change from last year to this year in Blueland's *nominal* exchange rate with Redland and in Blueland's *real* exchange rate with Redland. (Treat Blueland as the home country.) Relative to Redland, do you expect Blueland's exports to be helped or hurt by these changes in exchange rates? **LO1, LO5**

8. The following table provides, for each of the years from 1997 to 2005, the price levels for China and the United States, as well as the fixed nominal exchange rate of 0.12 U.S. dollars per Chinese yuan. **LO5**

   a. Find the real exchange rate for each of the years from 1997 to 2005.

   b. Did the real exchange rate appreciate or depreciate?

Year	Price level for China	Price level for the United States	Exchange Rate: U.S. Dollars per yuan
1997	100.00	100.00	0.12
1998	99.20	101.55	0.12
1999	97.81	103.77	0.12
2000	98.20	107.27	0.12
2001	98.91	110.29	0.12
2002	98.16	112.05	0.12
2003	99.30	114.62	0.12
2004	103.17	117.68	0.12
2005	105.03	121.65	0.12

c. If the real exchange rate was an equilibrium exchange rate in 1997, and assuming that all relevant factors other than relative inflation rates held constant, would we predict that the yuan would be undervalued or overvalued in 2005?

d. All else being equal, what would be the predicted consequences of the change in the real exchange rate from 1997 to 2005 for China's net exports and official foreign exchange reserves?

e. The price level data in the table is for the consumer price index. Why might the GDP deflator give different conclusions about relative inflation in the two countries? (To answer this part of the question, it may be helpful to review Chapter 6.)

9. Answer each of the following questions. LO5

a. Suppose that gold is $1050/ounce in the United States and 8400 pesos/ounce in Mexico. What nominal exchange rate between U.S. dollars and Mexican pesos is implied by the PPP theory? LO5

b. Mexico experiences inflation so that the price of gold rises to 12 600 pesos/ounce. Gold remains at $1050/ounce in the United States. According to the PPP theory, what happens to the exchange rate? What general principle does this example illustrate?

c. Gold is $1050/ounce in the United States and 12 600 pesos/ounce in Mexico. Crude oil (excluding taxes and transportation costs) is $70/barrel in the U.S. According to the PPP theory, what should a barrel of crude oil cost in Mexico?

d. Gold is $1050/ounce in the United States. The exchange rate between the United States and Canada is 0.95 U.S. dollars/Canadian dollar. How much does an ounce of gold cost in Canada?

ANSWERS TO IN-CHAPTER EXERCISES

13.1   The answer depends on current data. LO1

13.2   A decline in Canadian GDP reduces consumer incomes and hence imports. As Canadians are purchasing fewer imports, they supply fewer dollars to the foreign exchange market, so the supply curve for dollars shifts to the left. Reduced supply raises the equilibrium value of the dollar. LO2

13.3   At a fixed value for the yuan of 0.15 dollars, the demand for the yuan equals 25 000 − 50 000(0.15) = 17 500. The supply of the yuan equals 17 600 + 24 000(0.15) = 21 200. The quantity supplied at the official rate exceeds the quantity demanded by 3700. China will have to purchase 3700 yuan each period, so its balance-of-payments deficit will equal 3700 yuan, or 3700 × 0.15 = 555 dollars. This balance-of-payments deficit is larger than we found in Example 13.6. We conclude that the greater the degree of overvaluation, the larger the country's balance-of-payments deficit is likely to be. LO2, LO3

13.4 The figure above shows a situation in which the official value of the currency is *below* the market equilibrium value, as determined by the supply of and demand for the currency in the foreign exchange market, so the currency is undervalued. At the official value of the exchange rate, the quantity demanded of the domestic currency (point *B*) exceeds the quantity supplied (point *A*). To maintain the official value, the central bank must supply domestic currency to the foreign exchange market each period in the amount *AB*. In contrast to the case of an overvalued exchange rate, here the central bank is providing its own currency to the foreign exchange market and receiving foreign currency in return.

The central bank can print as much of its own currency as it likes, and so with an undervalued currency there is no danger of running out of international reserves. Indeed, the central bank's stock of international reserves increases in the amount *AB* each period, as it receives foreign currency in exchange for the domestic currency it supplies. **LO2, LO3**

13.5 The dollar price of the Canadian truck is \$24 000, and each dollar is equal to 75 yen. Therefore the yen price of the Canadian truck is (75 yen/dollar) × (\$24 000), or 1 800 000 yen. The price of the Japanese truck is 1 875 000 yen. Thus the conclusion that the Japanese vehicle is more expensive does not depend on the currency in which the comparison is made. **LO5**

13.6 Since the law of one price holds for gold, its price per ounce must be the same in New York and Tokyo:

$$\$1500 = 150\,000 \text{ yen.}$$

Dividing both sides by 1500, we get

$$\$1 = 100 \text{ yen.}$$

So the exchange rate is 100 yen/dollar. **LO5**

Practise and learn online with Connect.

PART 4

THE ECONOMY IN THE LONG RUN

For millennia, the great majority of the world's inhabitants eked out a spare existence by tilling the soil. Only a small proportion of the population lived above the level of subsistence, learned to read and write, or travelled more than a few miles from their birthplaces. Large cities grew up, serving as imperial capitals and centres of trade, but the great majority of urban populations lived in dire poverty, subject to malnutrition and disease.

Then, about three centuries ago, a fundamental change occurred. Spurred by technological advances and entrepreneurial innovations, a process of economic growth began that has transformed every aspect of how people live in most countries—from what we eat and wear to how we work and play. Economists recognize that this growth has been central to improvements in living standards, and they have been intensely concerned with the important questions it raises. What is necessary to sustain economic growth and improvements in living standards? Why have some countries enjoyed substantially greater growth than others?

The subject of Part 4 is the long-term behaviour of economies, including the factors that cause economies to grow. Chapter 14 begins by tackling directly the causes and consequences of economic growth. A key conclusion of the chapter is that improvements in average labour productivity are a key source of long-term improvements in living standards; hence, policies to improve living standards must be concerned with stimulating productivity growth. International trade theory and trade policy, including the issue of how trade relates to economic growth, are the topics of Chapter 15. Chapter 16 deals with the role of the financial system in the economy. It covers topics such as saving, investment in new capital goods, the pricing of bonds and stocks, and international capital flows.

CHAPTER 14
Economic Growth, Productivity, and Living Standards

At the time of Canadian Confederation in 1867, doctors lacked effective treatments for a wide range of communicable diseases that are now quite treatable; tuberculosis, typhoid fever, diphtheria, influenza, and pneumonia were once major killers. The shortcomings of healthcare in decades past were not limited to ineffective treatments for now-curable diseases. In addition, healthcare suffered because hospital administrators were slow to learn how much the health of medical patients depended on sanitary conditions and proper nursing care, a fact often illustrated with the story of Florence Nightingale (1820–1910). Nightingale became famous in mid-19th-century England after implementing sanitary reforms at a military hospital, thereby drastically reducing the mortality rates of patients there. She then used statistical evidence on the effectiveness of those reforms to campaign for their widespread adoption. Recognizing that the lack of training of nurses left them incapable of contributing to the recovery of patients, she campaigned successfully to establish nursing as a profession. Nightingale-trained nurses eventually came to Canada, and in 1881 a nursing school based on a modification of the Nightingale system was started at the Toronto General Hospital.

Healthcare is just one aspect of ordinary life where extraordinary progress has been made since the time of Confederation. No doubt you can think of other enormous changes in the conditions average Canadians face, even over the past few decades.

Computer technologies and the Internet have changed the ways people work and study in just a few years, for example. Though these changes are due in large part to scientific advances, such discoveries *by themselves* usually have little effect on most people's lives. New scientific knowledge leads to widespread improvements in living standards only when it is incorporated into widely used goods and services or production processes. Better understanding of the human immune system, for example, has little impact unless it leads to new therapies or drugs. And a new drug will do little to help unless it is affordable to those who need to buy it or is available to them through public healthcare.

Most improvements in living standards are the result not just of scientific and technological advances but of an economic system that makes the benefits of those advances available to the average person.

In this chapter, we will explore the sources of economic growth and rising living standards in the modern world. We will begin by reviewing the remarkable economic growth in the industrialized countries, as measured by real GDP per person. What explains rising living standards as indicated by rising real GDP per person? Generally speaking, rising living standards over long periods require a *continuing increase in average labour productivity*, which depends on several factors, including the equipment with which workers perform their tasks, the skills workers bring to their jobs, the transportation and communications infrastructure, and the legal and social environment. We will analyze each of these factors and discuss their implications for government policies to promote growth. We will also discuss the costs of rapid economic growth, special issues regarding growth and development in low- and middle-income countries, and consider whether there may be limits to the amount of growth a society can or should achieve.

14.1   THE REMARKABLE RISE IN REAL GDP PER CAPITA: THE RECORD

The advances in healthcare and computing mentioned in the beginning of this chapter illustrate only a few of the impressive changes that have taken place in people's living standards over the past two centuries, particularly in industrialized countries like Canada. To study the factors that affect living standards systematically, however, we must go beyond anecdotes and adopt a specific indicator of living standards in a particular country and time.

In Chapter 5, we introduced the concept of real GDP as a basic measure of the level of economic activity in a country. Recall that, in essence, real GDP measures the volume of goods and services produced within a country's borders during a specific period, such as a quarter or a year. Consequently, real GDP *per person* provides a measure of the quantity of goods and services available to the typical resident of a country at a particular time.[1] Moreover, although maximizing growth of real GDP per person may not be an appropriate normative goal for economic policy, as we saw in Chapter 5, real GDP per person is positively related to a range of basic indicators of human development, such as life expectancy, infant health, and years of schooling. Lacking a better alternative, economists have focused on real GDP per person as a rough indicator of a country's living standard and stage of economic development.

Figure 4.2 showed the remarkable growth in real GDP per person that occurred in Canada between 1926 and 2010. For comparison, Table 14.1 shows real GDP per person in seven countries in selected years from 1955 to 2009. Figure 14.1 displays the same data graphically for the eight countries.

The data in Table 14.1 and Figure 14.1 tell a dramatic story. For example, in Canada, real GDP per person grew almost three times larger between 1955 and 2009, which is quite impressive. But in Japan, real GDP per person grew more than 7 times larger over the same period, in South Korea more than 14 times larger, and in China it grew an amazing 26 times larger. On the other hand, it is possible for a country's real GDP per person to stagnate for an extended period. As Table 14.1 shows, Brazil's real GDP per capita barely changed from 1979 to 1999, and Ghana's real GDP per capita actually fell significantly over the two decades from 1979 to 1999.

In sections 14.2 to 14.7 of this chapter, we will primarily be concerned with analyzing the factors determining economic growth in high-income countries such as Canada,

---

1   If the income distribution is highly unequal, then real GDP per person considerably overstates the quantity of goods and services available to the typical resident.

TABLE 14.1

Real GDP per Person in Selected Countries, 1955–2009 (in 2005 U.S. Dollars)

2005$	1955	1969	1979	1989	1999	2009	Annual % change 1955–2009
Canada	12535	17723	23584	27957	32060	36208	1.96
United States	15148	20746	25564	31450	38190	41102	1.85
Japan	4341	13501	19961	27131	30097	31958	3.70
South Korea	1757	2860	5690	11437	17531	25029	5.00
Brazil	2379	4137	7596	7515	7613	9353	2.54
China	268	354	596	1205	2709	7012	6.05
Ghana	545	697	879	838	803	1239	1.52

SOURCE: Adapted from A. Heston, R. Summers, and B. Aten, Penn World Table Version 7.0, Center for International Comparisons of Production Income and Prices at the University of Pennsylvania, May 2011. PPP converted GDP per capita (chain series), at 2005 constant prices. Series rgdpch.

the United States, and Japan. In section 14.8, we will discuss some special issues regarding growth and development in middle-income countries such as Brazil and China, and in low-income countries such as Ghana.

14.2 WHY "SMALL" DIFFERENCES IN GROWTH RATES MATTER

The last column of Table 14.1 shows the annual growth rates of real GDP per person of the eight countries from 1955 to 2009. At first glance, some of these growth rates may not seem to differ much from country to country. For example, for the period, the highest growth rate is 6.05 percent for China, which may not seem that different from

FIGURE 14.1

Real GDP Per Person in Seven Countries, 1955–2009

The figure shows growth of real GDP per capita for seven countries. Among the highlights are the very high growth of Japan from 1955 to 1991, the very high growth of China since the 1980s, the stagnation of Brazil from 1980 to 2003, and the delay until 2008 of Ghana's return to the peak GDP per capita it had achieved in 1971. SOURCE: See Table 14.1.

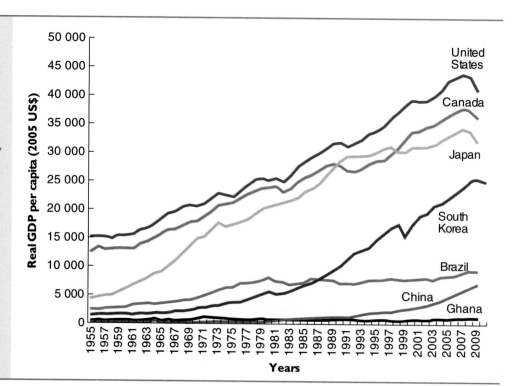

the 3.7 percent growth rate of Japan. And the 3.7 percent growth rate of Japan may not seem that different from the 1.96 percent growth rate of Canada. But these differences in growth rates resulted in large differences in how much real GDP per capita expanded in those three countries over the period from 1955 to 2009. As previously noted, Canada's 1.96 percent growth rate caused its real GDP per capita to grow almost three times larger between 1955 and 2009, but in Japan real GDP per person grew more than 7 times larger and in China it grew 26 times larger.

The fact that seemingly small differences in growth rates can have large long-run effects results from a general principle called the **power of compound growth,** a specific instance of which is the power of compound interest.

power of compound growth the fact that seemingly small differences in growth rates, maintained over long periods, will produce large differences in magnitude

EXAMPLE **14.1**

Compound interest (1)

Suppose that in 1955 your grandfather deposited $10 000 in a savings account at 4.1 percent interest. Interest is compounded annually (so that interest paid at the end of each year receives interest itself in later years). Grandpa's will specified that the account be turned over to you in the year 2012. If you withdrew the funds in 2012, how much would the account be worth? [2]

The account was worth $10 000 in 1955, $10 000 × 1.041 = $10 410 in 1956, $10 000 × 1.041 × 1.041 = $10 000 × $(1.041)^2$ = $10 836.81 in 1957, and so on. Since 57 years have elapsed between 1955 when the deposit was made, in the year 2012, when the account was closed, the value of the account was $10 000 × $(1.041)^{57}$, or $10 000 × 1.041 to the 57th power. Using a calculator, you will find that $10 000 times 1.041 to the 57th power is $98 785.13—a good return for a $10 000 deposit! In fact, if the original $10 000 was deposited at the beginning of 1955, then by about the middle of 2012 it would have undergone an increase in value to $100 000, a tenfold increase.

Compound interest is an arrangement by which interest is paid not only on the original deposit but on all previously accumulated interest. It is distinguished from *simple interest,* by which interest is paid only on the original deposit. If your grandfather's account had been deposited at 4.1 percent simple interest, it would have accumulated only 410 dollars each year (4 percent of the original $10 000 deposit), for a total value of $10 000 + (57 × $410) = $33 370 after 57 years.

compound interest the payment of interest not only on the original deposit but on all previously accumulated interest

EXAMPLE **14.2**

Compound interest (2)

Refer to Example 14.1. What would your grandfather's $10 000 deposit have been worth after 57 years if the annual interest rate had been 1 percent? 7 percent?

At 1 percent interest, the account would be worth $10 000 in 1955; $10 000 × 1.01 = $10 100 in 1956; $10 000 × (1.01) × (1.01) = $10 201 in 1957; and so on. In the year 2012 the value of the account would be $10 000 × $(1.01)^{57}$, or $17 632.68. If the interest rate were 7 percent, after 57 years the account would be worth $10 000 × $(1.07)^{57}$, or $473 015.45. Let's summarize the results of Examples 14.1 and 14.2.

Interest rate (%)	Value of $10 000 after 57 years
1	$17 632.68
4.1	$98 785.13
7	$473 015.45

2 This, of course, is a hypothetical example. It assumes that the savings account pays the same rate of interest for 57 years and that the interest generated by the account is not subject to taxation.

The power of compound interest is such that, even at relatively low rates of interest, any sum, compounded over a long enough period, can greatly increase in value. A more subtle point illustrated by this example is that seemingly small differences in interest rates matter a lot—hence the phrase "the power of compound interest." The difference between a 7 percent and a 4.1 percent interest rate may not seem tremendous, but over a long period of time it implies large differences in the amount of interest accumulated on an account. The 7 percent interest rate is less than twice as high, but after 57 years, it produced a balance more than 4.7 times as large.

As the term *power of compound growth* suggests, economic growth rates are similar to compound interest rates. Just as the value of a bank deposit grows each year at a rate equal to the interest rate, so the size of a nation's economy expands each year at the rate of economic growth. This analogy suggests that even a relatively modest rate of growth in output per person, 1 to 2 percent per year, will produce tremendous increases in average living standards over a long period. And relatively small *differences* in growth rates, as in the case of Canada versus Japan, will ultimately produce very different living standards if they persist for decades.

BOX 14.1

The Rule of 72

rule of 72 a rule of thumb stating that to find the number of years it takes a magnitude to double when it is growing at a constant rate, divide 72 by the growth rate

An often-used rule of thumb for examining differences in growth rates is known as the **rule of 72**. The rule states that to find how many years it takes for a magnitude to double when the magnitude is growing at a constant rate, divide 72 by the growth rate expressed in percentage terms. For example, if an economy's GDP per person is growing at 1 percent a year, it will take approximately 72 years for the economy's GDP per person to double. But if the economy's GDP per person is growing at the very high rate of 7.2 percent a year, it will only take about 10 years for GDP per person to double.

EXERCISE 14.1

Suppose that real GDP per person in Canada had grown at 3.70 percent per year, as Japan's did, instead of the actual 1.96 percent per year, from 1955 to 2009. How much larger would real GDP per person have been in Canada in 2009?

14.3 WHY NATIONS BECOME RICH: THE CRUCIAL ROLE OF AVERAGE LABOUR PRODUCTIVITY

What determines a nation's economic growth rate? To get some insight into this vital question, we find it useful to express real GDP per person as the product of two terms: average labour productivity and the share of the population that is working.

To do this, let Y equal total real output (as measured by real GDP, for example), N equal the number of employed workers, and POP equal the total population. Then real GDP per person can be written as Y/POP; average labour productivity, or output per employed worker, equals Y/N; and the share of the population that is working is N/POP. The relationship between these three variables is

$$\frac{Y}{POP} = \frac{Y}{N} \times \frac{N}{POP},$$

which, as you can see by cancelling out N on the right-hand side of the equation, always holds exactly. In words, this basic relationship is

Real GDP per person = Average labour productivity × Share of population employed.

This expression for real GDP per person tells us something very basic and intuitive: the quantity of goods and services produced per person depends on (1) how much each worker can produce and (2) how many people (as a fraction of the total population) are working. Furthermore, because real GDP per person equals average labour productivity times the share of the population that is employed, real GDP per person can *grow* only to the extent that there is *growth* in worker productivity and/or the fraction of the population that is employed.

Figures 14.2 and 14.3 show the Canadian figures for the three key variables in the relationship above for the period 1961–2010. Figure 14.2 shows both real GDP per person and real GDP per worker (average labour productivity) for 1961–2010. Figure 14.3 shows the portion of the entire Canadian population (not just the working-age population) that was employed for 1961–2010. Once again, we see that the expansion in output per person in Canada has been impressive. Between 1961 and 2010, real GDP per person in Canada grew by 182 percent. Thus, in 2010, output of goods and services per Canadian was 2.82 times as large as in 1961. Figures 14.2 and 14.3 show that increases in both labour productivity and the share of the population holding a job contributed to this rise in living standards (that is, in real GDP per capita).

Let's look a bit more closely at these two contributing factors, beginning with the share of the population that is employed. As Figure 14.3 shows, between 1961 and 2010, the number of people employed in Canada rose from 33 to 50 percent of the entire population, a remarkable increase. The growing number of women working outside the home was the most important reason for this rise in employment.

Although the rising share of the Canadian population with jobs contributed significantly to the increase in real GDP per person during the past four decades, this trend almost certainly will not continue in the future. Women's participation in paid employment, for example, seems unlikely to continue rising at the same rate as in the past four decades.

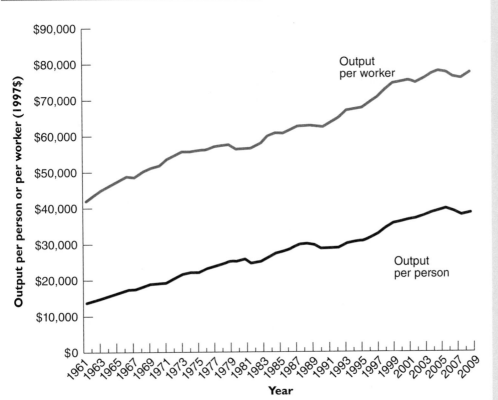

FIGURE 14.2

Output per Person and per Worker in the Canadian Economy, 1961–2010

Real output per person in Canada grew by 182 percent between 1961 and 2010, while real output per worker (average labour productivity) grew by 82 percent.

SOURCE: Adapted from Statistics Canada, CANSIM series v2461119, v466668, and v3860085; extraction date June 14, 2011; HSC series D129, A1, and F55.

FIGURE 14.3
Share of the Canadian Population in Paid Employment, 1961–2010
The share of the Canadian population holding a paid job increased from 33 percent in 1961 to 50 percent in 2010. SOURCE: Adapted from Statistics Canada, CANSIM series v2091072 and v466668. Extraction date, June 14, 2011.

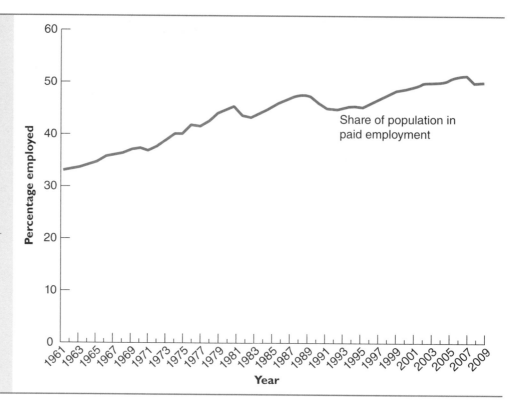

What about the other factor that determines output per person: average labour productivity? As Figure 14.2 shows, between 1961 and 2010, average labour productivity in Canada increased by 1.82 times, accounting for a sizable share of the overall increase in GDP per person. In other periods, the link between average labour productivity and output per person in Canada has often been even stronger, since in most earlier periods the share of the population holding jobs was more stable than it has been recently. (See Figure 4.2 for the behaviour of real GDP per person and average labour productivity in Canada over the period 1926–2010.)

This quick look at recent data supports a more general conclusion. *In the long run, increases in average labour productivity are important for increases in output per person.* To understand why economies grow, then, we must understand the reasons for increased labour productivity.

RECAP

ECONOMIC GROWTH AND PRODUCTIVITY

Real GDP per person, a rough indicator of living standards, has grown dramatically in many countries. This growth reflects the *power of compound growth:* even a modest growth rate, if sustained over a long period of time, can lead to large increases in the size of the economy.

Output per person equals average labour productivity times the share of the population that is employed. Since 1961, the share of the Canadian population with jobs has risen significantly, but it is unlikely to continue to increase in future decades. In coming decades, increases in output per person and, hence, living standards will depend primarily upon increases in average labour productivity.

14.4   THE DETERMINANTS OF AVERAGE LABOUR PRODUCTIVITY

What determines the productivity of the average worker in a particular country at a particular time? Popular discussions of this issue often equate worker productivity with the willingness of workers of a given nationality to work hard. Everything else being equal, a culture that promotes hard work certainly tends to increase worker productivity. But intensity of effort cannot explain the huge differences in average labour productivity that we observe around the world.

In this section we will examine six factors that appear to account for the major differences in average labour productivity, both between countries and between generations. It should be noted that contributions to productivity differences made by three of these factors—"human capital" (education and training), physical capital, and natural resources (including land)—are much easier to quantify than the contributions made by the other three factors—technology, entrepreneurship, and the legal and political environment. Later in the chapter, we will discuss how economic policies can influence these factors to spur productivity and growth.

HUMAN CAPITAL

To illustrate the factors that determine average labour productivity, we introduce two prototypical assembly line workers, Paris and Nicole.

EXAMPLE 14.3

Paris and Nicole on the assembly line

Paris and Nicole have jobs wrapping chocolate candies and placing them into boxes. Paris, a novice wrapper, can wrap only 100 candies/hour. Nicole, who has had on-the-job training, can wrap 300 candies/hour. Paris and Nicole each work 40 hours/week. Find average labour productivity, in terms of candies wrapped per week and candies wrapped per hour, (a) for Paris, (b) for Nicole, and (c) for Paris and Nicole as a team.

We have defined average labour productivity in general terms as output per worker. Note, though, that the measurement of average labour productivity depends on the time period that is specified. For example, the data presented in Figure 14.2 tell us how much the average worker produces *in a year*. In this example, we are concerned with how much Paris and Nicole can produce *per hour* of work or *per week* of work. All of these ways of measuring labour productivity are valid, as long as we are clear about the time unit we are using.

Paris and Nicole's hourly productivities are given in the problem: Paris can wrap 100 candies/hour and Nicole can wrap 300. Paris's weekly productivity is (40 hours/week) × (100 candies wrapped/hour) = 4000 wrapped candies/week. Nicole's weekly productivity is (40 hours/week) × (300 candies wrapped/hour), or 12 000 candies/week.

Together Paris and Nicole can wrap 16 000 candies/week. As a team, their average weekly productivity is (16 000 candies wrapped)/(2 weeks of work), or 8000 candies/week. Their average hourly productivity as a team is (16 000 candies wrapped)/(80 hours of work) = 200 candies/hour. Notice that, taken as a team, the two women's productivity lies midway between their individual productivities.

Nicole is more productive than Paris because she has had on-the-job training, which has allowed her to develop her candy-wrapping skills to a higher level than Paris's. Because of her training, Nicole can produce more than Paris can in a given number of hours.

EXERCISE 14.2   **Suppose Nicole attends additional classes in candy wrapping and learns how to wrap 500 candies/hour. Find the output per week and output per hour for Paris and Nicole, both individually and as a team.**

Many economists would explain the difference in the two women's performance by saying that Nicole has more human capital than Paris. *Human capital* is often used as a catch-all term for the talents, education, training, and skills of workers. Workers with a large stock of human capital are more productive than workers with less training. For example, a secretary who knows how to use a word processing program will be able to type more letters than one who does not; an auto mechanic who is familiar with computerized diagnostic equipment will be able to fix engine problems that a less well-trained mechanic could not.

COST-
BENEFIT

Education and training (human capital) require the investment of time and money. For example, to learn how to use a word processing program, a secretary might need to attend a technical school at night. The cost of going to school includes not only the tuition paid but also the *opportunity cost* of the secretary's time spent attending class and studying. The benefit of the schooling is typically the increase in wages the secretary will tend to earn when the course has been completed. If the secretary follows the *cost–benefit principle*, he or she will choose to learn word processing if the benefits exceed the costs, including the opportunity costs. The higher wages and other benefits that typically accrue to workers with more human capital provide an incentive for acquiring additional education and training.

PHYSICAL CAPITAL

Workers' productivity depends not only on their skills and effort but also on the tools they have to work with. Even the most skilled surgeon cannot perform open-heart surgery without sophisticated equipment, and an expert computer programmer is of limited value without a computer. These examples illustrate the importance of *physical capital*, such as factories and machines. More and better capital allows workers to produce more efficiently, as Example 14.4 illustrates.

EXAMPLE **14.4**
Paris and Nicole get automated

Refer to Example 14.3. Since that time, Paris and Nicole's boss has acquired an electric candy-wrapping machine, which is designed to be operated by one worker. Using this machine, an untrained worker can wrap 500 candies/hour. What are Paris and Nicole's hourly and weekly outputs now? Will the answer change if the boss gets a second machine? a third?

Suppose for the sake of simplicity that a candy-wrapping machine must be assigned to one worker only. (This assumption rules out sharing arrangements in which one worker uses the machine on the day shift and another on the night shift.) If the boss buys just one machine, she will maximize output by assigning it to Paris. (Why? See Exercise 14.3.) Now Paris will be able to wrap 500 candies/hour, while Nicole can wrap only 300/hour. Paris's weekly output will be 20 000 wrapped candies (40 hours × 500 candies wrapped/hour). Nicole's weekly output is still 12 000 wrapped candies (40 hours × 300 candies wrapped/hour). Together they can now wrap 32 000 candies/week, or 16 000 candies/week each. On an hourly basis, average labour productivity for the two women taken together is 32 000 candies wrapped/80 hours of work, or 400 candies wrapped/hour—twice their average labour productivity before the boss bought the machine.

With two candy-wrapping machines available, both Paris and Nicole could use a machine. Each could wrap 500 candies/hour, for a total of 40 000 wrapped candies/week. Average labour productivity for both women taken together would be 20 000 wrapped candies/week, or 500 wrapped candies/hour.

What would happen if the boss purchased a third machine? With only two workers, a third machine would be useless, adding nothing to either total output or average labour productivity.

The candy-wrapping machine is an example of a *capital good,* a long-lived good which is itself produced and used to produce other goods and services (as first explained in Chapter 2). Capital goods include machines and equipment (such as computers, earthmovers, or assembly lines) as well as buildings (such as factories or office buildings).

Capital goods like the candy-wrapping machine enhance workers' productivity. Table 14.2 summarizes the results from Examples 14.3 and 14.4. For each number of machines the boss might acquire (column 1), Table 14.2 gives the total weekly output of Paris and Nicole taken together (column 2), the total number of hours worked by the two women (column 3), and average output per hour (column 4) equal to total weekly output divided by total weekly hours.

INCREASING
OPPORTUNITY
COST

Table 14.2 demonstrates two important points about the effect of additional capital on output. First, for a given number of workers, adding more capital generally increases both total output and average labour productivity. For example, adding the first candy-wrapping machine increases weekly output (column 2) by 16 000 candies and average labour productivity (column 4) by 200 candies wrapped/hour.

TABLE 14.2
Capital, Output, and Productivity in the Candy-Wrapping Factory

(1) Number of machines (capital)	(2) Total number of candies wrapped each week (output)	(3) Total hours worked per week	(4) Candies wrapped per hour worked (productivity)
0	16 000	80	200
1	32 000	80	400
2	40 000	80	500
3	40 000	80	500

The second point illustrated by Table 14.2 is that, beyond some point, additional units of capital produce smaller and smaller benefits. In this particular example, the first machine adds 16 000 candies to total output, but the second machine adds only 8000. The third machine, which cannot be used since there are only two workers, does not increase output or productivity at all. The result, that additional units of a variable input eventually produce smaller and smaller benefits, illustrates a general principle of economics called the *law of diminishing returns.* When the variable input is capital, the general principle implies **diminishing returns to capital:** If the amount of labour and other inputs employed is held constant, then the amount an additional unit of capital adds to production eventually begins to decrease. In the case of the candy-wrapping factory, diminishing returns to capital are exhibited when the first candy-wrapping machine acquired adds more output than the second, which in turn adds more output than the third.

diminishing returns to capital if the amount of labour and other inputs employed is held constant, then, the greater the amount of capital already in use, the less an additional unit of capital will tend to add to production

Table 14.2 illustrates the link between units of capital and output at the level of a factory, but a similar relationship between units of capital and output seems to exist at the level of the economy as a whole. First, increasing the amount of capital available to the workforce will tend to increase output and average labour productivity. The more adequately equipped workers are, the more productive they will be. Second, the degree to which productivity can be increased by an expanding stock of capital is limited. An economy in which the quantity of capital available to each worker is already very high will typically benefit less dramatically from any further expansion of the capital stock than an economy in which the quantity of capital per worker is low.

FIGURE 14.4

FIGURE 14.4
Average Labour Productivity and Capital per Worker in 15 Countries, 1990
Countries with large amounts of capital per worker also tend to have high average labour productivity, as measured by real GDP per worker.
SOURCE: Adapted from Alan Heston, Robert Summers, and Bettina Aten, Penn World Table, Center for International Comparisons of Production, Income, and Prices at the University of Pennsylvania.

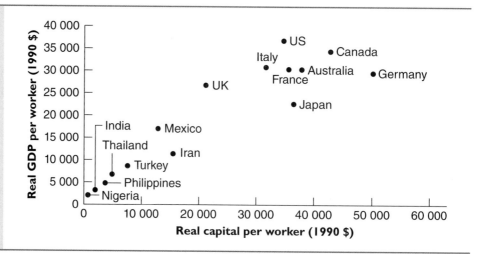

Is there empirical evidence that giving workers more capital makes them more productive? Figure 14.4 shows the relationship between average labour productivity and the amount of capital per worker in 15 major countries. The figure shows a strong relationship between the amounts of capital per worker and productivity.

BOX 14.2

Capital, Growth, and the PPC

We have made the argument that if an economy increases its physical capital, all else being equal, we would then expect the output of the economy to increase in future periods because of a higher capital to labour ratio. This argument is often represented by a production possibilities curve (PPC) because the image of the curve in your mind's eye can help you to remember the argument.

The discussion of PPCs in Chapter 2 noted that points inside a PPC were technically inefficient, points on the curve were technically efficient, and points outside the curve were unattainable at the current time. In Figure 2.6, the PPCs were used to illustrate the idea that increases in productive resources, such as labour and physical capital or improvements in knowledge and technology, cause the PPC to shift outward, a shift corresponding to (potential) growth of the economy.

In Figure 2.6, the PPCs were drawn for an economy producing two goods: sugar cane and nuts. Figure 14.5 presents a more general case; it shows the

FIGURE 14.5

output of physical capital goods along the vertical axis and the output of consumption goods along the horizontal axis.

A few simplifying assumptions help explain the connection between physical capital accumulation (real investment) and economic growth. The first is that all output can be divided into consumption goods and physical capital goods, as in Figure 14.5. Another assumption is that we have a closed economy, so that there will be a close match between the amount of physical capital produced in the economy and the amount of it employed. Labour, technology, and other factors affecting output are fixed.

The red curve in Figure 14.5 shows the PPC for the current period; that is, this year. Assume that our economy is currently operating at potential, producing a combination of consumption and capital goods shown by point X on the red curve.

Provided that X involves an output level of capital goods that is more than sufficient to offset the wearing out of the existing stock of capital goods, then next year the PPC will be further from the origin than is the red curve. The blue curve represents the PPC for next year if X is the output combination for this year.

If this year, instead of X, we had an output combination Y, representing a larger addition to the stock of capital goods (that is, more investment), then next year we would have a PPC that is further from the origin than the blue curve is. The green curve in Figure 14.5 represents a PPC for next year if this year's output combination is as shown by the point Y.

In summary, economic growth arising from additions to physical capital can be represented by PPC curve shifts. Figure 14.5 illustrates the idea that shifting output from consumption to investment—that is, adding to the stock of physical capital in the current period—causes the PPC in the future period to shift out more than it otherwise would.

LAND AND NATURAL RESOURCES

Besides capital goods, other inputs to production help to make workers more productive— among them are natural resources and land. An abundance of natural resources increases the productivity of workers in natural resource industries. The link between rich natural resources and labour productivity can be illustrated with data for Canada in the mid-1990s.[3] Annual output per worker in the natural resources sectors (essentially, the oil and gas industries) of Saskatchewan and Alberta was $360 000 and $290 000, respectively. These are many times higher than average output per worker for the Canadian economy as a whole (see Figure 14.2), even in 2010. The rich natural resource bases in these two provinces, not just high levels of capital intensity or worker skills, explain these high productivity levels.

Similarly, fertile land is essential to agriculture. A farmer can produce a much larger crop in a land-rich country like Canada or Australia than in a country where the soil is poor or arable land is limited in supply. With modern farm machinery and great expanses of land, today's Canadian farmers are so productive that even though they constitute less than 3 percent of the employed population, they provide enough of many agricultural commodities not only to feed the country but to export large quantities to the rest of the world. Of course, fertile farm land is most important to an economy at an early stage of economic development when most of the employed population is in agriculture.

Although there are limits to a country's supply of arable land, it is important to recognize that many natural resources, such as petroleum and metals, can be obtained through international markets. Thus, economies need not possess large quantities of natural resources within their own borders to achieve economic growth. Indeed, a number of

3 David Sabourin and Danielle Zietsma, "Interprovincial Productivity Differences," *Canadian Economic Observer*, Statistics Canada, August 2001.

economies have become rich without substantial natural resources of their own, including Japan, Hong Kong, Singapore, and Switzerland.

Also, some economists argue that countries that are abundant in natural resources can suffer from *Dutch disease*. The term **Dutch disease** refers to the tendency in an economy with a booming resource sector for the manufacturing sector to decline. The boom in the resource sector produces an appreciation of the currency that reduces the competitiveness of the manufacturing sector. Some economists have argued that Canada has been experiencing Dutch disease since 2003 or so.

Dutch disease the tendency in an economy with a booming natural resource sector for the manufacturing sector to decline

TECHNOLOGY

Besides human capital, physical capital, and natural resources, a country's ability to develop and apply new, more productive technologies helps to determine its productivity. Consider just one industry, transportation. Two centuries ago, even in the richest countries, the horse-drawn wagon was the primary means of transportation, a slow and costly method indeed. But in the 19th century, technological advances such as the steam engine supported the expansion of riverborne transportation and the development of national rail networks. In the 20th century, the invention of the internal combustion engine and the development of aviation, supported by the construction of an extensive infrastructure of roads and airports, have produced increasingly rapid, cheap, and reliable transport. Technological change has clearly been a driving force in the transportation revolution.

New technologies can improve productivity in industries other than the one in which they are introduced. At one time farmers could sell their produce only in their local communities, for example. Now rapid shipping and refrigerated transport allow farmers to sell their products internationally. With a broader market in which to sell, farmers can specialize in those products best suited to local land and weather conditions. Similarly, factories can obtain their raw materials wherever they are cheapest and most abundant, produce the goods they are most efficient at manufacturing, and sell their products wherever they will fetch the best price.

Numerous other technological developments have led to increased productivity, including advances in communication and medicine and the introduction of computer technology. All indications are that the Internet will have a major impact in many economies, not just in retailing but in many other sectors.

However, economic growth does not automatically follow from breakthroughs in basic science. To make the best use of new knowledge, an economy needs entrepreneurs who can implement scientific advances, as well as a legal and political environment that encourages the practical application of new knowledge.

EXERCISE 14.3   **A new kind of wrapping paper has been invented that makes candy-wrapping quicker and easier. The use of this paper increases the number of candies a person can wrap by hand by 200 per hour, and the number of candies a person can wrap by machine by 300 per hour. Using the data from Examples 14.3 and 14.4, construct a table like Table 14.2 that shows how this technological advance affects average labour productivity. Do diminishing returns to capital still hold?**

ENTREPRENEURSHIP

Increases in average labour productivity depend in part upon **entrepreneurship,** or innovative behaviour: that is, behaviour that results in new products, services, technological processes, or organizational innovations that are productivity enhancing. In a capitalist economy, much of entrepreneurial behaviour is associated with the owners and managers of capitalist enterprises. A classic example known throughout the world is that of Henry Ford, the American entrepreneur who developed mass production of automobiles. Mass production raised labour productivity and therefore lowered average costs enough to

entrepreneurship behaviour that results in new products, services, technological processes, or organizational innovations that are productivity enhancing bring automobiles within reach of the average household. Another example, dating from the 1970s and 1980s, is of Japanese companies whose new just-in-time production methods greatly increased the efficiency of their manufacturing plants.

But entrepreneurial behaviour is not exclusively limited to the owners or managers of capitalist enterprises. For example, Florence Nightingale exhibited entrepreneurial behaviour in campaigning to have nursing established as a profession in 19th-century England. The organizational innovation of replacing untrained servants with trained professionals greatly improved the efficiency of nursing in England's medical sector. Similarly, the politicians, civil servants, and others in Canada and the United States whose efforts resulted in the St. Lawrence Seaway project in the 1950s exhibited entrepreneurial behaviour. The system of locks and canals linking the Great Lakes with the Atlantic Ocean through the St. Lawrence River provided relatively low freight rates for bulk commodities and facilitated the development of both resource industries and manufacturing industries in much of Canada and the United States.

Entrepreneurial behaviour, then, can take place in the for-profit, non-profit, or government sectors. One common element is the exercise of creativity, typically combined with leadership skills, to produce new products, services, technological processes, or organizations. The other element is that these innovations serve to raise average labour productivity.

www.greatlakes-seaway.com
St. Lawrence Seaway System

Like any form of creativity or leadership skills, entrepreneurship is difficult to teach (although some of the supporting knowledge can be learned in university). How, then, does a society encourage entrepreneurship? History suggests that the entrepreneurial spirit will always exist; the challenge is to direct that spirit into economically productive channels.

For example, to encourage entrepreneurship in the for-profit sector, economic policymakers need to ensure that excessive regulations do not keep small businesses, some of which will eventually become big businesses, from getting off the ground. (Recent international surveys have ranked Canada as a country with relatively few barriers to establishing new businesses.) Sociological factors may play a role as well. Societies in which business and commerce are considered to be beneath the dignity of refined, educated people are less likely to produce successful entrepreneurs in the for-profit sector. Similarly, societies in which non-profit and government sectors are denigrated in favour of private business and the "free market" may suffer from a lack of entrepreneurial behaviour in those sectors.

THE LEGAL AND POLITICAL ENVIRONMENT

One of the key ways that government can foster productivity growth is to provide a legal and political environment that encourages people to behave in economically productive ways. The legal system should provide clear rules for determining who owns what resources (through a system of deeds and titles, for example) and how those resources can be used. Imagine living in a society in which a dictator, backed by the military and the police, could take whatever he wanted, and regularly did so. The incentive to invest in new enterprises or expand existing enterprises would be drastically impaired.

The political system can advance productivity growth by preventing extreme instability. Continuous civil unrest, terrorism, or guerrilla warfare are obviously detrimental to economic growth. Policies that promote social cohesion—that is, that reduce social conflicts between classes, ethnic groups, or linguistic communities—can contribute to economic growth by contributing to political stability.

At the same time, a political system that promotes the open exchange of ideas will speed the development of new technologies and products.

A Bangladeshi worker who immigrates to Canada is likely to find that his average labour productivity is much higher in Canada than it was at home. This worker is, of course, the same person he was when he lived in Bangladesh. How can the simple act of moving to Canada increase the worker's productivity?

EXERCISE 14.4

COMBINING AND QUANTIFYING THE DETERMINANTS

We have mentioned several determinants of average labour productivity. Given that average labour productivity times the amount of employment equals output, the determinants of average labour productivity are very similar to the determinants of output. Economists often use a mathematical expression called a *production function* in microeconomics to describe the determinants of output at the level of a firm. In other words, a production function is a function relating a firm's output to the inputs it employs. In macroeconomics, the corresponding concept is an *aggregate production function*. An **aggregate production function** shows the output of an economy as a function of various inputs including such determinants of average labour productivity as the skills and training of workers and the quantity of physical capital. Box 14.3 provides further information on aggregate production functions.

aggregate production function shows the output of an economy as a function of various inputs

---

BOX | **14.3**

Aggregate Production Functions

In its general form, an aggregate production function is written as

$$Y = f(K, L, M, A)$$

where
Y = the amount of output or real GDP
K = the amount of physical capital
L = the amount of labour, adjusted for the level of human capital
M = the amount of available land and other natural resources
A = the level of technology and other factors, such as the effectiveness of management and the social and legal environment
$f(\ )$ = some unspecified functional form.

In practice, there are a number of specific functional forms that are used to calculate the level of output. One simple but famous one that involves only Y, K, and L is

$$Y = K^{1/2}L^{1/2} = \sqrt{KL}.$$

For example, if $K = 25$ and $L = 100$, $Y = \sqrt{25 \times 100} = \sqrt{2,500} = 50$. This simple production function has two notable properties. First, if all the inputs K and L double, output also will double; that is, if $K = 50$ and $L = 200$, $Y = \sqrt{50 \times 200} = \sqrt{10,000} = 100$. Secondly, it exhibits diminishing returns to capital (as well as diminishing returns to labour), so that if we hold the level of labour constant and keep adding more capital, output will rise by smaller and smaller increments. Thus, if L remains equal to 100 and K rises from 25 to 26, output rises from 50 to $\sqrt{26 \times 100} = 50.99$, or by 0.99 unit. If K rises by one more unit to 27, output rises to $\sqrt{27 \times 100} = 51.96$, or by only 0.97 unit.

RECAP↑

DETERMINANTS OF AVERAGE LABOUR PRODUCTIVITY

Key factors determining average labour productivity in a country include the following:

- The skills and training of workers, called *human capital*.

- The quantity and quality of *physical capital*: machines, equipment, and buildings.

- The availability of land and other *natural resources*.

- The sophistication of the *technologies* applied in production.

- *Entrepreneurship.*

- The broad *legal and political environment.*

14.5 THE PRODUCTIVITY SLOWDOWN AND REAL WAGE STAGNATION

THE PRODUCTIVITY SLOWDOWN

During the 1950s and 1960s, most of the major industrialized countries saw rapid growth in real GDP, average labour productivity, and real wages. In the 1970s, however, productivity growth began to slow in the major industrialized countries. Slower growth in real GDP and in average living standards followed. In some countries, such as Canada, the reduction in the growth rate of real wages was even greater than the slowdown in productivity growth.

The slowdown in the growth of labour productivity is documented in Table 14.3, which gives data for Canada and the United States. Note the sharp decline in productivity growth in both countries during 1974–1979 compared with 1950–1973. In Canada, annual productivity growth fell to just 0.5 percent per year during 1974–1979.

The sudden decline in worldwide productivity growth around 1973 puzzles economists and policy-makers alike. What might have caused it? In the 1970s and 1980s, many economists thought that the fourfold increase in oil prices that followed the Arab-Israeli war (1973) might have caused the slowdown. The idea was that the dramatic increase in oil prices made many energy-intensive technologies obsolete. The negative impact of the dramatic oil price hikes on productivity growth now seems like a partial explanation. When oil prices (relative to the prices of other goods) dropped in the 1980s and later, productivity growth picked up somewhat from rate observed for the 1974–1979 period, but it did not return to the growth rate of the pre-1973 period.

One view of the slowdown in productivity growth since 1973 has been called the *technological depletion hypothesis.*[4] According to the **technological depletion hypothesis,** the high rates of productivity growth in the 1950s and 1960s reflected an unusual period of "catch up" after the Depression and Second World War. Although scientific and technical advances (many of which arose from military research during the Second World War) continued to be made during the 1930s and 1940s, depression and war hindered their application to civilian use. During the 1950s and 1960s, the backlog of technological breakthroughs was applied

technological depletion hypothesis the theory that the productivity slowdown after 1973 was due to the depletion of the backlog of technological advances made but not implemented during the 1930s and the Second World War

TABLE 14.3

Average Labour Productivity Growth Rates in Canada and the United States, 1950–2010

Country	Percentage growth, annual rates		
	1950–1973	1974-1979	1974–2010
Canada	2.7	0.5	0.9
United States	2.5	0.4	1.4

SOURCES: For Canada, the table uses the same sources as for Figure 14.2. For the United States, the average labour productivity growth rates are calculated from GDPCA series (real GDP) from the St. Louis Fed (http://research.stlouisfed.org/fred2/series/GDPCA/downloaddata?cid=106) and the civilian employment series from the Council of Economic Advisers, *Economic Report of the President 2011,* Table B-35, http://www.gpoaccess.gov/eop/2011/xls/ERP-2011-table35.xls. Extraction date, June 14, 2011.

4 See, for example, William Nordhaus, "Economic Policy in the Face of Declining Productivity Growth," *European Economic Review,* May/June 1982, pp. 131–158.

commercially, producing high rates of productivity growth at first and then a sharp decline in new technological opportunities. Once the catch-up period was over, productivity growth slowed. According to this hypothesis, then, the slowdown in productivity growth since the 1970s reflects a dearth of technological opportunities in the immediate postwar period. From this perspective, the 1950s and 1960s were the exception, and the period since the 1970s instead represents a return to more normal rates of productivity growth.

REAL WAGE STAGNATION

We have seen that in the 1970s labour productivity growth began to slow in many countries, including Canada, followed by slower growth in average living standards. What happened to real wages in Canada during this period of productivity growth slowdown?

Over most of the 20th century, real wages in Canada grew in line with labour productivity growth. So you might expect that during the period of productivity growth slowdown in Canada, real wage growth would have slowed in line with slower productivity growth. But, as shown in Figure 14.6, average real hourly wages in Canada stagnated from the late 1970s to 1996. Real wages did not just grow slowly—they did not grow at all. Canada's experience of real wage stagnation during the 1977–1996 period, despite 1 percent annual labour productivity growth, illustrates an important point: real wage growth can diverge from labour productivity growth for substantial periods.

How can we explain the stagnation of real wages from the late 1970s to 1996? It cannot be because the *human capital* of Canadian workers failed to improve. The average educational credentials of the Canadian workforce increased very substantially over the final quarter of the 20th century.

One hypothesis states that real wages stagnated because the bargaining power of labour deteriorated. Possible explanations as to why the bargaining power of labour deteriorated include the high unemployment rates of the 1980s and the first half of the 1990s.

FIGURE 14.6

Average Real Hourly Wage in Canada, 1914–2010 (2002$)

Real hourly wages in Canada increased five-fold between 1914 and 1977. From 1978 to 1996, real wages stagnated. Growth in real wages since 1997 has been positive but modest.

SOURCES: Adapted from the Statistics Canada, CANSIM series v2415197, v717706, and v41693271; extraction date, June 14, 2011; HSC series E198.

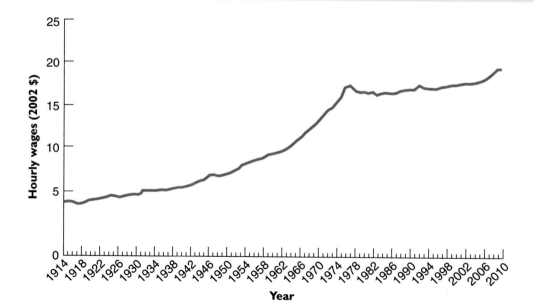

Since 1996, real wages have grown, although slowly. Even with relatively low unemployment rates for most of the 1996–2010, labour's bargaining power is increasingly constrained by global competition.

RECAP ↰

THE PRODUCTIVITY SLOWDOWN AND REAL WAGE STAGNATION

Beginning in the 1970s, the industrial world experienced a slowdown in average labour productivity growth. According to the technological depletion hypothesis, the slower growth in productivity beginning in the 1970s reflected a return to a normal rate of productivity growth following the abnormally high productivity growth of the 1950s and 1960s. From the late 1970s to 1996, a period of productivity growth slowdown in Canada, the growth of real wages stagnated. One hypothesis is that real wages stagnated because the bargaining power of labour was weak during the 1980s and the first half of the 1990s due to high unemployment rates.

14.6   TWO POSSIBLE OPPORTUNITY COSTS OF ECONOMIC GROWTH: CONSUMPTION AND LEISURE

Both this chapter and Chapter 5 emphasized the positive effects of economic growth on the average person's living standard. But even if we accept for the moment the idea that increased output per person is always desirable, maximization of the economic growth rate is a questionable economic goal. If the economy is already operating at or near capacity, then increasing the growth rate will require devoting more resources to investment as opposed to consumption, or increasing hours of work at the expense of leisure. In an economy operating at or near capacity, then, there are opportunity costs associated with increased investment and increased hours of work.

We know that by expanding the capital stock through investment, we can increase future productivity and output. But, to increase the capital stock, a society may have to divert resources that could otherwise be used to increase the supply of consumer goods. For example, to add more robot-operated assembly lines, a society must employ more of its skilled technicians in building industrial robots and fewer in designing video games. To build new factories, more carpenters and lumber must be assigned to factory construction and less to making furniture for homes. In short, a higher rate of investment in new capital would require fewer resources devoted to consumer goods—a real economic cost. (Alternatively, a higher rate of investment would require borrowing from abroad, which also has a real economic cost.)

Consumption sacrificed to capital formation is not the only cost of achieving higher growth. In Canada, in the 19th and early 20th centuries before the rise of industrial unions, periods of rapid economic growth were often times in which many people worked extremely long hours at dangerous and unpleasant jobs. While those workers helped to build the economy that Canadians enjoy today, the costs were great in terms of reduced leisure time and, in some cases, workers' health and safety. Many developing countries today are purchasing rapid economic growth at least partly at the same costs as Canada experienced in decades past.

As illustrated by Table 14.4, today there are notable differences in hours worked even among the high-income countries. For example, in 2008 average annual hours worked in Canada were about 21 percent greater than in Germany.

The fact that, in an economy operating at capacity, a higher living standard tomorrow must typically be purchased at the cost of current sacrifices is an example of the *scarcity*

COST-
BENEFIT

TABLE 14.4

Average Annual Hours Worked, Selected OECD Countries, 2008

Country	Hours	Hours relative to Germany
Germany	1430	100
France	1560	109
United Kingdom	1652	116
Canada	1727	121
Japan	1772	124
United States	1796	126
Italy	1807	126
Korea	2256	158

SOURCE: Organization for Economic Cooperation and Development, OECD.StatExtracts, Average annual hours actually worked per worker, http://stats.oecd.org/Index.aspx?DataSetCode=ANHRS.

problem: having more of one good thing usually means having less of another. Because achieving higher economic growth imposes real economic costs, we know from the *cost–benefit* principle that a rational approach to a welfare economics (that is, normative) issue of whether higher growth should be pursued involves weighing benefits and costs.

14.7 PROMOTING ECONOMIC GROWTH IN HIGH-INCOME COUNTRIES

If policy-makers in a high-income, industrialized economy such as Canada's decide to try to raise the rate of economic growth, what are some of the measures they might take to achieve this objective? We have mentioned a few broad considerations in our discussions of entrepreneurship and the legal and political environment. Here are some additional suggestions, based on our discussion of the factors that contribute to growth in average labour productivity and, thus, output per person.

POLICIES TO INCREASE HUMAN CAPITAL

Because skilled and well-educated workers are more productive than unskilled labour, governments in most countries try to increase the human capital of their citizens by supporting education and training programs. In Canada, provincial governments provide public education through high school and grant extensive support to post-secondary schools, including technical schools, colleges, and universities. To a lesser degree than some European countries, Canada also funds job training and supports retraining for workers whose skills no longer match available jobs.

POLICIES THAT PROMOTE INVESTMENT IN CAPITAL GOODS

Average labour productivity increases when workers can utilize a sizable and modern capital stock. One way that public policies can support the creation of new capital is to encourage a high rate of business investment (or, more precisely, what Statistics Canada calls non-residential business fixed capital formation). But how to encourage such investment is a controversial issue.

For example, some provincial governments have cut corporate income tax rates in recent years for the stated purpose of stimulating business investment. But there is some debate about whether corporate income tax cuts by provinces will actually stimulate investment at the national level or mainly just encourage some firms to relocate from higher-tax provinces to lower-tax ones. And questions have been raised about whether an investment tax credit to corporations, based upon new investment in plant and equipment in Canada, might have been more effective in stimulating new investment than income tax cuts awarded to corporations whether or not they expand their investment.

The federal government provides major tax breaks for Registered Retirement Savings Plans (RRSPs) for the stated purpose of encouraging personal saving. There is some doubt about whether tax breaks are even effective as a means of encouraging personal saving. More important, the empirical evidence (as we shall see in Chapter 16) suggests that the level of personal saving in Canada is not closely linked to the level of business investment.

In addition to encouraging business investment, public policies can contribute directly to capital formation through public investment, or the creation of government-owned capital. Public investment includes the building of roads, bridges, airports, dams, and so on, as explained in Chapter 5. As mentioned previously, the construction of the St. Lawrence Seaway, carried out in the 1950s by a federal Crown corporation (in conjunction with a U.S. counterpart), is often cited as an example of especially successful public investment. Today, the Internet, which received crucial public-sector funding in its early stages, is having a similar effect.

POLICIES THAT SUPPORT RESEARCH AND DEVELOPMENT

Productivity is enhanced by technological progress, which in turn requires investment in research and development (R&D). In many industries, private firms have adequate incentive to conduct research and development activities. There is no need, for example, for the government to finance research for developing a better underarm deodorant. But some types of knowledge, particularly basic scientific knowledge, may have widespread economic benefits that cannot be captured by a single private firm. The developers of the silicon computer chip, for example, were instrumental in creating huge new industries, yet they received only a small portion of the profits flowing from their inventions. Because society in general, rather than the individual inventors, may receive much of the benefit from basic research, government may need to support basic research, as it does through agencies such as the National Research Council of Canada and through support for research conducted at universities across the country. The federal government encourages applied research by the same institutions that conduct basic research, and it provides generous tax incentives to support the R&D activity of the private sector. Despite these generous tax incentives, the Canadian ratio of private-sector R&D investment to GDP is low compared to the ratios of other advanced economies, possibly because of the high degree of foreign ownership of Canadian industry. R&D tends to be conducted in head offices, and foreign ownership typically means that head offices are located abroad rather than in Canada.

The federal government also influences research and development by its laws regarding patent protection. Advocates of strong patent protection assert that if companies can patent their discoveries for long periods of time, they can charge high monopoly prices that result in large profits, and the lure of these large profits will encourage more R&D. Critics argue that long periods of patent protection encourage companies to engage in copycat R&D designed simply to get around the patents of other companies; for example, drug companies come up with second and third cures for the same disease. Critics also emphasize that high prices may hinder use of the inventions resulting from R&D (as when the high prices of patented AIDS drugs kept them out of reach of millions whose lives might have been saved by them).

www.nrc-cnrc.gc.ca
National Research Council of Canada

Why do almost all industrial countries provide free public education?

Industrial countries provide their citizens free public education through high school, and most subsidize college and other post-secondary schools. Why?

Canadians are so used to the idea of free public education that this question may seem odd. But why should the government provide free education when it does not provide even more-essential goods and services for free? Furthermore, educational services can be, and indeed commonly are, supplied and demanded in the private market, without the aid of the government.

An important argument for free or at least subsidized education is that the private demand curve for educational services does not include all the social benefits of education. For example, the democratic political system relies on an educated citizenry to operate effectively—a factor that an individual demander of educational services has little reason to consider. From a narrower economic

Why do almost all industrial countries provide free public education?

perspective, we might argue that individuals do not capture the full economic returns from their schooling. For example, people with high human capital, and thus high earnings, pay more taxes—funds that can be used to finance government services and aid the less fortunate. Because of income taxation, the private benefit to acquiring human capital is less than the social benefit, and the demand for education in the private market may be less than optimal from society's viewpoint. Similarly, educated people are more likely than others to contribute to technological development, and hence, to general productivity growth, which may benefit many other people besides themselves. Finally, another argument for public support of education is that poor people who would like to invest in human capital may not be able to do so because of insufficient income.[5]

14.8 GROWTH IN DEVELOPING COUNTRIES

World Bank a publicly funded international organization that provides assistance to low-income and middle-income countries to foster their development

The countries of the world are classified into the categories of low income, middle income, and high income by the *World Bank*. The **World Bank**, which was mentioned briefly in Chapter 13, is a publicly funded international organization headquartered in Washington, D.C., with a mandate to provide financial and technical assistance to low-income and middle-income countries to foster their development. As of 2011, the World Bank classified countries according to their 2009 output per capita in U.S. dollars as follows: low income, $995 or less; middle income, $996 to $12 195; and high income, $12 196 or more. This classification was followed in connection with Table 14.1 and Figure 14.1 earlier in this chapter where, for example, low income was used to describe Ghana, middle income to describe Brazil and China, and high income to describe Canada.[5]

The World Bank classification is one of several ways of classifying countries according to their output per capita or stage of economic development. For example, it is very common for economists and others to divide economies into *developed economies* and *developing economies* according to whether or not the economies are high income. There term **developing economies** then refers to low and middle-income economies.

developing economies a term widely used to refer to low and middle-income economies

The United Nations has promoted the term *least developed countries* or LDCs to recognize that some of the low-income countries, the LDCs, face particularly challenging circumstances, such as instability of agricultural production, which may be hindering them from developing. In the mid-1990s, the International Monetary Fund (IMF) and

5 For a more complete discussion of the external benefits associated with higher levels of education, see Barbara Wolfe and Robert Haveman, "Accounting for the Social and Non-Market Benefits of Education," in John Helliwell, ed., *The Contribution of Human and Social Capital to Sustained Economic Growth and Well Being* (Ottawa: HRDC and OECD, 2001), pp. 220–250.

the World Bank recognized the special issues facing a subset of low-income countries (currently numbering 36) with serious debt problems that are now known as *heavily indebted poor countries* or by the acronym HIPCs.

In the 1980s and earlier, it was common for the high-income countries to be called the *First World*, the Soviet Union and other middle-income Communist countries to be called the *Second World*, and other middle-income and especially low-income countries to be called the *Third World*. With the breakup of the Soviet Union and the shift of many formerly Communist economies to capitalism beginning in the early 1990s, the former Second World economies and other formerly Communist economies became known as *transition economies*.

In the 1980s the term *newly industrialized countries*, or NICs, became widely used to describe rapidly growing economies such as Singapore and South Korea as they moved from middle-income to high-income status. In the past decade, the term *emerging market economies* has been used to refer to a large number of rapidly growing middle-income countries.

Behind many of these classifications is the widely shared view that there is not a single set of policies suited to promoting growth in all economies. The challenges facing different economies certainly overlap, but some challenges differ according to the income level of the economy. The challenges facing low-income economies are particularly great.

GROWTH CHALLENGES IN LOW-INCOME COUNTRIES

The consequences of low income—or, more precisely, low GDP per capita—for indicators of living standards were discussed in connection with Table 5.4 of this textbook. Not only do citizens in low-income countries consume smaller quantities of goods and services, but their average life expectancy is much lower, they are much more likely to die as children, they are much more likely to be illiterate, and so on.

Nearly all of today's low-income countries are former colonies of European powers. Some were colonized as early as the 1500s during the so-called Age of Exploration from the 1500s to the 1700s. Many more were colonized in the latter half of the 1800s during what is sometimes known as the Age of Empire. In general, their role as colonies in the empire was to provide raw materials to the imperial power in Europe. Most of them gained independence in the period between the end of World War II and the early 1960s.

One challenge facing some low-income countries is high population growth and the resulting high population density. On average, population growth in low-income countries is about three times that in rich countries.[6] Most low-income countries have a large percentage of their populations engaged in agriculture. The increase in population relative to the land area—that is, the rise in population density—can make it difficult to raise output per person in agriculture. There is a situation of diminishing returns to labour applied to land (somewhat similar to the *diminishing returns to capital* mentioned in section 14.4). An extreme example is the country of Bangladesh in South Asia, which has a population of over 162 million people squeezed into an area not much larger than that occupied by the small Canadian provinces of New Brunswick and Nova Scotia.

There are various policies that can be used to control population growth, the one-child policy followed by China since the late 1970s being an example of very strict policy. With China's one-child policy, the general rule is that couples in urban areas should have no more than one child, and will be subject to fines if they have additional children. The policy has been subjected to various criticisms, but authorities in China, which has a population of 1.3 billion people, credit the one-child policy with having prevented roughly 400 million births.[7]

Another challenge facing some low-income countries is called the *resource curse*. The **resource curse** refers to the paradoxical finding that low-income countries with an abundance of natural resources such as minerals and fossil fuels do not necessarily achieve higher

resource curse a term widely used to refer to low and middle-income economies with an abundance of natural resources

---

6 See Partha Dasgupta, *Economics: A Very Short Introduction* (Oxford: Oxford University Press, 2007), p. 19.

7 See Jim Yardley, "China Sticking With One-Child Policy," *New York Times*, March 11 2008, http://www.nytimes.com/2008/03/11/world/asia/11china.html.

output levels than otherwise similar countries.[8] In Canada, the overall impact of abundant natural resources is to raise output per capita, as suggested in section 14.4. So how could an abundance of natural resources cause economic problems for a low-income country?

One reason is in common with Canada's experience—the Dutch disease whereby the export of natural resources may produce such a strong currency that other sectors of the economy have a difficult time competing against foreign producers. But there are three additional reasons, more specific to low-income countries, for the economic problems. First, if the economy is not very diversified, as is often the case in a low-income country, then the ups and downs of the natural resource sector can produce large and disruptive ups and downs in the economy as a whole, which can discourage investment in the economy, among other things. Another is that an abundance of natural resources can produce domestic conflict and even civil war over control of the resources and the economic gains from their exploitation. Domestic conflict reduces economic growth, as noted earlier in this chapter in connection with the legal and political environment. And third, economic gains from the exploitation of the natural resources may be "skimmed" off by foreign resource companies or by the local elite, with little being reinvested in the economy.

A high percentage of low-income countries are located in sub-Saharan Africa, and these countries face a range of special challenges, as outlined by development economist Jeffrey Sachs of Columbia University:

> Sub-Saharan Africa faces a constellation of special challenges, with greater or lesser impact in different parts of the region, including a climate and ecology especially burdened by infectious diseases such as … malaria and other vector-borne diseases; a rain-fed agriculture, much of it in sub-humid or arid zones that are prone to drought; high overland transport costs, including the greatest number of land-locked countries of any continent and a relative paucity of ocean-navigable rivers; low population densities in rural areas, characteristic of many rainforest and dry ecosystems, which make rural infrastructure relatively expensive; a historical legacy of colonial rule in which the colonial powers left behind relatively little infrastructure; and, of course, challenges of bad governance like Mr. Mugabe of Zimbabwe.[9]

While some low-income economies suffer from high population density, others from a resource curse, and still others from tropical diseases and land-locked geography, they are all characterized by low levels of capital per worker (as implied by Figure 14.4). Raising levels of capital per worker requires investment in machinery and equipment and so on, but the incentives for investment in low-income countries are often weak. The effective operation of modern machinery and equipment typically requires educated and healthy workers, but such workers may be in short supply. The operation of modern machinery and equipment also requires reliable power sources, but power sources may be unreliable. Access to larger markets requires transportation infrastructure, but transportation infrastructure may be underdeveloped. And so on.

One funding source in overcoming the various constraints that inhibit investment and otherwise hamper development in low-income countries is *official development assistance*. The term **official development assistance (ODA)** refers to grants or subsidized loans primarily provided by high-income countries and middle-income countries to low-income countries, with the stated purpose of promoting the development of the low-income countries. The high-income countries pledged to provide 0.7 percent of GNP to ODA in a 1970 United Nations General Assembly resolution, but few have lived up to their pledge. High-income countries such as Sweden, Luxembourg, Norway, the Netherlands, and Denmark have exceeded the goal, but most high-income countries fall

official development assistance (ODA) grants or subsidized loans primarily provided to low-income countries with the stated purpose of promoting their development

---

8 See, for example, Joseph Stiglitz, *Making Globalization Work* (New York: W.W. Norton, 2006), Chapter 5, "Lifting the Resource Curse," pp. 133–159.

9 Jeffrey Sachs, "No need to oversimplify poverty," *Huffpost World*, June 1 2009, www.huffingtonpost.com/jeffrey-sachs/no-need-to-oversimplify-p_b_209720.html. Note that low population densities in rural areas constitute a different challenge than the population density challenge faced, for example, by Bangladesh.

considerably short of the goal. Canada, for example, provided about 0.33 percent of GNP to ODA in 2010.[10]

Although low-income countries face special challenges, there have been periods during which they and other developing countries have achieved impressive improvements in living standards, as we will discuss in the section below.

THE EVOLUTION OF POLICIES AND PERFORMANCE IN DEVELOPING ECONOMIES

The economic performance of developing economies has varied from period to period over the past several decades. The general character of economic policies followed by developing economies and encouraged by the World Bank and the IMF has evolved as well.

Under the Bretton Woods system of international finance from the late 1940s to the early 1970s, most countries had fixed exchange rates, and international flows of capital were restricted. The Communist countries had widespread public ownership of industry and central planning and were seeking to recruit developing countries to the Communist camp. Even non-Communist middle-income and low-income countries often consciously pursued mixed economies with an important element of public ownership. Leaders such as Nasser of Egypt and Nyerere of Tanzania promoted Arab socialism and African socialism, respectively. Although international trade expanded with the assistance of tariff cuts implemented through the General Agreement on Tariffs and Trade (discussed in Chapter 15), "free trade" was not widely accepted as an ideal for the developing world. In many Latin American countries, for example, *import substitution policies* were vigorously pursued. An **import substitution policy** uses trade protection to develop local manufacturing of goods that can replace imported manufactured goods.

The average growth rate of real GDP per capita in developing countries during the 1960–1973 period was a healthy 2.5 percent. From the rule of 72 we can calculate that with a growth rate of 2.5 percent the real GDP per capita of a country will double in about 29 years. In the following two decades—that is, from 1974 to 1994—the average growth rate of real GDP per capita in developing countries fell to under 1 percent.[11] (See Figure 14.1 on the performance of Brazil and Ghana over this period.) With a growth rate of 1 percent, the real GDP per capita of a country will require about 72 years to double.

As in developed countries such as Canada (see section 14.5), the developing countries also generally experienced a productivity and growth slowdown beginning around 1973, when oil prices spiked upwards and inflation rose sharply in many countries. The Bretton Woods system of fixed exchange rates unravelled at about the same time, and it was followed by reduced restrictions on international capital flows and a massive expansion of lending from banks in high-income countries to borrowers in the developing countries, especially the middle-income developing countries. Much of the lending was described as *recycling of petrodollars* as it involved banks collecting deposits from oil exporters and lending to oil-importing developing economies. There was also significant lending by the World Bank, the IMF, and other public-sector institutions to the low-income developing countries.

During the high-interest-rate, strong-U.S.-dollar recession of the early 1980s, many developing countries found it increasingly difficult to repay their dollar-denominated external debts. Not only was the debt burden of the developing country borrowers increased by the strong U.S. dollar and high interest rates, but their debt servicing was also made more difficult by declining prices of commodities exported by developing countries and by slow growth in the high-income economies in the 1980s. The situation of many

import substitution policy uses trade protection to develop local manufacturing of goods that can replace imported manufactured goods

10 See http://oxfam.ca/news-and-publications/factsheets/gleneagles-commitments-and-07-target.

11 On the growth of real GDP per capita in developing countries, see Dani Rodrik, *The New Global Economy and Developing Countries: Making Openness Work* (Washington, D.C.: Overseas Development Council, 1999), p. 75.

developing countries having to devote large shares of their GDP to repaying external debt was called the *Third World debt crisis*.[12]

In parallel with the emergence of the Third World debt crisis, there was a general shift among policy-makers in many high-income countries, especially the United States under President Reagan and the United Kingdom under Prime Minister Thatcher, in favour of policies that political scientists have described as *neo-liberal*. **Neo-liberal policies** include reduced spending on social programs, lowered taxes, privatization of public enterprises, deregulation, trade liberalization, liberalization of international capital flows, and measures to achieve low inflation.

The view that such policies were appropriate to developing economies became known as the *Washington Consensus*. The **Washington Consensus** refers to the policy advice from the U.S. Treasury, the IMF, and the World Bank (all based in Washington, D.C.) to developing countries that they should privatize, liberalize, and pursue macroeconomic stability (interpreted to mean low inflation and balanced budgets). In many cases, acceptance of the policy advice was a condition for receiving loans from the IMF and the World Bank. Borrowing countries were required to adopt structural adjustment programs as a condition for borrowing.

The Washington Consensus approach to developing economies has been less influential since the late 1990s. It has been attacked by the antiglobalization movement. But it was also questioned by some prominent economists who argued that the greatest economic development success stories of recent decades—the newly industrialized economies of East Asia, such as South Korea (see Figure 14.1), Taiwan, and Singapore, and the Asian giants China (see Figure 14.1) and India—have been produced by policies somewhat at odds with the Washington Consensus. Washington Consensus policies have been associated by some with poor results for many transition economies in the 1990s.[13] Since the late 1990s, fewer and fewer developing countries have had to turn to the IMF for support, as noted in section 13.3, and they have had greater leeway to tailor their economic policies to domestic priorities. For example, in Latin America over the past decade, leftist or social democratic governments have been elected in a wide range of countries—at the time of writing, in Venezuela, Brazil, Paraguay, Argentina, Uruguay, Chile, Bolivia, Nicaragua, Honduras, Ecuador, and El Salvador—and are pursuing more egalitarian policies than in the 1980s and 1990s.

In 2000, the United Nations organized a Millennium Summit, which led to all United Nations member states and numerous international organizations including the World Bank and the IMF accepting the *Millennium Development Goals*. The **Millennium Development Goals** are eight international development goals that include eradicating extreme poverty, improving health and education, and developing a global partnership for development by the target year of 2015.[14]

---

neo-liberal policies include reduced taxes, privatization, deregulation, and trade liberalization

Washington Consensus the policy advice that developing countries should privatize, liberalize, and pursue low inflation and balanced budgets

Millennium Development Goals eight international goals, including the eradication of extreme poverty in the world by 2015

RECAP

GROWTH IN DEVELOPING COUNTRIES

The World Bank, a publicly funded international organization that provides assistance for development, classifies the countries of the world into the categories of high income, middle income, and low income. The high-income countries are called developed economies and the middle-income and low-income countries are called developing economies.

---

12 See Kenneth Rogoff, "Third World Debt," *The Concise Encyclopedia of Economics*, http://www.econlib.org/library/Enc1/ThirdWorldDebt.html.

13 See, for example, Dani Rodrik, *One Economics Many Recipes* (Princeton, New Jersey: Princeton University Press, 2007), especially Chapter 1.

14 See http://www.un.org/millenniumgoals/.

While some low-income economies suffer from high population density, others from a resource curse, and yet others from tropical diseases and land-locked geography, they are all characterized by low levels of capital per worker. Raising levels of capital per worker requires investment, but the incentives for investment in low-income countries are often weak. One source of funding to overcome the various constraints that inhibit investment and otherwise hamper development in low-income countries is official development assistance (ODA).

Although low-income countries face special challenges, many of them did achieve impressive improvements in living standards during the 1960s and early 1970s. In general, countries began to experience substantially lower growth after 1973. Following the emergence of the Third World debt crisis, the U.S. Treasury, IMF, and World Bank began to promote an approach to development policy called the Washington Consensus that encouraged developing countries to privatize, liberalize, and pursue low inflation and balanced budgets. Since the late 1990s, fewer and fewer developing countries have had to turn to the IMF for support, as noted in section 13.3, and they have had greater leeway to tailor their economic policies to domestic priorities. As well, the adoption of the Millennium Development Goals represents a different emphasis from the original Washington Consensus.

14.9 LIMITS TO GROWTH

Earlier in this chapter, we saw that even relatively low rates of economic growth, if sustained for a long period, will produce huge increases in the size of the economy. This fact raises the question of whether economic growth can continue indefinitely without depleting natural resources and causing massive damage to the global environment. Does the basic truth that we live in a finite world of finite resources imply that, ultimately, economic growth must come to an end?

The question is a complex one that requires expertise extending beyond economics. But economics can shed some light. On the one hand, most economists would agree that not all of the problems created by economic growth can be dealt with effectively through the market or through domestic politics. Global environmental problems, such as *global warming*, are a particular challenge for existing economic and political institutions. **Global warming** refers to the increase in the average temperature of the earth's surface since the mid-20th century, and its projected continuation. Achieving international cooperation to counter the trend to global warming is considered by many scientists to be the major international policy issue facing the world today.

global warming the increase in the average temperature of the earth's surface since the mid-20th century

Environmental quality is not bought and sold in markets and thus will not automatically reach its optimal level through market processes. Nor can local or national governments effectively address problems that are global in scope. Unless international mechanisms are established for dealing with global environmental problems, these problems may become worse as economic growth continues.

The Earth Summit organized by the United Nations in 1992 gave rise to the United Nations Framework Convention on Climate Change (UNFCC), an international environmental treaty. The **Kyoto Protocol**, adopted in 1997 and entering into force in 2005, is a refinement of the UNFCC that attempts to fight global warming by getting countries to commit to specific targets for reductions in emissions of greenhouse gases, such as carbon dioxide, which have been found to contribute to global warming. Among the many challenges facing the fight against global warming, however, is that many of the largest emitters of greenhouse gases—including the United States, China, India, and Brazil—have not committed to reducing greenhouse gas emissions. Economists may disagree about whether the Kyoto Protocol takes the right approach, but there is

Kyoto Protocol a refinement of the United Nations Framework Convention on Climate Change, attempting to fight global warming by getting countries to commit to specific targets for reductions in emissions of greenhouse gases quite widespread recognition among economists that the trend to global warming will tend to get worse unless effective international mechanisms of emissions control are established.

On the other hand, economists have long raised doubts about pessimistic arguments that economic growth must come to an end. In particular, economists were quick to point out flaws in an influential 1972 book, *The Limits to Growth*.[15] This book reported the results of computer simulations that suggested that unless population growth and economic expansion were halted, the world would soon run out of natural resources, drinkable water, and breathable air. One problem with the "limits to growth thesis," whether in its original form or recent restatements, lies in its underlying concept of economic growth. It assumes implicitly that economic growth will always take the form of still more of what we have now: smoky factories, polluting cars, fast-food restaurants. If that were indeed the case, then surely there would be limits to the growth the planet can sustain. But growth in real GDP does not necessarily take such a form. Increases in real GDP can also arise from new or higher-quality products and services, such as an expanded number of TV channels, higher-quality and more efficient vehicles, and environmentally benign human services (like education or child care). Thus, economic growth need not take the form of more and more of the same old stuff; it can mean newer, better, and perhaps cleaner and more efficient goods and services. If technological progress saves resources, GDP growth may mean reduced environmental impact.

A second problem with the limits to growth conclusion is that it overlooks the fact that increased wealth and productivity expand society's capacity to take measures to safeguard the environment. In fact, some of the most polluted countries in the world are not the richest but rather those that are in a relatively early stage of industrialization. At this stage, countries tend to devote the bulk of their resources to basic needs—food, shelter, and healthcare—and continued industrial expansion. In more economically developed countries, extra income is available to support environmental protection both at home and, through targeted foreign aid, in developing countries. (Whether the extra income is actually used for environmental protection at home and abroad, of course, depends upon the efforts of environmental activists and other political forces.)

A third problem with the limits to growth thesis is that it ignores the issue of how market participants will respond to temporary resource shortages (situations when demand outstrips supply). During the oil-supply disruptions of the 1970s, for example, newspapers were filled with headlines about the energy crisis and the imminent depletion of world oil supplies. But reduced oil supplies led to an increase in prices that changed the behaviour of both demanders and suppliers. Consumers insulated their homes, purchased more energy-efficient cars and appliances, and switched to alternative sources of energy. Suppliers engaged in a hunt for new reserves, opening up new sources in Latin America, China, and the North Sea. For a wide range of minerals and other natural resources, not just for oil, shortages will trigger price changes that induce suppliers and demanders to deal with the problem. Simply extrapolating current economic trends into the future ignores how market participants recognize shortages and tend to make the necessary corrections.

In short, economic growth does give rise to environmental problems, and those environmental problems requiring international political solutions may be particularly difficult to solve. But not all concerns about limits to growth are equally valid. Economics can help with the task of sorting out which concerns deserve attention and which are not well founded.

---

15 D. H. Meadows, D. L. Meadows, J. Randers, and W. W. Behrens III, *The Limits to Growth* (New York: New American Library, 1972).

SUMMARY

- Because of the power of *compound growth*, relatively small differences in growth rates, if continued over long periods, can produce large differences in real GDP per person and average living standards. The rule of 72—find how many years it takes for a magnitude to double when the magnitude is growing at a constant rate by dividing 72 by the growth rate expressed in percentage terms—is handy for examining differences in growth rates over time. **LO1**

- Real GDP per person is the product of average labour productivity (real GDP per employed worker) and the share of the population that is employed. Growth in real GDP per person can occur only through growth in average labour productivity, growth in the share of the population that is working, or both. Over the last four decades in Canada, roughly half the growth in real GDP per person came from increases in the employment-population ratio and half from growth in average labour productivity. In future years, however, higher labour productivity will be the main source of continuing improvements in real GDP per capita. **LO2**

- Among the factors that determine labour productivity are the education, training, and skills of workers, or human capital; the quantity and quality of the physical capital that workers use; the availability of land and other natural resources; the application of technology to the production and distribution of goods and services; entrepreneurship; and the broad political and legal environment. An aggregate production function shows the output of an economy as a function of various inputs, such as physical capital. **LO3**

- Since the 1970s, Canada and other high-income countries have experienced a slowdown in productivity growth. Some economists have suggested that the exploitation of a backlog of technological opportunities following the Great Depression and the Second World War led to unusually high growth rates in the 1950s and 1960s, a view called the *technological depletion hypothesis*. In Canada, during the period from the late 1970s to the late 1990s, the productivity slowdown was associated not just with a slowdown of real wage growth, but with stagnation of real wages. **LO4**

- Economic growth has costs as well as benefits. If the economy is already operating at or near capacity, then increasing the growth rate may require devoting more resources to investment as opposed to consumption or increasing hours of work at the expense of leisure. **LO5**

- Governments in high-income economies can stimulate economic growth by adopting policies that encourage the creation of human capital; promote investment, including public investment in infrastructure; support research and development, particularly in the basic sciences; and provide a legal and political framework that supports innovations in economic activity. **LO6**

- The World Bank, a publicly funded international organization that provides assistance to foster economic development, classifies countries into low-, middle- and high-income categories. Those in the low- and middle-income categories are called developing countries. The challenges facing different economies overlap, but the challenges facing low-income economies are particularly great. The general character of economic policies followed by developing economies has evolved over the past several decades. **LO6**

- Are there limits to growth? On the one hand, economic growth does give rise to environmental problems, and those environmental problems requiring international political solutions may be particularly difficult to solve. On the other hand, not all concerns about limits to growth are equally valid. Economic growth can take the form of cleaner and more-efficient goods and services. Higher productivity expands a society's capacity to take measures to safeguard the environment. And for a variety of natural resources, shortages will trigger price changes that induce suppliers and demanders to deal with the problem. **LO7**

KEY TERMS

aggregate production
   function (376)
compound interest (365)
developing economies (382)
diminishing returns to capital (371)
Dutch disease (374)
entrepreneurship (374)
global warming (387)

import substitution policy (385)
Kyoto Protocol (387)
Millennium Development
   Goals (386)
neo-liberal policies (386)
official development assistance
   (ODA) (384)
power of compound growth (365)

resource curse (383)
rule of 72 (366)
technological depletion
   hypothesis (377)
Washington Consensus (386)
World Bank (382)

REVIEW QUESTIONS

1. What has happened to real GDP per person in the industrialized countries over the past century? What implications does this have for the average person? **LO1**

2. What is the rule of 72?

3. Why do economists consider growth in average labour productivity to be the key factor in determining the growth of real GDP per capita in the long run? **LO2**

4. What is *human capital*? Why is it economically important? How is new human capital created? **LO3**

5. What is meant by *diminishing returns to capital*? **LO3**

6. What is an aggregate production function?

7. Discuss one explanation that has been offered for the slowdown in productivity growth observed in industrial countries since the early 1970s. **LO4**

8. Discuss the evolution of real wages in Canada since the late 1970s. What might explain the divergence between real wage growth and productivity growth in the period from the late 1970s to the late 1990s?

9. What major contributions can the government make to the goal of increasing average labour productivity in a high-income country? **LO6**

10. In connection with developing economies, what is meant by the resource curse? **LO6**

11. What is meant by the Washington Consensus? **LO6**

12. Discuss the following statement: "Because the environment is fragile and natural resources are finite, ultimately economic growth must come to an end." **LO7**

PROBLEMS

1. Richland's real GDP per person is $10 000, and Poorland's real GDP per person is $5000. However, Richland's real GDP per person is growing at 1 percent per year and Poorland's is growing at 3 percent per year. Compare real GDP per person in the two countries after ten years and after twenty years. Approximately how many years will it take Poorland to catch up to Richland? Using the rule of 72, calculate how many years it will take for real GDP per person to double in both Richland and Poorland. **LO1**

2. Refer to Table 14.3. Suppose that the growth of average labour productivity in Canada had continued at its 1950–1973 rate until 2010. Proportionally, how much higher would Canadian average labour productivity in 2010 have been, compared to its actual value? (*Note:* You do not need to know the actual values of average labour productivity in any year to solve this problem.) Does your answer shed light on why economists consider the post-1973 productivity slowdown to be an important issue? Explain. **LO2**

Year	GDP per capita	Average labour productivity	Share of population employed
1961	$14 096	$42 619	33.2%
2010	$38 600	$77 262	50.0%

3. Between 1961 and 2010, the rising share of the Canadian population in paid employment contributed to rising GDP per person. But suppose that the share of the Canadian population in paid employment had remained constant between 1961 and 2010. What would Canadian GDP per person have been in 2010? Make use of the relevant data from the table above. **LO2**

4 Here are approximate data for Canada and Japan on the ratio of employment to population in 1979 and 2009:

	1979	2009
Canada	0.45	0.50
Japan	0.47	0.49

Using data from Table 14.1 on real GDP per person, find average labour productivity for each country in 1979 and 2009. How much of the increase in output per person in each country over the 1979–2009 period is due to increased labour productivity? to increased employment relative to population? **LO2**

5. Joanne has just completed high school and is trying to determine whether to go to college for two years or go directly to work. Her objective is to maximize the savings she will have in the bank five years from now. If she goes directly to work, she will earn $20 000 per year for each of the next five years. If she goes to college, for each of the next two years she will earn nothing; indeed, she will have to borrow $6000 each year to cover tuition and books. This loan must be repaid in full three years after graduation. If she graduates from college, in each of the subsequent three years her wages will be $38 000 per year. Joanne's total living expenses and taxes, excluding tuition and books, equal $15 000 per year. **LO3**
   a. Suppose for simplicity that Joanne can borrow and lend at 0 percent interest. On purely economic grounds, should she go to college or work?
   b. Does your answer to (a) change if she can earn $23 000 per year with only a high school degree?
   c. Does your answer to (a) change if Joanne's tuition and books cost $8000 per year?
   d. (More difficult.) Suppose that the interest rate at which Joanne can borrow and lend is 10 percent per year, but other data are as in (a). Savings are deposited at the end of the year they are earned and receive (compound) interest at the end of each subsequent year. Similarly, the loans are taken out at the end of the year in which they are needed, and interest does not accrue until the end of the subsequent year. Now that the interest rate has risen, should Joanne go to college or go to work?

6. The Good'n'Fresh Grocery Store has two checkout lanes and four employees. Employees are equally skilled, and all are able either to operate a register (checkers) or bag groceries (baggers). The store owner assigns one checker and one bagger to each lane. A lane with a checker and a bagger can check out 40 customers per hour. A lane with a checker only can check out 25 customers per hour. **LO3**
   a. In terms of customers checked out per hour, what is total output and average labour productivity for the Good'n'Fresh Grocery Store?
   b. The owner adds a third checkout lane and register. Assuming that no employees are added, what is the best way to reallocate the workers to tasks? What

is total output and average labour productivity (in terms of customers checked out per hour) now?
   c. Repeat (b) for the addition of a fourth checkout lane, and a fifth. Do you observe diminishing returns to capital in this example?

7. Harrison, Carla, and Fred are housepainters. Harrison and Carla can paint 30 square metres per hour using a standard paintbrush, and Fred can paint 24 square metres per hour. Any of the three can paint 60 square metres per hour using a roller. **LO3**
   a. Assume Harrison, Carla, and Fred have only paintbrushes at their disposal. What is the average labour productivity, in terms of square metres per painter-hour, for the three painters taken as a team? Assume that the three painters always work the same number of hours.
   b. Repeat (a) for cases in which the team has one, two, three, or four rollers available. Are there diminishing returns to capital?
   c. An improvement in paint quality increases the area that can be covered per hour (by either brushes or rollers) by 20 percent. How does this technological improvement affect your answers to (b)? Are there diminishing returns to capital? Does the technological improvement increase or reduce the economic value of an additional roller?

8. Hester's Hatchery raises fish. At the end of the current season she has 1000 fish in the hatchery. She can harvest any number of fish that she wishes, selling them to restaurants for $5 apiece. Because fish reproduce, for every fish that she leaves in the hatchery this year she will have two fish at the end of next year. The price of a fish is expected to be $5 next year as well. Hester relies entirely on income from current fish sales to support herself. **LO3**
   a. How many fish should Hester harvest if she wants to maximize the growth of her stock of fish from this season to next season?
   b. Do you think maximizing the growth of her fish stock is an economically sound strategy for Hester? Why or why not? Relate to the text discussion on the costs of economic growth.
   c. How many fish should Hester harvest if she wants to maximize her current income? Do you think this is a good strategy?
   d. Explain why Hester is unlikely to harvest either all or none of her fish, but instead will harvest some and leave the rest to reproduce.

9. "For advances in basic science to translate into improvements in standards of living, they must be supported by favourable economic conditions." True or false, and discuss. Use concrete examples where possible to illustrate your arguments. **LO4**, **LO6**

10. Nominal GDP in South Africa was 482 billion rand in 1994 (at the beginning of the post-apartheid era) and 2 615 billion rand in 2010. The price level (base year 2005) in South Africa was 43.8 was 1994 and 142.6 in 2010. And the population of South Africa increased from 40.2 million in 1994 to 49.9 million in 2010. What was the percentage change in real GDP per capita in South Africa from 1994 to 2010? **LO6**

ANSWERS TO IN-CHAPTER EXERCISES

14.1   If Canada had grown at the Japanese rate of 3.7 percent for the period 1955–2009, real GDP per person in 2009 would have been $12 535 $\times$ $(1.037)^{54}$ = $89 163. Actual GDP per person in Canada in 2009 was $36 208 (in 2005 U.S. dollars), so at the higher rate of growth output per person it would have been $89 163/$36 208 = 2.5 times higher. **LO1**

14.2   As before, Paris can wrap 4000 candies/week, or 100 candies/hour. Nicole can wrap 500 candies/hour, and working 40 hours weekly she can wrap 20 000 candies/week. Together Paris and Nicole can wrap 24 000 candies/week. Since they work a total of 80 hours between them, their output per hour as a team is 24 000 candies wrapped/80 hours = 300 candies wrapped/hour, midway between their hourly productivities as individuals. **LO3**

14.3   Now, working by hand, Paris can wrap 300 candies/hour and Nicole can wrap 500 candies/hour. With a machine, either Paris or Nicole can wrap 800 candies/hour. As in Exercise 14.3, the benefit of giving a machine to Paris (500 candies/hour) exceeds the benefit of giving a machine to Nicole (300 candies/hour), so if only one machine is available, Paris should use it. **LO3**

The table analogous to Table 14.2 now looks like this:

Relationship of Capital, Output, and Productivity in the Candy-Wrapping Factory

Number of machines (K)	Candies wrapped per week (Y)	Total hours worked (N)	Average hourly labour productivity (Y/N)
0	32 000	80	400
1	52 000	80	650
2	64 000	80	800
3	64 000	80	800

Comparing this table with Table 14.2, you can see that technological advance has increased labour productivity for any value of *K*, the number of machines available.

Adding one machine increases output by 20 000 candies wrapped/week, adding the second machine increases output by 12 000 candies wrapped/week, and adding the third machine does not increase output at all (because there is no worker available to use it). So diminishing returns to capital still hold after the technological improvement. **LO3**

14.4   Although the individual worker is the same person he was in Bangladesh, by coming to Canada he gains the benefit of factors that enhance average labour productivity in this country compared with his homeland. These include factors such as more and better capital to work with, more natural resources per person, and more advanced technologies. **LO3**

Practise and learn online with Connect.

CHAPTER 15
International Trade and Trade Policy

Under the headline "Sudbury Goes Boom, Windsor Goes Bust," *The Toronto Star* business story of May 2008 told how two Canadian cities had opposite experiences in the past several preceding years.[1] In Sudbury, population and incomes had been growing; the unemployment rate of 5.7 percent was at its lowest level since the 1960s. As the business reporter put it, "Revellers crowd the nightclubs. Shoppers vie for elbow room in malls on weekends. Builders can't keep up." On the other hand, Windsor had lost 10 000 manufacturing jobs in the past six years and housing starts had plunged; the unemployment rate of 8.3 percent was one of the highest in the country. In the reporter's breathless prose, "Factories are lifeless. Stores keep shutting down. Cheques bounce. Movers are busy. Worry is everywhere."

Developments in international trade during that period explain the contrasting situations of Sudbury and Windsor. Sudbury is a hub for mining, particularly for nickel and copper; Windsor has, historically, depended on the auto industry. Sudbury's economy struggled when nickel prices hovered around US$3 per pound for many years. But nickel prices were in the $13 range on international commodity exchanges in mid-2008. Miners at Vale Inco were doing especially well because of a "nickel bonus" (incentives tied to company profits and the nickel price) negotiated by their United Steelworkers Union in 1985 when nickel prices were depressed. *The Toronto Star* article already quoted indicates that soaring nickel prices in preceding years could be traced to a surging worldwide demand for commodities as China and other Asian countries were hungry for copper and nickel, key elements in stainless steel and other products ranging from batteries to computers.

When the Canadian auto industry boomed in the late 1990s, thanks in part to the international competitive advantage provided by the low value of the Canadian dollar, Windsor thrived. Even as late as 2005, Windsor produced 360 000 vehicles, 1 000 000

1 Tony Van Alphen, "Sudbury Goes Boom, Windsor Goes Bust," *The Toronto Star*, 17 May 2008, http://www.thestar.com/article/426845. See also Tony Van Alphen, "Windsor is Falling Apart," *The Toronto Star*, 17 May 2008, http://www.thestar.com/article/426770; Tony Van Alphen, "Sudbury Booms on Soaring Metal Prices," *The Toronto Star*, 18 May 2008; and CAW Local 200, "What the Auto Industry Means to Windsor," http://www.caw.ca/en/campaigns-issues-ongoing-campaigns-issues-what-the-auto-industry-means-to-windsor-pdf.htm.

engines, and 885 000 transmissions. But Ford reduced its engine operations, and by May 2008, the Canadian Auto Workers Union had to negotiate a closeout agreement for its members at the General Motors Windsor transmission plant after the company announced the plant would close in 2010. The massive 47 percent appreciation of the Canadian dollar between 2002 and 2007 sharply reduced the international competitiveness of Canada's auto industry. The automakers demanded cost reductions from their suppliers and, as the business reporter states, "companies in China—one of the drivers of Sudbury's boom—South Korea, and the U.S. are producing some of the parts and tooling, putting operations like Kasko (a producer of equipment for automotive manufacturing, for Chrysler) in Windsor out of business." Within months of the publication of *The Toronto Star*'s business story, a global recession unfolded and the prices of commodites such as nickel and copper plummeted. The boom in Sudbury came to an end. The unemployment rate rose from 5.1 percent in July 2008 to a peak of 10.8 percent in February 2010.

The impact of shifts in international trade are more visible in cities such as Sudbury and Windsor than they would be in larger, more diversified cities such as Toronto, Montreal, and Vancouver or in the broader economy. But the impact of trade and changes in it is pervasive. It has been estimated, for example, that one in five paid jobs in Canada is directly linked to international trade.[2]

This chapter addresses international trade and trade policy as well as their effects on the broader economy. We begin by presenting statistics on Canada's position in the international trading system. The second section of the chapter provides a supply and demand perspective on winners and losers from trade. The third section provides background on the institutions of trade policy. In the final section, we conduct a quick review, especially as it relates to Chapter 8, of our treatment of international trade from a short-run, macroeconomic perspective.

15.1 CANADA IN THE INTERNATIONAL TRADING SYSTEM

Before we consider international trade theory and institutions, let us first examine some basic facts about Canada's place in the international trading system from a statistical perspective. As Figure 4.5 showed, trade is very important to modern-day Canada. In some recent years, exports and imports have each amounted to over 40 percent of Canadian GDP.[3]

To put Canada's reliance upon international trade in context, view Figure 15.1, which compares Canada's trade dependence to that of the other G7 countries (the United States, Japan, Germany, France, United Kingdom, and Italy) and to Australia. In Figure 15.1, trade dependence is measured by the value, expressed relative to GDP, of an economy's combined value of exports and imports. Of the high-income countries shown, Germany has the highest ratio of trade to GDP and Canada has the second highest.

Canada's characteristic feature of having a high level of dependence on trade is long-standing. Indeed, the great Canadian economic historian Harold Innis (1894–1952) analyzed Canada's economic development by focusing on a succession of leading exports: furs, fish, forestry products, grain, and oil and natural gas. Innis's *staples thesis* maintained that these natural resource, or staples, exports had a pervasive impact, not just on the Canadian economy, but on society and politics as well, because the staples affected everything from Canada's patterns of settlement to Canada's international relations. Although the importance of trade to the Canadian economy has not diminished, there have been major changes in Canada's trading partners and in the composition of Canada's exports since the days of Innis.

---

2 See "Trade Matters," at http://www.international.gc.ca/trade-agreements-accords-commerciaux/matters-important/index.aspx?lang=en&view=d.

3 Recall, however, that what counts as a component of GDP is the value of net exports—that is, exports *minus* imports.

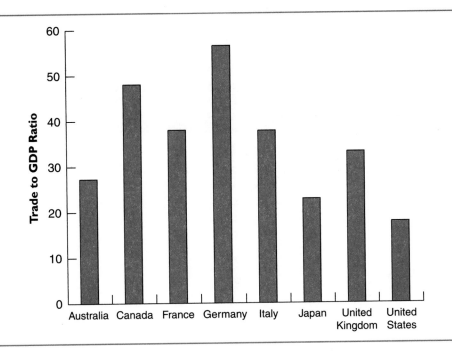

FIGURE 15.1
Trade to GDP Ratios for Selected Countries, 2004–2007
Canada and Germany are more heavily dependent upon international trade than many other high-income countries. The bars on the graph represent the value of each country's exports and imports in relation to its GDP.
SOURCE: OECD iLibrary, Key Tables from OECD— ISSN 2074-3920, OECD 2010, http://dx.doi.org/10.1787/20743920-2010-table1.

From the time of Confederation in 1867 until World War II, Canada had two major trading partners, the United Kingdom and the United States. But after World War II, the share of trade with the United States in the total of Canada's trade began a dramatic upward rise, and the share of trade with the United Kingdom began an equally dramatic decline. Figure 15.2 shows this trend by focusing on the export side of Canada's trade.

FIGURE 15.2
Canadian Exports to the United States and the United Kingdom, 1886–2010
Until the mid 1940s, the United States and the United Kingdom were of roughly equal importance as trading partners with Canada. The figure shows that since the late 1940s the United States has become the destination for the bulk of Canada's exports and the United Kingdom has become a minor export destination.
SOURCES: Adapted from CANSIM series v191334 (exports to U.S.), v191335 (exports to UK), and v191490 (total exports), and from *HSC* series G402, G401, G393, G390, and G389. Extraction date, June 14, 2011.

FIGURE 15.3

Canada's Five Major Trading Partners, 2010

The United States is Canada's most important trading partner by far, as measured by either the share of Canadian imports from it or the share of Canadian exports destined to it. The share of Canadian imports from each country is shown in red and the share of Canadian exports to each is shown in blue. If the blue bar for a country is larger than the red bar, then Canada runs a trade surplus with that country. China is Canada's second major source of imports but the United Kingdom is Canada's second major destination for exports.

SOURCE: Adapted from Department of Foreign Affairs and International Trade/ Office of the Chief Economist/Trade and Economic Statistics/Merchandise Trade. Extraction date, June 14, 2011.

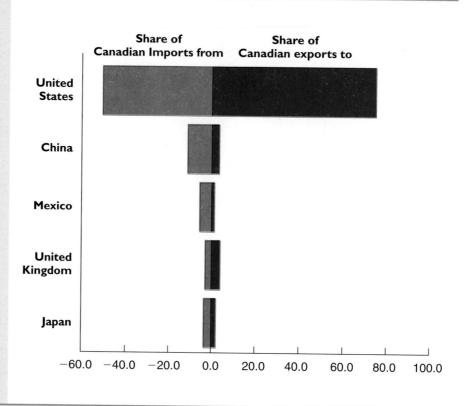

In recent decades, about 80 percent of Canada's exports have been destined for the United States compared with just a few percent for the United Kingdom. The rise in the U.S. share of Canada's trade has worried those who value Canada's independence, and for a period in the 1970s and early 1980s the Canadian government sought to boost the share of Canada's trade with Europe.

Today, Canada's other leading trading partners are China, Mexico, Japan, and the United Kingdom, as shown in Figure 15.3, but their importance pales in comparison to that of the United States. Japan had become an important trading partner for Canada by the 1980s. The major development in Canada's trade pattern in the past several years has been the rise of China as a source of imports, which will not surprise you if you have ever shopped at a "dollar" store and noticed where most of the goods are made. China, which accounted for only 1 percent of Canada's imports in 1989, accounted for 11 percent of Canada's imports by 2010. The rise of Mexico as a leading trading partner of Canada is very recent.

Figure 15.4 shows the pattern of Canada's exports and imports by broad categories of merchandise trade. In the past few years, natural resource exports have surged. Although the value of Canada's combined exports of industrial products, machinery and equipment, and automotive products ($243 billion) was double the value of Canadian exports of agricultural and fishing products, energy products, and forestry products ($124 billion) in 2003, by 2010 the value of industrial-type exports had dropped to $229 billion while the value of resource-type exports had risen to $150 billion.

Like many other countries, in the early stages of its development, Canada relied upon tariffs (taxes on imported goods) as an important source of government revenue and as a means of providing protection to domestic industries. Over the decades, however, other sources of government revenue—income, payroll, and sales taxes—have gained in relative importance, and Canada has become more open to imports.

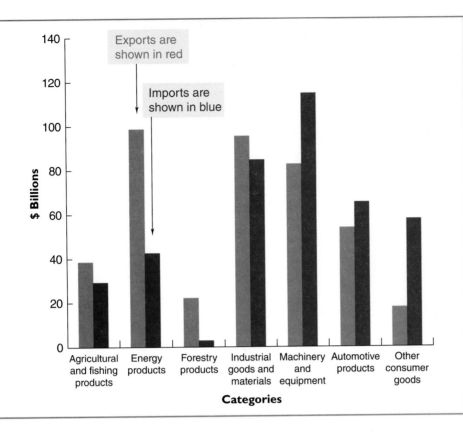

FIGURE 15.4

Canada's Exports and Imports by Major Product Category, Average 2008–2010

Canada's major export category in recent years has been energy products, which exceeded exports of industrial goods and materials. Natural resource exports have surged in the past several years, and Canada has become a net importer of automative products.
SOURCE: Adapted from Statistics Canada CANSIM Table 228-0043.

One indication of this is provided by Figure 15.5, which shows the evolution of Canada's average tariff rate—that is, the ratio of tariff revenue (also called import duties or custom duties) to the value of imports. Canada's average tariff rate, which peaked at 22 percent in 1888, had dropped below 1 percent by 1996. A high tariff rate was associated with the implementation in 1879 of the National Policy to protect domestic manufacturing, a policy that was maintained for most years until the late 1930s. Since the early 1950s, Canada's average tariff rate has shown a sharp downward trend, associated in part with the establishment of the General Agreement on Tariffs and Trade (GATT) and the various multilateral rounds of tariff reductions negotiated under the GATT (which we will examine further in section 15.3).

RECAP

CANADA IN THE INTERNATIONAL TRADING SYSTEM

- International trade is very important to the Canadian economy. Canada has the second highest trade to GDP ratio among the G7 countries.

- Canada's reliance upon trade with the United States increased over many decades. The share of Canadian exports to the United States peaked at about 84 percent in 2002. It has dropped to 73 percent in 2010.

- Natural resource exports are still an important component of Canada's international trade, and they have surged in the past several years. Energy products have surpassed industrial goods and materials as Canada's largest export category by value.

- Canada's average tariff rate, which peaked at 22 percent in 1888, has remained below 1 percent since 1996.

FIGURE 15.5

Average Tariff Rates for Canada, 1868–2008

Average tariff rates for Canada were high during the early stages of Canada's development, reaching a peak of 22 percent in 1888. Since the early 1950s, Canada's average rate has shown a sharp downward trend, and it dropped below 1 percent by 1996. The average tariff rate measures the ratio of tariff revenues to the value of imports. SOURCE: Adapted from Statistics Canada, CANSIM series V690200 and V646957; extraction date, June 14, 2011; and HSC series G485.

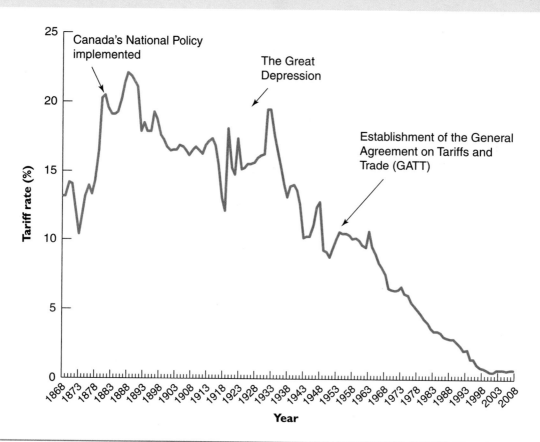

15.2 A SUPPLY AND DEMAND PERSPECTIVE ON TRADE

Economists study international trade theory to arrive at an awareness of what goes on in the real world of international trade. The comparative advantage theory we considered in Chapter 2 provides a starting point for standard international trade theory and understanding the real world of trade. Although there are various qualifications, standard international trade theory is used to show that the logic prompting individuals to specialize and to exchange is also the rationale that leads nations to specialize and trade with each other. Under certain assumptions, each trading partner can benefit from this, even though one may have an absolute advantage in each good. All else being equal, the output of an **open economy**, one that trades with other economies, should be greater than that of a **closed economy**, one that does not trade with others. The larger the difference between the trading partners' opportunity costs, the greater the benefits of trade tend to be.

This standard international trade theory provides a rationale for why a country such as Canada would reduce trade barriers over time, as is indicated by the declining average tariff rates shown in Figure 15.5. The theory, as typically presented, suggests that reducing trade barriers was in Canada's interest. But why has it taken Canada so many

open economy an economy that trades with other countries

closed economy an economy that does not trade with the rest of the world; also known as an autarky decades to reduce tariffs? Why do many countries continue to maintain tariffs that are much higher than Canada's? If it is possible for each partner to benefit from trade, why has Canada had a long-standing trade dispute with the United States over exports of softwood lumber?

In order to answer questions such as these, it is helpful to learn more about international trade theory. In certain situations some of the assumptions behind the standard international trade may not hold, so we have to qualify the conclusions of that chapter. But even if the standard international trade theory applies reasonably well in a given situation, there are still reasons for some groups to oppose freer trade.

In this section, we will develop a supply and demand model of international trade. With the aid of this model, we will see that opening up trade with other countries will generally create winners and losers, even if freer trade increases total output. In Figure 15.6 we see supply and demand for wine, one commodity in the markets for wine and lumber in the hypothetical economy we'll call Beaverland.

As usual, the price is shown on the vertical axis and the quantity on the horizontal axis. For now, think of the price of wine as being measured in terms of lumber rather than in terms of dollars (in other words, we measure the price of wine *relative* to the price of the other good in the economy). As usual, the upward-sloping curve in Figure 15.6 is the supply curve of wine, in this case for wine produced in Beaverland, and the downward-sloping curve is the demand curve for wine by Beaverland residents. The supply curve for wine in Beaverland reflects the opportunity cost of supplying wine (see Chapter 3 for a general explanation). Specifically, at any level of wine production, the relative price at which Beaverland firms are willing to supply an additional bottle of wine equals their opportunity cost of doing so. The demand curve, which tells us the number of bottles of wine Beaverland residents will purchase at each relative price, reflects the preferences and buying power of Beaverland residents.

If the Beaverland economy is closed to international trade, then market equilibrium occurs where the domestic supply and demand curves intersect, at point E in Figure 15.6. The equilibrium price will be p, and the equilibrium quantity will be q. We will ignore transportation and other trading costs.

If Beaverland opens its market to trade, however, the relevant price for wine becomes the **world price** of wine, the price at which wine is traded internationally. The world price for wine is determined by worldwide supply and demand. If we assume that Beaverland's wine market is too small to affect the world price for wine very much, the world price can be treated as fixed and represented by a horizontal line in the figure. Figure 15.6 shows the world price for wine as being lower than Beaverland's closed-economy price.

world price the price at which a good or service is traded on international markets

FIGURE 15.6
The Market for Wine in Beaverland
If Beaverland is closed to international trade, the equilibrium price and quantity of wine are determined by the intersection of the domestic supply and demand curves at point E. But if Beaverland is open to trade, the domestic price of wine must equal the world price. At that price, citizens will demand q_D wine, but domestic producers will supply only q_S wine. Thus $q_D - q_S$ wine must be imported from abroad.

If Beaverland residents are free to buy and sell wine on the international market, then the market price of wine in Beaverland must be the same as the world price. (The typical buyer in Beaverland will not pay a price above the world price, and the typical seller will not accept a price below the world price.) Figure 15.6 shows that at the world price, Beaverland consumers and firms demand q_D of wine but Beaverland wine producers will supply only q_S of wine. The difference between the two quantities, $q_D - q_S$, is the amount of wine that Beaverland must import from abroad. Figure 15.6 illustrates a general conclusion: *If the price of a good or service in a closed economy is greater than the world price, and that economy opens itself to trade, the economy will tend to become a net importer of that good or service.*

A different outcome occurs in Beaverland's lumber market shown in Figure 15.7.[4] The price of lumber (measured relative to the price of wine) is shown on the vertical axis, and the quantity of lumber on the horizontal axis. The downward-sloping demand curve in the figure shows how much lumber Beaverland purchasers want to buy at each relative price, and the upward-sloping supply curve how much lumber Beaverland producers are willing to supply at each relative price. If Beaverland's economy is closed to trade with the rest of the world, then equilibrium in the market for lumber will occur at point E, where the domestic demand and supply curves intersect. The quantity produced will be q and the price p.

Now imagine that Beaverland opens its lumber market to international trade. As in the case of wine, if free trade in lumber is permitted, then the prevailing price for lumber in Beaverland must be the same as the world price. Unlike the case of wine, however, the world price of lumber as shown in Figure 15.7 is *higher* than the domestic equilibrium price. How do we know that the world price of lumber will be higher than the domestic price? Recall that the price of lumber is measured relative to the price of wine, and vice versa. If the price of wine relative to the price of lumber is higher in Beaverland than in the world market, then the price of lumber relative to the price of wine must be lower, as

FIGURE 15.7

The Market for Lumber in Beaverland

With no international trade, the equilibrium price and quantity of lumber in Beaverland are determined by the intersection of the domestic supply and demand curves (point E). But if the country opens to trade, the domestic price of lumber must equal the world price. At the higher world price, Beaverland residents will demand the quantity of lumber q_D, which is less than the amount supplied by Beaverland producers, q_S. The excess lumber supplied by Beaverland producers, $q_S - q_D$, is exported.

4 In this example, the terms "buyers," "purchasers," and "consumers" are synonyms. For wine purchasers, the buyers are usually final consumers and for lumber purchases, the buyers are usually builders, and not final consumers. In any case, consumers, as used here, does not necessarily mean final consumers.

each price is the reciprocal of the other. More generally, as we saw in Chapter 2, when two people or two countries trade with each other, neither can have a comparative advantage in *every* good and service. Thus, in an example with only two goods, if non-Beaverland producers have a comparative advantage in wine, reflected in the lower cost of wine relative to lumber in the world market, then Beaverland producers must have a comparative advantage in lumber. By definition, this comparative advantage implies that the opportunity cost of lumber in terms of wine must be lower in Beaverland than in the rest of the world.

Figure 15.7 shows that at the world price for lumber, Beaverland producers are willing to supply q_S lumber, while Beaverland buyers want to purchase a smaller amount, q_D. The difference between domestic production and domestic purchases, $q_S - q_D$, is exported to the world market. The general conclusion of Figure 15.7 is this: *If the price of a good or service in a closed economy is lower than the world price, and that economy opens itself to trade, the economy will tend to become a net exporter of that good or service.*

WINNERS AND LOSERS FROM TRADE

Why do politicians so often resist "free trade" and "globalization"? As noted in the introduction to this section, one reason could be that the assumptions underlying our comparative advantage model of trade may not hold in specific real-world situations. For example, we have assumed that a country's comparative advantage in any industry is based upon the country's given endowments of resources used in producing the output of that industry. Taking endowments as given is a natural assumption when the key resource for an industry is, for example, huge expanses of arable land, but the assumption is more debatable when the key resource is something like computer programmers, the numbers of whom can be increased by changes in educational policy.[5]

Another reason for the resistance may be that what is being called free trade is not primarily about the trade of goods and services. In recent times, as we will see later in this chapter, free trade agreements have sometimes been significantly about such issues as the rights of multinational corporations and the protection of intellectual property rights. These issues are quite distinct from the trade in goods and services that has been the focus of our analysis of the comparative advantage model. It is possible to oppose the strengthening of corporate rights and intellectual property rights without being opposed to free trade in goods and services. But even if free trade is just about trade in goods and services, and even if it offers potential benefits for the economy as a whole, specific groups may not benefit. And politicians may respond to their concerns.

The supply and demand analyses shown in Figures 15.6 and 15.7 are useful for understanding who gains and who loses when an economy opens up to trade. Look first at Figure 15.6, which shows the market for wine in Beaverland. When Beaverland opens its wine market to international competition, Beaverland purchasers enjoy a larger quantity of wine at a lower price. Clearly, Beaverland wine buyers benefit from the free trade in wine. In general, *domestic consumers of imported goods benefit from trade.* However, Beaverland wine producers will not be so happy about opening their market to international competition. The fall in wine prices to the international level implies that less-efficient domestic producers will go out of business and that those who remain will earn lower profits. Unemployment in the wine industry will rise and may persist over time, particularly if displaced wine workers cannot easily move to a new industry.[6] We see that, in general, *domestic producers of imported goods are hurt by free trade* (although in this example they can console themselves with cheap wine).

---

5 To take a specific, real-world example, the endowments relevant to comparative advantage in the production of regional jets are not clearly given in the same way that huge expanses of arable land are, and countries like Canada and Brazil have had difficulty reaching agreement on which country has comparative advantage in the production of regional jets. On the trade dispute between Canada and Brazil over regional jets, see, for example, Kathryn Leger, "Canada, Brazil Both Claim Win in Subsidy War," *National Post*, 27 July 2001.

6 The real wages paid to Beaverland wine industry workers will also tend to fall, reflecting the lower relative price of wine.

Consumers are helped, and producers hurt, when imports increase. The opposite conclusions apply for an increase in exports (see Figure 15.7). In the example of Beaverland, an opening of the lumber market raises the domestic price of lumber to the world price and creates the opportunity for Beaverland to export lumber. Domestic producers of lumber benefit from the increased market (they can now sell lumber abroad as well as at home) and from the higher price of their product. In short, *domestic producers of exported goods benefit from free trade.* Beaverland lumber purchasers will be less enthusiastic, however, since they must now pay the higher world price of lumber and can therefore purchase less. Thus *domestic consumers of exported goods are hurt by free trade.*

TABLE 15.1
Trade Winners and Losers

Winners

- Consumers of imported goods
- Producers of exported goods

Losers

- Consumers of exported goods
- Producers of imported goods

TARIFFS AND QUOTAS

So far we have used our supply and demand model of international trade to examine the consequences, for both consumers and producers, of moving from a closed to an open economy. Next we will use the supply and demand model to examine two measures that are legal barriers to imports and are commonly employed to protect domestic markets: *tariffs* and *import quotas*. A **tariff** is a tax imposed on an imported good, and an **import quota** is a legal limit placed on the quantity of a good that may be imported.

Before we begin our supply and demand analysis of tariffs and quotas, however, two points are worth mentioning. First, it is a mistake to view tariffs simply as barriers to trade. The term **protective tariff** is used to describe a tariff that is intended to shield domestic industry from import competition. But there are also *revenue tariffs*. A **revenue tariff** is a tax imposed on imported goods for the purpose of collecting government revenue. For example, if a country such as Canada imposed a tariff on bananas it clearly would not be done to protect the domestic banana industry, because there is no such industry. Even protective tariffs generate revenue, provided that the tariff is not so high that it discourages imports altogether. As mentioned above in connection with Figure 15.5, countries such as Canada relied on tariffs as an important source of government revenue in their early stages of development.

A second point worth noting is that, although we will focus on the impact of tariffs and quotas on international trade, it should be recognized that the protection provided to an industry by a tariff (which raises the relative price of the imported good) can also be provided to an industry through a subsidy (which lowers the relative price of the domestically produced good). We will see in the following section how trade agreements that aim to reduce tariffs also aim to control subsidies for this very reason.

Tariffs

The effects of tariffs and quotas can be explained using supply and demand diagrams. Suppose that Beaverland wine makers, dismayed by the penetration of their market by imported wine, persuade their government to impose a tariff—that is, a tax—on every bottle of wine imported into the country. Wine produced in Beaverland will be exempt from the tax. Figure 15.8 shows the likely effects of this tariff on the domestic Beaverland wine market (assuming it does not affect the foreign exchange rate). The lower of the two horizontal lines

tariff a tax imposed on an imported good

import quota a legal limit placed on the quantity of a good that may be imported

protective tariff a tax on imported goods; the intention is to shield domestic industry from import competition

revenue tariff a tax imposed on imported goods; for the purpose of collecting government revenue

FIGURE 15.8

The Market for Wine After the Imposition of an Import Tariff

The imposition of a tariff on imported wine raises the price of wine in Beaverland to the world price plus tariff, p_T, represented by the upper horizontal line. Domestic production of wine rises from q_S to q'_S, domestic purchases of wine fall from q_D to q'_D, and wine imports fall from $q_D - q_S$ to $q'_D - q'_S$. Beaverland consumers are worse off and Beaverland wine producers are better off. The Beaverland government collects revenue from the tariff equal to the area of the pale blue rectangle.

in the figure indicates the world price of wine, not including the tariff. The higher of the two lines indicates the price Beaverland consumers will actually pay for imported wine, including the tariff. We refer to the price of wine including the tariff as p_T. The vertical distance between the two lines equals the amount of the tariff that is imposed on each imported bottle of wine.

From the point of view of domestic Beaverland producers and consumers, the imposition of the tariff has the same effects as an equivalent increase in the world price of wine. Because the price (including the tariff) of imported wine has risen, Beaverland wine producers will be able to raise the price they charge for their wine to the world price plus tariff, p_T. Thus, the price Beaverland consumers must pay—whether their wine is imported or not—equals p_T, represented by the upper horizontal line in Figure 15.8.

The rise in the price of wine created by the tariff affects the quantities of wine supplied and the quantities demanded by Beaverland residents. Domestic wine producers, facing a higher price for wine, increase their production from q_S to q'_S (see Figure 15.8). Beaverland consumers, also reacting to the higher price, reduce their wine purchases from q_D to q'_D. As a result, the quantity of imported wine, the difference between domestic purchases and domestic production, falls from $q_D - q_S$ to $q'_D - q'_S$.

Who are the winners and the losers from the tariff, then? The winners are the domestic wine producers, who sell more wine and receive a higher price for it. The clearest losers are Beaverland wine drinkers, who must now pay more for their wine. Another winner is the government, which collects revenue from the tariff. The pale blue area in Figure 15.8 shows the amount of revenue the government collects, equal to the quantity of wine imports after the imposition of the tariff, $q'_D - q'_S$, times the amount of the tariff.

EXAMPLE **15.1**

A tariff on imported wine[7]

Suppose the demand for wine by Beaverland consumers is given by

Demand = 3000 − 0.5(Price of wine).

---

7 If the price units in this example seem too high, think of the units as cents. If the quantities seem too low, think of them as quantities per hour.

The supply of wine by Beaverland producers is

Supply = 1000 + 0.5(Price of wine).

a. Assuming that the Beaverland economy is closed to trade, find the equilibrium price and quantity in the Beaverland wine market.
b. Assume the economy opens to trade. If the world price of Beaverland wine is 1500, find Beaverland consumption, production, and imports of wine.
c. At the request of domestic producers, the Beaverland government imposes a tariff of 300 per imported bottle of wine. Find Beaverland consumption, production, and imports of wine after the imposition of the tariff. How much revenue does the tariff raise for the government?

To find the closed-economy price and quantity, we set supply equal to demand:

1000 + 0.5(Price of wine) = 3000 − 0.5(Price of wine).

Solving this equation for the price of a bottle of wine gives the equilibrium price, equal to 2000. Substituting the equilibrium price into either the supply equation or the demand equation, we find the equilibrium quantity of wine in the Beaverland market, equal to 2000. This equilibrium price and quantity correspond to a point like point E in Figure 15.8.

If the economy opens to trade, the domestic price of wine must equal the world price, which is 1500. At this price, domestic demand for wine is 3000 − 0.5(1500), or 2250; domestic supply is 1000 + 0.5(1500), or 1750. These quantities correspond to q_D and q_S, respectively, in Figure 15.8. Imports equal the difference between domestic quantities demanded and supplied, equal to 2250 − 1750, or 500 bottles of wine.

The imposition of a tariff of 300 per bottle of wine raises the price from 1500 (the world price without the tariff) to 1800. To find Beaverland consumption and production at this price, we set the price equal to 1800 in the demand and supply equations. Thus, the domestic demand for wine is 3000 − 0.5(1800), or 2100 bottles of wine, the domestic supply is 1000 + 0.5(1800), or 1900 bottles. Imports, the difference between the quantity demanded by Beaverland residents and the quantity supplied by domestic firms, equal 2100 − 1900, or 200 bottles of wine, corresponding to $q'_D - q'_S$ in Figure 15.8. Thus the tariff has raised the price of wine by 300 and reduced imports by 300. The tariff revenue collected by the government equals 300 per imported bottle times 200 bottles, or 60 000.

EXERCISE 15.1   **Repeat parts (b) and (c) of Example 15.1 under the assumption that the world price of wine is 1200. What happens if the world price is 1800?**

Quotas

An alternative to a tariff is a quota, or legal limit, on the number or value of foreign goods that can be imported. One means of enforcing a quota is to require importers to obtain a licence or permit for each good they bring into the country. The government then distributes exactly the number of permits as the number of goods that may be imported under the quota.

How does the imposition of a quota on wine affect the domestic market for wine? To see the effect of a quota on imported wine, see Figure 15.9, which is similar to Figure 15.8. As before, assume that at first there are no restrictions on trade. Consumers pay the world price for wine, and $q_D - q_S$ bottles are imported. Now suppose once more that domestic wine producers complain to the government about competition from foreign wine makers, and the government agrees to act. However, this time, instead of a tariff, the government imposes a quota on the amount of wine that can be imported. For comparability

FIGURE 15.9

The Market for Wine after the Imposition of an Import Quota

The figure shows the effects of the imposition of a quota that permits only $q'_D - q'_S$ bottles to be imported. The total supply of wine to the domestic economy equals the domestic supply curve shifted to the right by $q'_D - q'_S$ units (the fixed amount of imports). Market equilibrium occurs at point F. The effects of the quota on the domestic market are identical to those of the tariff analyzed in Figure 15.8. The price rises to p_T, domestic production of wine rises from q_S to q'_S, purchases fall from q_D to q'_D, and imports fall from $q_D - q_S$ to $q'_D - q'_S$.

with the tariff analyzed in Figure 15.8, let's assume that the quota permits the same level of imports as entered the country under the tariff: specifically, $q'_D - q'_S$ bottles of wine. What effect does this ruling have on the domestic market for wine?

After the imposition of the quota, the supply of wine to the Beaverland market is the production of domestic firms plus the $q'_D - q'_S$ imported wine allowed under the quota. Figure 15.9 shows the supply of wine inclusive of the quota. The total supply curve, labelled "Domestic supply plus quota," is the same as the domestic supply curve except shifted $q'_D - q'_S$ units to the right. The domestic demand curve is the same as in Figure 15.8. Equilibrium in the domestic market for wine occurs at point F in Figure 15.9, at the intersection of the supply curve including the quota and the domestic demand curve. The figure shows that, relative to the initial situation with free trade, the quota (1) raises the domestic price of wine above the world price to the level marked p_T in Figure 15.9, (2) reduces domestic purchases of wine from q_D to q'_D, (3) increases domestic production of wine from q_S to q'_S, and (4) reduces imports to $q'_D - q'_S$, consistent with the quota. Like a tariff, the quota helps domestic producers by increasing their sales and the price they receive for their output, while hurting domestic consumers by forcing them to pay a higher price.

Interestingly, under our assumption that the quota is set so as to permit the same level of imports as the tariff, the effects on the domestic market of the tariff (Figure 15.8) and the quota (Figure 15.9) are not only similar, they are *equivalent*. Comparing Figures 15.8 and 15.9, you can see that the two policies have identical effects on the domestic price, purchases, and production, and on imports.

Although the market effects of a tariff and a quota are the same, there is one important difference between the two policies, which is that a tariff generates revenue for the government, while a quota does not.[8] A quota directs the revenue that would have gone to the government to those firms who hold the import licences instead. A holder of an import licence can purchase wine at the world price and resell it in the domestic market

8 This is true unless the government sells rather than gives away import licences. If a perfectly competitive auction of import licenses can be organized, a tariff and a quota are also equivalent in terms of government revenue.

at price p_T, pocketing the difference. Thus, with a tariff, the government collects the difference between the world price and the domestic market price of the good; with a quota, private firms or individuals collect that difference, unless they are required to bid for import licences in competitive auctions.

EXAMPLE **15.2**

Effects of an import quota

Suppose the supply of and demand for wine in Beaverland is as given in Example 15.1, and the government imposes an import quota of 200 bottles of wine. Find the equilibrium price in the domestic wine market, as well as the quantities produced by domestic firms and purchased by domestic consumers.

The supply of wine by domestic Beaverland producers was stated in Example 15.1 to be 1000 + 0.5(Price of wine). The quota allows 200 bottles of wine to be imported. Thus, the total supply of wine, including both domestic production and imports, is 1000 + 0.5(Price of wine) + 200, or 1200 + 0.5(Price of wine). Setting the quantity supplied equal to the quantity demanded, we get

$$1200 + 0.5(\text{Price of wine}) = 3000 - 0.5(\text{Price of wine})$$

Solving for the unknown, we find that the price of wine in the domestic Beaverland market is 1800. Domestic production of wine is 1000 + 0.5(1800), or 1900 bottles of wine, while domestic demand is 3000 − 0.5(1800), or 2100 bottles of wine. The difference between demand and domestic production, 200 bottles of wine, is made up by imports.

Note that the domestic price, domestic production, and domestic demand are the same as in Example 15.1 on the effect of a tariff. Thus, the tariff and the quota have the same effects on the domestic market for wine. The only difference between the two policies is that with a quota the government does not get the tariff revenue it got in Example 15.1. That revenue goes instead to the holders of import licences (assuming they get them for free rather than bidding for them) who can buy bottles of wine on the world market at 1500 and sell them in the domestic market at 1800.

RECAP ↑

A SUPPLY AND DEMAND PERSPECTIVE ON TRADE

- For a closed economy, the domestic supply of and demand for a good or service determine the equilibrium price and quantity of that good or service.

- In an open economy, the price of a good or service traded on international markets equals the *world price*. If the domestic quantity supplied at the world price exceeds the domestic quantity demanded, the difference will be exported to the world market. If the domestic quantity demanded at the world price exceeds the domestic quantity supplied, the difference will be imported.

- Generally, if the price of a good or service in a closed economy is lower than the world price, and the economy opens to trade, the country will become a net exporter of that good or service. If the closed-economy price is higher than the world price, and the economy opens to trade, the country will tend to become a net importer of the good or service.

- Consumers of imported goods and producers of exported goods benefit from trade, while consumers of exported goods and producers of imported goods are hurt by trade.

- The two most common types of trade barriers are *tariffs* and *import quotas*. A tariff raises the domestic price to the world price plus the tariff. The result is increased domestic production, reduced domestic consumption, and few imports. A quota has effects on the domestic market that are similar to a tariff. Although not analyzed here, subsidies can also duplicate the effects of tariffs.

- *Revenue tariffs* are taxes on imported goods designed to raise government revenue rather than to protect domestic industry from imports.

15.3 TRADE INSTITUTIONS

To analyze real world-trade issues, it is important to combine theoretical knowledge of trade with knowledge of trade institutions. In this section, we first examine two institutions with responsibility for Canada's international trade policy: the Department of Foreign Affairs and International Trade (DFAIT) and the Department of Finance. We then examine the evolution of international institutions affecting international trade.

DOMESTIC INSTITUTIONS: DFAIT AND THE DEPARTMENT OF FINANCE

We have seen that the Department of Finance is responsible for Canada's fiscal policy at the federal level and that the Bank of Canada is responsible for Canada's monetary policy. Canada's institutional arrangements for fiscal and monetary policy have close counterparts in most other countries. Institutional arrangements for international trade policy, however, vary considerably from one country to another.

In Canada, as of 2001, international trade policy is a responsibility of the **Department of Foreign Affairs and International Trade (DFAIT)**. Within DFAIT, the Minister of International Trade is responsible for international trade policy.

But trade policy is not solely the responsibility of the Minister of International Trade. The Department of Finance, among its other responsibilities, also plays a role in international trade policy. As the department's website has stated, the department "plays an important role in negotiating our trade arrangements with other nations and monitoring how those arrangements serve Canada's interests."[9] It has also declared, "One of the most important tools any government has for managing trade with other nations is the tariff. It's a kind of tax governments charge on imports of products and services. It's the job of Finance Canada to monitor our tariff policies and those of other nations, and to develop new policies that will best serve our economy."[10]

Department of Foreign Affairs and International Trade (DFAIT) a department of Canada's federal government led by multiple cabinet ministers; responsibility for international trade policy is shared between the Minister of International Trade and the Department of Finance

INTERNATIONAL INSTITUTIONS

In examining the international institutions that affect international trade, it is necessary to distinguish between the different levels of trade agreements: multilateral, regional, and those that are sector specific.

Multilateral Agreements and the WTO

A **multilateral agreement** typically refers to a document signed by representatives of many nations to express their acceptance of the principles set out in the document. One example is the Kyoto Protocol, the multilateral environmental agreement regarding

multilateral agreement a document signed by representatives of many nations to express their acceptance of the principles set out in the document

9 From http://www.fin.gc.ca/access/int_iss_e.html (May 2008). No longer active.
10 From http://www.fin.gc.ca/access/taxe.html (May 2008). No longer active.

General Agreement on Tariffs and Trade (GATT) a multilateral agreement dating back to the late 1940s that, through numerous rounds of trade negotiations, led to reduced tariffs and quotas among many countries

most-favoured nation (MFN) treatment an agreement that any special arrangement, such as a reduced tariff that is offered to one country in the interests of opening up a market, must be offered to all other members

national treatment once a good has entered a country it must be treated as equivalent to a domestically produced good of the same type for purposes of taxation and regulation

fair competition the practice of discouraging both export subsidies and the dumping of products on foreign markets at below cost in order to gain market share

World Trade Organization (WTO) official international trade body headquartered in Geneva that began operation in 1995; superseded the GATT as an unofficial, *de facto* trade organization

greenhouse gas emissions mentioned in Chapter 14. International trade today is governed in part by a multilateral trade agreement that was first signed several decades ago.

The **General Agreement on Tariffs and Trade (GATT),** which came about in 1947–1948 among 23 countries including Canada, was a multilateral agreement with a preamble describing its purpose as being the "substantial reduction of tariffs and other barriers to trade and to the elimination of discriminatory treatment in international commerce."[11] The GATT Treaty survived and evolved into an "unofficial, de facto international organization, also known informally as GATT."[12]

There are three particularly noteworthy GATT principles that still apply.[13] The first of these is *most-favoured nation treatment*. Under **most-favoured nation (MFN) treatment**, a special arrangement such as a reduced tariff offered to one country (the most-favoured nation) in the interests of opening up a market must be offered to all other members of the agreement as well.

The second GATT principle worthy of mention is *national treatment*. In the context of international trade, **national treatment** means that once a good has entered a country it must be treated as equivalent to a domestically produced good of the same type, for purposes of taxation and regulation. The rationale for this principle is prevention of the undermining of tariff reductions by domestic policy measures that discriminate against foreign-produced goods. For example, if a country applies more stringent safety standards to foreign-produced automobiles than it does to domestically produced ones it is in violation of the principle of national treatment.

The third noteworthy GATT principle is promotion of *fair competition*. Promoting **fair competition** means discouraging export subsidies and the dumping of products on foreign markets at below cost in order to gain market share. Under certain circumstances, the GATT permits its signatories to impose both *countervailing duties* on imports that have been subsidized and *antidumping duties* against imports that have been sold at a price below the one charged in the home market.

Over the years, the GATT went through eight rounds of negotiations that responded both to unresolved issues from previous negotiations as well as to new issues, and involved an ever-expanding set of countries.[14] The GATT, along with improvements in transportation and communication, among other factors, appears to have been an important contributor to ever rising trade-to-GDP ratios on a world level.[15]

Among other things, the Uruguay Round of the GATT produced an agreement to establish the *World Trade Organization*, which has headquarters in Geneva, Switzerland. The **World Trade Organization (WTO)** began operation in 1995 as an official international body governing world trade, and it superseded the role of the GATT as an unofficial, *de facto* trade organization. But the GATT, as an agreement, continues as the part of the WTO agreement dealing with trade in goods.

In addition to the GATT, the WTO agreement incorporated a new General Agreement on Trade in Services (GATS) and an Agreement on Trade-Related Aspects of Intellectual Property Rights (TRIPS). It also provided for a dispute-settlement mechanism, as well as for WTO reviews of governments' trade policies. Because of some of these measures, the WTO has been more controversial than the GATT ever was. The incorporation of GATS has raised concerns that domestic authority over services such as health, education, water, and electricity supply will be undermined. Likewise, critics see TRIPS as a tool by which certain rich countries will extract larger payments from other countries for patented and copyrighted material.

---

11 See http://www.wto.org/english/docs_e/legal_e/gatt47_01_e.htm.

12 See http://www.wto.org/English/thewto_e/whatis_e/tif_e/fact1_e.htm.

13 These and other principles are discussed at http://www.wto.org/english/thewto_e/whatis_e/tif_e/fact2_e.htm; the GATT legal text is available online at http://www.wto.org/english/docs_e/legal_e/gatt47_01_e.htm.

14 Details about the evolution of the GATT can be found at http://www.wto.org/English/thewto_e/whatis_e/tif_e/fact4_e.htm.

15 For a graph showing the growth of merchandise trade relative to the growth of GDP at the world level, see http://www.wto.org/English/thewto_e/whatis_e/tif_e/fact3_e.htm.

Regional Trade Agreements

The WTO reported that, as of May 2008, all of its 152 members but one, Mongolia, were also members of *regional trade agreements*. A **regional trade agreement** aims to reduce restrictions on international trade between two or more countries, usually within a certain region. These trade agreements need not be limited to trade in goods and services; they may also deal with issues such as foreign investment and intellectual property protection.

Regional trade agreements have resulted in four major forms of regional trade arrangements, of which the least comprehensive is a *free trade area*. A **free trade area** involves two or more countries that agree to eliminate tariffs and other trade restrictions on most or all mutual trade of their own goods and services, but, at the same time, each may have different tariffs on imports from outside countries. They must agree on *rules of origin* that prevent goods from outside countries from entering the member country with the lowest external tariff and from there being transported free of any additional tariff to the member with a higher tariff. Otherwise, if transport costs are negligible, the member with the higher tariff would collect no revenue from the evaded tariff and the volume of the good imported to this higher-tariff member would be the same as it would be if the tariff were reduced to the level of the member country with the lowest tariff.

The Canada-U.S. Free Trade Agreement (CUSFTA) that came into effect in 1989 joined the United States and Canada into a free trade area. In 1994, the CUSFTA was replaced by the North American Free Trade Agreement (NAFTA) under which Canada, the United States, and Mexico formed the world's largest free trade area.

A *customs union* is characterized by a higher degree of trade integration than a free trade area. A **customs union** involves two or more countries that not only agree to eliminate tariffs and other trade restrictions on most or all mutual trade of their own goods and services, but which also agree to a common set of trade barriers against imports from non-member countries. Members of a customs union have less freedom to set trade policy than members of a free trade area have. But because of their common set of trade barriers against non-member imports, they do not have to bother with rules of origin.

The third major type of regional trade arrangement, a *common market*, is characterized by an even higher degree of economic integration than a customs union imposes. A **common market** involves two or more countries that have agreed to eliminate trade restrictions on most or all mutual trade, to maintain a common set of trade barriers against imports from non-member countries, and to permit mobility of capital and labour among member countries.

A common market taken to the next level of economic integration, an *economic and monetary union*, is the fourth major type of regional trade arrangement. An **economic and monetary union** is a common market with a single currency. The process of economic integration among member countries is ongoing, but the European Union countries that have adopted the euro as their currency can be said to constitute an economic and monetary union.

Regardless of the type of regional trade arrangement that binds them, groups of countries that have joined together under a regional trade agreement are known as *trade blocs*. When a new trade bloc is formed, outsider countries often worry that they will suffer from *trade diversion*. **Trade diversion** occurs when a reduction of trade barriers among members of a trade bloc causes trade between them to take the place of trade with countries outside the bloc. The lowest-cost supplier for a particular product may exist outside of the trade bloc but be unable to compete with a higher-cost supplier within the bloc because of a tariff applying only to outside suppliers.

Sector-Specific Trade Agreements

The trade agreements considered above, whether multilateral or regional, are broad ones covering wide ranges of goods and, in some cases, services. Some international trade

regional trade agreement aims to reduce restrictions on international trade between two or more countries, usually within a certain region

free trade area involves two or more countries that agree to eliminate tariffs and other trade restrictions on most or all mutual trade of their own goods and services; they may each have different tariffs for imports from non-member countries

customs union two or more countries that not only agree to eliminate tariffs and other trade restrictions on most or all mutual trade, but also agree to a common set of trade barriers to imports from non-member countries

common market two or more countries eliminating trade restrictions on most or all mutual trade, maintaining a common set of trade barriers against imports from non-member countries, and permitting mobility of capital and labour among member countries

economic and monetary union a common market with a single currency but made up of any number of member countries

trade diversion a reduction of trade barriers among members of a trading bloc causes trade among them to take the place of trade with countries outside the bloc

sector-specific trade agreement international trade agreement for the products of a particular economic sector, such as the softwood lumber industry

agreements that have been important to Canada, however, were *sector-specific*. A **sector-specific trade agreement** deals with international trade in the products of a particular economic sector, such as the clothing and textile sector, the automotive industry, or the softwood lumber industry.

The Canada–United States Automotive Products Trade Agreement (1965–2001), popularly known as the Auto Pact, is an example of a bilateral sector-specific trade agreement and also an example of managed trade. Basically, under it, for every vehicle sold in Canada the auto companies had to assemble a vehicle in Canada. The Auto Pact resulted in larger, more efficient auto plants that exported freely to both countries, as opposed to smaller plants largely restricted by tariffs to producing for their domestic market only. Given our much smaller market, Canada's gains from the Auto Pact were particularly large. The losers were foreign auto producers such as the British who saw sharp reductions in their Canadian market share after the implementation of the Auto Pact. In 2001, the Auto Pact was abolished by the federal government in response to a WTO dispute panel ruling following a complaint by Japan and the European Union that the Auto Pact discriminated against vehicles produced outside North America.

A more recent example of a bilateral sector-specific trade agreement is the Canada–U.S. Softwood Lumber Agreement of 2006, the latest attempt to solve a trade dispute over softwood lumber exports from Canada to the United States that began back in the early 1980s. The dispute began with the U.S. lumber industry's argument that the Canadian system of forestry managment, under which forestry companies pay stumpage fees set by governments rather than by competitive auction as is typical in the United States, constituted a form of export subsidy that should be offset by countervailing duties. These countervailing duties mainly benefited the U.S. lumber industry. The Canadian lumber industry suffered, of course, but groups representing U.S. buyers such as the National Association of Home Builders and American Consumers for Affordable Homes have also seen themselves as losing through the restrictions on Canadian lumber exports.

RECAP

TRADE INSTITUTIONS

Canada's international trade policy is the joint responsibility of the Department of Foreign Affairs and International Trade (DFAIT), particularly the Minister of International Trade, and of the Department of Finance.

The General Agreement on Tariffs and Trade (GATT) refers to a series of multilateral trade agreements but also to an unofficial, de facto international trade organization that was superseded by the World Trade Organization (WTO) in 1995. The GATT trade principles of most-favoured nation (MFN) treatment, national treatment, and fair competition continue to exist within the WTO. In addition to the GATT, the World Trade Organization (WTO) agreement incorporated a new General Agreement on Trade in Services (GATS) and a new Agreement on Trade-Related Aspects of Intellectual Property Rights (TRIPS), and it provided for a dispute-settlement mechanism.

Regional trade arrangements take four major forms: free trade areas, customs unions, common markets, and economic and monetary unions. Under the NAFTA, Canada forms a free trade area with the United States and Mexico. The Auto Pact (1965–2001) and the Canada–U.S. Softwood Lumber Agreement of 2006 are examples of sector-specific trade agreements.

FIGURE 15.10

An Increase in Net Exports Eliminates a Recessionary Gap

The economy is initially at point E, with a recessionary gap of 50. A 10-unit increase in net exports raises autonomous expenditure by 10 units, shifting the expenditure line up and raising the equilibrium point from E to F. At point F, where output equals potential output ($Y = Y^* = 4800$), the output gap has been eliminated. (The figure is not drawn to scale.)

15.4 RELEVANT SHORT-RUN MACROECONOMIC THEORY

The comparative advantage theory of international trade presented in Chapter 2 and the supply and demand perspective on international trade presented in this chapter are both important for understanding real-world trade issues. But the short-run macroeconomic theory that we covered in Chapters 8 and 9 is also relevant to an understanding of international trade issues.

The Keynesian cross diagram of Chapter 8 is useful for analyzing an economy suffering from a recessionary gap. For example, Figure 8.5 showed how an increase in government purchases could be used to close a recessionary gap. Figure 15.10 is a similar diagram showing how an increase in net exports closes a recessionary gap.

In Figure 15.10, the expenditure line is given by PAE (planned aggregate expenditure) = $950 + 0.8Y$, and it intersects the 45-degree line at E, equilibrium. The output associated with E is 4750 units. Potential output, Y^*, is 4800. Thus, there is a recessionary gap of 50 units. If net exports, NX, increase by 10, however, the expenditure line will shift upwards to $PAE = 960 + 0.8Y$ and the new equilibrium will be given by F. The increase in planned aggregate expenditure will eliminate the recessionary gap.

Figure 15.10 applies regardless of the reason that net exports increase. It could be, for example, that net exports increase because income in a trading partner goes up, causing that trading partner to increase its imports from the economy in question. But it could also be that the economy in question raises tariffs against the imports of its trading partners. All else being equal, the higher tariffs should cause its net exports to increase.

As these principles will also operate in reverse, they can be used to determine what monetary or fiscal measures need to be adopted in order to prevent a recessionary gap that otherwise might occur as the result of changes in trade policy. Suppose, for example, that an economy is initially in equilibrium with no recessionary gap, and it drops tariffs against the imports of its trading partners. All else being equal, the lower tariffs should cause net exports to decline, planned aggregate expenditure to fall, and a recessionary gap to develop. Hence a policy of trade liberalization may require the simultaneous adoption of expansionary monetary and/or fiscal policy measures to ensure against a recessionary gap.[16] The Canada–U.S. Free Trade Agreement (FTA) of 1989 was, however, introduced

---

16 This point has been emphasized many times by Joseph Stiglitz, a recipient of the Nobel Prize in Economics, in his role as a development economist.

at the same time that the Bank of Canada was engaged in an extremely contractionary monetary policy to bring down the rate of inflation, and during the early stages of FTA implementation, the federal government introduced the GST, widely seen as a contractionary fiscal policy measure as well.

We saw in Figure 15.5 that Canada's average tariff rate jumped during the Great Depression. Many countries raised their tariff rates during this period as they generally did not have a good grasp of how fiscal and monetary policy could be used to improve the economic situation. Many of them had the idea that if they could boost their net exports through trade protection they could stimulate their economies. Figure 15.10 suggests that this could work for one country. But if many countries try to boost net exports through trade protection they will fail: increased net exports for one country would mean reduced net exports for another. The belief that every country could increase net exports at once is an example of the *fallacy of composition*. This is one reason why economists generally oppose the use of trade protection as a means of increasing net exports and refer to it as a *beggar-thy-neighbour* policy.

We close this chapter with an Economic Naturalist that is an example of the use of short-run macroeconomic analysis in predicting the consequences of trade policy actions.

ECONOMIC NATURALIST 15.1

Correctly predicting Argentina's growth performance

Suppose a country that had been gradually moving towards freer trade suddenly reversed the process of trade liberalization. Would this increase in trade protection result in reduced economic growth?

The microeconomic reasoning about trade that we have studied with the production possibilities curve diagram suggests that an increase in trade protection would tend to reduce output. Another possibility, however, is suggested by the short-run macroeconomic reasoning we studied with the Keynesian cross diagram. If the economy is suffering from underutilization of resources—that is, if there is a recessionary gap—then it is possible to increase actual output to the level of potential output by increasing planned aggregate expenditure. One way to increase planned aggregate expenditure is to increase net exports. And an increase in trade protection that, say, reduces imports while not reducing exports will increase net exports. So macroeconomic reasoning suggests that increased trade protection, though it may not be the best approach, could increase output.

During the 1990s, Argentina gradually moved towards freer trade. The country was sliding further and further into a deep recessionary gap when, in a *New York Times* column of January 1, 2002, economist Paul Krugman reasoned that Argentina would soon turn to greater trade protection. His comment was, "Turning your back on the world market is bad for long-run growth; Argentina's own history is the best proof."[17] With these words, he was recognizing

the microeconomic reasoning we have studied with the production possibilities curve diagram in Chapter 2.

Krugman predicted, however, that Argentina would impose "import quotas, turning its back on world markets", and he added that "...these retrograde policies will work, in the sense that they will produce a temporary improvement in the economic situation—just as similar policies did back in the 1930s." These words, on the other hand, are a recognition of the short-run macroeconomic reasoning we studied with the Keynesian cross diagram. With them, Krugman was also suggesting that the macroeconomic reasoning was more relevant for predicting what would happen to Argentina's output in the short run than the microeconomic reasoning was.

In general terms, Krugman's prediction proved to be accurate. An index of Argentina's trade freedom (with 100 as a theoretical maximum) dropped from 65, before Krugman made his prediction and to 53 after it was made, as shown in column 2 of Table 15.2. Argentina's trade balance (net exports), which had averaged 1 percent of GDP from 1994–2001 and 14 percent of GDP in 2002–2003, as shown in column 3. In 2003, Argentina's real GDP per capita grew by 7.8 percent, and it continued to grow at over 7 percent per year from 2004 to 2006, as shown in column 4. Argentina real GDP per capita has continued to grow, as shown in Figure 15.11.

17 Paul Krugman, "Crying with Argentina," *New York Times*, 1 January 2002, http://www.pkarchive.org/column/010102.html.

TABLE 15.2
Key Economic Indicators, Argentina, 1994–2009

1. Year	2. Trade Freedom Index	3. Trade balance as % of GDP	4. Growth of Real GDP Per Capita	5. U.S.$/peso Forex Rate	6. Real interest rate
1994	n.a.	−3.1	4.5	1.00	5.8
1995	58.4	−0.4	−4.0	1.00	14.6
1996	60.0	−0.7	4.3	1.00	10.8
1997	60.0	−2.2	6.9	1.00	8.5
1998	60.0	−2.5	2.7	1.00	10.1
1999	61.2	−0.3	−4.4	1.00	12.2
2000	62.0	0.9	−1.8	1.00	12.0
2001	65.0	2.7	−5.4	1.00	28.8
2002	53.0	16.7	−11.7	0.35	25.8
2003	54.0	13.0	7.9	0.34	5.7
2004	61.6	8.7	7.9	0.34	2.4
2005	56.2	7.2	8.1	0.34	−3.5
2006	67.4	6.5	7.4	0.32	−2.3
2007	61.4	5.1	7.6	0.32	2.2
2008	69.6	4.7	5.7	0.31	10.9
2009	70.0	6.0	−0.1	0.27	9.4

SOURCES: Trade Freedom Index, http://www.heritage.org/index/trade-freedom; U.S.$/peso foreign exchange rate, 1999–2009, adapted from monthly data, http://fx.sauder.ubc.ca/data.html; inflation, real GDP, and real GDP per capita, International Monetary Fund World Economic Outlook Database, April 2011; trade balance and nominal interest rate data, http://data.un.org.

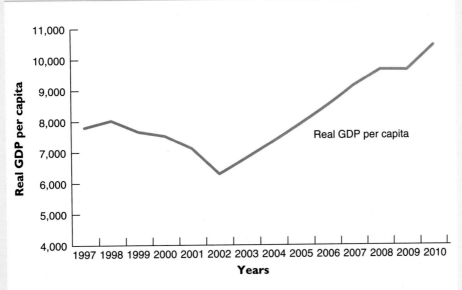

FIGURE 15.11
Argentina's Dramatic Economic Recovery Since 2002
Some observers predicted that Argentina's move to increased trade protection in 2002 would harm its economic growth. Argentina, however, has experienced strong growth of real GDP per capita since 2002. SOURCE: Adapted from International Monetary Fund, World Economic Outlook Database, April 2011.

However, factors other than increased trade protection also contributed to Argentina's strong economic recovery, and probably much more than increased trade protection did. The exchange rate, which had been pegged at US$1/peso, was allowed to depreciate to about US$0.34/peso, as shown in column 5. As we have seen in Chapter 12, exchange rate depreciation tends to boost net exports and, hence, planned aggregate expenditure and output also. Real interest rates, which averaged almost 30 percent in 2001, averaged less than 1 percent for the 2003–2006 period, as shown in column 6. We have seen in Chapters 10, 11, and 12 that lower real interest rates also boost planned aggregate expenditure (or aggregate demand) and, hence, output also.

Nevertheless, Krugman correctly predicted Argentina's economic recovery. He recognized the contribution that open trade can make to long-run growth. But at the same time he did not allow that recognition to cloud his short-run macroeconomic prediction about what a boost to net exports could do to eliminate a severe recessionary gap.

SUMMARY

- Canada had a long-standing dependence on international trade, and today it has the second highest ratio of trade to GDP among the G7 countries. Until the mid 1940s, the United States and the United Kingdom were of roughly equal importance as trading partners of Canada, but since then, the U.S. role has grown to the point where the great bulk of Canadian trade is with the United States. Natural resource exports continue to be an important component of Canadian trade, but in recent years machinery and equipment has been Canada's largest export category. In the early stages of Canadian development, tariffs were an important source of government revenue but today the value of tariff revenues is less than 1 percent of the value of imports. **LO1**

- In a closed economy, the relative price of a good or service is determined at the intersection of the supply curve of domestic producers and the demand curve of domestic consumers. In an open economy, the relative price of a good or service equals the world price—the price determined by supply and demand in the world economy. If the price of a good or service in a closed economy is greater than the world price, and the country opens its market to trade, it will become a net importer of that good or service. But if the closed-economy price is below the world price, and the country opens itself to trade, it will become a net exporter of that good or service. **LO2**

- Some groups are hurt by free trade. Groups that are hurt by trade may be able to induce the government to impose tariffs or quotas. A *tariff* is a tax on an imported good that has the effect of raising the domestic price of the good. A higher domestic price increases domestic supply, reduces domestic demand, and reduces imports of the good. A *quota*, which is a legal limit on the amount of a good that may be imported, has the same effects as a tariff, except that the government collects no tax revenue. **LO2**

- Canada's international trade policy is the joint responsibility of the Department of Foreign Affairs and International Trade (DFAIT), particularly the Minister of International Trade, and of the Department of Finance. **LO3**

- The General Agreement on Tariffs and Trade (GATT) refers to a series of multilateral trade agreements but also to an unofficial, de facto international trade organization that was superseded by the World Trade Organization (WTO) in 1995. **LO3**

- The GATT continues to exist as an agreement featuring the principles of *most-favoured nation (MFN) treatment*, *national treatment*, and *fair competition*. **LO3**

- Regional trade arrangements take four major forms: *free trade areas, customs unions, common markets, and economic and monetary unions.* Under NAFTA, Canada forms a free trade area with the United States and Mexico. **LO3**

- The Auto Pact (1965–2001) and the Canada–U.S. Softwood Lumber Agreement of 2006 are examples of *sector-specific trade agreements.* **LO3**

- A policy of trade liberalization may require the simultaneous adoption of expansionary macroeconomic policy measures to ensure against a recessionary gap. **LO4**

- If many countries try to boost net exports through trade protection, they will encounter the problem that increased net exports for one country would mean reduced net exports for another. **LO4**

KEY TERMS

closed economy (398)
common market (409)
customs union (409)
Department of Foreign Affairs and International Trade (DFAIT) (407)
economic and monetary union (409)
fair competition (408)
free trade area (409)

General Agreement on Tariffs and Trade (GATT) (408)
import quota (402)
most-favoured nation (MFN) treatment (408)
multilateral agreement (407)
national treatment (408)
open economy (398)
protective tariff (402)
regional trade agreement (409)

revenue tariff (402)
sector-specific trade agreement (410)
tariff (402)
trade diversion (409)
world price (399)
World Trade Organization (WTO) (408)

REVIEW QUESTIONS

1. Which two countries were Canada's leading trade partners during and prior to World War II and which five countries are Canada's major trade partners today? **LO1**

2. Show, graphically, the effects of a tariff on imported automobiles on the domestic market for automobiles. Who is hurt by the tariff, and why? Who benefits, and why? **LO2**

3. Show, graphically, the effects of a quota on imported automobiles in the domestic market for automobiles.

   Who does the quota hurt and who benefits? Explain. **LO2**

4. Explain why a free trade area requires rules of origin. **LO2**

5. Discuss the winners and losers from the application of countervailing duties on Canadian lumber exports to the United States. **LO2, LO3**

6. Use a Keynesian cross diagram to explain how a decrease in net exports would reduce an expansionary gap. **LO4**

PROBLEMS

1. Suppose that a Canadian worker can produce 1000 pairs of shoes or 10 industrial robots per year. For simplicity, assume there are no costs other than labour costs and firms earn zero profits. Initially, the Canadian economy is closed. The domestic price of shoes is $30 per pair, so a Canadian worker can earn $30 000 annually by working in the shoe industry. The domestic price of a robot is $3000, so a Canadian worker can also earn $30 000 annually working in the robot industry.

   Now suppose that Canada opens trade with the rest of the world. Foreign workers can produce 500 pairs of shoes or one robot per year. The world price

   of shoes after Canada opens its markets is $10 per pair, and the world price of robots is $5000. **LO2**

   a. What do foreign workers earn annually, in dollars?

   b. When it opens to trade, which good will Canada import and which will it export?

   c. Find the real income of Canadian workers after the opening to trade, measured in (1) the number of pairs of shoes annual worker income will buy and (2) the number of robots annual worker income will buy. Compare to the situation before the opening of trade. Does trading in goods produced by "cheap foreign labour" hurt Canadian workers?

d. How might your conclusion in (c) be modified if it is costly for workers to change industries?

2. The demand for automobiles in a certain country is given by

$$D = 12\,000 - 200P,$$

where P is the price of a car. Supply by domestic automobile producers is

$$S = 7000 + 50P. \text{ LO2}$$

a. Assuming that the economy is closed, find the equilibrium price and production of automobiles.

b. The economy opens to trade. The world price of automobiles is 18. Find the domestic quantities demanded and supplied, and the quantity of imports or exports. Who will favour the opening of the automobile market to trade, and who will oppose it?

c. The government imposes a tariff of 1 unit per car. Find the effects on domestic quantities demanded and supplied and on the quantity of imports or exports. Also find the revenue raised by the tariff. Who will favour the imposition of the tariff, and who will oppose it?

d. Can the government obtain the same results as you found in (c) by imposing a quota on automobile imports? Explain.

3. Suppose the domestic demand and supply for automobiles is as given by Problem 2. The world price of automobiles is 16. Foreign car firms have a production cost of 15 per automobile, so they earn a profit of 1 per car. **LO2**

a. How many cars will be imported, assuming this country trades freely?

b. Now suppose foreign car producers are asked "voluntarily" to limit their exports to the home country to half of free-trade levels. What will be the equilibrium price of cars in the domestic market if foreign producers comply? Find domestic quantities of cars supplied and demanded.

c. How will the voluntary export restriction affect the profits of foreign car producers?

ANSWER TO IN-CHAPTER EXERCISE

15.1 If the world price of wine is 1200, domestic demand for wine is $3000 - 0.5(1200)$, or 2400 bottles. Domestic supply is $1000 + 0.5(1200)$, or 1600 bottles. The difference between the quantity demanded and the quantity supplied, 800 bottles of wine, is imported.

A tariff of 300 raises the domestic price of wine to 1500. Now domestic demand is $3000 - 0.5(1500)$, or 2250, and domestic supply is $1000 + 0.5(1500)$, or 1750. The difference, 500 bottles of wine, equals imports. Revenue for the government is 300 per bottle times 500 imported bottles, or 150 000.

If the world price of wine is 1800 and there is no tariff, domestic demand is $3000 - 0.5(1800)$, or 2100; domestic supply is $1000 + 0.5(1800)$, or 1900; and imports are 200. A tariff of 300 raises the world price to 2100, which is greater than the domestic price when there is no trade (2000). No wine is imported in this case, and no tariff revenue is raised. **LO2**

CHAPTER 16
Saving, Capital Formation, and Financial Markets

At your mother's or father's knee you probably heard the fable of the ant and the grasshopper. All summer the ant worked hard laying up food for the winter. The grasshopper mocked the ant's efforts and contented himself with basking in the sunshine, ignoring the ant's earnest warnings. When winter came the ant was well fed, while the grasshopper starved. Moral: When times are good, the wise put aside something for the future.

Saving is certainly important, both for individuals and nations. People need to save to provide for their retirement and for other future needs, such as their children's education or a new home. Individual or family savings can provide a crucial buffer in the event of an economic emergency, such as the loss of a job. At the national level, the production of new capital goods—factories, equipment, and office buildings—is an important factor promoting economic growth and higher living standards. As we will see in this chapter, the resources necessary to produce new capital come primarily from a nation's collective saving.

Because saving is required for creating new capital goods, some people have expressed concern over the decline in Canada's personal saving rate since the early 1980s. Figure 16.1 shows Canada's personal saving rate (the percentage of personal disposable income saved) for the period from 1982, when the personal saving rate was at a peak of 20.1 percent, until 2010, when it was at 4.8 percent.

What was the significance of this precipitous decline? Alarmists saw the data as evidence of "grasshopperish" behaviour, and a threat to Canadians' future prosperity. The reality, as we will see, is more complex. Many Canadian families save very little and have accumulated little in the way of financial wealth. On the other hand, personal saving (more precisely, net saving by persons and unincorporated businesses) is only one domestic source of saving available to the Canadian economy. Corporations and governments also save, and they have saved considerably more than households in some years. Furthermore, the level of domestic saving in Canada does not set an upper limit to the level of investment in Canada; non-resident saving (essentially, net borrowing from abroad) can be used to finance investment in Canada, and it has been used to do so throughout much of Canadian history. In the global economy over the past decade, much attention has been focused on the role of China's savings serving to finance investment in the United States economy.

We saw in Chapter 14 the importance of investment (or capital formation) for increasing labour productivity and improving living standards. What we did not do was examine the role of the financial system—banks, bond markets, and stock markets—in channelling saving into capital formation. A healthy economy channels savings into capital formation in a productive way, and it is important to understand how a financial system works when it is functioning productively.

But this transformation of savings into productive investment by the financial system is not automatic. It is important to recognize how the financial system can fail to do its job. History is full of examples of "white elephants" or capital projects in which millions, and even billions, of dollars were invested with little economic benefit: nuclear power plants that were never opened, massive dams whose main effect was to divert water supplies and disrupt the local agriculture, dot-com companies that never amounted to anything. In the early and mid-2000s, as mentioned repeatedly in this textbook, many countries experienced massive increases in both housing prices and investments in housing, aided and abetted by their financial systems. By the late 2000s, the housing bubbles burst in many countries, including the United States, the United Kingdom, Ireland, and Spain. House prices tumbled, and housing construction plummeted. One consequence was the global recession of 2008–2009 and another, a key concern of this chapter, is evident in the sprawling subdivisions of luxury homes, sitting empty and gradually falling apart—a visible symbol of investment not allocated in a productive way.

The evidence shows that the domestic saving of the Canadian economy, which economists call Canada's national saving, has climbed steadily since the 1990–1992 recession. In fact, from 1999 to 2008, national saving was sufficiently high to cover all investment in Canada and leave some over for lending to the rest of the world.

In this chapter, we will look at saving and its links to investment, including the role of the financial system in connecting saving with investment. We begin by defining the

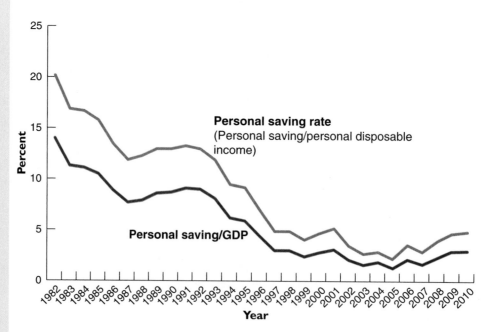

FIGURE 16.1
Personal Saving in Canada, 1982–2010
The personal saving rate, shown by the red line, is personal saving expressed as a percentage of personal disposable income. The decline in the personal saving rate from a peak of 20.1 percent in 1982 to a low of 1.5 percent in 2007 raised concern in some circles. The saving rate rose in the recession of 2008–2009. For some purposes, it is convenient to consider the ratio of personal saving to GDP, as shown by the blue line.
SOURCE: Adapted from Statistics Canada, CANSIM series V498187, V647354, and V498086.

concepts of saving and wealth and exploring the connection between them through simple examples concerning one individual. We will consider why people choose to save, rather than spend all their income. We then turn saving by corporations, governments, and non-residents, and the link between saving and the formation of national wealth.

After examining national wealth, we discuss fixed capital formation. Most decisions to invest in fixed capital are made by firms. As we will see, a firm's decision to invest is in many respects analogous to its decision about whether to increase employment; firms will choose to expand their capital stocks when the benefits of doing so exceed the costs.

In the latter part of this chapter, we discuss some major financial markets and institutions and their role in directing investment funds into real investments.

16.1 SAVING AND WEALTH

In general, the **saving** of an economic unit—whether a household, a business, a university, or a nation—may be defined as its *current income* minus its *spending on current needs*. For example, if Avril earns $300 per week, spends $280 weekly on living expenses such as rent, food, clothes, and entertainment, and deposits the remaining $20 in the bank, her saving is $20 per week. The **saving rate** of any economic unit is its saving divided by its income. Since Avril saves $20 of her weekly income of $300, her saving rate is $20/$300, or 6.7 percent.

The saving of an economic unit measured over time contributes to its **wealth**; that is, the net value of all its assets minus all its liabilities, measured at a point in time. **Assets** are anything of value that one *owns*, either *financial* or *real*. Examples of financial assets that you or your family might own include cash, a chequing account, stocks, and bonds. Examples of real assets include a home or other real estate, jewellery, and consumer durables, such as cars. **Liabilities**, on the other hand, are the debts one *owes*. Examples of liabilities are credit card balances, student loans, and mortgages.

Accountants list the assets and liabilities of a family, a university, or any other economic unit on a *balance sheet*. Comparing the values of the assets and liabilities helps them to determine the economic unit's wealth, also called its *net worth*.

saving current income minus spending on current needs; a flow

saving rate saving divided by income

wealth the value of assets minus liabilities; also called net worth

assets anything of value that one owns

liabilities the debts one owes

EXAMPLE 16.1

Avril constructs her balance sheet

To take stock of her financial position, Avril lists her assets and liabilities on a balance sheet. The result is shown in Table 16.1. What is Avril's wealth?

TABLE 16.1
Avril's Balance Sheet

Assets		Liabilities	
Cash	$ 80	Student loan	$3000
Chequing account	1200	Credit card balance	250
Shares of stock	1000		
Car (market value)	3500		
Furniture (market value)	500		
Total	**$6280**		**$3250**
		Net worth	**$3030**

Avril's financial assets are the cash in her wallet, the balance in her chequing account, and the current value of some shares of stock her parents gave her. Together, her financial assets are worth $2280. She also lists $4000 in real assets, the sum of the market values of her car and furniture. Avril's total assets, both financial and real, come to $6280. Her liabilities are the student loan she owes the bank and the balance due on her credit card, which total $3250. Avril's wealth, or net worth, then, is the value of her assets ($6280) minus the value of her liabilities ($3250), or $3030.

EXERCISE 16.1

What would Avril's net worth be if her student loan were for $6500 rather than $3000? Construct a new balance sheet for her.

Saving and wealth are related, because saving adds to wealth. To understand this relationship better, we must recognize the distinction between *stocks* and *flows* mentioned previously in this textbook, including Chapter 4.

STOCKS AND FLOWS

Saving is an example of a flow, a measure that is defined *per unit of time*. For example, Avril's saving is $20 *per week*. Wealth, in contrast, is a stock, a measure that is defined *at a point in time*. Avril's wealth of $3030, for example, is her wealth on a particular date—say, January 1, 2012.

EXAMPLE 16.2

The link between saving and wealth

Avril saves $20 per week. How does this saving affect her wealth? Does the change in her wealth depend on whether Avril uses her saving to accumulate assets or to pay down her liabilities?

Avril could use the $20 she saved this week to increase her assets (e.g., add the $20 to her chequing account) or reduce her liabilities (e.g., pay down her credit card balance). Suppose she adds the $20 to her chequing account, increasing her assets by $20. Since her liabilities are unchanged, her wealth also increases by $20, to $3050 (see Table 16.1).

CAPITAL GAINS AND LOSSES

Though saving increases the wealth of an individual or household, it is not the only factor that determines wealth. Wealth can also change because of changes in the values of the real or financial assets one owns. Suppose Avril's shares of stock rise in value, from $1000 to $1500. This increase in the value of Avril's stock raises her total assets by $500 without affecting her liabilities. As a result, Avril's wealth rises by $500, from $3030 to $3530 (see Table 16.2).

TABLE 16.2
Avril's Balance Sheet after an Increase in the Value of Her Stocks

Assets		Liabilities	
Cash	$ 80	Student loan	$3000
Chequing account	1200	Credit card balance	250
Shares of stock	1500		
Car (market value)	3500		
Furniture (market value)	500		
Total	**$6780**		**$3250**
		Net worth	**$3530**

Changes in the value of existing assets are called **capital gains** when an asset's value increases and **capital losses** when an asset's value decreases.[1] Just as capital gains increase wealth, capital losses decrease it. Capital gains and losses are not counted as part of saving, however (which is in keeping with the fact that they are not counted as part of income in GDP accounting). Therefore, the total change in a person's wealth during any period equals the saving done during the period plus capital gains or minus capital losses during that period. In terms of an equation,

$$\text{Change in wealth} = \text{Saving} + \text{Capital gains} - \text{Capital losses}$$

capital gains increases in the value of existing assets

capital losses decreases in the value of existing assets

How would each of the following actions or events affect Avril's saving and her wealth?
a. **Avril deposits $20 in the bank at the end of the week, as usual. She also charges $50 on her credit card, raising her credit card balance to $300.**
b. **Avril uses $300 from her chequing account to pay off her credit card bill.**
c. **Avril's furniture falls in value from $500 to $200.**

E X E R C I S E   1 6 . 2

We have seen how saving is related to the accumulation of wealth. To understand why people save, however, we need to examine their motives for saving.

> ## RECAP
>
> ### SAVING AND WEALTH
>
> In general, *saving* is current income minus spending on current needs. *Wealth*, also called net worth, is the value of assets, anything of value that one owns, minus liabilities, the debts one owes. Saving is measured per unit of time (e.g., dollars per week) and thus is a *flow*. Wealth is measured at a point in time and thus is a *stock*. In somewhat the same way the flow of water through the faucet increases the stock of water in a bathtub, the flow of saving increases the stock of wealth.
>
> Wealth can also be increased by *capital gains* (increases in the value of existing assets) or reduced by *capital losses* (decreases in asset values).

16.2 WHY DO PEOPLE SAVE?

As mentioned in the introduction, the total saving available to the Canadian economy comes from four different sectors or sources: persons (like Avril in our examples) and unicorporated businesses, corporations, governments, and non-residents. The savings of different sectors are generally determined by distinctive factors. The factors determining the saving of people (individuals or households) have been intensively studied by economists, and we will consider them first.

Economists have identified at least three broad reasons for saving. First, people save to meet certain long-term objectives, such as a more comfortable retirement. Some people save during their working years in the hope that in their retirement years they will be able to supplement their public pensions. Other long-term objectives might include college tuition for one's children and the purchase of a new home or car. Since many of these needs occur at fairly predictable stages in one's life, economists call this type of saving **life-cycle saving**.

A second reason to save is to protect oneself and family against unexpected setbacks—the loss of a job, for example. Personal financial advisors typically suggest that families maintain an emergency reserve (a "rainy-day fund") equal to three to six months' of income. Saving for protection against potential emergencies is called **precautionary saving**.

life-cycle saving saving to meet long-term objectives such as retirement, university attendance, or the purchase of a home

precautionary saving saving for protection against unexpected setbacks, such as the loss of a job

1 Capital gains and losses typically relate to changes in the value of financial assets or real estate. The normal decrease over time (related to quality deterioration or obsolescence) in the value of a real asset like a car is known as *depreciation*, which differs from a capital loss. To simplify matters, we ignore depreciation for now.

bequest saving saving done for the purpose of leaving an inheritance

A third reason to save is to accumulate an estate to leave to one's heirs, usually one's children but possibly a favourite charity or other worthy cause. Saving for the purpose of leaving an inheritance, or bequest, is called **bequest saving**. Bequest saving is done primarily by people at the higher end of the income ladder. But because these people control a large share of the nation's wealth, bequest saving is an important part of overall saving.

To be sure, people usually do not mentally separate their saving into these three categories; rather, all three reasons for saving motivate most savers to varying degrees. The amount they choose to save, however, may depend on the economic environment. An economic variable of some relevance to saving decisions is the real interest rate.

SAVING AND THE REAL INTEREST RATE

Most people don't save by putting cash in a mattress. Instead, they make financial investments that they hope will provide a good return on their saving. For example, a savings account may pay interest on the account balance.

The rate of return that is most relevant to saving decisions is the *real interest rate, r*. Recall from Chapter 6 that the real interest rate equals the market, or nominal, interest rate (i) minus the inflation rate (π). The real interest rate is relevant to savers because it is the "reward" for saving. While a higher real interest rate increases the reward for saving, which tends to strengthen people's willingness to save, another force counteracts that extra incentive. Recall that a major reason for saving is to attain specific goals. If the goal is a specific amount, say, $25 000 for a down payment on a home, then a higher rate of return means that households can save *less* and still reach their goal, because funds that are put aside will grow more quickly. To the extent that people are *target savers* who save to reach a specific goal, higher interest rates actually decrease the amount they need to save.

In sum, a higher real interest rate has both positive and negative effects on saving—a positive effect because it increases the reward for saving and a negative effect because it reduces the amount people need to save each year to reach a given target. Empirical evidence suggests that, in practice, higher real interest rates lead to modest increases in saving.

SAVING, SELF-CONTROL, AND DEMONSTRATION EFFECTS

The reasons for saving we just discussed are based on the notion that people are rational decision makers who choose their saving rates to maximize their welfare over the long run. Yet many psychologists, and some economists, have argued instead that people's saving behaviour is based as much on psychological as on economic factors. They stress that people sometimes lack the *self-control* to do what is in their own best interest. Many people have good intentions about saving, for example, but they lack the self-control to put aside as much as they ought to each month.

One way to strengthen self-control is to remove temptations from the immediate environment. A person who is not saving enough might arrange to use a payroll saving plan, through which a predetermined amount is deducted from each paycheque and set aside in a special account from which withdrawals are not permitted until retirement. Making saving automatic and withdrawals difficult reduces the temptation to spend all of current earnings or squander accumulated savings. In Canada, employer-sponsored pension plans (known as RPPs, for Registered Pension Plans) are an especially important way of making saving automatic.

One implication of the self-control hypothesis is that consumer credit arrangements which make borrowing and spending easier may reduce the amount that people save. For example, in recent years banks have encouraged people to borrow against the *equity* in their homes; that is, the value of the home less the value of the outstanding mortgage. Such financial innovations, by increasing the temptation to spend, may have reduced the personal saving rate. The increased availability of credit cards with high borrowing limits is another temptation.

*"These are hard times for retailers, so we should
show them our support in every way we can"*

Downward pressure on the saving rate may also occur when additional spending by some consumers stimulates additional spending by others. Such *demonstration effects* arise when people use the spending of others as a yardstick by which to measure the adequacy of their own living standards. When satisfaction depends in part on *relative* living standards, an upward spiral may result in which household spending is higher, and saving lower, than would be best for either the individual families involved or for the economy as a whole.

The idea that relative living standards or income levels affect personal saving rates was first developed into a formal theory by the Harvard economist James Duesenberry in the 1950s. He explained why aggregate personal saving rates do not increase with average disposable income, all else being equal, even though higher-income households have higher savings rates than do lower-income households.[2]

> ## RECAP ⬆
>
> ### WHY DO PEOPLE SAVE?
>
> Motivations for personal saving include saving to meet long-term objectives such as retirement (*life-cycle saving*), saving for emergencies (*precautionary saving*), and saving to leave an inheritance or bequest (*bequest saving*). The amount that people save also depends on macroeconomic factors, such as the real interest rate. A higher real interest rate stimulates saving by increasing the reward for saving, but it can also depress saving by making it easier for savers to reach a specific savings target. On net, a higher real interest rate appears to lead to modest increases in saving.
>
> Psychological and sociological factors may also affect personal saving rates. If people have *self-control* problems, then financial arrangements (such as automatic payroll deductions) that make it more difficult to spend will increase their saving. People's saving decisions may also be influenced by *demonstration effects,* as when people feel compelled to spend at the same rate as their neighbours, even though they may not be able to afford to do so.

2 Robert Frank, "The Mysterious Disappearance of James Duesenberry," *New York Times*, June 9, 2005.

16.3 ECONOMY-WIDE SAVING AND WEALTH

Thus far we have been examining the concepts of saving and wealth from an individual's perspective. But macroeconomists are interested primarily in saving and wealth for the economy as a whole. In this section we will study the four major components of economy-wide saving published by Statistics Canada: personal, corporate, government, and non-resident saving.[3] We will also study Statistics Canada's economy-wide measures of wealth.

The economy-wide measure of saving employed by Statistics Canada is **gross saving,** and by definition it equals **gross investment**.[4] The concept of gross investment employed by Statistics Canada in connection with gross saving is broader than the concept of private-sector investment that we encountered in Chapter 5 as a component of expenditure-based GDP, and for good reason.

As discussed in Chapter 14, both private-sector investment (particularly non-residential business fixed capital formation) and government investment contribute to the long-run growth of the economy. For example, if an airport is constructed by private-sector firms at the request of a government airport operator, the construction of the airport would count as government investment. If the same airport had been constructed by the same private-sector firms on behalf of a private airport operator, the airport would count as private-sector investment. But regardless of whether it is the government or the private sector that pays to have the airport built, the construction of the airport is infrastructure investment for the economy. Furthermore, both private-sector investment and government investment contribute to the stock of capital that is part of national wealth.

gross saving the sum of household, corporate, government, and non-resident saving

gross investment the sum of private-sector and government investment

THE COMPONENTS OF GROSS SAVING

To understand all the sources of saving that are available to support gross investment in the Canadian economy, it is first necessary to distinguish gross saving from net saving.

How does net saving differ from gross saving? The personal saving rate shown in Figure 16.1, for example, is based upon the net saving of the persons and unincorporated businesses sector (or household sector). This net saving amounted to $48.2 billion in 2010, as shown in Table 16.3. It was actually smaller than another form of saving associated with the household sector—a capital consumption allowance of $52.8 billion. In general, a capital consumption allowance is an allowance for the using up of capital in the production of income; that is, for the depreciation of business and government fixed assets (and people's housing). Roughly speaking, it is the counterpart on the saving side to *replacement investment* on the investment side. For the household sector, major housing renovations are an important form of replacement investment. For the economy as a whole, net saving of the different sectors of the economy (including non-resident saving) plus their capital consumption allowances add up to gross saving, as Table 16.3 shows.

For many purposes it is useful to consider a large subset of gross saving known as *national saving*. **National saving** is the sum of gross saving by the household sector, corporations and government business enterprises sector (also called the corporate sector), and government sector. Note that the government sector includes not just the federal government, but also provincial and territorial governments, local governments, and public institutions like hospitals and universities.

Figure 16.2 shows trends in the three components of national saving (expressed as a percentage of GDP) for the period 1961–2010. Gross corporate saving is currently the most important component of national saving.

national saving the sum of gross saving by the household sector, the corporate sector, and the government sector

---

3 We focus on gross saving by these four sectors of the economy and, to keep things relatively simple, we ignore the concept of net lending by different sectors.

4 In practice, gross saving and gross investment are made equal by Statistics Canada using the same statistical discrepancy required to make the income-based measure of GDP equal to the expenditure-based measure.

TABLE 16.3

Gross Saving and Gross Investment, Canada, 2010

Components and Subcomponents	$ (billions)	Percent of gross saving or gross investment
I. GROSS SAVING (A + B + C + D)	360.7	100.0
A. Net domestic saving (1 + 2 + 3)	70.4	19.5
1. Persons and unincorporated business	48.2	13.4
2. Corporations and government business	77.9	21.6
3. Government	−55.7	−15.5
B. Capital consumption allowances (4 + 5 + 6)	229.3	63.6
4. Persons and unincorporated businesses	52.8	14.6
5. Corporations and government business enterprises	140.3	38.9
6. Government	36.2	10.0
C. Saving of non-residents	61.4	17.0
D. Statistical discrepancy	−0.4	−0.1
II. INVESTMENT IN FIXED CAPITAL AND INVENTORIES (E + F + G)	360.7	100.0
E. Persons and unincorporated businesses	119.7	33.2
F. Corporations and government business enterprises	173.8	48.2
G. Government	67.3	18.7

SOURCE: Adapted from the Statistics Canada publication *National Income and Expenditure Accounts,* Catalogue 13-001, Table 15, http://www.statcan.gc.ca/pub/13-019-x/2011001/t/tab0015-eng.htm. Extraction date, July 12, 2011.

Sometimes economists divide national saving into two categories. *Private saving* is used to describe the sum of gross saving by the household and the corporate sectors. *Public saving* can then be used to mean gross government saving.

The difference between gross saving and national saving is known as *non-resident saving.* In general, **non-resident saving** is the balance between saving provided to the Canadian economy by non-residents and saving provided to foreign economies by residents of Canada. In 2010, as shown in Table 16.3, saving by non-residents amounted to

non-resident saving the balance between saving provided to the Canadian economy by non-residents and saving provided to foreign economies by residents of Canada

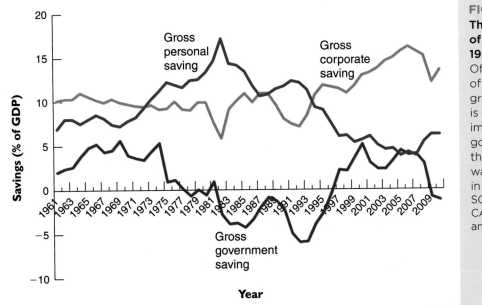

FIGURE 16.2

The Three Components of National Saving, 1961–2010

Of the three components of national saving, gross corporate saving is currently the most important. The rise in government saving from the mid-1990s to 2007 was offset by the decline in personal saving. SOURCE: Adapted from CANSIM table 380-0032 and series v498187.

FIGURE 16.3

Gross Saving, National Saving, and Non-Resident Saving, 1961–2010

Gross saving (which equals gross investment) as a percentage of Canadian GDP has tended to drop during economic slowdowns but has not exhibited any pronounced long-term trend. Non-resident saving as a percentage of GDP has traditionally been positive, but from 1999 to 2008 it was negative. National saving is the difference between gross saving and non-resident saving.

SOURCE: Adapted from the Statistics Canada CANSIM Table 380-0032.

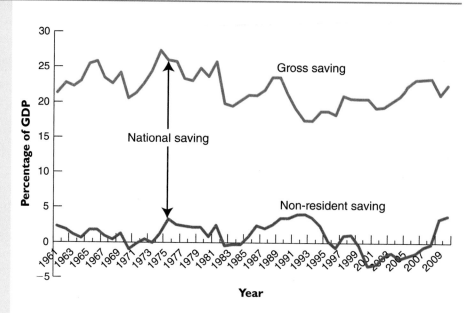

$61.4 billion. But non-resident saving can also be negative, as it was for Canada during the period 1999–2008, for example.

Figure 16.3 shows trends in gross saving, national saving, and non-resident saving for 1961–2010. All variables are expressed as percentages of GDP. As a percentage of Canadian GDP, gross saving (which equals gross investment, as we have mentioned) has tended to fluctuate within the 20–25 percent range. Non-resident saving has tended to fluctuate in the 0–4 percent range, with no particular trend. Positive non-resident saving for most years means Canada typically experienced capital inflows for the 1961–1999 period. In other words, Canada was a capital importer because national saving was insufficient to develop our infrastructure and build our capital stock. In Figure 16.3, the gap between gross saving and non-resident saving in any given year gives national saving for the year.

To summarize saving terminology, suppose that we represent gross saving by S_{gross}, gross household saving by $S_{household}$, gross corporate saving by $S_{corporate}$, gross government or public saving by $S_{government}$, national saving by $S_{national}$, private saving by $S_{private}$, and non-resident saving by $S_{non\text{-}resident}$. Then we can decompose gross saving as follows:

$$S_{gross} = S_{household} + S_{corporate} + S_{government} + S_{non\text{-}resident} \qquad (16.1)$$

$$S_{gross} = S_{private} + S_{government} + S_{non\text{-}resident} \qquad (16.2)$$

$$S_{gross} = S_{national} + S_{non\text{-}resident} \qquad (16.3)$$

$$S_{gross} = S_{net} + \text{Capital consumption allowances} \qquad (16.4)$$

The determinants of personal saving were explained in some detail earlier in this chapter. Now we need to explain a few details about the other two components of gross saving—gross corporate and government saving. We will then deal with some details about non-resident saving.

MORE ABOUT CORPORATE AND GOVERNMENT SAVING

Most of us have no problem conceptualizing personal saving. Indeed, many of us learned about personal saving at a very young age, putting coins in a piggybank to save up for some special purchase. But the concepts of corporate and government saving seem a bit strange to people who think of saving as being conducted by individuals and investment being carried out by corporations. People find it surprising both that corporate saving could be the most important form of saving in the Canadian economy in 2010 (as shown in Figure 16.2) and that even government saving could exceed personal saving.

Corporate Saving

We have already mentioned one component of gross corporate saving—capital consumption allowances. The Statistics Canada estimates for capital consumption allowances are indirectly based upon business records employing the standard accounting practice that part of the revenue a firm receives cannot prudently be treated as profit because it represents reimbursement for the cost of capital goods that depreciate in value over time and will have to be replaced. The largest component of net corporate saving is undistributed profits (or unremitted profits, in the case of government business enterprises). Undistributed profits are typically, but not necessarily, plowed back into investment within the firm. If the corporate sector has a bad year—that is, if profits drop—then undistributed profits will drop, and with them net corporate savings.

Figure 16.4 shows gross corporate saving as a percentage of gross corporate investment for Canada during the period 1961–2010. When the percentage equals 100, gross corporate saving equals gross corporate investment. When the percentage exceeds 100, then gross corporate saving exceeds gross corporate investment.

In most years, the Canadian corporate sector has relied upon external funding to finance its gross investment, shown in Figure 16.4 by a percentage less than 100. But even during recession years, when gross corporate saving has plummeted, the Canadian corporate sector has always financed the bulk of its investment with internal funding. Since the end of the 1990–1992 recession, gross corporate saving has tended to exceed gross corporate investment, and by a large amount in some years.

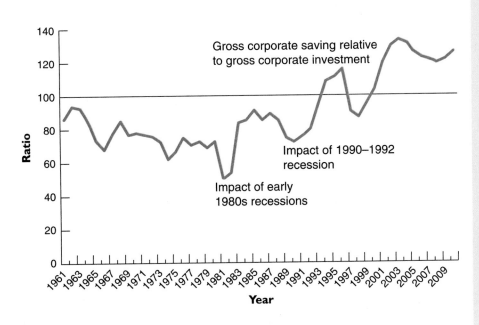

FIGURE 16.4
Ratio of Corporate Saving to Corporate Investment, 1961–2010
In most years, particularly during recessions, the Canadian corporate sector has relied upon external funding to finance its gross investment. But even during recession years, the Canadian corporate sector has always financed the bulk of its investment with internal corporate funding. Since the end of the 1990–1992 recession, gross corporate saving has tended to exceed gross corporate investment.
SOURCE: Adapted from Statistics Canada CANSIM series v647355, v647360, and v647369.

Government Saving

Like gross corporate saving, gross government saving consists of a capital consumption allowance component and a net saving component shown in Table 16.4. The *net saving* component is closely related to the more widely known concept of the *government budget balance*.[5]

We first encountered the concept of the government budget balance in connection with Figure 4.7, which showed deficits when the federal government budget balance was zero and then surpluses more recently when the federal government budget balance has been positive. Roughly speaking, positive government saving corresponds to government surpluses and negative government saving corresponds to deficits.

Like corporate saving, government saving tends to decline during recessions. If personal incomes and corporate profits fall in a recession, then personal and corporate income taxes fall automatically, even without any change in income tax rates. Similarly, when unemployment rises in a recession, more people will end up drawing employment insurance benefits and social assistance, and government transfers will rise. So in a recession, for example, government revenue tends to decline and government transfers tend to rise, a combination that spells a decline in government saving. (In Part 3, which dealt with short-run macroeconomics, we explained that budget items like income taxes and employment insurance are known as *automatic stabilizers*.)

Cyclical fluctuations in the economy are not the only economic influence on government saving. Another key influence is the level of interest rates. The government sector carries a substantial amount of debt (a stock) as a consequence of past deficits (flows). For the federal, provincial and territorial, and local governments of Canada, net debt

TABLE 16.4

Government Revenue, Expenditure, and Saving, Canada, 2010

Components	$ (billions)	Percent of GDP
Revenue	625.0	38.5
Taxes on incomes	240.5	14.8
Contributions to social insurance plans	75.3	4.6
Taxes on production and imports	191.2	11.8
Other current transfers from persons	11.5	0.7
Investment income	49.4	3.2
Sales of goods and services	57.1	3.5
Expenditure	680.8	42.0
Gross current expenditure on goods and services	410.7	25.3
Current transfers	209.9	12.9
Interest on public debt	60.2	3.7
Net saving = Revenue − Expenditure	−55.8	−3.4
Capital consumption allowances	36.2	2.2
Gross saving = Net saving + CCA	−19.5	−1.2

SOURCE: Adapted from the Statistics Canada publication *National Income and Expenditure Accounts*, Catalogue 13-001, Table 9, http://www.statcan.gc.ca/pub/13-019-x/2011001/t/tab0009-eng.htm. Extraction date, July 12, 2011.

---

5 The value of net government saving exceeds the value of the government budget surplus by the value of government investment. For example, if the government budget surplus is $25 billion, and government investment is $15 billion, then net government saving amounts to $40 billion. Net government saving, then, equals the amount of money the government makes available for investment, whether it is investment in other sectors of the economy (made possible by the budget surplus) or investment in the government sector.

amounted to $740 billion as the end of March 2008 (equivalent to 45.5 percent of GDP produced during 2008).

When interest rates rise, any debt that has to be refinanced is subject to the higher rates, and so there is an increase in interest payments on the public debt, a category of government expenditures. All else being equal, a rise in interest rates will produce a decline in government saving.[6]

But a rise in the government debt-to-GDP ratio beyond some threshold level can also affect government saving. At the provincial level, especially high government debt-to-GDP ratios tend to result in higher borrowing costs to governments, as financial market participants demand an interest rate premium to cover the risk of default by the government. The higher borrowing costs provide governments with an incentive (or at least an excuse) to increase government saving.

Of course, levels of government saving do not just depend on economic factors. Politics also plays a role. For example, while strong economic growth from 1997 to 2000 helped produce a dramatic increase in federal government saving (specifically, a transformation from negative to positive saving), the expenditure cuts launched by then Finance Minister Paul Martin in his February 1995 federal budget also played an important role.

NET CAPITAL INFLOWS AND THE CURRENT ACCOUNT: MORE ABOUT NON-RESIDENT SAVING

Non-resident saving, like government saving and corporatge saving, is more mysterious to most people than is personal saving. Non-resident saving relates to *international capital flows*. **International capital flows** are purchases or sales of real and financial assets across international borders (economically equivalent to lending and borrowing across international borders). From the perspective of a particular country, say, Canada, purchases of domestic (Canadian) assets by foreigners are called **capital inflows**, and purchases of foreign assets by domestic (Canadian) households and firms are called **capital outflows**. To remember these terms, it may help to keep in mind that capital inflows represent funds "flowing in" to the country (foreign savers buying domestic assets), while capital outflows are funds "flowing out" of the country (domestic savers buying foreign assets). The difference between the two flows can be expressed as the **net capital inflows**—capital inflows minus capital outflows. When non-resident saving is positive, net capital inflows are positive, and when non-resident saving is negative, net capital inflows are negative.

From a macroeconomic perspective, international capital flows play two important roles. First, they allow countries whose real investment opportunities are greater than domestic saving to fill in the gap by borrowing from abroad. Second, they allow countries to run trade imbalances—situations in which the country's exports of goods and services do not equal its imports of goods and services—and, more generally, current account imbalances. While international capital flows play these important roles, they also pose risks for both borrowing and lending countries (as illustrated, for example, by the 1997–1998 Asian currency crisis discussed in Chapter 13).

The current account balance and net capital inflows

In the economic news, you are more likely to read about the current account balance than about non-resident saving or net capital inflows. These different concepts are closely related. When non-resident saving is positive, net capital inflows are positive, and there is a current account deficit. When non-resident saving is negative, net capital inflows are negative, and there is a current account surplus. What is this current account balance?

The *current account balance* is a broader record of international payments and receipts than the trade balance (introduced in Chapter 4). In addition to the trade balance, the

international capital flows purchases or sales of real and financial assets across international borders

capital inflows purchases of domestic assets by foreign households and firms

capital outflows purchases of foreign assets by domestic households and firms

net capital inflows capital inflows minus capital outflows

---

6 Recessions such as those in the early 1980s and during 1990–1992 were particularly hard on government saving because they were triggered by sharp rises in interest rates that continued well into the recessions.

TABLE 16.5

Canada's Current Account Balance, 2010 ($ millions)

Goods and services balance	− 31 757
Investment income balance	−16 436
Transfers balance	−2 671
Current account balance	−50 864

SOURCE: Adapted from Statistics Canada CANSIM Table 376-0001, and http://www40. statcan.ca/l01/cst01/ECON01A-eng.htm. Extraction date, July 12, 2011.

current account balance
the record of payments and receipts arising from trade in goods and services, from international investment income and from international transfers

current account balance includes net international investment income and net international transfers. Table 16.5 shows Canada's balances on goods and services (another term for *trade balance*; *net exports* is yet another), investment income, and transfers for 2010. As can be seen, the current account balance was negative in 2010, reflecting a negative trade balance (goods and services balance), a negative investment income balance, and a negative transfers balance.

We asserted that when non-resident saving is posiive, net capital inflows are positive and there is a current account deficit, and when non-resident saving is negative, net capital inflows are negative and there is a current account surplus. Why?

First, by definition, *the current account balance and net capital inflows sum to zero.* Let's write this relationship as an equation:

$$CA + KI = 0, \tag{16.5}$$

where CA is the current account balance and we use KI to stand for net capital inflows. The relationship given by Equation 16.5 is an identity, meaning that it is true by definition.

Next, recall that gross saving in the economy must equal gross investment, and gross saving can be divided into national saving and non-resident saving. National saving is saving that originates within Canada from household, corporate, or government sources and can be denoted by $S_{national}$ or S, for simplicity. If non-resident saving is positive, then foreigners are bringing more funds into Canada than Canadians are taking out of the country. If non-resident saving is negative, then Canadians are taking more funds out of Canada than foreigners are bringing into the country. Non-resident saving is thus equal to net capital inflows. We can therefore denote non-resident saving by KI. If we denote gross investment by GI, then our statement that national saving plus non-resident saving equals gross investment can also be written as

$$S + KI = GI. \tag{16.6}$$

Equation 16.6, a key result, states that in an open economy the pool of saving available for gross investment (GI) may include not only national saving (S) but funds from savers abroad as well (if KI is positive).

We now have the necessary background to answer an important question: what causes current account deficits?

Economists argue that *a low rate of national saving relative to investment* (or, equivalently, a high rate of investment relative to national saving) *is the primary cause of current account deficits.* To see the link between national saving, investment, and the current account deficit, recall the identity $CA + KI = 0$ of Equation 16.5, and $S + KI = GI$ of Equation 16.6. Together, these two equations imply that

$$S - GI = CA. \tag{16.7}$$

The conclusion from Equation 16.7 is that, holding domestic investment (GI) constant, low national saving (S) tends to be associated with a current account deficit ($CA < 0$), and high national saving is associated with a current account surplus ($CA > 0$).

How could Canada have a current account deficit but a trade surplus?

As shown by Figure 16.5, over many years of the the last few decades, Canada's current account balance has tended to be negative even while its net exports have tended to be positive. How can this be?

Recall that the current account balance includes not only net exports, but also net investment income and net transfers. Net transfers represent foreign aid as well as private remittances across borders and are a small part of the current account. The primary reason for the current account deficits must, therefore, lie in net investment income, which has been strongly negative throughout Canada's history: from—$208 million in 1926 to −$16.4 billion in 2010.

Investment income is composed of profits, interest, and dividends on *past* investments. If net investment income is negative, then more of these kinds of payments are leaving Canada than are entering. This would occur because of prior sales of Canadian assets to foreign residents. These sales entail the future repatriation of profits, interest, and dividends to the foreign owners of the Canadian assets.

If Canada's net exports are positive but relatively low, then negative net investment income will be sufficient to pull the current account into deficit. During the 1999–2008 period, the sharp rise in Canada's net exports was adequate to bring the current account into surplus, but the decline in Canada's net exports in 2009 and 2010 brought the current account balance back into deficit.

FIGURE 16.5
Canada's Net Exports and Current Account Balance as a Percentage of GDP, 1971–2010
In the past, Canada's current account balance has often been negative even while its net exports were positive, due to negative investment income pulling down the current account balance. From the late 1990s to 2008, the strong performance of net exports was sufficient to make the current account balance positive. SOURCES: Adapted from Statistics Canada CANSIM series v113713, v113714, and v646937.

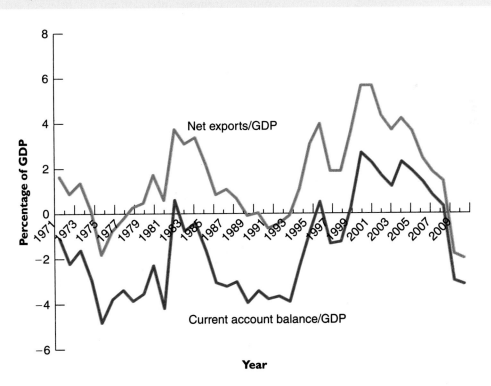

ECONOMY-WIDE WEALTH AND STOCK MEASURES

Recall that earlier in this chapter we examined the wealth of an imaginary individual named Avril. Using a balance sheet, we calculated her wealth. Statistics Canada calculates a national balance sheet for the economy as a whole. The non-financial (or "real") assets in the balance sheet are residential structures, non-residential structures, machinery and equipment, consumer durables, inventories, and land found in Canada.[7] The value of this stock of real assets is related to the value of past investment flows (or, alternatively, the sum of past gross saving). Note, however, that while consumer durables count as real assets in the national balance sheet, their purchase does not count as investment in the national income and expenditure accounts. Also, land simply exists as a real asset and is not the product of investment. The value of these real assets is called the **national wealth** of Canada. As shown in Table 16.6, in 2010 Canada's national wealth totalled about $6.5 trillion.

The **national net worth** of Canadians is calculated by adding up the value of real and financial assets and subtracting from the value of these assets the value of financial liabilities. Canada's national net worth in 2010 totalled about $6.3 trillion.

If there were no financial transactions with the rest of the world, the financial assets and liabilities summed up over the whole economy would add to zero because the financial assets of some are always the financial liabilities of others; the national wealth of Canada and the national net worth of Canadians would be equal. But Canada has **net international liabilities** (also called net foreign debt). These are the value of financial claims of non-residents on Canadian wealth net of the value of financial claims of Canadian residents against foreign wealth. Net international liabilities are a stock measure, and the corresponding flow measure is the current account balance. More precisely, current account surpluses add to net international liabilities, and current account deficits subtract from net international liabilities. In 2010, Canada's net international liabilities amounted to about $186 billion (expressed in Table 16.5 as a negative number, because it represents a claim against a portion of real wealth in Canada). Net foreign liabilities are subtracted from national wealth to get national net worth.

national wealth the total value of the real assets in a country

national net worth the total value of the real assets of a country adjusted for its net foreign liabilities

net international liabilities the value of financial claims of non-residents on Canadian wealth net of the value of financial claims of Canadian residents against foreign wealth

TABLE 16.6
National Balance Sheet, Canada, 2010

Assets ($ billions)		Liabilities ($ billions)	
National wealth **(Non-financial or "real" assets)**	6 510.5	Financial liabilities owed to Canadian residents	14 721.7
		Financial liabilities owed to non-residents	−185.8
Financial assets	14 536.0		
Total	21 046.3	**Total**	**14 536.0**
		Net worth = Total assets − Liabilities	**6 324.7**
		Net foreign liabilities = Net worth − National wealth	**−185.8**

SOURCE: Adapted from Statistics Canada Summary Tables, National Balance Sheet, Market Value, http://www40.statcan.gc.ca/l01/cst01/ECON02b-eng.htm. Extraction date, July 12, 2011.

7 Recall that in Chapter 5 we mentioned that economists sometimes use the term "real investment" to describe formation of new physical capital and inventories, and to contrast it with financial investment. The "real assets" that make up national wealth are the stock counterparts to the flow of real investment.

16.4 FACTORS AFFECTING BUSINESS INVESTMENT IN FIXED CAPITAL

From the point of view of the economy as a whole, gross saving is important because it provides the funds needed for gross investment. Gross investment is important because it is associated with the accumulation of wealth, as mentioned above. It is also important because it is critical to increasing average labour productivity and improving standards of living.

But not all components of gross investment are equally critical to increasing average labour productivity. Inventory investment, for example, tends to account for a small share of gross investment (2.4 percent for Canada in 2010, and it turns negative when inventories decline) and is relatively unimportant for explaining differences in average labour productivity across countries and time periods.

Residential investment accounts for a significant share of gross investment (36.5 percent for Canada in 2010). But increases in residential investment are not closely associated with increases in average labour productivity. Spending on new housing is much like consumer spending on consumer durables like cars, household appliances, and furniture; increased spending is more a result of rising productivity than a cause of it.

As mentioned in Chapter 14, research has shown that government investment in fixed capital is important for increases in labour productivity. Buiness investment in non-residential structures (such as factory and office buildings, shopping malls, and warehouses) and machinery and equipment (such as assembly lines, mining and transportation equipment, computers, cash registers, and photocopiers) is larger than government fixed capital formation as a share of gross investment. And, as with government fixed capital formation, research shows that it is clearly critical to increasing average labour productivity. We will, therefore, focus on determinants of non-residential business fixed capital formation; that is, on investment by firms in non-residential structures, machinery, and equipment.

COST-BENEFIT

What factors determine whether and how much firms choose to invest? Firms acquire new capital goods for the same reason they hire new workers: they expect that doing so will be profitable. According to the *cost–benefit principle*, the profitability of employing an extra worker depends primarily on two factors: the cost of employing the worker and the value of the worker's marginal product. In the same way, firms' willingness to acquire new factories and machines depends on the expected *cost* of using them and the expected *benefit*, equal to the value of the marginal product, they will provide.

EXAMPLE 16.3

Does it pay Larry to buy a riding lawn mower?

Larry is thinking of going into the lawn care business. He can buy a $4000 riding mower by taking out a loan at 6 percent annual interest. With this mower and his own labour, Larry can net $6000 per summer, after deducting costs such as gasoline and maintenance. Of the $6000 net revenues, 20 percent must be paid to the government in taxes. Assume that Larry could earn $4400 after taxes by working at another job. Assume also that the lawn mower can always be resold for its original purchase price of $4000. Does it pay Larry to buy the lawn mower?

To decide whether to invest in the capital good (the lawn mower), Larry would typically compare the financial benefits and costs. With the mower he can earn revenue of $6000, net of gasoline and maintenance costs. However, 20 percent of that, or $1200, must be paid in taxes, leaving Larry with $4800. Larry could earn $4400 after taxes by working at another job, so the financial benefit to Larry of buying the mower is the difference between $4800 and $4400, or $400; $400 is the value of the marginal product of the lawn mower.

Since we have assumed that the mower does not lose value over time and since gasoline and maintenance costs have already been deducted, the only remaining cost

Larry should take into account is the interest on the loan for the mower. Larry must pay 6 percent interest on $4000, or $240 per year. Since this financial cost is less than the financial benefit of $400, the value of the mower's marginal product, Larry should buy the mower.

Larry's decision might change if the costs and benefits of his investment in the mower change, as Example 16.4 shows.

EXAMPLE **16.4**

Does it pay Larry to buy a riding lawn mower? (continued)

With all other assumptions the same as in Example 16.3, decide whether Larry should buy the mower if the

a. interest rate is 12 percent rather than 6 percent.
b. purchase price of the mower is $7000 rather than $4000.
c. tax rate on Larry's net revenues is 25 percent rather than 20 percent.

In each case, Larry must compare the financial costs and benefits of buying the mower.

a. If the interest rate is 12 percent, then the interest cost will be 12 percent of $4000, or $480, which exceeds the value of the mower's marginal product ($400). Larry would not buy the mower.
b. If the cost of the mower is $7000, then Larry must borrow $7000 instead of $4000. At 6 percent interest, his interest cost will be $420—too high to justify the purchase, since the value of the mower's marginal product is $400.
c. If the tax rate on net revenues is 25 percent, then Larry must pay 25 percent of his $6000 net revenues, or $1500, in taxes. After taxes, his revenues from mowing will be $4500, which is only $100 more than he could make working at an alternative job. Furthermore, the $100 will not cover the $240 in interest that Larry would have to pay. So again, Larry would not buy the mower.

EXERCISE 16.3   **Repeat Example 16.3, but assume that, over the course of the year, wear and tear reduces the resale value of the lawn mower from $4000 to $3800. Does it pay Larry to buy the mower?**

The examples involving Larry and the lawn mower illustrate most of the main factors firms must consider when deciding whether to invest in new capital goods. On the cost side, two important factors are the *price of capital goods* and the *real interest rate.* Clearly, the more expensive new capital goods are, the more reluctant firms will be to invest in them. Buying the mower was profitable for Larry when its price was $4000, but not when its price was $7000.

Why is the real interest rate a factor in investment decisions? The most straightforward case is when a firm has to borrow (as Larry did) to purchase its new capital. The real interest rate then determines the real cost to the firm of paying back its debt. Since financing costs are a major part of the total cost of owning and operating a piece of capital, much as mortgage payments are a major part of the cost of owning a home, increases in the real interest rate make the purchase of capital goods less attractive to firms, all else being equal.[8]

On the benefit side, the key factor in determining business investment is the *value of the marginal product* of the new capital, which should be calculated net of both operating and maintenance expenses and taxes paid on the revenues the capital generates. The

---

8 It should be recognized that statistical studies have generally found that business investment in plant and equipment is much less sensitive to changes in real interest rates than residential investment

value of the marginal product is affected by several factors. For example, a technological advance that allows a piece of capital to produce more goods and services would increase the value of its marginal product, as would lower taxes on the revenues produced by the new capital. An increase in the relative price of the good or service that the capital is used to produce will also increase the value of the marginal product and, hence, the desirability of the investment. For example, if the going price for lawn mowing services were to rise, then, all else being equal, investing in the mower would become more profitable for Larry.

While these examples illustrate most of the main factors that firms consider in making decisions about fixed capital formation, there are other potentially important factors. For example, we have considered the impact of government taxation but not the impact of government expenditure. Yet provision of a subsidy to firms in the lawn care business (an increase in government expenditure falling under the category of transfers to business, sometimes called corporate welfare) could have the same impact on their investment as providing them with a tax cut. Increased government expenditure on roads could reduce the time Larry spends getting from one lawn care job to another, thereby enabling him to earn more revenue per year. Increased government expenditure on education could increase the pool of potential qualified employees Larry could draw upon to expand his business (putting the lawn mower to use in the evenings, say, after he has finished working for the day).

In general, the purpose of imposing taxes is to support government expenditures. It can be misleading to consider the impact of taxes without also considering the impact of the government expenditures that the taxes make possible. As the *scarcity problem* states, having more of one good thing (in this case, lower taxes) usually means having less of another (government expenditure).

> **RECAP**
>
> **FACTORS THAT AFFECT INVESTMENT IN FIXED CAPITAL**
>
> Any of the following factors will increase the willingness of firms to invest in new capital:
>
> 1. A decline in the price of new capital goods.
>
> 2. A decline in the real interest rate.
>
> 3. Technological improvement that raises the marginal product of capital.
>
> 4. Lower taxes on the revenues generated by capital.
>
> 5. A higher relative price for the firm's output.
>
> This list of factors is not exhaustive, however. Increases in certain forms of government expenditure, for example, will also increase investment by firms in new capital.

THE FINANCIAL SYSTEM AND THE ALLOCATION OF FUNDS TO REAL
16.5 INVESTMENT: BANKS, BONDS, STOCKS

We have emphasized the importance of a high rate of real (as opposed to financial) investment for economic growth and increased productivity.[9] A high rate of real investment (involving purchases of new factories and equipment, and so on) is not sufficient,

---

9 Recall from Chapters 5 and 15 that economists sometimes use the term "real" in contrast to "financial" to distinguish investment in the national accounts sense (private and public investment in physical capital and inventories) from financial investment (purchases of stocks and bonds). The other use of the term "real," which was particularly emphasized in Chapter 6, means "inflation-adjusted."

however. A successful economy not only invests vigorously but it applies its limited funds to investment projects that, on average, have a high rate of return.

In a capitalist economy like that of Canada, some investment funds are allocated by public sector decision-makers to government fixed capital formation, as discussed in seciton 16.4. But most investment funds are allocated either by private businesses reinvesting their profits or by the financial system. The Canadian financial system consists both of financial institutions, such as banks, and financial markets, such as bond markets and stock markets.

The financial system ideally performs two major functions on behalf of financial investors (savers). First, it provides information to financial investors about which of the many possible uses of their funds are likely to prove most profitable, and, hence, pay the highest return. For example, financial intermediaries such as banks develop expertise in evaluating prospective borrowers, making it unnecessary for small financial investors to do that on their own. Similarly, stock and bond analysts evaluate the business prospects of a company issuing shares of stock or bonds, which affects the price the stock will sell for or the interest rate the company will have to offer on its bond.

Second, financial markets help financial investors share the risks of lending by permitting them to diversify their financial investments. When capital markets have not been developed, as in much of the least-developed world, the only way a person can save for the future is by acquiring real assets—as, for example, when a peasant farmer invests in a bigger barn or in more livestock. A central problem with such direct investments is that the risk is not diversified. When everything that a person owns is tied up in their farm, a single fire or other disaster would wipe them out financially. Where capital markets have been developed, such as in countries like Canada, savers are able to buy a share in many different investments; thus, no single event can wipe out the entire value of their portfolio.

Although it is important to recognize these two major functions that the financial system performs on behalf of financial investors, it is also important to recognize that even in well-regulated financial systems, financial investors may not always get particularly good advice and may even be swindled from time to time, and this can have consequences for the whole economy. It is not easy to achieve a financial system that motivates its agents to provide quality service to investor customers but at the same time cuts off all opportunities for those agents to profit at the customer's expense. Sound financial decisions require reliable information, but reliable financial information can be difficult to obtain. In numerous corporate scandals, for example, financial investors have been duped by corporations engaging in deceptive accounting practices. In the subprime mortgage debacle in which financial investors around the world bought U.S. mortage-backed securities, financial investors were misled by ratings agencies into believing that extremely risky securities were actually extremely safe. Many analysts attribute the global recession of 2008–2009 to problems in the financial systems of the United States and other countries.[10]

In this section, we briefly discuss three key components of the financial system: the banking system, the bond market, and the stock market. In doing so we elaborate on the role of the financial system as a whole in providing information about investment projects and in helping financial investors to share the risks of lending.

THE BANKING SYSTEM

Canada's banking system is based upon commercial banks (also known in Canada as chartered banks). The six largest domestic banks, with their country-wide branch networks, are particularly important, as they account for about 90 percent of the assets of Canada's banking system.

---

10 For a fascinating analysis of the problems financial investors have in obtaining reliable information, see Robert Shiller, *Irrational Exuberance,* 2nd ed., (Princeton, N.J.: Princeton University Press, 2006). For a critical view of Canada's financial system, see Jim Stanford, *Paper Boom* (Ottawa: James Lorimer, 1999). Dozens of excellent books have been written on the financial aspects of the 2008–2009 global recession; a particularly informative one is John Cassidy, *How Markets Fail* (New York: Picador, 2010).

Commercial banks are privately owned firms that accept deposits from individuals and businesses and use those deposits to make loans. Banks are the most important example of a class of institutions called **financial intermediaries**—firms that extend credit to borrowers using funds raised from savers. Other examples of financial intermediaries are trust companies, credit unions, and caisses populaires.

Why are financial intermediaries such as banks, which "stand between" financial investors and business borrowers, necessary? Why don't individual investors just lend directly to borrowers who want to invest in new capital projects? The main reason is that, through specialization, banks and other intermediaries develop a *comparative advantage* in evaluating the quality of borrowers—the information-gathering function that we referred to a moment ago. Most savers, particularly small investors, do not have the time or the knowledge to determine for themselves which borrowers are likely to most productively use the funds they receive.

Banks help financial investors by eliminating their need to gather information about potential borrowers and by directing their funds toward higher-return, more productive investments. Banks help borrowers as well by providing access to credit that might otherwise not be available.

financial intermediaries
firms that extend credit to borrowers using funds raised from savers

COMPARATIVE ADVANTAGE

BONDS AND STOCKS

Large and well-established corporations wishing to obtain funds for investment will sometimes go to banks. Unlike the typical small borrower, however, a larger firm usually has alternative ways of raising funds, notably through the corporate bond market and the stock market. We will therefore discuss some of the mechanics of bonds and stocks, and then return to the role of bond and stock markets in allocating funds. To understand bonds and stocks, it is first necessary to understand the time value of money.

The Time Value of Money

The *time value of money* implies that if money can be invested in an interest-bearing account a given dollar amount today is equivalent to a larger dollar amount in the future. A dramatic example of the time value of money was provided by the case of an Ontario resident who made the news when it was reported that he had decided to stash a winning $30 million lottery ticket in a safe-deposit box for almost a year before cashing it in. What was the opportunity cost of this decision? One financial reporter put it this way: "How about earnings of $675,000 in a one-year cashable guaranteed investment certificate with an annual interest rate of 2.25 per cent at the Royal Bank of Canada?"[11]

In general, what is the amount of money that would be required in the future to equal a given dollar amount today? Suppose you have $100, and you can get a 2 percent annual interest rate if you invest the $100 in an interest-bearing account. After one year the balance in the account will have a value of $102: the original sum of $100 plus the $2 of interest. If the interest rate remains at 2 percent, then the $102 to which the balance grew after one year will grow by 2 percent over the second year, to $104.04.

The logic of this example can be generalized. We can refer to *present discounted value* or, more succinctly, **present value (PV)**, as the value of a sum of money today. This can be contrasted with *future value*. **Future value (FV)** refers to how much a sum of money grows when it compounds at a given rate. If the interest rate is symbolized by i and the number of compounding periods by n, the relationship between present value and future value can now be represented by Equation 16.8:

$$FV = PV \times (1 + i)^n \qquad (16.8)$$

Does Equation 16.10 fit with the example of $100 growing to $104.04 after two years when the interest rate is 2 percent? Let's check. The $100 corresponds to PV, the 2 percent

present value (PV) the value of a sum of money today; that is, the value in the current or initial period

future value (FV) the value a sum of money grows to at some date in the future, when it compounds at a given interest rate

11 Rob Ferguson, "Long Wait Cost Lottery Winner Big Bucks," *The Toronto Star*, April 3, 2004.

(.02) corresponds to i, and the two years corresponds to n, the number of compounding periods. Substituting for PV, i, and n in Equation 16.8 indeed yields FV of $104.04—that is, $104.04 = \$100 \times (1.02)^2$.

Another way to express the relationship between present value and future value is to divide both sides of Equation 16.8 by $(1 + i)^n$ to get

$$FV = PV/(1 + i)^n \tag{16.9}$$

To take a concrete example, what is the present value (PV) of $100 received three years from now when the interest rate is 2 percent? From Equation 16.9, we conclude that $PV = \$100/(1.02)^3 = \$94.23$.

EXAMPLE **16.5**

When is a million dollars not worth a million dollars?

A few years ago, the McDonald's fast food chain advertised that on one weekend it would give out 15 prizes of one million dollars each to lucky customers. The fine print of the advertising, however, revealed that each one million dollar prize would be paid out in installments of $50 000 a year over a period of 20 years. What is the present value of such a prize?

To calculate the present value of the "one million dollar" prize you would add together the present values of each of the 20 installments. If the relevant interest rate is 2.25 percent and if payments are made at the end of each year, then the value of the first installment is $50 000/(1.0225)$, the value of the second installment is $50 000/(1.0225)^2$, and so on, with the value of the final installment being worth $50 000/(1.0225)^{20}$. It turns out that the present value of the "one million dollar" prize would be $798 186.

If you can grasp the time value of money, you should have no trouble understanding bond and stock price determination: both bond prices and stock prices involve present values of expected future payments.

Bonds

bond a legal promise to repay a debt, usually including both the principal amount and regular interest payments

principal amount the amount originally lent

coupon rate the interest rate promised when a bond is issued

coupon payments regular interest payments made to the bondholder

A **bond** is a legal promise to repay a debt, usually including both the **principal amount**, which is the amount originally lent, and regular interest payments. The promised interest rate when a bond is issued is called the **coupon rate**. The regular interest payments made to the bondholder are called **coupon payments**. The coupon payment of a bond that pays interest annually equals the coupon rate times the principal amount of the bond. For example, if the principal amount of a bond is $1 000 000 and its coupon rate is 5 percent, then the annual coupon payment made to the holder of the bond is (0.05)($1 000 000), or $50 000.

Corporations and governments frequently raise funds by issuing bonds and selling them to savers or financial investors. The coupon rate that a newly issued bond has to promise in order to be attractive to financial investors depends on a number of factors, including the bond's term and its credit risk. The *term* of a bond is the length of time before the debt it represents is fully repaid, a period that can range from 30 days to 30 years or more. Generally, lenders will demand a higher interest rate to lend for a longer term. *Credit risk* is the risk that the borrower will go bankrupt and thus not repay the loan. A borrower viewed as risky will have to pay a higher interest rate, to compensate lenders for taking the chance of losing all or part of their financial investment. For example, so-called high-yield bonds, less formally known as "junk bonds," are bonds issued by firms judged to be risky by credit-rating agencies; these bonds pay higher interest rates than bonds issued by companies thought to be less risky.

Bondholders are not required to hold bonds until *maturity*, the time at which they are supposed to be repaid by the issuer, but are always free to sell their bonds in the *bond market,* an organized market run by professional bond traders.[12] The market value of a particular bond at any given point in time is called the *price* of the bond. As it turns out, there is a close relationship between the price of a bond at a given point of time and the interest rate prevailing in financial markets at that time, as is illustrated by Example 16.6.

EXAMPLE 16.6

Bond prices and interest rates

On January 1, 2009, Tanya purchases a newly issued, two-year government bond with a principal amount of $1000. The coupon rate on the bond is 5 percent, paid annually. Hence Tanya, or whoever owns the bond at the time, will receive a coupon payment of $50 (5 percent of $1000) on January 1, 2010, and $1050 (a $50 coupon payment plus repayment of the original $1000 lent) on January 1, 2011.

On January 1, 2010, after receiving her first year's coupon payment, Tanya decides to sell her bond to raise the funds to take a vacation. She offers her bond for sale in the bond market. How much can she expect to get for her "used" bond if the prevailing interest rate in the bond market is 6 percent? if the prevailing interest rate is 4 percent?

As we mentioned, the price of a "used" bond at any point in time depends on the prevailing interest rate. Suppose first that, on January 1, 2010, when Tanya takes her bond to the bond market, the prevailing interest rate on newly issued one-year bonds is 6 percent. Would another financial investor be willing to pay Tanya the full $1000 principal amount of her bond? No, because the purchaser of Tanya's bond will receive $1050 in one year, when the bond matures; whereas if he uses his $1000 to buy a new one-year bond paying 6 percent interest, he will receive $1060 ($1000 principal repayment plus $60 interest) in one year. So Tanya's bond is not worth $1000 to another financial investor.

How much would another investor be willing to pay for Tanya's bond? Since newly issued one-year bonds pay a 6 percent return, he will buy Tanya's bond only at a price that allows him to earn at least that return. As the holder of Tanya's bond will receive $1050 ($1000 principal plus $50 interest) in one year, the price for her bond that allows the purchaser to earn a 6 percent return must satisfy the equation

$$\text{Bond price} \times 1.06 = \$1050.$$

Solving the equation for the bond price, we find that Tanya's bond will sell for $1050/1.06, or just under $991. To check this result, note that in one year the purchaser of the bond will receive $1050, or $59 more than he paid. His rate of return is $59/$991, or 6 percent, as expected.

What if the prevailing interest rate had been 4 percent rather than 6 percent? Then the price of Tanya's bond would satisfy the relationship (bond price × 1.04) = $1050, implying that the price of her bond would be $1050/1.04, or almost $1010. What happens if the interest rate when Tanya wants to sell is 5 percent, the same as it was when she originally bought the bond? You should show that in this case the bond would sell at its face value of $1000.

This example illustrates a general principle: *bond prices and interest rates are inversely related.* When the interest rate being paid on newly issued bonds rises, the prices financial investors are willing to pay for existing bonds falls, and vice versa.

Three-year government bonds are issued at a face value (principal amount) of $100 and a coupon rate of 7 percent, interest payable at the end of each year. One year prior to the maturation of these bonds, a newspaper headline reads,   EXERCISE 16.4

---

12 The analysis in the text does not apply to the special cases of Canada Savings Bonds and Canada Premium Bonds, two categories of federal government "bonds" that cannot be resold in markets but can only be redeemed at financial institutions for principal and accumulated interest. Neither of these are true "bonds" but, actually, savings certificates.

"Bond Prices Plunge," and the story reveals that these three-year bonds have fallen in price to $96. What has happened to interest rates? What is the one-year interest rate at the time of the newspaper story?

Issuing bonds is one means by which a corporation or a government can obtain funds from financial investors. Another important way of raising funds, but one restricted to corporations, is by issuing stock to the public.

Stocks

stock (or equity) a claim to partial ownership of a firm

dividend a regular payment received by stockholders for each share that they own

A share of **stock** (or **equity**) is a claim to partial ownership of a firm. For example, if a corporation has one million shares of stock outstanding, ownership of one share is equivalent to ownership of one-millionth of the company. Stockholders receive returns on their financial investment in two forms. First, stockholders receive a regular payment called a **dividend** for each share of stock they own. Dividends are determined by the firm's management and usually depend on the firm's recent profits. Second, stockholders receive returns in the form of *capital gains* when the price of their stock increases (we discussed capital gains and losses in section 16.1).

Prices of stocks are determined through trading on a stock exchange, such as the Toronto Stock Exchange. A stock's price rises and falls as the demand for the stock changes. Demand for stocks in turn depends on factors such as news about the prospects of the company. For example, the stock price of a pharmaceutical company that announces the discovery of an important new drug is likely to rise on the announcement, even if actual production and marketing of the drug is some time away, because financial investors expect the company to become more profitable in the future. Example 16.7 gives a numerical illustration of some key factors that affect stock prices.

EXAMPLE 16.7

How much should you pay for a share of FortuneCookie.com?

You have the opportunity to buy shares in a new company called FortuneCookie.com, which plans to sell gourmet fortune cookies over the Internet. Your stockbroker estimates that the company will pay $1 per share in dividends a year from now, and that in a year the market price of the company will be $80 per share. Assuming that you accept your broker's estimates as accurate, what is the most that you should be willing to pay today per share of FortuneCookie.com? How does your answer change if you expect a $5 dividend? if you expect a $1 dividend but an $84 stock price in one year?

Based on your broker's estimates, you conclude that in one year each share of FortuneCookie.com you own will be worth $81 in your pocket—the $1 dividend plus the $80 you could get by reselling the stock. Finding the maximum price you would pay for the stock today therefore boils down to asking how much you would invest today to have $81 a year from today. Answering this question, in turn, requires one more piece of information—what is the expected rate of return that you require in order to be willing to buy stock in this company.

How would you determine your required rate of return to hold stock in FortuneCookie.com? For the moment, let's imagine that you are not too worried about the potential riskiness of the stock, either because you think that it is a "sure thing" or because you are a devil-may-care type who is not bothered by risk. In that case, your required rate of return to hold FortuneCookie.com should be about the same as you can get on other financial investments, such as government bonds. The available return on other financial investments gives the *opportunity cost* of your funds. So, for example, if the interest rate currently being offered on government bonds is 6 percent, you should be willing to accept a 6 percent return to hold FortuneCookie.com as well. In that case, the maximum price you would pay today for a share of FortuneCookie.com satisfies the equation

$$\text{Stock price} \times 1.06 = \$81.$$

This equation defines the stock price you should be willing to pay if you are willing to accept a 6 percent return over the next year. Solving this equation yields stock price = $81/1.06 = $76.42. If you buy FortuneCookie.com for $76.42, then your return over the year will be ($81 − $76.42)/$76.42 = $4.58/$71.42 = 6 percent, which is the rate of return you required to buy the stock.

If, instead, the dividend is expected to be $5, then the total benefit of holding the stock in one year, equal to the expected dividend plus the expected price, is $5 + $80, or $85. Assuming, again, that you are willing to accept a 6 percent return to hold FortuneCookie.com, the price you are willing to pay for the stock today satisfies the relationship (stock price × 1.06) = $85. Solving this equation for the stock price yields stock price = $85/1.06 = $80.19. Comparing with the previous case, we see that a higher expected dividend in the future increases the value of the stock today. That's why good news about the future prospects of a company—such as the announcement by a pharmaceutical company that it has discovered a useful new drug—affects its stock price immediately.

If the expected future price of the stock is $84, with the dividend at $1, then the value of holding the stock in one year is once again $85, and the calculation is the same as the previous one. Again, the price you should be willing to pay for the stock is $80.19.

These examples show that an increase in the future dividend or in the future expected stock price raises the stock price today, whereas an increase in the return a financial investor requires to hold the stock lowers today's stock price. Since we expect required returns in the stock market to be closely tied to market interest rates, this last result implies that increases in interest rates tend to depress stock prices (as well as bond prices) and vice versa.

Our examples also took the future stock price as a given. But what determines the future stock price? Just as today's stock price depends on the dividend shareholders expect to receive this year and the stock price a year from now, the stock price a year from now depends on the dividend expected for next year and the stock price two years from now, and so on. Ultimately, then, today's stock price is affected not only by the dividend expected this year but future dividends as well. A company's ability to pay dividends depends on its earnings. Thus, as we noted in the example of the pharmaceutical company that announces the discovery of a new drug, news about future earnings, even earnings quite far in the future, is likely to affect a company's stock price immediately.

As in Example 16.7, you expect shares of FortuneCookie.com to be worth $80 per share in one year, and also to pay a dividend of $1 in one year. What should you be willing to pay for the stock today if the prevailing interest rate, equal to your required rate of return, is 4 percent? What if the interest rate is 8 percent? In general, how would you expect stock prices to react if economic news arrives that implies that interest rates will rise in the very near future?

EXERCISE 16.5

In Example 16.7, we assumed that you were willing to accept a return of 6 percent to hold FortuneCookie.com, the same return that you could get on a government bond. However, financial investments in the stock market are quite risky in that returns to holding stocks can be quite variable and unpredictable. For example, although you expect a share of FortuneCookie.com to be worth $80 in one year, you also realize that there is a chance it might sell for as low as $50 or as high as $110 per share. Most financial investors dislike risk and unpredictability and, thus, have a higher required rate of return for

risk premium the rate of return that financial investors require to hold risky assets minus the rate of return on safe assets

holding risky assets like stocks than for holding relatively safe assets like government bonds. The difference between the required rate of return to hold risky assets and the rate of return on safe assets, like government bonds, is called the **risk premium**. Example 16.8 illustrates the effect of financial investors' dislike of risk on stock prices.

EXAMPLE **16.8**

Riskiness and stock prices

Continuing Example 16.7, suppose that FortuneCookie.com is expected to pay a $1 dividend and have a market price of $80 per share in one year. The interest rate on government bonds is 6 percent per year. However, to be willing to hold a risky asset like a share of FortuneCookie.com, you require an expected return four percentage points higher than the rate paid by safe assets like government bonds (a risk premium of 4 percent). Hence you require a 10 percent expected return to hold FortuneCookie. com. What is the most you would be willing to pay for the stock now? What do you conclude about the relationship between perceived riskiness and stock prices?

As a share of FortuneCookie.com is expected to pay $81 in one year and the required return is 10 percent, we have (stock price × 1.10) = $81. Solving for the stock price, we find the price to be $81/1.10 = $73.64, less than the price of $76.42 we found when there was no risk premium and the required rate of return was 6 percent (Example 16.7). We conclude that financial investors' dislike of risk, and the resulting risk premium, lowers the prices of risky assets like stocks.

To give a real-world example, in the spring of 2000, North American investors began to fear the risks associated with Internet-related (or "dot-com") companies, the real-world counterparts to our hypothetical FortuneCookie.com. Some observers have said that investors began to see through the hype that had been fed to them by dot-com entrepreneurs and by biased stock market analysts and brokers. In any case, the perceived riskiness of Internet-related shares rose, and this rise in perceived risk was one reason why share prices began to fall. The Forbes Internet index of 300 companies, for example, corresponded to a market value of over US$1 trillion in early 2000, but by December 2000 its market value had dropped to under US$400 billion, a fall of more than 60 percent. (Broad-based stock indices fell during the same period, but not by nearly as much as indices of Internet-related stocks.)

WHAT TYPE OF FINANCIAL SYSTEM?

To conclude this chapter and the textbook as a whole, let us refer to two major issues about financial systems: whether the financial system is bank-based or market-based and whether the system is strongly or lightly regulated and supervised.

Bank-based or Market-based Finance?

Having explained how bonds and stocks are priced, let us briefly consider the significance of bond and stock finance versus bank finance. Like banks, bond and stock markets provide a means of channelling funds from savers or financial investors to borrowers with investment opportunities.

In most developing economies, the financial systems depend heavily upon bank financing of real investment projects and financial markets, that is, bonds and stocks, have a minor role. Financial markets begin to play a greater role as the economies become more advanced. Some research indicates that "bank-led finance may be inevitable at certain stages of development, and that efforts to develop stock exchanges in some countries may have been premature. . . ."[13]

---

13 Erik Berglof and Patrick Bolton, "The Great Divide and Beyond: Financial Architecture in Transition," http://wdi.umich.edu/files/publications/workingpapers/wp414.pdf.

Bank-led finance, also called bank-based finance, has also been more characteristic of some advanced economies, such as Japan's, than of others, such as the United States', the leading example of financial marketed-based finance. When Japan was growing rapidly in the 1980s and the United States seemed to be falling behind, the strengths of a bank-based financial system were widely noted. When Japan stagnated in the 1990s, however, the weaknesses of bank-based finance were highlighted, and in recent years the relative importance of bank finance in Japan has declined somewhat.

Strictly Regulated or Lightly Regulated Finance?

Most countries had strictly regulated financial systems in the period after World War II and into the 1970s. The regulation was partly in response to the financial system problems experienced during the Great Depression. A central concern of regulation was to prevent banks from taking on risks that could possibly bring down the broader banking and financial system. But by the 1980s, those who believed that financial market regulation was excessive became more influential in many countries, and there was a strong trend to financial market deregulation. This trend to deregulation was stronger in some countries, such as the United States, Ireland, and Iceland, than in others, such as Canada and Australia.

The global recession of 2008–2009, however, triggered a renewed debate on the merits of financial regulation. To many it seemed that not only was financial market regulation in the United States the ultimate factor behind the global recession, but the countries which had most aggressively pursued financial market degulation were among those worst hit by the recession. Canada, which had been widely criticized for excessive caution on financial matters, including on the decision to disallow mergers of the largest banks in the late 1990s, suddenly became the subject of widespread praise for its sound financial regulation symbolized by a story about Canada's financial regulation in the *The Economist* newsweekly subtitled "A country that got things right."[14]

Another view, however, is that Canada had started to adopt similar financial deregulation measures as the United States, but the dramatic failure of financial institutions in the United States took place before Canadian financial deregulation had gone very far and served to put a halt to the trend there. It remains to be seen whether the halt is temporary and the trend will resume. That will depend in part on the decisions of voters, including ones who have completed a course in macroeconomics and hence have a better foundation for many of the decisions they will face as citizens.

RECAP

THE FINANCIAL SYSTEM AND THE ALLOCATION OF FUNDS TO REAL INVESTMENT

- The financial system ideally performs two major functions on behalf of financial investors: first, it provides information about which uses of their funds are likely to prove most profitable and, second, it facilitates diversification of risk.

- Although it is important to recognize these functions, it is also important to recognize that financial systems can malfunction, and this can have consequences for the whole economy.

- Bond prices and interest rates are inversely related. That is, when the interest rate being paid on newly issued bonds rises, the price financial investors will pay for existing bonds falls, and vice versa.

---

14 See "Don't blame Canada: A country that got things right," *The Economist*, May 14, 2009. For the view that disallowing the bank mergers in the late 1990s was actually wise, see Brian K. MacLean, ed., *Out of Control: Canada in an Unstable Financial World* (Ottawa: Lorimer, 1999).

- An increase in expected future dividends or in the expected future market price of a stock raises the current price of the stock.

- An increase in interest rates, implying an increase in the required rate of return to hold stocks, lowers the current price of stocks.

- An increase in perceived riskiness, as reflected in an increase in the risk premium, lowers the current price of stocks.

- Greater reliance on banks than on financial markets is characteristic of developing countries but some successful advanced economies have also been characterized by bank-based finance.

- The trend in high-income countries from the 1980s until the great recession of 2008–2009 was towards less regulation of the financial system, but the events leading to the recession led to a wider appreciation of the merits of financial regulation.

SUMMARY

- In general, *saving* equals current income minus spending on current needs; the *saving rate* is the percentage of income that is saved. *Wealth*, or net worth, equals the market value of assets (real or financial items of value) minus liabilities (debts). Saving is a *flow*, being measured in dollars per unit of time, while wealth is a *stock*, measured in dollars at a point in time. As the amount of water in a bathtub changes according to the rate at which water flows in, the stock of wealth increases at the saving rate. Wealth also increases if the value of existing assets rises (*capital gains*) and decreases if the value of existing assets falls (*capital losses*). **LO1**

- Individuals and households save for a variety of reasons, including *life-cycle* objectives, such as saving for retirement or a new home; the need to be prepared for an emergency (*precautionary saving*); and the desire to leave an inheritance (*bequest saving*). The amount people save is also affected by the real interest rate, which is the "reward" for saving. Evidence suggests that higher real interest rates lead to modest increases in saving. Saving can also be affected by psychological factors, such as the degree of self-control and the desire to consume at the level of one's neighbours (demonstration effects). **LO2**

- The *gross saving* of an economy is equal to its *gross investment*. Gross saving minus *national saving* equals non-resident saving, which can be positive or negative. Throughout most of the 20th century, the non-resident sector was a net supplier of saving to the Canadian economy. But at the beginning of the 21st century, Canada's national saving exceeded its gross saving, meaning that Canada was a net supplier of saving to the rest of the world. The three components of national saving are personal (or household) saving, corporate saving, and government (or public) saving. Public saving refers to the saving of the government sector as a whole, not just saving associated with the federal government. The sum of household and corporate saving is called private saving. In recent years, the level of household saving has been lower than the level of corporate saving, and the level of corporate saving has exceeded the level of real investment by the corporate sector. In the latter half of the 1990s, government saving turned positive, after about two decades of being negative. More recently, reflecting tax cuts and the 2008–2009 recession effects, it turned negative again. LO3

- The *current account* is the record of payments and receipts arising from trade in goods and services from international investment income and from international transfers. Trade takes place in assets as well as goods and services. Purchases of domestic assets (real or financial) by foreigners are called *capital inflows,* and purchases of foreign assets by domestic savers are called *capital outflows.* Because imports that are not financed by sales of exports must be financed by sales of assets, the current account balance and net capital inflows sum to zero. LO4

- A low rate of national saving relative to domestic investment (or a high rate of investment relative to national saving) is the primary cause of current account deficits. A country with low savings relative to investment opportunities will attract net capital inflows. Because the sum of the current account balance and capital inflows is zero, a high level of net capital inflows is consistent with a large current account deficit. LO4

- The *national balance sheet* records assets and liabilities for Canada as a whole. Canada's *national wealth* corresponds to the value of real assets in Canada. Canada's *national net worth* is less than Canada's national wealth because Canada has *net international liabilities.* LO5

- Firms will invest in new capital goods if the benefits of doing so outweigh the costs. Two factors that determine the cost of investment are the price of new capital goods and the real interest rate. The higher the real interest rate, the more expensive it is to borrow, and the less likely firms are to invest. The benefit of investment is the value of the marginal product of new capital, which depends on factors such as the productivity of new capital goods and the relative price of the firm's output. LO6

- In addition to borrowing from banks, corporations can obtain financing by issuing bonds or stocks. A bond is a legal promise to replay a debt, including both the principal amount and regular interest payments. The prices of previously issued bonds decline when interest rates rise. A share of stock is a claim to partial ownership of a firm. The price of a stock depends positively on the dividend the stock is expected to pay and the expected future price of the stock, and negatively on the rate of return required by financial investors to hold the stock. LO7

- The financial system performs two major functions on behalf of financial investors. First, it provides information to financial investors about which of the many possible uses of their funds are likely to prove most profitable, and, thus, pay the highest return. Second, financial markets help financial investors share the risks of lending by permitting them to diversify their financial investments—they allow financial investors to avoid having all their "eggs in one basket." LO8

- Although it is important to recognize these functions, it is also important to recognize that financial systems can malfunction, and this can have consequences for the whole economy. LO8

- Some countries are characterized by bank-led finance; others rely more heavily upon financial markets (bonds and stocks) for channelling funds to investment. LO8

- The trend in many countries from the 1980s until the great recession of 2008–2009 was towards less regulation of the financial system, but the events leading to the recession led to a wider appreciation of the merits of financial regulation, and Canada was widely praised for its strict financial supervision and regulaton. LO8

KEY TERMS

assets (419)
bequest saving (422)
bond (438)
capital gains (421)
capital inflows (429)
capital outflows (429)
capital losses (421)
coupon payments (438)
coupon rate (438)
current account (430)
dividend (440)

financial intermediaries (437)
future value (FV) (437)
gross investment (424)
gross saving (424)
international capital flows (429)
liabilities (419)
life-cycle saving (421)
national net worth (432)
national saving (424)
national wealth (432)
net capital inflows (429)

net international liabilities (432)
non-resident saving (425)
precautionary saving (421)
present value (PV) (437)
principal amount (438)
risk premium (442)
saving (419)
saving rate (419)
stock (or equity) (440)
wealth (419)

REVIEW QUESTIONS

1. Explain the relationship between an individual's saving and wealth using the concepts of flows and stocks. Is saving the only means by which wealth can increase? Explain. **LO1**

2. Give three basic motivations for saving. Illustrate each with an example. What other factors would psychologists cite as possibly being important for saving? **LO2**

3. Define gross saving, national saving, and non-resident saving. How do these concepts relate to national wealth, national net worth, and net international liabilities? **LO3, LO5**

4. Canadian household saving rates were low in the latter half of the 1990s. What implications would low saving rates have for individual households? What implications, if any, would they have for the Canadian economy as a whole? **LO3**

5. What are the sources of gross corporate saving? What are some key economic factors influencing the level of government saving? **LO3**

6. From the point of view of a given country, say, India, give an example of a capital inflow and a capital outflow. **LO4**

7. Explain how a country could simultaneously run a trade surplus and a current account deficit. **LO4**

8. What are some key determinants of business investment? Could government spending on infrastructure influence the level of business investment? **LO6**

9. Arjay plans to sell a bond that matures in one year and has a principal value of $1000. What factors determine the price he can expect to get for the bond? **LO7**

10. Stock prices surge but the prices of government bonds remain stable. What can you infer from the behaviour of bond prices about the possible causes of the increase in stock values? **LO7**

11. Suggest two ways that the financial system can work on behalf of financial investors. Illustrate with examples. **LO8**

12. Discuss how the financial system can negatively impact the productivity of investment and the stability of the economic system. **LO8**

PROBLEMS

1. a. Corey has a mountain bike worth $300, credit card debt of $150, $200 in cash, a Wayne Gretzky hockey card worth $400, $1200 in a chequing account, and an electric bill due for $250. Construct Corey's balance sheet and calculate his net worth.

   For each remaining part, explain how the event affects Corey's assets, liabilities, and wealth. **LO1**

   b. Corey goes to a hockey card convention and finds out that his hockey card is a worthless forgery.

   c. Corey uses $150 from his paycheque to pay off his credit card balance. The remainder of his earnings is spent.

   d. Corey writes a $150 cheque on his chequing account to pay off his credit card balance.

   Of the events in parts (b) to (d), which, if any, correspond to saving on Corey's part?

2. State whether each of the following is a stock or a flow, and explain. **LO1**

   a. The gross domestic product.

b. National saving.

c. The value of the Canadian housing stock on January 1, 2009.

d. The amount of Canadian currency in circulation as of this morning.

e. The government budget surplus or deficit.

f. The quantity of outstanding government debt on January 1, 2009.

3. Ellie and Vince are a married couple, both with university degrees and jobs. How would you expect each of the following events to affect the amount they save each month? Explain your answers in terms of the basic motivations for saving. **LO2**

a. Ellie learns she is pregnant.

b. Vince reads in the paper about possible layoffs in his industry.

c. Vince had hoped that his parents would lend financial assistance toward the couple's planned purchase of a house, but he learns that they can't afford it.

d. Ellie announces that she would like to go to law school in the next few years.

e. A boom in the stock market greatly increases the value of the couple's retirement funds.

f. Vince and Ellie agree that they would like to leave a substantial amount to local charities in their wills.

4. Use the economic data given to find national saving, private saving, public saving, and national saving as a percentage of GDP. Assume that saving amounts for all sectors represent gross rates, and assume that the government budget balance equals public saving. There is no government investment. **LO3**

Household saving = 200   Corporate saving = 400
Government purchases of goods and services = 100
Government transfers and interest payments = 100
Tax collections = 150   GDP = 2200

5. How do each of the following transactions affect (1) the current account surplus or deficit and (2) capital inflows or outflows for Canada? Show that in each case the identity that the current account balance plus net capital inflows equals zero applies. **LO4**

a. A Canadian exporter sells software to Israel. She uses the Israeli shekels received to buy stock in an Israeli company.

b. A Mexican firm uses proceeds from its sale of oil to Canada to buy Canadian government debt.

c. A Mexican firm uses proceeds from its sale of oil to Canada to buy oil drilling equipment from a Canadian firm.

d. A Mexican firm receives Canadian dollars from selling oil to Canada. A French firm accepts the dollars as payment for drilling equipment. The French firm uses the dollars to buy Canadian government debt.

e. A British financial investor writes a cheque on his bank account in Toronto to purchase shares of Bombardier stock (Bombardier is a Canadian company).

6. A country's domestic supply of saving, domestic demand for saving for purposes of capital formation, and supply of net capital inflows are given by the following equations: **LO4**

$$S = 1500 + 2000r,$$

$$GI = 2000 - 4000r,$$

$$KI = -100 + 6000r.$$

a. Assuming that the market for saving and investment is in equilibrium, find national saving, net capital inflows, domestic investment, and the real interest rate.

b. Repeat part (a), assuming that desired national saving declines by 120 at each value of the real interest rate. What effect does a reduction in domestic saving have on capital inflows?

c. Concern about the economy's macroeconomic policies causes capital inflows to fall sharply so that now $KI = -700 + 6000r$. Repeat part (a). What does a reduction in capital inflows do to domestic investment and the real interest rate?

7. Ellie and Vince are trying to decide whether to purchase a new home. The house they want is priced at $200 000. Annual expenses such as maintenance, taxes, and insurance equal 4 percent of the home's value. If properly maintained, the house's real value is not expected to change. The real interest rate in the economy is 6 percent, and Ellie and Vince can qualify to borrow the full amount of the purchase price (for simplicity, assume no down payment) at that rate. **LO6**

a. Ellie and Vince would be willing to pay $1500 monthly rent to live in a house of the same quality as the one they are thinking about purchasing. Should they buy the house?

b. Does the answer to part (a) change if they were willing to pay $2000 monthly rent?

c. Does the answer to part (a) change if the real interest rate is 4 percent instead of 6 percent?

d. Does the answer to part (a) change if the developer offers to sell the house to Ellie and Vince for $150 000?

e. Why do home-building companies dislike high interest rates?

8. The builder of a new movie theatre complex is trying to decide how many screens she wants. Below are her estimates of the number of patrons the complex will attract each year, depending on the number of screens available.

Number of screens	Total number of patrons
1	40 000
2	75 000
3	105 000
4	130 000
5	150 000

After paying the movie distributors and meeting all other non-interest expenses, the owner expects to net $2 per ticket sold. Construction costs are $1 000 000 per screen. LO6

a. Make a table showing the value of marginal product for each screen from the first through the fifth. What property is illustrated by the behaviour of marginal product?

b. How many screens will be built if the real interest rate is 5.5 percent?

c. If the real interest rate is 7.5 percent?

d. If the real interest rate is 10 percent?

e. If the real interest rate is 5.5 percent, how far would construction costs have to fall before the builder would be willing to build a five-screen complex?

9. Simon purchases a bond, newly issued by the Amalgamated Corporation, for $1000. The bond pays $60 to its holder at the end of the first and second years and pays $1060 upon its maturity at the end of the third year. LO7

a. What are the principal amount, the term, the coupon rate, and the coupon payment for Simon's bond?

b. After receiving the second coupon payment (at the end of the second year), Simon decides to sell his bond in the bond market. What price can he expect for his bond if the one-year interest rate at that time is 3 percent? 8 percent? 10 percent?

c. Can you think of a reason that after two years the price of Simon's bond might fall below $1000, even though the market interest rate equals the coupon rate?

10. Shares in Brothers Grimm Inc., manufacturers of gingerbread houses, are expected to pay a dividend of $5 in one year and to sell for $100 per share at that time. How much should you be willing to pay today per share of Grimm LO7

a. If the safe rate of interest is 5 percent and you believe that investing in Grimm carries no risk?

b. If the safe rate of interest is 10 percent and you believe that investing in Grimm carries no risk?

c. If the safe rate of interest is 5 percent but your risk premium is 3 percent?

d. Repeat parts (a) to (c), assuming that Grimm is not expected to pay a dividend but the expected price is unchanged.

11. Your financial investments consist of Canadian government bonds maturing in 10 years and shares in a start-up company doing research in pharmaceuticals. How would you expect each of the following news items to affect the value of your assets? Explain. LO7

a. Interest rates on newly issued government bonds rise.

b. Inflation is forecasted to be much lower than previously expected (*Hint*: Recall the Fisher effect from Chapter 6.) Assume for simplicity that this information does *not* affect your forecast of the dollar value of the pharmaceutical company's future dividends and stock price.

In parts (c) to (f), interest rates on newly issued government bonds are assumed to remain unchanged.

c. Large swings in the stock market increase financial investors' concerns about market risk.

d. The start-up company whose stock you own announces the development of a valuable new drug. However, the drug will not come to market for at least five years.

e. The pharmaceutical company announces that it will not pay a dividend next year.

f. The federal government announces a system of price controls on prescription drugs.

12. You have $1000 to invest and are considering buying some combination of the shares of two U.S. companies, Donkey Inc and Elephant Inc. Shares of Donkey Inc will pay a 10 percent return if the Democrats are elected, an event you believe to have a 60 percent probability; otherwise, the shares pay a zero return. Shares of Elephant Inc will pay 8 percent if the Republicans are elected (a 40 percent probability), and zero otherwise. Either the Democrats or the Republicans will be elected. LO7

a. If your only concern is maximizing your average expected return in U.S. dollars, with no regard for risk, how should you invest your $1000?

b. What is your expected return if you invest $500 in each stock? (*Hint*: Consider what your return will be if the Democrats win and if the Republicans win, then weight each outcome by the probability that event occurs.)

c. The strategy of investing $500 in each stock does *not* give the highest possible average expected return. Why might you choose it anyway?

d. Devise an investment strategy that guarantees at least a 4.4 percent return, no matter which party wins.

e. Devise an investment strategy that is riskless, that is, one in which the return on your $1000 does not depend at all on which party wins.

ANSWERS TO IN-CHAPTER EXERCISES

16.1 If Avril's student loan were for $6500 instead of $3000, her liabilities would be $6750 (the student loan plus the credit card balance) instead of $3250. The value of her assets, $6280, is unchanged. In this case, Avril's wealth is negative, since assets of $6280 less liabilities of $6750 equals −$470. Negative wealth or net worth means one owes more than one owns. **LO1**

16.2 a. Avril has set aside her usual $20, but she has also incurred a new liability of $50. So her net saving for the week is *minus* $30. Since her assets (her chequing account) have increased by $20 but her liabilities (her credit card balance) have increased by $50, her wealth has also declined by $30. **LO1**

b. In paying off her credit card bill, Avril reduces her assets by $300 by drawing down her chequing account and reduces her liabilities by the same amount by reducing her credit card balance to zero. Thus, there is no change in her wealth. There is also no change in her saving (note that Avril's income and spending on current needs have not changed).

c. The decline in the value of Avril's furniture is a capital loss of $300. Her assets and wealth fall by $300. Changes in the value of existing assets are not treated as part of saving, however, so her saving is unchanged.

16.3 The loss of value of $200 over the year is another financial cost of owning the mower, which Larry should take into account in making his decision. His total cost is now $240 in interest costs plus $200 in anticipated loss of value of the mower (known as depreciation), or $440. This exceeds the value of marginal product, $400, so now Larry should not buy the mower. **LO6**

16.4 Since bond prices fell, interest rates must have risen. To find the interest rate, note that bond investors are willing to pay only $96 today for a bond that will pay back $107 (a coupon payment of $7 plus the principal amount of $100) in one year. To find the one-year return, divide $107 by $96 to get 1.115. Thus the interest rate must have risen to 11.5 percent. **LO7**

16.5 The share of stock will be worth $81 in one year—the sum of its expected future price and the expected dividend. At an interest rate of 4 percent, its value today is $81/1.04 = $77.88. At an interest rate of 8 percent, the stock's current value is $81/1.08 = $75. Recall from Example 16.7 that when the interest rate is 6 percent, the value of a share of FortuneCookie.com is $76.42. Since higher interest rates imply lower stock values, news that interest rates are about to rise should cause the stock market to fall. **LO7**

Practise and learn online with Connect.

GLOSSARY

100 percent reserve banking. a situation in which banks' reserves equal 100 percent of their deposits

A

absolute advantage. the advantage of taking fewer hours to perform a task than another person does

accelerating inflation. when the inflation rate rises from one year to the next

Adam Smith. (1723-1790) Scottish economist who wrote *The Wealth of Nations* (1776), probably the most influential economics book ever written

adaptive expectations of inflation. a method of forming expectations about the inflation rate that involves looking to past experience, especially recent past experience

aggregate demand curve. a relationship between overall spending in the economy and the aggregate price level

aggregate demand (ADI) curve. shows the relationship between short-run equilibrium output Y and the rate of inflation π

aggregate demand-aggregate supply model (AS-AD). a model of real output and overall price level determination

aggregate production function. shows the output of an economy as a function of various inputs

aggregate supply shock. either an inflation shock or a shock to potential output; adverse aggregate supply shocks of both types reduce output and increase inflation

aggregation. the adding up of individual economic variables to obtain economywide totals

Alfred Marshall. (1842-1924) an economist of the nineteenth and early twentieth century who published *Principles of Economics* (1890) and whose influence on economics continues to this day

allocative efficiency. occurs when it is impossible to reorganize economic resources so that at least one person is better off while nobody is worse off

anticipated inflation. when the rate of inflation turns out to be roughly what most people had expected

appreciation. an increase in the value of a currency relative to another currency

asset price bubble. occurs when the price of a financial or real asset or asset category rises much more rapidly than prices in general and by much more than can be explained by fundamental factors

assets. anything of value that one owns

attainable point. any combination of goods that can be produced using currently available resources

automatic stabilizers. provisions in the law that imply automatic increases in government spending or decreases in taxes when real output declines

autonomous expenditure. the portion of planned aggregate expenditure that is independent of output

average benefit. total benefit of undertaking n units of an activity divided by n

average cost. total cost of undertaking n units of an activity divided by n

average labour productivity. output per employed worker

average propensity to consume (APC). consumption divided by disposable income

B

balance-of-payments deficit. the net decline in a country's stock of international reserves over a year

balance-of-payments surplus. the net increase in a country's stock of international reserves over a year

bank rate. the interest rate that the Bank of Canada charges commercial banks for overnight loans, it corresponds to the upper limit of the Bank of Canada's operating band for the overnight rate; for decades, it was the Bank's official interest rate

bank reserves. cash or similar assets held by commercial banks for the purpose of meeting depositor withdrawals and payments

bank run. occurs when the depositors of a particular bank respond to news or rumours of impending bankruptcy of that particular bank by rushing to withdraw their deposits from the bank

banking panic. a rush of withdrawals from the banking system made by depositors responding to news or rumours of impending bankruptcy of one or more banks

barter. the direct trade of goods or services for other goods or services

basis point. one hundredth of a percentage point; term often used in describing interest rates

benchmark rate. an interest rate upon which other interest rates are based

bequest saving. saving done for the purpose of leaving an inheritance

bond. a legal promise to repay a debt, usually including both the principal amount and regular interest payments

boom. a particularly strong and protracted phase of an expansion

Bretton Woods system. an international monetary system under which most countries pegged their currencies to the U.S. dollar; it operated from the end of World War II until 1971

C

capital. any durable goods (buildings, machinery, tools) produced by other factors of production for use in a production process. Any durable inputs to the production process, such as tools, machinery, and buildings

capital controls. taxes or rules such as constraints on foreign exchange transactions that impede money flows between economies; they are sometimes used to prevent exchange rate fluctuations

capital gains. increases in the value of existing assets

capital good (or physical capital). a long-lived good, which is itself produced and used to produce other goods and services

capital inflows. purchases of domestic assets by foreign households and firms

capital losses. decreases in the values of existing assets

capital outflows. purchases of foreign assets by domestic households and firms

ceteris paribus. a Latin phrase meaning "all else equal"

change in demand. a shift of the entire demand curve

change in supply. a shift of the entire supply curve

change in quantity demanded. a movement along the demand curve that occurs in response to a change in price

change in quantity supplied. a movement along the supply curve that occurs in response to a change in price

circular flow diagram. an illustration of exchange relationships in a monetary economy highlighting the mutual dependence of incomes and expenditures

closed economy. an economy that does not trade with the rest of the world; also know as an autarky

commodity money. an asset with intrinsic value, such as a gold or silver coin, that is generally accepted as a means of payment for purchases and settling debts

common market. two or more countries eliminating trade restrictions on most or all mutual trade, maintaining a common set of trade barriers against imports from non-member countries, and permitting mobility of capital and labour among member countries

comparative advantage. the advantage of having a lower opportunity cost of performing a task than another person does for the same task

complements. a relationship between two goods such that an increase in the price of one causes a leftward shift in the demand curve for the other

compound interest. the payment of interest not only on the original deposit but on all previously accumulated interest

constant (or parameter). a quantity that is fixed in value

consumer price index (CPI). for any period, measures the cost in that period of a standard basket of goods and services relative to the cost of the same basket of goods and services in a fixed year, called the base year

consumption. spending by households on goods and services, such as food, clothing, and entertainment

consumption function. the relationship between consumption spending and its determinants, such as disposable (after-tax) income

contractionary policies. government policy actions designed to reduce planned spending and output

core CPI. measure of the price level that excludes the most volatile components of the total CPI

core CPI inflation. rate of change of the core CPI

coupon payments. regular interest payments made to the bondholder

coupon rate. the interest rate promised when a bond is issued

credit easing. the unconventional monetary policy of the central bank purchasing private-sector financial assets in order to reduce interest rate spreads

currency. refers to bank notes and coins

current account balance. the record of payments and receipts arising from trade in goods and services, from international investment income, and from international transfers

customs union. two or more countries that not only agree to eliminate tariffs and other trade restrictions on most or all mutual trade but also agree to a common set of trade barriers to imports from non-member countries

cyclical unemployment. the extra unemployment brought about by periods of recession

D

deflating (a nominal quantity). the process of dividing a nominal quantity by a price index (such as the CPI) to express the quantity in real terms

deflation. a situation in which the prices of most goods and services are falling over time so that inflation is negative

demand curve. a curve or schedule showing the total quantity of a good of uniform quality that buyers want to buy at each price during a particular period of time provided that all other things are held constant

Department of Foreign Affairs and International Trade (DFAIT). a department of Canada's federal government led by multiple cabinet ministers

dependent variable. a variable in an equation whose value is determined by the value taken by another variable in the equation

deposit insurance. is provided to financial institutions such as banks so that the deposits of their customers are insured in case the financial institution goes bankrupt

deposit rate. the interest rate that the Bank of Canada pays commercial banks for overnight deposits; it corresponds to the lower limit of the Bank of Canada's operating band for the overnight rate

depreciation. a decrease in the value of a currency relative to another currency

depression. a particularly severe or protracted recession

devaluation. a reduction in the official value of a currency (in a fixed-exchange-rate system)

developing economies. a term widely used to refer to low and middle-income economies

diminishing returns to capital. if the amount of labour and other inputs employed is held constant, then the greater the amount of capital already in use, the less an additional unit of capital will tend to add to production

discouraged workers. people who say they would like to have a job but have not made an effort to find one in the past four weeks

discretionary fiscal policy. changes in government spending and taxation deliberately made to stabilize aggregate expenditure

disinflation. when the inflation rate falls from one year to the next

disposable income. refers to income that includes the addition of transfers and the deduction of taxes

dividend. a regular payment received by stockholders for each share that they own

downward inflation shock. a sudden decrease in the inflation rate, unrelated to the economy's output gap

downward nominal wage rigidity hypothesis. the claim that low levels of inflation will reduce efficiency because real wage cuts will then typically require nominal wage cuts, which will be resisted

Dutch disease. the tendency in an economy with a booming natural resource sector for the manufacturing sector to decline

E

econometrics. a branch of economics that involves the application of statistical techniques to economic data and the development of statistical techniques for analyzing such data

economic and monetary union. a common market with a single currency but made up of any number of member countries

economic model. a representation of economic reality that highlights particular variables and the relationships among them

economic naturalist. someone who uses insights from economics to help make sense of observations from everyday life

economics. the study of how people make choices under conditions of scarcity and of the results of those choices for society

economy-wide marginal tax rate. the amount by which taxes rise when income rises by $1

effective lower bound. the lowest practically feasible level for a central bank's key policy rate

efficient point. any combination of goods for which currently available resources do not allow an increase in the production of one good without a reduction in the production of the other

employment rate. a measure of the employed relative to the working-age population

entrepreneurship. behaviour that results in new products, services, technological processes, or organizational innovations that are productivity-enhancing

equation. a mathematical expression that describes the relationship between two or more variables

equilibrium. a state that occurs when all of the forces that act on all the variables in a system are in balance, exactly offsetting each other so that none of the variables in the system has any tendency to change

equilibrium price and equilibrium quantity. the price and quantity of a good at the intersection of the supply and demand curves for the good

excess demand, or shortage. the difference between the quantity supplied and the quantity demanded when the price of a good lies below the equilibrium price; leaves some buyers dissatisfied

excess supply, or surplus. the difference between the quantity supplied and the quantity demanded when the price of a good exceeds the equilibrium price; leaves some sellers dissatisfied

expansion. a period in which the economy is growing at a rate significantly above normal

expansionary gap. a negative output gap, which occurs when actual output is higher than potential output

expansionary policies. government policy actions intended to increase planned spending and output

expectations-augmented Phillips curve model. distinguishes between a short-run and a long-run Phillips curve and argues that the short-run version shifts when expectations about the inflation rate change

F

fallacy of composition. the argument that because something is true for a part, it also is true for the whole; the mistake of falsely assuming that what is true at the level of a particular individual, household, firm, or industry is necessarily true at a higher aggregate level

fair competition. the practice of discouraging both export subsidies and the dumping of products on foreign markets at below cost in order to gain market share

fiat money. an asset with no intrinsic value, such as paper currency, that is generally accepted as a means of payment for purchases and the settling of debts

final goods or services. consumed by the ultimate user; because they are the end products of the production process, they are counted as part of GDP

financial intermediaries. firms that extend credit to borrowers using funds raised from savers

fiscal policy. decisions that determine the government's budget, including the amount and composition of government expenditures and government revenues

Fisher effect. the tendency for nominal interest rates to be high when inflation is high and low when inflation is low

fixed exchange rate. an exchange rate whose value is set by official government policy

flexible exchange rate. an exchange rate whose value is not officially fixed but varies according to the supply of and demand for the currency in the foreign exchange market

foreign exchange market. the market on which currencies of various nations are traded for one another

foreign trade effect. the hypothesis that net exports will be inversely related to the overall price level, and therefore that aggregate demand and the price level will be inversely related

fractional-reserve banking system. a banking system in which bank reserves are less than deposits so that the reserve-deposit ratio is less than 100 percent

free trade area. involves two or more countries that agree to eliminate tariffs and other trade restrictions on most or all mutual trade of their own goods and services; they may each have different tariffs for imports from non-member countries

frictional unemployment. the short-term unemployment associated with the process of matching workers with jobs

future value (*FV*). the value a sum of money grows at some date in the future, when it compounds at a given interest rate

G

GDP deflator. a measure of the price level of goods and services included in GDP

General Agreement on Tariffs and Trade (GATT). a multilateral agreement dating back to the late 1940s that, through numerous rounds of trade negotiations, led to reduced tariffs and quotas among many countries

global warming. the increase in the average temperature of the earth's surface since the mid-20th century

government budget balance. the difference between government revenues and expenditures; it equals zero when revenues equal expenditure, is positive when revenues exceed expenditures, and is negative when revenues fall short of expenditures

government budget deficit. when government revenues fall short of expenditures; this is, the government budget balance is negative

government budget surplus. when government revenues exceed expenditures; that is, the government budget balance is positive

government debt. the sum of past government deficits and surpluses; a stock measure that is calculated at a point in time

government debt stability. the condition that the government debt-to-GDP ratio does not change

government deposit shifting. the transfer of government deposits by the central bank between the government's account at the central bank and the government's accounts at commercial banks

government purchases. purchases by federal, provincial, and municipal governments of final goods and services; does not include government transfer payments or interest paid on the public debt

gross domestic product (GDP). the market value of the final goods and services produced in a country during a given period

gross investment. the sum of private-sector and government investment

gross national product (GNP). the market value of goods and services produced by factors of production owned by the residents of a country; equivalent in magnitude to gross national income (GNI)

gross saving. the sum of household, corporate, government, and non-resident saving

H

high inflation. typically means inflation greater than 6 percent per year

hyperinflation. typically means inflation greater than 500 percent per year

I

import quota. a legal limit placed on the quantity of a good that may be imported

import substitution policy. uses trade protection to develop local manufacturing of goods that can replace imported manufactured goods

income effect. a change in quantity of a good demanded because a change in the price of the good has changed the real income of the person who purchases it

income-expenditure multiplier. the effect of a one-unit increase in autonomous expenditure on short-run equilibrium output

independent variable. a variable in an equation whose value determines the value taken by another variable in the equation

indexing. the practice of increasing a nominal quantity each period by an amount equal to the percentage increase in a specified price index; prevents the purchasing power of the nominal quantity from being eroded by inflation

induced expenditure. the portion of planned aggregate expenditure that depends on output Y

inefficient point. any combination of goods for which currently available resources enable an increase in the production of one good without a reduction in the production of the other

inferior good. a good whose demand curve shifts leftward when the incomes of buyers increase

inflation adjustment (*IA*) curve. a horizontal line showing the current rate of inflation, as determined by past expectations and pricing decisions

inflation-control target. refers either to the range of annual inflation rates within which the central bank aims to keep actual inflation or to the midpoint of the target range

inflation shock. a sudden change in the normal behaviour of inflation, unrelated to the nation's output gap

inputs. goods or services used in the process of producing a different good or service

interest rate spread. the difference, often measured in basis points, between a benchmark interest rate and a related market interest rate (such as between an overnight rate and a mortgage lending rate)

intermediate goods or services. used up in the production of final goods and services and therefore not counted as part of GDP

international capital flows. purchases or sales of real and financial assets across international borders

international reserves. foreign currency assets held by a government for the purpose of purchasing the domestic currency in the foreign exchange market

J

John Maynard Keynes. (1883-1946) a British economist (whose surname is pronounced as pronounced "Kains") whose *The General Theory of Employment, Interest and Money* (1936) is widely-regarded as the seminal work in modern macroeconomics

K

key policy rate. a general term for the interest rate that the central bank controls to achieve its monetary policy objective

Kyoto Protocol. a refinement of the United Nations Framework Convention on Climate Change, attempting to fight global warming by getting countries to commit to specific targets for reductions in emissions of greenhouse gases

L

labour force. the total number of employed and unemployed people in the economy

Large Value Transfer System (LVTS). an electronic wire system overseen by the Bank of Canada that allows major financial institutions operating in Canada to send large payments back and forth to each other

law of one price. if transportation costs are relatively small, the price of an internationally traded commodity will be the same in all locations

lender of last resort. an institution, typically a central bank, that will extend credit to financial institutions

during a financial panic to keep the payments system operating smoothly

liabilities. the debts one owes

life-cycle saving. saving to meet long-term objectives, such as retirement, university attendance, or the purchase of a home

liquidity. refers to the ease with which an asset can be converted into cash

long-run aggregate supply (*LRAS*) curve. a relationship between potential output and the inflation rate, a vertical curve indicating that potential output is independent of the inflation rate

long-run aggregate supply (*LRAS*) line. a vertical line showing the economy's potential output Y*

long-run equilibrium. a situation in which actual output equals potential output and the inflation rate is stable; graphically, occurs when the *ADI* curve, the *IA* curve, and the *LRAS* line all intersect at a single point

long-run Phillips curve. a relationship between the inflation rate and the unemployment rate in the long run; the vertical curve is drawn at the natural rate of unemployment

low inflation. typically means inflation between 1 and 3 percent per year

M

M1. sum of currency outside banks and balances held in chequing accounts

M2. all the assets in M1 plus some additional assets that are usable in making payments but at greater cost or inconvenience than currency or chequing accounts

macroeconomic policies. government actions designed to affect the performance of the economy as a whole

macroeconomics. the study of the performance of national economies and the policies that governments use to try to improve that performance

marginal benefit. the increase in total benefit that results from carrying out one more unit of an activity

marginal cost. the increase in total cost that results from carrying out one additional unit of an activity

marginal propensity to consume (*mpc*). the amount by which consumption rises when disposable income rises by \$1; we assume that $0 < MPC < 1$

marginal propensity to import. the amount by which imports rise when income rises by \$1

market. the context in which potential buyers and sellers of a good or service can negotiate exchanges

market equilibrium. occurs when all buyers and sellers are satisfied with their respective quantities at the market price

market equilibrium value of the exchange rate. the exchange rate that equates the quantities of the currency supplied and demanded in the foreign exchange market

medium of exchange. an asset used in purchasing goods and services

menu costs. the costs of changing prices

microeconomics. the study of individual choice under scarcity, and its implications for the behaviour of prices and quantities in individual markets

Millennium Development Goals. eight international goals, including the eradication of extreme poverty in the world by 2015

moderate inflation. typically means inflation between 3 and 6 percent per year

modern central banking theory. the view that the central bank changes its key policy (that is, official interest rate) directly and commercial banks respond by changing market interest rates

monetary policy. central bank management of interest rates to achieve macroeconomic objectives

monetary policy instrument. a tool or technique that a central bank uses to achieve a monetary policy objective

monetary policy objective. a central bank goal regarding a macroeconomic indicator that the bank influences

monetary policy rule. describes how the action a central bank takes in response to changes in the state of the economy depends on the state of the economy

money. any asset that can be used as a means of payment for purchases and to settle debts

most-favoured nation (MFN) treatment. an agreement that any special arrangement, such as a reduced tariff that is offered to one country (the most-favoured nation), in the interests of opening up a market must be offered to all other members

multilateral agreement. a document signed by representatives of many nations to express their acceptance of the principles set out in the document

N

national net worth. the total value of the real assets of a country adjusted for its net foreign liabilities

national saving. the sum of gross saving by the household sector, the corporate sector, and the government sector

national treatment. once a good has entered a country it must be treated as equivalent to a domestically produced good of the same type for purposes of taxation and regulation

national wealth. the total value of the real assets in a country

natural rate of unemployment (or u^*). the part of the total unemployment rate that is attributable to frictional, structural, and seasonal unemployment; equivalently, the unemployment rate that prevails when cyclical unemployment is zero, so the economy has neither a recessionary nor an expansionary output gap

neo-liberal policies. include reduced taxes, privatization, deregulation, and trade liberalization

net capital inflows. capital inflows minus capital outflows

net capital outflows. capital outflows minus capital inflows

net exports. exports minus imports

net international liabilities. the value of financial claims of non-residents on Canadian wealth net of the value of financial claims of Canadian residents against foreign wealth

net investment. investment that adds to the total capital stock of the economy

net taxes. refers to taxes minus transfers

nominal exchange rate. the rate at which two currencies can be traded for each other

nominal GDP. a measure of GDP in which the quantities produced are valued at current-year prices; measures the current dollar value of production

nominal interest rate. the type of interest rate you usually encounter in everyday life—the price paid per dollar borrowed per year

nominal quantity. a quantity that is measured in terms of its current dollar value

non-resident saving. the balance between saving provided to the Canadian economy by non-residents and saving provided to foreign economies by residents of Canada

normal good. a good whose demand curve shifts rightward when the incomes of buyers increase

O

official development assistance (ODA). grants or subsidized loans primarily provided to low-income countries with the stated purpose of promoting their development

official interest rate. a general term for the interest rate which the central bank controls to achieve its monetary policy objective; a term for the key policy rate of a central bank

Okun's law. states that each extra percentage point of cyclical unemployment is associated with about a 2-percentage-point increase in the output gap, measured in relation to potential output

open economy. an economy that trades with other countries

open-market operations. open-market purchases and open-market sales

open-market purchase. the purchase of government bonds from the public by the central bank for the purpose of increasing the supply of bank reserves

open-market sale. the sale by the central bank of government bonds for the purpose of reducing bank reserves

operating band. a term used by the Bank of Canada to describe the range of possible overnight interest rates: from 0.25 percentage points below the overnight rate target to 0.25 percentage points above the target

opportunity cost. the value of the next-best alternative that must be forgone in order to undertake the activity

output gap (or $Y^* - Y$). the difference between the economy's potential output and its actual output at a point in time

overnight rate. the market interest rate that financial institutions charge each other for overnight loans

overnight rate target. the interest rate that the Bank of Canada wants to prevail in the financial market where major Canadian institutions borrow and lend funds to settle daily transactions with one another

overvalued exchange rate. an exchange rate that has an officially fixed value greater than its fundamental value

P

parity. the situation when one unit of one currency trades on the foreign exchange market for one unit of another currency; frequently abbreviated to "par"

participation rate. the labour force divided by the working-age population

parameter (or constant). a quantity that is fixed in value

peak. the beginning of a recession, the high point of economic activity prior to a downturn

Phillips curve. a term that typically refers to a statistical relationship between the inflation rate and the unemployment rate

planned aggregate expenditure (*PAE*). total planned spending on final goods and services

positive economics. economic analysis offering cause-and-effect explanations of economic relationships; its propositions or hypotheses can, in principle, be confirmed or refuted by data; in principle, data can also be used to measure the magnitude of effects that it predicts

potential output (or potential GDP or full-employment output or Y^*). the amount of output (real GDP) that an economy can produce when using its resources, such as capital and labour, at normal rates

power of compound growth. the fact that small differences in growth rates, maintained over long periods, will produce large differences in magnitude

precautionary saving. saving for protection against unexpected setbacks, such as the loss of a job

present value (*PV*). the value of a sum of money today—that is, the value in the current or initial period

price index. a measure of the average price of a given class of goods or services relative to the price of the same goods and services in a base year

price level. the overall level of prices at a point in time as measured by a price index such as the CPI

price signal distortion hypothesis. the claim that any substantial amount of change in the price level will make it difficult for market participants to interpret the extent to which price changes involve relative price changes

principal amount. the amount originally lent

prime business rate. the interest rate that commercial banks charge to their least risky business borrowers; also called the prime rate

private-sector investment. spending by firms on final goods and services, primarily capital goods and housing

production possibilities curve. a graph that describes the maximum amount of one good that can be produced for every possible level of production of the other good

productive efficiency. occurs when an economy is using all of its economic resources in their technically most effective way

productivity. units of output per hour divided by units of input per hour

protective tariff. a tax on imported goods; the intention is to shield domestic industry from import competition

purchasing power parity (PPP). the theory that nominal exchange rates are determined as necessary for the law of one price to hold

Q

quantitative easing. the unconventional monetary policy of actively creating central bank reserves for the purchase of financial assets

quantity demanded. the total amount of a good of uniform quality purchased at a single, specific price by all buyers during a particular period of time

quantity equation. an amount of money times its velocity equals nominal GDP; $M \times V = P \times Y$

quantity supplied. the total amount of a good of uniform quality that all sellers are willing to produce and sell at a single, specific price during a particular period of time

R

rate of inflation. the annual percentage rate of change in the price level as measured, for example, by the CPI

rational decision maker. someone with clear objectives who behaves logically to achieve those objectives

real-balances effect. the hypothesis that overall wealth in the economy will be inversely related to the overall price level, and therefore that aggregate demand and the price level will be inversely related

real exchange rate. the price of the average domestic good or service relative to the price of the average foreign good or service, when prices are expressed in terms of a common currency

real GDP. a measure of GDP in which the quantities produced are valued at the prices in a base year rather than at current prices

real interest rate. the nominal interest rate minus the inflation rate

real quantity. a quantity that is measured in constant dollar terms

real wage. the wage paid to workers measured in terms of real purchasing power

recession (or contraction). a period in which the economy is growing at a rate significantly below normal

recessionary gap. a positive output gap, which occurs when potential output exceeds actual output

regional trade agreement. aims to reduce restrictions on international trade between two or more countries, usually within a certain region

relative price. the price of a specific good or service in comparison to the prices of other goods and services

reserve requirements. set by some central banks, the minimum values of the ratio of bank reserves to bank deposits that commercial banks are allowed to maintain; not set by the Bank of Canada

reserve-deposit ratio. bank reserves divided by deposits

resource curse. a term widely used to refer to low and middle-income economies with an abundance of natural resources

revaluation. an increase in the official value of a currency (in a fixed-exchange-rate system)

revenue tariff. a tax imposed on imported goods; for the purpose of collecting government revenue

rise. vertical distance a straight line travels between any two points

risk premium. the rate of return that financial investors require to hold risky assets minus the rate of return on safe assets

rule of 72. a rule of thumb stating that to find the number of years it takes a magnitude to double when it is growing at a constant rate, divide 72 by the growth rate

run. horizontal distance a straight line travels between any two points

S

saving. current income minus spending on current needs; a flow

saving rate. saving divided by income

sector-specific trade agreement. international trade agreement for the products of a particular economic sector, such as the softwood lumber industry

seasonal unemployment. unemployment associated with the seasons and/or weather

seigniorage. the profit gained from the issue of paper money or coins

settlement balances. accounts held at the Bank of Canada by financial institutions for the purpose of settling their net payment obligations to one another

shortage. the difference between the quantity supplied and the quantity demanded when the price of a good lies below the equilibrium price; some buyers are dissatisfied when there is excess demand

short-run aggregate supply (*SRAS*) curve. a relationship between real output and the overall price level in the short run: a horizontal version of the curve indicates that firms in the short run meet demand, on average, at existing prices

short-run equilibrium. a situation in which inflation equals the value determined by past expectations and pricing decisions, and output is consistent with output of that inflation rate; graphically, the intersection of the *ADI* curve and the *IA* curve

short-run equilibrium output. the level of output at which output *Y* equals planned aggregate expenditure; the level of output that prevails during the period in which prices are predetermined

short-run Phillips curve. a relationship between actual unemployment and the inflation rate for given inflationary expectations

slope. in a straight line, the ratio of the vertical distance the straight line travels between any two points (rise) to the corresponding horizontal distance (run)

speculative attack. a massive selling of domestic currency assets by financial investors

special purchase and resale agreement (SPRA). a financial transaction, used to reinforce the overnight rate target, in which the Bank of Canada buys Government of Canada bonds in the overnight market with an agreement to sell them back the next business day; SPRAs are initiated by the Bank when overnight funds are trading above the target rate

spurious correlation. a case in which two variables move together but are otherwise unrelated

stabilization policies. government policies that are used to affect planned aggregate expenditure, with the objective of eliminating output gaps

stable inflation. when the inflation rate stays roughly constant from one year to the next

stagflation. the combination of a recessionary gap and a rising price level

stock. a claim to partial ownership of a firm

store of value. an asset that serves as a means of holding wealth

structural policy. government policies aimed at changing the underlying structure, or institutions, of the nation's economy

structural unemployment. unemployment that occurs when workers are unable to fill available jobs because they lack the skills, or do not live where jobs are available

substitutes. a relationship between two goods such that an increase in the price of one causes a rightward shift in the demand curve for the other

sunk cost. a cost that is beyond recovery at the moment a decision must be made

supply curve. a curve or schedule showing the total quantity of a good of uniform quality that all sellers want to sell at each price during a particular period of time provided that all other things are held constant

surplus. the difference between the quantity supplied and the quantity demanded when the price of a good exceeds the equilibrium price; some sellers are dissatisfied when there is excess supply

T

tariff. a tax imposed on an imported good

technology. the stock of knowledge, useful in producing goods and services, that is available to a society

technological depletion hypothesis. the theory that the productivity slowdown after 1973 was due to the depletion of the backlog of technological advances made but not implemented during the 1930s and the Second World War

total CPI. synonym for the CPI or Consumer Price Index; the adjective "total" emphasizes that is a broad measure of the price level

total CPI inflation. rate of change of the total CPI

trade diversion. a reduction of trade barriers among members of a trading bloc causes trade among them to take the place of trade with countries outside the bloc

trough. the end of a recession, the low point of economic activity prior to a recovery

U

unanticipated inflation. when the rate of inflation turns out to be substantially different from what most people had expected

unattainable point. any combination of goods that cannot be produced using currently available resources

unconventional monetary policy. refers to measures, such as loaning money to troubled financial institutions and buying long-term government debt, that central banks utilize in abnormal times to supplement conventional monetary policy

undervalued exchange rate. an exchange rate that has an officially fixed value less than its fundamental value

unemployment duration. the length of a period during which an individual is continuously unemployed

unemployment rate. the number of unemployed people divided by the labour force

unit of account. a basic measure of economic value

upward inflation shock. a sudden increase in the inflation rate, unrelated to the economy's output gap

V

value added. for any firm, the market value of its product or service minus the cost of inputs purchased from other firms

variable. a quantity that is free to take a range of different values

velocity of money. a measure of the speed at which money changes hands in transactions involving final goods and services; $V = (P \times Y)/M$

vertical intercept. in a straight line, the value taken by the dependent variable when the independent variable equals zero

W

Washington Consensus. the policy advice that developing countries should privatize, liberalize, and pursue low inflation and balanced budgets

wealth. the value of assets minus liabilities, also called net worth

wealth effect. the tendency of changes in asset prices to affect households' wealth and thus their spending on consumption goods and services

welfare economics. economic analysis that is concerned not only with prediction or facts but also involves the evaluation of economic outcomes or situations according to ethical or value standards (which may be either explicit or implicit)

World Bank. a publicly funded international organization that provides assistance to low-income and middle-income countries to foster their development

world price. the price at which a good or service is traded on international markets

World Trade Organization (WTO). official international trade body headquartered in Geneva that began operation in 1995; superseded the GATT as an unofficial, *de facto* trade organization

Z

zero bound on nominal interest rates hypothesis. the claim that because interest rates cannot go below zero, a central bank may be unable to stimulate the economy with rate cuts if the official interest rate is low to begin with

zero inflation. when the price level stays roughly constant from one year to the next

zero interest rate commitment. a promise made by a central bank that it will maintain its key policy rate at the effective lower bound for an extended periods

INDEX

CANADIAN MACROECONOMIC DATA TABLE, 1976–2010

What's happening to our standard of living? Are jobs readily available? Are we investing enough? Is our wealth increasing? Is the cost of living under control? These are examples of macroeconomic questions. From the millions of time series in Statistics Canada's CANSIM database, here are 28 of the most important ones for answering such questions.

		1976	1977	1978	1979	1980	1981	1982	1983	1984	1985	1986	1987	1988	1989	1990	1991
1	Consumption expenditure, $B	107.8	120.2	134.4	150.1	168.5	190.4	204.1	224.1	244.2	266.7	288.6	312.3	338.5	365.5	385.4	398.3
	(Share of GDP, %)	*53.9*	*54.4*	*54.9*	*53.7*	*53.6*	*52.8*	*53.7*	*54.5*	*54.3*	*54.9*	*56.3*	*55.9*	*55.2*	*55.6*	*56.7*	*58.1*
2	Private-sector investment, $B	42.4	45.0	48.2	60.5	63.0	78.7	61.1	69.4	79.2	86.9	93.5	108.2	123.6	134.6	121.9	108.5
	(Share of GDP, %)	*21.2*	*20.3*	*19.7*	*21.6*	*20.0*	*21.8*	*16.1*	*16.9*	*17.6*	*17.9*	*18.2*	*19.4*	*20.2*	*20.5*	*17.9*	*15.8*
3	Government purchases, $B	50.2	56.7	61.2	67.2	76.3	87.2	99.2	105.4	111.1	120.7	126.0	133.1	144.4	157.0	171.7	182.5
	(Share of GDP, %)	*25.1*	*25.6*	*25.0*	*24.0*	*24.3*	*24.2*	*26.1*	*25.6*	*24.7*	*24.9*	*24.6*	*23.8*	*23.6*	*23.9*	*25.3*	*26.6*
4	Net exports, $B	−1.4	−0.4	0.9	1.6	5.8	2.6	14.8	13.4	15.8	11.3	5.0	6.6	4.7	0.2	0.9	−3.9
	(Share of GDP, %)	*−0.7*	*−0.2*	*0.4*	*0.6*	*1.9*	*0.7*	*3.9*	*3.3*	*3.5*	*2.3*	*1.0*	*1.2*	*0.8*	*0.0*	*0.1*	*−0.6*
5	GDP at market prices, $B	200.0	221.0	244.9	279.6	314.4	360.5	379.9	411.4	449.6	485.7	512.5	558.9	613.1	657.7	679.9	685.4
6	GNP at market prices, $B	196.4	216.3	238.8	271.9	305.8	348.3	366.6	399.2	435.4	470.6	495.1	541.6	593.3	635.2	655.5	662.5
	(Percentage of GDP)	*98.2*	*97.9*	*97.5*	*97.3*	*97.3*	*96.6*	*96.5*	*97.0*	*96.8*	*96.9*	*96.6*	*96.9*	*96.8*	*96.6*	*96.4*	*96.7*
7	Personal disposable income, $B	127.8	141.7	160.1	180.7	205.6	238.6	263.5	275.5	299.2	323.0	340.4	362.2	395.2	432.8	457.4	472.5
	(Percentage of GDP)	*63.9*	*64.1*	*65.4*	*64.6*	*65.4*	*66.2*	*69.4*	*67.0*	*66.5*	*66.5*	*66.4*	*64.8*	*64.5*	*65.8*	*67.3*	*68.9*
8	Personal saving, $B	17.5	18.9	22.8	26.5	32.1	41.6	53.1	46.5	49.9	50.9	45.8	43.1	48.7	56.3	59.3	62.7
	(Share of gross saving, %)	*35.6*	*36.1*	*40.7*	*38.6*	*44.4*	*46.5*	*72.5*	*57.2*	*54.2*	*50.1*	*42.3*	*34.9*	*34.7*	*36.7*	*41.7*	*48.7*
9	Corporate saving, $B	8.0	6.7	6.9	10.0	10.2	2.9	−4.7	9.2	14.8	19.0	13.9	22.4	26.3	19.7	6.3	0.5
	(Share of gross saving, %)	*16.3*	*12.9*	*12.4*	*14.5*	*14.1*	*3.2*	*−6.4*	*11.3*	*16.0*	*18.7*	*12.9*	*18.1*	*18.8*	*12.8*	*4.4*	*0.4*
10	Government saving, $B	−2.1	−4.4	−6.8	−5.7	−8.5	−4.5	−19.0	−25.0	−26.6	−31.3	−28.2	−22.7	−17.9	−21.4	−30.1	−48.4
	(Share of gross saving, %)	*−4.3*	*−8.4*	*−12.1*	*−8.3*	*−11.8*	*−5.0*	*−26.0*	*−30.8*	*−28.8*	*−30.8*	*−26.0*	*−18.4*	*−12.7*	*−14.0*	*−21.1*	*−37.6*
11	Non-resident saving, $B	5.2	5.3	5.5	6.3	2.8	9.6	−1.4	−0.7	−0.8	4.7	12.9	11.9	16.1	23.5	24.5	28.1
	(Share of gross saving, %)	*10.6*	*10.1*	*9.9*	*9.2*	*3.8*	*10.7*	*−1.9*	*−0.9*	*20.9*	*4.7*	*11.9*	*9.6*	*11.5*	*15.3*	*17.2*	*21.8*
12	Capital consumption, $B	22.5	24.9	27.8	32.1	37.2	43.0	46.7	49.6	53.3	58.4	62.6	66.3	70.5	75.9	82.2	85.9
	(Share of gross saving, %)	*45.7*	*47.7*	*49.7*	*46.7*	*51.5*	*48.1*	*63.8*	*61.0*	*57.8*	*57.5*	*57.9*	*53.7*	*50.3*	*49.6*	*57.8*	*66.7*
13	Gross investment, $B	49.2	52.3	55.9	68.6	72.3	89.4	73.3	81.3	92.2	101.6	108.1	123.5	140.1	153.1	142.2	128.7
	(Share of GDP, %)	*24.6*	*23.6*	*22.8*	*24.5*	*23.0*	*24.8*	*19.3*	*19.8*	*20.5*	*20.9*	*21.1*	*22.1*	*22.9*	*23.3*	*20.9*	*18.8*
14	National wealth, $B	738.4	822.4	924.5	1061.1	1210.5	1366.8	1453.1	1515.9	1598.7	1686.8	1815.3	1966.5	2140.2	2326.6	2423.7	2489.8
	(Percentage of GDP)	*369.2*	*372.2*	*377.5*	*379.5*	*385.0*	*379.2*	*382.5*	*368.5*	*355.6*	*347.3*	*354.2*	*351.8*	*349.1*	*353.7*	*356.5*	*363.3*
15	Current account balance, $B	−7.5	−7.4	−9.4	−9.8	−7.1	−15.0	2.3	−3.1	−1.7	−7.8	−15.5	−17.8	−18.3	−25.8	−23.1	−25.6
	(Percentage of GDP)	*−3.8*	*−3.4*	*−3.8*	*−3.5*	*−2.3*	*−4.2*	*0.6*	*−0.8*	*−0.4*	*−1.6*	*−3.0*	*−3.2*	*−3.0*	*−3.9*	*−3.4*	*−3.7*
16	Net int'l investment position, $B	−61.3	−68.7	−88.1	−103.2	−110.3	−135.7	−136.6	−144.3	−154.4	−177.8	−196.8	−212.6	−215.9	−232.1	−252.5	−267.4
	(Percentage of GDP)	*−30.7*	*−31.1*	*−36.0*	*−36.9*	*−35.1*	*−37.7*	*−36.0*	*−35.1*	*−34.3*	*−36.6*	*−38.4*	*−38.0*	*−35.2*	*−35.3*	*−37.1*	*−39.0*
17	National net worth, $B	673.7	749.9	830.5	951.2	1093.3	1224.6	1306.2	1361.0	1433.2	1491.9	1595.8	1729.6	1901.8	2073.8	2164.3	2209.6
	(Percentage of GDP)	*336.9*	*339.4*	*339.2*	*340.2*	*347.7*	*339.7*	*343.9*	*330.8*	*318.8*	*307.2*	*311.3*	*309.4*	*310.2*	*315.3*	*318.3*	*322.4*
18	Net federal debt–GDP ratio (%)	14.3	14.8	18.7	21.1	23.1	23.9	26.2	31.2	36.6	43.2	47.8	49.5	49.8	50.7	53.0	57.8
19	CPI inflation rate (%)	7.2	8.0	8.9	9.3	10.0	12.5	10.9	5.8	4.3	4.0	4.1	4.4	3.9	5.1	4.8	5.6
20	Short-term interest rate (%)	8.9	7.4	8.6	11.6	12.7	17.8	13.8	9.3	11.1	9.5	9.0	8.2	9.4	12.0	12.8	8.8
21	Exchange rate (U.S.$ per C$)	1.01	0.94	0.88	0.85	0.86	0.83	0.81	0.81	0.77	0.73	0.72	0.75	0.81	0.84	0.86	0.87
22	Population (millions)	23.4	23.7	24.0	24.2	24.5	24.8	25.1	25.4	25.6	25.8	26.1	26.4	26.8	27.3	27.7	28.0
23	Working-age population (millions)	17.1	17.4	17.8	18.1	18.5	18.8	19.1	19.4	19.6	19.8	20.1	20.3	20.6	20.9	21.2	21.5
24	Labour force (millions)	10.5	10.8	11.1	11.5	11.9	12.2	12.3	12.5	12.7	13.0	13.3	13.5	13.8	14.0	14.2	14.3
25	Employment (millions)	9.8	9.9	10.2	10.7	11.0	11.3	10.9	11.0	11.3	11.6	12.0	12.3	12.7	13.0	13.1	12.9
26	Labour productivity (2002$, 1000s)	56.2	57.2	57.7	57.6	56.7	56.8	57.0	58.1	59.9	61.2	61.0	61.8	63.0	63.2	63.0	62.9
27	Unemployment rate (%)	7.1	8.0	8.3	7.5	7.5	7.6	11.0	12.0	11.3	10.7	9.7	8.8	7.8	7.6	8.1	10.3
28	Growth of real GDP per capita (%)	4.1	2.2	3.0	3.2	0.1	1.8	−4.0	1.8	4.7	4.5	1.6	2.8	3.6	0.8	−1.2	−3.1
		1976	1977	1978	1979	1980	1981	1982	1983	1984	1985	1986	1987	1988	1989	1990	1991

Note: Series 1 to 17 are in billions of *current* (or *nominal*) dollars. For any given year, the data series numbered 1 through 4 sum to the series numbered 5 (except for a statistical discrepancy). They are also expressed as shares of GDP. Series 8 through 12 sum to series 13 (except for a statistical discrepancy). They are also expressed as shares of gross saving (which equals gross investment). Series 14, 16, and 17 measure stocks (at a point in time). They are also expressed as percentages of GDP. Series 18 compares a stock (debt) to a *flow* (GDP). Estimates listed below are as presented by Statistics Canada as of mid-October 2011; current estimates may differ. Further details are provided in the table of explanatory notes.

1992	1993	1994	1995	1996	1997	1998	1999	2000	2001	2002	2003	2004	2005	2006	2007	2008	2009	2010
411.2	428.2	445.9	460.9	480.4	510.7	531.2	560.9	596.0	620.6	655.7	686.6	719.9	759.0	801.7	851.6	890.6	898.2	940.6
58.7	*58.9*	*57.8*	*56.9*	*57.4*	*57.9*	*58.1*	*57.1*	*55.4*	*56.0*	*56.9*	*56.6*	*55.8*	*55.2*	*55.3*	*55.7*	*55.5*	*58.7*	*57.9*
104.8	110.0	123.8	130.6	131.6	162.9	166.5	176.4	193.3	185.2	193.9	212.4	235.0	266.2	292.8	310.1	322.4	261.9	293.4
15.0	*15.1*	*16.1*	*16.1*	*15.7*	*18.5*	*18.2*	*18.0*	*18.0*	*16.7*	*16.8*	*17.5*	*18.2*	*19.4*	*20.2*	*20.3*	*20.1*	*17.1*	*18.1*
188.7	191.0	193.2	193.9	191.7	191.9	199.3	209.1	224.6	239.0	253.0	268.5	279.9	297.0	318.7	338.9	368.1	394.9	420.9
26.9	*26.3*	*25.1*	*23.9*	*22.9*	*21.7*	*21.8*	*21.3*	*20.9*	*21.6*	*21.9*	*22.1*	*21.7*	*21.6*	*22.0*	*22.2*	*23.0*	*25.8*	*25.9*
−2.6	−0.0	9.1	25.9	33.7	17.3	18.3	36.0	61.9	63.6	50.9	45.6	55.7	51.2	36.4	29.7	24.4	−25.8	−30.5
−0.4	*−0.0*	*1.2*	*3.2*	*4.0*	*2.0*	*2.0*	*3.7*	*5.8*	*5.7*	*4.4*	*3.8*	*4.3*	*3.7*	*2.5*	*1.9*	*1.5*	*−1.7*	*−1.9*
700.5	727.2	770.9	810.4	836.9	882.7	915.0	982.4	1076.6	1108.2	1152.9	1213.2	1290.9	1373.8	1450.4	1529.6	1603.4	1529.0	1624.6
675.1	702.0	742.9	781.9	808.5	855.0	884.6	949.2	1048.5	1076.7	1124.0	1184.6	1264.6	1348.1	1436.2	1510.0	1583.2	1505.3	1596.4
96.4	*96.5*	*96.4*	*96.5*	*96.6*	*96.9*	*96.7*	*96.6*	*97.4*	*97.2*	*97.5*	*97.6*	*98.0*	*98.1*	*99.0*	*98.7*	*98.7*	*98.5*	*98.3*
483.4	494.9	501.7	519.6	527.8	546.2	568.8	596.2	639.6	669.2	694.0	720.9	760.5	794.3	853.2	901.6	953.6	966.3	1013.8
69.0	*68.1*	*65.1*	*64.1*	*63.1*	*61.9*	*62.2*	*60.7*	*59.4*	*60.4*	*60.2*	*59.4*	*58.9*	*57.8*	*58.8*	*58.9*	*59.5*	*63.2*	*62.4*
62.9	58.7	47.4	47.9	37.0	26.6	27.6	23.9	29.9	34.5	24.0	19.1	24.1	16.9	30.0	25.4	37.5	44.3	48.2
50.4	*45.2*	*32.6*	*31.5*	*24.3*	*14.5*	*14.8*	*12.0*	*13.7*	*16.2*	*10.8*	*7.9*	*9.0*	*5.6*	*9.0*	*7.2*	*10.1*	*13.9*	*13.4*
−3.2	5.2	23.0	32.9	29.8	28.7	23.9	34.1	52.2	51.6	59.1	72.3	83.5	99.6	100.1	100.3	113.7	50.6	77.9
−2.6	*4.0*	*15.8*	*21.6*	*19.6*	*15.7*	*12.8*	*17.1*	*24.0*	*24.3*	*26.6*	*29.8*	*31.2*	*32.8*	*30.0*	*28.2*	*30.5*	*15.8*	*21.6*
−56.7	−58.0	−46.3	−38.2	−20.7	1.3	0.3	16.1	34.8	11.9	4.6	6.3	21.6	35.7	40.9	40.0	15.0	−47.9	−55.7
−45.5	*−44.7*	*−31.8*	*−25.2*	*−13.6*	*0.7*	*0.2*	*8.1*	*16.0*	*5.6*	*2.1*	*2.6*	*8.1*	*11.8*	*12.2*	*11.2*	*4.0*	*−15.0*	*−15.5*
29.1	25.9	19.4	2.8	−6.0	9.7	11.3	−3.5	−35.0	−33.9	−22.0	−16.8	−28.7	−23.1	−20.7	−8.1	−3.2	52.2	61.4
23.4	*20.0*	*13.3*	*1.9*	*−4.0*	*5.3*	*6.0*	*−1.8*	*−16.1*	*−15.9*	*−9.9*	*−6.9*	*−10.7*	*−7.6*	*−6.2*	*−2.3*	*−0.9*	*16.4*	*17.0*
89.6	94.0	99.6	105.0	110.8	116.6	122.7	129.0	137.4	147.5	155.6	161.8	167.8	176.2	185.2	196.3	209.3	219.4	229.3
71.8	*72.5*	*68.5*	*69.1*	*72.8*	*63.7*	*65.8*	*64.7*	*63.1*	*69.4*	*69.9*	*66.7*	*62.7*	*58.1*	*55.5*	*55.2*	*56.2*	*68.8*	*63.6*
124.7	129.8	145.5	152.0	152.2	183.0	186.5	199.5	217.8	212.5	222.5	242.5	267.5	303.3	333.9	355.5	372.6	319.0	360.7
17.8	*17.8*	*18.9*	*18.8*	*18.2*	*20.7*	*20.4*	*20.3*	*20.2*	*19.2*	*19.3*	*20.0*	*20.7*	*22.1*	*23.0*	*23.2*	*23.2*	*20.9*	*22.2*
2546.8	2654.6	2783.8	2852.9	2942.2	3077.4	3218.5	3382.3	3564.3	3737.3	3965.8	4167.5	4484.6	4826.7	5286.6	5732.1	6113.2	6265.9	6510.0
363.6	*365.0*	*361.1*	*352.0*	*351.6*	*348.6*	*351.8*	*344.3*	*331.1*	*337.2*	*344.0*	*343.5*	*347.4*	*351.3*	*364.5*	*374.7*	*381.3*	*409.8*	*400.7*
−25.4	−28.1	−17.7	−6.1	4.6	−11.4	−11.4	2.6	29.3	25.1	19.8	14.6	29.8	25.9	20.5	12.8	5.3	−45.2	−50.9
−3.6	*−3.9*	*−2.3*	*−0.8*	*0.5*	*−1.3*	*−1.2*	*0.3*	*2.7*	*2.3*	*1.7*	*1.2*	*2.3*	*1.9*	*1.4*	*0.8*	*0.3*	*−3.0*	*−3.1*
−298.1	−323.7	−333.1	−324.2	−311.4	−290.2	−299.7	−243.7	−208.8	−203.4	−208.7	−216.7	−190.4	−164.9	−90.9	−129.8	−48.3	−110.4	−196.2
−42.6	*−44.5*	*−43.2*	*−40.0*	*−37.2*	*−32.9*	*−32.8*	*−24.8*	*−19.4*	*−18.4*	*−18.1*	*−17.9*	*−14.8*	*−12.0*	*−6.3*	*−8.5*	*−3.0*	*−7.2*	*−12.1*
2244.7	2314.1	2459.3	2514.7	2620.4	2780.4	2917.4	3174.3	3402.1	3593.1	3769.2	3973.5	4309.3	4712.0	5316.7	5699.3	6086.7	6185.0	6324.7
320.5	*318.2*	*319.0*	*310.3*	*313.1*	*315.0*	*318.8*	*323.1*	*316.0*	*324.2*	*326.9*	*327.5*	*333.8*	*343.0*	*366.6*	*372.6*	*379.6*	*404.5*	*389.3*
62.2	66.6	68.4	68.9	69.2	66.1	62.0	58.6	51.7	46.3	45.2	42.2	40.1	37.5	34.6	32.3	30.2	32.4	34.4
1.4	1.9	0.1	2.2	1.5	1.7	1.0	1.8	2.7	2.5	2.2	2.8	1.8	2.2	2.0	2.2	2.3	0.3	1.8
6.5	4.9	5.4	7.0	4.3	3.2	4.7	4.7	5.5	3.9	2.5	2.9	2.2	2.7	4.0	4.2	2.4	0.4	0.6
0.83	0.78	0.73	0.73	0.73	0.72	0.67	0.67	0.67	0.65	0.64	0.71	0.77	0.83	0.88	0.93	0.94	0.88	1.0
28.4	28.7	29.0	29.3	29.6	29.9	30.2	30.4	30.7	31.0	31.4	31.6	31.9	32.2	32.6	32.9	33.3	33.7	34.1
21.9	22.2	22.4	22.7	23.0	23.4	23.7	24.0	24.3	24.6	24.9	25.3	25.4	25.8	26.2	26.6	26.9	27.3	27.7
14.4	14.5	14.6	14.8	14.9	15.2	15.4	15.7	16.0	16.2	16.7	17.0	17.2	17.3	17.6	17.9	18.2	18.3	18.5
12.8	12.9	13.1	13.4	13.5	13.8	14.1	14.5	14.9	15.1	15.4	15.7	15.9	16.2	16.5	16.9	17.1	16.8	17.0
64.1	65.3	67.0	67.6	68.1	69.6	70.7	72.9	74.5	75.0	75.2	75.3	76.0	77.5	78.0	78.0	76.1	76.1	77.5
11.2	11.4	10.4	9.4	9.7	9.1	8.3	7.6	6.8	7.2	7.7	7.6	7.2	6.8	6.3	6.0	6.1	8.3	8.0
−0.3	*1.2*	*3.7*	*1.7*	*0.5*	*3.4*	*3.2*	*4.6*	*4.3*	*0.5*	*1.9*	*1.0*	*2.0*	*2.1*	*1.7*	*0.9*	*−1.4*	*−3.1*	*1.7*
1992	1993	1994	1995	1996	1997	1998	1999	2000	2001	2002	2003	2004	2005	2006	2007	2008	2009	2010

CANADIAN MACROECONOMIC DATA: EXPLANATORY NOTES

Key variables from the Statistics Canada CANSIM Database	Meaning and Significance of the Key Variables
	These comments highlight the meaning and significance of the variables in the data table. Chapter listings below indicate the textbook chapters in which variables are introduced or most extensively discussed.
1. Consumption expenditure v498087	Largest of the four components of expenditure-based GDP. It consists of spending on durable goods, semi-durable goods, non-durable goods, and services. It depends on personal disposable income and the real interest rate, and is represented by the symbol **C**. Chapters 5 & 8
2. Private-sector investment v498097, v498096, and v498100	Consists of *non-residential business fixed capital formation, residential investment,* and *inventory investment.* Residential investment is especially sensitive to real interest rate changes. Private-sector investment involves "real" (i.e., non-financial) investment in factories, equipment, and the like, and does not refer to purchases of stocks and bonds. It is represented by the symbol **I**. Chapters 5 & 10
3. Government purchases v498092, v498093, and v498094	Can be divided into *government current purchases* and *government investment.* Government purchases differ from government budgetary expenditures, a broader category including both government purchases and two types of transfers (transfer payments and interest payments on the public debt). Government purchases are represented by the symbol **G**. Chapters 5 & 8
4. Net exports v498103 minus v498106	Canadian exports of goods and services to the rest of the world minus Canadian imports of goods and services from the rest of the world. Net exports for Canada have traditionally been positive, but were negative in 2009 and 2010. Net exports are represented by the symbol **NX**. Chapters 5, 8, 10, 11, 12, 13, 15 & 16
5. GDP at market prices v498086	Nominal *Gross Domestic Product* is a measure of the total output of the Canadian economy. It is the annual market value of all final goods and services produced in Canada. Expenditure-based GDP is theoretically the sum of **C + I + G + NX** (*Table 5.2*). GDP can also be calculated by the *income* and *value-added* approaches. The concept of production underlying GDP is the same as the concept of production under-lying employment in the *Labour Force Survey*. GDP and its subcomponents are *flows,* not stocks. Chapter 5
6. GNP at market prices v499688	*Gross National Product* is the annual market value of all final goods and services produced by factors of production owned by the residents of Canada. *GNP − net international investment income = GDP*. For Canada, net international investment income is always negative; hence, for Canada GDP is always greater than GNP (subtracting a negative number from a magnitude adds to the magnitude). The term *gross national income* (GNI) is sometimes used instead of GNP. Chapter 5
7. Personal disposable income v498186	A measure of income available to households for personal saving or for buying consumer goods and services. It does not include the value of public services received by households. Income taxes and social insurance contributions are deducted from personal income to get personal disposable income. Chapters 5 & 8
8. Personal saving v647354	Decisions about *net personal saving* have been explained by economists in terms of life-cycle, precautionary, and bequest motives. The term *personal saving rate* usually refers to personal saving expressed relative to personal disposable income, but personal saving is also expressed relative to GDP. Personal saving relative to GDP rose during the 2008–2009 recession. Chapter 16
9. Corporate saving v647355	The largest component of *net corporate saving* is undistributed profits (or *retained earnings*) that are typically, but not necessarily, invested back into the firm. If the corporate sector has a bad year—that is, if profits drop—then undistributed profits will tend to drop, and with them net corporate saving. Chapter 16
10. Government saving v647356	Because of *automatic stabilizers*, government revenue tends to decline in recessions and government transfers tend to rise. Hence, government saving tends to decline during recessions. Canada's *net government saving*, which is calculated for all levels of government, turned negative in 2009 after many years of being positive. Chapter 16
11. Non-resident saving v647357	Has traditionally added to the funds available for gross investment in Canada—that is, the Canadian economy has usually experienced *net capital inflows. Net* capital inflows add to Canada's net international liabilities. Net *capital outflows*, as Canada experienced during the 1999–2007 period, reduce the funds available for gross investment in Canada but act to reduce Canada's net international debt. Chapter 16
12. Capital consumption v647358	*Capital consumption allowances.* They are accounting allowances for depreciation—the using up of capital in the production of income. Gross measures (e.g., gross corporate saving) exceed their corresponding net measures (e.g., net corporate saving) by the amount of the relevant capital consumption allowances. (This usage of "net" differs from "net" used to describe the balance of positive and negative entries, as in net capital inflows or net international debt.) Chapters 5 & 16
13. Gross investment v647367	Total or economy-wide investment. It includes both private-sector and government "real" (or non-financial) investment. Except for a minor statistical discrepancy, it equals *gross saving*—personal, corporate, government, and non-resident saving, plus capital consumption allowances. Gross investment is a flow, not a stock. It is an extremely important category for the analysis of long-run economic growth. Chapters 5 & 16

14. National wealth v52229141

The value of the stock of non-financial (or "real") assets—factories, equipment, office buildings, shopping malls, warehouses, residential dwellings, inventories, land, and so on—located in Canada. It is stock that is largely the result of past flows of gross investment. Chapter 16

15. Current account balance v113713

The sum of net exports, net international investment income, and net transfers, as shown in *Table 16.5*. It is linked to non-resident saving. Canada's current account balance has tended to be negative while its net exports of goods and services have tended to be positive. During the 1999–2007 period, however, net exports were strongly positive and the current account balance turned positive. Chapter 16

16. Net international investment position v235422

A country's *net international investment position* represents the value of the financial claims of non-residents on domestic wealth, net of the value of financial claims of domestic residents against foreign wealth, and the position can be positive or negative. Canada's position has been persistently negative so it is common to refer to the position as Canada's *net international debt* or *net international liabilities*. When the current account balance (a flow) is positive, net international debt (a stock) tends to decline. Chapter 16

17. National net worth v52229183

The value of the stock of non-financial (or "real") assets located in Canada minus the value of Canada's net international debt. Because Canada has net international debt, Canada's national net worth is less than Canada's national wealth. *Table 16.6* shows how the *national balance sheet* categories of national wealth, net international debt and national net worth are related. Chapter 16

18. Net federal debt–GDP ratio v52020763

Although *consolidated government debt* is a more comprehensive measure of government debt for Canada than *federal debt*, federal debt statistics become available more quickly. This ratio fell sharply during the 1997–2006 period due to federal surpluses and solid growth of nominal GDP. Reduction of the ratio does not require surpluses, but only that nominal GDP grow more rapidly than net federal debt. Usually it is the debt-to-GDP ratio that matters, not the absolute amount of the debt. Chapters 4 & 16

19. CPI inflation rate v41693271

Percentage change in the consumer price index (CPI). In Canada, inflation rates in the 1–3 percent range are typically called *low*, those from 3 to 6 percent are called *moderate*, and those 6 percent or higher are called *high*. When the inflation rate goes up and up, a country experiences *accelerating inflation*. *Disinflation* is the term for a declining rate of inflation. *Deflation*, or negative inflation, refers to a drop in the price level, the CPI. Canada's CPI has not dropped on an annual basis for decades. Chapters 6, 10, 11 & 12

20. Short-term interest rate v122484

The short-term interest rate is represented by the *nominal* interest rate on 3-month treasury bills (federal bonds). It changes, for example, when the Bank of Canada changes its overnight rate target. For a given inflation rate, changes in the nominal interest rate produce equal changes in the *real* (in the sense of "inflation-adjusted"; not in the sense of "non-financial") interest rate. Short-term interest rates vary more with the overnight rate target than do long-term rates. Chapters 6, 9, 10, 11, 12 & 13

21. Exchange rate reciprocal of v37426

For Canada, the most important foreign exchange rate is that between the U.S. and Canadian dollars. Canada had a *fixed exchange rate* during the 1962–1970 period, but has had a *flexible exchange rate* since then. An increase in Canadian real interest rates relative to U.S. rates will tend to cause the Canadian dollar to appreciate. Chapters 10, 11, 12 & 13

22. Population v466668

Refers to the total population of Canada—34.1 million people in 2010. Population estimates provide the denominator for calculations like real GDP per capita. With positive population growth, growth of total output will exceed growth of output per capita. Population estimates from Statistics Canada exceed the Census counts (e.g., by 3.2% for 2006) due to under-enumeration in the Census. Chapters 4 & 14

23. Working-age population v2461077

The working-age population is that part of the Canadian population aged 15 and over. It divides into those in the *labour force* and those *not in the labour force*. Note that although Canadians aged 65 and over are typically retired, they are considered part of the working-age population. If they are retired, they are classified as *not in the labour force*. Chapter 5

24. Labour force v2461098

The labour force is the sum of the employed plus the unemployed, as shown in *Table 5.5*. The labour force divided by the working-age population gives the *labour force participation rate*, which is still somewhat higher for men than for women in Canada. Chapter 5

25. Employment v2461119

Total employment—that is, the total number of employed persons—exceeds the number of employees. In addition to employees, total employment includes employers and self-employed persons without paid help. For calculating the employment total, part-time workers are treated no differently than full-time workers. Employment divided by the working-age population gives the *employment-population ratio*, a measure of job creation. Chapter 5

26. Labour productivity v41707175 and v2461119

The level of average labour productivity is most simply measured by dividing real GDP by the level of employment. High-income countries have high average labour productivity levels. This series makes use of real GDP measured in constant 2002 dollars. Chapters 4 & 14

27. Unemployment rate v2461224

Calculated by dividing the unemployed by the labour force. Someone of working age is unemployed if he or she lacks a job but is looking for work. The unemployed and those not in the labour force are mutually exclusive categories. In recent years, less than half of Canada's unemployed have received employment insurance benefits. The unemployment rate rises during recessions. Chapter 5

28. Growth of real GDP per capita v41707175 and v466668

The most widely used indicator of the pace of improvement in living standards. Even small long-term differences between two countries in their growth rates of real GDP per capita will result in large differences between the living standards of the two countries. Chapter 14